AMNESTY INTERNATIONAL

Amnesty International is a global movement of more than 7 million people who campaign for a world where human rights are enjoyed by all. Our vision is for every person to enjoy all the rights enshrined in the Universal Declaration of Human Rights and other international human rights standards. We are independent of any government, political ideology, economic interest or religion and are funded mainly by our membership and public donations.

First published in 2018 by Amnesty International Ltd

Peter Benenson House,
1, Easton Street,
London WC1X 0DW
United Kingdom

© Amnesty International 2018

Index: POL 10/6700/2018

ISBN: 978-0-86210-499-3

A catalogue record for this book is available from the British Library.

Original language: English

This report documents Amnesty International's work and concerns through 2017.

The absence of an entry in this report on a particular country or territory does not imply that no human rights violations of concern to Amnesty International have taken place there during the year. Nor is the length of a country entry any basis for a comparison of the extent and depth of Amnesty International's concerns in a country.

AMNESTY INTERNATIONAL

REPORT 2017/18

THE STATE OF THE WORLD'S HUMAN RIGHTS

CONTENTS
ANNUAL REPORT 2017/18

ABBREVIATIONS

ASEAN
Association of Southeast Asian Nations

AU
African Union

CEDAW
UN Convention on the Elimination of All Forms of Discrimination against Women

CEDAW Committee
UN Committee on the Elimination of Discrimination against Women

CERD
International Convention on the Elimination of All Forms of Racial Discrimination

CERD Committee
UN Committee on the Elimination of Racial Discrimination

CIA
US Central Intelligence Agency

ECOWAS
Economic Community of West African States

EU
European Union

European Committee for the Prevention of Torture
European Committee for the Prevention of Torture and Inhuman or Degrading Treatment or Punishment

European Convention on Human Rights
(European) Convention for the Protection of Human Rights and Fundamental Freedoms

ICC
International Criminal Court

ICCPR
International Covenant on Civil and Political Rights

ICESCR
International Covenant on Economic, Social and Cultural Rights

ICRC
International Committee of the Red Cross

ILO
International Labour Organization

International Convention against Enforced Disappearance
International Convention for the Protection of All Persons from Enforced Disappearance

LGBTI
lesbian, gay, bisexual, transgender and intersex

NATO
North Atlantic Treaty Organization

NGO
non-governmental organization

OAS
Organization of American States

OSCE
Organization for Security and Co-operation in Europe

UK
United Kingdom

UN
United Nations

UN Convention against Torture
Convention against Torture and Other Cruel, Inhuman or Degrading Treatment or Punishment

UN Refugee Convention
Convention relating to the Status of Refugees

UN Special Rapporteur on freedom of expression
UN Special Rapporteur on the promotion and protection of the right to freedom of opinion and expression

UN Special Rapporteur on racism
Special Rapporteur on contemporary forms of racism, racial discrimination, xenophobia and related intolerance

UN Special Rapporteur on torture
Special Rapporteur on torture and other cruel, inhuman or degrading treatment or punishment

UN Special Rapporteur on violence against women
Special rapporteur on violence against women, its causes and consequences

UNHCR, the UN refugee agency
Office of the United Nations High Commissioner for Refugees

UNICEF
United Nations Children's Fund

UPR
UN Universal Periodic Review

USA
United States of America

WHO
World Health Organization

PREFACE

The *Amnesty International Report 2017/18* shines a light on the state of the world's human rights during 2017.

The foreword, five regional overviews and a survey of 159 countries and territories from all regions document the struggle of many people to claim their rights, and the failures of governments to respect, protect and fulfil human rights.

Yet there are also glimpses of hard-won progress, demonstrating that the defence of human rights does yield positive developments. This report pays tribute to the human rights defenders who continue to fight for change, sometimes risking their own lives in the process.

In a year when austerity measures and natural disasters pushed many into deeper poverty and insecurity, this year's report also shines a spotlight on economic, social and cultural rights.

While every attempt is made to ensure accuracy, information may be subject to change without notice.

AMNESTY INTERNATIONAL REPORT 2017/18

PART 1: FOREWORD, SPOTLIGHT AND REGIONAL OVERVIEWS

FOREWORD

"As we enter the year in which the Universal Declaration of Human Rights turns 70, it is abundantly clear that none of us can take our human rights for granted."

SALIL SHETTY, SECRETARY GENERAL

Throughout 2017, millions across the world experienced the bitter fruits of a rising politics of demonization. Its ultimate consequences were laid bare in the horrific military campaign of ethnic cleansing against the Rohingya people in Myanmar. This caused an exodus of some 655,000 people into neighbouring Bangladesh in a matter of weeks, the fastest-growing refugee crisis of 2017. At the end of the year, their prospects for the future remained very unclear, and the enduring failure of world leaders to provide real solutions for refugees left little reason for optimism.

This episode will stand in history as yet another testament to the world's catastrophic failure to address conditions that provide fertile ground for mass atrocity crimes. The warning signs in Myanmar had long been visible: massive discrimination and segregation had become normalized within a regime that amounted to apartheid, and for long years the Rohingya people were routinely demonized and stripped of the basic conditions needed to live in dignity. The transformation of discrimination and demonization into mass violence is tragically familiar, and its ruinous consequences cannot be easily undone.

The appalling injustices meted out to the Rohingya may have been especially visible in 2017, but the trend of leaders and politicians demonizing whole groups of people based on their identity reverberated across the globe. The past year showed us once again what happens when the politics of demonization become mainstream, with grim consequences for human rights.

As we enter 2018, the year in which the Universal Declaration of Human Rights turns 70, it is abundantly clear that none of us can take any of our human rights for granted. We certainly cannot take for granted that we will be free to gather together in protest or to criticize our governments. Neither can we take for granted that social security will be available when we are old or incapacitated; that our babies can grow up in cities with clean, breathable air; or that as young people we will leave school to find jobs that enable us to buy a home.

The battle for human rights is never decisively won in any place or at any point in time. The frontiers shift continually, so there can never be room for complacency. In the history of human rights, this has perhaps never been clearer. Yet, faced with unprecedented challenges across the world, people have shown repeatedly that their thirst for justice, dignity and equality will not be extinguished; they continue to find new and bold ways of expressing this, while often paying a heavy price. In 2017, this global battle of values reached a new level of intensity.

Assaults on the basic values underpinning human rights – which recognize the dignity and equality of all people – have assumed vast proportions. Conflicts, fuelled by the international arms trade, continue to exact a cataclysmic toll on civilians, often by design. Whether in the humanitarian catastrophe of Yemen, exacerbated by Saudi Arabia's blockade, or government and international forces' indiscriminate killing of civilians used as human shields by the armed group calling itself Islamic State in Iraq and Syria, or crimes under international law driving a huge outflow of refugees from South Sudan – at times, parties to the world's numerous conflicts have abdicated even the pretence of respect for their obligations to protect civilians.

Leaders of wealthy countries have continued to approach the global refugee crisis with a blend of evasion and outright callousness, regarding refugees not as human beings with rights but as problems to be deflected. The efforts of US President Donald Trump to ban entry to all citizens of several Muslim-majority countries based on their nationality was a transparently hateful move. Most European leaders have been unwilling to grapple with the big challenge of regulating migration safely and legally, and have decided that practically nothing is off limits in their efforts to keep refugees away from the continent's shores. The inevitable consequences of this approach were evident in the shocking abuses suffered by refugees in Libya, with the full knowledge of European leaders.

Across parts of Europe and Africa, the spectre of hatred and fear loomed throughout a succession of significant elections. In Austria, France, Germany and the Netherlands, some candidates sought to transpose social and economic anxieties into fear and blame, especially against migrants, refugees and religious minorities. In Kenya, presidential elections in August and October were marred by intimidation and violence, including on the basis of ethnic identity.

However, 2017 also demonstrated the enduring willingness of people to stand up for their rights and for the values they want to see in the world. New and severe threats gave fresh oxygen to the spirit of protest. In Poland, serious threats to the independence of the judiciary brought large numbers of people onto the streets. In Zimbabwe, tens of thousands marched with determination in November, consummating their decades-long struggle against strongman politics and demanding a genuine election in 2018 – one in which the people's will is freely expressed. In India, rising Islamophobia and a wave of lynchings of Muslims and Dalits provoked outrage and protest as people said: "Not in my name". A vast women's march, centred on the USA but with many offshoots around the world, became one of the largest protest events in history. And globally, the #MeToo phenomenon drew enormous attention to the appalling extent of sexual abuse and harassment.

But the cost of speaking out against injustice continues to grow. In Turkey, the ruthless and arbitrary assault on civil society in the wake of the failed coup in 2016 continued at a furious pace, sweeping up the Chair and Director of Amnesty International Turkey among thousands of others. China unleashed unprecedented crackdowns on individuals and organizations perceived to be critical of the government, in the name of "national security". Following large, widespread protests in Russia, hundreds of peaceful protesters, bystanders and journalists were arrested; many faced ill-treatment, arbitrary detention and heavy fines following unfair trials. Across much of Africa, the intolerance of public protest was alarmingly apparent, from arbitrary bans in Angola and Chad, to heavy-handed crackdowns in the Democratic Republic of the Congo, Sierra Leone, Togo and Uganda. In Venezuela, hundreds of people were arbitrarily detained and many more suffered the consequences of excessive and abusive force used by security forces in response to widespread public protests against rising inflation and shortages of food and medical supplies. In Egypt, authorities severely curbed the freedom to criticize the government by closing down or freezing the assets of NGOs, enacting draconian legislation that provided for five years' imprisonment for publishing research without government permission, and sentencing journalists and hundreds of political opponents to prison terms. As the year drew to a close, a wave of anti-establishment demonstrations began in Iran, the like of which had not been seen since 2009. Reports emerged that security forces killed and injured unarmed protesters by using firearms and other excessive force. Hundreds were arrested and detained in jails notorious for torture and other ill-treatment.

2018 will mark 20 years since the UN adopted by consensus the Declaration on Human Rights Defenders, which provides for their protection and support and encourages everyone to stand up for human rights. Yet two decades later, those who take up the mantle of defending human rights often face the gravest of consequences. In 2017, the tragic death of Nobel Laureate Liu Xiaobo in China was emblematic of the contempt in which too many governments hold human rights defenders. He died in custody from liver cancer on 13 July, after the Chinese authorities refused to allow him to receive medical treatment abroad.

Meanwhile, narratives of national security and counter-terrorism have continued to provide justification to governments seeking to reconfigure the balance between state powers and individual freedoms. States have a clear responsibility to protect people from acts of violence that are designed to terrorize; yet, increasingly, they have done so at the expense of rights rather than to protect rights. Europe has continued to slip towards a near-permanent state of securitization. France, for example, ended its state of emergency in November, but only after adopting a new anti-terror law, which embedded in ordinary law many of the provisions of the emergency regime.

However, despite the gravity of these assaults on human rights, an understanding of the global struggle for the values of human dignity and equality demands that we resist any simple equation of repressive government versus principled people-power. Today's public spaces are contested between often-polarized extremes. While both Poland and the USA saw significant rallies calling for human rights protections not to be undermined, a large-scale nationalist march with xenophobic slogans in Warsaw and a white supremacist rally in Charlottesville called for policies that are profoundly antithetical to human rights. Abusive policies and practices that deny human rights to certain groups enjoyed popular support in many countries.

Today, many of our most important public spaces exist online, where the tools for addressing emerging challenges have at times proved wholly inadequate to the task. The avalanche of online abuse, particularly against women, and the incitement of hatred against minorities, drew weak and inconsistent responses from social media companies and scant action from governments. The impact of "fake news" as a tool for manipulating public opinion was widely discussed throughout 2017. Technological capabilities to blur the distinction between reality and fiction are only likely to grow in future, raising significant questions about people's access to information. These concerns are compounded by the extreme concentration of control in only a handful of companies over the information people view online, and by the huge power asymmetry between individuals and the companies and governments who control vast amounts of data. The capabilities deriving from this to shape public attitudes are immense, including virtually unchecked potential for incitement to hatred and violence.

As we approach the 70th anniversary of the Universal Declaration of Human Rights in December 2018, the challenge ahead is clear. This is a moment to reclaim the essential idea of the equality and dignity of all people, to cherish those values, and demand that they become a foundation for policy-making and practice. The artificial boundaries erected by a politics of demonization lead us only towards conflict and brutality, a nightmarish vision of humanity governed by naked self-interest and blinded to the plight of others. Too many leaders in the world have allowed the exponents of vilification to set the agenda, and failed to articulate an alternative vision.

It is time for this to change. We must refuse to accept narratives of demonization and build instead a culture of solidarity. We must hone our capacity for generosity towards others. We must assert the right of all people to participate in building the societies to which they belong. And we must seek constructive answers – rooted in human rights – to the frustrations, anger and alienation that provide a ready context for toxic political narratives of blame.

The coming year provides a vital opportunity for a renewed commitment to the transformative idea of human rights, as we ask what kind of societies we want to live in. We must not squander it.

SPOTLIGHT ON AUSTERITY

"I feel alone, like I've been left in the dark without anywhere to get help... I'm scared about what that will mean for my kids."

– Sarah

When the UK government cut legal aid support in 2012, Sarah was left without the support she needed to fight a complex legal case regarding access to her children. She is one of countless millions affected worldwide by government austerity policies. Yet the sheer scale of austerity and the statistics surrounding it can blind us to the day-to-day toll it is having on the lives of individual people and families.

Since the financial crisis of 2008, austerity has become a familiar term and experience for millions of people. This phenomenon – in which a government seeks to reduce a deficit in public finances, typically to reduce public debt – usually involves cuts to government spending, sometimes coupled with tax rises which often hit the poorest hardest by raising prices of basic necessities such as food.

Austerity is a human rights issue. It affects people's access to education, health, housing, social security and other economic and social rights. It also leads to abuses of civil and political rights, as governments respond to protests and other dissent in draconian ways or cut services that affect access to justice, such as legal aid. All too often, governments dismiss these rights and make decisions that put the greatest burden on those living in poverty while threatening the welfare of society as a whole. Austerity is a global issue. In 2017, widespread austerity measures were applied in countries from every region, particularly restricting people's economic and social rights.

In Europe, people took to the streets to protest against the detrimental effects of austerity measures in Greece, Serbia, Spain and the UK. In the case of the latter, research in England linked roughly 120,000 deaths to cuts to health and social care.

Amnesty International is researching the impact of austerity policies on the protection and realization of socio-economic rights in selected countries. The next piece of research, to be published in the first half of 2018, focuses on the impact of austerity measures on the right to health in Spain. A nurse working in the Spanish public health system told Amnesty International: "We have all suffered because of the cuts: nurses, doctors, patients, families, everyone."

In Sub-Saharan Africa, subsidies for the poor and social welfare have all been cut at a time when consumption taxes such as Value Added Tax (VAT) have been increased, often hitting hardest those living in poverty. Countries including Botswana, Burundi, Mauritius, Mozambique, Namibia and Togo continued to be "advised" by the International Monetary Fund (IMF) to keep on implementing austerity measures – despite the IMF's own admission in 2012 that such an approach is not always warranted and can undermine the economic growth needed to pay for services. In North Africa, Algeria's response to the fall in oil prices saw its government implement deep spending cuts in its 2017 budget, combined with a rise in VAT from 2% to 19%. IMF lending policies also prompted the Egyptian government to raise the prices of essential goods and services.

In Brazil, the unprecedented decision to impose a 20-year fiscal spending cap at the end of 2016 drew strong criticism from both inside and outside the country. In condemning the measure, the UN Special Rapporteur on extreme poverty and human rights stated: "Logic dictates that it is virtually inevitable that the progressive realization of economic and social rights [will] become impossible."

Economies in the Asia-Pacific and Middle East regions were similarly hamstrung by austerity measures. During 2017, Indonesia, Mongolia and Sri Lanka witnessed cuts to public spending. Even the budgets of resource-rich Qatar and Saudi Arabia shrank in moves to reduce state deficits, prioritizing economic efficiency over social protection.

In the absence of appropriate social safety nets, such measures risk violating governments' human rights obligations as well as commitments under the global 2030 Agenda for Sustainable Development and its 17 Sustainable Development Goals.

Looking ahead, even in the short term some commentators are forecasting an "austerity apocalypse". Regions such as Southeast Asia and Sub-Saharan Africa are predicted to be particularly badly affected. One report forecasts that during the next three years more than two-thirds of all countries will be impacted by austerity, affecting more than 6 billion people and wiping 7% off global Gross Domestic Product. The human cost is estimated to include millions being put out of work, including 2.4 million people in low-income countries, with few prospects of alternative employment.

How should governments respond and what do they have to do to fulfil their human rights obligations? These obligations do not prohibit austerity per se, but do require that other options also be considered by governments making economic and fiscal decisions. Above all, human rights underline the importance of governmental accountability when making such decisions. Rights holders should be asking key questions of their governments when confronted by austerity: What levels of scrutiny were employed? How participatory and transparent was the process? What potential impacts, particularly on the most socially and economically marginalized, were considered and what mitigation measures were put in place?

Human rights standards require that measures are put in place to ensure that nobody is allowed to fall below the minimum safety net needed to guarantee a dignified life. Unfortunately, this is routinely being ignored in even the largest economies as we see ever-increasing numbers of homeless people and the growth of food banks; charities and communities are responding to welfare cuts by stepping in to prevent people going hungry.

There is no question that many national budgets are under strain. But are governments making the maximum use of all the potential resources at their disposal, as they are required to do under human rights law? The November 2017 release of the so-called "Paradise Papers" revealed the vast extent of tax evasion and aggressive tax avoidance around the world, demonstrating the systematic failure of governments to close loopholes and monitor and address abuses. It has been estimated that Brazil alone is losing up to USD80 billion a year as a result of tax evasion (which calls into question the need for a 20-year spending cap), while African countries could collectively claw back at least the same amount annually. In addition to the well-known tax havens, a 2017 study showed that countries including Ireland, the Netherlands, Singapore, Switzerland and the UK are facilitating tax evasion by people in other countries. Globally it is estimated that the annual figure could be as high as USD10 trillion.

Extraordinary times require the consideration of radical alternatives. A number of ideas have been gaining traction during 2017. They include the introduction of a universal basic income – already being piloted in some countries – which would guarantee everyone enough money to live on, regardless of circumstances. Another proposal would involve the state paying for all key basic services rather than leaving it to the market. Of course such ideas have their critics: Where will the money come from? Will it simply encourage people to live off the state, even if they are in a position to work? Nevertheless, proponents point to the potential longer-term social and economic cost savings for societies, as well as the need to recognize that nobody should be left behind even in the most straitened of times. Governments should seriously consider these ideas as possible ways to meet their human rights obligations.

As austerity continues to bite worldwide, individuals and communities are fighting back and defending human rights. Their voices and the alternative vision they articulate need to be heard.

AFRICA REGIONAL OVERVIEW

Africa's human rights landscape was shaped by violent crackdowns against peaceful protesters and concerted attacks on political opponents, human rights defenders and civil society organizations. Meanwhile, relentless violence against civilians in long-standing conflicts was compounded by the stagnation of political efforts to resolve these crises. The cycle of impunity for human rights violations and abuses committed in conflicts – including crimes under international law – continued.

Intolerance of peaceful dissent and an entrenched disregard for the right to freedom of peaceful assembly were increasingly the norm. From Lomé to Freetown, Khartoum to Kampala and Kinshasa to Luanda, there were mass arrests of peaceful protesters, as well as beatings, excessive use of force and, in some cases, killings.

Political deadlock and failures by regional and international bodies to address long-standing conflicts and their underlying causes were also in danger of becoming normalized, and leading to more violations, with impunity.

These trends occurred within a context of slow and intermittent success in reducing poverty, and limited progress in human development. According to the Africa Sustainable Development Report, the rate of decline in extreme poverty was slow; women and young people bore the brunt of poverty.

However, there were signs of hope and progress that rarely made global headlines: the courage of ordinary people and human rights defenders who stood up for justice, equality and dignity in the face of repression.

Significant reforms emerged in a few countries. Gambia rescinded its decision to withdraw from the International Criminal Court (ICC), freed political prisoners and promised to abolish the death penalty. Burkina Faso's draft Constitution included provisions to strengthen human rights protection.

Notable too were landmark judicial decisions on human rights. Kenya's High Court decision to block the government's planned closure of Dadaab, the world's largest refugee camp, prevented the forcible return of more than a quarter of a million refugees to Somalia, where they were at risk of serious abuses. In Nigeria, two judgments declared threats of forced evictions without the service of statutory notices to be illegal, and found that forced evictions and the threat of such evictions amounted to cruel, inhuman and degrading treatment.

Angola's Constitutional Court declared legislation designed to stifle the work of civil society organizations to be unconstitutional.

REPRESSION OF DISSENT

CRACKDOWN ON PROTEST

In over 20 countries, people were denied their right to peaceful protest, including through unlawful bans, use of excessive force, harassment and arbitrary arrests. The right to freedom of assembly was the exception rather than the rule.

In Angola, Chad, Democratic Republic of the Congo (DRC), Ethiopia, Sudan, Togo and elsewhere, legal, administrative and other measures were used to impose unlawful restrictions and bans on peaceful protests.

In Angola, authorities frequently prevented peaceful demonstrations, even though no prior authorization was required in law. In Chad, at least six peaceful assemblies were banned, and many organizers and participants were arrested. In DRC, peaceful protests, particularly those related to the political crisis sparked by delayed elections, were banned and repressed. Civil society organizations, political opposition and Darfuri students in Sudan were prevented from holding events.

Use of excessive force and other abuses to disperse peaceful protests resulted in deaths, injuries and unlawful arrests in many countries. In Angola, the few demonstrations that proceeded were met with arbitrary arrests, detention and ill-treatment by police and security forces. Cameroon's security forces violently repressed demonstrations in Anglophone regions. Kenyan police used excessive force against opposition protesters following the general election – including with live ammunition and tear gas, leaving dozens dead, at least 33 of whom were shot by police, including two children.

In Togo, at least 10 people, including three children and two members of the armed forces, were killed during a crackdown by security forces, who frequently beat and fired tear gas and live ammunition at protesters. Sierra Leone's security forces opened fire on students demonstrating against a lecturers' strike in the city of Bo, killing one and injuring others. Uganda's government used raids, arrests, intimidation and harassment to stop peaceful gatherings and silence opposition to an amendment to remove the presidential age limit from the Constitution.

ATTACKS ON HUMAN RIGHTS DEFENDERS, JOURNALISTS AND OPPOSITION ACTIVISTS

Widespread repression of dissent also manifested itself through attacks on human rights defenders, civil society organizations, journalists and bloggers.

In Cameroon, civil society activists, journalists, trade unionists and teachers were arbitrarily arrested, and some faced military court trials. The government banned the activities of political parties and civil society organizations. Many remained in detention on spurious charges relating to national security.

Chad's authorities arrested and prosecuted human rights defenders, activists and journalists to silence criticism of the government, including in response to rising anger at the economic crisis.

In Equatorial Guinea, police detained activists, highlighting the authorities' willingness to abuse laws to intimidate and silence dissent.

In Eritrea, thousands of prisoners of conscience and political prisoners were detained without charge or access to lawyers or family members, many having been held for over 10 years.

In Ethiopia, arbitrary detentions continued under the state of emergency declaration, until it was lifted in June. The government ordered the release of 10,000 of the 26,000 detained in 2016 under the declaration. Meanwhile, hundreds were detained under the draconian Anti-Terrorism Proclamation, often used to target government critics.

In Mauritania, Mohamed Mkhaïtir, a blogger accused of apostasy, had his death sentence commuted but remained in detention even after he had served his sentence. Meanwhile two anti-slavery activists remained in jail.

The authorities in Madagascar intimidated and harassed journalists and human rights defenders in an attempt to silence them. Those daring to speak out against illegal trafficking and exploitation of natural resources were increasingly targeted through the use of criminal charges.

Sudan's government persisted in stifling dissent, with opposition political party members, trade union activists, human rights defenders and students increasingly targeted by the security forces; they faced arbitrary arrests and detention on trumped-up charges, and routine torture and other ill-treatment.

In Zambia, the Public Order Act was used to repress the rights to freedom of expression, association and peaceful assembly, particularly against critical civil society activists and opposition political party leaders. Police used excessive force against peaceful protesters while ignoring violence by ruling party loyalists against civil society activists.

In Zimbabwe, Pastor Evan Mawarire – founder of the #Thisflag movement – suffered political persecution and harassment, until he was acquitted following the change in government in November.

Ugandan academic Stella Nyanzi was detained for over one month for Facebook posts criticizing the President and his wife, who was the Minister for Education.

EMERGING REGRESSIVE LAWS AND SHRINKING POLITICAL SPACE

Some governments moved to introduce new laws to restrict the activities of human rights defenders, journalists and opponents.

Angola's Parliament adopted five bills containing provisions restricting freedom of expression, establishing a media regulatory body with broad oversight powers.

Legislation adopted in Côte d'Ivoire contained provisions curtailing the right to freedom of expression – including in relation to defamation, offending the President and disseminating false news.

A draft bill in Nigeria and draft amendments to Malawi's NGO law introduced excessive, intrusive and arbitrary controls on the activities of NGOs, including human rights groups.

MEDIA FREEDOM

In at least 30 countries – more than half the countries monitored – media freedom was curtailed and journalists faced criminalization.

Misuse of the justice system to silence dissent was common in Angola where the government used defamation laws, especially against journalists and academics.

In Uganda, journalist Gertrude Uwitware was arrested for supporting Stella Nyanzi.

In Botswana, journalists faced continued harassment and intimidation for their investigative journalism; three journalists were detained and threatened with death by security agents in plain clothes after they investigated the construction of President Ian Khama's holiday home.

Cameroon and Togo blocked the internet to prevent journalists from doing their jobs and closed media outlets.

Activists including journalists and bloggers were detained in Ethiopia and many were convicted under the Anti-Terrorism Proclamation which provided vague definitions of terrorist acts.

A military court in Cameroon sentenced Radio France Internationale journalist Ahmed Abba to 10 years' imprisonment after an unfair trial, for exercising his right to freedom of expression. He was released in December following a decision by an appellate tribunal which reduced his sentence to 24 months.

POLITICAL REPRESSION AND VIOLATIONS IN THE CONTEXT OF ELECTIONS

Fear, intimidation and violence marred Kenya's presidential elections. Police used excessive force against opposition protesters following the elections leaving dozens dead, including at least 33 shot by the police. Senior ruling party officials repeatedly threatened the independence of the judiciary after the Supreme Court annulled the election results. The NGOs Coordination Board threatened human rights and governance organizations with closure and other punitive measures after they criticized the electoral process.

In Rwanda's August presidential election, incumbent Paul Kagame won a landslide victory, following constitutional changes that allowed him to contest a third term; the election took place in a climate of fear created by two decades of attacks on political opposition, independent media and human rights defenders. Potential presidential candidates were also targeted, including by smear campaigns.

The run-up to Angola's elections in August was marked by human rights abuses – journalists and human rights defenders were repeatedly intimidated for exposing corruption and human rights violations. Protesters faced arrest and excessive use of force by police.

Political repression was rife in Burundi, with unlawful killings, arbitrary arrests, and enforced disappearances across the country.

ARMED CONFLICT AND VIOLENCE

Although the nature and intensity of Africa's conflicts varied, they were generally characterized by gross human rights violations and violations of international humanitarian law – including acts constituting crimes under international law.

Amid the paralysis of regional efforts to resolve the political deadlock, intense suffering and loss of life continued in South Sudan's four-year armed conflict, which forced millions from their homes. In the Upper Nile region, tens of thousands of civilians were forcibly displaced as government forces burned, shelled and systematically looted homes; sexual violence continued unabated. A cessation of hostilities agreement was signed in December following the forum launched by the intergovernmental Authority on Development (IGAD) to revitalize the previous peace agreement. However, soon after, renewed fighting broke out in different parts of the country.

In Sudan, the security and humanitarian situation in Darfur, Blue Nile and South Kordofan states remained dire, with widespread violations of international humanitarian and human rights law.

There was renewed conflict in the Central African Republic (CAR), which led to large-scale human rights violations and abuses and crimes under international law. Outside the government-controlled capital, armed groups carried out a range of abuses, and reports of sexual exploitation and abuses by UN peacekeeping troops continued.

In DRC, unprecedented violence in the Kasaï region left thousands dead and as of 25 September 1 million were internally displaced; over 35,000 people fled to neighbouring Angola. Congolese army soldiers used excessive force, killing scores of suspected members and sympathizers of the armed insurgent group Kamuena Nsapu, which, in turn, recruited children and carried out attacks on civilians and government forces. The government proxy-militia group Bana Mura was responsible for dozens of ethnic-based attacks including killings, rapes and destruction of civilian property.

In response to threats by the armed group Boko Haram and its ongoing commission of war crimes, security forces in Cameroon and Nigeria continued to commit gross human rights violations and crimes under international law. These included extrajudicial executions, enforced disappearances, arbitrary arrests, incommunicado detentions, torture and other ill-treatment, which, in some cases, led to deaths in custody. People accused of supporting Boko Haram were sentenced to death in Cameroon following unfair trials in military courts, although none were executed during the year. In Nigeria, the military arbitrarily arrested and detained incommunicado thousands of women, men and children in harsh conditions. In Niger – where the government declared a state of emergency in the western areas bordering Mali and renewed the state of emergency in the Diffa region – more than 700 suspected Boko Haram members went on trial.

ABUSES BY ARMED GROUPS

Armed groups including al-Shabaab and Boko Haram perpetrated abuses and attacks against civilians in countries including Cameroon, CAR, DRC, Mali, Niger, Nigeria and Somalia. In some cases, the attacks constituted serious abuses of international humanitarian and human rights law.

In the Lake Chad basin region, Boko Haram committed war crimes on a large scale. Boko Haram attacks targeted civilians, caused deaths and led to an increase in displacement of civilians. Resurgent attacks in Cameroon and Nigeria left hundreds of civilians dead. While 82 of the abducted schoolgirls from Chibok, northeast Nigeria, were released in May, thousands of abducted women, girls and young men were unaccounted for and faced horrific abuses, including rape. Across northeast Nigeria, 1.7 million people were displaced, bringing many to the brink of starvation.

In Mali, attacks by armed groups on civilians and peacekeepers spread from the north to the centre, and a state of emergency was extended in October for another year.

In October, al-Shabaab carried out the deadliest attack against civilians in recent times in Somalia's capital, Mogadishu; it left over 512 people dead.

TORTURE AND OTHER ILL-TREATMENT

Torture and other ill-treatment was reported in several countries including Burkina Faso, Cameroon, Eritrea, Ethiopia, Mauritania, Nigeria and Sudan.

Cameroon's security forces perpetrated torture against people suspected – often without evidence – of supporting Boko Haram; these violations amounted to war crimes and the crimes were carried out with impunity.

In Ethiopia, detainees accused of terrorism repeatedly complained to the courts that police tortured and ill-treated them during interrogations. Although, in some cases, judges ordered the Ethiopian Human Rights Commission to investigate the allegations, the investigations failed to adhere to international human rights standards.

On the positive side, the Anti-Torture Bill – intended to prohibit and criminalize the use of torture – was signed into law in Nigeria in December.

PEOPLE ON THE MOVE

Protracted conflicts, along with recurring humanitarian crises and persistent human rights violations, forced millions to flee their homes in search of protection. Refugees and migrants faced widespread abuses and violations. Millions of refugees hosted by African countries were inadequately supported by the international community.

The ongoing conflict and drought in Somalia left half the country's population in need of humanitarian assistance, according to UNHCR, the UN Refugee Agency. Over a million people were internally displaced by conflict and drought during the year – adding to 1.1 million internally displaced people living in deplorable conditions in unsafe informal settlements.

In Kenya, over 285,000 refugees and asylum-seekers from Somalia remained in urgent need of protection. In February, a High Court ruling blocked the Kenyan government's unilateral decision to shut Dadaab refugee camp, which – in violation of international law – had put more than 260,000 Somali refugees at risk of forcible return. Although Dadaab remained open, the Kenyan government continued to refuse to register new arrivals from Somalia. Over 74,000 refugees were repatriated from Dadaab to Somalia between December 2014 and November 2017 under the voluntary repatriation framework. The repatriations took place despite ongoing concerns about the "voluntary" nature of returns and despite concerns that the conditions to ensure returns in safety and dignity were not yet in place in Somalia, due to ongoing conflict and severe drought.

Hundreds of thousands of people from CAR sought refuge from conflict in neighbouring countries or were internally displaced, living in makeshift camps.

Military operations and the conflict with Boko Haram in the Lake Chad basin region forced millions from their homes. In Nigeria, at least 1.7 million were internally displaced in the northeastern states of Borno, Yobe and Adamawa. UNHCR said that 5.2 million people in the northeast were in urgent need of food assistance and 450,000 children under five were in urgent need of nutrition. In Chad, over 408,000 refugees from CAR, DRC, Nigeria and Sudan lived in dire conditions in refugee camps.

Botswana denied refugees freedom of movement, the right to work and local integration; asylum-seekers faced lengthy refugee status determination procedures and detention.

Thousands continued to flee Eritrea, where the human rights situation and the imposition of indefinite military national service created major difficulties for many. They faced serious abuses in transit and in some destination countries, and many were subjected to arbitrary detention, abduction, sexual abuse and ill-treatment on their way to Europe. In August, Sudan forcibly returned more than 100 refugees to Eritrea, where they were at risk of serious human rights violations, in violation of international law.

In South Sudan, around 340,000 fled an escalation of the fighting in the Equatoria region, which led to atrocities and starvation between January and October. Mainly government – but also opposition – forces in the southern region committed crimes under international law and other serious violations and abuses, including war crimes, against civilians. More than 3.9 million people – approximately one third of the population – had been displaced since the beginning of the conflict in December 2013.

Other states did little to help neighbouring countries hosting more than 2 million refugees from South Sudan. Uganda hosted over 1 million refugees, mostly children, and encountered difficulties in implementing its progressive and widely respected refugee policy, due to chronic underfunding by the international community. Consequently, the Ugandan government, UNHCR and NGOs struggled to meet refugees' basic needs.

IMPUNITY

Failure to ensure justice, redress and the holding of suspected perpetrators to account remained a key driver of human rights violations and abuses in a wide range of contexts and countries.

In CAR, some progress was made towards operationalizing the Special Criminal Court, which was established to try individuals suspected of serious human rights violations and crimes under international law committed during the country's 14-year conflict. The Court's Special Prosecutor took office in May, but the Court was not yet operational and impunity remained the norm.

In South Sudan, three transitional justice bodies provided for in the 2015 peace agreement had still not been established. In July, a joint roadmap for the establishment of the Hybrid Court for South Sudan was agreed between the African Union (AU) Commission and the government; discussions continued on the instruments for the establishment of the Court, but nothing was formally adopted.

In Nigeria – amid concerns about independence and impartiality – a Special Board of Inquiry, established by the army to investigate allegations of gross human rights violations, cleared senior military officers of crimes under international law. Its report was not made public. In August, the acting President set up a presidential investigation panel to probe allegations of human rights violations carried out by the military; the panel held public hearings between September and November but there was no outcome by the end of the year. Meanwhile, the Nigerian authorities held mass secret trials for Boko Haram suspects; 50 defendants were sentenced to various terms of imprisonment in a trial that took place over four days.

In DRC, the killing of two UN experts and the disappearance of their Congolese interpreter and three of their drivers, in Kasaï Central Province in March, illustrated the urgent need to end violence in the region. The Congolese authorities' investigation was not transparent or credible. In June, the UN Human Rights Council decided to dispatch a team of international experts to DRC to help in investigations. In July, the UN High Commissioner for Human Rights appointed a team of three experts whose findings were expected in June 2018.

In Ethiopia, the police and army continued to enjoy impunity for violations committed in 2015 and 2016. The government rejected calls for independent and impartial investigations into violations committed in the context of protests in various regional states.

The Extraordinary African Chambers in Senegal upheld the conviction and sentence of life imprisonment of former Chadian President Hissène Habré for war crimes, crimes against humanity and torture.

INTERNATIONAL CRIMINAL COURT

Burundi became the first State Party to withdraw from the Rome Statute of the ICC in October. Despite this, in November, the Pre-Trial Chamber made public its decision to authorize the ICC Prosecutor to open an investigation regarding crimes within the jurisdiction of the Court allegedly committed in Burundi – or by nationals of Burundi outside the country – between April 2015 and October 2017.

However, developments in Africa suggested a tempering of the rhetoric calling for withdrawal from the ICC. The AU adopted a decision in January, which despite its misleading title, outlined plans for engagement with the ICC and other stakeholders. More encouragingly, member states – including Senegal, Nigeria, Cape Verde, Malawi, Tanzania, Tunisia, Zambia and Liberia – expressly stated their support for the ICC and rejected any notion of mass withdrawal.

Gambia's new government revoked its withdrawal from the Rome Statute, while Botswana's Parliament passed a bill incorporating the Rome Statute into domestic law.

In March, the South African government announced it would revoke its 2016 notice of intention to withdraw from the Rome Statue after the North Gauteng High Court decision held that withdrawal from the ICC without consulting Parliament was unconstitutional and invalid. However, a draft bill to repeal the Rome Statue Domestication Act was introduced to Parliament in early December 2017, signalling the government's intention to pursue its decision to leave the ICC.

Meanwhile, the ICC's Pre-Trial Chamber ruled that South Africa should have executed the arrest warrant against Sudanese President Omar Al-Bashir during his 2015 visit to the country. The ruling confirmed that President Al-Bashir did not have immunity from arrest and that any states party to the Rome Statute were obliged to arrest him if he entered their territory, and hand him over to the Court.

In its December preliminary report, the Office of the Prosecutor of the ICC announced that it was continuing its analysis of the potential eight crimes it had previously identified as having been allegedly committed in Nigeria, as well as gathering evidence on new crimes, but was yet to reach a decision on whether to open an investigation.

DISCRIMINATION AND MARGINALIZATION

Discrimination, marginalization and abuse of women and girls – often arising from cultural traditions and institutionalized by unjust laws – continued in a number of countries. Women and girls were subjected to rape and other sexual violence, including in the context of conflicts and in countries with large numbers of refugee and internally displaced populations.

Pregnant girls continued to be excluded from school in countries including Sierra Leone and Equatorial Guinea. In June, Tanzania's President announced a ban on pregnant girls returning to public-funded schools – fuelling stigma and discrimination against girls and victims of sexual violence.

Gender-based violence against women and girls was prevalent in several countries including Liberia, Malawi, Mozambique, South Africa and Swaziland.

In countries including Burkina Faso, lack of medical equipment, medication and staffing in hospitals left pregnant women and infants at serious risk of birth complications, infection and death. Female genital mutilation rates decreased; however, despite being outlawed, the practice remained widespread.

Unsafe abortions contributed to one of Africa's highest rates of maternal death and injury in Liberia, where affordable and accessible abortion services were largely unavailable to rape survivors.

Despite its progressive abortion laws, women and girls faced substantial barriers to legal abortion services in South Africa and faced serious risks to health, and even death, from unsafe abortions. The government failed to address the refusal of health care professionals to provide abortions.

In Angola, the government proposed an amendment to the Penal Code, which would decriminalize abortion in certain limited cases, but Parliament rejected the proposal. After a public outcry, the parliamentary vote on the legislation was postponed indefinitely.

PEOPLE WITH ALBINISM

Superstitions about the magical powers of people with albinism fuelled a surge of attacks against them; in Malawi and Mozambique, they were abducted and killed for their body parts. In Mozambique, a seven-year-old boy was murdered when unidentified men abducted him from his home. Despite public outcry, the government took little action.

RIGHTS OF LESBIAN, GAY, BISEXUAL, TRANSGENDER AND INTERSEX PEOPLE

LGBTI people faced discrimination, prosecution, harassment and violence, including in Senegal, Ghana, Malawi and Nigeria. In Ghana, the parliamentary Speaker called for a constitutional amendment to make homosexuality illegal and punishable by law. In Liberia, a man arrested in 2016 and charged with "voluntary sodomy" under the Penal Code, remained in detention awaiting trial. In Nigeria, arrest, public shaming, extortion of and discrimination against individuals based on their sexual orientation were reported.

In a landmark decision in Botswana, a High Court ordered the government to change the gender marker in the identity document of a transgender woman, ruling that its refusal to do so was unreasonable and in violation of her rights.

RIGHT TO HOUSING AND FORCED EVICTIONS

Amid increasing urbanization, unemployment, poverty and inequality, many countries failed to ensure accessible, affordable and habitable housing.

A landslide at a vast rubbish dump on the outskirts of Ethiopia's capital caused 115 deaths. Most of the victims lived next to the site and supported themselves by recycling rubbish.

At least 10 people, including two children, were also killed in a landslide at a rubbish dump in Guinea.

In Lagos state in Nigeria, authorities forcibly evicted at least 5,000 people from the Otodo-Gbame and Ilubirin waterfront neighbourhoods, while security services fired tear gas and live bullets to clear the area. The forced evictions were in violation of a High Court order restraining authorities from carrying out demolitions in these communities.

On the other hand, a High Court ruling in Nigeria declared the planned demolition of Mpape settlement in Abuja illegal, thereby offering relief to hundreds of thousands of residents. The Court ruled that the authorities were obliged to refrain from forced evictions and should develop policies to implement the right to adequate housing.

BUSINESS AND CORPORATE ACCOUNTABILITY

In DRC, children and adults risked their lives and health working in cobalt mines for a dollar a day. In South Africa, Lonmin Plc, a UK-based platinum mining giant, allowed its workforce to live in squalor in Marikana, in spite of making legally binding commitments to build 5,500 new houses over 10 years before. No one was held to account for the killing in 2012 of 34 people protesting against poor conditions at the mine.

At the same time, there were growing signs of public pressure, action and demands for corporate accountability in various countries.

In June, a landmark civil case was launched against Shell in the Netherlands – accusing it of complicity in the unlawful arrest, detention and execution of the Ogoni nine, hanged by Nigeria's military government in 1995. International organizations called for Shell to be investigated for its part in these serious human rights violations committed by the Nigerian security forces in Ogoniland in the 1990s.

Some governments took positive steps. The DRC government committed to end child labour in the mining sector by 2025, in what could be a significant step towards eradicating the use of children as young as seven in dangerous mining work. Ghana ratified the UN Minamata Convention on Mercury, which aims to protect workers from toxic liquid metal by reducing mercury use in artisanal and small-scale gold mining and to protect children from exposure.

LOOKING AHEAD

While 2017 saw protracted and, in some cases, deepening challenges to the state of human rights in Africa, it also offered hope and opportunities for change. A key source of hope lay in the countless people across the region who stood up for human rights, justice and dignity – often risking their lives and freedoms.

Africa's regional bodies remained key to the realization of positive change; they too are presented with many opportunities. During the year, the AU endorsed an ambitious plan to realize its commitment to "silence the guns" by 2020. It embarked on a major institutional reform agenda, which includes mobilizing significant resources for its operations and for peace and security interventions. This holistic approach and the AU's ambition to address the root causes of conflict offer real opportunities to mobilize an effective regional response for better protection of civilians, respect for human rights and tackling the entrenched culture of impunity.

The year also marked the 30th anniversary of the establishment of the African Commission on Human and Peoples' Rights, which – despite many challenges – made significant contributions towards the promotion and protection of human rights, including by formulating an impressive list of instruments and standards. In 2017 alone, the Commission adopted at least 13 such instruments; these gave specific content to the broad provisions of the African Charter on Human and Peoples' Rights and the Protocol to the African Charter on Human and Peoples' Rights on the Rights of Women in Africa.

The Commission should build on these successes and work towards refining and strengthening its processes and mechanisms; it needs to develop a single set of consolidated state reporting guidelines and to apply consistently the Commission's procedure for following up the implementation of its decisions and recommendations to states.

AMERICAS REGIONAL OVERVIEW

Discrimination and inequality continued to be the norm across the continent. High levels of violence continued to ravage the region, with waves of killings, enforced disappearances and arbitrary detentions. Human rights defenders experienced increasing levels of violence. Impunity remained pervasive. Politics of demonization and division increased. Indigenous Peoples faced discrimination and continued to be denied their economic, social and cultural rights, including their rights to land and to free, prior and informed consent on projects affecting them. Governments made little headway in protecting the rights of women and girls, and of lesbian, gay, bisexual, transgender and intersex (LGBTI) people.

Huge numbers of people across the Americas region faced a deepening human rights crisis, fuelled by the downgrading of human rights in law, policy and practice, together with increasing use of the politics of demonization and division. Such regression risked becoming endemic in many countries. It exacerbated a lack of trust in the authorities – manifested in low levels of participation in elections and referendums – and in institutions such as national justice systems.

Rather than using human rights as a way to secure a more just and sustainable future, many governments fell back on tactics of repression – misusing their security forces and justice systems to silence dissent and criticism; allowing widespread torture and other ill-treatment to go unpunished; and presiding over rampant inequality, poverty and discrimination sustained by corruption and failures in accountability and justice.

Major regression in human rights was also driven by a series of executive orders issued by US President Donald Trump, including what became known as the "Muslim ban" and plans to build a wall along the US border with Mexico.

Extreme and persistent violence was commonplace in countries including Brazil, El Salvador, Honduras, Mexico and Venezuela. Violence across the region was frequently driven by the proliferation of illicit small arms and the growth of organized crime. Violence against LGBTI people, women and girls, and Indigenous Peoples was widespread.

According to a UN report, Latin America and the Caribbean remained the most violent region in the world for women, despite strict laws aimed at addressing the crisis. The region had the world's highest rate of non-intimate partner violence against women, and the second highest rate of intimate partner violence.

Mexico witnessed a wave of killings of journalists and human rights defenders. Venezuela faced its worst human rights crisis in modern history. Killings of Indigenous people and Afro-descendant leaders in Colombia exposed shortcomings in the implementation of the country's peace process.

Land rights activists were targeted with violence and other abuses in many countries. The region continued to suffer from an alarming rise in the number of threats and attacks against human rights defenders, community leaders and journalists, including through misuse of the justice system.

Huge numbers of people fled their homes to escape repression, violence, discrimination and poverty. Many suffered further abuses while in transit or upon reaching other countries in the region.

The pardon granted to Peru's former president Alberto Fujimori, who in 2009 was sentenced for crimes against humanity, sent a worrying signal about Peru's willingness to confront impunity and respect the rights of victims.

States' failure to uphold human rights increased the space for non-state actors to commit crimes under international law and other abuses. These included organized criminal entities, which in some cases controlled entire territories, often with the complicity or acquiescence of security forces. National and transnational corporations sought to take control of the land and territory of groups including Indigenous Peoples and – in countries like Peru and Nicaragua – peasant farmers.

Failures to uphold economic, social and cultural rights caused widespread suffering. A reversal of political rhetoric by the USA under President Trump reduced the chances of the US Congress passing legislation to lift the economic embargo on Cuba – and so perpetuated the embargo's adverse impacts on Cubans. Paraguay's authorities failed to ensure the right to adequate housing following forced evictions. There were thousands of new cases of cholera in Haiti.

Tens of thousands of people were displaced from their homes and struggled with badly damaged infrastructure in countries in the Caribbean, including in the Dominican Republic and Puerto Rico, following two major hurricanes, among other natural disasters. In Mexico, two devastating earthquakes that cost hundreds of lives compromised people's rights to adequate housing and education.

At the Organization of American States (OAS) General Assembly, held in Cancún, Mexico, in June, there was a clear lack of political leadership to address some of the region's most pressing human rights issues. A group of countries tried to condemn the crisis in Venezuela, without acknowledging their own failures to respect and protect human rights. After the previous year's financial crisis, the OAS took a step forward by doubling the budget allocation for the Inter-American human rights system – although the funding was to be allocated under certain conditions, which could limit the ability of the Inter-American Commission on Human Rights and the Inter-American Court of Human Rights to hold states accountable for human rights violations.

In the USA, President Trump wasted little time in putting his anti-rights rhetoric of discrimination and xenophobia into action, threatening a major rollback on justice and freedoms – including by signing a series of repressive executive orders that threatened the human rights of millions, at home and abroad.

This included abusive USA-Mexico border enforcement practices such as the increased detention of asylum-seekers and their families; extreme restrictions on women's and girls' access to sexual and reproductive health services in the USA and elsewhere; repeal of protections for LGBTI workers and transgender students; and permission for the Dakota Access Pipeline to be completed – threatening the water source of the Standing Rock Sioux Tribe and other Indigenous Peoples, as well as violating their right to free, prior and informed consent.

Yet growing disenfranchisement did not equate to disengagement. Emerging social discontent inspired people to take to the streets, stand up for their rights and demand an end to repression, marginalization and injustice. Examples included the massive demonstrations in support of activist Santiago Maldonado, who was found dead after going missing in the context of a demonstration marred by police violence in a Mapuche community in Argentina, and the massive social movement of "Ni Una Menos" ("not one less woman") – denouncing femicide and violence against women and girls – in various countries in the region.

Massive grassroots and political opposition in the USA resisted some of the policies and decisions by the Trump administration that undermined human rights, including attempts to ban people from several Muslim-majority countries from entering the USA and to reduce the number of refugees eligible for admission; threats to increase the number of detainees at the US detention centre in Guantánamo Bay; and an attempt to take away health care coverage from millions in the USA.

PUBLIC SECURITY AND HUMAN RIGHTS

VENEZUELA CRISIS

Venezuela faced one of the worst human rights crises in its recent history, fuelled by an escalation of government-sponsored violence. There were growing protests due to rising inflation and a humanitarian crisis caused by shortages of food and medical supplies. Rather than address the food and health crisis, the authorities instituted a premeditated policy of violent repression of any form of dissent. The security forces used abusive and excessive force against protesters, including by throwing tear gas and firing rubber bullets, leading to more than 120 deaths. Thousands of people were arbitrarily detained and there were many reports of torture and other ill-treatment. The judicial system was used to silence dissent, including through the use of military courts to prosecute civilians, and to target and harass human rights defenders.

VIOLENCE AND IMPUNITY IN MEXICO

Mexico's human rights crisis continued, exacerbated by increases in violence and homicides, including a record number of killings of journalists. Arbitrary arrests and detentions remained widespread – often leading to further human rights violations, most of which were not properly investigated. More than 34,000 people remained subject to enforced disappearance, and extrajudicial executions were rife. Torture and other ill-treatment continued to be widespread and were committed with impunity by the security forces, with people routinely forced to sign false "confessions". However, the Senate's approval of a new law on enforced disappearances – following a national public outcry over the case of 43 forcibly disappeared students whose fate and whereabouts remained undisclosed – was a potential step forward, although its eventual implementation will require serious political commitment to ensure justice, truth and reparations. Congress also finally passed a new general law on torture. More concerning was the enactment of a law on interior security that would enable the prolonged presence of the armed forces in regular policing functions, a strategy that has been linked to an increase in human rights violations.

UNLAWFUL KILLINGS

Authorities in Brazil ignored a deepening human rights crisis of their own making. In the city of Rio de Janeiro, a spike in violence saw a surge in unlawful killings by the police, with soaring rates of killings and other human rights violations elsewhere in the country. Little was done to reduce the number of homicides, to control the use of force by the police or to guarantee Indigenous Peoples' rights. The chaotic, overcrowded and dangerous state of Brazil's prisons resulted in more than 120 deaths of inmates during riots reported in January.

Despite the homicide rate falling in Honduras, there were serious concerns about high levels of violence and insecurity; prevalent impunity undermined public trust in the authorities and the justice system. Massive protests took place throughout the country – denouncing the lack of transparency around the presidential election held in November – and were violently repressed by security forces, leading to at least 31 people being killed, dozens arbitrarily detained and others injured.

Dozens of unlawful killings by the security forces were reported in the Dominican Republic, which endured a persistently high homicide rate. Jamaica's police continued to commit unlawful killings – some potentially amounting to extrajudicial executions – with impunity.

PROTESTS

Protests were met with unnecessary and excessive use of force by the authorities in countries including Colombia, Paraguay and Puerto Rico.

In Paraguay, protests erupted after a secret attempt by senators to amend the Constitution to allow presidential re-elections was exposed. The Congress building was set on fire by some protesters, and opposition activist Rodrigo Quintana was killed by police. Dozens of people were injured, more than 200 were detained, and local organizations reported torture and other ill-treatment by security forces.

In Nicaragua, police officers prevented rural communities and Indigenous Peoples from participating in peaceful demonstrations against the construction of the Grand Interoceanic Canal.

In Argentina, more than 30 people were arbitrarily detained by police in the capital, Buenos Aires, for taking part in a demonstration following the death of activist Santiago Maldonado. In December, excessive force was used against protesters in Buenos Aires taking part in massive demonstrations against governmental reforms.

ACCESS TO JUSTICE AND THE FIGHT TO END IMPUNITY

Impunity remained pervasive and a key driver of human rights violations and abuses in many countries.

Ongoing impunity and corruption in Guatemala eroded public trust in the authorities and hampered access to justice. There were large protests in August and September and the country faced a political crisis when members of the government resigned in response to President Jimmy Morales' attempt to expel the head of the International Commission against Impunity in Guatemala, an independent body established by the government and the UN in 2006 to strengthen the rule of law post-conflict.

Impunity for past and present human rights violations remained a concern in Chile. The closure by the authorities of an investigation into the alleged abduction and torture reported by Mapuche leader Víctor Queipul Hueiquil sent a chilling message to human rights defenders across the country, while it appeared that no comprehensive and impartial investigation was carried out. Indigenous leader Machi Francisca Linconao and 10 other Mapuche people were acquitted of terrorism charges, due to a lack of evidence to implicate them in the deaths of two people in January 2013. However, in December the Court of Appeals declared the judgment null. A new trial was due to start in 2018.

CONFRONTING PAST HUMAN RIGHTS VIOLATIONS

Efforts to address unresolved human rights violations often remained slow and sluggish, hampered by a lack of political will.

In Peru, President Pedro Pablo Kuczynski granted a medical pardon and grace to former president Alberto Fujimori, who had been sentenced in 2009 to 25 years' imprisonment for his responsibility for crimes against humanity committed by his subordinates, and was still facing other charges for his alleged responsibility for other human rights violations that could constitute crimes against humanity. Thousands took to the streets to protest against the decision.

In Uruguay, human rights defenders investigating human rights violations that took place during the military regime (1973-1985) reported receiving death threats, the sources of which were not investigated. In November the Supreme Court found that crimes committed during the regime did not amount to crimes against humanity and were, therefore, subject to statutes of limitations.

Yet there was some progress. In Argentina, 29 people were sentenced to life imprisonment for crimes against humanity committed during the 1976-1983 military regime, and a federal court issued a historic decision under which four former members of the judiciary were sentenced to life in prison for contributing to the commission of crimes against humanity during those years.

In Bolivia a Truth Commission was established to investigate serious human rights violations committed under military governments from 1964 to 1982.

There was progress in prosecuting some crimes against humanity committed during Guatemala's internal armed conflict (1960-1996), with five former members of the military sent to trial on charges of crimes against humanity, rape and enforced disappearance. After several failed attempts since 2015, the trials of former military head of state José Efraín Ríos Montt and former intelligence chief José Rodríguez Sánchez finally resumed in October.

REFUGEES, MIGRANTS AND STATELESS PEOPLE

DENIAL OF PROTECTION BY THE USA

Amid a global refugee crisis in which more than 21 million people have been forced to flee their homes due to war and persecution, the USA took extreme steps to deny protection to people in need. In the first few weeks of his administration, President Trump issued executive orders to suspend the country's refugee resettlement programme for 120 days, impose an indefinite ban on the resettlement of refugees from Syria, and reduce the annual refugee admission cap to 50,000.

President Trump also signed an executive order vowing to build a wall along the USA-Mexico border. His order, which pledged to put in place 5,000 additional border patrol agents, carried the risk that more migrants – including many in need of international protection – would be unlawfully pushed back at the border or deported to places where their lives are at risk. The injustice of President Trump's actions was emphasized by Central America's ongoing refugee crisis, and by the appalling situation in Venezuela, which led to an increase in the number of Venezuelans seeking asylum abroad. As conditions for refugees and migrants in the USA deteriorated, there was a significant increase in numbers of asylum-seekers irregularly crossing the border from the USA into Canada.

REFUGEE CRISIS

According to UNHCR, the UN refugee agency, more than 57,000 people from Honduras, Guatemala and El Salvador sought asylum in other countries. Many were forced back home, where a lack of an effective system to protect them meant they faced the same dangers and conditions from which they had fled. Thousands of families and unaccompanied children from those countries migrated to the USA through Mexico and were apprehended at the US border.

Mexico received a record number of asylum applications, mostly from nationals of El Salvador, Honduras, Guatemala and Venezuela, but repeatedly failed to provide protection to those who needed it – instead pushing people back to highly dangerous and even life-threatening situations.

Argentina's reception system for asylum-seekers remained slow and insufficient, and there was no integration plan in place to help asylum-seekers and refugees access basic rights such as education, work and health care.

Cubans continued to leave the country in large numbers, pushed by low wages and undue restrictions on freedom of expression.

STATELESS AND INTERNALLY DISPLACED PEOPLE

The Dominican Republic's statelessness crisis continued to affect tens of thousands of people of Haitian descent who were born in the country but were left stateless after being retroactively and arbitrarily deprived of their Dominican nationality in 2013. Those affected were denied a range of human rights and were prevented from accessing higher education, formal employment or adequate health care.

In Haiti, almost 38,000 people remained internally displaced because of the 2010 earthquake. There was a reported increase in deportation cases at the Dominican-Haitian border.

INDIGENOUS PEOPLES' RIGHTS

Indigenous Peoples' rights continued to be violated in countries including Argentina, Bolivia, Canada, Chile, Colombia, Ecuador, Honduras, Nicaragua and Peru.

VIOLENCE AGAINST INDIGENOUS PEOPLES

Indigenous Peoples continued to be criminalized and discriminated against in Argentina, where the authorities used legal proceedings to harass them; there were reports of police attacks, including beatings and intimidation. Rafael Nahuel of the Mapuche community was killed in November during an eviction conducted by security forces.

In Colombia, a wave of killings of Indigenous people from communities historically affected by the armed conflict highlighted shortcomings in the implementation of the peace agreement. The killing of Gerson Acosta – leader of the Kite Kiwe Indigenous council in Timbío, Cauca, who was shot repeatedly while leaving a community meeting – was a tragic example of the ineffectiveness of the authorities' measures to safeguard the lives and safety of community leaders and other Indigenous people.

The Inter-American Commission on Human Rights documented the different forms of discrimination faced by Indigenous women in the Americas and highlighted how their political, social and economic marginalization contributed to permanent structural discrimination, leaving them at increased risk of violence.

LAND RIGHTS

In Peru, new laws weakened the protection of Indigenous Peoples' rights related to land and territory and undermined their right to free, prior and informed consent. The government neglected the right to health of hundreds of Indigenous Peoples whose only water sources were contaminated with toxic metals, and who lacked access to adequate health care.

In Ecuador, the right to free, prior and informed consent of Indigenous Peoples continued to be violated, including after intrusions of the state into their territories for future oil extraction.

Indigenous Peoples in Paraguay also continued to be denied their rights to land and to free, prior and informed consent on projects affecting them. Despite rulings from the Inter-American Court of Human Rights, the government failed to provide the Yakye Axa community access to their lands, or to resolve a case regarding the ownership of land expropriated from the Sawhoyamaxa community.

Guatemala's Supreme Court recognized the lack of prior consultation with the Xinca Indigenous People of Santa Rosa and Jalapa, who were negatively affected by mining activities.

In Brazil, conflicts over land, and invasion by illegal loggers and mine workers into Indigenous Peoples' territory, resulted in violent attacks against Indigenous communities.

HUMAN RIGHTS DEFENDERS AND JOURNALISTS

The extreme risks and dangers of defending human rights were apparent in numerous countries in the region, with human rights defenders facing threats, harassment and attacks including in Bolivia, Brazil, Chile, Ecuador, Honduras, Mexico, Nicaragua and Paraguay.

KILLINGS AND HARASSMENT IN MEXICO

In Mexico, human rights defenders were threatened, attacked and killed, with digital attacks and surveillance especially common. During the year, at least 12 journalists were killed – the largest number recorded since 2000 – many in public places in daylight, with the authorities making no notable progress in investigating and prosecuting those responsible. Victims included prize-winning journalist Javier Valdez, who was killed in May near the office of the newspaper *Ríodoce*, which he founded. It became apparent that a network of people was using the internet to harass and threaten journalists throughout Mexico. Evidence also emerged of surveillance against journalists and human rights defenders, using software that the government was known to have purchased.

HUMAN RIGHTS DEFENDERS AT RISK IN HONDURAS

Honduras remained one of the region's most dangerous countries for human rights defenders – especially those working to protect land, territory and the environment. They were targeted by both state and non-state actors, subjected to smear campaigns to discredit their work, and regularly faced intimidation, threats and attacks. Most attacks registered against human rights defenders went unpunished. There was little progress in the investigation into the March 2016 killing of Indigenous environmental defender Berta Cáceres. Since her murder, several other Honduran environmental and human rights activists have been harassed and threatened.

INCREASED ATTACKS IN COLOMBIA

There was an increase in the number of attacks against human rights defenders in Colombia, especially community leaders, defenders of land, territory and the environment, and those campaigning in favour of the peace agreement. According to the Office of the UN High Commissioner for Human Rights, almost 100 human rights defenders were killed during the year. Many death threats against activists were attributed to paramilitary groups, but in most cases the authorities failed to identify who was responsible for the killings that resulted from the threats.

ARBITRARY DETENTIONS, THREATS AND HARASSMENT

In Cuba, large numbers of human rights defenders and political activists continued to be harassed, intimidated, dismissed from state employment and arbitrarily detained to silence criticism. Online and offline censorship undermined advances in education. Prisoners of conscience included the leader of the pro-democracy Christian Liberation Movement, Eduardo Cardet Concepción, who was jailed for three years for publicly criticizing former president Fidel Castro.

Human rights defenders in Guatemala, especially those working on land, territorial and environmental issues, faced ongoing threats and attacks, and were subjected to smear campaigns. The justice system was also frequently misused to target, harass and silence human rights defenders.

A ruling by Peru's Supreme Court confirming the acquittal of human rights defender Máxima Acuña Atalaya after five years of unfounded criminal proceedings for land seizure was a landmark decision for environmental defenders.

RIGHTS OF WOMEN AND GIRLS

Women and girls across the region continued to be subjected to a wide range of violations and abuses, including gender-based violence and discrimination and violations of sexual and reproductive rights.

VIOLENCE AGAINST WOMEN AND GIRLS

Violence against women and girls remained prevalent. Impunity for crimes such as rape, killings and threats was widespread and entrenched, often underpinned by weak political will, limited resources to investigate and bring perpetrators to justice, and an unchallenged patriarchal culture.

Ongoing gender-based violence in the Dominican Republic resulted in an increase in the number of killings of women and girls. Gender-based violence against women and girls was also a major concern in Mexico and worsened in Nicaragua.

In Jamaica, women's movements and survivors of gender-based and sexual violence took to the streets to protest against impunity for such crimes.

There was an increase in the number of killings of women in leadership roles in Colombia, and no clear progress in ensuring access to justice for women survivors of sexual violence. However, women's organizations ensured that the Peace Agreement established that people suspected of having committed crimes of sexual violence would be required to appear before transitional justice tribunals.

In Cuba, The Ladies in White – a group of female relatives of prisoners detained on politically motivated grounds – remained a key target of repression by the authorities.

Canada's federal government released a strategy to combat gender-based violence, and committed to placing women's rights, gender equality and sexual and reproductive rights at the core of its foreign policy. A law to combat violence against women entered into force in Paraguay in December, although it remained unclear how it would be funded.

SEXUAL AND REPRODUCTIVE RIGHTS

THE USA'S "GLOBAL GAG RULE"

In January, two days after massive worldwide demonstrations for equality and against discrimination, US President Trump put at risk the lives and health of millions of women and girls around the world by reinstating the so-called "global gag rule". This blocked US financial assistance to any hospitals or organizations that provide abortion information about, or access to, safe and legal abortion care, or that advocate the decriminalization of abortion or the expansion of abortion services.

In Latin America alone – where experts estimate that 760,000 women are treated annually from complications of unsafe abortion – President Trump's stance put many more lives at risk.

CRIMINALIZATION OF ABORTION

A ruling by Chile's Constitutional Tribunal to support the decriminalization of abortion in certain cases left just seven countries worldwide persisting with a total ban on abortion, even when the life or health of the woman or girl is at risk. Six of those countries were in the Americas region: the Dominican Republic, El Salvador, Haiti, Honduras, Nicaragua and Suriname.

In El Salvador, 19-year-old Evelyn Beatriz Hernández Cruz was jailed for 30 years on charges of aggravated homicide, after suffering obstetric complications resulting in a miscarriage. In December, a court confirmed the 30-year sentence of Teodora, a woman who suffered a stillbirth in 2007.

The Dominican Republic's Senate voted against a proposal that would have decriminalized abortion in certain circumstances. In Honduras, Congress also maintained the ban on abortion in all circumstances in the new Criminal Code.

In Argentina, women and girls faced obstacles in accessing legal abortion when the pregnancy posed a risk to their health or resulted from rape; full decriminalization of abortion was pending in Parliament. In Uruguay, sexual and reproductive health services were difficult to access in rural areas, and objectors to providing abortion continued to obstruct access to legal abortions.

In October, the Ministry of Education and Science of Paraguay issued a resolution banning the inclusion in educational materials of basic information about human rights, sexual and reproductive health education and diversity, among other subjects.

In Bolivia – where unsafe abortions were one of the main causes of maternal mortality – the Criminal Code was amended to significantly expand access to legal abortion.

RIGHTS OF LESBIAN, GAY, BISEXUAL, TRANSGENDER AND INTERSEX PEOPLE

LGBTI people faced persistent discrimination, harassment and violence in the region, including in Haiti, Honduras and Jamaica.

In Bolivia the Constitutional Court invalidated part of a law which granted civil marriage rights to transgender people who had changed their gender on their identity documents. The country's Ombudsman proposed an amendment to the Criminal Code to make hate crimes against LGBTI people a criminal offence.

In the Dominican Republic the body of a transgender woman, Jessica Rubi Mori, was found dismembered in wasteland. By the end of the year, no one had been brought to justice for her killing.

In Uruguay there remained no comprehensive anti-discrimination policy protecting LGBTI people from violence in schools and public spaces, or ensuring their access to health services.

ARMED CONFLICT

Despite the opportunities presented by the Peace Agreement in Colombia, legislation remained unimplemented on most of its points, and there were serious concerns around impunity for crimes committed during the conflict.

Ongoing human rights violations and abuses also demonstrated that the internal conflict between the Revolutionary Armed Forces of Colombia (FARC) and the security forces was far from over, and in some areas it appeared to intensify. Civilian populations continued to be the main victims of the conflict – especially Indigenous Peoples, Afro-descendant and peasant farmer communities, and human rights defenders.

A spike in the number of human rights activists killed at the beginning of the year highlighted the dangers faced by those exposing ongoing abuses in Colombia.

ASIA-PACIFIC REGIONAL OVERVIEW

The human rights landscape of the Asia-Pacific region was mostly characterized by government failures. However, these frequently contrasted with an inspiring and growing movement of human rights defenders and activists.

Many countries saw a shrinking space for civil society. Human rights defenders, lawyers, journalists and others found themselves the target of state repression – from an unprecedented crackdown on freedom of expression in China to sweeping intolerance of dissent in Cambodia and Thailand and enforced disappearances in Bangladesh and Pakistan.

Impunity was widespread – breeding and sustaining violations including unlawful killings and torture, denying justice and reparation to millions, and fuelling crimes against humanity or war crimes in countries such as Myanmar and Afghanistan.

The global refugee crisis worsened. Hundreds of thousands in the region were forced to flee their homes and faced uncertain, often violent, futures. Their numbers were swelled by the Myanmar military's crimes against humanity in northern Rakhine State where the army burned entire Rohingya villages, killed adults and children, and raped women and girls. The mass violations forced more than 655,000 Rohingya to escape persecution by fleeing to Bangladesh. Those who remained continued to live under a systematically discriminatory system amounting to apartheid which severely restricted virtually every aspect of their lives and segregated them from the rest of society.

ASEAN, chaired by the Philippines during 2017, marked its 50th anniversary. ASEAN governments and institutions remained silent over the massive violations in the Philippines, Myanmar and elsewhere in the region.

Against this backdrop, growing calls to respect and protect human rights in Asia-Pacific, increasingly by young people, delivered some progress and hope. There were advances in policing in the Republic of Korea (South Korea), and positive court rulings on corporate accountability in South Korea; on marriage equality in Australia and Taiwan; and on the right to privacy in India.

EAST ASIA

The authorities in Japan, Mongolia and South Korea all failed to adequately protect human rights defenders. Human rights defenders were specifically targeted and persecuted in China. A notable shrinking of space for civil society was especially apparent in China, and was of increasing concern in Hong Kong and Japan.

Human rights protection was diluted in Japan where parliament adopted an overly broad law targeting "terrorism" and other serious crimes, despite harsh criticism from civil society and academics. This law gave the authorities broad surveillance powers that could be misused to curtail human rights.

Following a change of government in South Korea, the national police accepted recommendations for a change in the overall approach of policing in order to allow the full and free exercise of the right to freedom of peaceful assembly. Also in South Korea, while hundreds of conscientious objectors were imprisoned, an increasing number of lower courts handed down decisions recognizing the right to conscientious objection, and court rulings acknowledged the responsibility of multinational corporations for work-related death or illness of employees.

The consecration of President Xi Jinping as China's most powerful leader for many years took place against the backdrop of a stifling of freedom of expression and information. Authorities increasingly used "national security" as justification for restriction of human rights and detention of activists; the tactic escalated significantly in the Xinjiang Uighur Autonomous Region (XUAR) where, under the leadership of new regional Communist Party Secretary Chen Quanguo, authorities put new emphasis on "social stability" and increased technological surveillance, armed street patrols and security checkpoints and implemented an array of intrusive policies violating human rights. Authorities set up detention facilities within the XUAR, variously called "counter extremism centres", "political study centres" or "education and transformation centres", in which people were arbitrarily detained for unspecified periods and forced to study Chinese laws and policies.

Citizens of the Democratic People's Republic of Korea (North Korea) continued to face a series of grave human rights violations, some of which amounted to crimes against humanity. The rights to freedom of expression and movement were severely restricted, and up to 120,000 people continued to be arbitrarily detained in political prison camps, where they were subjected to forced labour, torture and other ill-treatment.

HUMAN RIGHTS DEFENDERS

The Chinese authorities continued their unprecedented crackdown on dissent with a ruthless campaign of arbitrary arrests, detention, imprisonment and torture and other ill-treatment of human rights lawyers and activists. The authorities persisted in the use of "residential surveillance in a designated location", a form of secret incommunicado detention that allowed the police to hold individuals for up to six months outside the formal detention system, without access to legal counsel of their choice, their families or others, and placed suspects at risk of torture and other ill-treatment. This form of detention was used to curb the activities of human rights defenders, including lawyers, activists and religious practitioners.

The government also continued to imprison those trying to commemorate peacefully the Tiananmen Square crackdown of 3-4 June 1989 in the capital, Beijing, in which hundreds, if not thousands, of protesters were killed or injured after the People's Liberation Army opened fire on unarmed civilians. Nobel Peace Prize laureate Liu Xiabo died in custody in July.

In Hong Kong, the repeated use of vague charges against prominent pro-democracy movement figures appeared to be an orchestrated and retaliatory campaign by the authorities to punish and intimidate those advocating democracy or challenging the authorities.

PEOPLE ON THE MOVE

In Japan, while asylum applications continued to increase, the government reported in February that it had approved 28 out of 10,901 claims in 2016, which was a 44% increase in claims from the previous year. Meanwhile, to address the country's labour shortage, Japan began to accept the first of 10,000 Vietnamese nationals to be admitted over three years under a labour migration programme harshly criticized by human rights advocates for facilitating a wide range of abuses.

In South Korea, deaths of migrant workers raised concerns about safety in the workplace. North Korean authorities continued to dispatch workers to other countries, including China and Russia, although some countries stopped renewing or issuing additional work visas to North Koreans in order to comply with the new UN sanctions on North Korea's economic activities abroad in response to the country's missile tests.

DISCRIMINATION

In China, religious repression remained particularly severe in the XUAR and in Tibetan-populated areas.

Discrimination against LGBTI people remained prevalent in public life in South Korea. Gay men faced violence, bullying and verbal abuse during compulsory military service. A serving soldier was convicted of same-sex sexual activity.

Although pervasive discrimination based on real or perceived sexual orientation and gender identity continued in Japan, there was some progress in local municipalities. For the first time in the city of Osaka, the authorities approved a same-sex couple as foster parents, and two other municipalities took positive steps towards recognizing same-sex partnerships.

A landmark ruling by its highest court saw Taiwan close to becoming the first Asian country to legalize same-sex marriage, in a major step forward for LGBTI rights. The judges ruled the country's marriage law unconstitutional as it discriminated against same-sex couples, and gave lawmakers two years to amend or enact relevant laws. A bill on same-sex marriage was being considered by Taiwan's legislature.

DEATH PENALTY

China remained the world's leading executioner, although capital punishment statistics continued to be classified as state secrets.

Taiwan's Supreme Court rejected the Prosecutor General's extraordinary appeal for the retrial of the longest-serving death row inmate in Taiwan's modern history; Chiou Ho-shun, on death row since 1989, claimed that he was tortured and forced to "confess" during police interrogations.

In July, Mongolia became the 105th country worldwide to abolish the death penalty for all crimes, yet in November the President proposed its reintroduction to the Ministry of Justice in response to two violent rape and murder cases.

SOUTH ASIA

Across South Asia, governments invoked law and order, national security and religion as they engaged in attacks against religious minorities, criminalization of freedom of expression, enforced disappearances, prolific use of the death penalty, and assaults on refugee rights. Impunity was widespread.

Freedom of expression was under attack across South Asia. Using vague concepts such as "the national interest" as an excuse to silence people, governments targeted journalists, human rights defenders and others for peacefully expressing their beliefs.

A new trend involved criminalizing online freedom of expression. In Pakistan, five bloggers critical of the government were subjected to enforced disappearance. Other bloggers were arrested for comments criticizing the military or allegedly expressing remarks deemed "anti-Islamic". Criticism of the Bangladesh government or the family of the Prime Minister also triggered criminal cases. The government proposed a new Digital Security Act, which would place even greater restrictions on the right to freedom of expression and impose heavier penalties. In Afghanistan, where internet penetration is among the lowest in the Asia-Pacific region, a new Cyber Crime Law was passed criminalizing freedom of expression.

Failures to uphold economic, cultural and social rights had major impacts. As a result of Pakistan failing to bring its laws into line with international standards, the population suffered widespread discrimination, curtailed workers' rights, and meagre social security. India ratified two ILO core conventions on child labour, but activists remained critical of amendments to the country's child labour laws that allowed children to work in family enterprises. Two years after a massive earthquake shook Nepal, the government was still failing thousands of marginalized earthquake survivors who languished in flimsy temporary shelters.

In October, Pakistan was elected to the UN Human Rights Council, pledging commitment to human rights. Yet it failed to address directly Pakistan's serious human rights issues, including enforced disappearances; the death penalty; blasphemy laws; the use of military courts to try civilians; women's rights; and threats to the work of human rights defenders.

Killings, abductions and other abuses were committed by armed groups in Afghanistan, Bangladesh, India and Pakistan, among others. Civilian casualties, particularly of religious minorities, continued to be high in Afghanistan. In Pakistan, armed groups targeted Shi'a Muslims, including by bombing a Shi'a mosque in Quetta, killing at least 18 people.

Violations around Nepal's historic local elections included arbitrary arrests and detention, and the security forces opening fire on protesters at an election rally.

In the Indian state of Jammu and Kashmir, security forces killed eight people following protests during a by-election for a parliamentary seat; one voter was beaten by army personnel, strapped to the front of an army jeep and driven around for over five hours, seemingly as a warning to other protesters. The security forces also persisted in their use of inherently inaccurate pellet-firing shotguns during protests – blinding and otherwise injuring several people.

HUMAN RIGHTS DEFENDERS

In India, the authorities were openly critical of human rights defenders, contributing to a climate of hostility and violence against them. Repressive laws were used to stifle freedom of expression, and journalists and press freedom came under increasing attack.

Human rights defenders in Afghanistan faced constant threats to their life and security from armed groups and state actors, and journalists faced violence and censorship.

Pakistan authorities failed to protect journalists, bloggers, and civil society and activists who faced constant harassment, intimidation, threats, smear campaigns and attacks from non-state actors. Instead, the authorities increased restrictions on the work of scores of NGOs, and subjected many activists to attacks, including torture and enforced disappearances.

In Bangladesh, the government intensified its crackdown on public debate and criticism. Media workers were harassed and prosecuted under draconian laws. The government failed to hold accountable armed groups that carried out a high-profile spate of killings of secular bloggers. Activists regularly received death threats, forcing some to leave the country.

In Maldives, restrictions on public debate intensified. The authorities harassed journalists, activists and media outlets. The government was apparently behind a relentless assault on the rule of law that compromised the judiciary's independence.

IMPUNITY

Impunity was widespread and entrenched across South Asia. However, in Nepal, a district court sentenced three army officers to life imprisonment for the murder in 2004 of Maina Sunuwar, a 15-year-old girl; she died after being tortured in army custody during the decade-long armed conflict between Maoists and government forces that ended in 2006. The convictions were an important development in the justice system's ability to deal with grave conflict-era abuses, and offered the first sign of justice for victims.

In India, the Supreme Court directed the Central Bureau of Investigation to investigate more than 80 alleged extrajudicial executions by police and security force personnel in the state of Manipur between 1979 and 2012, ruling that cases should not go uninvestigated merely because of the passage of time.

ENFORCED DISAPPEARANCES

Enforced disappearances continued in Pakistan; the victims were at considerable risk of torture and other ill-treatment, and even death. No perpetrators were known to have been brought to justice for the hundreds or thousands of cases reported across the country in recent years.

Despite the Sri Lankan government's 2015 pledge to deliver truth, justice and reparation to victims of the armed conflict in the country, and to deliver reforms to prevent violations, progress was slow. Impunity for enforced disappearances remained. The government stalled on its commitment to repeal the draconian Prevention of Terrorism Act that enabled incommunicado and secret detention. However, the parliament passed an amended Office on Missing Persons Act, intended to assist families of the disappeared seek missing relatives.

Enforced disappearances were committed in Bangladesh; the victims often belonged to opposition political parties.

PEOPLE ON THE MOVE

In different parts of South Asia, refugees and migrants were denied their rights.

Bangladesh had opened its borders to more than 655,000 members of the Rohingya community fleeing a campaign of ethnic cleansing in Myanmar. However, if the Rohingya refugees were forced to return to Myanmar, they would be at the mercy of the same military that drove them out and would continue to face the entrenched system of discrimination and segregation amounting to apartheid that made them so vulnerable in the first place.

The number of internally displaced people in Afghanistan rose to more than 2 million, while about 2.6 million Afghan refugees lived outside the country.

DISCRIMINATION

Across South Asia, dissenting voices and members of religious minorities were increasingly vulnerable to attacks from mobs. In India, several cases of lynching of Muslims were reported, sparking outrage against the wave of rising Islamophobia under the Hindu nationalist government. Demonstrations against attacks on Muslims were held in several cities, but the government did little to show that it disapproved of the violence. Indigenous Adivasi communities in India continued to be displaced by industrial projects.

In Bangladesh, attacks against religious minorities were met with near-indifference by the government. Those who sought help from the authorities after they received threats were often turned away.

Sri Lanka saw a rise in Buddhist nationalist sentiment, including attacks against Christians and Muslims. The Maldives government used religion to cloak its repressive practices, including attacks against members of the opposition and plans to reintroduce the death penalty.

Marginalized communities in Pakistan faced discrimination in law, policy and practice because of their gender, religion, nationality, sexual orientation or gender identity. Pakistan's blasphemy laws, which carry a mandatory death penalty for "blasphemy against the Prophet Muhammad", remained incompatible with a range of rights. The frequently misused laws were disproportionately applied to religious minorities and others targeted with accusations that were often false and violated international human rights law. A man was sentenced to death for allegedly posting content on Facebook deemed "blasphemous" – the harshest sentence handed down to date in Pakistan for a cyber crime-related offence.

GENDER-BASED DISCRIMINATION

Although India's Supreme Court banned the practice of triple talaq (Islamic instant divorce), other court rulings undermined women's autonomy. The Supreme Court weakened a law enacted to protect women from violence in marriage. Several rape survivors, including girls, approached the courts for permission to terminate pregnancies over 20 weeks, as required under Indian law; although courts approved some abortions, they refused others. The central government instructed states to set up permanent medical boards to decide such cases promptly.

In Pakistan, the rape of a teenage girl ordered by a so-called village council in "revenge" for a rape allegedly committed by her brother was one in a long series of horrific cases. Although people from the council were arrested for ordering the rape, the authorities failed to end impunity for sexual violence and abolish so-called village councils that prescribed crimes of sexual violence as revenge. Pakistan also continued to criminalize same-sex consensual relationships.

Violence against women and girls persisted in Afghanistan, where an increase was reported in the number of women publicly punished in the name of Shari'a law by armed groups.

DEATH PENALTY

Against the backdrop of a worsening political crisis, the authorities in Maldives announced that executions would resume after more than 60 years. None had been carried out by the end of the year.

Pakistan had executed hundreds of people since it lifted an informal moratorium on executions in 2014, often with serious additional concerns that those executed were denied the right to a fair trial. In violation of international law, courts imposed the death penalty on people with mental disabilities, individuals aged below 18 when the crime was committed, and those whose convictions were based on "confessions" extracted through torture or other ill-treatment.

ARMED CONFLICT

The situation in Afghanistan continued to deteriorate, with the number of civilian casualties remaining high, a growing internal displacement crisis, and the Taliban controlling more territory than at any point since 2001. Since 2014, tens of thousands of Afghan refugees have been returned against their will from Pakistan, Iran and EU countries.

The Afghanistan government and the international community showed too little concern for the plight of civilians. When crowds protested against violence and insecurity following one of the deadliest attacks – a bombing in Kabul on 31 May that claimed the lives of more than 150 people and injured hundreds – the security forces opened fire on the crowds, killing several protesters.

In a welcome development, the Prosecutor of the International Criminal Court requested that a preliminary investigation be opened into crimes alleged to have been committed by all parties to the ongoing armed conflict in Afghanistan. The decision was an important step towards ensuring accountability for crimes under international law committed since 2003, and providing truth, justice and reparation for the victims.

SOUTHEAST ASIA AND THE PACIFIC

Many of those taking action to demand respect for human rights and accountability for violations were demonized and criminalized, leading to shrinking civic space. Police and security forces persecuted human rights defenders. Extrajudicial killings, torture and other ill-treatment, and enforced disappearances persisted with impunity.

The Myanmar security forces' campaign of violence against the Rohingya people in northern Rakhine State, which amounted to crimes against humanity, created a human rights and humanitarian crisis in the country and in neighbouring Bangladesh.

Lawlessness and violence increased further in the Philippines. The President's contempt for human rights in the "war on drugs" was characterized by mass killings, mostly of people from poor and marginalized groups, including children. The scope of the killings and rampant impunity led to growing calls for an investigation at the international level. The extension of martial law in the island of Mindanao in December led to concerns that military rule could be used to justify further human rights abuses. The government attempted to reintroduce the death penalty.

In Indonesia, police killings of suspected drug dealers rose sharply.

Australia continued to pay lip service to human rights while subjecting asylum-seekers and refugees to cruel, inhuman and degrading treatment.

Governments in Southeast Asia and the Pacific failed to uphold economic, social and cultural rights. Villagers in Laos were forced to relocate due to development projects; the right to adequate housing in Cambodia was undermined by land grabbing; and housing conditions for foreign workers in Singapore were criticized as poor by NGOs.

National elections were held in Papua New Guinea, amid allegations of corruption and heavy-handed actions by the authorities, including violence and arbitrary arrests.

HUMAN RIGHTS DEFENDERS

Human rights defenders, peaceful political activists and religious followers were subjected to violations including arbitrary detention; they faced vaguely worded charges; and they were tried in trials that did not meet internationally defined standards of fairness. Prisoners of conscience were tortured and otherwise ill-treated.

In Cambodia, the government's relentless crackdown on civil society and political activists intensified ahead of a general election scheduled for 2018. Human rights defenders were monitored, arrested and imprisoned; media outlets were shut; harassment of civil society through misuse of the criminal justice system escalated; and an amendment to existing legislation provided the authorities with additional powers over political parties. The judiciary was used as a political tool to silence dissent, and in a blatant act of political repression the Supreme Court ruled to dissolve the main opposition party ahead of the election.

Thailand's military government continued its systematic suppression of dissent, preventing people from speaking or assembling peacefully, and criminalizing and targeting civil society. Dozens of human rights defenders, pro-democracy activists and others faced investigation and prosecution under draconian laws and decrees, many facing lengthy, unfair proceedings before military courts.

An ongoing crackdown on civil and political rights by Malaysia's government included harassment, detention and prosecution of critics through the use of restrictive laws; an increase in open-ended, arbitrary travel bans that violated human rights defenders' freedom of movement; and the arrest and investigation of Indigenous rights activists and journalists for peacefully demonstrating against abuses.

Fiji's government used restrictive legislation to stifle the media and curtail freedom of expression and peaceful assembly. Charges against staff members of the *Fiji Times* were changed to sedition, in a politically motivated move designed to silence one of the country's few remaining independent media outlets.

Amendments to Singapore's Public Order Act gave the authorities greater powers to restrict or ban public assemblies, and human rights defenders were investigated by police for taking part in peaceful protests. Charges were brought against lawyers and academics who criticized the judiciary, and restrictions placed on media freedom.

In Laos, the rights to freedom of expression, association and peaceful assembly remained severely curtailed and criminal code provisions were used to imprison peaceful activists.

A crackdown on dissent in Viet Nam intensified, forcing numerous activists to flee the country.

Erosion of the space for a free press increased in Myanmar, where journalists and other media workers faced intimidation and at times arrest, detention and prosecution in connection with their work.

IMPUNITY

Impunity for deaths in custody and unnecessary or excessive use of force and firearms persisted in Malaysia. There were several deaths in custody, including that of S. Balamurugan who was reportedly beaten by police during interrogation.

In Indonesia's Papua province there was a lack of accountability for unnecessary or excessive use of force during mass protests or other security operations. Fiji's government failed to ensure accountability for torture and other ill-treatment of detainees by the security forces.

In Timor-Leste, victims of serious human rights violations committed during the Indonesian occupation (1975-1999) continued to demand justice and reparations.

MYANMAR'S CAMPAIGN OF VIOLENCE AGAINST THE ROHINGYA

The security forces launched a targeted campaign of ethnic cleansing, including unlawful killings, rape and burning of villages – amounting to crimes against humanity – against the Rohingya people in northern Rakhine State. The atrocities – an unlawful and disproportionate response to attacks on security posts by an armed Rohingya group in August – created the worst refugee crisis in decades in Southeast Asia. Severe restrictions imposed by Myanmar on aid groups working in Rakhine State worsened the suffering.

More than 655,000 Rohingya people fled to Bangladesh. By the end of the year, nearly 1 million Rohingya refugees were scattered across Bangladesh's Cox's Bazar District, including those who had fled earlier waves of violence. Those who remained in Myanmar continued to live under a regime amounting to apartheid in which their rights, including to equality before the law and freedom of movement, as well as access to health, education and work, were severely restricted.

The Myanmar security forces were primarily responsible for the violence against the Rohingya. However, the civilian administration led by Aung San Suu Kyi failed to speak out or intervene. Instead it maligned humanitarian workers, accusing them of aiding "terrorists" while denying the violations.

Despite mounting evidence of atrocities in Myanmar, the international community, including the UN Security Council, failed to take effective action or send a clear message that there would be accountability for the military's crimes against humanity.

PEOPLE ON THE MOVE

Australia maintained its hardline policies of confining hundreds of people seeking asylum in offshore processing centres in Papua New Guinea and Nauru, and turning back those attempting to reach Australia by boat – failing in its international obligation to protect them.

Refugees and asylum-seekers remained trapped on Nauru, forcibly sent there by the Australian government – most more than four years previously – despite widespread reports of physical, psychological and sexual abuse. Several hundred people living in the offshore processing facility, including dozens of children, faced humiliation, abuse, neglect and poor physical and mental health care. More than 800 others living in the community faced serious security risks as well as inadequate access to health care, education and employment opportunities.

The Australian government withdrew services from its facility on Manus Island in Papua New Guinea at the end of October in order to force refugees to move closer to town where refugees and asylum-seekers had well-founded fears for their safety. Refugees were forcibly moved to new but unfinished facilities in November. They continued to face challenges with inadequate health care, violence in the community and no clear plans for their future.

Fiji forcibly returned people to countries where they might be at risk of serious violations.

Cambodia rejected 29 applications for refugee status by Montagnard asylum-seekers, forcibly returning them to Viet Nam where they faced possible persecution.

DISCRIMINATION

Australia's justice system continued to fail Indigenous people, especially children – with high rates of incarceration and reports of abuse and deaths in custody. Ill-treatment of Indigenous children in the Northern Territory, including tear gassing, choking, restraints and solitary confinement, was exposed by leaked footage.

LGBTI people suffered discrimination in Malaysia, Papua New Guinea and Singapore. Reports of hate speech against members of Australia's lesbian, gay, bisexual, transgender, intersex and questioning (LGBTIQ) community increased, despite newly introduced penalties. In Indonesia's Aceh province two men were publicly caned 83 times each for consensual same-sex sexual activity.

Numerous women defending human rights faced harassment, threats, imprisonment and violence.

Papua New Guinea remained one of the world's most dangerous countries to be a woman, with increased reports of violence against women or girls, sometimes following sorcery accusations.

There were convictions under Indonesia's blasphemy laws of people belonging to minority religious communities who had been peacefully practising their beliefs.

The Australian Parliament passed legislation to create marriage equality in December. The postal survey process chosen by the government failed to acknowledge that marriage equality is a human right and generated divisive and damaging public debate.

DEATH PENALTY

At least four executions took place in Malaysia. In Singapore execution by hanging continued to be carried out for murder and drug trafficking; among those executed was Malaysian national Prabagaran Srivijayan whose execution was carried out despite an appeal pending in Malaysia.

ARMED CONFLICT

Although receiving less international attention than the situation in Rakhine State, there were similar patterns of violations by Myanmar's military in northern Myanmar. War crimes and human rights violations were committed against civilians in Kachin and northern Shan States, including extrajudicial executions, enforced disappearances, torture, indiscriminate shelling, forced labour, and restrictions on humanitarian access. Ethnic armed groups committed abuses including abductions and forced recruitment. Both the army and armed groups used landmine-like weapons that harmed civilians.

In the Philippines, a five-month battle in Marawi between the military and an alliance of militants aligned with the armed group calling itself Islamic State (IS), caused the displacement of hundreds of thousands of civilians, dozens of civilian deaths, and widespread destruction of homes and infrastructure. The militants targeted Christian civilians for extrajudicial killings and mass hostage-taking, and the armed forces detained and ill-treated fleeing civilians.

CORPORATE RESPONSIBILITY

Communities living close to the giant Letpadaung copper mine in Myanmar continued to call for a halt to its operations. Thousands of families living near the mine were at risk of being forcibly evicted from their homes or farmland, and the authorities used repressive laws to harass activists and villagers.

In Indonesia there was labour exploitation on plantations owned by suppliers and subsidiaries of Wilmar International, the world's largest palm oil trader. Abuses included women being forced to work long hours under threat of having their already meagre pay cut, children as young as eight doing hazardous physical work, and workers injured by toxic chemicals. Wilmar International's subsequent campaign to cover up the abuses, including by intimidating staff into denying the allegations, was aided by the Indonesian government's failure to investigate claims against the company.

EUROPE AND CENTRAL ASIA REGIONAL OVERVIEW

The space for civil society continued to shrink across Europe and Central Asia region. In Eastern Europe and in Central Asia, a discourse hostile to human rights remained prevalent. Human rights defenders, activists, the media and political opposition were frequently targeted by authorities. Across the region, the rights to freedom of association and peaceful assembly and the right to freedom of opinion and expression came under attack. Public protests were met with a range of restrictive measures and excessive use of force by police. Governments continued to implement a range of counter-terrorism measures disproportionately restricting people's rights in the name of security. Millions of people faced an erosion of their economic, social and cultural rights, which led to diminished social protection, increased inequality and systemic discrimination. States repeatedly failed to meet their protection responsibilities towards refugees and migrants. Women and girls continued to experience systemic human rights violations and abuses, including torture and other ill-treatment, and faced widespread gender-based violence. Discrimination and stigmatization of minorities remained common with groups facing harassment and violence. Some prisoners of conscience were released.

In 2017, for the first time in Amnesty International's almost 60 years of existence, both the chair and director of an Amnesty International section became prisoners of conscience themselves. In June, Taner Kılıç, Chair of Amnesty International Turkey, was arrested. In July, 10 other human rights defenders, known as the "Istanbul 10", including Idil Eser, Director of Amnesty International Turkey, were detained while attending a routine workshop in Istanbul. The Istanbul 10 and Taner Kılıç were later put on trial for terrorism-related offences, their arrests falling into a broader pattern of repression against civil society following the failed coup attempt of July 2016. By the end of the year, the Istanbul 10 had been released pending trial, but Taner Kılıç remained in detention. Although the prosecutor failed to provide any incriminating evidence against them, they remained at serious risk, facing an ongoing trial on absurd charges carrying up to 15 years' imprisonment.

The crackdown on dissenting voices in Turkey was part of a broader trend of shrinking space for civil society across Europe and Central Asia. Human rights defenders faced huge challenges, and the rights to freedom of association and assembly in particular came under attack.

In the east, a discourse hostile to human rights remained prevalent, frequently leading to the repression of human rights defenders, political opposition, protest movements, anti-corruption campaigners and sexual minorities. This hostile discourse also inched westward and found its first legislative expression in Hungary with the adoption of a law effectively stigmatizing NGOs that received foreign funding.

Violent attacks caused deaths and injuries, including in Barcelona, Brussels, London, Manchester, Paris, Stockholm, St Petersburg and multiple locations across Turkey. In response, governments continued to implement a range of counter-terrorism measures disproportionately restricting people's rights in the name of security.

Millions of people faced an erosion of their economic, social and cultural rights. This led to diminished social protection, exacerbated inequality and systemic discrimination in many countries. Those most affected by higher levels of poverty included women, children, young or low-paid workers, people with disabilities, migrants and asylum-seekers, ethnic minorities, and retired and single people.

Across the region, governments repeatedly failed to meet their responsibilities towards refugees and migrants. The number of irregular arrivals of refugees and migrants in the EU dropped significantly in the second half of the year, largely as a result of co-operation agreements with Libyan authorities that turned a blind eye and even contributed to the abuses faced by those trapped in the country. Those who did make it to the EU faced an increased risk of forcible return to countries such as Afghanistan, where their life or liberty were at risk.

At the UN Security Council, Russia used its veto for the ninth time to shield the Syrian government from the consequences of war crimes and crimes against humanity. Russia's routine use of its veto had become the equivalent of acquiescence in war crimes, allowing all parties in Syria's conflict to act with impunity, with civilians paying the ultimate price.

FREEDOM OF EXPRESSION

Across Eastern Europe and across Central Asia, civil society faced a range of harassment and restrictions. Dozens of individuals were jailed for their peaceful activism and became prisoners of conscience in Belarus and Russia, amid ongoing legislative restrictions on media, NGOs and public assemblies.

The deterioration of the respect for freedom of opinion and expression in Tajikistan became further entrenched with the authorities imposing sweeping restrictions to silence critical voices. The police and security services intimidated and harassed journalists. Human rights lawyers endured arbitrary arrests, politically motivated prosecutions, harsh prison sentences and harassment.

In Kazakhstan, journalists and activists faced politically motivated prosecutions and attacks. Having all but strangled independent media already, the authorities used increasingly elaborate and aggressive methods to stamp out dissenting voices on the internet and social media. A targeted cyber campaign was being waged against critical voices in Azerbaijan.

The Uzbekistani government used unlawful surveillance on its citizens at home and abroad – reinforcing a hostile environment for journalists and activists, and fostering a climate of fear for Uzbekistani nationals in Europe. Human rights defenders and journalists continued to be summoned for questioning at police stations, placed under house arrest and beaten by the authorities.

In Crimea, the de facto authorities continued to suppress dissenting opinion. Leaders of the Crimean Tatar community who spoke out against the Russian occupation and illegal annexation of the peninsula faced exile or prison.

Turkey continued to detain tens of thousands of perceived government critics in the aftermath of the 2016 coup attempt. Criticism of the government largely disappeared from mainstream media. More than 100 journalists languished in jail – more than in any other country – many for months on end, on spurious charges.

The primary positive developments in Eastern Europe and in Central Asia involved releases of prisoners of conscience and other long-term prisoners, notably in Uzbekistan. In Azerbaijan, some prisoners of conscience were released; however, new ones took their places in the never-ending policy of repression. In Russia, prisoner of conscience Ildar Dadin – the first and so far only person imprisoned under a recent law criminalizing repeated violation of Russia's draconian restrictions on public assembly – was released and cleared of conviction following a Constitutional Court ruling.

RESTRICTIVE LAWS

Across Europe and Central Asia, restrictive laws were passed. Drawing inspiration from similar legislation adopted in Russia in 2012, Hungary adopted a law on the transparency of organizations funded from abroad, which forced NGOs receiving more than EUR24,000 direct or indirect funding from abroad to re-register as a "civic organization funded from abroad" and to put this label on every publication. The move was accompanied by highly stigmatizing government rhetoric. Similar legislation was tabled in Ukraine and in Moldova, but was withdrawn in Moldova due to objections from civil society and international organizations.

In November, there were protests throughout Poland when MPs voted on two legislative amendments threatening the independence of the judiciary and placing the right to a fair trial and other rights at risk. President Andrzej Duda vetoed the amendments in July, but subsequently redrafted and submitted them to Parliament in September.

FREEDOM OF ASSOCIATION AND ASSEMBLY

In Eastern Europe and in Central Asia, the authorities clamped down on peaceful protesters. In Russia, during mass anti-corruption protests across the country in March, police used excessive force and arrested hundreds of overwhelmingly peaceful demonstrators in the capital, Moscow, and well over a thousand across the country, including opposition leader Aleksei Navalny. Hundreds of people were again detained and ill-treated during anti-corruption protests across the country in June, and on 7 October, President Vladimir Putin's birthday.

In Kazakhstan, organizing or participating in a peaceful demonstration without the authorities' prior authorization remained an offence. Police in Kyrgyzstan disrupted a peaceful demonstration in the capital, Bishkek, organized to protest against deterioration of freedom of expression, and arrested several participants. The Belarusian authorities violently suppressed mass demonstrations against a tax on the unemployed.

A discriminatory amendment to a law in Poland led to bans of certain demonstrations and favoured pro-government assemblies. People participating in demonstrations against the government policies were prosecuted, harassed by law enforcement officials and political opponents, and prevented from exercising their right to freedom of peaceful assembly.

In several countries of Western Europe, public protests were met with a range of restrictive measures and abuses. In Germany, France, Poland and Spain, governments' response to public assemblies against restrictive policies or human rights abuses included sealing off public spaces, excessive use of force by police, containment of peaceful protesters or "kettling", surveillance, and threats of administrative and criminal sanctions. France's government continued to resort to emergency measures to ban public assemblies and to restrict freedom of movement to prevent individuals from participating in demonstrations.

In October, Spanish security forces that were ordered to prevent the holding of the Catalan independence referendum used unnecessary and disproportionate force against demonstrators, injuring hundreds of them. This included evidence of police beating peaceful demonstrators.

COUNTER-TERROR AND SECURITY

In Western Europe, a raft of disproportionate and discriminatory counter-terrorism laws continued to be rushed through. The adoption of the EU Directive on Combating Terrorism in March looked set to lead to a proliferation of such measures in 2018, as states were to transpose the Directive into domestic law.

Broad definitions of terrorism in the law, and the misapplication of counter-terrorism laws to a wide group of people – human rights defenders, environmental activists, refugees, migrants, and journalists – continued, notably in Turkey but also throughout Western Europe. Vague laws punishing "glorification" or "apology" of terrorism were used to prosecute activists and civil society groups for opinions expressed on the internet and social media, including in France, Spain and the UK.

France's state of emergency ended in November, having lasted almost two years. In October, France adopted a new counter-terrorism law embedding in ordinary law many of the measures permitted under the emergency regime.

Instead of investigating and prosecuting suspected perpetrators of violent attacks, many states implemented administrative control measures limiting everyone's rights and often applied these based on vague grounds, often connected to religious belief or associations. Detention without charge or trial was proposed in several countries, including France, the Netherlands and Switzerland, and introduced in Bavaria, Germany.

Many EU member states also attempted to draw links between the refugee crisis and terrorism-related threats. Although a Hungarian court's conviction on spurious terrorism charges of "Ahmed H", a Syrian resident in Cyprus, was annulled, Ahmed H remained in detention while his new trial unfolded. The trial was ongoing at the end of the year. He had been convicted of an "act of terror" for throwing stones and speaking to a crowd through a megaphone during clashes with border police.

A number of states in Europe and in Central Asia intensified their focus on online activity as a perceived potential driver for terrorism-related or "extremist" activity. The UK proposed criminalizing repeated viewing of "terrorism-related" content online with a maximum 15-year prison sentence. Similar measures already existed, and were deemed unconstitutional, in France.

In Eastern Europe and in Central Asia, government responses to the real and perceived threats posed by terrorism and extremism followed an all-too-familiar pattern. Extraditions and renditions of suspects to destinations where they were at risk of torture and other ill-treatment were frequent and swift, individuals being forcibly returned, in contravention of international law. In Russia's North Caucasus, enforced disappearances, unlawful detention, torture and other ill-treatment of detainees, and extrajudicial executions were reported in the context of security operations. In Russia-occupied Crimea, the de facto authorities pursued all forms of dissent and continued to arbitrarily target the Crimean Tatar community under anti-extremism and counter-terrorism legislation.

REFUGEES AND MIGRANTS

During 2017, 171,332 refugees and migrants arrived in Europe by sea, compared to 362,753 in 2016. The decrease was mainly due to EU states' co-operation with Libya and Turkey. At least 3,119 people died attempting to cross the Mediterranean Sea to Europe. EU states intensified their efforts to prevent irregular entry and increased returns, including through policies that exposed migrants and those in need of protection to ill-treatment, torture and other abuses in countries of transit and origin.

By using aid, trade and other leverage, European governments encouraged and supported transit countries – even those where widespread and systematic violations against refugees and migrants were documented – to implement stricter border control measures, without adequate human rights guarantees. This trapped thousands of refugees and migrants in countries where they lacked adequate protection and where they were exposed to serious human rights violations.

NGOs, which performed more rescues in the central Mediterranean in the first half of 2017 than any others, were discredited and attacked by public commentators and politicians, and faced restrictions on their activities by a new code of conduct imposed by the Italian authorities.

Russia continued to return asylum-seekers and refugees to countries where they were at risk of torture and other ill-treatment, as did other countries in Europe and Central Asia.

EUROPEAN COLLABORATION WITH LIBYA

With most refugees and migrants crossing the sea into Europe embarking from Libya, the EU and European governments, with Italy at the forefront, sought to close down this route by co-operating with the Libyan coastguard and other actors in the country. They entered into a string of co-operation agreements with Libyan authorities responsible for grave human rights violations, in particular the Libyan Coast Guard and Libya's General Directorate for Combating Illegal Migration (DCIM).

Italy and other governments failed to include key human rights guarantees in these agreements and turned a blind eye to the abuses, including torture and extortion, against refugees and migrants by the very institutions they were co-operating with. The actions of European countries were leading to increasing numbers of people being stopped or intercepted. In so doing, European governments, and Italy in particular, were breaching their own international obligations and becoming complicit in the violations committed by the Libyan authorities they were sponsoring and co-operating with.

EU-TURKEY MIGRATION DEAL, CONDITIONS IN GREECE

The March 2016 EU-Turkey migration deal remained in place and continued to restrict access to territory and asylum in the EU. The deal aimed at returning asylum-seekers to Turkey, on the pretence of it being a "safe country" of transit. European leaders maintained the fiction that Turkey provided protection equivalent to that of the EU, even though Turkey had become even more unsafe for refugees since the 2016 coup attempt. The removal of procedural safeguards under Turkey's state of emergency put refugees there at heightened risk of *refoulement*, the forcible return to countries where they were at risk of facing serious human rights violations.

Throughout 2017, the deal left thousands exposed to overcrowded, squalid and unsafe conditions on Greek islands that were transformed into de facto holding pens and condemned them to extended asylum procedures. Some suffered violent hate crimes. Compared to 2016, arrivals on the Greek islands dropped sharply, mainly due to the deal,but a relative increase in arrivals during the summer stretched the islands' already insufficient reception capacity once again. In December, around 13,000 asylum-seekers remained in limbo, stranded on the islands.

Reception conditions both on the islands and in mainland Greece, meanwhile, continued to be inadequate, with many still forced to sleep in tents unfit for winter and women and girls particularly vulnerable in unsafe camp facilities.

In September, Greece's highest administrative court paved the way for forcible returns of Syrian asylum-seekers under the EU-Turkey migration deal by endorsing decisions by the Greek asylum authorities that deemed Turkey safe for two Syrian nationals.

RELOCATION SCHEMES

Solidarity with frontline countries receiving the majority of arrivals continued to be in short supply. European countries failed to relocate their committed numbers of asylum-seekers from Greece and Italy under the emergency relocation scheme adopted in September 2015. As of November, European states had fulfilled just 32% of their legal commitment. At the end of

2017, 21,703 asylum-seekers out of 66,400 had been relocated from Greece, and 11,464 out of around 35,000 from Italy.

Among the worst offenders were Poland and Hungary, both having refused to accept a single asylum-seeker from Italy and Greece by the year's end.

The European Court of Justice rejected Slovakia's and Hungary's complaint against the mandatory refugee relocation scheme. The European Commission also opened infringement proceedings against Poland, Hungary and the Czech Republic for failing to comply with their relocation obligations.

CURTAILING ACCESS TO ASYLUM AND PUSHBACKS

Hungary reached a new low by passing legislation allowing pushbacks of all people found in an irregular situation in the country and by introducing the automatic detention of asylum-seekers, in blatant breach of EU law. The authorities locked up in containers asylum-seekers arriving at its borders. Hungary's systematic flouting of the rights of refugees, asylum-seekers and migrants also included severely restricting access by limiting admission to two operational border "transit zones" in which only 10 new asylum applications could be submitted each working day. This left thousands of people in substandard camps in Serbia, at risk of homelessness and forcible return further south to Macedonia and Bulgaria.

Abuses and pushbacks continued at the EU external borders, from Bulgaria, Greece, Spain, and Poland. Poland's government proposed legislation to legalize pushbacks, a regular practice at a crossing between Poland and Belarus. In a landmark ruling, the European Court of Human Rights condemned Spain for breaching the prohibition of collective expulsions and for violating the right to an effective remedy in the case of two migrants who were summarily returned from the Spanish enclave of Melilla to Morocco.

Slovenia adopted legislative amendments under which it could deny entry to people arriving at its borders and automatically expel migrants and refugees who entered irregularly, without assessing their asylum claims.

FORCED RETURNS

EU member states also continued to put pressure on other governments to accept readmissions – in some cases without including adequate guarantees against *refoulement*.

At a time when civilian casualties in Afghanistan were at some of their highest levels on record, European governments forced increasing numbers of Afghan asylum-seekers back to the dangers from which they fled in Afghanistan. Forced returns to Afghanistan were made from countries including Austria, the Netherlands and Norway.

IMPUNITY AND ACCOUNTABILITY IN THE FORMER YUGOSLAVIA

The International Criminal Tribunal for the former Yugoslavia delivered its final judgment on 29 November 2017, bringing to a close its largely successful 23-year effort to hold perpetrators of war crimes to account. Also in November, it sentenced Bosnian Serb war leader Ratko Mladić to life imprisonment for crimes under international law, including genocide, war crimes, and crimes against humanity.

At the national level, with the exception of Bosnia and Herzegovina, in which some modest progress was made, impunity remained the norm, with courts continuing to have limited capacity and resources, and facing undue political pressure. Prosecutors across the region lacked the support of the executive and their work was compromised by a climate of nationalist rhetoric and lack of political commitment to sustained regional co-operation.

By the end of the year, the authorities had made no progress in establishing the fate of over 11,500 people disappeared during the armed conflicts in the Balkans. Victims of enforced disappearance and their families continued to be denied access to justice, truth and reparation. Nominal improvements in the laws regulating reparation for victims of wartime sexual violence continued to be made in several countries.

DISCRIMINATION

THE "TRADITIONAL VALUES" PRETENCE IN EASTERN EUROPE AND IN CENTRAL ASIA

Governments across Eastern Europe and across Central Asia continued to prop up repression and discrimination by promoting and increasingly invoking the rhetoric of a discriminatory interpretation of so-called "traditional values". The "traditional values" referred to were selective xenophobic, misogynistic and homophobic interpretations of cultural values. In Tajikistan, this discourse and its application was used to punish LGBTI communities for "amoral" behaviours and enforce "norms" for dress code, language and religion primarily against women and religious minorities, including through new legislation. In Kazakhstan and Russia, there was an increasing number of criminal prosecutions and other harassment of religious minorities, on arbitrary grounds, under "anti-extremism" legislation. The said interpretation assertion of "traditional values" reached a terrifying dimension with the secret torture and killing of gay men in Chechnya by authorities.

WOMEN'S RIGHTS

Following sexual harassment allegations against US Hollywood producer Harvey Weinstein and others in the show business industry, millions of women worldwide used the online hashtag #MeToo to break the silence about their experiences as survivors of sexual violence. This became a rallying cry for challenging victim blaming and holding offenders to account. The year also saw the women's and feminist movements mobilizing thousands – including during January's Women's Marches across Europe, and Black Monday protests in Poland that successfully pushed the government not to further restrict access to safe and legal abortion. Yet, throughout Europe and Central Asia, women and girls continued to experience systemic human rights violations and abuses, including torture and other ill-treatment, denial of the right to health and bodily autonomy, inequality of opportunity, and widespread gender-based violence.

Access to abortion remained criminalized in most circumstances in Ireland and Northern Ireland and severely restricted in practice. In Poland, there were systemic barriers in accessing safe and legal abortion. Abortion remained criminalized in all circumstances in Malta.

The EU and Moldova signed the Council of Europe Convention on preventing and combating violence against women and domestic violence (Istanbul Convention). It was ratified by Cyprus, Estonia, Georgia, Germany, Norway and Switzerland – bringing to 28 the number of states to have done so. Ukraine signed it in 2011 but failed to ratify the Convention.

Despite increasingly strong legislative protections, gender-based violence against women remained pervasive, including in Albania, Croatia and Romania. In Russia, under the cover of the so-called "traditional values" narrative, and encountering little public criticism, the Parliament adopted legislation decriminalizing some forms of domestic violence which President Putin signed into law. In Norway and Sweden, gender-based violence, including sexual violence, remained a serious problem with inadequate state response.

MINORITY RIGHTS

Discrimination and stigmatization of minorities remained pervasive across Europe and Central Asia with several groups facing harassment, violence, and obstacles to meaningful participation in society.

Discrimination against Roma remained widespread in Slovakia. The European Commission continued an infringement procedure against Slovakia and Hungary for systematic discrimination and segregation of Roma children in schools. Segregated camps, discrimination in access to social housing and forced evictions remained a daily reality for thousands of the 170,000 Roma estimated to be living across Italy, around 40,000 of them in camps in squalid conditions. The European Commission still failed to take effective action towards ending discrimination against Roma.

Muslims faced discrimination, particularly when looking for work, at work, and when accessing public or private services such as education and health care.

In Austria, a new law banned any kind of full-face covering in public spaces, disproportionately restricting the rights to freedom of expression and of religion or belief. Tajikistan's authorities forced thousands of women to remove their Islamic headscarves (hijabs) in public places to comply with the law on traditions.

RIGHTS OF LESBIAN, GAY, BISEXUAL, TRANSGENDER AND INTERSEX PEOPLE

LGBTI people faced growing abuse and discrimination across the east, including violence, arbitrary arrests and detention. In Azerbaijan, over 100 LGBTI people were arbitrarily arrested on one day in the capital Baku. In Uzbekistan and Turkmenistan, consensual sex among men remained a crime punishable by prison. Georgia's new Constitution restricted the definition of marriage to exclude same-sex couples. Lithuania's Parliament adopted legislation discriminating against LGBTI people. In Russia, the "gay propaganda law" continued to be used, despite being ruled discriminatory by the European Court of Human Rights.

Reports emerged in April that the Chechen authorities were secretly and arbitrarily detaining, torturing and killing gay men. In response to the international outcry, the authorities claimed that gay men did not exist in Chechnya, while the federal authorities failed to carry out an effective investigation.

There were also positive developments and examples of human courage and solidarity. The Russian LGBT Network organized a hotline and facilitated the evacuation to safety of LGBTI people from Chechnya and elsewhere in the North Caucasus. The biggest-ever Pride rally in Ukraine was held. Malta's parliament approved same-sex marriage legislation and extended full marriage rights to same-sex couples. Germany granted marriage rights to all, regardless of their gender or sexual orientation, and equal rights to adoption for married people.

TRANSGENDER PEOPLE AND PEOPLE WITH VARIATIONS OF SEX CHARACTERISTICS

Transgender people in Europe and Central Asia faced hurdles seeking legal recognition of their gender identity. Children and adults with variations in sex characteristics continued to face human rights violations, perpetrated in the course of non-emergency, invasive and irreversible medical interventions which often had harmful consequences on physical and psychological health, especially for children. In 18 European countries, transgender people were required to undergo sterilization, and in 35 countries they had to receive a mental health diagnosis in order to change their gender.

There was progress in Belgium and Greece; they were the latest European countries to abolish sterilization and mental health diagnosis requirements, although legal gender recognition reforms in both countries still fell short of establishing a quick, transparent and accessible administrative procedure.

MIDDLE EAST AND NORTH AFRICA REGIONAL OVERVIEW

Journalists and human rights defenders were targeted in government crackdowns, and online expression was heavily controlled in several countries. Civil society activists managed to halt further tightening of restrictions on free expression in some places. Freedom of religion and belief came under attack from armed groups and governments alike. The struggle of women's rights movements successfully led to the amendment of laws that had entrenched discrimination and violence against women in some countries. However, systematic discrimination remained in law and practice across the region and women were still inadequately protected against gender-based violence. Authorities arrested and prosecuted people for their real or perceived sexual orientation in some countries, and consensual same-sex sexual relations were still criminalized in many, in a handful of cases punishable by death. There were severe restrictions on trade unions in some countries, and migrant workers continued to face exploitation and abuse. However, reforms in a couple of countries gave migrant workers greater employment protections. Armed conflicts took a heavy toll on beleaguered civilians and were characterized by serious violations, including the use of banned weapons, unlawful sieges, and direct attacks on civilians and civilian infrastructure. Death sentences were imposed in a number of countries across the region, and hundreds of executions were carried out. Impunity persisted for historical and recent crimes; however, some progress was made towards securing truth and justice for victims.

FREEDOMS OF EXPRESSION, ASSOCIATION AND ASSEMBLY

Governments across the Middle East and North Africa repressed civil society both offline and online in an attempt to prevent or punish reporting on human rights violations or other criticism directed at them or their allies, often on the pretext that they were combating threats to national security or corruption. They also used excessive force in an attempt to quell protest movements that had taken to the streets.

CRACKDOWNS IN EGYPT AND SAUDI ARABIA

In some countries, increased clampdowns accompanied a global trend that saw political strongmen attempting to establish their credentials in the eyes of the international community. In President Abdel Fattah al-Sisi's Egypt, the authorities continued to curb the work of human rights defenders in an unprecedented manner, shutting down or freezing the assets of NGOs; they enacted a draconian new law that gave them broad powers to dissolve NGOs and provided for five years' imprisonment for publishing research without government permission. The Egyptian authorities also sentenced at least 15 journalists to prison terms on charges related solely to their writing, including publication of what the authorities deemed "false information"; they blocked more than 400 websites, including those of independent newspapers and human rights organizations. Meanwhile, security forces arrested hundreds of individuals based on their membership or perceived membership of the Muslim Brotherhood. To punish political dissidents, the authorities used prolonged pre-trial detention, often for periods of more than two years, placed those imprisoned in indefinite and prolonged solitary confinement, and subjected many of those released to probation periods in which they were forced to spend up to 12 hours per day in a police station, amounting to arbitrary deprivation of liberty.

Saudi Arabia witnessed the promotion of Mohammed bin Salman to the role of Crown Prince in June as part of a broader re-engineering of the political landscape. In the months that followed, the authorities intensified their crackdown on freedom of expression, detaining more than 20 prominent religious figures, writers, journalists, academics and activists in one week in September. They also put human rights defenders on trial on charges related to their peaceful activism before the Specialized Criminal Court, a tribunal set up to try terrorism-related cases. At the end of the year, despite the image the palace wished to portray of a more tolerant country, the majority of Saudi Arabia's human rights defenders were either in prison or facing grossly unfair trials.

ATTACKS ON JOURNALISTS AND HUMAN RIGHTS DEFENDERS

Elsewhere, human rights advocacy and journalistic reporting, as well as criticism of official institutions, led to prosecution and imprisonment and, in some cases, smear campaigns orchestrated by the government or its supporters.

In Iran, the authorities jailed scores of peaceful critics including women's rights activists, minority rights and environmental activists, trade unionists, lawyers, and those seeking truth, justice and reparation for the mass executions of the 1980s.

In Bahrain, the government arbitrarily detained human rights defenders and government critics and subjected others to travel bans or the stripping of their nationality, dissolved the independent *al-Wasat* newspaper and the opposition political group Waad, maintained a ban on demonstrations in the capital, Manama, and used unnecessary and excessive force to disperse protests elsewhere.

In Morocco and Western Sahara, the authorities prosecuted and imprisoned a number of journalists, bloggers and activists who criticized officials or reported on human rights violations, corruption or popular protests, such as those that took place in the northern Rif region, where security forces conducted mass arrests of largely peaceful protesters, including children, and sometimes used excessive or unnecessary force.

The Kuwaiti authorities imprisoned several government critics and online activists under legal provisions that criminalized comments deemed offensive to the Emir or damaging to relations with neighbouring states.

In the Kurdistan Region of Iraq, a number of journalists and online activists were subjected to arbitrary arrest, death threats and smear campaigns, a pattern that escalated in the run-up to an independence referendum in September called by the region's president.

In Yemen, the Huthi armed group arbitrarily arrested and detained critics, journalists and human rights defenders in the capital, Sana'a, and other areas they controlled.

Meanwhile, the Israeli authorities banned entry into Israel or the Occupied Palestinian Territories to individuals supporting or working for organizations that had issued or promoted a statement which the authorities deemed to be a call to boycott Israel or Israeli entities, including settlements, targeted both Palestinian and Israeli human rights NGOs through harassment and campaigns to undermine their work, and deployed forces that used rubber-coated metal bullets and live ammunition against Palestinian protesters in the West Bank and Gaza Strip, killing at least 20 and injuring thousands.

ONLINE REPRESSION

Governments other than Egypt also made efforts to increase their control of expression on the internet. The State of Palestine adopted the Electronic Crimes Law in July, permitting the arbitrary detention of journalists, whistle-blowers and others who criticize the authorities online. The law allowed for prison sentences and up to 25 years' hard labour for anyone deemed to have disturbed "public order", "national unity" or "social peace". Several Palestinian journalists and human rights defenders were charged under the law.

Jordan continued to block access to certain websites, including online forums. Oman blocked the online publication of *Mowaten* newspaper, and the effect of trials against *Azamn* newspaper and some of its journalists continued to reverberate following its publication in 2016 of allegations of corruption in the government and the judiciary. In Iran, judicial officials attempted to block the popular messaging application Telegram, but failed because of opposition from the government; other popular social media websites including Facebook, Twitter and YouTube were still blocked.

GULF POLITICAL CRISIS

The political crisis in the Gulf triggered in June, when Saudi Arabia, the United Arab Emirates (UAE), Bahrain and Egypt severed relations with Qatar and accused it of financing and harbouring terrorists and interfering in the domestic affairs of its neighbours, had an impact beyond the paralysis of the Gulf Cooperation Council. Bahrain, Saudi Arabia and the UAE announced that they would treat criticism of the measures taken against Qatar, or sympathy with Qatar or its people, as a criminal offence, punishable by a prison term.

CIVIL SOCIETY FIGHT-BACK

Civil society did, however, make significant efforts to stem the tide of measures attempting to restrict freedom of expression. In Tunisia, activists put the brakes on a new bill that could bolster impunity for security forces by criminalizing criticism of police conduct and granting officers immunity from prosecution for unnecessary use of lethal force. In Palestine, the authorities agreed to amend the Electronic Crimes Law following huge pressure from civil society.

FREEDOM OF RELIGION AND BELIEF

ABUSES BY ARMED GROUPS

Armed groups targeted religious minorities in several countries. The armed group calling itself Islamic State (IS) and other armed groups killed and injured scores of civilians across Iraq and Syria in suicide bombings and other deadly attacks that targeted Shi'a religious shrines and other public spaces in predominantly Shi'a neighbourhoods. The UN reported in January that nearly 2,000 Yazidi women and children remained in IS captivity in Iraq and Syria. They were enslaved and subjected to rape, beatings and other torture. In Egypt, IS claimed responsibility for the bombing of two churches which left at least 44 dead in April, and unidentified militants launched a bomb and gun attack at a mosque in North Sinai during Friday prayers in November, killing more than 300 Sufi Muslim worshippers – the deadliest attack by an armed group in Egypt since 2011.

In Yemen, the Huthis and their allies subjected members of the Baha'i community to arbitrary arrest and detention.

RESTRICTIONS BY GOVERNMENTS

In Algeria, the authorities were engaged in a new clampdown against the Ahmadi religious movement; during the year more than 280 Ahmadis were prosecuted because of their religious beliefs and practices.

Elsewhere, government restrictions followed a familiar pattern. In Saudi Arabia, the authorities discriminated against members of the Shi'a Muslim minority because of their faith, limiting their right to religious expression and their access to justice, and arbitrarily restricting their right to work and access to state services. Shi'a activists continued to face arrest, imprisonment and – in some cases – the death penalty following unfair trials.

In Iran, freedom of religion and belief was systematically violated, in law and practice. Widespread and systematic attacks continued to be carried out against the Baha'i religious minority. These included arbitrary arrests, lengthy imprisonment, torture and other ill-treatment, forcible closure of Baha'i-owned businesses, confiscation of Baha'i properties, bans on employment in the public sector and denial of access to universities. Other religious minorities not recognized under the Constitution, such as Yaresan (Ahl-e Haq), also faced systematic discrimination, including in education and employment, and were persecuted for practising their faith. The right to change or renounce religious beliefs continued to be violated. A number of Christian converts received prison sentences ranging from 10 to 15 years.

WOMEN'S RIGHTS

Long-term struggles by women's rights movements resulted in some positive developments during the year.

Laws were amended in Jordan, Lebanon and Tunisia to stop rapists escaping prosecution (or benefiting from reduced penalties) if they married their victim. However, legislation in many other countries retained such a loophole. Jordan also struck out a provision that allowed reduced sentences for men found guilty of killing a female relative in a "fit of rage caused by an unlawful or dangerous act on the part of the victim", but kept one that granted leniency for "honour" killings of female relatives found in an "adulterous situation". Tunisia's parliament adopted the Law on Eliminating Violence against Women, which brought in several guarantees for the protection of women and girls from gender-based violence, and its president repealed a decree prohibiting marriage between a Tunisian woman and a non-Muslim man.

In Qatar, a draft law was approved to provide permanent residency rights for the children of Qatari women married to non-Qataris, but discrimination persisted, with women unable to pass on their nationality and citizenship to their children.

In Saudi Arabia, a royal order was issued in September allowing women to drive from mid-2018, although there were questions about how it would be implemented in practice. In April, another royal order had instructed all government agencies that women should not be denied access to government services if they did not have a male guardian's consent, unless existing regulations required it. However, the order appeared to keep in place regulations that explicitly require a guardian's approval, such as for women to travel abroad, obtain a passport, or marry.

Despite the positive developments, entrenched discrimination against women in law and in practice, notably in matters of marriage and divorce, inheritance and child custody, remained in these and many other countries in the region. Women were inadequately protected against sexual and other gender-based violence, as well as forced and early marriage.

RIGHTS OF LESBIAN, GAY, BISEXUAL, TRANSGENDER AND INTERSEX PEOPLE

While sexual orientation and gender identity issues were increasingly on the agendas of mainstream human rights movements in the region, governments continued to heavily limit the enjoyment of the rights of LGBTI people in law and practice.

In Egypt, in the worst crackdown in over a decade, the authorities rounded up and prosecuted people for their perceived sexual orientation after a rainbow flag was displayed at a concert in Cairo in September performed by Lebanese band Mashrou' Leila, who had been banned from playing in Jordan earlier in the year. Security forces arrested at least 76 people and subjected at least five to anal examinations, a practice which amounts to torture. Courts sentenced at least 48 people to prison terms of between three months and six years on charges that included "habitual debauchery". In October, parliamentarians proposed a deeply discriminatory law explicitly criminalizing same-sex sexual relations and any public promotion of LGBTI gatherings, symbols or flags.

Countries including Morocco and Tunisia continued to arrest people and sentence them to terms of imprisonment under laws criminalizing consensual same-sex sexual relations. In Tunisia, while the police subjected men accused of such relations to forced anal examinations, the government accepted a recommendation under the UN Universal Periodic Review process in September to end their use. Elsewhere, in countries including Iran and Saudi Arabia, some consensual same-sex sexual conduct remained punishable by death.

RIGHT TO WORK

TRADE UNIONS

Some governments heavily curtailed trade union rights.

In Egypt, the authorities subjected dozens of workers and trade unionists to arrest, military trial, dismissal and a range of disciplinary measures solely for exercising their rights to strike and to form independent trade unions. In December, parliament passed a law tripling the number of members (from 50 to 150) that independent trade unions need to obtain legal recognition.

In Algeria, the authorities continued to deny registration to the independent, cross-sector General Autonomous Confederation for Algerian Workers – it first filed its application in 2013 – and banned the National Autonomous Electricity and Gas Trade Union by withdrawing its recognition.

MIGRANT WORKERS' RIGHTS

Across the Gulf and in other countries such as Jordan and Lebanon, migrant workers, including those in the domestic, construction and other sectors, continued to face exploitation and abuse. However, there were some positive developments. In Qatar, the government passed two new laws in August. One established a labour dispute mechanism, which could address some of the barriers to migrant workers accessing justice. The other provided legal protections for domestic workers' labour rights for the first time, including paid holidays and a limit to working hours. However, the law was open to abuse of a provision allowing domestic workers to work beyond the legal limit if they "agreed". In October, the Qatari government announced new reform plans, including a minimum wage and a fund to pay unpaid workers, and the International Labour Organization published details of a package it had agreed with Qatar to reform the *kafala* sponsorship system, which prevents migrant workers from changing jobs or leaving the country without their employers' permission.

In the UAE, a law came into effect in September limiting working hours and providing paid leave and the right to retain personal documents.

RIGHTS TO HOUSING, WATER AND HEALTH

ISRAEL AND THE OCCUPIED PALESTINIAN TERRITORIES

The year marked the 50th anniversary of Israel's occupation of the Palestinian Territories and the 10th anniversary of its illegal blockade of the Gaza Strip. Israeli authorities intensified the expansion of settlements and related infrastructure across the West Bank, including East Jerusalem, and carried out a large number of demolitions of Palestinian property, forcibly evicting more than 660 people. Many of these demolitions were in Bedouin and herding communities that the Israeli authorities planned to forcibly transfer.

Israel's air, land and sea blockade of the Gaza Strip continued the long-standing restrictions on the movement of people and goods, collectively punishing Gaza's entire population of approximately 2 million inhabitants. Combined with Egypt's almost total closure of the Rafah border crossing, and the West Bank authorities' punitive measures, Israel's blockade triggered a humanitarian crisis with power cuts, reducing access to electricity to a few hours per day, affecting the supply of clean water and sanitation and reducing access to health services.

Elsewhere in the region, Palestinian refugees, including many long-term residents, remained subject to discriminatory laws. In Lebanon, they continued to be excluded from many types of work, owning or inheriting property and from accessing public education and health services.

WATER, SANITATION AND HEALTH

Civil society raised a number of cases before the Lebanese judiciary related to violations of the rights to health and clean water, including cases related to the sale of expired drugs in public hospitals and to waste mismanagement.

In Tunisia, water shortages became acute. The government admitted it did not have a national strategy for water distribution, thereby making it impossible to ensure equitable access. Marginalized regions were disproportionately affected by water cuts, leading to local protests throughout the year.

COUNTER-TERROR AND SECURITY

Serious human rights violations accompanied counter-terrorism measures in several countries.

In Egypt, where more than 100 members of the security forces were killed in attacks by armed groups, mostly in North Sinai, the National Security Agency continued to forcibly disappear and extrajudicially execute individuals suspected of political violence. The Ministry of the Interior claimed that more than 100 individuals were shot dead in exchanges of fire with security forces throughout the year. However, in many of these cases the people killed were already in state custody after having been forcibly disappeared. Torture and other ill-treatment remained routine in official places of detention and was systematic in detention centres run by the National Security Agency. Hundreds were sentenced, including to death, after grossly unfair mass trials.

In Iraq, suspects prosecuted on terrorism-related charges were routinely denied the rights to adequate time and facilities to prepare a defence, to not incriminate themselves or confess guilt, and to question prosecution witnesses. Courts continued to admit into evidence "confessions" that were extracted under torture. Many of those convicted after these unfair and hasty trials were sentenced to death. Iraqi and Kurdish government forces and militias also carried out extrajudicial executions of men and boys suspected of being affiliated with IS.

Complaints of torture in custody against defendants accused of national security-related offences were reported in countries including Bahrain, Israel and Kuwait. In general, the allegations were not investigated. Saudi Arabia introduced a new counter-terrorism law that allowed for the death penalty for some crimes. In Tunisia, the government continued to restrict freedom of movement through arbitrary and indefinite orders that confined hundreds to their governorate of residence, justifying this as a measure to prevent Tunisians from travelling to join armed groups.

DEATH PENALTY

Iran, Iraq and Saudi Arabia remained among the world's most prolific users of the death penalty, carrying out hundreds of executions between them, many after unfair trials. In Iran, Amnesty International was able to confirm the execution of four individuals who were under 18 at the time the crime was committed, but several executions of other juvenile offenders were postponed at the last minute because of public campaigning. The Iranian authorities continued to describe peaceful campaigning against the death penalty as "un-Islamic", and harassed and imprisoned anti-death penalty activists. In Saudi Arabia, courts continued to impose death sentences for drugs offences and for conduct that under international standards should not be criminalized, such as "sorcery" and "adultery". In Iraq, the death penalty continued to be used as a tool of retribution in response to public outrage after attacks claimed by IS.

Bahrain and Kuwait both resumed executions in January, the first since 2010 and 2013 respectively; the death sentences had been imposed for murder. Egypt, Jordan, Libya and the Hamas de facto administration in the Gaza Strip also carried out executions. Except for Israel and Oman, all other countries in the region continued a long-standing practice of imposing death sentences but not implementing them.

ARMED CONFLICT

Fuelled by the international arms trade, conflict in the region continued to blight the lives of millions of individuals, particularly in Yemen, Libya, Syria and Iraq. In each conflict, multiple parties committed war crimes and other serious violations of international law, including indiscriminate attacks that killed and injured civilians, direct attacks against civilians or civilian infrastructure. In Syria and Yemen, government and allied forces used internationally banned weapons such as cluster munitions and, in the case of Syria, chemical weapons.

YEMEN CONFLICT

The situation in Yemen, the poorest country in the Middle East and North Africa even before the outbreak of conflict in March 2015, became the world's worst humanitarian crisis, according to the UN, with three quarters of its population of 28 million in need of help. The country faced the biggest cholera epidemic in modern times, exacerbated by a lack of fuel for water-pumping stations, and was on the verge of the world's most severe famine for decades. The conflict has shattered the water, education and health systems. The Saudi Arabia-led coalition supporting the internationally recognized Yemeni government held up shipments of food, fuel and medicine. In November it cut off Yemen's northern ports completely for more than two weeks. The coalition's air strikes hit funeral gatherings, schools, markets, residential areas and civilian boats. Huthi rebel forces, allied with forces loyal to former president Ali Abdullah Saleh until splits between them led to his killing in December, indiscriminately shelled civilian residential areas in Ta'iz city and fired artillery indiscriminately across the border into Saudi Arabia, killing and injuring civilians.

INTERNATIONAL RESPONSE TO ISLAMIC STATE

In both Syria and Iraq, a US-led international coalition refocused its attention on combating IS, which was responsible for gross abuses. Hundreds of civilians were killed as a result. In Mosul, Iraq's second city, IS forcibly displaced thousands of civilians into zones of active hostilities in an attempt to shield their own fighters, and deliberately killed civilians fleeing the fighting and hung their bodies in public areas as a warning to others. In the battle to drive IS out of west Mosul, Iraqi and coalition forces launched a series of disproportionate or otherwise indiscriminate attacks to devastating effect; hundreds of civilians were killed. Iraqi forces consistently used explosive weapons which affected a large area, such as improvised rocket-assisted munitions, which cannot be precisely targeted at military objectives or used lawfully in densely populated civilian areas.

In Syria, IS lost control of Raqqa governorate following a military campaign by the Syrian Democratic Forces, consisting of Syrian-Kurdish and Arab armed groups, and the US-led coalition. IS prevented residents from fleeing and used civilians as human shields, as well as carrying out direct attacks on civilians and indiscriminate attacks, killing and injuring civilians. The coalition's air strikes also caused hundreds of civilian casualties. Syrian government forces, supported by Iranian and Hezbollah fighters on the ground and Russian air power, captured other areas previously held by IS and other armed groups. In doing so, they killed and injured civilians in indiscriminate attacks and direct attacks on civilians and civilian objects, including homes, hospitals and medical facilities.

SIEGES AND DISPLACEMENT OF CIVILIANS IN SYRIA

The Syrian government continued to maintain lengthy sieges of predominantly civilian areas, depriving some 400,000 people of access to medical care, other basic goods and services and humanitarian assistance, while subjecting them to repeated air strikes, artillery shelling and other attacks. Armed opposition groups were also responsible for besieging thousands of civilians and carrying out indiscriminate rocket and mortar attacks on government-controlled neighbourhoods, killing and injuring civilians. Thousands of civilians experienced the harsh impact of forced displacement following "reconciliation" agreements in the second half of 2016 and early 2017. They were only some of the 6.5 million people displaced within Syria between 2011 and 2017. More than half a million people fled Syria during the year, taking the total number of Syrian refugees to more than 5 million.

KURDISTAN REGION OF IRAQ

Government forces responded to the referendum on independence for the Kurdistan Region of Iraq by launching an operation that quickly retook the disputed city of Kirkuk, as well as most of the territory captured by Kurdish Peshmerga forces in the fight against IS. In October, tens of thousands of civilians were forced to flee their homes after fierce clashes erupted between Iraqi government forces, supported by affiliated militias, and Peshmerga forces in the multi-ethnic city of Tuz Khurmatu; at least 11 civilians were killed in indiscriminate attacks.

LAWLESSNESS IN LIBYA

Three rival governments and hundreds of militias and armed groups continued to compete for power and control over territory, lucrative trade routes and strategic military locations in Libya. Militias and armed groups carried out indiscriminate attacks in heavily populated areas leading to deaths of civilians; executed captured fighters from rival groups; and abducted and unlawfully detained hundreds of people, including political and human rights activists, because of their origin, opinions, perceived political affiliations or perceived wealth. Up to 20,000 refugees and migrants were held arbitrarily and indefinitely in overcrowded, unsanitary detention centres and exposed to torture, forced labour, extortion and unlawful killings at the hands of the authorities and militias who ran the centres. The assistance provided by EU member states, particularly Italy, to the Libyan Coast Guard and migrant detention centres made them complicit in the abuses.

IMPUNITY

Impunity for grave violations of the past remained a live concern.

Victims of crimes committed in recent and ongoing conflicts generally faced entrenched impunity at a national level. In Iraq, the authorities announced investigations in response to some allegations of serious violations committed by Iraqi forces and pro-government militias – such as torture, extrajudicial execution and enforced disappearance. However, they consistently failed to make any findings public. In Libya, the judicial system was hamstrung by its own dysfunctionality, with magistrates often failing to pursue accountability for abuses because of fears of reprisal. In Syria, the judicial system lacked independence, and failed to investigate and prosecute crimes by state forces. In Yemen, the National Commission to Investigate Alleged Violations of Human Rights, established by the government, failed to conduct investigations consistent with international standards into alleged violations committed by all parties to the conflict in Yemen.

SLOW PROGRESS

The region's only ongoing national transitional justice mechanism, Tunisia's Truth and Dignity Commission – mandated to address human rights violations committed between July 1955 and December 2013 – held 11 public sessions during which victims and perpetrators testified on a range of violations including election fraud, enforced disappearance and torture. However, there was no progress on an agreement to refer cases to specialized judicial chambers, and security agencies continued to fail to provide the Commission with the information it requested for its investigations.

At the international level, some significant initiatives continued but moved slowly. The Office of the Prosecutor of the International Criminal Court continued its preliminary examination of alleged crimes under international law committed in the Occupied Palestinian Territories since 13 June 2014, including during the 2014 Gaza-Israel conflict. In Libya, it broadened its investigations from political and military leaders to consider the wider systematic mistreatment of migrants.

Other initiatives had positive aspects, but were tarnished or undermined. The UN Security Council passed a resolution in September that was aimed at ensuring accountability for war crimes and human rights abuses committed by IS in Iraq, but crucially failed to include any provisions to ensure accountability for crimes committed by Iraqi forces, militias and the US-led coalition. The Joint Investigative Mechanism of the UN and the Organisation for the Prohibition of Chemical Weapons made progress on determining accountability for chemical weapons use in Syria, but an extension of its mandate was vetoed by Russia at the Security Council.

Two developments raised particular hope in the longer term for truth and justice for victims of violations in two seemingly intractable ongoing conflicts. The International Impartial and Independent Mechanism to assist in the investigation and prosecution of the most serious crimes under international law committed in Syria since March 2011 took shape during the year after its formal establishment in December 2016 by the UN General Assembly. And the UN Human Rights Council passed a resolution in September to establish a panel of experts to investigate abuses by all parties in Yemen. Both developments followed concerted advocacy by human rights organizations.

AMNESTY
INTERNATIONAL
REPORT 2017/18

PART 2: A-Z COUNTRY ENTRIES

AFGHANISTAN

Islamic Republic of Afghanistan
Head of state and government: **Muhammad Ashraf Ghani**

The civilian population suffered widespread human rights abuses as a result of the continuing conflict. Conflict-related violence led to deaths, injuries and displacement. Civilian casualties continued to be high; the majority were killed or injured by armed insurgent groups, but a significant minority by pro-government forces. The number of people internally displaced by conflict rose to more than 2 million; about 2.6 million Afghan refugees lived outside the country. Gender-based violence against women and girls persisted by state and non-state actors. An increase in public punishments of women by armed groups applying Shari'a law was reported. Human rights defenders received threats from both state and non-state actors; journalists faced violence and censorship. Death sentences continued to be imposed; five people were executed in November. Members of the Hazara minority group and Shi'a continued to face harassment and increased attacks, mainly by armed insurgent groups.

BACKGROUND

In March, the UN Security Council renewed the mandate of the UN Assistance Mission in Afghanistan (UNAMA) for another year, under the leadership of Tadamichi Yamamoto.

Gulbuddin Hekmatyar, leader of the country's second largest insurgent group, Hezb-i-Islami, joined the Afghan government. On 4 May, after two years of negotiations, the draft peace agreement signed in September 2016 between the government and Gulbuddin Hekmatyar was finalized, granting him amnesty for past offences, including war crimes, and permitting the release of certain Hezb-i-Islami prisoners.

By the end of June, UNAMA had documented 12 incidents of cross-border shelling from Pakistan into Afghanistan, in which at least 10 civilians were killed and 24 injured. This was a substantial increase on the same period in 2016.

The government made amendments to the Penal Code. Some provisions of the Rome Statute of the ICC were incorporated into law and some offences which previously carried the death penalty became punishable by life imprisonment.

ARMED CONFLICT

The non-international armed conflict between "anti-government elements" and pro-government forces continued. The Taliban and the armed group Islamic State (IS) were among the "anti-government elements" but more than 20 armed groups operated inside the country. The Taliban and other armed opposition groups were responsible for the majority of civilian casualties (64%) in the first nine months of the year, according to UNAMA.

By the end of September, UNAMA had documented 8,019 civilian casualties (2,640 killed and 5,379 injured), a small overall decrease compared to the same period in 2016, although there was a 13% increase in the number of women killed or injured. About 20% of the casualties were attributed to pro-government forces, including Afghan national security forces, the Afghan Local Police, pro-government armed groups and international military forces.

While acknowledging that Afghan government forces made some efforts to mitigate civilian casualties, especially during ground engagement, UNAMA also noted that the number of civilians killed or injured in aerial attacks increased by some 50% over 2016; about two-thirds of these were women and children.

ABUSES BY PRO-GOVERNMENT FORCES

In January, according to UNAMA, Afghan National Border Police in Paktika province sexually abused a 13-year-old boy, then shot him; the boy died from his injuries. Those suspected of criminal responsibility were prosecuted by the Afghan National Police, convicted of murder and sentenced to six years' imprisonment.

According to UNAMA, more than a dozen civilians were shot at checkpoints. In one such incident on 16 March, Afghan Local Police at a checkpoint in Jawzjan province shot and injured a man and his mother after mistaking them for insurgents. In April, Afghan National Police shot a 65-year-old man returning from feeding his cows; he later died in hospital. In May, an Afghan National Army soldier shot dead a 13-year-old boy as he collected grass close to a checkpoint in Badghis province.

In June, according to UNAMA, three young children in Saydebad district were killed in their home by a mortar round fired by the Afghan National Army. The same month, pro-government forces on patrol shot dead a father and his two young sons (aged five and 12) outside the brick factory where they worked; there was no known military activity in the area at the time. UNAMA requested updates on any investigation or follow-up action on these cases, but by July had received no information from the Ministry of the Interior.

During the first six months of the year, according to UNAMA, 95 civilians, half of them children, were killed in air strikes.

ABUSES BY ARMED GROUPS
In January, in Badakhshan province, five armed men dragged a pregnant woman from her home and shot her dead in front of her husband and six children; witnesses said her attackers accused her of being a government supporter. On 8 March, armed men entered an Afghan National Army military hospital in central Kabul and killed at least 49 people, including patients. In August, armed groups attacked the village of Mirza Olang, in Sar-e-Pul province, killing at least 36 people, including civilians.

Suicide attacks by armed groups in civilian areas caused at least 382 deaths and 1,202 injuries. In one such attack in December, at least 41 people, including children, were killed in a suicide bomb attack on a Shi'a cultural organization in Kabul.

On 25 August, a Shi'a mosque in Kabul was attacked by IS, killing at least 28 people and injuring dozens more. On 20 October, similar attacks were carried out against two more Shi'a mosques – one in western Kabul and the other in Ghor province – leaving more than 60 people dead and dozens injured.

VIOLENCE AGAINST WOMEN AND GIRLS
The Ministry of Women's Affairs of Afghanistan (MoWA) reported an increase in cases of gender-based violence against women, especially in areas under Taliban control.

In the first half of the year, the Afghanistan Independent Human Rights Commission reported thousands of cases of violence against women and girls across the country, including beatings, killings and acid attacks. Against the backdrop of impunity for such crimes and a failure to investigate, cases of violence against women remained grossly under-reported due to traditional practices, stigmatization and fear of the consequences for the victims.

Armed groups perpetrated gender-based violence, torture and other ill-treatment and other human rights abuses, imposing corporal punishments on women for having sex outside of marriage or engaging in sex work. In one instance, according to UNAMA, men severely beat a woman in her home in Darah-i-Suf Payin district, Samangan province, after accusing her of having sex outside of marriage and engaging in sex work.

UNAMA also noted that armed groups tried to restrict girls' access to education. In February, threats forced the closure of girls' schools in several villages in Farah province, temporarily denying education to more than 3,500 girls. When the schools reopened 10 days later, the vast majority of the girls were initially afraid to return.

The head of the women's affairs department in Badakhshan reported that in March the Taliban stoned a woman to death and whipped a man on charges of having sex outside of marriage in Wardoj district, northeastern Badakhshan province.

In August, a woman named Azadeh was shot dead by Taliban members in Jawzjan province. According to the governor's spokesman, the woman had fled some months earlier to a safe house in Sheberghan city due to domestic violence. She returned after local mediation, but was then dragged from her house and shot by Taliban members.

REFUGEES AND INTERNALLY DISPLACED PEOPLE

Some 2.6 million Afghan refugees were living in more than 70 countries around the world during 2017. Around 95% were hosted in just two countries, Iran and Pakistan, where they faced discrimination, racial attacks, lack of basic amenities and the risk of mass deportation.

Between 2002 and 2017, more than 5.8 million Afghans were returned home, many of them involuntarily by other governments.

The UN Office for the Coordination of Humanitarian Affairs (OCHA) said that some 437,907 people were displaced by the conflict in 2017 alone, bringing the total number of internally displaced people (IDPs) to more than 2 million. Despite the promises made by successive Afghan governments, IDPs continued to lack adequate housing, food, water, health care and opportunities to pursue education and employment. Most were forced to make long daily trips to fetch water and struggled to obtain one daily meal. Most IDPs lacked access to basic health care facilities. Private health care was unaffordable for most IDPs, and mobile clinics, operated by NGOs or the government, were only available sporadically.

IDPs also faced repeated threats of forced eviction from both government and private actors.

HUMAN RIGHTS DEFENDERS

Human rights defenders faced constant threats to their life and security. In June, at least four people were killed when police opened fire on demonstrators protesting deteriorating security conditions in Kabul following a 31 May truck bombing that killed more than 150 people. No investigations appeared to have been conducted into the police shootings. Relatives of the victims subsequently staged a sit-in for several weeks in Kabul, which the police broke up by force. One person was killed and at least five others were reported to have been arbitrarily detained in a private house and questioned by plain-clothes officers before being released the next day. In July, the government proposed amendments to the laws on associations, strikes and demonstrations, which would limit the rights to freedom of association and expression by introducing new restrictions on the organization of demonstrations and strikes. The proposed amendments would also give police enhanced authority to stop or prevent demonstrations or strikes, further undermining the right to peaceful assembly.

Women human rights defenders continued to face threats and intimidation by both state and non-state actors across Afghanistan. Most cases were not reported to police because of lack of trust in the security agencies, which consistently failed to investigate and address these threats. Some who did report threats were not given support or protection.

FREEDOM OF EXPRESSION

A string of violent attacks and intimidation against journalists, including killings, further underlined the steady erosion of freedom of expression.

Media freedom watchdog Nai reported more than 150 attacks against journalists, media workers and media offices during the year. These included killings, beatings, detention, arson, attacks, threats and other forms of violence by both state and non-state actors.

In March, a reporter working for Ariana TV in Sar-e-Pul province was beaten by police after trying to report on excessive use of force against civilians. Officers seized the reporter's camera and other equipment; he sought refuge in the governor's office.

In August, a prominent reporter from Zabul province received death threats from Taliban members, followed by attempts on his life.

Security officials made little effort to protect him after he reported the incidents, and he left the province for his safety.

In November, IS fighters attacked Shamshad TV's station in Kabul; one staff member was killed and others wounded.

Nai reported that in 2016 it had submitted to the authorities at least 240 cases of violence against media workers, including reporters and journalists. One year later the government had taken no action in response and no one had been brought to justice.

TORTURE AND OTHER ILL-TREATMENT

Afghans across the country remained at risk of torture and other ill-treatment, with little progress towards curbing impunity. The UN Committee against Torture found "widespread acceptance and legitimation of torture in Afghan society".

Many of those suspected of criminal responsibility continued to hold official executive positions, including in government. The Committee also found that detainees held by the National Directorate of Security, the Afghan National Police and the Afghan Local Police were subject to "beatings, electric shocks, suspensions, threats, sexual abuse, and other forms of mental and physical abuse". UNAMA and OHCHR investigators who had interviewed 469 detainees said that 39% of them gave credible accounts of torture and other ill-treatment during their arrest and interrogation.

In March the government enacted an Anti-Torture Law, which criminalized torture but did not provide for restitution or compensation to victims.

Armed groups including the Taliban continued to commit crimes under international law, including killings, torture and other abuses as punishment for perceived crimes or offences. The executions and severe punishments imposed by the parallel justice system amounted to criminal acts under the law, and in some circumstances could amount to war crimes.

DEATH PENALTY

In a revision to the Penal Code, life imprisonment replaced the death penalty for some offences.

Five executions were carried out in November at Pul-e-Charki prison in Kabul. The Ministry of the Interior said that the five had been convicted in 2016 of murder and kidnapping, and that they had been executed despite their sentences being under review by three appeal courts.

ALBANIA

Republic of Albania
Head of state: **Ilir Meta (replaced Bujar Nishani in July)**
Head of government: **Edi Rama**

Impunity persisted for past killings and enforced disappearances. Measures protecting women from domestic violence were inadequately implemented. Women and children were trafficked for forced prostitution and labour. Albania's path to EU membership was hindered by slow progress in combating corruption and organized crime.

BACKGROUND

A political crisis preceded elections in June. The opposition Democratic Party, which organized street protests in February, boycotted the election process until May, when an EU and US-supported agreement promised them representation in government and state agencies. The ruling Socialist Party was returned with an increased majority. International observers reported incidents of voter intimidation and alleged vote-buying.

Under a new mechanism established in January, by August 183 people, including author Ismail Kadare, applied to access secret police files held on them during the Communist period. In September, the International Commission on Missing Persons agreed to assist with the identification of bodies recovered from mass graves from the same period.

JUSTICE SYSTEM

Measures to ensure judicial independence were partially implemented. In June, two judicial associations appealed to the Constitutional Court against a vetting law, which sought to ensure judges' and prosecutors' independence from organized crime.

IMPUNITY

In a case brought before the European Court of Human Rights, in April the government agreed to reopen proceedings in the case of four protesters killed during January 2011 demonstrations. A total payment of just over EUR100,000 as a form of compensation was divided between relatives of two of the victims.

ENFORCED DISAPPEARANCES

No measures were taken to locate the body of Remzi Hoxha, a Macedonian Albanian who was forcibly disappeared by National Intelligence Service officials in 1995. No progress was reported towards the exhumation of the remains of around 6,000 people who had disappeared between 1945 and 1991.

FREEDOM OF EXPRESSION – JOURNALISTS

Physical attacks against investigative journalists were perpetrated by organized criminals, or owners of private companies. In March, journalist Elvi Fundo was beaten in the capital, Tirana, by assailants believed to be associated with organized crime. In June, TV channel owner Erven Hyseni was shot dead in Vlora, along with a government official.

In July, journalists claimed that defamation proceedings brought against two media outlets by High Court Judge Gjin Gjoni and his wife, businesswoman Elona Caushi, aimed to intimidate investigative journalists and encourage self-censorship.

RIGHTS OF LESBIAN, GAY, BISEXUAL, TRANSGENDER AND INTERSEX PEOPLE

In February two NGOs filed a complaint with the European Court of Human Rights, requesting an amendment to the Family Code which prohibits cohabitation rights for same-sex couples. An August survey found widespread discrimination in employment in both the public and private sectors.

MIGRANTS' RIGHTS

In May, a UK court found that hundreds of lesbian and gay people, trafficking victims and domestic violence survivors may have been wrongly deported to Albania since 2011 because UK courts had relied on incorrect guidance. Some 4,421 Albanian asylum-seekers voluntarily returned from EU countries; 2,500 rejected asylum-seekers were deported from Germany.

Unaccompanied minors and families with children were sometimes detained in the Irregular Foreigners Centre at Karreç, a closed centre for irregular migrants due for deportation.

ECONOMIC, SOCIAL AND CULTURAL RIGHTS

In September, 20 children's NGOs protested against the abolition of the Labour and Social Welfare Ministry, which threatened to put social services at risk.

The Ministry of Urban Development reconstructed 300 Roma and Egyptian houses, and improved sanitation. However, most Roma lacked clean water and many were at risk of forced evictions.

VIOLENCE AGAINST WOMEN AND GIRLS

Reports of domestic violence increased; 420 immediate protection orders had been issued by 1 June. In August, Judge Fildeze Hafizi was shot and killed in her car by her former husband. She had been granted a protection order in 2015 after he had beaten her. He was convicted and imprisoned in April 2016, but released in early 2017 under a general amnesty.

ALGERIA

People's Democratic Republic of Algeria
Head of state: **Abdelaziz Bouteflika**
Head of government: **Ahmed Ouyahia (replaced
Abdelmadjid Tebboune in August, who replaced
Abdelmalek Sellal in May)**

The authorities continued to arbitrarily
detain peaceful demonstrators, human
rights defenders, activists and journalists.
Associations continued to face undue
restrictions, and legislation that restricted
the right to form trade unions remained in
place. Members of the Ahmadi Muslim
religious minority group were unjustly
prosecuted. Impunity for past abuses
prevailed. Migrants faced mass expulsions.
Courts handed down death sentences; no
executions were carried out.

BACKGROUND

In January, new austerity measures
announced by the government triggered
protests and strikes, particularly in the
northern Kabylia and Chaouia regions. In
February, a presidential decree established
Algeria's new national human rights
institution, the National Human Rights
Council, replacing the National Consultative
Commission for the Promotion and Protection
of Human Rights. In May, Algeria was
examined under the UN UPR process for the
third time.[1] Also in May, legislative elections
characterized by low participation brought
limited change to party representation in
parliament and Abdelmadjid Tebboune briefly
became Prime Minister after a government
reshuffle, before Ahmed Ouyahia replaced
him in August.

Low-level sporadic clashes took place
between security forces and armed
opposition groups in several areas. In August,
a suicide bomber killed himself and two
policemen in an attack on a police station in
Tiaret, west of the capital Algiers, which was
later claimed by both the armed group
Islamic State (IS) and al-Qa'ida in the Islamic
Maghreb (AQIM).

FREEDOMS OF EXPRESSION AND ASSEMBLY

The authorities continued to arrest and
prosecute peaceful activists, including those
protesting about unemployment and public
services. Those protesting in solidarity with
detained activists, as well as journalists and
bloggers covering protests on social media,
were also detained.

In January, police arrested renowned
blogger Merzoug Touati in Bejaia, Kabylia
region, following anti-austerity protests in
Kabylia. The authorities kept him in detention
while investigating him for interviewing an
Israeli Ministry of Foreign Affairs spokesman
on his blog, and for posts about the protests.

In June, police arrested journalist Said
Chitour on suspicion of espionage and selling
classified documents to foreign diplomats. In
November his case was transferred to the
Penal Court.

The authorities maintained a protest ban in
Algiers under a decree from 2001.

FREEDOM OF ASSOCIATION

The authorities kept many associations,
including Amnesty International Algeria and
other human rights groups, in legal limbo by
failing to respond to registration applications
under the highly restrictive Associations Law.
Local authorities denied authorization to the
Algerian League for the Defence of Human
Rights (LADDH) to hold a human rights
meeting in October and a public event
celebrating the Universal Declaration of
Human Rights in December. The government
had yet to produce a new draft law respecting
freedom of association, as required by the
constitutional amendments of 2016.

HUMAN RIGHTS DEFENDERS

Human rights defender Hassan Bouras was
released in January after a court reduced his
one-year prison term to a six-month
suspended sentence. Police had arrested
him for posting a video on the YouTube
channel of the El Bayadh branch of LADDH
alleging corruption among high-ranking
officials in the city of El Bayadh.

In March, a court in Ghardaia referred human rights lawyer Salah Dabouz of LADDH to trial in relation to comments he made on television about unrest in Ghardaia and for allegedly carrying a computer and camera during a visit to detained activists. The court had kept him under judicial supervision from July 2016 until March 2017, forcing him to travel more than 600km twice a week to report to the court in Ghardaia from his home in Algiers.

In April, the investigative judge at a court in Medea transferred a case against human rights lawyer Noureddine Ahmine of the Network of Lawyers for the Defence of Human Rights (RADDH) to a court in Ghardaia for trial on charges of "insulting a public institution" and "falsely" reporting an offence. The charges related to a complaint of torture that he had filed, apparently on behalf of someone else, in 2014.

UNFAIR TRIALS

In May, a court in Medea unfairly convicted the founder of the Movement for the Autonomy of the Mzab (MAM), Kamaleddine Fekhar, and 21 of his 41 co-defendants of murder, terrorism and other serious offences, for their alleged role in communal violence in Ghardaia province between 2013 and 2015 which left an estimated 25 people dead.[2] They were sentenced to prison terms of between three and five years, partially suspended. All were then released between May and July 2017 after having served their sentence. Among the 41 defendants, 37 had been in pre-trial detention, many since 2015.

In July, the Spanish authorities detained MAM activists Salah Abbouna and Khodir Sekkouti after Algerian authorities filed an extradition request against them, citing their criticism of Algerian authorities on Facebook. In October the Spanish authorities released both activists on bail awaiting the National High Court's decision on extradition.

FREEDOM OF RELIGION AND BELIEF

More than 280 members of the minority Ahmadi religious movement were prosecuted in relation to their religious beliefs and practices during the year.[3] From April onwards, courts released 16 Ahmadis after reducing or suspending their sentences, while dozens of others remained under investigation or on trial and five remained in detention. In August, authorities rearrested Mohamed Fali, head of the Ahmadi community in Algeria, in Ain Safra, Naama province, before trying him before the Ain Tedles Court of First Instance for collecting donations without a licence, "denigrating Islamic dogma", and "membership of an unauthorized association". By the end of the year, he faced six cases pending before different courts arising from the peaceful practice of his faith.

IMPUNITY

The authorities took no steps to open investigations and counter the impunity for grave human rights abuses and possible crimes against humanity, including unlawful killings, enforced disappearances, rape and other forms of torture committed by security forces and armed groups in the 1990s during Algeria's internal conflict, which left an estimated 200,000 people killed or forcibly disappeared.

In January, the Swiss judiciary shelved a war crimes investigation against retired Algerian Minister of Defence Khaled Nezzar for events between 1992 and 1994 in Algeria, citing inadmissibility due to the absence of armed conflict in Algeria at the time.

In February, the UN Human Rights Committee found that the Algerian authorities had violated the right to remedy, the right to life, and the prohibition against torture with regard to Mohamed Belamrania, who was forcibly disappeared and extrajudicially executed in 1995. Days after the UN finding was published, police detained his son, Rafik Belamrania, and charged him with "advocating terrorism on Facebook". He had filed his father's case before the UN body and documented other cases of enforced disappearance, arbitrary detention and extrajudicial executions by Algeria's security forces against suspected supporters of the

Islamic Salvation Front (FIS) party during the 1990s. In November he was sentenced to five years' imprisonment and fined 100,000 Algerian dinars (around USD870).

REFUGEES' AND MIGRANTS' RIGHTS

From April to June, a group of 25 Syrian refugees, including 10 children, were stranded in the buffer zone of Morocco's desert border area with Algeria.[4] In June, the Algerian authorities announced they would permit them to enter Algeria and would allow UNHCR, the UN refugee agency, to provide them with assistance. However, the Algerian authorities later refused to let them in through an unofficial crossing point. The refugees remained stranded in the desert until Morocco granted them protection.

Between August and December the authorities arbitrary arrested and forcibly expelled more than 6,500 sub-Saharan African migrants to neighbouring Niger and Mali on the basis of racial profiling.[5]

In February, a court in Annaba convicted 27 people, including Algerians, for irregular exit from Algeria after they attempted to leave the country by boat. They were fined 20,000 Algerian dinars (about USD180) each.

WORKERS' RIGHTS

The Labour Code continued to unduly restrict the right to form trade unions by limiting trade union federations and confederations to single occupational sectors; allowing only Algerian-born people or those who had held Algerian nationality for a minimum of 10 years to create trade union organizations; and imposing restrictions on foreign funding for trade unions. Authorities continued to deny registration to the independent, cross-sector General Autonomous Confederation for Algerian Workers, since it first filed its application in 2013.

In May, the Ministry of Labour banned the National Autonomous Electricity and Gas Trade Union by withdrawing its recognition. A government official publicly denied the ban during an International Labour Conference session in June.

DEATH PENALTY

Courts continued to impose death sentences. No executions have been carried out since 1993.

1. Human Rights Council adopts Universal Periodic Review outcome on Algeria (MDE 28/7152/2017)

2. Algeria: Ensure fair trial for minority rights activists (News story, 29 May)

3. Algeria: Wave of arrests and prosecutions of hundreds of Ahmadis (News story, 19 June)

4. Morocco: Syrian refugees trapped in desert on Moroccan border with Algeria in dire need of assistance (News story, 7 June)

5. Algeria: Mass racial profiling used to deport more than 2,000 sub-Saharan migrants (News story, 23 October)

ANGOLA

Republic of Angola
Head of state and government: **João Manuel Gonçalves Lourenço (replaced José Eduardo dos Santos in September)**

Agri-business mega projects displaced communities from their land. Although the restrictive NGO law was repealed, the space for individuals to exercise their civil and political rights continued to shrink. Peaceful protesters were met with violent repression; government critics faced criminal defamation suits. Attempts by Parliament to criminalize abortion in all circumstances were defeated.

BACKGROUND

Historic elections were held on 23 August. João Lourenço of the ruling People's Movement for the Liberation of Angola (MPLA) became President. According to the Electoral Commission, the MPLA obtained 61% of the vote, down from 81% in 2012. Opposition parties – National Union for the Total Independence of Angola (UNITA), Broad Convergence for the Salvation of Angola-Electoral Coalition (CASA-CE), and National Front for the Liberation of Angola (FNLA) – contended that the election results were illegitimate, but took their seats in Parliament.

The continuing economic crisis precipitated popular discontent with the MPLA. Because of the economic crisis, the government adopted a development model for agri-business mega projects, large-scale land acquisition, and dispossession of rural communities, which put community livelihoods at risk.

Political intolerance was increasingly normalized due, in part, to government indifference to sectarian violence in Monte Belo in Benguela province. Following the signing in 2002 of the peace agreement between the government and UNITA, the area became an enclave of political conflict with increasing polarization of and violence between MPLA and UNITA supporters. Monte Belo residents continued to suffer persecution, violence, death threats, intimidation and looting on grounds of suspected allegiance to one or other of the political parties. Despite public objections from civil society, the government allowed a culture of impunity and violent political intolerance to develop.

FREEDOM OF EXPRESSION

To silence critics, particularly journalists and academics, the authorities used defamation laws among others, restricting freedom of expression and access to information. The misuse of the justice system and other state institutions in order to silence critics remained commonplace. The "Press Law Pack" of five bills was passed by Parliament in January; it included Press Law, Journalist's Statute, Radio Broadcasting Law, Television Law and Social Communications Regulatory Body Law.

The laws contained provisions that restricted freedom of expression, particularly press freedoms, through a series of prohibitive regulations on social communication and by establishing a communications regulatory body with oversight competencies, including the power to determine whether or not a given communication met good journalistic practices; this amounted to prior censorship

and hindrance of the free flow of ideas and opinions.

The majority of the regulatory body's members were nominated by MPLA, the party with the most seats in the National Assembly, which caused concerns as to the body's independence and impartiality.

On 20 June, Rafael Marques de Morais, investigative journalist and editor of the online publication Maka Angola, and Mariano Brás Lourenço, journalist and editor for O Crime newspaper, were charged with "defamation of a public authority" and causing "outrage to a sovereign body" in relation to an article they published questioning the acquisition of public land by the General Public Prosecutor.

FREEDOM OF ASSEMBLY

The authorities frequently refused to allow peaceful demonstrations to take place, even though prior authorization was not required in law. When demonstrations did take place, police often arbitrarily arrested, detained and ill-treated peaceful protesters. However, no investigations were initiated into the police actions.

On 24 February, police violently repressed two peaceful protests by the Angolan Revolutionary Movement taking place simultaneously in Luanda, the capital, and Benguela. The protesters demanded the resignation of Bornito de Sousa, Minister of Territorial Administration, who was in charge of electoral registration for the August election and was also the MPLA's vice-presidential candidate; these roles were seen as amounting to a conflict of interests and to a violation of the electoral law. After handcuffing and forcing the protesters to lie down, the police beat them with batons.

On 24 June, security forces violently dispersed a peaceful demonstration organized by the Lunda-Tchokwe Protectorate Movement, which campaigned for autonomy for the eastern and southeastern regions in Lunda Norte province. Security forces used live ammunition against demonstrators, killing a bystander, and injuring 13 protesters. They arrested 70 people; on 28 June, they were sentenced each to 45 days' imprisonment and a fine of 22,000 kwanzas (USD135). Those who paid the fines had their sentences suspended and were released immediately while the others served their full prison terms. The protesters were calling for, among other things, an end to persecution and arbitrary imprisonment of their members, and for the release of political prisoners in Kakanda Prison in Lunda Norte.

FREEDOM OF ASSOCIATION

Repression of the right to freedom of association persisted. The space in which human rights defenders, political activists, journalists, broadcasters and civil society organizations could exercise their civil and political rights was increasingly restricted. On 11 July, however, the Constitutional Court struck down the NGO law which had been passed by presidential decree No. 74/15 in 2015. The law had restricted the legal framework within which NGOs could operate, and empowered the Public Prosecutor's Office to suspend national and international NGO activities on suspicion of money laundering, or illegal or harmful acts against "Angola's sovereignty and integrity". The decree imposed burdens on civil society organizations, including excessive requirements and unwieldly procedures for NGO registration; excessive control over NGO activities; funding restrictions and sanctions.

UNFAIR TRIALS

On 25 September, six people, five of whom had been held in prolonged pre-trial detention for one year, were brought to trial before Luanda Provincial Court on charges of "organizing terrorism". However, the trial was adjourned the same day when the Public Prosecutor failed to appear in court alleging health reasons. The Court granted the substitute prosecutor's plea to be allowed more time so that he could familiarize himself with the case. Five of the accused remained in detention while a sixth, the wife of one of the detained, remained under house arrest at the end of the year.

SEXUAL AND REPRODUCTIVE RIGHTS

In March, the government proposed an amendment to legislation under the Penal Code which would de-criminalize abortion in cases where a woman's pregnancy was the result of rape, or when the pregnant woman's health was at risk. Parliament rejected the proposal. The final parliamentary vote on the legislation was scheduled for later the same month, but was postponed indefinitely following a public outcry against Parliament's rejection of the government's proposal to liberalize the abortion laws.

LAND DISPUTES

Ongoing land acquisition for business, mainly in southern provinces of Cunene and Huíla, continued to devastate local communities who relied on the land for their livelihoods.

In April and May, the government of Huíla presented its Transhumance Project, which included plans to appropriate a water fountain used by the community of Capela de Santo António in the Kahila area of Gambos municipality. Capela de Santo António is home to 600 families who depended on the fountain for drinking water, and for their livestock and irrigation. The community was not consulted over the plans and the authorities did not conduct an environmental impact assessment. The government of Huíla remained determined to seize the community's water fountain in violation of the Constitution and laws including the Land Law and the Environmental Law.

In June, it came to light that the Angolan government had authorized the Agro-Industrial Horizonte 2020 mega project to appropriate 76,000 hectares of fertile land without the free, prior and informed consent of the affected communities. The land is in the west of Ombadja municipality and the south of Curoca municipality, both in Cunene province. It is home to 39 communities of 2,129 families with 10,675 children who live by the Cunene River. They have historically relied on agriculture and livestock for their livelihoods. By the end of the year, vegetation on 15,000 hectares had been destroyed, including trees used for food and firewood, grass for cattle grazing, and burial sites; 19 families had been expelled from the land and forced into vagrancy with diminishing access to food and water.

ARGENTINA

Argentine Republic
Head of state and government: **Mauricio Macri**

Women and girls faced obstacles in accessing legal abortions. Indigenous Peoples continued to be criminalized and discriminated against. Migrants' rights suffered significant setbacks.

BACKGROUND

Argentina's human rights situation was reviewed under the UN UPR process and by the UN Committee against Torture. The UN Working Group on Arbitrary Detention (WGAD), the UN Independent Expert on sexual orientation and gender identity and the Rapporteur on Argentina for the Inter-American Commission on Human Rights visited Argentina during the year.

In November, Congress approved the national law on gender parity.

SEXUAL AND REPRODUCTIVE RIGHTS

Women and girls continued to encounter barriers to accessing legal abortion when the pregnancy posed a risk to their health, or when it resulted from rape. Full decriminalization of abortion was pending in parliament.

VIOLENCE AGAINST WOMEN

According to civil society information, at least 254 femicides occurred between January and November. The National Women's Institute and the National Plan of Action for the Prevention, Assistance and Eradication of Violence against Women for 2017-2019 appeared to lack the necessary resources to be fully implemented.

INDIGENOUS PEOPLES' RIGHTS

The majority of Indigenous communities still lacked legal recognition of their land rights, despite the Constitution recognizing their right to ancestral lands and natural resources.

In January, local police and members of the Argentine National Gendarmerie (GNA) – a militarized federal police – closed off all access points to the Indigenous land inhabited by the Mapuche community Pu Lof en Resistencia in Chubut province. The community reported attacks by the police, including beatings and intimidation of children.[1] At least 10 community members and their supporters were arrested. In August the GNA conducted an illegal raid in the same community, during which Santiago Maldonado – a non-Indigenous supporter of the Mapuche community – disappeared. In October his body was found in a river in the territory. The judicial investigation into his death was ongoing at the end of the year.

The Neuquén provincial government, oil unions and industry created an investment plan for the Vaca Muerta oilfield, located partly on the land of the Lof Campo Maripe Indigenous community, without the community's participation.

Authorities used legal proceedings to intimidate Indigenous Peoples, including accusations of sedition, resisting authority, theft, attempted assaults and killings. Agustín Santillán, an Indigenous leader of the Wichí people in Formosa province, spent 190 days in pre-trial detention from April to October with more than 28 criminal proceedings against him.

REFUGEES' AND MIGRANTS' RIGHTS

Bypassing parliamentary debate, the government modified the 2004 Migration Act, limiting entry and residency rights and potentially hastening deportations.

The Asylum Act had not yet been fully implemented, 11 years after its adoption, and the National Committee for Refugees had no specific budget. The reception system for asylum-seekers remained slow and insufficient and there was no integration plan in place to help asylum-seekers and refugees access basic rights such as education, work, health care and language training.

Despite Argentina's commitment in 2016 to receive 3,000 Syrian refugees, no resettlement programme had been created. Fewer than 400 Syrian refugees had benefited from a private sponsorship and humanitarian visa scheme.

IMPUNITY

Trials before ordinary civilian courts continued to be held for crimes against humanity during the 1976-1983 military regime. Between 2006 and May 2017, 182 rulings were issued, bringing the total number of convictions to 756 and acquittals to 74.

In July, the Federal Court of Mendoza issued a historic decision under which four former members of the judiciary were sentenced to life in prison and barred from holding public office for contributing to the commission of crimes against humanity during the military regime.

The Supreme Court ruled in the case of Luis Muiña – who was found guilty of crimes against humanity – that one day served in pre-trial detention must be considered as two, if the person has been detained without sentence for more than two years. Congress then passed a law clarifying that the so-called "2x1 formula" may not be applied to crimes against humanity, genocide or war crimes.[2]

Public hearings continued in the case of the cover-up of the investigation into the 1994 attack on the Jewish Mutual Association of Argentina building. A government decree issued in April 2017 transferred classified documents from the Prosecution Unit to the Ministry of Justice, compromising the independence of the investigation and restricting complainants' access to evidence.

FREEDOMS OF EXPRESSION AND ASSEMBLY

Indiscriminate detentions took place during an International Women's Day demonstration on 8 March. Many women reported that they were mistreated, detained and humiliated by police; some said they were forced to undress completely.

In April, teachers were violently repressed while demonstrating for fair wages. Participants reported that police used tear gas and beat them while the military stood by. At least four teachers were arrested.

In September, 31 people were violently detained and held at several police stations in the capital, Buenos Aires, for more than 48 hours for participating in a mass demonstration following the disappearance of Santiago Maldonado. Those detained reported that they were beaten and some women were forced to undress.

In December, many protesters took to the streets in Buenos Aires to express their disagreement with a legislative reform proposed by the government. The police used excessive force and there were reports of arbitrary detentions during the demonstrations.[3]

The call by WGAD to national authorities to immediately release social leader and activist Milagro Sala was not implemented. In August, the Inter-American Commission on Human Rights requested that Argentina offer Milagro Sala house arrest or other alternatives to prison. This request was only partially implemented since its conditions did not comply with domestic and international standards.

1. Argentina: Violent repression of Mapuche Peoples (AMR 13/5477/2017)

2. Argentina: Amnistía Internacional repudia la aplicación del 2x1 a delitos de lesa humanidad y estará presente en Plaza de Mayo (News story, 9 May)

3. Argentina: Autoridades deben garantizar protesta pacífica e investigar violaciones a derechos humanos tras represión frente al Congreso de la Nación (News story, 15 December)

ARMENIA

Republic of Armenia
Head of state: **Serzh Sargsyan**
Head of government: **Karen Karapetyan**

Lack of accountability continued for the use of unnecessary and excessive force by police during protests in the capital, Yerevan, in 2016. The trials of opposition members accused of hostage-taking and other violent crimes violated the right to a fair trial. A human rights defender faced criminal charges. The parliamentary and Yerevan city council elections were accompanied by incidents of violence.

BACKGROUND

On 2 April, the ruling Republican Party won a parliamentary majority, in the first elections since the 2015 constitutional referendum approved the transition from a presidential to a parliamentary republic. Monitors from the OSCE reported that the elections were "tainted by credible information about vote-buying, and pressure on civil servants and employees of private companies" to vote for the ruling party.

In November, Armenia and the EU signed a Comprehensive and Enhanced Partnership Agreement, a looser form of co-operation than the Association Agreement which Armenia rejected in 2013 in favour of joining the Russian-led customs union.

IMPUNITY

There was limited accountability for the unnecessary and excessive use of force by police against largely peaceful anti-government protesters in Yerevan in July 2016, when hundreds of individuals were injured and arbitrarily arrested. Dozens of protesters faced criminal charges for allegedly violating public order and other offences. The criminal investigation into allegations of abuse of power by police officers did not lead to any criminal charges.

UNFAIR TRIALS

Members of the opposition group that occupied a police station in the run-up to the 2016 protests stood trial on charges of a range of violent crimes, including hostage-taking and killing of police officers. Several defendants reported being beaten in detention, while their defence lawyers reported that they themselves were subjected to pressure and harassment to obstruct their work.

Arayik Papikyan, Mushegh Shushanyan, Nina Karapetyants and other defence lawyers in the case complained that the detention facility's administration prevented them from visiting the accused men and holding confidential meetings with them, and unlawfully confiscated and destroyed some of the case-related materials they were carrying. Several lawyers also reported being subjected to lengthy and intrusive security searches when arriving at court. Lawyers who refused to undergo searches were denied entry to the courtrooms and subjected to disciplinary proceedings by the Bar Association.

The lawyers also reported that, on 28 June, five defendants were forcibly removed from the courtroom, taken to the basement and beaten by several police officers while the court was in session. The defendants showed signs of ill-treatment, including bruises and scratches on their faces and legs, documented by prison medical staff. The police claimed these injuries were self-inflicted when the defendants deliberately hit their heads and feet against walls and fences in protest. At the end of the year, investigations were ongoing into the allegations of the beatings and the harassment of the lawyers.

HUMAN RIGHTS DEFENDERS

In January, court hearings commenced in the case against Marina Poghosyan, a human rights defender and director of the NGO Veles, known for exposing government corruption and providing legal aid to victims of human rights violations. She had been charged with extortion in 2015 after she alleged that former government officials were running a money laundering scheme. Local human rights defenders linked the trial to her work exposing corruption. On 30 April, Marina Poghosyan reported that a fake Facebook profile had been created under her name and used to send sexually explicit photos and videos to her contacts to smear her reputation.

FREEDOM OF EXPRESSION

The parliamentary and Yerevan city council elections, in April and May respectively, and the preceding electoral campaigns were accompanied by isolated incidents of violence against journalists and others attempting to expose violations of the electoral process.

On 2 April, two journalists were attacked in Yerevan's Kond neighbourhood while investigating allegations of vote-buying at the local Republican Party's campaign office. Supporters of the Party took away one reporter's video equipment as she was filming people leaving the campaign office. An investigation into the incident was ongoing at the end of the year.

ECONOMIC, SOCIAL AND CULTURAL RIGHTS

The CERD Committee raised concerns over the absence of data on the enjoyment of economic, social and cultural rights by minority groups, refugees and asylum-seekers. It also raised concern over the lack of information available on small minority ethnic groups – such as the Lom (also known as Bosha) and the Molokans – and requested that the authorities collect data on economic and social indicators disaggregated by ethnicity, nationality and country of origin.

AUSTRALIA

Australia
Head of state: **Queen Elizabeth II, represented by Peter Cosgrove**
Head of government: **Malcolm Turnbull**

The justice system continued to fail Indigenous people, particularly children, with high rates of incarceration, reports of abuse and deaths in custody. Australia maintained hardline policies by confining people seeking asylum in offshore processing centres in Papua New Guinea and Nauru, and turning back those attempting to reach Australia by boat. In October, Australia was elected to the UN Human Rights Council, attracting calls for improvement of its human rights record, including cutting all ties to the Myanmar military.

INDIGENOUS PEOPLES' RIGHTS

Indigenous children were 25 times more likely to be imprisoned than non-Indigenous children.

Leaked footage exposed abuses of children in prison in the Northern Territory, including tear gassing, restraints, choking and solitary confinement. In response, a Royal Commission into the Protection and Detention of Children in the Northern Territory was established and reported on 17 November.

An independent review of youth detention centres in Queensland released in April found abuses including solitary confinement, use of dogs to intimidate, missing CCTV footage, and children at risk of self-harm being sedated and hogtied. Further alleged abuses emerged in Victoria, New South Wales, the Australian Capital Territory and Western Australia.

Indigenous adults were 15 times more likely to be jailed than non-Indigenous adults. At least eight Indigenous people died in police custody.

The government did not adopt a national plan to ensure Australia meets its obligations in protecting the rights of Indigenous children. However, on 15 December, it ratified the Optional Protocol to the Convention against Torture (OPCAT), which mandates that youth detention centres and police lockups are subject to independent oversight and monitoring.

REFUGEES AND ASYLUM-SEEKERS

On 9 April, the government announced that the Australian-run facility on Manus Island, Papua New Guinea (PNG), would be closed by 31 October following the PNG Supreme Court ruling in 2016 that the centre was "illegal" and "unconstitutional". On 14 April, PNG Defence Force personnel fired into the centre injuring nine people.

The men in detention were forcibly moved into "transit" centres on Manus Island on 24 November. By the end of the year there was no clear plan for the settlement of refugees in a safe country.

As of December there were approximately 800 adult males in detention on Manus Island (see Papua New Guinea entry).

The Australian government was forced to pay a settlement in June to nearly 2,000 refugees and asylum-seekers held on Manus Island, for illegally detaining them in horrific conditions between 2012 and 2016.

As of 30 November, there were 339 people living in the offshore processing facility on Nauru, including 36 children. They were subjected to humiliation, neglect, abuse and poor physical and mental health care. At least 820 additional refugees lived in the community on Nauru; these people faced serious security risks and inadequate access to health care, education and employment.

Approximately 435 people transferred to Australia for medical treatment remained at risk of return to either Nauru or Manus Island.

Australia continued its "turnback" policy. In May the government reported that since 2013, 30 boats had been returned either to Indonesia or to their country of departure. During 2017 people were directly returned to their country of nationality on three known occasions: from a boat containing 25 Sri

Lankan nationals in March; five Chinese nationals who landed in northern Australia in August; and a boat containing 29 Sri Lankan nationals in December.

Australia continued its policy of mandatory indefinite detention of people arriving by plane without a visa. As of 30 November, there were 1,301 people in immigration detention onshore (including on Christmas Island). Of these, 19.8% had been detained for over 730 days.

Australia's resettlement and humanitarian intake was 16,250 for its financial year beginning in June. This decreased from almost 22,000 for the previous financial year, with an additional intake of Syrian and Iraqi refugees ending.

RIGHTS OF LESBIAN, GAY, BISEXUAL, TRANSGENDER AND INTERSEX PEOPLE

Following an overwhelming vote in favour of same-sex marriage, Parliament passed legislation to create marriage equality in December. The postal survey process chosen by the government failed to acknowledge that marriage equality is a human right and generated divisive and damaging public debate.

AUSTRIA

Republic of Austria
Head of state: **Alexander Van der Bellen (replaced Heinz Fischer in January)**
Head of government: **Sebastian Kurz (replaced Christian Kern in December)**

The number of asylum-seekers continued to fall. Authorities continued to deport rejected asylum-seekers to Afghanistan despite the security situation in the country. Amendments to the law on public assemblies increased the potential for restrictions on the right to peaceful assembly.

REFUGEES' AND MIGRANTS' RIGHTS – FORCIBLE RETURN

Between January and August, 17,095 people requested asylum; the number fell by nearly half compared to 32,114 people for the same period in 2016.

In October, Parliament amended the asylum law to automatically add a return order to any decision concerning the revocation of asylum or subsidiary protection status, for example upon conviction for a criminal offence, increasing the risk of *refoulement* – forcible return of an individual to a country where they would risk serious human rights violations.

The authorities continued to deport rejected asylum-seekers and undocumented migrants to Afghanistan despite the deterioration of the security situation in the country. In the first half of the year, 67 people were forcibly returned there.

In September, the Minister of the Interior announced the non-renewal of the Humanitarian Admission Programme pointing to the large number of asylum cases that were still pending. Since 2013, 1,900 vulnerable refugees had been successfully resettled through the Programme.

During the year, asylum-seekers brought six individual complaints before the UN Human Rights Committee alleging that their return under the Dublin III Regulation (an EU law that establishes the criteria and mechanisms for determining the EU member state responsible for examining an asylum application) to Bulgaria and Italy would violate their human rights. In March the authorities deported a Syrian family to Bulgaria and in June a Somalian woman to Italy, despite the Human Rights Committee requesting Austria to refrain from doing so.

FREEDOM OF ASSEMBLY

In June, Parliament amended the law on public assemblies, which gave the authorities new vaguely formulated grounds to prohibit public assemblies, including where an assembly is "against a foreign policy interest". Shortly after, the Minister of the Interior suggested the introduction of further far-reaching amendments to the law, including fines and other administrative measures against organizers not complying with the law, and a cap on the number of public assemblies taking place in shopping streets. There were no steps to further amend the law at the end of the year.

COUNTER-TERROR AND SECURITY

In July, the government tabled an amendment to the Criminal Procedure Code that would introduce several new far-reaching surveillance methods. The amendment gave rise to concern regarding the right to privacy. The methods included software to access data from smartphones and techniques to intercept mobile phone traffic. The authorities would be able to use many of those techniques without seeking prior judicial authorization.

DISCRIMINATION

In October, a new law entered into force banning any kind of full-face covering in public spaces. Despite its purpose of "promoting active participation in society", the law disproportionately restricted the rights to freedom of expression and of religion or belief.

In June, the Austrian National Council rejected a motion that would open a discussion on equal marriage irrespective of sexual orientation and gender identity. Same-sex couples could enter a civil partnership but were not allowed to marry. In December, the Constitutional Court repealed discriminatory passages of the Marriage Act and the Registered Partnership Act. The repeal was to take effect from 1 January 2019, thus enabling same-sex couples to marry and heterosexual couples to enter registered partnerships.

AZERBAIJAN

Republic of Azerbaijan
Head of state: **Ilham Aliyev**
Head of government: **Artur Rasizade**

Authorities intensified the crackdown on the right to freedom of expression, particularly following revelations of large-scale political corruption. Independent news outlets were blocked and their owners arrested. Critics of the government continued to face politically motivated prosecution and imprisonment following unfair trials. LGBTI individuals were arbitrarily arrested and ill-treated. Suspicious deaths in custody were still not effectively investigated.

BACKGROUND

In July, renewed hostilities in the breakaway region of Nagorno-Karabakh resulted in the death of at least two ethnic Azerbaijani civilians, including a minor, following shelling by the Armenian-backed forces.

Azerbaijan received international attention following a report by the Organized Crime and Corruption Reporting Project, published in September, which accused members of Azerbaijan's political elite of operating a large international money laundering scheme. Part of the money was allegedly used to pay European politicians to help whitewash Azerbaijan's human rights reputation, among other things. On 11 October, the Parliamentary Assembly of the Council of Europe (PACE) adopted two critical resolutions on Azerbaijan following allegations that some members of the PACE had benefited from the money laundering scheme.

On 5 December, the Committee of Ministers of the Council of Europe triggered infringement proceedings against Azerbaijan under Article 46.4 of the European Convention on Human Rights. This followed its repeated failure to implement the decision of the European Court of Human Rights (ECtHR) in the case of opposition leader Ilgar Mammadov to immediately release him; he had been arbitrarily detained since 2013.

The EU and Azerbaijan proceeded with negotiations over a new strategic partnership agreement to deepen their economic relationship. In October, the European Bank for Reconstruction and Development (EBRD) approved a USD500 million loan for the construction of a government-owned gas pipeline. This was despite Azerbaijan's suspension from the EBRD-endorsed international oil and gas transparency initiative in March 2017, due to its repression of civil society.

FREEDOM OF ASSOCIATION

Leading human rights organizations remained unable to resume their work. The authorities continued using restrictive regulations and arbitrary prosecution to close down the few remaining critical organizations.

On 2 May, Aziz Orujev, head of the independent online TV channel Kanal 13, was arrested by a police officer who claimed he looked like a wanted fugitive and remanded him to 30 days of administrative detention for purportedly disobeying police orders. On the day of his release, Aziz Orujev was remanded on fabricated charges of illegal entrepreneurship and abuse of office, and ordered to pre-trial detention. On 15 December Baku Court on Grave Crimes sentenced him to six years' imprisonment.

In August, the prosecution opened an investigation into Azerbaijan's only remaining independent news agency, Turan, and arrested its director, Mehman Aliyev, on fabricated charges of illegal entrepreneurship. Following international pressure, Mehman Aliyev was transferred to house arrest on 11 September. On 2 November, the prosecution dropped the charges against him and closed the investigation against Turan.

FREEDOM OF EXPRESSION

All mainstream media remained under effective government control, with independent media outlets facing undue restrictions and media workers facing harassment. Access to opposition newspaper websites was blocked.

Radio Azadliq (Radio Free Europe/Radio Liberty Azerbaijani service), Meydan TV, and Azerbaycan SAATI, remained blocked following a claim by the prosecutor's office that they posed a threat to national security. On 12 May, a court in the capital, Baku, ruled in favour of keeping the websites blocked.

PROSECUTION OF CRITICS

The authorities continued to arbitrarily arrest and detain independent journalists and bloggers. According to Azerbaijani human rights defenders more than 150 people remained in prison on politically motivated charges, and the number of such cases continued to grow.

On 9 January, police officers detained and held blogger Mehman Huseynov overnight in incommunicado detention. He reported that he was beaten by the police and subjected to electric shocks while in custody. On 3 March, a court in Baku sentenced him to two years in prison for "defaming" police officers.

On 12 January, Afgan Sadygov, a journalist and blogger from Jalilabad District, was sentenced to two and a half years in prison. He was prosecuted under hooliganism charges, after writing about government corruption and refusing to remove his articles from the internet.

On 14 June, Fikret Faramazoglu, editor of the independent news website Journalistic Research Centre, was sentenced to seven years in prison and banned from his profession for a further two years. He had been detained on 30 June 2016 for allegedly extorting money from a restaurant owner, charges that he denied.

FORCIBLE RETURNS

The authorities intensified their clampdown on critics who had fled the country, and unlawfully transferred many of them back to Azerbaijan and harassed their families.

Investigative journalist Afgan Mukhtarli was abducted in Tbilisi, the capital of Georgia, on 29 May, and reappeared in the custody of Azerbaijani border police the following day. He said he had been abducted and trafficked across the border by security services, who accused him of a range of offences including smuggling. He remained in detention and his trial was ongoing at the end of the year.

Russian-Israeli-Ukrainian blogger Aleksandr Lapshin, who published critical posts on the situation in Azerbaijan's breakaway Nagorno-Karabakh region, was arrested in Belarus, and extradited to Azerbaijan in February. In July, a court in Baku sentenced him to three years in prison for entering the breakaway region illegally. He was released on 11 September after a presidential pardon.

RIGHTS OF LESBIAN, GAY, BISEXUAL, TRANSGENDER AND INTERSEX PEOPLE

On 22 September, more than 100 LGBTI individuals were rounded up by the police in public spaces and detained. Some were released, but at least 48 were sentenced to administrative detention, ranging from 10 to 20 days. They were accused of "resisting police's legitimate orders", and found guilty on the basis of police officers' allegations, without any further evidence. The summary hearings fell short of international trial standards. The detainees said they had been beaten by the police and subjected to other ill-treatment while in custody. All were released on 2 October.

UNFAIR TRIALS

Unfair trials were commonplace, particularly in politically motivated proceedings, during which suspects were typically detained and charged without access to a lawyer of their choice. Police continued using torture and other ill-treatment to extract forced confessions which were later used by judges as incriminating evidence. Allegations of torture and other ill-treatment were not effectively investigated.

On 25 January, the Baku Serious Crimes Court sentenced 18 men associated with the Shi'ite Muslim Unity Movement (MUM) in Nardaran to lengthy prison terms. Their trial did not meet international standards of fairness and was marred by numerous torture allegations. During the trial, the defendants complained of having been tortured into signing confessions. Witnesses called by the prosecution also said that they had been threatened by police into incriminating MUM defendants. The forced testimonies were admitted by court and used by the prosecution throughout the trial.

Elgiz Garhaman, a NIDA Youth movement activist, was sentenced to five and a half years in prison on fabricated drug-related charges following an unfair trial. He was denied access to lawyers of his choice, and kept incommunicado for a week following his detention. During the trial, he told the judge the police had beaten, threatened and humiliated him into signing a confession. The judge refused to order an investigation into his allegations, dismissing them as groundless.

On 1 December, the amendments to the Code of Civil and Administrative Procedure excluded lawyers without Bar Association (Collegium of Lawyers) membership from court proceedings.

DEATHS IN CUSTODY

The authorities repeatedly failed to promptly and effectively investigate reported deaths in custody.

On 4 May, the ECtHR ruled that the Azerbaijani government violated the right to life of Mahir Mustafayev for its failure to protect his life while in custody and to conduct an effective investigation into the circumstances of his death. Mahir Mustafayev died from his burns caused by a fire in his cell in December 2006.

On 28 April, activist and blogger Mehman Qalandarov was found hanged in his prison cell in Kurdakhani. Police arrested him on drug-related charges for his Facebook posts in support of two other activists who had been arrested for spraying political graffiti. According to local human rights defenders, Mehman Qalandarov had been tortured and was buried in secret to conceal the evidence. The prison administration announced his death on 29 April, and an investigation was ongoing at the end of the year.

BAHRAIN

Kingdom of Bahrain
Head of state: King Hamad bin Issa al-Khalifa
Head of government: Shaikh Khalifa bin Salman al-Khalifa

The government launched a large-scale campaign to clamp down on all forms of dissent by repressing the rights to freedom of expression and association of human rights defenders and government critics. This campaign was marked by travel bans; the arrest, interrogation and arbitrary detention of human rights defenders; the dissolution of the opposition group Waad and the closure of the newspaper *al-Wasat*; as well as the continued imprisonment of opposition leaders. Scores of people were sentenced to long prison terms after unfair trials. Authorities stripped at least 150 people of their Bahraini nationality, rendering the majority stateless. Mass protests were met with excessive force, resulting in the deaths of five men and one child and the injury of hundreds. Executions resumed after a hiatus of nearly seven years.

BACKGROUND

Bahrain joined Saudi Arabia, the UAE and Egypt in severing ties with Qatar. Bahrain remained part of the Saudi Arabia-led coalition engaged in armed conflict in Yemen (see Yemen entry).

In January, Decree 1 of 2017 authorized the National Security Agency (NSA) to conduct arrests and interrogations in cases linked to "terrorist crimes", reversing a Bahrain Independent Commission of Inquiry recommendation. In April, the King reversed another such recommendation by ratifying a constitutional amendment that re-enabled military courts to try civilians. In December, six men were sentenced to death in the first trial of civilians by a military court, which had begun in October. In June, Bahrain's lower house approved a decree ending retirement rights and benefits of those who had their citizenship revoked, or who lost or were granted foreign citizenship without permission.

In March, the US administration approved the sale to Bahrain of new F-16 fighter jets and upgrades for older jets, which under the previous US administration had been conditional on the improvement of human rights in Bahrain.

International NGOs, including Amnesty International, and journalists critical of Bahrain, were denied access to Bahrain throughout the year.

FREEDOM OF EXPRESSION

Freedom of expression remained severely restricted throughout the year. The authorities arrested, detained, interrogated and prosecuted human rights defenders, political activists and Shi'a clerics who expressed criticism of government policies, or criticism of Saudi Arabia or the Saudi-led coalition in Yemen. The government announced that it would be illegal to express sympathy with Qatar following the severance of ties in June, and arrested and detained one lawyer on that basis. Human rights defenders and opposition leaders arbitrarily detained in previous years for their peaceful opposition remained held as prisoners of conscience.

In May, human rights defender Ebtisam al-Saegh was arrested and interrogated in NSA custody, during which she said she was tortured, including by being sexually assaulted. She was arrested again in July and remanded in custody for a further six months pending completion of the investigation. She was released in October without knowing the legal status of the case against her. In July, human rights defender Nabeel Rajab was sentenced to two years in prison for "spreading false information and rumours with the aim of discrediting the state". The sentence was upheld on appeal in November.

The media continued to be restricted and journalists were targeted. The only independent newspaper in Bahrain, *al-Wasat*, was temporarily suspended and then shut down after it reported on protests in Morocco. In May, journalist Nazeeha Saeed was convicted for working without renewing her press licence, issued by the Information Affairs Authority, and fined 1,000BD (USD2,650). The court of appeal upheld the fine in July.

FREEDOM OF ASSOCIATION

The authorities maintained undue restrictions on freedom of association. Leaders of al-Wefaq and other opposition parties remained in detention and political activists and members of opposition parties were harassed. Several political activists and members of opposition parties reported that they were threatened, tortured or otherwise ill-treated by NSA agents in May.

In February, the dissolution of al-Wefaq was upheld by the Court of Cassation. In March, the Minister of Justice filed a lawsuit against the secular opposition group Waad for violating the Law on Political Associations. In May, the High Administrative Court ordered the dissolution of Waad and the liquidation of its assets. In October the Appeal Court upheld the verdict.

Opposition leaders and prisoners of conscience Sheikh Ali Salman and Fadhel Abbas Mahdi Mohamed remained arbitrarily detained. In April, Sheikh Ali Salman's prison sentence was reduced to four years; in November he was charged with spying for Qatar in 2011, which he denied, and at the end of the year his trial was ongoing. In March, former Secretary General of Waad, Ebrahim Sharif, was charged over a series of posts on Twitter, including an Amnesty International graphic and a tweet criticizing the lack of democracy in Bahrain.

FREEDOM OF ASSEMBLY

Protests remained banned in the capital, Manama, and the authorities used unnecessary and excessive force to disperse protests. Peaceful protesters continued to be arrested and detained on charges of "illegal gathering". In January, mostly peaceful mass protests took place in 20 villages following the execution of three men. In Duraz, security forces used live ammunition and semiautomatic rifles, injuring hundreds, including Mustapha Hamdan, who later died of his wounds. In February, hundreds of protesters again took to the streets in several villages when the authorities refused to allow the funeral of three men who were killed by coastguard forces after escaping from Jaw prison a month earlier.

The authorities continued to restrict access to Duraz village until May, where a peaceful daily sit-in continued outside the home of Sheikh Isa Qassem, the spiritual leader of al-Wefaq. On 23 May, security forces entered Duraz with hundreds of armoured vehicles, beating protesters, firing tear gas from armoured vehicles or helicopters and firing birdshot. Four men and a 17-year-old child were killed.

In February, human rights defender Nader Abdulemam was arrested to serve a six-month sentence for participating in an "illegal gathering" and having called on people on Twitter to join a protest in Manama in January 2013. He was held as a prisoner of conscience until his release in June.

In May, the Court of Appeal reduced Dr Taha Derazi's six-month prison sentence to three months for taking part in an "illegal gathering" in Duraz in July 2016. He was held as a prisoner of conscience until his release in August.

FREEDOM OF MOVEMENT

The authorities maintained administrative travel bans that prevented scores of human rights defenders and other critics from travelling abroad, including to attend meetings of the UN Human Rights Council. In April, days ahead of the UN UPR of Bahrain, 32 activists were summoned by the Public Prosecution. The majority were charged with "illegal gathering" and banned from travelling. Most bans were lifted in July, after the UPR had been conducted. Similar tactics were used in September ahead of the UN Human Rights Council session in which the outcome of the UPR on Bahrain was adopted.

DEPRIVATION OF NATIONALITY

Authorities obtained court orders to strip at least 150 people of their Bahraini nationality. The majority were effectively rendered stateless as they had no other nationality. No forced expulsions took place.

TORTURE AND OTHER ILL-TREATMENT

There continued to be reports of torture and other ill-treatment in custody, in particular of those interrogated about terrorism-related offences. In May alone, eight human rights defenders and political activists in NSA custody were reportedly tortured or otherwise ill-treated. Unfair trials continued and courts relied on allegedly coerced "confessions" to convict defendants on terrorism-related charges.

Reports of ill-treatment in Dry Dock prison and Jaw prison continued, including the use of prolonged solitary confinement and lack of adequate medical care. After the escape of 10 prisoners from Jaw prison in January, new arbitrary regulations were introduced, including that prisoners must remain locked in their cells for most of the day. Prisoners' legs and ankles were shackled whenever they left their cells, including to go to the medical clinic. Eleven opposition activists who remained in prison, including Abdulhadi al-Khawaja, refused to attend medical appointments to protest the mandatory prison uniform, shackles and full body strip search required to attend the appointment. In March, the prison administration also reduced the length of family visits from one hour to 30 minutes and separated prisoners from visitors by a glass barrier.

Student Ali Mohamed Hakeem al-Arab reported that he was tortured throughout 26 days of interrogation in February and March, including by having his toenails pulled out, being subjected to electric shocks and beatings, and being forced to sign a "confession". In May, Ebtisam al-Saegh and seven other peaceful critics reported that they were tortured and otherwise ill-treated in NSA custody. (See above, Freedom of expression.)

IMPUNITY

A climate of impunity persisted. The authorities continued to fail to hold senior officials accountable for torture and other human rights violations committed during and since the 2011 protests. No investigation or prosecution was known to have taken place into the deaths of six people, including one child, killed by security forces in Duraz between January and May 2017.

WORKERS' RIGHTS – MIGRANT WORKERS

Migrant workers continued to face exploitation. In March and June, migrant workers participated in marches to peacefully protest against unpaid salaries.

DEATH PENALTY

Bahrain resumed executions after a hiatus of nearly seven years, executing three Bahrainis in January. The courts continued to hand down death sentences for offences including murder and terrorism-related charges.

BANGLADESH

People's Republic of Bangladesh
Head of state: Abdul Hamid
Head of government: Sheikh Hasina

Bangladesh received more than 655,000 Rohingya refugees who were forced out of Myanmar's Rakhine State. Members of the opposition Jamaat-e-Islami were arbitrarily arrested. Human rights defenders were harassed and intimidated. The rights to freedom of peaceful assembly and association remained restricted. Enforced disappearances persisted. The strategy to combat violence by armed groups continued to be marked by human rights violations. LGBTI people continued to be harassed and arrested. Security forces in the Chittagong Hill Tracts failed to protect Indigenous people from violence. On a positive note, a decade of steady economic growth helped to reduce extreme poverty.

FREEDOM OF EXPRESSION

Attacks against journalists continued, with a number of physical assaults on journalists reported, including the killing of Abdul Hakim Shimul.

The government continued to use repressive laws to unduly restrict the right to freedom of expression, and to target and harass journalists and human rights defenders. Key punitive provisions of the Information and Communications Technology (ICT) Act remained intact, despite repeated calls by human rights mechanisms to repeal its abusive clauses. The government reiterated its intention to introduce the Digital Security Act, which would restrict further the right to freedom of expression online.

Investigations into killings during 2015 and 2016, which were claimed by the armed group Ansar al-Islam and targeted secular activists, were still ongoing. The group was banned in March 2017 but ongoing delays in criminal prosecutions continued to have a chilling impact on civil society.

RIGHTS OF LESBIAN, GAY, BISEXUAL, TRANSGENDER AND INTERSEX PEOPLE

LGBTI activists continued to be routinely harassed and subject to arbitrary detention by state and non-state actors. The killings of activists in 2016 by Ansar al-Islam intensified existing fears of the LGBTI community; many activists remained in hiding. In May, 28 men believed to have been targeted for their perceived sexual orientation were arrested in Keraniganj, a neighbourhood of the capital, Dhaka, and charged with violating the Narcotics Control Act 1990. The arrests were made at a regular gathering known to be frequented by gay men.

No one was brought to justice for the 2016 killing of LGBTI activists Xulhaz Mannan, Mahbub Rabbi Tanoy, Avijit Roy and Niladry Niloy, although at least one arrest was made in 2017.

FREEDOM OF ASSEMBLY

The right to freedom of peaceful assembly continued to be severely restricted. Political opponents were denied the right to organize campaign meetings and political rallies.The activities of NGOs continued to be restricted through the Foreign Donation (Voluntary Activities) Regulation Act.

ENFORCED DISAPPEARANCES

Enforced disappearances were routinely carried out by security forces, mainly targeting supporters of the opposition. Some of the disappeared were subsequently found dead. In a statement to the authorities in February, the UN Working Group on Enforced or Involuntary Disappearances said that the number of enforced disappearances had risen considerably in recent years. Reports suggested that more than 80 people were forcibly disappeared during the year.

In March, Hummam Quader Chowdhury, son of an executed leader of the opposition Bangladesh Nationalist Party, was released after six months' incommunicado detention. Concerns increased for the safety of Mir Ahmad Bin Quasem and Abdullahil Amaan Azmi, also sons of executed opposition leaders; they disappeared in August 2016 and their whereabouts remained unknown at the end of 2017. In April, Swedish Radio published an interview – recorded undercover – in which a senior member of the Rapid Action Battalion described how the unit carried out enforced disappearances and extrajudicial executions. In October, academic Mubashar Hasan was allegedly abducted by members of military intelligence; he returned home after 44 days.

JUSTICE SYSTEM

Concerns increased about the growing interference by the government in the judiciary. In July, the Chief Justice presided over a ruling overturning a controversial constitutional amendment (16th Amendment) which allowed parliament to impeach judges if charges against them of misconduct or incapability were upheld. The Prime Minister criticized the Chief Justice after the ruling. Subsequently in November, Chief Justice Sinha resigned from his post and left the country under circumstances that indicated executive interference following the 16th Amendment decision.

REFUGEES AND ASYLUM-SEEKERS

An acute humanitarian crisis began in August when more than 655,000 of Myanmar's mainly Muslim Rohingya fled to the district of Cox's Bazar after fleeing violence inflicted by the Myanmar military in northern Rakhine State. The Myanmar military's campaign of ethnic cleansing amounted to crimes against humanity under international law (see Myanmar entry). Cox's Bazar already hosted approximately 400,000 Rohingya refugees who had fled earlier episodes of violence and persecution at the hands of the Myanmar military.

Bangladesh continued to refuse to formally recognize Rohingya as refugees. Reports of severe malnutrition were rife; children comprised 61% of the new arrivals and were particularly affected.

Rohingya women and girls were at heightened risk of sexual and gender-based violence and human trafficking, both by the local population and other refugees. Risk factors included inadequate protection or camp management mechanisms, poor living conditions, lack of a civil administration and police presence, as well as lack of access to the formal justice system and other services. Newly arrived Rohingya lived in squalid conditions and were not permitted to leave the camp.

In November, the governments of Bangladesh and Myanmar signed a repatriation agreement to facilitate the return of newly arrived Rohingya to Myanmar. The conditions of the agreement could violate international standards on voluntary repatriation and the international legal principle of *non-refoulement*, paving the way for forcible return of hundreds of thousands of Rohingya to Myanmar where they were at serious risk of human rights violations.

TORTURE AND OTHER ILL-TREATMENT

Torture and other ill-treatment in custody remained widespread and complaints were rarely investigated. The 2013 Torture and

Custodial Death (Prevention) Act continued to be inadequately enforced due to a lack of political will and awareness among law enforcement agencies.

DEATH PENALTY

Scores of people were sentenced to death and executions took place.

In April, two people were sentenced to death after being convicted of crimes against humanity by the International Crimes Tribunal, a Bangladeshi court established to investigate the events of the 1971 independence war. The Tribunal also concluded the hearing of arguments in the trial of six alleged war criminals in Gaibandha for mass killings, abductions, looting and arson during the 1971 war. The trial remained ongoing. Serious concerns regarding the fairness of the trial were raised about the Tribunal proceedings, such as denial of adequate time for defence lawyers to prepare their cases and arbitrary limitation of the number of witnesses.

CHITTAGONG HILL TRACTS

In June, at least one person was killed and hundreds of homes were burned during a mob attack on Indigenous people in the town of Langadu, Rangamati Hill District. Police and soldiers reportedly failed to protect Indigenous villagers. Those made homeless had not been rehoused by the end of the year. A video posted on social media appeared to show soldiers using excessive force against students peacefully protesting against the violence and the 1996 disappearance of Indigenous rights activist Kalpana Chakma. Mithun Chakma, an Indigenous rights campaigner, denounced a "situation of suffocation" in which he was forced to attend court up to eight times a month to answer criminal charges relating to 11 separate cases, some of which were under the ICT Act and concerned articles he had posted on social media about human rights violations, thus preventing him from carrying out his work as a human rights defender.

BELARUS

Republic of Belarus
Head of state: **Alyaksandr Lukashenka**
Head of government: **Andrey Kabyakou**

Between February and April, the authorities violently cracked down on peaceful protests. The government continued to refuse to accept the mandate of the UN Special Rapporteur on human rights in Belarus. Several individuals seeking international protection were returned to countries where they were at risk of torture and other ill-treatment. Heavy legislative restrictions on media, NGOs, political parties and public assemblies remained in place. One person was executed and four were sentenced to death.

BACKGROUND

After several years with no large protests, mass demonstrations took place in February and March against a tax on the unemployed, introduced by a Presidential Decree in 2015. The authorities clamped down on the protests. In March, they accused 35 men of plotting mass disturbances supported with foreign funding, and hinted that these were linked to the demonstrations. The arrests were widely televised; by July, all men had been released.

The rapprochement between Belarus and its western neighbours continued. In July, the OSCE Parliamentary Assembly was held in Minsk, the capital.

DEATH PENALTY

In April, Siarhei Vostrykau, who had been on death row since May 2016, was executed. Homel Regional Court received confirmation of his execution on 29 April. The last letter his mother received from him was dated 13 April.

Five men remained on death row. They included Aliaksei Mikhalenya, whose sentence on 17 March was upheld by the Supreme Court on 30 June; Ihar Hershankou and Siamion Berazhnoy, both sentenced on

21 July and whose appeals were rejected by the Supreme Court on 20 December, and Viktar Liotau who was sentenced on 22 September. Kiryl Kazachok, who was sentenced on 28 December 2016, chose not to appeal.

PRISONERS OF CONSCIENCE

Dozens of protesters were sentenced for their peaceful activism. On 7 April, Zavodski District Court in Minsk changed Dzmitry Paliyenka's conditional sentence from 2016 to two years' imprisonment after he received two administrative penalties. His first administrative penalty on 10 March 2017 – a seven-day detention for "minor hooliganism" and "disobedience to lawful police demands" – was imposed after he vocally criticized the verdict at a trial he was observing. His second administrative penalty on 20 March 2017 – a 15-day detention for "organizing or participating in unsanctioned mass events" – was imposed for his peaceful protest on 25 February against the construction of a building in central Minsk. Dzmitry Paliyenka received the two-year suspended sentence for purportedly assaulting a police officer during a peaceful cyclists' protest in Minsk in April 2016.

FREEDOM OF ASSEMBLY

In February and March, thousands of people attended a series of peaceful rallies across the country to protest against the tax on the unemployed. Some of the organizers and participants reported harassment by the police, including brief detentions and police summons for questioning. On 25 March, police prevented peaceful protesters from assembling in central Minsk and arrested hundreds; some arrests were made using excessive force. Some protesters were severely beaten by law enforcement officials during arrest and in police custody.

Between February and April, over 900 people were arrested in connection with the protests, including political activists who were prevented from attending the protests and journalists. At least 177 were found guilty of purported administrative offences and fined

or detained for five to 25 days. All but one arrested individual were found guilty in summary trials; courts uniformly accepted police reports as evidence against them without any questioning.

FREEDOM OF ASSOCIATION

Heavy restrictions on NGOs remained in place. Under Article 193.1 of the Criminal Code, the founding, or participation in, the activities of an unregistered organization remained a crime punishable by up to two years' imprisonment.

On 25 March, masked police officers raided the office of human rights group Vyasna and arrested all 57 people present. Among them were local and international human rights defenders and journalists who were attending training on how to monitor demonstrations. They were held for three hours at the local police station and released without charge or explanation. One detainee was hospitalized for head injuries sustained during the arrest.

FREEDOM OF EXPRESSION

Official accreditation remained compulsory for anyone working for a foreign media outlet and continued to be routinely and arbitrarily denied. More than 100 print, radio and TV journalists and bloggers were arrested for not having obtained accreditation, some repeatedly, leading to fines. In at least eight cases, journalists reporting from protests were arrested as participants and sentenced to administrative detention of between five and 15 days.

Journalist Larysa Schyryakova, from the city Homel in southeastern Belarus, was arrested and fined repeatedly for reporting on protests. She reported that police warned her that she could be found "socially irresponsible" if she committed further administrative offences and that her 11-year-old son might be placed in a children's home.

LEGAL, CONSTITUTIONAL OR INSTITUTIONAL DEVELOPMENTS

The tax on the unemployed remained in place; failure to comply continued to incur administrative fines and compulsory community service. In March, after the protests against the tax, the President mandated the government to suspend the tax collection until 2018; in August, he promised to waive the tax for "people with many children, the sick and invalids". Respective changes were introduced in October.

REFUGEES AND ASYLUM-SEEKERS

Belarus lacked a functioning asylum system and repeatedly handed over individuals seeking international protection to authorities of countries where they were at real risk of torture or other ill-treatment.

FORCIBLE RETURN

Ethnic Chechen Imran Salamov, who claimed to have been repeatedly tortured in Chechnya, was forcibly returned to Russia on 5 September. He was in the process of appealing against his rejected asylum application. On 11 September, the Chechen authorities confirmed that he was in police custody in Grozny, capital of Chechnya. Since that date, he had had no contact with his lawyer or family and his whereabouts remained undisclosed at the end of the year. Following his forcible return, the Belarusian authorities opened an investigation which concluded that there had been a violation of Belarusian law and that Imran Salamov had been prematurely expelled from Belarus. Disciplinary action was taken against a number of officials linked to his case and was ongoing at the end of the year.

Russian-Ukrainian-Israeli blogger Aleksandr Lapshin was detained in Belarus in December 2016 on request from Azerbaijan, and extradited to Azerbaijan in February where he was detained arbitrarily and prosecuted in connection with his blog posts criticizing the Azerbaijani authorities. Aleksandr Lapshin was sentenced to three years' imprisonment and released under a presidential pardon on 11 September (see Azerbaijan entry).

BELGIUM

Kingdom of Belgium
Head of state: **King Philippe**
Head of government: **Charles Michel**

Prison conditions remained poor; hundreds of offenders with mental health problems or mental disabilities continued to be detained in inadequate prison wards. Several laws on professional secrecy introduced requirements for social workers to share private information regarding potential suspects of terrorism-related offences. Parliament introduced a number of restrictions to asylum and migration laws. A new law on legal gender recognition improved the rights of transgender people.

COUNTER-TERROR AND SECURITY

In July, Parliament adopted a new law establishing a special status and compensation system for victims of terrorism-related offences. However, the law failed to ensure swift and full compensation. Victims could access state compensation only after a burdensome and lengthy process.

In May, Parliament passed a law requiring employees of welfare institutions to report to prosecutors, or provide upon their request, information on people who could be involved in the perpetration of terrorism-related offences. In June a new law passed that allowed the sharing of confidential information previously protected by professional secrecy obligations to prevent the commission of terrorism-related offences.

In October, Parliament amended the Constitution to increase the maximum duration of pre-charge detention from 24 to 48 hours. The provision applies to suspects of any crime, although the initial proposed scope was restricted to suspects of terrorism-related offences.

Authorities failed to effectively monitor the human rights impact of measures against terrorism and radicalization.

DETENTION

Prisons continued to be overcrowded, facilities dilapidated and there was insufficient access to basic services. Several hundred offenders with mental health problems or mental disabilities remained in detention in regular prisons with insufficient health care and treatment.

In May, the European Court of Human Rights (ECtHR) found that the conditions of detention of two detainees in two different prisons amounted to inhuman or degrading treatment.

In July, the European Committee for the Prevention of Torture raised concerns regarding the consequences of the repeated strikes by prison officials in recent years which worsened the poor detention conditions.

In September, the ECtHR ruled that Belgium had violated the right to life of Michael Tekin, an offender with a mental health problem who died in custody in a regular section of Jamioulx prison on 8 August 2009. The Court found that the restraining technique used by three prison officers was unnecessary and disproportionate.

REFUGEES AND ASYLUM-SEEKERS

The authorities resumed the transfers of asylum-seekers to Greece under the Dublin III Regulation – EU law that determines the EU member state responsible for examining an application for asylum.

In November, laws were adopted widening the scope for detention of asylum-seekers and curtailing the right to appeal negative asylum decisions.

In September, the government invited a delegation of Sudanese government officials to identify dozens of undocumented Sudanese nationals with the intention of returning them to Sudan. Several judicial proceedings were started challenging forcible returns on the basis of the principle of *non-refoulement* – the forcible return of individuals to countries where they risk serious human rights violations. Ten Sudanese nationals were reportedly returned

in the context of this operation. In December, testimonies surfaced of returnees who stated that upon return they had been detained by Sudanese government agents, interrogated and subjected to ill-treatment or torture. The government announced an investigation into the allegations.

DISCRIMINATION

On 14 March, the Court of Justice of the EU failed to uphold Muslim women's right to non-discrimination by ruling that a private Belgian employer had not breached EU anti-discrimination law in dismissing a woman for wearing a headscarf.

RIGHTS OF LESBIAN, GAY, BISEXUAL, TRANSGENDER AND INTERSEX PEOPLE

On 24 May, Parliament adopted a law allowing transgender people to seek legal gender recognition without imposing on them any psychiatric assessment or sterilization requirements.

ARMS TRADE

The Walloon regional government continued to license weapon transfers to parties of the Saudi-Arabia-led coalition in Yemen. In June, the Flemish regional Parliament improved the compliance of its legislation with the Arms Trade Treaty by, among other things, amending the legal definition of transit. However, it failed to address the control of the end-use of parts and components that could be used to produce arms.

BENIN

Republic of Benin
Head of state and government: **Patrice Athanase Guillaume Talon**

The authorities continued to restrict the rights to freedom of expression and peaceful assembly. Fourteen prisoners remained on death row although the death penalty had been abolished. Civil society groups' access to prisons was restricted.

Benin joined the AU campaign to end child marriage.

BACKGROUND

In April, the National Assembly rejected a presidential bill which aimed to amend the Constitution. It contained provisions which limited the President's tenure to one six-year non-renewable term and provided immunity from police custody or pre-trial detention for the President and members of the government.

In November, Benin's human rights record was examined under the UN UPR process. The government accepted 191 recommendations and made note of seven others including calls to strengthen efforts to prevent the use of arbitrary detention, extrajudicial executions and the excessive use of force by security forces; and to ensure that all national legislation complied with international standards on the rights to freedom of expression and media freedom, and to take steps to prevent the arbitrary suspension of media outlets.

FREEDOMS OF EXPRESSION AND ASSEMBLY

In January, Radio Soleil FM, E-Tele and Eden TV reopened. They were three of the seven media outlets which the High Authority of Audiovisual Communication (HAAC) closed in November 2016. Four other outlets which broadcast from abroad – Sikka TV, la Chrétienne TV, Unafrica TV and La Béninoise – remained closed. In May, the Court of First Instance in Cotonou fined HAAC President 50 million CFA francs (around USD89,648) for closing Sikka TV.

On 17 February police used tear gas to disperse hundreds of University of Abomey-Calavi students. They had gathered at a hotel in Abomey-Calavi, a suburb of Cotonou, for a general assembly and press conference, and to peacefully protest against the October 2016 ban on all student union activities.

DETENTION

Prisons remained overcrowded; Abomey Civil Prison in the de Zou district held three times as many detainees as its intended capacity, and Kandi Civil Prison held twice as many. Around 4,500 of the country's 7,179 detainees awaited trial.

In April, the Ministry of Justice issued an order restricting the access of NGOs, religious and civil society groups to detention centres. Authorization for group visits was issued for periods of three months. Authorization could not be renewed without groups presenting a report of their activities for sign-off by the prison director who could make observations for the Minister of Justice's attention, or even refuse to sign the report.

DEATH PENALTY

The government failed to adopt laws to remove the death penalty from legislation despite its abolition by the Constitutional Court in 2016. However, it accepted a recommendation made under the UN UPR process to commute all death sentences and expedite the adoption of provisions under the new Criminal Code to abolish the death penalty. Fourteen prisoners remained on death row at the end of the year. Their detention conditions improved slightly during the year when restrictions on outdoor activities were relaxed.[1]

CHILDREN'S RIGHTS

In June, Benin became the 20th country to join the AU Campaign to End Child Marriage. The campaign's objectives included educating communities about the negative effects of child marriage. Despite legislation prohibiting marriage before the age of 18, 32% of girls continued to marry under 18 years, and 9% married before the age of 15. In November, the government accepted a recommendation under the UN UPR process to fast-track the implementation of legislation which would address harmful practices against children, including in relation to forced early and child marriages.

---

1. Living in limbo: Benin's last death row prisoners (ACT 50/4980/2017)

BOLIVIA

Plurinational State of Bolivia
Head of state and government: **President Evo Morales Ayma**

A Truth Commission was created to investigate serious human rights violations committed under military governments (1964-1982). Progress was made in protecting the rights of transgender people. Concerns remained regarding threats against and harassment of human rights organizations, and Indigenous Peoples' rights.

BACKGROUND

In November, the Constitutional Court ruled to lift the limits on candidates standing in presidential re-elections thereby allowing President Morales to stand for a fourth consecutive term in 2019.

The country office of the UN High Commissioner for Human Rights closed down on 31 December after the government decided not to renew its mandate.

IMPUNITY

In August, a Truth Commission was established to investigate serious human rights violations committed under the military governments between 1964 and1982. It is due to submit a report in two years. The armed forces created a working group composed of military officers to provide support for the Commission, including by granting access to their archives.

PERSONS WITH DISABILITIES

In August, the Plurinational Legislative Assembly passed a law to facilitate the inclusion in the labour market of people with disabilities and the provision of financial assistance for people with severe disabilities. For years, disability rights activists have called for a monthly disability allowance which has yet to be granted.

INDIGENOUS PEOPLES' RIGHTS

In August, the President promulgated Law 969, allowing the construction of a road that will cut across the Isiboro Sécure National Park and Indigenous Territory (TIPNIS), one of the country's main water reserves and home to approximately 14,000 people, mainly from Indigenous communities. This Law repealed legislation under which the TIPNIS was a protected area, raising concerns about possible development of other infrastructure and extractive projects in the area.

RIGHTS OF LESBIAN, GAY, BISEXUAL, TRANSGENDER AND INTERSEX PEOPLE

In June, the Supreme Electoral Tribunal granted civil marriage rights to people who had legally changed their gender. Nevertheless, same-sex marriage remained officially unrecognized. In the same month, the Ombudsman proposed an amendment to the Criminal Code to make hate crimes against LGBTI people a criminal offence. In the past decade, the authorities had failed to hold perpetrators accountable for the killings of LGBTI people.

SEXUAL AND REPRODUCTIVE RIGHTS

Unsafe abortions continued to be one of the main causes of maternal mortality.

HUMAN RIGHTS DEFENDERS

On 6 February, leaders of the Federation of Bolivian Mineworkers took over the Permanent Human Rights Assembly for several hours in the capital, La Paz, and demanded the removal of its president. Meanwhile, human rights organizations and Indigenous leaders held a press conference at the Assembly, where they announced that the Inter-American Commission on Human Rights had asked the government to provide information on their request for precautionary measures. The organizations had submitted the request on behalf of Indigenous Peoples in voluntary isolation whose survival they alleged would be at risk due to proposed oil extraction in their territories.

In March, the Bolivian Documentation and Information Centre (CEDIB), an NGO based at the Universidad Mayor de San Simón, a public university in Cochabamba, reported that the Dean of the university had harassed them and threatened them with eviction. Despite the CEDIB director's request that safety guarantees be provided to his staff and archives, he received no response from the authorities. In November, CEDIB reported that its bank accounts were frozen as a result of a judicial administrative procedure which had been filed by the Dean.

BOSNIA AND HERZEGOVINA

Bosnia and Herzegovina
Head of state: **Rotating presidency – Bakir Izetbegović, Dragan Čović, Mladen Ivanić**
Head of government: **Denis Zvizdić**

Minorities continued to face widespread discrimination. Threats and attacks against journalists and media freedom persisted. Access to justice and reparations for civilian victims of war remained limited.

DISCRIMINATION

Social exclusion and discrimination – in particular of Roma; lesbian, gay, bisexual, transgender and intersex (LGBTI) people; and of people with disabilities – remained widespread, despite the adoption of a progressive Law on Prevention of Discrimination in 2016.

Efforts continued to reduce the number of Roma without identity documents and to increase the number of Roma children enrolled in primary schools. However, Roma continued to face systemic barriers to education, housing, health services and employment. In July, the Council of Ministers adopted a new three-year Action Plan for Roma Integration specifically aimed at improving employment opportunities and easing access to housing and health services. The Plan's implementation was hampered

after the Council of Ministers removed a portion of its funding for the second consecutive year.

Police failures to thoroughly investigate acts of violence and discrimination against LGBTI people continued. No indictments were issued against those suspected of criminal responsibility for the 2014 attack on the organizers of the Merlinka Queer Film Festival, or the 2016 incident in Sarajevo, the capital, in which a group of young men harassed and physically threatened visitors of a café and cinema popular with the LGBTI community. In May, a planned public gathering to mark the International Day against Homophobia and Transphobia could not take place as Sarajevo Canton Ministry of Traffic failed to provide the necessary permits in time, although it received a formal application in advance.

People with disabilities, in particular women and children, continued to face systemic social exclusion, including severely limited access to health services and mainstream education. According to legislation, people with disabilities whose impairment was not a consequence of war were treated differently and received lower allowances and social benefits than war veterans and civilian victims of war.

The 2009 judgment of the European Court of Human Rights in *Sejdić-Finci v. Bosnia and Herzegovina* which found the power-sharing arrangements set out in the Constitution to be discriminatory, remained unimplemented. Under the arrangements, citizens who would not declare themselves as belonging to one of the three main constituent peoples of the country (Bosniaks, Croats and Serbs) were still excluded from running for legislative and executive office.

FREEDOM OF EXPRESSION

The pattern of threats, political pressure and attacks against journalists continued. In July and August, Dragan Bursać, a journalist with Al Jazeera Balkans, received a series of death threats after publishing a piece in which he condemned public gatherings in Banja Luka city in support of a charged war criminal. Local journalist associations documented nearly 40 cases of direct pressure, verbal threats and physical attacks against journalists by the end of the year.

CRIMES UNDER INTERNATIONAL LAW

In November, the International Criminal Tribunal for the former Yugoslavia (ICTY) issued the first-instance verdict in the case of former Bosnian Serb leader, General Ratko Mladić. The ICTY found him guilty of genocide, war crimes, and crimes against humanity committed during the 1992-1995 conflict and sentenced him to life imprisonment.

Also in November, the ICTY confirmed earlier sentences against six former Bosnian Croat political and military leaders. This was the final verdict passed by the tribunal prior to permanently shutting down in December, after 23 years of operation.

The domestic prosecution of war crimes remained slow, with a backlog of several hundred cases pending before various courts at the end of the year. Despite recent progress, the prosecutions continued to suffer from lack of capacity and resources, ineffective case-management and persistent political obstruction. A revision of the 2008 National War Crimes Strategy to address key institutional deficiencies and to establish new deadlines for the completion of cases was under way at the end of the year.

Some progress was made in harmonizing entity laws regulating the rights of civilian victims of war, including victims of wartime sexual violence. However, public aid for victims of wartime sexual violence remained fragmented and dependent on residency; victims residing in Republika Srpska (RS) were excluded from the system of social benefits for civilian victims of war. The Draft Law on Protection of Victims of Wartime Torture in RS, intended to recognize victims' rights, was adopted by the government in December, but it included provisions which could potentially discriminate against non-Serb victims. There was no progress in the adoption of the Law on Protection of Victims of Torture at the state level by the end of the

year. The Law would guarantee a specific set of rights and entitlement for victims of war on the whole territory of Bosnia and Herzegovina.

Criminal courts continued the recent practice of granting financial compensation to victims of wartime rape, bringing the number of final judgments awarding financial reparation for war crimes in criminal proceedings to four. However, the compensations had not been paid by the end of the year. The convicted perpetrators lacked funds and there was no alternative mechanism to compensate survivors of criminal acts in cases where convicted perpetrators were not able to pay damages.

Most victims continued to be required to pursue compensation claims in separate civil proceedings, where they had to reveal their identity and incur additional costs. The 2016 Constitutional Court ruling that the statute of limitations applied to reparation claims directed against the perpetrators and not the state – even in war crimes cases – resulted in widespread dismissal of claims in 2017, further limiting victims' ability to claim compensation and leaving them liable for high court fees.

Although over 75% of missing persons from the war had been exhumed and identified, there were still 8,000 people missing in connection with the conflict. The process of exhumations continued to encounter significant challenges, including reduced funding and limited expertise. The Law on Missing Persons remained unimplemented, with the Fund for Families of the Missing still awaiting dedicated resources.

BOTSWANA

Republic of Botswana
Head of state and government: **Seretse Khama Ian Khama**

The right to freedom of expression continued to be restricted. Asylum-seekers whose asylum claims were rejected continued to face detention. A landmark

ruling in the Lobatse High Court upheld the rights of transgender people. Two men were sentenced to death.

FREEDOM OF EXPRESSION

Journalists continued to be intimidated and harassed by the authorities. On 8 March, three journalists from the INK Centre for Investigative Journalism were briefly detained and threatened by plain-clothes security agents in the village of Mosu. The journalists had tried to access the area where the new home of President Khama was allegedly being constructed amid allegations of corruption. The security agents told them that the building site was a "restricted area" and that they would be shot on sight if they tried to return.

On 19 April, the Court of Appeal upheld an earlier decision by the High Court and turned down the application of a teacher who had challenged his dismissal from employment on the grounds that it violated his constitutional right to freedom of expression. The teacher was dismissed after he published an opinion piece in a newspaper in May 2011 on the country's political situation, following a national strike by public sector employees. In February 2012, a disciplinary hearing had found the teacher guilty of contravening section 34(a) of the Public Service Act.

Outsa Mokone, editor of the *Sunday Standard*, continued to face a criminal sedition charge following his arrest in 2014 after publishing articles alleging President Khama's involvement in a road accident. In December 2016, he was released on bail and asked to appear at the magistrate's court every two months and to seek permission before leaving the country. His legal case challenging the constitutionality of the sedition law was still pending at the end of the year.

REFUGEES AND ASYLUM-SEEKERS

Botswana's restrictive encampment policy continued, denying refugees freedom of movement, work and local integration. Asylum-seekers faced lengthy refugee status

determination procedures and asylum-seekers – with both pending and denied applications – continued to be detained in the Francistown Centre for Illegal Immigrants. The duration of detention averaged between six months and five years, far beyond the detention period stipulated in the Refugee Act.

On 13 April, the High Court ordered the release of two Somali asylum-seekers from the Francistown Centre for Illegal Immigrants. They had been detained in the Centre since being denied refugee status in October 2015, having arrived separately in Botswana in June 2014. On 15 April, following their release, they were taken into custody at the Tlokweng police station after attempting to enter the Dukwe Refugee Camp, Botswana's only refugee camp. On 25 April, President Khama declared them to be prohibited immigrants; they were subsequently detained at the first offenders prison in Gaborone, the capital, and have allegedly since been deported.

On 23 November, the Court of Appeal set aside the High Court ruling that the detention of 165 asylum-seekers and their relatives was illegal. As a result, the asylum-seekers sought refuge in Zimbabwe, Namibia and South Africa. Members of the group had arrived in Botswana between January 2014 and October 2016 and, after their asylum applications were denied, they had remained in detention in the Francistown Centre for Illegal Immigrants. The Attorney General made an appeal on 4 August.

RIGHTS OF LESBIAN, GAY, BISEXUAL, TRANSGENDER AND INTERSEX PEOPLE

In a landmark decision on 29 September, the Lobatse High Court ruled that the government's refusal to change the gender marker in the identity document of a transgender man was unreasonable and in violation of his rights, including the right to dignity, freedom of expression and freedom from discrimination, and ordered the government to change the gender marker.

On 12 December, the Gaborone High Court ruled in favour of Tshepo Ricki Kgositau, a transgender woman who successfully challenged the government's refusal to change her gender from male to female in her identity document as unconstitutional. Tshepo Ricki Kgositau had unsuccessfully applied to the Civil and National Registration Office in Gaborone to change her gender identity. The Office advised her to seek a court order after denying her application.

INTERNATIONAL JUSTICE

On 17 July, Parliament passed a bill which incorporated the Rome Statute of the International Criminal Court into domestic law, including the offences of genocide, crimes against humanity and war crimes. This followed Botswana's ratification of the Rome Statute in 2000.

DEATH PENALTY

Tshiamo Kgalalelo and Mmika Mpe were sentenced to death on 13 December; they were convicted of murder and other charges, including theft and abduction, in the Lobatse High Court in May.

BRAZIL

Federative Republic of Brazil
Head of state and government: **Michel Temer**

A number of proposals which threatened human rights and represented huge setbacks to existing law and policy made their way through the legislative process. Violence and killings increased, mostly affecting young black males. Conflicts over land and natural resources resulted in dozens of killings. Human rights defenders were not effectively protected. Police responded to most protests with unnecessary and excessive force.

LEGAL, CONSTITUTIONAL OR INSTITUTIONAL DEVELOPMENTS

Up to 200 different proposals for constitutional amendments, new laws and changes to existing legislation threatened a range of human rights. Among other retrogressive measures, proposals were introduced to reduce the age at which children can be tried as adults to below 18; change or revoke the Disarmament Bill, facilitating licensing and purchasing of firearms; restrict the right to peaceful assembly and to criminalize social protests; impose a full ban on abortion, violating the sexual and reproductive rights of women and girls; change the land demarcation process and requirements for free, prior and informed consent of Indigenous Peoples and Afro-descendant communities; and reduce the protection of labour rights and access to social security.

Law 13.491/2017, signed by President Temer on 13 October, provided that human rights violations, including murder or attempted murder, committed by military personnel against civilians would be tried by military courts.[1] The Law violated the right to a fair trial, as military courts in Brazil did not guarantee judicial independence.

Despite these setbacks, in May a new migration law (Law 13.445/2017) came into effect, representing improvements to migrants' rights.

INTERNATIONAL SCRUTINY

Brazil's human rights record was examined for the third time under the UN UPR process.[2] Brazil received 246 recommendations, including on Indigenous Peoples' rights to land; killings by the police; torture and degrading conditions in prisons; and protection of human rights defenders. Brazil accepted all but four recommendations; however, there remained concerns about their implementation in the context of the retrogressive laws and policies adopted during the year.

In May the Inter-American Court of Human Rights issued a ruling against Brazil for its failure to grant justice for the killing by police of 26 people in Favela Nova Brasília, in Complexo do Alemão, city of Rio de Janeiro, in October 1994 and May 1995.

POLICE AND SECURITY FORCES

The deployment of the armed forces for policing and law and order increased.

The authorities failed to adopt measures to reduce the homicide rate, which remained high for young black males. The number of homicides increased in major cities, especially in the northeast. National data compiled and published during the year by the Brazilian Public Security Forum revealed that 61,619 people were killed during 2016, of which 4,657 were women. Public security policies continued to rely on highly militarized police interventions, motivated mainly by the so-called "war on drugs".

In January the Ministry of Justice announced a Public Security National Plan which was to focus on reducing homicides, tackling drug trafficking and conducting a review of the prison system. A detailed and comprehensive plan was never presented or implemented and the public security situation deteriorated during the year.

Instances of "multiple homicides" (single events with more than three victims) and "chacinas" (multiple killings characteristic of executions) increased in several cities; the authorities often failed to properly investigate. On 5 January, eight men were killed by a group of armed men in Porto Seguro, Bahia state. On 3 June, six men were killed inside a house by armed hooded men in Porto das Dunas in Fortaleza, Ceará state. On 6 June, four men and a woman were killed and nine other people were injured by a group of 10 hooded gunmen in a bar in Belem, Pará state. On 22 September, six young men aged between 16 and 23 were killed in Grande Natal, Rio Grande do Norte state. In Bom Jardim neighbourhood in Fortaleza, Ceará state, five people were killed and three others injured on 20 February, and four young males aged between 14 and 20 were killed inside a house on 8 October. In most cases, the perpetrators were unidentified.

Police interventions in favelas and marginalized areas often resulted in intensive shoot-outs and deaths. Data about people killed by the police remained inaccurate as states kept poor records using different methodologies; however, official numbers indicated that such killings increased across Brazil. Official figures showed that on-duty police officers killed 494 people in São Paulo state between January and September and, between January and November, 1,035 in Rio de Janeiro state and 148 in Ceará state.

On 13 February, four people were killed and others injured by military police during a police intervention in the favela of Chapadão, Rio de Janeiro city.

In February, a 21-day strike by the military police in Espírito Santo state resulted in chaos. Armed forces and national security forces were called in to police the state.

On 12 July, a homeless man was killed by a military police officer in the neighbourhood of Pinheiros, city of São Paulo.

In August, at least seven people were killed by the police during police interventions that continued for several days in the favela Jacarezinho, Rio de Janeiro city. Residents reported that police officers were violent and committed a number of abuses, such as assaults, unlawful raids on homes, and unlawful killings. The police interventions may have been in retaliation for a police officer being killed in the area.

On 3 September, 10 men were killed by civil police officers during a police intervention attempting to prevent an armed robbery in the neighbourhood of Morumbi, São Paulo city.

Early in the year, military police from the Pacification Police Unit raided several houses in the favela Complexo do Alemão, Rio de Janeiro city. These unlawful actions by police continued even after a court ruled that the police should leave the area. Those denouncing the police violations were threatened and intimidated. After months of mobilization, the Public Prosecutor's Office brought charges against two police officers who were in command of the operation and responsible for the area.

On 11 November, seven men were killed during a joint security operation of the Civil Police and the Army in São Gonçalo, Rio de Janeiro state. Civilian authorities said they had no competence to investigate the killings after a new law expanded the jurisdiction of military courts to try crimes committed by military personnel. The military denied using firearms, and did not announce whether it had opened an investigation into the killings.

DETENTION

The prison system remained overcrowded and prisoners suffered inhuman and degrading conditions. The prison population reached 727,000 people, 55% of whom were aged between 18 and 29 and 64% of whom were Afro-descendant, according to the Ministry of Justice. A significant proportion – 40% nationally – of those imprisoned were in pre-trial detention, where detainees often waited several months to face trial.

In January, riots took place in prisons in several states resulting in at least 123 deaths: 64 in Amazonas state; 31 in Roraima; 26 in Rio Grande do Norte; and two in Paraíba.[3]

In May, 32 people escaped from Pedrinhas prison in Maranhão state; two escapees were killed by prison guards.

As a result of extreme overcrowding in prisons in Rio Grande do Sul state, some people detained by police were held for more than 48 hours in unsuitable areas in police stations and cars, while waiting for space in the prison system.

In October, a man died after being detained for a day and a night in an outdoor cage-like cell in a police station in Barra do Corda, Maranhão state. The cell had no protection from the sun or extremely high temperatures, leaving detainees at risk of dehydration and other dangerous consequences of exposure.

In Rio de Janeiro state, inhumane prison conditions were further degraded by the financial crisis, putting at risk the supply of food, water and medicines for more than 50,800 prisoners. Tuberculosis and skin diseases reached epidemic levels inside the state's prisons.

The 25th anniversary of the Carandiru massacre, in which 111 people were killed by the police in Carandiru prison, São Paulo, was on 2 October. Those responsible for the massacre had yet to be held accountable.

FREEDOM OF ASSEMBLY

On 31 March, thousands of people protested in major cities against proposed reforms to labour laws and social security policies. On 28 April, social movements, students and trade unions called for a "general strike" and tens of thousands of people protested throughout the country after the labour reforms were approved. In many areas, including Rio de Janeiro city, the police used unnecessary and excessive force against peaceful protesters.

On 24 May at least 49 people were injured, including eight military police officers and one man who was shot with a firearm, after police used excessive force against protesters in the capital, Brasilia. Tens of thousands of people protested against President Temer in a demonstration that ended in clashes with the police and damage to public buildings. The federal government called in the military to police the area in the following days.

HUMAN RIGHTS DEFENDERS

Human rights defenders, especially those in rural areas, continued to be threatened, attacked and killed. The states of Pará and Maranhão were among those where defenders were at the highest risk. According to the civil society coalition Brazilian Committee for Human Rights Defenders, 62 defenders were killed between January and September, an increase from the previous year. Most were killed in conflicts over land and natural resources. Budget cuts and lack of political will to prioritize the protection of human rights defenders resulted in the dismantling of the National Programme of Protection, leaving hundreds exposed to a higher risk of attacks.

LAND DISPUTES

On 20 April at least nine men were killed and others injured in Colniza, Mato Grosso state, after gunmen attacked rural workers in the settlement of Taquaruçu do Norte. The decade-long trend of frequent, violent attacks by gunmen hired by large-scale farmers and illegal loggers in the area continued.

On 24 May, 10 rural workers who were camping in the margins of Santa Lucia farm in Pau D'Arco, Pará state, were shot dead during a joint operation between military and civil police officers. On 7 July, one of the leaders of the group of rural workers, Rosenildo Pereira de Almeida, was shot dead. Survivors of the massacre continued to fear for their lives following the killings.

In September a group of armed mine workers threatened smallholders in the rural settlement of Montanha e Mangabal, in the Tapajós river region, municipality of Itaituba, Pará state.

INDIGENOUS PEOPLES' RIGHTS

Conflicts over land and invasion by illegal loggers and mine workers into Indigenous Peoples' territory continued, resulting in several episodes of violence against Indigenous people. The government and courts undermined the institutional framework and national policies, introducing further delays in the already slow land demarcation process, aggravating conflicts over land in Indigenous territories. Data published by the Indigenous Missionary Council during the year revealed that at least 118 Indigenous people were killed in 2016.

In January, the Ministry of Justice issued a decree changing the land demarcation process, making it even slower and more vulnerable to pressure from landlords.

In April, at least 22 Indigenous Gamela people were attacked by gunmen in Viana, Maranhão state; some were shot at, others beaten, and two had their hands cut off.

The Parliamentary Commission of Inquiry into the National Indigenous Foundation (FUNAI) and the National Institute for Colonization and Agrarian Reform, two independent institutions set up by the government to protect Indigenous Peoples' rights and promote access to land, presented its final report, which was approved by the House of Representatives in May. The report was a clear attack on Indigenous Peoples' rights and had a direct intent to criminalize (including by requesting criminal indictment of dozens of people) Indigenous leaders, civil society organizations and governmental technical bodies working for Indigenous Peoples' rights. Budget cuts to FUNAI impacted negatively on its work for the protection of Indigenous Peoples' rights.

Indigenous people from Vale do Javari, Amazonas state, reported that members of isolated Indigenous groups in the area were killed during the year. The killings were not investigated. Demarcated Indigenous land in Vale do Javari was subjected to invasions by miners.

RIGHTS OF LESBIAN, GAY, BISEXUAL, TRANSGENDER AND INTERSEX PEOPLE

According to Bahia Gay Group, 277 LGBTI people were killed in Brazil between 1 January and 20 September, the highest number since the group began compiling data in 1980.

On 15 February, transgender woman Dandara dos Santos was beaten to death in Bom Jardim neighbourhood in Fortaleza city. According to investigators, at least 12 people were involved in her killing. Two men were arrested in connection with her killing during the year.

In September, a Federal District judge authorized psychologists to use unethical and harmful so-called "conversion therapies" in an attempt to alter individuals' sexual orientation. The decision flouted a resolution of the Federal Psychology Council confirming that psychologists cannot take any action that would "pathologize homosexuality". The judge's decision contributed to increasing stigma and violence against LGBTI people.

A number of proposals at city, state and national level sought to prohibit gender and sexual orientation-related issues from being included in educational materials.

FREEDOM OF RELIGION AND BELIEF

Throughout the year, religious centres (*terreiros*) of the Afro-descendant religions Umbanda and Candomblé in Rio de Janeiro state suffered several attacks by private individuals, criminal gangs and members of other religions. In August and September, at least eight centres were attacked and destroyed, most of them in Rio de Janeiro city and surrounding municipalities in the Baixada Fluminense region.

CHILDREN'S RIGHTS

Juvenile detention facilities remained overcrowded and detainees suffered inhuman and degrading conditions.

In Ceará state, torture by state officials was recurrent inside juvenile detention facilities. During the year, there were at least 20 riots and 37 escapes from units in Ceará. Out of 200 formal reports of torture of adolescents inside juvenile detention units in Ceará between 2016 and September 2017, only two reports resulted in a formal inquiry by the state for further investigation. Reports of the chaotic state of the juvenile justice system in Ceará resulted in a formal visit by Brazil's National Human Rights Council in September.

Early in the year, Espirito Santo state held 1,198 juvenile detainees in a system with capacity for only 754, a rate of overcrowding of more than 39%. Of the state's 13 detention facilities, only four were operating within their intended capacity.

On 3 June, seven boys aged between 15 and 17 were killed by other teenage detainees during a riot in a juvenile detention facility in Lagoa Seca, Paraíba state.

On 13 November, four young boys were killed by hooded men who entered a juvenile justice system facility where the boys were detained.

---

1. Brazil: Law leading to military impunity sanctioned (AMR 19/7340/2017)

2. Brazil: Police killings, impunity and attacks on defenders: Amnesty International submission for the UN Universal Periodic Review – 27th session of the UPR working group, May 2017 (AMR 19/5467/2016)

3. Brazil: Over 90 men killed in Brazilian prison riots (AMR 19/5444/2017)

BRUNEI DARUSSALAM

Brunei Darussalam
Head of state and government: **Sultan Hassanal Bolkiah**

Lack of transparency made independent monitoring of the human rights situation difficult. Phased amendments to the Shari'a Penal Code, if implemented, would provide for the death penalty and corporal punishment, such as caning and stoning which amount to torture and other ill-treatment, for a range of offences. The amendments would further restrict the rights to freedom of thought, conscience and religion and discriminate against women.

BACKGROUND

Several amendments to the Shari'a Penal Code remained pending and were subject to phased implementation. Brunei completed phase one of the amendments which dealt with crimes punishable by prison sentences and fines. If implemented, phase two will cover crimes punishable by amputation; while phase three will deal with crimes carrying the penalty of stoning to death.

FREEDOM OF EXPRESSION

On 27 July, government employee Shahiran Sheriffudin bin Shahrani Muhammad was removed from his post and charged under Section 4(1)(c) of the Sedition Act for posting comments on Facebook deemed "offensive" to the Ministry of Religious Affairs. Journalists and online activists continued to self-censor for fear of prosecution.

WOMEN'S RIGHTS

Shari'a Penal Code amendments included provisions which, if implemented, would further discriminate against women, including by criminalizing pregnancy outside marriage and forcing unmarried Muslim women to live in their guardian's home.

DEATH PENALTY

Although abolitionist in practice, death by hanging was maintained as punishment for several offences including murder, terrorism and drug-related crimes. Penal Code amendments, if implemented during phase three, would impose death by stoning as punishment for offences including "adultery", "sodomy" and rape. Stoning to death or 100 lashes, depending on the offender's marital status, would be imposed on Muslims and non-Muslims who commit "adultery" with a Muslim.

RIGHT TO EDUCATION

Stateless children and children who were not citizens of Brunei faced barriers to basic rights, including education. While primary education was free and accessible to citizens, stateless and non-citizen children had to apply for permission to enrol and were often required to pay monthly fees.

RIGHTS OF LESBIAN, GAY, BISEXUAL, TRANSGENDER AND INTERSEX PEOPLE

Consensual same-sex sexual relations remained a criminal offence with "intercourse against the order of nature" punishable by up to 10 years' imprisonment under Article 377 of the Penal Code. Amendments to the Penal Code would, if implemented, allow a mandatory punishment of death by stoning for consensual same-sex activity (see above).

COUNTER-TERROR AND SECURITY

Suspects were detained without trial under the Internal Security Act. In February, four Indonesian nationals were detained under the law for alleged links with the armed group Islamic State (IS) and subsequently deported.

BULGARIA

Republic of Bulgaria
Head of state: **Rumen Radev (replaced Rosen Plevneliev in January)**
Head of government: **Boyko Borisov**

Summary detentions, pushbacks and abuses at the border continued. The necessary services were not provided to migrants and refugees, including to unaccompanied children. A climate of xenophobia and intolerance sharply intensified. Roma continued to be at risk of pervasive discrimination.

REFUGEES' AND MIGRANTS' RIGHTS

The number of refugees and migrants entering Bulgaria declined, but reports of frequent pushbacks, excessive use of force and theft by border police continued. Irregular border crossing remained criminalized resulting in administrative detention of migrants and refugees, including unaccompanied children, who arrived in greater numbers. Human rights organizations documented numerous allegations of ill-treatment of refugees and asylum-seekers and substandard conditions in detention facilities.

In February, local authorities in the town of Elin Pelin refused to receive a Syrian family that had been granted humanitarian status in Bulgaria. The Mayor publicly warned that "Muslims from Syria [were] not welcome" and refused to register the family or issue them with identity documents. Other municipalities expressed a similar unwillingness to accommodate refugees.

In July, the government adopted the Regulation on Integration of Refugees; however, this fell short of providing an effective mechanism for integration. According to UNHCR, the UN refugee agency, the Regulation failed to address the persistent problem of unco-operative municipalities or to propose measures to create more favourable conditions for integration in local communities. It also failed to address the gaps in refugees' access to social housing, family benefits for children or language training, which limited their enjoyment of social and economic rights.

The government issued an order restricting freedom of movement for registered asylum-seekers. Adopted in September, it imposed territorial limits for asylum-seekers in refugee centres, prohibiting them from moving out of prescribed areas.

Although Bulgaria committed to accept 1,302 asylum-seekers from Greece and Italy under the EU emergency relocation scheme, it had only resettled 50 people from Greece by the end of the year. It did not receive any Syrian refugees from Turkey under the EU-Turkey "one-for-one" resettlement deal although it had originally committed to accept 100 people under the scheme.

CHILDREN'S RIGHTS

Reception conditions for unaccompanied refugee and migrant children remained inadequate. Children were routinely denied adequate access to legal representation, translation, health services and psychosocial support. Basic education was not available in the centres and most children were not enrolled in local schools. Limited social and educational activities were available several days a week and organized exclusively by NGOs and humanitarian organizations.

The authorities lacked developed systems for early identification, assessment and referral mechanisms for unaccompanied children. Children often did not have access to qualified legal guardians and legal representation. In February, mayors and residents of several towns refused to accommodate two unaccompanied refugee children in facilities in their communities. The boys were moved several times and finally separated, causing the younger boy to abscond.

In September, the National Assembly adopted, in the first reading, amendments to the Law on Foreigners. They included an obligation to provide legal representation for all unaccompanied children and to increase the authority of the Social Assistance Directorate in all proceedings involving unaccompanied children who had not applied for international protection. The amendments, however, proposed repealing the requirement for an individual assessment of the best interests of the child before placing children in short-term immigration detention. Human rights organizations warned that the proposals would legitimize the practice of "attaching" unaccompanied children to often unrelated adults travelling in the same group in order to avoid the prohibition of detention of children.

DISCRIMINATION

Hate speech and hate crimes continued, directed at minority groups, including Turks and Roma; refugees, asylum-seekers and migrants remained vulnerable to violence and harassment. Discriminatory or xenophobic statements were made during the campaign for parliamentary elections held in March, by candidates and political parties as well as by the coalition of far-right parties, the Patriotic Front, which gained enough seats to enter the government.

Marginalization and widespread discrimination against Roma persisted. They faced systemic obstacles in all aspects of life, including education, health care, housing and employment. Roma children were enrolled in special schools and denied access to mainstream education. High numbers of Roma lacked health insurance and faced persistent barriers to adequate health care and services. The authorities continued the practice of forced evictions without the provision of adequate alternative housing, leaving many families homeless. Human rights organizations documented numerous cases involving ill-treatment and physical abuse of Roma by police. Roma remained over-represented in places of detention. In July, mass anti-Roma demonstrations organized by the Patriotic Front took place in the towns of Asenovgrad and Byala, following a violent incident between a sports youth team and several Roma.

People with disabilities, particularly children, continued to face discrimination and systemic social exclusion, including limited access to education, health services and employment. Those with intellectual disabilities and psychosocial problems were deprived of their legal capacity and the right to independent living and were frequently placed under guardianship or social care institutions without their consent.

Despite numerous threats and simultaneous counter-demonstrations organized by far-right groups, Sofia Gay Pride took place in June under heavy police presence.

FREEDOM OF EXPRESSION
JOURNALISTS AND MEDIA

A pattern of threats, political pressure and attacks against journalists continued; a significant portion of the media remained under the tight control of political parties and local oligarchs. In October, Deputy Prime Minister Valeriy Simeonov and MP Anton Todorov publicly threatened TV journalist Victor Nikolaev that he would be fired unless he stopped investigating the government's purchase of a fighter aircraft. The incident was widely condemned by civil society, but no action was taken against the public officials.

Bulgaria remained the lowest ranking EU member state on the World Press Freedom Index. The NGO Reporters without Borders ranked Bulgaria 109th out of 180 countries in terms of press freedom.

BURKINA FASO

Head of state: **Roch Marc Christian Kaboré**
Head of government: **Paul Kaba Thiéba**

The draft Constitution included provisions which, if implemented, would strengthen human rights protection. There were reports of torture and other ill-treatment and prison conditions remained poor. Rates of maternal mortality as well as early and forced marriage remained high. Armed groups committed human rights abuses.

LEGAL, CONSTITUTIONAL OR INSTITUTIONAL DEVELOPMENTS

In December, a draft Constitution was submitted to the President for approval, following which it will either be approved by referendum or adopted by Parliament. It included provisions to strengthen human rights protection, including economic, social and cultural rights, gender equality, protection for women and girls from violence, abolition of the death penalty, and to increase the independence of the judiciary.

In June, the National Assembly adopted a law to protect human rights defenders.

In July, legislation was adopted which would give the High Court of Justice jurisdiction to try members of the government for crimes committed in the course of, or in connection with, their duties. In the same month, the government adopted a law allowing the military prosecutor to initiate public prosecutions against civilians in proceedings which would operate independently of the High Council of Magistrates which, among other things, was responsible for overseeing the independence of the judiciary.

TORTURE AND OTHER ILL-TREATMENT

There were complaints at the main prison of Ouagadougou, the capital: detainees at MACO prison (Maison d'Arrêt et de Correction de Ouagadougou) complained of torture and other ill-treatment, mainly during arrest or in police custody, often in order to extract "confessions". Several prisoners said they were held in custody for over two weeks without charge. Four prisoners said that courts took no action when they reported that they had been tortured.

Several soldiers who were tried in April for conspiracy to raid an arms depot in Yimdi in January complained in a military court in Ouagadougou that they were tortured during detention in custody either at the gendarmerie or at MACO prison.

DETENTION

Many prisons remained overcrowded: 1,900 detainees were held in MACO prison which has a capacity for 600. Conditions remained poor, with inadequate food and medical provisions. In June, however, Ministry of Justice representatives said that they were developing a strategic plan to improve prison conditions.

IMPUNITY

The trial of former President Blaise Compaoré and 32 former ministers before the High Court of Justice was repeatedly delayed; in June it was temporarily suspended by the Constitutional Council. Blaise Compaoré was charged with acts of wilful assault, complicity in assault, assassination and complicity in assassination in relation to the October 2014 uprising. An international arrest warrant for him and his former Chief of Security, Hyacinthe Kafando, remained in place.

In May, an international arrest warrant was issued against Blaise Compaoré's brother, François Compaoré, in relation to the murder of investigative journalist Norbert Zongo in December 1998. François Compaoré was placed under court supervision in France, where he was living, pending a decision on his extradition to Burkina Faso.

Fourteen people awaited trial in connection with the murder of former President Thomas Sankara, three of whom remained in detention.

The findings of an investigation into the attempted coup in September 2015 were referred to the Indictments Division for a decision in October. At least 106 people – including 40 civilians, one of whom was a foreign national – were charged, including with threatening state security, crimes against humanity and murder during the coup attempt. More than 20 of them remained in detention at the end of the year while another, General Djibril Bassolé, remained under house arrest having been transferred from detention in October. In December the UN Working Group on Arbitrary Detention called for his release.

WOMEN'S AND GIRLS' RIGHTS

Lack of medical equipment, medication and staffing in hospitals left women and newborn babies at serious risk of birth complications, infection and death. There were at least 100 maternal deaths in the first half of the year at one of the two main public hospitals in Ouagadougou. In one hospital, overworked midwives carried out up to 25 caesarean sections a day, while shortages forced women patients to sleep on the floor, sometimes without bedding.

No progress was made towards implementing the government's pledge in 2016 to increase the legal marriage age of girls and women. Over 50% of girls between 15 and 17 were married in the Sahel region in the north of the country. Rates of female genital mutilation continued to lessen although it remained widespread despite being outlawed.

ABUSES BY ARMED GROUPS

The self-defence militia called "Kogleweogo", mainly comprising farmers and cattle breeders, continued to commit human rights abuses including beatings and abductions, despite the Justice Minister's pledge in December 2016 to regulate the militia's activities.

Justice Ministry officials said that Kogleweogo members beat a man to death in the town of Tapoa in January over an alleged chicken theft. In May, six people died, including four Kogleweogo members, in clashes between locals and Kogleweogo in Goundi. In the same month, the regional governor banned "self-defence groups" in Boulkiemdé and Sanguié.

There were reports that trials were postponed when Kogleweogo held demonstrations in order to protect their members from prosecution in Fada N'Gourma and Koupela.

Armed groups carried out attacks close to the Mali and Niger border, killing dozens of civilians. They also attacked police and military personnel. Repeated attacks in the Sahel region led to public officials temporarily vacating the region.

In late January, armed men went to several schools in the north and threatened teachers to make them adopt Islamic teaching.

Consequently, hundreds of schools closed, including in Soum, Oudalan and Loroum.

Ansaroul Islam claimed responsibility for attacking police stations in Baraoulé and Tongomaël on 27 and 28 February.

On 3 March, an armed group killed a school principal and another local person in Kourfayel, a village in Soum.

In August, at least 19 people were killed and more than 22 injured in an attack against a restaurant in Ouagadougou. No group claimed responsibility.

On two occasions in September and November, armed groups carried out attacks in Soum, killing at least nine people.

BURUNDI

Republic of Burundi
Head of state and government: **President Pierre Nkurunziza**

Restrictions on the rights to freedom of expression and assembly continued. The security forces, among others, carried out unlawful killings, enforced disappearances, torture and other-ill-treatment, arbitrary arrests and detention.

BACKGROUND

In October, the Council of Ministers approved revisions of the Constitution. The proposed constitutional amendments would allow President Nkurunziza to stand for at least two more seven-year terms, and reduce the size of the majority required to pass legislation in Parliament. In December, the President of the National Independent Electoral Commission announced that a referendum on the constitutional amendments was planned for May 2018.

Efforts by the East African Community (EAC) to find a mediated solution to the political crisis sparked by the President's decision in 2015 to stand for a third term continued to stall. Michel Kafando, former President of Burkina Faso, was appointed as UN Secretary-General Special Envoy to Burundi in May. His role included providing assistance to the EAC's political dialogue efforts.

The government declared a malaria epidemic in March. Between January and mid-November, 6.89 million cases and 3,017 deaths were recorded.

UNLAWFUL KILLINGS

Unlawful killings continued. Bodies were regularly discovered in the streets of the capital, Bujumbura, and throughout the country. Several Burundians who were living as refugees in neighbouring countries said that they left Burundi after their relatives were killed, primarily by the Imbonerakure – the increasingly militarized youth wing of the ruling National Council for the Defence of Democracy-Forces for the Defence of Democracy. Others witnessed the killings of their family members by the Imbonerakure as they tried to flee the country.

ENFORCED DISAPPEARANCES

Reports of enforced disappearances continued, and cases from 2015 and 2016 remained unresolved. The UN Commission of Inquiry on Burundi highlighted several cases where there were reasonable grounds to believe or to fear that people had been forcibly disappeared. Pacifique Birikumana, driver for the Ngozi diocese, was believed to have been forcibly disappeared on 8 April after he returned from driving a group of soldiers to Gitega province. The Commission received information that he may have been arrested by the National Intelligence Services (SNR); his whereabouts remained unknown. Former senator and businessman Oscar Ntasano went missing with two of his employees on 20 April after meeting a man said to work for the SNR. Witnesses told the Commission that Oscar Ntasano received threats from state officials in connection with a contract he was negotiating with the UN to rent office space. One state official was said to have threatened him with death if he refused to split the proceeds.

TORTURE AND OTHER ILL-TREATMENT

Reports of torture and other ill-treatment by, among others, the SNR, police and the army, of detainees suspected of opposing the government continued. Torture methods included beating men with cables, iron reinforcing bars (rebar) and batons, as well as hanging heavy weights from genitals. Imbonerakure members were frequently accused of beating detainees during arrest.

Impunity for such violations continued. Burundi had not yet established a National Preventive Mechanism against torture as set out in the Optional Protocol to the UN Convention against Torture.

SEXUAL AND GENDER-BASED VIOLENCE

The Commission of Inquiry interviewed 49 survivors of sexual violence that took place between 2015 and 2017. Most of the cases involved rape of women and girls by police, often while arresting a male family member. The Commission also documented sexual violence against men in detention. It concluded that sexual violence appeared to be used as a way to assert dominance over people linked to opposition parties or movements.

ARBITRARY ARRESTS AND DETENTIONS

Arbitrary arrests and detentions continued, including during police searches in the so-called opposition neighbourhoods of Bujumbura. People were often arrested without warrants and only later informed of the accusations against them. Police and Imbonerakure sometimes used excessive force during arrests and attempted arrests. Former detainees said that they or their family had to pay vast sums of money to members of the SNR, police or Imbonerakure in exchange for their release.

FREEDOMS OF EXPRESSION AND ASSEMBLY

Restrictions on freedom of expression and peaceful assembly continued at all levels. University students in Bujumbura went on strike in March to protest against a new student loan and grant system; several of them were arrested and six student leaders were charged with rebellion.

On 4 April, Joseph Nsabiyabandi, editor-in-chief of Radio Isanganiro, was summoned for questioning by the SNR, and accused of collaborating with two radio stations set up by Burundian journalists in exile.

On 9 June, the Mayor of Bujumbura refused to allow Amizero y'Abarundi, the parliamentary opposition coalition, composed of representatives from the National Liberation Forces and Union for National Progress, to hold a press conference on the grounds that the coalition did not have "legal personality".

HUMAN RIGHTS DEFENDERS

In January, the Bujumbura Court of Appeal overturned a decision by the Bar Association's president not to disbar four lawyers following a request to do so by a prosecutor in 2016. Three of the lawyers were, therefore, disbarred while another was suspended for one year. The prosecutor had called for them to be struck off after they contributed to a report to the UN Committee against Torture.

Germain Rukuki was arrested on 13 July; he was president of the community organization Njabutsa Tujane, an employee of the Burundian Catholic Lawyers Association and a former member of ACAT-Burundi (Action by Christians for the Abolition of Torture, ACAT). The SNR held and interrogated him without a lawyer present, before transferring him to prison in Ngozi city on 26 July. On 1 August, he was charged with "undermining state security" and "rebellion", for collaborating with ACAT-Burundi, which was banned in October 2016. The Public Prosecutor presented as evidence against him an email exchange from a period when ACAT-Burundi was legally registered in Burundi. Germain Rukuki was denied bail and remained in detention at the end of the year.

Nestor Nibitanga, former member of the deregistered Association for the Protection of Human Rights and Detained Persons (APRODH), was arrested in Gitega on 21

November. He was charged with undermining state security and rebellion. This appeared to be in retaliation for his human rights activities. Following a hearing on 28 December, the Mukaza court in session at Rumonge decided to keep Nestor Nibitanga in provisional detention. He remained in detention at the Murembwe central prison in Rumonge at the end of the year.

REFUGEES AND ASYLUM-SEEKERS

People trying to flee the country reported abuses including rape, killings, beatings and extortion by members of the Imbonerakure. Many tried to leave by informal routes, as they did not have official travel documents; they were afraid of being accused of joining the rebellion, being refused permission to leave or being arrested at the border for trying to leave.

The number of Burundian refugees in relation to the current crisis reached over 418,000 in September but fell to 391,111 by the end of 2017. Most of them were hosted by Tanzania, Rwanda, Democratic Republic of the Congo (see Democratic Republic of the Congo entry) and Uganda. In an operation led by the Tanzanian government and supported by UNHCR, the UN refugee agency, organized returns began in September with 8,836 refugees assisted to return to Burundi by 20 November. Many refugees cited harsh conditions in their countries of asylum as their main reason for return. In August, the World Food Programme warned that without urgent funding from donors, insufficient food rations to refugees in Tanzania would be further reduced. The UNHCR-led Burundi Regional Refugee Response received only 20% of the funding required for 2017.

In January, Tanzania stopped automatically recognizing Burundian asylum-seekers as refugees. Uganda followed suit in June. On 20 July 2017, President Nkurunziza visited Tanzania in an attempt to convince Burundian refugees that it was safe to return.

INTERNALLY DISPLACED PEOPLE

The International Organization for Migration said that 187,626 people were internally displaced as of November; 19% were displaced in 2017. Two thirds of the total were displaced by natural disasters and one third as a result of the socio-political situation.

RIGHT TO PRIVACY

Couples cohabiting without being married risked prosecution under a 2016 law which banned "free unions" or cohabitation and carried a prison sentence of one to three months, and a fine of up to 200,000 francs (USD114). In May, following President Nkurunziza's call for a nationwide "moralization" campaign, the Interior ministry spokesperson gave cohabiting couples until 31 December to "regularize" their situation.

ECONOMIC, SOCIAL AND CULTURAL RIGHTS

In October, the Minister of Justice presented proposed amendments to the Penal Code which were unanimously adopted by the National Assembly and the Senate. The amendments would criminalize begging and "vagrancy". Able-bodied people found guilty of begging would face a prison sentence of between two weeks and two months, and/or a fine of up to 10,000 francs (USD6). The same sentence was proposed for "vagrancy".

Burundian refugees living outside the country claimed that increased local taxation was affecting their livelihoods. The extent to which fees were formally imposed or were simply acts of extortion was not always clear especially where they were collected by members of the Imbonerakure.

INTERNATIONAL SCRUTINY

On 4 September, the Commission of Inquiry report concluded that there were reasonable grounds to believe that crimes against humanity had been committed since April 2015. On 28 September, the UN Human Rights Council adopted a resolution mandating a team of three experts "to collect and preserve information […] in cooperation with the Government of Burundi", and "to make recommendations for technical assistance and capacity building". On 29 September, the Council also renewed the Commission of Inquiry's mandate for another year. Discussions between the UN and the government on the reopening of the UN Office of the High Commissioner for Human Rights in Burundi had not reached a conclusion by the end of the year.

Burundi's withdrawal from the ICC came into effect on 27 October. Two days earlier, the Pre-Trial Chamber authorized an investigation into the situation in Burundi, a decision made public in November.

The AU Peace and Security Council did not meet to discuss Burundi in 2017, despite the continued presence of AU human rights observers and military experts in the country at the Council's request.

CAMBODIA

Kingdom of Cambodia
Head of state: **King Norodom Sihamoni**
Head of government: **Hun Sen**

The crackdown on human rights defenders, media, civil society and the political opposition intensified ahead of elections scheduled for July 2018. The authorities' misuse of the justice system continued. New criminal charges were brought against serving and former leaders of the main opposition party. The authorities increased pressure on civil society including by conducting surveillance of human rights workers and restricting or shutting down organizations monitoring elections. Media freedom and diversity were dramatically reduced. Human rights defenders continued to be monitored, threatened, arrested and imprisoned. Montagnard asylum-seekers faced forcible return to Viet Nam.

BACKGROUND

The prospect of a close general election in 2018 led to an unstable political environment and threats to human rights. In February,

Sam Rainsy stood down as leader of the opposition Cambodia National Rescue Party (CNRP) to avoid party dissolution because of his 2016 conviction on criminal charges. The lead-up to the June 2017 commune elections was marked by threatening rhetoric from the Prime Minister and other senior government and military officials. The ruling Cambodian People's Party (CPP) won control of 70% of communes. In September, the UN Human Rights Council extended the mandate of the Special Rapporteur on the situation of human rights in Cambodia for a further two years. On 16 November, the CNRP was dissolved amid allegations of being part of a purported US-funded "colour revolution" to topple the current regime.

FREEDOMS OF EXPRESSION AND ASSOCIATION

Harassment of the political opposition and civil society through misuse of the criminal justice system escalated in an apparent attempt to hamper activities ahead of the 2018 general election.[1] Amendments to the Law on Political Parties in February and July gave the Ministry of Interior and courts new powers over political parties and barred individuals convicted of a criminal offence from holding leadership positions.

In March, Sam Rainsy was convicted of "defamation and incitement to commit a felony" for claiming on social media that the July 2016 murder of political commentator Kem Ley was an act of "state-sponsored terrorism". Political commentator Kim Sok was convicted on the same charges in August for allegedly linking the government to the murder in a radio interview. Following the commune elections, the Ministry of Interior ordered a local election monitoring coalition to cease its activities.

In August, the US-based National Democratic Institute was expelled from Cambodia for alleged regulatory violations. Also in August, more than 30 FM radio frequencies were silenced. Radio stations were alleged to have violated their contracts with the government by "overselling" air time to broadcasting programmes from the US-based Radio Free Asia (RFA) and Voice of America, as well as Cambodian radio programme Voice of Democracy. In September, the long-running English language newspaper *The Cambodia Daily* shut down after the authorities gave its publishers 30 days to pay a USD6.3 million tax bill, a move widely viewed as arbitrary. The same month, RFA ceased operations in Cambodia, citing the restrictive media environment. In November, two former RFA reporters were arrested on trumped-up charges of "espionage" and faced up to 15 years in jail.

On 3 September, new CNRP leader Kem Sokha was arrested at his home in the capital, Phnom Penh, and later charged with "conspiracy with a foreign power" in relation to a 2013 speech in which he discussed international advice he had received regarding democratic change. CPP lawmakers later voted to strip him of the parliamentary immunity he had been granted under the Constitution.

The Ministry of Interior ordered local land rights organization Equitable Cambodia (EC) to suspend its activities for 30 days for alleged regulatory violations. Although the suspension lapsed on 15 November, EC was not allowed to resume activities. At least three individuals were arrested throughout the year for posting comments on Facebook that were regarded by authorities as insulting to the Prime Minister. On 26 November, the Cambodian Centre for Human Rights was threatened by the Prime Minister with closure; it was allowed to remain open after investigation by the Ministry of Interior and an announcement by the Prime Minister on 2 December.

HUMAN RIGHTS DEFENDERS

Human rights defenders were harassed and prosecuted for their peaceful human rights work. In February, Tep Vanny, a prominent land rights activist from the Boeung Kak Lake community, was convicted of "intentional violence with aggravating circumstances" in relation to a 2013 protest, and sentenced to two years and six months' imprisonment. In December, the Supreme Court upheld a six-month prison sentence against Tep Vanny and two other community members stemming from a protest in 2011. Human rights defenders Am Sam Ath and Chan Puthisak were investigated in February for allegedly instigating violence at an October 2016 demonstration in Phnom Penh. They were beaten by para-police during the demonstration; however, their formal complaint of assault appeared to have been ignored.

In June, five serving and former staff members of the Cambodian Human Rights and Development Association (ADHOC) were released on bail after being held for more than a year in pre-trial detention on charges of bribing a witness. Three of the five – Ny Sokha, Nay Vanda and Yi Soksan – were arbitrarily denied access to medical care for two months prior to their release. The charges remained pending at the end of the year.

In September, two activists from the environmental organization Mother Nature were arrested while filming sand-dredging boats off the coast of Koh Kong in an attempt to highlight alleged illegal smuggling. They were charged with incitement to commit a felony and making an unauthorized recording.

UNLAWFUL KILLINGS

On 23 March Oeuth Ang was sentenced to life imprisonment after being convicted by the Phnom Penh Municipal Court of the 2016 murder of prominent political commentator Kem Ley. The trial lasted only half a day. The authorities did not respond to calls for an independent, impartial and effective investigation into the killing of Kem Ley.

WOMEN'S RIGHTS

Cambodia failed to submit its report, due in October, on implementation of the recommendations of the 2013 UN CEDAW Committee, or to follow up with requested information regarding sexual and gender-based violence – in particular redress and protection for victims. Women continued to be under-represented in politics. Although the number of women commune chiefs elected during the 2017 commune elections increased, the total number of women councillors decreased.

RIGHT TO HOUSING AND FORCED EVICTIONS

Land grabbing, land concessions granted to private stakeholders for agri-industrial use, and major development projects continued to impact the right to adequate housing for communities around the country. A report released in January by the Land Management Ministry showed an increase in land dispute complaints received in 2016 compared to the previous year. Work on the Lower Sesan II hydropower dam in the northeast province of Stung Treng progressed; Indigenous people who refused to leave their ancestral lands faced forcible relocation. Those who accepted relocation were moved to substandard and flooding-affected resettlement sites.

REFUGEES AND ASYLUM-SEEKERS

The government rejected 29 applications for refugee status by Montagnard asylum-seekers from Viet Nam, who faced possible *refoulement*. UNHCR, the UN refugee agency, stated that they had legitimate grounds. They remained in Cambodia at the end of the year.

INTERNATIONAL JUSTICE

In February, the Co-Investigating Judges issued a joint closing order dismissing the case against Im Chaem in Case 004/1 at the Extraordinary Chambers in the Courts of Cambodia (ECCC). She was found not to fall within the ECCC's personal jurisdiction of being a senior leader or one of the most responsible officials during the Khmer Rouge regime.

In June, closing statements were made in a second trial of Nuon Chea and Khieu Samphan in Case 002. The case against them had been severed by the Trial Chamber of the ECCC in 2011, resulting in two trials on different charges. They faced charges of crimes against humanity, genocide and grave breaches of the Geneva Conventions.

---

1. Cambodia: Courts of injustice – suppressing activism through the criminal justice system (ASA 23/6059/2017)

CAMEROON

Republic of Cameroon
Head of state: **Paul Biya**
Head of government: **Philémon Yang**

The armed group Boko Haram continued to commit serious human rights abuses and violations of international humanitarian law in the Far North region, including looting and destroying properties and killing and abducting civilians. In response, the authorities and security forces committed human rights violations and crimes under international law, including arbitrary arrests, incommunicado detentions, torture and deaths in custody. As a result of the conflict, around 240,000 people in the Far North region had fled their homes between 2014 and the end of 2017. Freedoms of expression, association and peaceful assembly continued to be restricted throughout the country. Security forces violently repressed demonstrations in Anglophone regions in January and September. Civil society activists, journalists, trade unionists and teachers were arrested and some faced trial before military courts.

ABUSES BY ARMED GROUPS

The armed group Boko Haram committed crimes under international law and human rights abuses, including suicide bombings in civilian areas, summary executions, abductions, recruitment of child soldiers, and looting and destruction of public and private property. During the year, the group carried out at least 150 attacks, including 48 suicide bombings, killing at least 250 civilians. The crimes were part of a widespread and systematic attack on the civilian population across the Lake Chad basin. Boko Haram deliberately targeted civilians in attacks on markets, mosques, commercial areas and other public places. On 12 July a female suicide bomber detonated explosives in a crowded video-game shop in the town of Waza, killing at least 16 civilians and injuring more than 30. On 5 August, a suicide bomber in the village of Ouro Kessoum, near Amchide, killed eight children and injured four more.

TORTURE AND OTHER ILL-TREATMENT

Security forces continued to arbitrarily arrest individuals accused of supporting Boko Haram, often with little or no evidence and sometimes using unnecessary or excessive force. Those arrested were frequently detained in inhumane, life-threatening conditions. At least 101 people were detained incommunicado between March 2013 and March 2017 in a series of military bases run by the Rapid Intervention Battalion (BIR) and facilities run by the intelligence agency. They were subjected to torture and other ill-treatment.[1] These routine and systematic practices continued throughout 2017, although at least 20 people were reported to have been transferred from the BIR military base in Salak to the central prison in Maroua in late August.

It was highly likely that senior military officers based in Salak were aware of the torture, but they did nothing to prevent it. US military personnel also had a regular presence at the BIR's base at Salak and an investigation was launched into their possible knowledge of human rights violations at the base; its outcomes were not published during the year.

No investigations were known to have been conducted by the Cameroonian authorities into the allegations of incommunicado detention, torture and other ill-treatment, nor efforts made to prevent such occurrences or to prosecute and punish the perpetrators.

In December the UN Committee against Torture expressed deep concern about the use of torture and incommunicado detention, and criticized the failure by Cameroonian authorities to clarify whether investigations were being carried out.

FREEDOMS OF EXPRESSION, ASSOCIATION AND ASSEMBLY

Human rights defenders, including civil society activists, journalists, trade unionists, lawyers and teachers continued to be intimidated, harassed and threatened.

On 17 January, following protests in the English-speaking regions of the country, the Minister of Territorial Administration banned the activities of the political party Southern Cameroons National Council (SCNC) and the Cameroon Anglophone Civil Society Consortium (CACSC).[2] The same day, the president of the CACSC, barrister Nkongho Felix Agbor-Balla, and its Secretary General, Dr Fontem Aforteka'a Neba, were arrested after signing a statement calling for non-violent protests. Held incommunicado at the State Defence Secretariat, they were charged under the 2014 anti-terrorism law, without any basis. They were transferred to the Prison Principale in the capital, Yaoundé, before eventually being released following a presidential decision on 30 August, along with 53 other Anglophone protesters who had been arrested between late October 2016 and February 2017.

Between January and April, and in early October, telephone and internet services were cut in the English-speaking regions, with no official explanation.

On 24 May, authorities shut down an Amnesty International press conference scheduled to take place in Yaoundé. Amnesty International staff had planned to present more than 310,000 letters and petitions asking President Biya to release three students imprisoned for 10 years for sharing a joke by text message about Boko Haram. No written administrative justification was provided for the prohibition of the press conference.

More than 20 protesters were shot by security forces in the Anglophone regions between 1 and 2 October, and more than 500 arrested. Others wounded in the protests were forced to flee hospitals where they sought life-saving treatment out of fear of arrest. In addition, dozens of members of the security forces, including soldiers and gendarmes, were killed in attacks perpetrated by Anglophone insurgents in the South and North West regions during the year.

UNFAIR TRIALS
Unfair trials continued before military courts, which were often marred by irregularities.

On 10 April, Radio France Internationale correspondent Ahmed Abba was sentenced to 10 years' imprisonment, convicted by the Yaoundé Military Court of "complicity with and non-denunciation of terrorist acts". The trial was marred by irregularities, including documents not being disclosed to defence lawyers. Ahmed Abba had been arrested in Maroua in July 2015 and was tortured while held incommunicado for three months at a facility run by the General Directorate of External Research. On 21 December the Appeal Court of the Yaoundé Military Court ordered his initial sentence to be reduced to 24 months, which he had already served. The Court upheld the charge of "non-denunciation of terrorism".

The appeal of Fomusoh Ivo Feh, who was arrested in December 2014 for forwarding a sarcastic text message about Boko Haram and sentenced to 10 years in prison, had not begun at the end of the year. Scheduled to begin in December 2016, his hearings had been adjourned at least seven times.

On 30 October, journalists Rodrigue Tongué, Felix Ebole Bola and Baba Wamé were acquitted by the Yaoundé Military Court, having been initially charged in October 2014 with "non-denunciation of information and sources". Facing trial alongside the journalists were opposition party leader Aboubakary Siddiki, and Abdoulaye Harissou, a well-known notary detained since August 2014. The Yaoundé Military Court sentenced Aboubakary Siddiki to 25 years' imprisonment on charges including hostility against the homeland, revolution, and contempt of the President. Abdoulaye Harissou was sentenced to three years' imprisonment, and subsequently released

having already served this sentence. Their trial was marred by irregularities. During their initial period of detention, the two men had been held incommunicado for more than 40 days in an illegal facility run by the General Directorate of External Relations and subjected to torture.

DETENTION
Prison conditions remained poor, marked by chronic overcrowding, inadequate food, limited medical care, and deplorable hygiene and sanitation. Maroua prison housed around 1,500 detainees, more than four times its intended capacity. The population of the central prison in Yaoundé was approximately 4,400, despite a maximum capacity of 1,500. The main factors contributing to overcrowding included the mass arrests since 2014 of people accused of supporting Boko Haram, the large number of detainees held without charge, and the ineffective judicial system. The government finalized the construction of at least 10 new cells for the prison in Maroua.

REFUGEES AND ASYLUM-SEEKERS
At least 250,000 refugees from the Central African Republic lived in harsh conditions in crowded camps or with host families along border areas of southeastern Cameroon. Some 60,000 refugees from Nigeria lived in the UN-run Minawao camp in the Far North region; around 30,000 others struggled to cope outside the camp, facing food insecurity, lack of access to basic services, harassment by the security forces and the risk of *refoulement* as they were perceived to be supporters of Boko Haram.

On 2 March, Cameroon, Nigeria and UNHCR, the UN refugee agency, signed a "Tripartite Agreement for the Voluntary Repatriation of Nigerian Refugees Living in Cameroon". However, between January and September, Cameroon forcibly returned at least 4,400 Nigerians. These forced returns were part of a larger deportation operation carried out by Cameroon. Human Rights Watch estimated that, since 2015, Cameroonian authorities and security forces had summarily deported more than 100,000 Nigerians living in areas located along the Cameroon-Nigeria border, often with unnecessary and excessive use of force. Some of those forcibly returned, including children, weakened by living for months or years with limited or no access to food and health care, died during the deportations.

In December, UNHCR reported having registered more than 5,000 Cameroonians, mainly women and children, who had fled the Anglophone areas of Cameroon to Nigeria.

RIGHT TO AN ADEQUATE STANDARD OF LIVING

The conflict with Boko Haram led to the internal displacement of around 240,000 people in the Far North region and exacerbated the hardships experienced by communities, limiting their access to basic social services, and disrupting trade, farming and pastoralism. In December, almost 3.3 million people, of whom 61% were in the Far North region, were in need of humanitarian assistance, including food and medical care. Humanitarian access continued to be restricted by the ongoing conflict.

RIGHT TO EDUCATION

Dozens of schools were closed in the English-speaking regions between November 2016 and September 2017, following strikes and boycotts called for by trade unions and members of civil society. Extreme elements within Anglophone pro-secession groups carried out attacks on education facilities that "breached the boycott".

Between January and September 2017, more than 30 schools were burned and severely damaged. In the Far North region, 139 primary schools in the departments of Logone and Chari, Mayo Sava and Mayo Tsanaga remained closed because of insecurity and at least eight were occupied by security forces, affecting almost 40,000 children.

DEATH PENALTY

People accused of supporting Boko Haram continued to be sentenced to death following unfair trials in military courts; none were executed during the year. The cases were all prosecuted under the deeply flawed 2014 anti-terrorism law.

---

1. Cameroon's secret torture chambers: Human rights violations and war crimes in the fight against Boko Haram (AFR 17/6536/2017)

2. Cameroon: Arrests and civil society bans risk inflaming tensions in English-speaking regions (Press release, 20 January)

CANADA

Canada
Head of state: **Queen Elizabeth II, represented by Julie Payette (replaced David Johnston in October)**
Head of government: **Justin Trudeau**

Discrimination against Indigenous Peoples continued, in particular the failure to protect their rights to lands and resources. Urgent measures were required to ensure the safety of Indigenous women and girls while a national inquiry was under way. There was a substantial increase in numbers of asylum-seekers crossing the border from the USA irregularly.

INDIGENOUS PEOPLES' RIGHTS

Government commitments to respect and protect the rights of Indigenous Peoples were contradicted by the failure to address violations of treaty-protected Indigenous hunting and fishing rights by the planned flooding of the Peace River Valley in the province of British Columbia for the Site C dam.

The Canadian Human Rights Tribunal issued three non-compliance orders against the federal government for discrimination in services for First Nations children and families.

The Public Inquiry Commission on Relations between Indigenous Peoples and Certain Public Services in Québec held hearings throughout the year.

In June the province of Ontario agreed to fund the clean-up of a river system contaminated with mercury. In November the federal government agreed to provide specialized medical care for mercury poisoning as long sought by members of the Grassy Narrows First Nation.

In July the Supreme Court of Canada, in a case brought by the Inuit hamlet of Clyde River, ruled that the government has an obligation to intervene when regulatory agencies fail to protect Indigenous rights.

In August the UN CERD Committee expressed concern about Indigenous land rights violations and Canada's failure to respect the right of free, prior and informed consent. The Committee asked Canada to report back within one year on measures to address the impacts of the Site C dam. In December the provincial government in British Columbia announced that construction of the Site C dam would continue, despite the objections of affected First Nations.

In November the government announced support for a bill to develop a legislative framework for implementing the UN Declaration on the Rights of Indigenous Peoples.

In November, the Supreme Court rejected a potentially groundbreaking legal challenge by the Ktunaxa Nation in British Columbia which sought to apply constitutional protection of religious freedom to the preservation of Indigenous Peoples' sacred sites.

WOMEN'S RIGHTS

In June, the federal government launched a Feminist International Assistance Policy and committed to placing women's rights, gender equality and sexual and reproductive rights at the core of its foreign policy. In November the government released its second National Action Plan on women, peace and security.

In June, the federal government released a strategy to combat gender-based violence, but without a national action plan.

The National Inquiry into Missing and Murdered Indigenous Women and Girls proceeded throughout the year. A growing number of relatives of missing and murdered women and girls expressed frustration about the Inquiry's slow progress and poor communication, and several staff and one of five Commissioners resigned. Community hearings commenced in June and an interim report was issued in November.

In October, Quebec passed the Act to Foster Adherence to State Religious Neutrality requiring everyone, including Muslim women wearing a niqab, to uncover their faces to use or provide government services, including on public transit and in libraries. A court ruling in December suspended application of the Act until a constitutional challenge is heard.

RIGHTS OF LESBIAN, GAY, BISEXUAL, TRANSGENDER AND INTERSEX PEOPLE

In June, Parliament passed legislation adding gender identity and expression as prohibited grounds for discrimination in Canada's Human Rights Act and Criminal Code.

COUNTER-TERROR AND SECURITY

In January, six worshippers were killed and 19 others injured when a gunman opened fire in a mosque in Quebec City.

In March, parliament adopted a motion calling for a committee study to develop a new approach for addressing Islamophobia and religious discrimination.

In March, Canadian citizens Abdullah Almalki, Ahmad Abou-Elmaati and Muayyed Nureddin received compensation and an apology for the role of Canadian officials in their unlawful arrest, imprisonment and torture in Syria and Egypt between 2001 and 2004.

In June, national security legal reforms were proposed, including improved review and oversight of national security agencies. Continuing concerns included insufficient information-sharing safeguards, inadequate appeal provisions for people named on "no-fly lists", and expanded mass surveillance and data-mining powers.

In June, legislation was passed reversing 2014 Citizenship Act reforms which had allowed dual nationals convicted of terrorism and other offences to be stripped of Canadian citizenship.

In July, Canadian citizen Omar Khadr received compensation and an apology for the role of Canadian officials in violations against him at the US detention facility at Guantánamo Bay, Cuba, for 10 years from 2002.

In September, revised guidelines strengthened safeguards against complicity in torture in intelligence sharing with other governments, but failed to absolutely prohibit the use of information obtained through torture by other governments.

JUSTICE SYSTEM

In June, federal legislation was tabled proposing to establish a 20-day limit on solitary confinement, to be reduced to 15 days once the law has been in force for 18 months. The draft law did not prohibit holding people suffering from mental illness in solitary confinement. A court ruling in December declared existing solitary confinement provisions to be unconstitutional because of inadequate safeguards and provided the government with one year to adopt new standards.

In October the Journalistic Source Protection Act was passed, establishing a "shield law" to protect journalists and their sources.

REFUGEES' AND MIGRANTS' RIGHTS

More than 18,000 asylum-seekers irregularly crossed from the USA into Canada during the year, as conditions for refugees and migrants in the USA deteriorated. Asylum-seekers crossed irregularly to avoid the ban on making claims at official border posts, pursuant to the 2004 Canada-US Safe Third Country Agreement. A legal challenge to the Agreement was launched jointly by civil society groups and individual asylum-seekers in July.

In August, the CERD Committee pressed Canada to set a maximum time frame for immigration detention, end the immigration detention of minors and provide access to essential health care for all people in Canada, regardless of immigration status. New guidelines released in November required that minors only be held in immigration detention in "extremely limited circumstances".

Annual government refugee resettlement targets declined to pre-2016 levels of 7,500, following an increase to 25,000 in 2016 as part of the government's Syrian refugee resettlement programme.

CORPORATE ACCOUNTABILITY

The British Columbia Conservation Officer Service concluded its investigation into the 2014 Mount Polley Mining Corporation (MPMC) tailings pond collapse, without bringing charges. A federal level investigation for violations of the Fisheries Act was ongoing. In April, against the wishes of Indigenous and other communities, British Columbia authorities approved MPMC's plan to discharge mine waste water that does not meet provincial drinking water guidelines into Quesnel Lake. In June the UN Working Group on Business and Human Rights supported British Columbia Auditor General's recommendation to establish a compliance and enforcement unit independent of the Ministry of Energy and Mines. In August, a private prosecution was filed against MPMC. Also in August, the CERD Committee called on Canada to report within one year on action to address the 2014 disaster.

In January the British Columbia Court of Appeal ruled that a lawsuit against Tahoe Resources regarding the shooting of protesters outside its mine in Guatemala could be heard in Canada. In November the Court upheld a lower court ruling that a lawsuit against Nevsun Resources for complicity in forced labour at its mine in Eritrea could proceed.

In December, the government announced plans to establish, in early 2018, a human rights Ombudsperson for Canadian extractives companies operating abroad.

Negotiations to revise the North American Free Trade Agreement between Canada, Mexico and the USA, including Canadian proposals on gender equality and Indigenous Peoples, were under way.

Talks regarding a potential free trade deal with China continued, amid concerns over possible implications for human rights protection in China.

LEGAL, CONSTITUTIONAL OR INSTITUTIONAL DEVELOPMENTS

In June the government tabled legislation to accede to the UN Arms Trade Treaty, but without it applying to arms transfers to the USA, the primary market for Canadian arms sales.

In October the Justice for Victims of Corrupt Foreign Officials Act was passed, strengthening redress and sanctions in designated cases of serious human rights violations.

In December, federal, provincial and territorial ministers responsible for human rights met for the first time since 1988 and committed to establish a "senior level mechanism" to more effectively co-ordinate implementation of Canada's international human rights obligations.

CENTRAL AFRICAN REPUBLIC

Central African Republic
Head of state: **Faustin-Archange Touadéra**
Head of government: **Simplice Sarandji**

The government had minimal control outside the capital, Bangui. Armed groups continued to fight for territorial control, and targeted civilians, humanitarian workers and peacekeepers. Widespread impunity further fuelled instability and conflict. Increasing numbers sought refuge in neighbouring countries or were internally displaced, in dire conditions. At least 2.4 million people depended on humanitarian assistance and 1.4 million remained food insecure.

BACKGROUND

There was a resurgence of violence mainly in and around the Ouaka, Basse-Kotto and Haute-Kotto prefectures (districts). Ex-Seleka and Anti-balaka armed groups controlled much of the country.

The mandate of the UN Multidimensional Integrated Stabilization Mission in the Central African Republic (MINUSCA) was renewed until 15 November 2018. Its forces were strengthened following criticism of its capacity to protect civilians and respond to attacks. In June, the UN agreed to reduce the MINUSCA budget by USD18.8 million, and the budgets of 14 peacekeeping missions.

US and Ugandan troops, deployed under the African Union-led Regional Task Force to eliminate the Lord's Resistance Army (LRA), withdrew from the country between April and May.

In May, the national assembly presented a peace roadmap, which included a national committee of victims and excluded amnesties for war crimes, to the government.

In June, the government and 13 of the 14 armed groups signed a peace agreement which included an immediate ceasefire, political representation for armed groups and the creation of a Truth and Reconciliation Commission. It also incorporated the potential for pardons.

In July, the AU produced the Roadmap for Peace and Reconciliation in the Central African Republic, which launched a joint mediation.

ABUSES BY ARMED GROUPS AND CRIMES UNDER INTERNATIONAL LAW

Armed groups were responsible for killings, torture and other ill-treatment, sexual assaults, abductions, arrests, extortion and looting, recruitment and exploitation of children and attacks on humanitarian workers and premises; they also prevented access to humanitarian assistance.

The International NGO Safety Organisation reported that over 390 security incidents targeted relief agencies and at least 15 local humanitarian workers were killed.

Between 20 and 21 March, at least 20 people, including civilians, were killed in clashes between ex-Seleka and Anti-balaka in the towns of Bakouma and Nzako, Mbomou prefecture.

In April, 11 civilians were killed in fighting between Anti-balaka and the Union for Peace in the Central African Republic (UPC) in loose alliance with herders along the Bangassou-Rafai road.

On 2 May, Return, Reclamation and Rehabilitation (3R) killed 12 people in Niem-Yelewa and occupied the town for 12 days.

Between 7 and 25 May, UPC's attacks killed hundreds of civilians and displaced thousands in the southeast including in the towns of Alindao, Nzangba and Mobaye. At least 130 civilians died in Alindao; women were systematically raped.

Between 12 and 13 May, Anti-balaka attacked the predominantly Muslim neighbourhood of Tokoyo in Bangassou, Mbomou prefecture, and the MINUSCA base. The UN estimated that at least 72 people were killed, 76 injured and 4,400 displaced, while the national Red Cross estimated at least 115 deaths.

From 16 to 18 May, at least 17 civilians were killed in clashes between ex-Seleka and Anti-balaka in the town of Bria, and some 15,000 displaced.

On 6 June, at least 18 civilians were killed when Popular Front for the Rebirth of Central African Republic (FPRC) elements attacked Anti-balaka positions in Nzako.

From 20 to 23 June, over 80 civilians died during fights between Anti-balaka and FPRC in Bria.

Between 27 and 30 June, at least 22 people were killed when Anti-balaka attacked Muslim neighbourhoods in Zemio town, and the local population retaliated.

On 1 July, at least 10 people were killed in fighting between the Central African Patriotic Movement (MPC) and Anti-balaka in Kaga-Bandoro, Nana-Gribizi province.

Between 29 July and 1 August, clashes between ex-Seleka and Anti-balaka in the town of Batangafo resulted in at least 14

civilian deaths and over 24,000 people displaced.

In August, clashes between Anti-balaka and UPC in the town of Gambo, near Bangassou, resulted in at least 36 civilian deaths including six national Red Cross workers.

In September, clashes between rival FPRC factions left 10 people dead in Bria.

Hundreds of Muslims returned home in the southwest but continued to be persecuted; fear of attacks forced them to restrict their movements and, in some cases, hide their religion.

In the southeast, international NGOs reported 113 attacks by the LRA and at least 12 civilian casualties and 362 kidnappings.

On 10 October, at least 25 people were killed in a mosque when Anti-balaka attacked Kembe town, in the Basse-Kotto province. On 18 October, clashes between Anti-balaka and UPC fighters in Pombolo, in Mbomou province, led to at least 26 deaths.

In November, four people were killed when unidentified assailants threw a grenade at a concert in Bangui.

VIOLATIONS BY PEACEKEEPING FORCES

Reports of sexual exploitation and abuses ("SEA") by UN peacekeeping troops continued. In January, the UN Secretary-General announced a new task force to prevent and respond to SEA. However, the UN registered 21 SEA cases, including against six children, involving peacekeepers. In June, the Republic of the Congo withdrew nearly 650 troops in light of sexual abuse and misconduct allegations.

On 30 September, at least one Mauritanian peacekeeper allegedly drugged and raped a woman in the town of Bambari. MINUSCA rapidly deployed investigators and committed to pursuing the issue.

Several SEA complaints involving French forces, deployed under Operation Sangaris, were dismissed following investigations. In March, the Paris Prosecutor requested the dismissal of a rape case which allegedly occurred between 2013 and 2014 at an internally displaced people's settlement in M'Poko in Bangui. At least 14 Operation

Sangaris soldiers and five soldiers of the African-led International Support Mission to the Central African Republic (MISCA), AU troops, and peacekeepers, were allegedly involved. The Prosecutor's decision was that the victims' testimonies did not sufficiently establish the facts.

REFUGEES AND INTERNALLY DISPLACED PEOPLE

The number of people seeking refuge in neighbouring countries increased due to an escalation of violence in April and May. By the end of the year, at least 538,000 people had fled the country for neighbouring countries Chad, Cameroon, DRC and Republic of the Congo; while 601,000 were internally displaced, living in poor conditions in makeshift camps with inadequate access to food, water, health care and sanitation.

IMPUNITY

Many suspected perpetrators of human rights abuses and violations, including armed groups and security forces, were not investigated or tried. Impunity was exacerbated by the collapse of the national justice system and its slow reconstruction.

On 26 February, MINUSCA arrested six FPRC and MPC members. Central African authorities detained them from 1 March and opened investigations. Suspects had not been brought to trial by the end of the year.

Between November and December, eight Anti-balaka members were sentenced in four cases, in a court in the western town of Bouar, to up to 20 years' imprisonment for crimes including criminal association, unlawful possession of homemade arms, murder and theft. Others were sentenced in their absence.

The Central African authorities failed to implement an asset freeze which was extended by the UN Security Council on 27 January until 31 January 2018 along with an arms embargo and travel ban. Several listed individuals continued to collect their state salaries.

Between April and December, the US imposed financial sanctions including against Abdoulaye Hissène, a leading FPRC member, and Maxime Mokom, an Anti-balaka leader. In June, Chad announced that it had frozen Abdoulaye Hissène's assets and banned him from crossing the Chadian borders.

INTERNATIONAL JUSTICE

Progress was made in operationalizing the Special Criminal Court (SCC) which will try individuals suspected of serious human rights violations and crimes under international law committed since 2003. The SCC Special Prosecutor took office in May after which five national magistrates and two international magistrates were nominated, and a committee to select judicial police officers was created.

The ICC investigations on the "Central African Republic II situation" continued but no arrest warrants were issued. In March, the ICC increased Jean-Pierre Bemba Gombo's 18-year prison sentence to 19 years after he and his legal team were convicted of attempting to bribe witnesses in 2016.

NATURAL RESOURCES

On 20 July, the General Court of the European Union upheld the asset freeze against the Belgium-based diamond companies BADICA and KARDIAM, which had procured diamonds from the Central African Republic despite a ban.

RIGHT TO AN ADEQUATE STANDARD OF LIVING

The UN reported that nearly half the population (2.4 million) needed humanitarian assistance, and 1.4 million were food insecure.

The health system collapsed due to the conflict and the population depended almost entirely on humanitarian organizations for basic services. Escalating violence led humanitarian organizations to temporarily withdraw staff from cities and villages.

The UN said that about a third of the population had access to safe drinking water and adequate sanitation facilities.

CHAD

Republic of Chad
Head of state: **Idriss Déby Itno**
Head of government: **Albert Pahimi Padacké**

The armed group Boko Haram continued to commit abuses around Lake Chad. Chadian authorities repeatedly banned peaceful assemblies and arrested and prosecuted human rights defenders, activists and journalists, some of whom became prisoners of conscience. The right to freedom of association was violated with unlawful restrictions on the right to organize freely, including the criminalization of certain citizens' associations. More than 408,000 refugees continued to live in dire conditions in camps including in Baga Sola.

BACKGROUND

Revisions to the Criminal Code were promulgated by President Déby, repealing the death penalty except for "terrorism", and increasing the minimum age for marriage to 18 years.

New powers, including the power to arrest, were provided to the National Security Agency (ANS).

A severe economic crisis, following a sharp drop in the price of petrol in recent years, led to austerity measures, public discontent and strikes in sectors including health, education and justice.

ABUSES BY ARMED GROUPS

The armed group Boko Haram continued to kill, abduct and injure civilians, and to destroy property.

On 5 May, Boko Haram members killed at least four civilians and burned 50 houses in Kaiga Kindjiria. On the night of 25 May, a Boko Haram attack on Kirnatchoulma village, in the west of Kaiga Kinjiria, resulted in at least three people being killed and three wounded. On 26 and 27 May, Boko Haram carried out several attacks on the villages of Konguia, Wangui and Kagrerom, in the area of Tchoukoutalia.

On 30 May a woman was abducted by Boko Haram about 4km from Kaiga Kindjiria. Similar attacks were reported in May and June in other areas including Bodou-Doloum in the Baga Sola sub-prefecture, which resulted in the killing of three people and the abduction of three others.

FREEDOM OF ASSEMBLY

During the year, the authorities banned at least six peaceful assemblies, and those organizing and participating in protests were arrested.

On 6 and 15 April respectively, Nadjo Kaina and Bertrand Solloh, leaders of the citizen movement IYINA ("We are tired"), were arrested by ANS agents for calling on citizens to wear red on the anniversary of the 2016 presidential election as a protest against corruption and impunity. They were detained by the ANS without access to their families or lawyers, before being handed over to the judicial police. They were charged with attempted conspiracy and organizing an unauthorized gathering and given a six-month suspended sentence. The two men reported being tortured while in detention, including by being suffocated with plastic bags containing chili.

On 12 April, Dingamnayal Nely Versinis, president of the organization Collectif Tchadien Contre la Vie Chère, was arrested by ANS agents at the city hall in the capital, N'Djamena. He had called on traders at the N'Djamena Millet Market to strike in protest at an increase in market fees. He was detained without access to his family or lawyer and charged with fraud and using a false identity, before being released on 27 April by the Public Prosecutor on the grounds that he had committed no offence.

FREEDOM OF ASSOCIATION

Certain social movements and civil society platforms were banned and the right to strike was restricted in contravention of international law.

The citizens' movement IYINA remained banned and, on 6 January, the Minister of Territorial Administration banned the activities of the National Movement of Citizen Awakening (MECI), a movement bringing together civil society organizations, trade unions and political parties, describing it as "unnatural" and "without any legal basis". On 27 May the police interrupted and banned MECI's General Assembly.

The rights of trade unions were violated in response to the strike action they initiated from September 2016 to January 2017. They remained subject to a decree introduced in 2016 limiting the right to strike, and their requests to protest were rejected.

In January the authorities interfered in the internal affairs of the trade union representing researchers and university teachers, SYNECS, to force the removal of its president and end its strike. The same month, visas were denied to representatives of the General Confederation of Labour, an international partner of Chadian trade unions.

FREEDOM OF EXPRESSION

Journalists critical of the government received threats and were subject to surveillance, while defamation and contempt laws continued to be used in an attempt to silence them.

Between 22 and 24 February, Eric Kokinagué, the Director of Publication of the newspaper Tribune Info, received more than a dozen anonymous, threatening calls from different numbers after he published an article heavily critical of President Déby. On 25 February, the columnist who wrote the article, Daniel Ngadjadoum, was abducted by armed men, detained for up to 24 hours in what he believes was an ANS facility, and forced to write a letter of apology to the President.

In June, Déli Sainzoumi Nestor, editor of the bi-monthly newspaper Eclairages, was charged with defamation after Daoussa Déby Itno, former minister and brother of President Déby, filed a complaint about an article alleging his involvement in fraud in the sugar industry.

On 4 September, radio journalist Mbairaba Jean Paul was arrested and accused of defamation after he reported on a communal conflict between herders and farmers in Doba. He was released the following day and the prefect who ordered his arrest was removed from office.

PRISONERS OF CONSCIENCE

The authorities continued to arrest and detain journalists for doing their work and activists and human rights defenders for exercising their freedoms of expression and opinion.

Online activist Tadjadine Mahamat Babouri (also known as Mahadine), who was arrested on 30 September 2016, remained in detention. He was arrested by ANS agents after posting several videos on Facebook criticizing the government's alleged mismanagement of public funds. He was later charged with undermining the constitutional order, threatening territorial integrity and national security, and collaborating with an insurrectional movement. He reported that, while detained by the ANS, he was deprived of food and water for three days, electrocuted and beaten.

On 5 May, Maoundoe Decladore, spokesperson of the organization Ça doit changer ("It must change"), was arrested at night by four armed men in plain clothes in Moundou. He was detained for 25 days without any access to his family or lawyer, in what he believes was an ANS facility. He was transferred to the judicial police on 30 May and charged with public disorder. Maoundoe Decladore was released on bail due to his deteriorating health and was awaiting trial at the end of the year.

On 20 June, Sylver Beindé Bassandé, a journalist and director of community radio Al Nada FM in Moundou, was sentenced to two years in prison and fined XAF100,000 (USD180) by the High Court of Moundou for complicity in contempt of court and undermining judicial authority. He had been charged after airing a radio interview with a municipal councillor, who had criticized judges after having been convicted with two other councillors in a separate proceeding. Sylver Beindé Bassandé lodged an appeal and was released on bail on 19 July. On 26

September, the Court of Appeal overruled the decision by the High Court of Moundou, sentencing Sylver Beindé Bassandé to complicity in defamation and fined him XAF100,000 (USD180). He appealed to the Supreme Court.

REFUGEES AND INTERNALLY DISPLACED PEOPLE

More than 408,000 refugees from the Central African Republic, the Democratic Republic of the Congo, Nigeria and Sudan continued to live in poor conditions in refugee camps. Insecurity caused by Boko Haram attacks and military operations resulted in the displacement of more than 174,000 people including at least 25,000 in 2017 alone.

In June, nearly 5,000 people fled a wave of Boko Haram attacks on villages around Kaiga Kindjiria and Tchoukoutalia, creating two new sites for internally displaced people: Kengua (Kiskra canton, Fouli department) and Kane Ngouboua (Diameron). Since July, around 6,700 people arrived in Baga Sola from Niger after the withdrawal of Chadian troops from the country and in fear of attacks from Boko Haram.

RIGHT TO FOOD

The Chadian military continued to impose restrictions on the movement of people and goods along the shores of Lake Chad, hampering the livelihoods of communities and heightening the risk of food insecurity.

According to the UN, severe acute malnutrition increased from 2.1% to 3.4% in the region during the year. Countrywide, the UN estimated that 2.8 million people were food insecure, including more than 380,000 people at crisis or emergency level.

CHILE

Republic of Chile
Head of state and government: **Michelle Bachelet Jeria**

Impunity for past and present human rights violations remained a concern. Police continued to use excessive force, especially against Mapuche Indigenous Peoples. The Anti-Terrorism Law was used against Mapuche people, despite violating international standards on due process guarantees. A law decriminalizing abortion in three specific circumstances entered into force; abortion continued to be otherwise criminalized.

BACKGROUND

Presidential and congressional elections were held between November and December, and Sebastián Piñera Echenique was elected President. The President-elect and new members of Congress were due to begin their mandates in March 2018.

REFUGEES' AND MIGRANTS' RIGHTS

Congress considered a bill proposed by the executive for a new immigration law.

The first 14 Syrian families (66 people) arrived in October under a resettlement programme announced in 2014.

POLICE AND SECURITY FORCES

There were continuing reports of excessive use of force by the police.

In June, police used tear gas in close proximity to a school in the Temucuicui Mapuche community where young children were attending class. The action was deemed "proportionate" by the Supreme Court.

In November, a judge in Collipulli, Malleco Province, opened an investigation against a police officer for shooting 17-year-old Brandon Hernández in December 2016; he received more than 100 pellet wounds in his back. The hearing was rescheduled three times because the accused police officer did not appear in court.

The Supreme Court reopened the case of Alex Lemún, who was shot and killed by a police officer in Ercilla, Malleco Province in 2002. A military court had closed the case in 2004 without finding anyone responsible.

IMPUNITY

Victims of human rights violations during Chile's military regime continued to demand truth, justice and reparation. Although courts had heard hundreds of cases, most of those convicted did not serve prison sentences, and many victims continued to lack access to institutional mechanisms to demand reparation.

Congress discussed a bill to make information gathered by former truth commissions available to prosecutors and parties to relevant judicial proceedings.

In May the government filed a bill before Congress to establish a National Mechanism for the Prevention of Torture.

INDIGENOUS PEOPLES' RIGHTS

In June the government announced the Plan for the Recognition and Development of Araucanía to promote Indigenous Peoples' participation, economic development and protection of victims of violence.

President Bachelet extended a formal apology to the Mapuche People for "errors and horrors" perpetrated by the state against them. A bill was under discussion to create a Ministry of Indigenous Issues.

As part of the process of developing a new Constitution, scheduled to be completed in 2018, a consultation was conducted with Indigenous Peoples' representatives. The process was criticized by some representatives for excluding some key issues brought forth by Indigenous Peoples.

The Attorney General's Office and the government continued to misuse the Anti-Terrorism Law to prosecute Mapuche people in violation of due process guarantees. In 2014, similar applications of the Anti-Terrorism Law against Mapuche activists were found by the Inter-American Court of Human Rights – in *Norín Catrimán et al v. Chile* – to be in violation of the American Convention on Human Rights.

In October, 11 Mapuche people, including Machi Francisca Linconao, who had been charged with "terrorism" for a fire that killed landowners Werner Luchsinger and Vivian Mackay in January 2013, were acquitted. The 11 defendants had been held in pre-trial detention or under house arrest for 18 months. Upon appeal by the Attorney General's Office in December, the trial and acquittal were declared null and void. The trial was due to be repeated in 2018.

The government and Attorney General's Office also brought "terrorism" charges against four Mapuche men for a fire that destroyed a church in the city of Padre las Casas in June 2016. No one was hurt in the fire. The men were arrested, detained and indicted on the day of the incident and continued to be held in pre-trial detention at the end of 2017. After the four accused held a prolonged hunger strike, the government filed a request for reclassification of the crime. However, the prosecution decided to continue pursuing terrorism charges.

In September the government implemented "Operation Hurricane", arresting and charging eight people with conspiracy to commit terrorist acts in connection with burning and planning to burn dozens of cargo vehicles. No one was hurt in these incidents. The eight accused were held in pre-trial detention until October when the Supreme Court declared their detention unlawful and ordered their release, since the judge had not sufficiently justified the need for pre-trial detention. Investigation of the alleged crimes was ongoing.

HUMAN RIGHTS DEFENDERS

In April, Rodrigo Mundaca and other leaders of the Movement for the Defence of Water, Land and the Environment (MODATIMA) in the province of Petorca received death threats. An investigation was ongoing into the harassment and intimidation that MODATIMA's leaders had been subjected to for a number of years.

In May the Temuco Public Prosecutor's Office announced the closure of the investigation into the abduction and torture of Víctor Queipul Hueiquil, a Mapuche lonko (traditional community authority) in the Autonomous Community of Temucuicui in June 2016. He had been threatened with death if he continued his work as a leader and supporter of the Mapuche People. The Public Prosecutor said that the investigation could not proceed because Víctor Queipul did not collaborate with the investigation. In

May, the National Human Rights Institute filed a new lawsuit relating to the torture of Víctor Queipul; the investigation for the second case was ongoing.

SEXUAL AND REPRODUCTIVE RIGHTS

In September a law entered into force decriminalizing abortion in three circumstances: when the pregnancy poses a risk to the life of the pregnant woman or girl; when the foetus is not viable; or when pregnancy is a result of rape. It also established the right to conscientious objection for medical professionals and institutions who choose not to perform abortions even in those circumstances. Guidelines for the implementation of the law were approved in December. Abortion continued to be criminalized in all other circumstances.

RIGHTS OF LESBIAN, GAY, BISEXUAL, TRANSGENDER AND INTERSEX PEOPLE

In August a criminal case filed against a judge for allowing the change of name and gender markers for a transgender girl was closed with all charges dropped.

In June the Senate approved the Gender Identity Bill, which established the right of people over the age of 18 to have their gender identity legally recognized by changing their name and gender markers on official documents through an administrative process, without requiring gender reassignment surgery or medical certification. The bill was pending before Congress at the end of the year.

In August the government filed a bill in the Senate establishing marriage and adoption rights for same-sex couples in equality with different-sex couples.

CHINA

People's Republic of China
Head of state: **Xi Jinping**
Head of government: **Li Keqiang**

The government continued to draft and enact new laws under the guise of "national security" that presented serious threats to human rights. Nobel Peace Prize laureate Liu Xiaobo died in custody. Activists and human rights defenders were detained, prosecuted and sentenced on the basis of vague and overbroad charges such as "subverting state power" and "picking quarrels and provoking trouble". Police detained human rights defenders outside formal detention facilities, sometimes incommunicado, for long periods, which posed additional risk of torture and other ill-treatment to the detainees. Controls on the internet were strengthened. Repression of religious activities outside state-sanctioned churches increased. Repression conducted under "anti-separatism" or "counter-terrorism" campaigns remained particularly severe in the Xinjiang Uighur Autonomous Region and Tibetan-populated areas. Freedom of expression in Hong Kong came under attack as the government used vague and overbroad charges to prosecute pro-democracy activists.

LEGAL, CONSTITUTIONAL OR INSTITUTIONAL DEVELOPMENTS

Sweeping national security-related laws and regulations continued to be drafted and enacted, giving greater powers to the authorities to silence dissent, censor information and harass and prosecute human rights defenders.

On 1 January the foreign NGO management law, whose provisions impeded independent operations of registered NGOs, came into effect. Foreign NGOs that had not yet registered and continued to operate in China could face a freeze on bank accounts, sealing of venues, confiscation of assets, suspension of activities and detention of staff.

In June, the National Intelligence Law was adopted and entered into force. These laws were part of a national security legal architecture introduced in 2014 – which also included the Anti-espionage Law, Criminal Law Amendment (9), National Security Law, Anti-terrorism Law and Cyber Security Law – and presented serious threats to the protection of human rights. The National Intelligence Law used similarly vague and overbroad concepts of national security, and granted effectively unchecked powers to national intelligence institutions with unclear roles and responsibilities. All lacked safeguards to protect against arbitrary detention and to protect the right to privacy, freedom of expression and other human rights.[1]

The draft Supervision Law, which opened for consultation in November, would, if enacted as is, legalize a new form of arbitrary detention, named *liuzhi*, and create an extrajudicial system with far-reaching powers with significant potential to infringe human rights.[2]

The authorities continued to use "residential surveillance in a designated location", a form of secret incommunicado detention that allowed the police to hold individuals for up to six months outside the formal detention system, without access to legal counsel of their choice, their families or others, and placed suspects at risk of torture and other ill-treatment. This form of detention was used to curb the activities of human rights defenders, including lawyers, activists and religious practitioners.

HUMAN RIGHTS DEFENDERS

On 13 July, Nobel Peace Prize laureate Liu Xiaobo died in custody from liver cancer. The authorities had refused a request from Liu Xiaobo and his family that he travel abroad to receive medical treatment.[3] At the end of the year, his wife Liu Xia remained under surveillance and illegal "house arrest" which had continued since Liu Xiaobo was awarded the Nobel Peace Prize in 2010. At least 10 activists were detained for holding memorials for him.

In November, writer and government critic Yang Tongyan, who had spent nearly half his life in detention, died shortly after his release on medical parole.

Among the nearly 250 targeted individuals who were questioned or detained by state security agents following the unprecedented government crackdown on human rights lawyers and other activists that started in July 2015, nine were convicted of "subverting state power", "inciting subversion of state power" or "picking quarrels and provoking trouble". Three people were given suspended sentences and one "exempted from criminal punishment" while remaining under surveillance and five remained imprisoned. In April, Beijing lawyer Li Heping, detained since the beginning of the crackdown, was given a three-year suspended prison sentence for "subverting state power". He claimed that he was tortured during pre-trial detention, including being force-fed medicine. Yin Xu'an was sentenced in May to three and a half years' imprisonment. Wang Fang was sentenced in July to three years' imprisonment. Beijing lawyer Jiang Tianyong, who went missing in November 2016 and "confessed" at a trial in August to fabricating the torture account of lawyer Xie Yang by Chinese police and attending overseas workshops to discuss changing China's political system, was sentenced in November to two years' imprisonment for "inciting subversion of state power". Hu Shigen and Zhou Shifeng, convicted in 2016, remained imprisoned. Beijing human rights lawyer Wang Quanzhang, held in incommunicado detention since the beginning of the crackdown, was still awaiting trial at the end of the year, charged with "subverting state power". In January, an interview transcript with Xie Yang was published in which he said he faced torture and other ill-treatment during detention. Xie Yang was released on bail without a verdict in May after his trial. On 26 December, the court announced his conviction on the charge of "inciting subversion of state power" but ruled that he was "exempt from criminal punishment". He remained under surveillance.

In July, Beijing lawyer Wang Yu, whose detention on 9 July 2015 marked the beginning of the crackdown, wrote in an article published online that she was ill-treated during detention. She was released on bail in mid-2016 but remained under close surveillance. Lawyers Li Shuyun, Ren Quanniu and Li Chunfu, and activist Gou Hongguo, reported that they were drugged during detention.[4]

In addition to the 250 targeted individuals, activist Wu Gan, who worked in a law firm later targeted by the authorities in the crackdown, was tried in August in a closed hearing for "subverting state power" after nearly 27 months' pre-trial detention. On 26 December, he was sentenced to eight years' imprisonment.

In March, Guangdong activist Su Changlan was sentenced to three years' imprisonment for "inciting subversion of state power" for her online criticism of the Chinese Communist Party and the Chinese socialist system. She was detained in 2014 after expressing support for Hong Kong's 2014 pro-democracy Umbrella Movement. She was released in October after serving the full sentence but with health concerns aggravated by poor conditions in detention.

On 19 March, Lee Ming-Cheh, manager of a Taiwan NGO, was detained by state security officers when he entered mainland China from Macao. In September, he was tried in Hunan Province for "subverting state power" and sentenced to five years' imprisonment in November.[5]

At least 11 activists were detained in June for commemorating the 1989 Tiananmen crackdown; most were accused of "picking quarrels and provoking trouble". Li Xiaoling and Shi Tingfu remained in detention, and Ding Yajun was sentenced to three years' imprisonment in September.

In August, lawyer Gao Zhisheng went missing from an isolated village in Shaanxi province, where he had lived under tight surveillance since his release from prison in 2014. The family later learned he was in authorities' custody but his location and condition remained unknown.

Lawyer Li Yuhan was detained in October and claimed she was tortured and ill-treated during detention.

WORKERS' RIGHTS

In May, labour activists Hua Haifeng, Li Zhao and Su Heng were detained in Jiangxi province while investigating work conditions at Huajian shoe factories. The activists were released on bail in June but remained under close surveillance.

In July, a Guangzhou court sentenced labour activist Liu Shaoming to four and a half years' imprisonment for publishing his reflections about joining the pro-democracy movement and becoming a member of China's first independent trade union in 1989, and experiences during the 1989 Tiananmen crackdown.

FREEDOM OF EXPRESSION – INTERNET

Thousands of websites and social media services remained blocked, including Facebook, Instagram and Twitter. On 1 June, the Cybersecurity Law came into effect, making it obligatory for internet companies operating in China to censor users' content. In August, the Cyberspace Administration of China and the Guangdong Provincial Cyberspace Administration launched an investigation into internet service providers Tencent's WeChat, Sina Weibo and Baidu's Tieba because their platforms contained user accounts which "spread information that endangers national security, public security and social order, including violence and terror, false information and rumours and pornography". In September, China's dominant messaging service WeChat introduced new terms of service to collect a wide range of personal information, and made data on its over 900 million users available to the government.

Huang Qi, co-founder of 64tianwang.com, a website that reports on and documents protests in China, was accused of "leaking state secrets". He was allowed to meet his lawyer only eight months after he was detained and claimed that he was ill-treated in detention. At the end of 2017, 10 journalists of 64tianwang.com were in prison: Wang Jing, Zhang Jixin, Li Min, Sun Enwei, Li Chunhua, Wei Wenyuan, Xiao Jianfang, Li Zhaoxiu, Chen Mingyan and Wang Shurong.

Liu Feiyue, founder of human rights website Civil Rights and Livelihood Watch, was detained in late 2016 and charged with "inciting subversion of state power". His lawyer said that the charge was mostly related to opinions he had expressed publicly and posted on the website.

In August, Lu Yuyu, who documented protests in China on Twitter and in a blog, was convicted of "picking quarrels and provoking trouble" and sentenced to four years' imprisonment.

In September, Zhen Jianghua, executive director of online platform Human Rights Campaign in China, was criminally detained on suspicion of "inciting subversion of state power" and later placed under residential surveillance at a designated location. Police confiscated numerous documents related to his website which contained reports from grassroots rights activists.

FREEDOM OF RELIGION AND BELIEF

In June, the State Council passed the revised Regulations on Religious Affairs, to come into effect on 1 February 2018. It codified far-reaching state control over every aspect of religious practice, and extended power to authorities at all levels of the government to monitor, control and potentially punish religious practice. The revised law, which emphasized national security with a goal of curbing "infiltration and extremism", could be used to further suppress the right to freedom of religion and belief, especially for Tibetan Buddhists, Uighur Muslims and unrecognized churches.[6]

Falun Gong practitioners continued to be subjected to persecution, arbitrary detention, unfair trials and torture and other ill-treatment. Chen Huixia remained detained since 2016 for suspicion of "using an evil cult to undermine law enforcement". In May, her trial was adjourned after her lawyer requested the court exclude evidence extracted through torture.

DEATH PENALTY

In March, the President of the Supreme People's Court announced that over the last 10 years, since the Court regained the authority to review and approve all death sentences, capital punishment "had been strictly controlled and applied prudently" and only applied "to an extremely small number of criminals for extremely severe offences". However, the government continued to conceal the true extent of the use of the death penalty, despite more than four decades of requests from UN bodies and the international community for more information, and despite the Chinese authorities' own pledges to bring about greater openness in the criminal justice system.[7]

TIBET AUTONOMOUS REGION AND TIBETAN-POPULATED AREAS IN OTHER PROVINCES
ECONOMIC, SOCIAL AND CULTURAL RIGHTS

In June, in his report of a 2016 visit to China, the UN Special Rapporteur on extreme poverty and human rights stated that while achievements towards alleviating poverty were generally "impressive", the situation of Tibetans and Uighurs was deeply problematic, and "that most ethnic minorities in China are exposed to serious human rights challenges, including significantly higher poverty rates, ethnic discrimination and forced relocation".

Tashi Wangchuk, a Tibetan education advocate, remained in detention awaiting trial at the end of the year, without access to his family. He was taken away in early 2016 for giving an interview to the *New York Times* in which he expressed fears about the gradual extinction of the Tibetan language and culture.

FREEDOM OF EXPRESSION

Ethnic Tibetans continued to face discrimination and restrictions on their rights to freedom of religion and belief, of opinion and expression, of peaceful assembly and of association.

At least six people set themselves on fire in Tibetan-populated areas during the year in protest against repressive policies, bringing the known number of self-immolations since February 2009 to 152. On 18 March, Pema Gyaltsen set himself on fire in Ganzi (Tibetan: Kardze) Tibetan Autonomous Prefecture in Sichuan Province. Tibetan sources said that he was believed to be alive when he was taken away by the police. His relatives were detained and beaten when they approached the authorities asking for his whereabouts. Tibetan NGOs abroad said that Lobsang Kunchok, a Tibetan monk detained after surviving a self-immolation attempt in 2011, was released from prison in March.[8] On 26 December, Tibetan filmmaker Dhondup Wangchen was reunited with his family in the USA, almost 10 years after he was first detained in China for making an independent documentary about the views of ordinary Tibetans ahead of the 2008 Beijing Olympics.

XINJIANG UIGHUR AUTONOMOUS REGION

Under the leadership of new regional Communist Party Secretary Chen Quanguo, the Xinjiang Uighur Autonomous Region (XUAR) authorities put new emphasis on "social stability" and increased security. Media reports indicated that numerous detention facilities were set up within the XUAR, variously called "counter extremism centres", "political study centres", or "education and transformation centres", in which people were arbitrarily detained for unspecified periods and forced to study Chinese laws and policies.

In March, the XUAR enacted the "De-extremification Regulation" that prohibits a wide range of behaviours labelled "extremist", such as spreading "extremist thought", denigrating or refusing to watch public radio and TV programmes, wearing burkas, having an "abnormal" beard, resisting national policies, and publishing, downloading, storing or reading articles, publications or audio-visual materials containing "extremist content".

In April, the government published a list of prohibited names, most of which were Islamic in origin, and required all children under 16 with these names to change them.

In May, there were media reports that the Chinese authorities in the XUAR had initiated a policy to compel all Uighurs studying abroad to return to China. Six Uighurs who had studied in Turkey but had returned to the XUAR were given prison sentences ranging from 5 to 12 years on undefined charges. In April, Chinese authorities detained relatives of several students in Egypt to coerce them to return home by May. Reports were received that some who returned were tortured and imprisoned. In July, the Egyptian authorities began a massive round-up of hundreds of Chinese nationals in Egypt, mainly Uighurs. Of these, at least 22 Uighurs were forcibly returned to China.

Buzainafu Abudourexiti, a Uighur woman who returned to China in 2015 after studying for two years in Egypt, was detained in March and sentenced in June to seven years' imprisonment after a secret trial.[9]

In August, international media reported that education authorities had issued an order in June in the largely Uighur-populated Hotan Prefecture to ban the use of the Uighur language in schools, including for "collective activities, public activities and management work of the education system". Media reports stated that families across the region were required to hand copies of the Qur'an and any other religious items to the authorities or risk punishment.

HONG KONG SPECIAL ADMINISTRATIVE REGION

A series of actions taken throughout the year by the Hong Kong authorities increased concerns about whether freedom of expression and freedom of peaceful assembly were at risk.

In March, the founders of the Occupy Central campaign – Benny Tai, Chan Kin-man and Rev Chu Yiu-Ming – were charged with "public nuisance"-related offences, carrying a maximum penalty of seven years' imprisonment, for their involvement in the Umbrella Movement.

In July, the High Court disqualified four elected pro-democracy legislators – Nathan Law, Leung Kwok-hung, Lau Siu-lai and Yiu Chung-yim – for failing to meet the requirements specified in the National People's Congress Standing Committee's interpretation of the Hong Kong Basic Law when they took their oaths of office in October 2016.

In August, the Court of Appeal sentenced Joshua Wong, Alex Chow and Nathan Law to six, seven and eight months' imprisonment respectively for their part in a student-led demonstration in September 2014 which triggered the Umbrella Movement. Joshua Wong and Alex Chow had been found guilty in 2016 of "taking part in an unlawful assembly" and Nathan Law of "inciting others to take part in an unlawful assembly". A magistrates' court originally ordered community service or suspended sentences but prosecutors successfully appealed, seeking harsher penalties.[10] Joshua Wong and Nathan Law were released on bail in October and Alex Chow in November pending their appeals.

The District Court sentenced seven police officers to two years' imprisonment in February for assaulting protester Ken Tsang during the Umbrella Movement protests. After the sentencing, China's state mouthpieces initiated an orchestrated campaign attacking Hong Kong's judiciary. Appeals were pending at year end.

RIGHTS OF LESBIAN, GAY, BISEXUAL, TRANSGENDER AND INTERSEX PEOPLE

In April, the Court of First Instance ruled that the government's refusal to extend work benefits to the same-sex husband of a civil servant was discrimination based on sexual orientation.

In September, the Court of Appeal ruled that the Immigration Department's refusal to grant a dependant visa to the same-sex civil partner of a foreign professional on a work visa was discriminatory. The government appealed against the decisions in both cases.

MACAO SPECIAL ADMINISTRATIVE REGION

In August, the Macao government stopped four Hong Kong journalists from entering Macao to report on the destruction and clean-up work of Typhoon Hato, which media reported caused 10 deaths. In December, Macao's legislature voted to suspend pro-democracy lawmaker Sulu Sou and to remove his legislative immunity. He was elected in September and charged in November for taking part in a May 2016 peaceful protest against Macao's Chief Executive.

1. China: Submission on the draft "National Intelligence Law" (ASA 17/6412/2017)

2. China: Submission on the draft "Supervision Law" (ASA 17/7553/2017)

3. Liu Xiaobo: A giant of human rights who leaves a lasting legacy for China and the world (Press release, 13 July)

4. Further information: China – lawyer on bail remains under tight surveillance: Xie Yang (ASA 17/6307/2017)

5. China: Taiwanese activist sentenced to five years in jail (Press release)

6. Why China must scrap new laws that tighten the authorities' grip on religious practice (News story, 31 August)

7. China's deadly secrets (ASA 17/5849/2017)

8. China: Disclose the whereabouts of two Tibetans who attempted self-immolation (ASA 17/6098/2017)

9. China: Uighur woman incommunicado after secret trial – Buzainafu Abudourexiti (ASA 17/7168/2017)

10. Hong Kong: Freedom of expression under attack as scores of peaceful protesters face "chilling" prosecutions (News story, 26 September)

COLOMBIA

Republic of Colombia
Head of state and government: **Juan Manuel Santos Calderón**

The civilian population, especially Indigenous Peoples, Afro-descendant and peasant farmer communities, and human rights defenders, continued to be the main victims of the ongoing armed conflict. Although official figures indicated that there was a decrease in the number of civilians killed in military actions involving the Revolutionary Armed Forces of Colombia (FARC) and the Colombian security forces from the start of the negotiations to signing of the Peace Agreement in 2016, the armed conflict persisted in 2017 and in some parts of the country it seemed to have intensified. Concerns remained about impunity for crimes committed during the armed conflict. Security forces used excessive force, sometimes causing civilian deaths. Violence against women, particularly sexual violence, persisted.

INTERNAL ARMED CONFLICT
PEACE PROCESS
On 11 October, the Constitutional Court gave backing to the Peace Agreement signed by the Colombian government and the FARC guerrilla group on 24 November 2016. However, at the end of 2017 legislation had yet to be implemented for most of the points in the Peace Agreement.

During separate negotiations in Quito, Ecuador, between the National Liberation Army (ELN) guerrilla group and the Colombian government, the parties declared on 4 September that a bilateral ceasefire would take effect from 1 October until early 2018. The ceasefire was declared in principle for a period of four months, after which the Colombian government and the ELN would begin to discuss a possible peace agreement. However, from October there were various reports of ELN attacks against civilians in contradiction of the ceasefire agreement. ELN acknowledged one such attack: the killing of Aulio Isaramá Forastero, an Indigenous leader from Chocó, by ELN members on 24 October. Civil society organizations in the Department of Chocó issued a call for a "Humanitarian Agreement Now", directed at the national government and the ELN guerrillas, in order to implement concrete humanitarian actions to stop ethnic communities in Chocó continuing to be put at risk by confrontations in their territories.

Between 28 January and 18 February, 6,803 FARC guerrillas moved into 26 demobilization zones with the support of the UN Monitoring and Verification Mission in Colombia established by UN Security Council resolution 2261 (2016). The process to verify FARC disarmament, which was due to be completed in 180 days, began on 1 March. On 27 June, the process of surrendering of weapons by individuals ended, and on 15 August the process of removing arms and munitions from the 26 FARC camps was completed. In accordance with the Peace Agreement, the UN Security Council adopted resolution 2377 (2017) approving a second verification mission on the political, economic and social reintegration of FARC members, which commenced on 26 September.

Despite the stipulations in the "Ethnic Chapter" of the Peace Agreement, there were complaints about the lack of guarantees for the effective participation of Indigenous Peoples and Afro-descendant communities in the implementation of the Agreement. On 21 September, members of the Permanent Bureau for Co-ordination with Indigenous Peoples and Organizations declared themselves to be in a state of emergency and permanent assembly to demand that the provisions of the Peace Agreement be fully complied with.

CIVILIAN VICTIMS OF THE ARMED CONFLICT
The Unit for the Victims' Assistance and Reparation, created in 2011 by Law 1148, recorded a total 8,532,636 victims for the five-decade duration of the armed conflict. This included 363,374 victims of threats, 22,915 victims of sexual offences, 167,809 victims of enforced disappearance, 7,265,072 victims of forced displacement and 11,140 victims of anti-personnel mines. Crimes against 31,047 victims of the armed conflict were recorded for the first time between January and October 2017.

In the departments of Chocó, Cauca, Antioquia and Norte de Santander, among others, crimes under international law and human rights violations persisted, including targeted killings of members of Afro-descendant communities and Indigenous Peoples, collective forced displacements, the forced confinement of communities within their territories (limiting their freedom of movement and access to essential services and food), the forced recruitment of children, sexual violence, and the use of anti-personnel mines.

Despite the signing of the Peace Agreement, the armed conflict intensified in some areas of Colombia as a result of armed confrontations between ELN guerrillas, paramilitary groups and state forces seeking to fill the power vacuum left by the demobilized FARC guerrillas. On 27 November, 13 people were killed as a result of a confrontation between FARC dissidents and ELN members in Magüí Payán Nariño department. There were complaints about the weak state presence in areas that were historically controlled by the FARC, which facilitated incursions and control by other illegal armed groups, putting Afro-descendant and peasant farmer communities and Indigenous Peoples at risk.

Paramilitary structures continued to operate in various parts of the country, despite their supposed demobilization under the terms of Law 975, passed in 2005. There were reports of paramilitary attacks and threats against leaders of the Peace Community of San José de Apartadó in the department of Antioquia.[1] On 29 December, armed men attempted to kill Germán Graciano Posso, the legal representative of the community. Other community members disarmed them, but were injured in the process. The Peace Community had sought to distance itself from the armed conflict by formally refusing to allow state security forces, guerrilla groups or paramilitary groups to enter their territory. Despite their efforts to remain neutral, people living in San José de Apartadó continued to be victims of attacks, torture, sexual abuse and forced displacement at the hands of all parties to the conflict.

There were reports of paramilitary incursions in the department of Chocó, in northwestern Colombia, particularly affecting Afro-descendant communities and Indigenous Peoples. On 8 February, a group of paramilitaries belonging to the Gaitanista Self-Defence Forces entered the Humanitarian Zone of Nueva Esperanza en Dios, in the Cacarica River Basin, department of Chocó, searching for several people said to be on a "death list".[2] On 6 March, a paramilitary incursion was reported in the town of Peña Azul, municipality of Alto Baudó, Chocó, which resulted in the large-scale displacement of families and the forced confinement of many people within their communities near Peña Azul.[3] On 18 April, residents of Puerto Lleras in the Jiguamiandó collective territory, Chocó, reported that they had received threats and that there had been a paramilitary incursion into the Humanitarian Zone of Pueblo Nuevo that put all the inhabitants at risk.[4]

Indigenous Peoples and Afro-Colombian communities continued to be at risk from anti-personnel mines on their territory; the laying of such mines is a grave violation of international humanitarian law. On 11 July, Sebastián Carpio Maheche, from the Wounaan Indigenous community of Juuin Duur in the Embera Wounaan Katio de Quiparadó Reserve in the municipality of Riosucio, Chocó, was injured by an exploding anti-personnel mine.[5]

Clashes between ELN guerrillas, the security forces and paramilitary groups put Indigenous Peoples and Afro-Colombian communities at serious risk.[6] According to the National Indigenous Organization of Colombia, between 1 November 2016 and 31 July 2017, 3,490 Indigenous people were victims of mass forced displacements, 827 were subjected to forced confinement, 115 received threats and 30 were killed, including community leaders.

The ELN abducted two Dutch journalists on 19 June in the area of El Tarra, Norte de Santander. Both were released on 24 June. According to the Office of the Ombudsperson, hostage-taking by ELN guerrillas continued.

REPARATION FOR VICTIMS

Point 5 of the Peace Agreement created the "Truth, Justice, Reparation and Non-repetition System", which included the Special Jurisdiction for Peace and judicial mechanisms such as a unit for investigating and dismantling the criminal organizations that succeeded paramilitarism. Point 5 also defined the position regarding reparations for the victims of the armed conflict. In this context, victims of the armed conflict demanded guarantees of access to justice, as well as guarantees of the right to truth and reparation and, especially, of non-repetition of abuses such as forced displacement and sexual violence, for Indigenous, Afro-descendant and peasant farmer communities at risk. These demands had yet to be met, and the long-term viability of the Peace Agreement was threatened due to the perpetrators of crimes under international law, including war crimes, crimes against humanity and human rights abuses not being brought to justice.

In April Legislative Act No.1 of 2017 was adopted, to ensure Congress would pass legislation implementing Point 5 of the Peace Agreement. One of its provisions provided for the separate – and privileged – treatment of state agents before the law, to the detriment of the rights of victims of crimes by the state in the context of the armed conflict. The law also provided for the possibility that the state would not pursue criminal prosecutions in certain cases – although how this would be implemented was not clear – potentially breaching the obligation of the state to investigate, prosecute and punish grave violations of human rights, undermining the rights of victims to truth and full reparation. On 27 November, Congress approved the Special Jurisdiction for Peace.

POLICE AND SECURITY FORCES

There were allegations of deliberate killings by state forces and allegations of excessive use of force by the Mobile Anti-Riot Squad (ESMAD) during protests in Chocó, Valle del Cauca, Cauca and Catatumbo.

Inhabitants of Buenaventura on the Pacific coast reported police repression of peaceful demonstrations which were part of the "Civic Strike" declared on 16 May to demand that the Colombian government guarantee economic, social and cultural rights and the right of the city's inhabitants to participate in the implementation of the Peace Agreement

with the FARC. Police, army and navy officers were present in the area. Protesters reported that tear gas was used against peaceful demonstrators. The Ombudsperson reported that approximately 205 children as well as 10 pregnant women and 19 elderly people suffered health complications as a result. In total, health problems as a result of exposure to tear gas were reported by 313 people, and 16 people sustained gunshot injuries or trauma from blunt objects. The "Civic Strike" ended on 7 June.

One Indigenous man, Felipe Castro Basto, was reported to have died in the municipality of Corinto, in the North of Cauca, when ESMAD opened fire on a demonstration by 200 Indigenous people.

The Association of Community Councils Mira, Nulpe and Mataje (Asominuma) reported that, on 5 October, security forces killed nine peasant farmers by indiscriminately firing at a peaceful demonstration in Tumaco (Nariño).

HUMAN RIGHTS DEFENDERS

Human rights defenders continued to be the victims of threats and targeted killings. The Office of the UN High Commissioner for Human Rights reported that at least 105 human rights defenders were killed in Colombia during the year. There was continuing concern over the increase in the number of attacks against defenders, especially community leaders; defenders of land, territory and the environment; and those campaigning in favour of the signing of the Final Agreement with the FARC. There continued to be an alarming rate of attacks against defenders of the rights of Indigenous and Afro-descendant people, peasant farmers and women, calling into question the implementation of the Peace Agreement.

According to the organization Somos Defensores, the number of killings of defenders increased by 31% in the first half of the year compared to the same period in 2016. The killings of women exercising any kind of leadership role increased compared to 2016, with seven such killings occurring in the first six months of 2017.

There were reports of killings of Afro-descendant leaders. On 8 June, Afro-descendant human rights defender Bernardo Cuero Bravo of the National Association of Displaced Afro-Colombians in Malambo, Atlántico, was killed. He had been threatened and attacked many times on account of his work for the community and as a defender of those who had been forcibly displaced. Despite his repeated requests, he had not been granted any protection measures by the National Protection Unit.

In November and December, two land claimant leaders from collective Afro-descendant territories were killed by paramilitaries from the Gaitanistas Self-Defence Forces of Colombia. There were reports of at least 25 other leaders being threatened by paramilitaries in these areas during the year.

Many death threats against human rights defenders and other activists were attributed to paramilitary groups, but in most cases of killings it was difficult to identify which groups were responsible. However, the nature of the work carried out by the victims, many of whom were community leaders or land and environmental rights activists, suggested that several of them may have been killed because of their human rights work. Moreover, it appeared that denouncing abuses was perceived as a threat by regional and local economic and political interests, as well as by various armed groups, including paramilitaries.[7]

VIOLENCE AGAINST WOMEN AND GIRLS

The efforts of women's organizations ensured that the Peace Agreement established that people suspected of committing crimes of sexual violence would be required to appear before transitional justice tribunals. In addition, the Agreement confirmed that such crimes would not be subject to amnesties or pardons, although human rights groups had serious reservations as to whether this provision would be genuinely implemented.

Official statistics showed no progress in access to justice for women survivors of sexual violence, despite repeated allegations by women's organizations of serious cases of sexual violence perpetrated during the year. According to the organization Sisma Mujer, between 1 January 2016 and 31 July 2017, the Ombudsperson issued 51 statements warning of the risk of sexual violence, including six reports and notes associated with women defenders/leaders, in which he highlighted the extraordinary risks faced by women leaders and human rights defenders.

Due to weak protection mechanisms, there was a heightened risk of gender-based violence, particularly domestic violence against women, in the context of the transition towards peace. Official figures recognized that following the demobilization of the United Self-Defence Forces of Colombia (AUC) in 2005 there was a 28% increase in cases of sexual violence in the communities where ex-combatants from the AUC were reintegrated. However, the government had yet to implement mechanisms for prevention and for ensuring care, assistance, protection and access to justice for women survivors of sexual violence, notably in communities where FARC guerillas were to be reintegrated during the year. There were also weaknesses in mechanisms to ensure that survivors of sexual violence are heard and can participate equally in all bodies responsible for implementing the Peace Agreement.

1. Colombia: Paramilitary build-up in peace community (AMR 23/5614/2017); Colombia: Spike in attacks against peace community shows conflict still alive (News story, 21 March)

2. Colombia: Paramilitary incursion in humanitarian zone (AMR 23/5685/2017)

3. Colombia: Over 300 displaced due to paramilitary incursion (AMR 23/5826/2017)

4. Colombia: Further information: Continued paramilitary presence in Chocó (AMR 23/6082/2017)

5. Colombia: Wounaan Indigenous community in danger (AMR 23/6774/2017)

6. Colombia: Recent collective displacements and violence indicate the lack of non-repetition guarantees for Chocó's Indigenous Peoples and Afro-Colombian communities (AMR 23/6946/2017)

7. The human rights situation in Colombia – Amnesty International's written statement to the 34th Session of the UN Human Rights Council (27 February-24 March 2017) (AMR 23/5573/2017)

CONGO (REPUBLIC OF THE)

Republic of the Congo
Head of state: **Denis Sassou Nguesso**
Head of government: **Clément Mouamba**

Dozens of political opponents remained in detention; some were prisoners of conscience. There were no investigations into allegations of torture and other ill-treatment by security forces and prison guards. Armed conflict between security forces and armed groups continued in Pool; around 81,000 internally displaced people (IDPs) from the area continued to live in appalling conditions; and the rate of acute malnutrition reached alarming levels.

BACKGROUND

The government conducted military operations, including air strikes, in the southeastern department of Pool. Government restrictions and the continuing armed conflict limited access to the area.

The Congolese Labour Party won 90 of the 151 National Assembly seats in legislative elections in July while elections in Pool had been postponed indefinitely due to the conflict. On 23 December, the government and armed groups led by Frédéric Bintsamou (also known as Reverend Ntumi) signed up to a ceasefire in Pool.

On 31 March, the Republic of the Congo ratified the International Convention on the Protection of the Rights of All Migrant Workers and Members of Their Families.

FREEDOMS OF ASSEMBLY AND EXPRESSION

The authorities used restrictive legislation, relating to public gatherings and assemblies, to curtail the right to freedom of assembly. On 23 March, the Prefect of Brazzaville, the capital, rejected a request to hold a peaceful demonstration from the Congolese Observatory of Human Rights, the Association for Human Rights and Prison Conditions, and the United Forces for Freedom and Democracy. The organizations had intended, during the demonstration, to give the Prime Minister a letter raising concerns about the human rights situation.

The right to freedom of expression was restricted. On 11 January, Ghys Fortuné Dombé Bemba, editor of the *Talassa* newspaper, was summoned by the judicial police in connection with charges of "complicity in undermining state security". This followed his publishing a statement by Reverend Ntumi, leader of the "Ninjas", an armed group operating in the Pool department.

PRISONERS OF CONSCIENCE

In November Paulin Makaya completed a two-year prison sentence for participating in an unauthorized protest. However, he remained in prison at the end of the year as a result of additional charges brought against him on 6 January 2017 which included "undermining national security, complicity in a plan to escape from detention, and complicity in the unlawful possession of arms and munitions of war". The charges related to a shooting in Brazzaville central prison in December 2016 in which, according to witnesses, he played no part.

POLITICAL PRISONERS

Little progress was made in judicial proceedings involving opposition leaders and members detained since 2015 for opposing changes to the Constitution, or the presidential election results.

The opposition Initiative for Democracy in the Republic of Congo – Republican Front for the Respect of Constitutional Order and Democratic Change (FROCAD-IDC) – said that over 100 political prisoners remained in detention in Brazzaville central prison at the end of the year. Local human rights organizations compiled a list of names of 90 political prisoners held during the year. They included opposition leaders Okouya Rigobert of the Convention for Action, Democracy and Development (CADD); Jean-Marie Michel Mokoko, a presidential candidate and retired army general; and Jean Ngouabi, a member of the latter's campaign team. In January,

André Okombi Salissa, former member of the National Assembly and president of CADD, was arrested and detained at the General Directorate of Territorial Surveillance after spending almost a year in hiding.

Also in January, Noël Mienanzambi Boyi, president of the Association for the Culture of Peace and Non-Violence and a broadcaster for a community radio station, was arrested in Kinkala, the main town in Pool. The authorities claimed that he was transporting medicine and food to Reverend Ntumi, and charged him with "complicity in undermining state security". Local NGOs said that he was arrested after he agreed to organize mediation between the authorities and Reverend Ntumi on the government's request. They also alleged that he was tortured in various detention centres before being transferred to Brazzaville central prison in June where he remained at the end of the year.

TORTURE AND OTHER ILL-TREATMENT

Several cases of torture and other ill-treatment by security services were reported. No investigations or judicial proceedings into these allegations were conducted by the authorities.

On 24 January, Modeste Boukadia, president of the opposition Congolese Circle of Democrats and Republicans, was admitted to Clinique Guénin in Pointe Noire city as a result of injuries he sustained when prison guards beat him at Pointe Noire prison in November 2016. The beating resulted in two fractured bones, and caused him to have high blood pressure and a heart condition.

INTERNALLY DISPLACED PEOPLE

Following fighting between government forces and the Ninjas armed group, around a third of residents in Pool fled their homes. An estimated 81,000 people were IDPs; 59,000 of them were registered displaced in 2017. IDPs were in dire need of shelter, food, water, basic health services and adequate sanitation. They were forced to live with families in host communities, on church grounds, in public buildings, or in overcrowded makeshift sites.

REFUGEES AND ASYLUM-SEEKERS

The refugee status of around 10,000 Rwandan refugees expired on 31 December, under the Cessation Clause for Rwandan refugees, on the grounds that Rwanda was a safe country. Some of the refugees may be permitted to choose between voluntary repatriation and residency in their host countries, or otherwise retain their refugee status if they fulfill certain criteria.

RIGHT TO FOOD

According to the UN, 138,000 people in Pool required humanitarian assistance, and over 50% of families were food insecure.

Global Acute Malnutrition – the measurement of the nutritional status of those in long-term refugee situations – affected between 17.3 and 20.4% of IDP children aged under five who fled from Pool.

CÔTE D'IVOIRE

Republic of Côte d'Ivoire
Head of state: **Alassane Dramane Ouattara**
Head of government: **Amadou Gon Coulibaly (replaced Daniel Kablan Duncan in January)**

Around 200 detainees, loyal to former President Laurent Gbagbo, awaited trial in connection with post-electoral violence in 2010 and 2011. Killings in the context of mutinies and clashes between demobilized soldiers and security forces were uninvestigated. The rights to freedom of expression, association and peaceful assembly were restricted; some protests were prohibited. Simone Gbagbo, wife of former President Gbagbo, was acquitted of crimes against humanity and war crimes. The ICC tried Laurent Gbagbo and Charles Blé Goudé.

BACKGROUND

The UN Operation in Côte d'Ivoire (UNOCI) concluded its mission in June, 13 years after its establishment by the UN Security Council. The UN Independent Expert praised Côte d'Ivoire's gradual progress towards national reconciliation and stability which, he warned, was fragile given the unrest in January.

The government launched an investigation, supported by UN investigators, into the discovery of an arms cache in a house owned by a close aide of the President of the National Assembly.

In July, there were several attacks by armed groups. Three soldiers were killed when armed men attacked a military camp in Korhogo in the north.

FREEDOM OF EXPRESSION

Legislation which contained provisions that curtailed the right to freedom of expression, including in relation to defamation, offending the President and disseminating false news, was adopted.

In February, six journalists were detained for two days in the city of Abidjan, accused of divulging false information on army mutinies. They were not charged but continued to be summoned by authorities for questioning.

In August, two Le Quotidien journalists were arrested over an article they wrote about the National Assembly President's finances.

FREEDOMS OF ASSOCIATION AND ASSEMBLY

In February, the police used tear gas and rubber bullets to repress a peaceful protest by cocoa planters and National Agricultural Union members in Abidjan.

In July, demobilized soldiers held peaceful protests in Bouaké city calling on the government to deliver on promises made after protests in May (see below). Amadou Ouattara, Mégbè Diomandé and Lassina Doumbia, members of "Cellule 39" (an association of demobilized soldiers), were arrested and charged with public disorder and organizing an unauthorized protest.

At least 40 students were arrested in September after FESCI (Fédération estudiantine et scolaire de Côte d'Ivoire) organized protests across the country against police violence and increased university fees.

One student said the police arrested her with her friends in her room, and beat her. Some of those arrested had thrown stones at the police, but others were peaceful. All were charged with disruption of public order and provisionally released after 20 days.

IMPUNITY

People suspected of supporting former President Gbagbo were tried for human rights violations committed during and after the 2010 election. In contrast, none of President Ouattara's supporters were arrested or tried in connection with human rights violations.

In May Simone Gbagbo was acquitted of crimes against humanity and war crimes by the Assize Court of Abidjan. Victims of human rights violations were denied their legal right to participate in the hearing. New lawyers, appointed by the head of the bar after her lawyers withdrew in 2016, also pulled out in March saying the Court was irregularly constituted because a judge was appointed after the trial had begun.

Around 200 supporters of Laurent Gbagbo, arrested since 2011 for crimes allegedly committed during the post-electoral violence, were still detained awaiting trial. Two of them – Assi Jean Kouatchi and Bonfils Todé – died in custody in 2017.

Some detainees were provisionally released and awaited trial. They included Antoinette Meho, a member of civil society organization Solidarité Wé, released in May. She was charged with undermining state security. In December Hubert Oulaye, a former minister who was provisionally released in June, and Maurice Djire, were sentenced to 20 years in prison for the murder of, and complicity in the murder of, UN soldiers in 2012. Despite defence lawyers' requests, the court did not provide testimonies from two prosecution witnesses during their trial.

In July, Adou Assoa, another former minister was sentenced to four years' imprisonment for public disorder but cleared of charges of undermining state security.

David Samba, opposition activist and president of the NGO Coalition des Indignés de Côte d'Ivoire, completed his six-month sentence for public disorder in March 2016. Prior to completing that sentence, he was charged with a new offence of undermining state security in relation to an attempted uprising in Dabou in 2015 and was held pending trial at the end of the year.

MUTINIES

At least 10 people were killed and dozens wounded in mutinies and clashes between the security forces and demobilized soldiers. Four people were killed between 12 and 14 May during a mutiny in Bouaké which spread to other cities. It was led by soldiers who had been integrated into the army in 2011 and were demanding the payment of bonuses. On 13 May a group of mutineers went to the office of "Cellule 39" and shot at them, in response to "Cellule 39" condemning the munity. Issoufou Diawara was killed after he was shot in the back, and several were wounded. The violence ended when the government agreed to meet the mutineers' payment demands.

On 22 May, four demobilized soldiers were killed in clashes with police when they held protests calling for an agreement equivalent to the one obtained by the mutineers. They said they were unarmed when police fired on them. (The demobilized soldiers were former members of armed groups who fought on the side of President Ouattara during the 2010-2011 election violence.)

There was no indication that suspected perpetrators, including security forces, would be brought to justice for human rights violations by the end of the year.

INTERNATIONAL JUSTICE

The ICC trial of Laurent Gbagbo and Charles Blé Goudé for crimes against humanity, including murder and rape during the post-electoral violence, continued. In July, the ICC Appeals Chamber ordered the Trial Chamber to review its ruling to deny Laurent Gbagbo's provisional release.

CORPORATE ACCOUNTABILITY

The UN Environment Programme (UNEP) delayed until 2018 the publication of its assessment of lasting pollution at the 18 sites where 540,000 litres of toxic waste were dumped in Abidjan in 2006. The waste had been produced by the company Trafigura. The authorities had still not assessed the long-term health risks to individuals of exposure to the chemicals in the waste or monitored victims' health. Compensation claims against the company continued although many had not received payments.

CROATIA

Republic of Croatia
Head of state: **Kolinda Grabar-Kitarović**
Head of government: **Andrej Plenković**

Discrimination against ethnic and sexual minorities persisted. Refugees and migrants entering irregularly were returned without access to an effective asylum process. Croatia accepted less than a 10th of the refugees and asylum-seekers it had committed to relocate and resettle under EU schemes. Access to abortion remained restricted.

CRIMES UNDER INTERNATIONAL LAW

Of the over 6,000 people who went missing during the 1991-1995 war, the fate and whereabouts of more than 1,500 remained unclarified. The International Commission on Missing Persons reported that Croatia failed to make significant steps towards fulfilling the rights to truth, justice and reparation for victims, including by failing to account for over 900 unidentified mortal remains in its mortuaries.

DISCRIMINATION

Discrimination against ethnic and sexual minorities remained widespread.

Civil society organizations criticized new government proposals for a national strategy and action plan to fight discrimination that were presented in March. The policies subsequently adopted by the government in December failed to reflect and adequately address human rights violations faced by Serbs, Roma and sexual minorities.

In February, the European Court of Human Rights found in *Škorjanec v. Croatia* that the authorities had failed to guarantee the applicant's right to be free from torture and other inhuman or degrading treatment by failing to adequately investigate and prosecute the racist motives of the assailants who violently attacked and beat the applicant and her partner, who is Roma, in 2013.

REFUGEES AND ASYLUM-SEEKERS

Croatia continued to return to Serbia refugees and migrants who entered the country irregularly, without granting them access to an effective asylum process. These push-backs by police, sometimes from deep inside Croatian territory, routinely involved coercion, intimidation, confiscation or destruction of private valuables and the disproportionate use of force by the police.

In July, the Court of Justice of the European Union ruled that Croatia had acted against the rules of the Dublin Regulation (which defines which EU member state has the obligation to evaluate the asylum claims) by allowing transit for refugees and migrants through the country in 2015 without examining applications for international protection.

The NGOs Are You Syrious and Centre for Peace Studies documented that between January and April, at least 30 asylum applications – including those from families with children – had been dismissed on the grounds of "security concerns" during a routine security check carried out by the Security and Intelligence Agency as part of the asylum process. The notes of these applications were marked as "classified" and could not be seen and thus could not be rebutted or challenged on appeal by those seeking asylum or their legal representatives. Cases with classified notes led to an automatic rejection by the Ministry of Interior. Subsequently, the failed asylum-seekers were at risk of expulsion from the country and at heightened risk of *refoulement* – a measure forcing an individual to return to a country where they would risk serious human rights violations.

Unaccompanied minors represented a quarter of all asylum-seekers in the country. By the end of the year, fewer than 200 asylum-seekers had been granted international protection.

Croatia committed to accept 1,600 refugees and asylum-seekers under the EU resettlement and relocation schemes by the end of the year; by mid-November, fewer than 100 people had been relocated, and none had been resettled.

In June, amendments introduced to the Law on Foreigners forbade the provision of assistance in accessing basic needs, such as housing, health, sanitation or food, to foreign nationals irregularly residing in Croatia, except in cases of medical and humanitarian emergencies or life-threatening situations.

VIOLENCE AGAINST WOMEN AND GIRLS

The criminal justice system continued to fail many victims of domestic abuse by routinely treating abuse as a minor offence.

In June, the European Court of Human Rights found in *Ž.B. v. Croatia* that the authorities violated the right to respect for private and family life of a victim of multiple instances of domestic violence. The authorities had failed to criminally prosecute the alleged perpetrator and establish the facts, suggesting that the victim should have acted by herself as a subsidiary prosecutor and pursued private prosecution.

Croatia had yet to ratify the Council of Europe Convention on preventing and combating violence against women and domestic violence.

RIGHT TO HEALTH

In April, the UN Special Rapporteur on the right of everyone to the enjoyment of the highest attainable standard of physical and mental health noted with concern the renewed and pending revision of the 1978 Act on Health Care Measures for Exercising the Right to a Free Decision on Giving Birth, which could potentially restrict access to abortion. Individual doctors, and in some cases health care institutions, continued to refuse abortions on grounds of conscience, forcing women to undergo clandestine and unsafe abortions. In March, the Constitutional Court ruled against a challenge seeking the 1978 Act to be declared unconstitutional and called on the national assembly to refrain from adopting any laws which would effectively ban abortions. In pharmacies, women and girls continued to be assessed against a questionnaire for which they had to reveal personal information about their sexual behaviour and reproductive health as a condition of accessing emergency contraceptives that were available without prescription, in violation of their right to privacy.

Roma children and women continued to be disadvantaged in accessing health care, and one fifth of this group lacked access to it altogether.

CUBA

Republic of Cuba
Head of state and government: **Raúl Castro Ruz**

Arbitrary detentions, discriminatory dismissals from state jobs, and harassment in self-employment continued to be used to silence criticism. Advances in education were undermined by ongoing online and offline censorship. Cuba remained mostly closed to independent human rights monitors.

BACKGROUND

Lifting of travel restrictions on Cubans in 2013, removal of limits on receiving remittances, and the draw of visa-free countries continued to be important push factors for emigration. Cubans continued to leave in large numbers, despite the country's changing international diplomacy, pushed by exceptionally low salaries and a tight web of control on freedom of expression.

In June, the administration of US President Donald Trump made an almost complete reversal of the USA's political rhetoric towards Cuba. This reduced the chance of US Congress passing legislation to lift the economic embargo on Cuba, which continued to undermine economic, social and cultural rights.

At least 12 lawyers from the human rights organization Cubalex received asylum in the USA after being harassed, intimidated and threatened with imprisonment for their peaceful human rights work.

Cuba had not ratified the ICCPR or the ICESCR, both of which it signed in February 2008, nor the Rome Statute of the ICC.

In December the government announced that President Raúl Castro would step down in April 2018.

ARBITRARY ARRESTS AND DETENTIONS

Human rights and political activists continued to be harassed, intimidated and arbitrarily detained in high numbers. The Cuban Commission for Human Rights and National Reconciliation, a Cuban NGO not officially recognized by the state, recorded 5,155 arbitrary detentions in 2017, compared to 9,940 in 2016.

The Ladies in White, a group of female relatives of prisoners detained on politically motivated grounds, remained one of the primary targets of repression by the authorities. During detention, the women were often beaten by law enforcement officials and state security agents dressed as civilians.

In January, Danilo Maldonado Machado, known as El Sexto, was released from a maximum security prison. He had been arrested in November 2016, hours after the announcement of Fidel Castro's death, for having written Se fue ("He's gone") on a wall in the capital, Havana.[1]

In August, Yulier Perez, a graffiti artist known for painting dilapidated walls in Havana, was arbitrarily detained after months of intimidation and harassment from the authorities for freely expressing himself through his art.[2]

PRISONERS OF CONSCIENCE

The leader of the pro-democracy Christian Liberation Movement, Dr Eduardo Cardet Concepción, remained in prison having been handed a three-year sentence in March for publicly criticizing Fidel Castro.[3]

A family of four human rights defenders were detained in Holguín, southeast Cuba, for allegedly leaving their house during the period of state mourning for Fidel Castro in 2016. The three siblings were given one-year prison sentences for "defamation of institutions, organizations and heroes and martyrs of the Republic of Cuba" and "public disorder".[4] Their mother was sentenced to house arrest. On 2 April, after a prolonged hunger strike, the three siblings were freed under conditional release, but they continued to be intimidated by the authorities.

Jorge Cervantes, a member of the political opposition group Patriotic Union of Cuba (UNPACU), was detained for approximately three months between May and August. Weeks before, UNPACU had published on its YouTube channel a video called "Horrors in jail" in which Jorge Cervantes interviewed a man who had allegedly been ill-treated in a Cuban prison, and a series of videos which alleged corruption by public officials.[5]

The authorities continued to present trumped-up charges for common crimes as a way to harass and detain political opponents, meaning there were likely many more prisoners of conscience than documented.

WORKERS' RIGHTS

The state continued to use its control – as the biggest employer in the country, and as a regulator of the private sector – as a way to stifle even the most subtle criticism of the government.[6] Politically motivated and discriminatory dismissals continued to be used against those who criticized the government's economic or political model. Workers pushed out of employment in the public sector for freely expressing themselves were often further harassed after entering the emerging but highly regulated self-employment sector.

The de facto prohibition on independent trade unions limited workers' ability to independently organize and appeal against discriminatory dismissals. The executive's strong influence over the judiciary and lawyers limited effective recourse through the courts.

RIGHT TO EDUCATION

Undue restrictions in access to information and freedom of expression online followed decades of offline censorship, undermining Cuba's advances in education.

Between May and mid-June, the Open Observatory of Network Interference conducted testing on a sample of websites in Cuba and found 41 sites blocked by the authorities. All the blocked sites expressed criticism of the Cuban government, reported on human rights issues, or discussed techniques to bypass censorship.

While the government continued to expand access to the internet, it prioritized access to the highly censored, government-curated national intranet. Access to the global internet remained prohibitively expensive for most Cubans.[7]

INTERNATIONAL SCRUTINY

In April, the UN Special Rapporteur on trafficking in persons conducted a visit to Cuba, and in July the country received the UN independent expert on human rights and international solidarity.

Most independent human rights organizations continued to be denied access to the country and to its prisons. Cuba remained the only country in the Americas region to deny access to Amnesty International.

1. Cuban graffiti artist released (AMR 25/5545/2017)

2. Urban artist at risk in Cuba (AMR 25/7000/2017)

3. Cuba: Activist sentenced to three years in jail after criticizing Fidel Castro (News story, 21 March)

4. Cuba: Prisoners of conscience on hunger strike (AMR 25/6001/2017)

5. Cuba: Opposition activist in maximum security prison (AMR 25/6671/2017)

6. Cuba: "Your mind is in prison" – Cuba's web of control over free expression and its chilling effect on everyday life (AMR 25/7299/2017)

7. Cuba's internet paradox: How controlled and censored internet risks Cuba's achievements in education (News story, 29 August)

CYPRUS

Republic of Cyprus
Head of state and government: **Nicos Anastasiades**

UN-backed peace talks for the reunification of the island collapsed in early July. Reception conditions for asylum-seekers remained a cause of concern.

BACKGROUND

After intense negotiations, high-level peace talks for the reunification of Cyprus failed to reach an agreement in early July. The Greek-Cypriot and Turkish-Cypriot leaders could not agree on security, including the withdrawal of Turkish troops, and property issues.

REFUGEES' AND MIGRANTS' RIGHTS

In February, the Supreme Court rejected an application challenging the detention and extradition of Seif el-Din Mostafa, an Egyptian national accused of hijacking an EgyptAir plane in March 2016. Despite concerns he would be at real risk of torture or other ill-treatment if returned to Egypt, the Supreme Court decided not to accept additional evidence regarding the risk of torture. The Court held that the applicant could be extradited regardless of his not having had a final decision in his asylum claim. In November, the Supreme Court also rejected an appeal lodged against its previous decision. However, on the same day the European Court of Human Rights halted Seif el-Din Mostafa's extradition to Egypt.

In May, the CERD Committee expressed concerns about the limited employment options for asylum-seekers living on the island, the insufficient amount of social assistance they received and the limited reception facilities. The Committee also raised concern about the insufficient access to services for those asylum-seekers staying at the Kofinou Reception and Accommodation Center for Applicants for International Protection, the only official centre hosting asylum-seekers on the island.

In September, the NGO Future Worlds Center warned of the need for a contingency reception plan, especially in case of an increase in refugees arriving by boat. According to the UN Migration Agency, 851 people arrived by boat on Cyprus between January and November 2017 in comparison to 345 in the previous year.

ENFORCED DISAPPEARANCES

Between January and the end of December, the Committee of Missing Persons in Cyprus exhumed the remains of 46 people, bringing the total number of exhumations since 2006 to 1,217. Between 2007 and 31 December 2017, the remains of 855 missing individuals (645 Greek Cypriots and 210 Turkish Cypriots) were identified.

DISCRIMINATION – PEOPLE WITH DISABILITIES

In May, the UN Committee on the Rights of Persons with Disabilities expressed concerns about the insufficient access to health care by people with disabilities, the high level of unemployment among them and the insufficient measures to promote their access to employment in an open labour market.

TORTURE AND OTHER ILL-TREATMENT

In April, the European Court of Human Rights found that the Cypriot Ombudsperson and the national police complaints mechanism had failed to investigate effectively the alleged ill-treatment of a Kenyan national during his deportation in March 2007 (*Thuo v. Cyprus*). The Court also held that the applicant's detention conditions in Nicosia Central Prison amounted to degrading treatment.

At the end of August, a 60-year-old Turkish national claimed to have been ill-treated by a police officer outside and inside a police station near a designated crossing point of the UN Buffer Zone. The incident was being investigated by the national police complaints mechanism at the end of the year.

CZECH REPUBLIC

Czech Republic
Head of state: **Miloš Zeman**
Head of government: **Andrej Babiš (replaced Bohuslav Sobotka in December)**

The government refused to participate in the EU mandatory refugee relocation quotas. Despite reforms, Roma pupils continued to be segregated in schools. An amendment allowing municipalities to declare zones of "socially pathological behaviour" with restricted access to housing benefits entered into force.

DISCRIMINATION – ROMA
RIGHT TO EDUCATION

One year after the reform of the primary education system that aimed to facilitate the inclusion of pupils from disadvantaged backgrounds into mainstream schools, Roma children continued to face discrimination in access to education. In July, the government published data which showed that over 24% of Roma pupils continued to be educated in ethnically segregated schools.

In March, a district court ordered a primary school in the city of Ostrava to apologize to two Roma pupils. The school had refused to register the pupils in 2014, claiming that it had reached full capacity. Legal guardians of the pupils complained that the director justified his decision by claiming that non-Roma parents could start removing their children from the school as there were already nine Roma pupils registered in that grade. The court held that a fear of "white flight" could not justify the treatment of pupils on the basis their ethnicity.

RIGHT TO HOUSING

In July, an amendment to the law on welfare benefits entered into force and dozens of municipalities announced that they would restrict access to housing allowances. The amendment allows municipalities to declare zones of "socially pathological behaviour" where residents would be barred from claiming some housing allowances. This will affect new tenants or those who move to or within these zones. NGOs raised concerns that the new regulation would disproportionately affect Roma and poor people.

REFUGEES AND ASYLUM-SEEKERS

The Czech Republic accepted only 12 asylum-seekers out of the 2,691 it had been assigned under the 2015 EU Emergency Relocation Scheme – which aimed to relocate refugees from EU member states such as Greece and Italy – by the end of the year. In June, the European Commission started infringement procedures against the Czech Republic, as well as Poland and Hungary, for refusing to participate in the scheme. In July, the government stated it would not accept any further asylum-seekers. In December, the European Commission decided to step up the action against all three countries and referred them to the Court of Justice of the European Union over their refusal to accept the asylum-seekers under the scheme.

There were 974 applications made for international protection by the end of the year. Thirteen people were successful in their applications; 79 applications were rejected. Sixteen asylum-seekers from Afghanistan were refused an extension to their temporary protection. The government continued to base such asylum decisions on its arbitrary designation of certain areas in Afghanistan as "safe", despite evidence to the contrary and with violence continuing to escalate in Afghanistan during the year.

RACISM AND XENOPHOBIA

High-level government officials, including the President, made xenophobic statements about refugees and migrants. During the pre-election campaign, the Minister of Interior presented as a success the restrictive policies that led refugees to avoid the Czech Republic.

In February, the police discontinued their investigation into the 2016 death of a Roma man at a pizzeria in Žatec, determining that no crime had been committed. The man died after he was restrained by municipal police officers and some customers as a result of his allegedly aggressive behaviour. The victim's family had filed a complaint against the police in January, alleging that the investigation was not thorough; their lawyer criticized the police for failing to secure the scene and evidence.

In May, the Council of Europe Commissioner for Human Rights urged the Czech authorities to remove a pig farm from the site of a former Nazi concentration camp, where most of the victims were Roma, in the village of Lety u Písku. While appreciating the government's efforts to buy the land, the Commissioner was concerned over the length of the process, and the government's repeated failure to remove the pig farm and create a memorial as a measure of reparation for the Roma who suffered and died there during the Second World War. In November, the government signed a contract to buy off the land from the owner of the pig farm and made a commitment to build a memorial on the site.

SECURITY AND HUMAN RIGHTS

The Czech Republic continued to export arms to countries where there was a substantial risk that such arms could be used to commit or facilitate serious human rights violations, including the unlawful use of force against protesters or opposition groups. In May, during an arms fair in the city of Brno, the President stated that the Czech arms industry needed to "export globally", denying that the country had responsibility to prevent the re-export of its equipment to countries which are "not safe".

DEMOCRATIC REPUBLIC OF THE CONGO

Democratic Republic of the Congo
Head of state: **Joseph Kabila**
Head of government: **Bruno Tshibala Nzenze** (replaced **Samy Badibanga Ntita** in April)

The human rights situation further deteriorated. Violence in the Kasaï region left thousands dead, at least 1 million internally displaced, and caused more than 35,000 people to flee for neighbouring Angola. In the east, armed groups and government forces continued to target civilians and engage in illegal exploitation of natural resources with impunity. Police, intelligence services and courts continued to crack down on the rights to freedom of expression, association and peaceful assembly. Human rights defenders and journalists were harassed, intimidated, arbitrarily arrested, expelled or killed.

BACKGROUND

President Kabila remained in post although his second constitutional term ended on 19 December 2016. A political agreement was signed in December 2016 by the ruling coalition, the opposition and some civil society organizations. It provided that President Kabila would remain in power, and a government of national unity would be appointed, led by a Prime Minister designated by the Rassemblement, the main opposition, with the task of organizing the elections by December 2017. The agreement established the National Council for the Implementation of the Accord and the Electoral Process (CNSA) to monitor progress, led by Rassemblement leader Etienne Tshisekedi. The agreement included a commitment by President Kabila to adhere to the constitutional two-term limit and not undertake a revision or change of the Constitution. Implementation of the agreement stalled over the appointment and distribution of political posts to the transitional institutions. In February Etienne Tshisekedi died. In April, President Kabila unilaterally appointed Bruno Tshibala as Prime Minister; the Rassemblement refused to recognize the appointment. In July, Joseph Olenghankoy was also unilaterally appointed as chairman of the CNSA. The main opposition leaders, the Catholic Church and the international community denounced these appointments as violating the agreement.

Voter registration in the run-up to the elections was significantly delayed. In July, the president of the Independent National Electoral Commission announced that elections could not be held in December 2017, on grounds including the security situation in the Kasaï region.

Violence that erupted in 2016 over the killing of Chief Kamuena Nsapu spread to five provinces, triggering an unprecedented humanitarian crisis. In the east, several armed groups stepped up their attacks to expel President Kabila. Both the Democratic Republic of the Congo (DRC) security forces and the UN Organization Stabilization Mission in the DRC (MONUSCO) were unable to tackle the insecurity and neutralize more than 40 local or foreign armed groups that remained active.

The annual inflation rate increased by around 50% in 2017, contributing to deepening levels of poverty. Strikes were held demanding salary increases for teachers, university professors, doctors, nurses and civil servants. A cholera epidemic affected at least 24,000 people; over 500 died between January and September.

FREEDOM OF EXPRESSION

Press freedom and the right to information were restricted. The granting of visas and accreditations to foreign correspondents was drastically limited. At least one journalist, a Belgian national, was expelled in September; a French national and a US national were unable to renew accreditation in June and August respectively. On at least 15 occasions,

Congolese and foreign journalists were intimidated, harassed and arbitrarily arrested and detained while carrying out their work. In many cases, their equipment was confiscated or they had to erase recorded data. The Minister of Communication issued a decree in July introducing new rules requiring foreign correspondents to obtain authorization from the Minister to travel outside the capital, Kinshasa.

In August, the day before a two-day protest, organized by the opposition, calling on people across the country to stay at home to encourage the publication of an electoral calendar, the Post and Telecommunications Regulatory Authority ordered telecommunication companies to strictly limit all social media activity and communication.

FREEDOM OF ASSEMBLY

Authorities continued to ban and repress public dissent and peaceful assemblies organized by civil society organizations and the opposition, especially protests concerning the political crisis and elections. Opposition peaceful protesters were intimidated, harassed and arrested by security forces; government supporters' demonstrations took place without interference from the authorities.

On 31 July, more than 100 people, including 11 Congolese and foreign journalists, were arrested during country-wide demonstrations organized by the Struggle for Change (LUCHA), to demand the publication of the electoral calendar. A journalist was charged in connection with the protest and remained in detention in Lubumbashi; four demonstrators received prison sentences. The others were released without charge the same or following day.

EXCESSIVE USE OF FORCE

Protests other than those organized by government supporters were often met with excessive and sometimes lethal force.

On 15 September, in Kamanyola, the army and police fired at a crowd of Burundian refugees protesting the detention and deportation of four refugees by DRC intelligence services; 39 protesters were killed, including at least eight women and five children, and at least 100 were injured. No legal action was known to have been taken against the perpetrators by the end of the year.

HUMAN RIGHTS DEFENDERS

Human rights defenders and youth activists were targeted by security forces and armed groups for their work; they included Alex Tsongo Sikuliwako and Alphonse Kaliyamba, killed in North Kivu.

In May, the Senate passed a bill purporting to strengthen protection for human rights defenders. However, the bill contained a restrictive definition of what constituted a human rights defender. It strengthened the state's control over human rights organizations, and threatened to curtail their activities. It could result in the non-recognition of human rights organizations.

CONFLICT IN THE KASAÏ REGION

Violence in the region, which erupted in 2016, spread to five provinces and left thousands dead, and by 25 September, 1 million were internally displaced; there was widespread destruction of social infrastructure and villages. Militias emerged, which increasingly attacked people on the basis of their ethnicity, namely those perceived to support the Kamuena Nsapu uprising.

Followers of Kamuena Nsapu were suspected of human rights abuses in the region, including recruitment of child soldiers, rapes, killings, destruction of over 300 schools and of markets, churches, police stations and government buildings.

The Bana Mura militia was formed around March by individuals from the Tshokwe, Pende and Tetela ethnic groups with the support of local traditional leaders and security officials. It launched attacks against the Luba and Lulua communities whom it accused of supporting the Kamuena Nsapu uprising. Between March and June, there were reports that in Kamonia territory, the Bana Mura and the army killed around 251

people; 62 were children, 30 of them aged under 8.

VIOLATIONS BY SECURITY FORCES

The Congolese police and army carried out hundreds of extrajudicial killings, rapes, arbitrary arrests and acts of extortion. Between February and April, internet videos showed soldiers executing alleged Kamuena Nsapu followers, including young children. The victims were armed with sticks or defective rifles, or were simply wearing red headbands. The government initially dismissed the accusations, saying they were "fabricated" to discredit the army. However, in February it acknowledged that "excesses" had taken place and pledged to prosecute those suspected of serious human rights violations and abuses in the region, including its security forces.

LACK OF ACCOUNTABILITY

On 6 July, seven army soldiers were given sentences of between one year and life imprisonment in connection with extrajudicial executions in Mwanza-Lomba, a village in Kasaï Oriental province. The sentences followed a trial in which the victims were not identified and nor were their relatives given the opportunity to testify before the court or seek reparations.

On 12 March, Swedish national Zaida Catalan and US national Michael Sharp, both members of the UN Security Council DRC Sanctions Committee's Group of Experts, were executed during an investigative mission in the Kasaï Central province. Their bodies were found 16 days later, near Bunkonde village. Zaida Catalan had been beheaded. Three of their drivers and an interpreter who accompanied them disappeared and had not been found by the end of the year. In April, the authorities showed diplomats and journalists in Kinshasa a video of the execution of the two experts; the origins of the video remained unknown. The video, which claimed that Kamuena Nsapu "terrorists" were the perpetrators, was shared on the internet and admitted as evidence in the ongoing military court trial of the people accused of the killings. The trial began on 5 June in the city of Kananga.

In June, the UN Human Rights Council established an independent international inquiry, which was opposed by the government, to investigate serious human rights violations in the Kasaï province. In July, the UN High Commissioner for Human Rights announced the appointment of an international team of experts, which in September began investigating the incidents and is expected to issue its findings in June 2018.

CONFLICT IN EASTERN DRC

Chronic instability and conflict continued to contribute to grave human rights violations and abuses. In the Beni region, civilians were targeted and killed. On 7 October, 22 people were killed on the Mbau-Kamango road by unidentified armed men.

Kidnappings increased in North Kivu; at least 100 cases were recorded in Goma city. In North Kivu, South Kivu and Ituri, dozens of armed groups and security forces continued to commit murder, rape, extortion, and to engage in illegal exploitation of natural resources. The conflict between the Hutu and Nande in North Kivu resulted in deaths, displacement and destruction, especially in the Rutshuru and Lubero areas.

In the Tanganyika and Haut-Katanga provinces, communal violence between the Twa and the Luba continued. In Tanganyika the number of internally displaced people (IDPs) reached 500,000. Between January and September, over 5,700 Congolese fled to Zambia to escape the conflict.

Despite the security situation, the authorities continued to close IDP camps around the town of Kalemie, forcing displaced people to return to their villages or to live in even worse conditions.

DETENTION

There was an unprecedented number of prison breakouts across the country; thousands escaped, and dozens died. On 17 May, an attack was carried out on Makala Penitentiary and Rehabilitation Centre, Kinshasa's main prison. The attack, which the authorities blamed on the political group Bundu dia Congore, resulted in the escape of over 4,000 prisoners. On 11 June, 930 prisoners escaped from the Kangbayi central prison in Beni city, including dozens convicted a few months earlier for killing civilians in the Beni area. Hundreds of other detainees escaped from prisons and police detention centres in Bandundu-ville, Kasangulu, Kalemie, Matete (Kinshasa), Walikale, Dungu, Bukavu, Kabinda, Uvira, Bunia, Mwenga and Pweto.

Prisons were overcrowded, and conditions remained dire, with inadequate food and drinking water, and poor health care. Dozens of prisoners died of starvation and disease.

CORPORATE ACCOUNTABILITY

In August, the Ministry of Mines validated a National Strategy to Combat Child Labour in Mining. National and international civil society groups were given the opportunity to provide feedback. The government announced that it would "progressively" implement many of their recommendations and eradicate child labour by 2025.

DENMARK

Kingdom of Denmark
Head of state: **Queen Margrethe II**
Head of government: **Lars Løkke Rasmussen**

The government annulled an agreement with UNHCR, the UN refugee agency, to accept refugees for resettlement. The classification of transgender identities as a "mental disorder" was ended.

REFUGEES AND ASYLUM-SEEKERS

Denmark failed to accept any refugees for resettlement. The government annulled its standing agreement with UNHCR to receive 500 refugees annually for resettlement. From January 2018, the government, not Parliament, will decide each year if Denmark is to accept refugees for resettlement.

Individuals granted subsidiary temporary protection status had to wait three years before being eligible to apply for family reunification. In May, the High Court of Eastern Denmark ruled that the postponement of family reunification of a Syrian refugee with his wife was not in violation of the right to family life under the European Convention on Human Rights. In November, the Supreme Court confirmed this ruling.

In January, the Supreme Court ruled that the compulsory overnight stay and twice daily reporting regime at a centre for individuals on "tolerated stay" (those excluded from protection but who could not be deported), constituted a disproportionate measure amounting to custody when extended beyond a period of four years. The government implemented the ruling, but also decided that any person leaving the centre to live with their family would lose their right to health care and financial assistance for food.

In March, the Parliamentary Ombudsman concluded that government policy to separate asylum-seeking couples when one partner was under the age of 18 was a violation of the Danish Act on Public Administration and possibly a violation of the right to family life. The policy did not provide for a process to determine whether the separation was in the interest of the younger spouse and did not consider their opinion.

VIOLENCE AGAINST WOMEN

In April, a proposal by the opposition to introduce a consent-based definition of rape, in line with the Council of Europe Convention on Preventing and Combating Violence against Women and Domestic Violence (Istanbul Convention) ratified by Denmark in 2014, was rejected in Parliament. In November, the Council of Europe's Group of Experts on Action against Violence against Women and Domestic Violence (GREVIO) encouraged the Danish authorities to change the current sexual violence legislation and base it on the notion of freely given consent as required by the Istanbul Convention.

RIGHTS OF LESBIAN, GAY, BISEXUAL, TRANSGENDER AND INTERSEX PEOPLE

In January, Parliament's landmark 2016 resolution to end the pathologization of transgender identities was implemented. However, existing procedural rules on access to hormone treatment and gender-affirming surgery continued to unreasonably prolong the gender recognition process for transgender people.

No national guidelines from the Danish Health Authority outlined how doctors should treat children with variations of sex characteristics and the approach was not human rights-based. This allowed non-emergency invasive and irreversible medical procedures to be carried out on children, typically under the age of 10, in violation of the UN Convention on the Rights of the Child. These procedures can be carried out despite the lack of medical research to support the need for surgical intervention, and despite documentation of the risk of lifelong harmful effects.[1] In October the UN Committee on the Rights of the Child raised concerns regarding surgical interventions on intersex children.

---

1. Europe: First, do no harm – ensuring the rights of children with variations of sex characteristics in Denmark and Germany (EUR 01/6086/2017)

DOMINICAN REPUBLIC

Dominican Republic
Head of state and government: **Danilo Medina Sánchez**

Limited progress was made in solving the statelessness crisis. Abortion remained criminalized in all circumstances. Excessive use of force by the police and gender-based violence continued.

BACKGROUND

The Dominican Republic suffered from a series of natural disasters that hit the Caribbean during the year, including two major hurricanes in September. This, along with previous flooding earlier in the year, left tens of thousands of people temporarily displaced and badly damaged infrastructure. Like many small, developing island states, the Dominican Republic remained very vulnerable to climate change, which scientists linked to the increasingly extreme weather. On 21 September, the Dominican Republic ratified the UN Paris Agreement on climate change.

Allegations that several Dominican officials were bribed by the Brazilian construction company Odebrecht triggered massive country-wide demonstrations against corruption under the Green March movement. In September, the Inter-American Commission on Human Rights (IACHR) held a public hearing on the issue of "human rights and reports of impunity and corruption in the Dominican Republic".

In May, the UN Special Rapporteur on the sale and sexual exploitation of children visited the country. She urged the government to put child protection at the core of any tourism strategy.

DISCRIMINATION – STATELESS PERSONS

The Dominican Republic continued to fail to uphold its international human rights obligations with respect to the large number of stateless people born in the country who were retroactively and arbitrarily deprived of their Dominican nationality in September 2013.[1]

Law 169-14, adopted in May 2014 to address the statelessness crisis, continued to be poorly implemented. According to official statistics, only 13,500 people of the so-called "Group A" created by the law (out of an official estimate of 61,000 individuals) were able to access some sort of Dominican identity document proving their Dominican nationality. In the meantime, many had their original birth certificates nullified and their new ones transferred to a separate civil registry without the necessary measures in place to avoid further discrimination.

The naturalization plan established by Law 169-14 for people in "Group B" (those whose birth was never registered in the Dominican Civil Registry) had made little or no progress during the year. Of the 8,755 individuals who were able to register under the new plan (16% of the estimated 53,000 people in Group B, according to the government), it was believed that as few as 6,545 had had their files approved by the authorities by the end of the year. The law required a two-year waiting period after the approval of the registration for them to be able to formally request their naturalization as Dominicans. By the end of the year no one was known to have been naturalized under the new plan. Most of the individuals affected remained stateless in the absence of another nationality.

During the year, the authorities failed to discuss, design or implement new solutions to guarantee the right to nationality for the tens of thousands of Dominican-born people who could not benefit from Law 169-14, in particular the remaining 84% of those in Group B, and all those who were left out of the scope of the 2014 legislation.

Responding to this situation, in April the IACHR incorporated the Dominican Republic in Chapter IV.B of its annual report that included countries in need of special human rights attention.

By the end of the year, no public official had been held accountable for discriminatory practices in granting registration and identity documents, including for the 2013 mass arbitrary deprivation of nationality. Affected people continued to be denied a range of human rights and were prevented from accessing higher education, formal employment or adequate health care, among other things.

POLICE AND SECURITY FORCES

The Office of the Prosecutor General reported 110 killings by security forces between January and October. The circumstances around many of the killings suggested that they may have been unlawful. The homicide rate remained high, at nearly 16 per 100,000 inhabitants during the first half of the year.

The media reported allegations of the repeated use of unnecessary and excessive force by the police during social protests.

REFUGEES' AND MIGRANTS' RIGHTS

The authorities remained unable to process most of the cases of irregular migrants that they received during the National Regularization Plan for Foreigners with Irregular Migration Status that operated between 2014 and 2015. As a result, in July the authorities renewed for a further year the temporary "regularization carnets" issued to registered individuals, allowing them to stay in the country.

SEXUAL AND REPRODUCTIVE RIGHTS

The Dominican Republic remained one of the few countries worldwide that criminalized abortion without exception.

In May the Senate voted against a proposal, supported by President Medina, to decriminalize abortion.[2] On 11 July the Senate's vote was rejected by the Chamber of Deputies, providing the possibility of future reforms that would protect the rights of women and girls.[3]

In August, a petition was presented to the IACHR seeking justice and reparation for the death in 2012 of 16-year-old Rosaura Almonte Hernández, publicly known as "Esperancita". Because of the country's restrictive legislation on abortion, Rosaura Almonte Hernández, who was seven weeks pregnant, was denied life-saving treatment for leukaemia for several days and died shortly after.

An investigation published in August by the NGO Women's Link Worldwide found that one woman died every two days in the Dominican Republic during the first half of 2017 from pregnancy-related causes due to the lack of access to quality maternal health services.

VIOLENCE AGAINST WOMEN AND GIRLS

According to official statistics, the first half of the year saw a 21% increase in the number of killings of women and girls, compared with the same period in 2016.

RIGHTS OF LESBIAN, GAY, BISEXUAL, TRANSGENDER AND INTERSEX PEOPLE

The Dominican Republic continued to lack legislation to combat hate crimes. In June, the body of a transgender woman, Rubi Mori, was found dismembered in wasteland.[4] By the end of the year, no one had been brought to justice for her killing.

1. Dominican Republic: What does it take to solve a statelessness crisis? (News story, 23 May)

2. Dominican Republic: Vote against decriminalization of abortion, a betrayal to women (Press release, 1 June)

3. República Dominicana: Amnistía Internacional y Oxfam llaman a Cámara de Diputados a garantizar derechos de las mujeres (AMR 27/6605/2017); Dominican Republic: Further information - Congress rejects regressive abortion reform (AMR 27/6724/2017); Dominican Republic: Further information: Abortion vote pending after President's veto (AMR 27/5478/2017)

4. Dominican Republic: Horrifying killing of transgender woman highlights need for protection against discrimination (News story, 6 June)

ECUADOR

Republic of Ecuador
Head of state and government: Lenín Boltaire Moreno Garcés (replaced Rafael Vicente Correa Delgado in May)

Indigenous leaders, human rights defenders and staff of NGOs faced persecution and harassment amid continuing restrictions on the rights to freedom of expression and association. The right to free, prior and informed consent of Indigenous Peoples continued to be restricted. The Bill to Prevent and Eliminate Violence against Women was pending revision by the National Assembly.

BACKGROUND

On 24 May, Lenín Moreno Garcés became President. Shortly afterwards he called for a referendum and a popular consultation, to be held in February 2018, for Ecuadorians to decide on matters including the amendment of the Constitution to eliminate indefinite re-election of authorities, the banning of mining in protected areas, and reducing the area of oil exploitation in the Yasuní National Park.

INTERNATIONAL SCRUTINY

In May, Ecuador's human rights record was examined under the UN UPR process. Ecuador accepted recommendations to adopt a national action plan on business and human rights, create an effective consultation mechanism for Indigenous Peoples, align national laws on freedoms of expression and assembly with international standards, ensure the protection of journalists and human rights defenders, and guarantee protection from discrimination based on sexual orientation and gender identity. Ecuador pledged to lead on creating an international legally binding instrument on transnational corporations and human rights. Ecuador received a total of 182 recommendations of which it accepted 159, noted 19, and left four for further review.

In July, the Inter-American Commission on Human Rights (IACHR) held hearings on violence and harassment against human rights defenders, and on extractive industries and the right to cultural identity of Indigenous Peoples in Ecuador. The IACHR expressed concern over the absence of state representatives at both hearings.

FREEDOMS OF EXPRESSION AND ASSOCIATION

In January, the Ministry for the Environment rejected a complaint filed by the Ministry of the Interior aimed at shutting down the NGO Ecological Action Corporation, based on a lack of evidence linking the NGO to violence that occurred in 2016 in Morona Santiago province.

VIOLENCE AGAINST WOMEN AND GIRLS

In November the National Assembly approved a Bill to Prevent and Eliminate Violence against Women. In December, President Moreno partially vetoed the Bill and proposed a series of modifications, which were pending revision by the National Assembly at the end of the year.

INDIGENOUS PEOPLES' RIGHTS

In July, Indigenous and human rights organizations denounced before the IACHR intrusions of the state into the territory of the Sápara People for future oil extraction. They also denounced government bids for oil extraction in the territory of the Kichwa People of Sarayaku without obtaining their free, prior and informed consent, despite the Inter-American Court of Human Rights ruling that the Kichwa People must be consulted.

In April, Shuar Indigenous leader Agustín Wachapá was released on parole after four months in pre-trial detention on charges of inciting violence in Morona Santiago in 2016. The Shuar People continued to face a dispute over the development of two copper mines in their territory.

HUMAN RIGHTS DEFENDERS

NGOs denounced before the IACHR the lack of an adequate protection system or specialized institution responsible for investigating attacks against and criminalization of human rights defenders. They also denounced the frequent misuse of the charge of attacking or resisting authority to prosecute human rights defenders.

ENFORCED DISAPPEARANCES

The UN Committee on Enforced Disappearances noted in March that no criminal responsibility had been established for 17 cases of enforced disappearances from 1984 to 2008 identified by the Truth Commission, and that the whereabouts of 12 of those victims remained undisclosed.

EGYPT

Arab Republic of Egypt
Head of state: **Abdel Fattah al-Sisi**
Head of government: **Sherif Ismail**

Egypt's human rights crisis continued unabated. The authorities used torture and

other ill-treatment and enforced disappearance against hundreds of people, and dozens were extrajudicially executed with impunity. The crackdown on civil society escalated with NGO staff being subjected to additional interrogations, travel bans and asset freezes. Arbitrary arrests and detentions followed by grossly unfair trials of government critics, peaceful protesters, journalists and human rights defenders were routine. Mass unfair trials continued before civilian and military courts, with dozens sentenced to death. Women continued to be subjected to sexual and gender-based violence and were discriminated against in law and practice. The authorities brought criminal charges for defamation of religion and "habitual debauchery" on the basis of people's real or perceived sexual orientation.

BACKGROUND

In June, President al-Sisi ceded sovereignty over two uninhabited Red Sea islands to Saudi Arabia, leading to widespread public criticism. In July, EU-Egypt Association council meetings resumed for the first time since 2011 and the priorities of the Association were finalized.

In February a member of parliament proposed a constitutional amendment to extend the presidential term from four to six years. In April, President al-Sisi passed a new set of legislative amendments weakening fair trial guarantees and facilitating arbitrary arrests, indefinite pre-trial detention, enforced disappearances and the passing of more sentences. The amendments also allowed criminal courts to list people and entities on "terrorism lists" based solely on police information. Also in April, President al-Sisi approved the Judicial Bodies Law 13 of 2017, granting him the authority to appoint the heads of judicial bodies, including the Court of Cassation and the State Council, two courts that had hitherto been regarded as the most independent judicial bodies in holding the executive to account.[1]

At least 111 security agents were killed, mostly in North Sinai. The armed group Willayet Sinai, affiliated to the armed group Islamic State (IS), claimed responsibility for most of the attacks across the country, with smaller attacks claimed by other armed groups, such as Hasm, Liwaa al-Thawra and Ansar al-Islam. In April, IS claimed responsibility for the bombing of two churches in Tanta and Alexandria which left at least 44 dead. In October, at least 16 officials from the Ministry of the Interior were killed in an ambush in the western desert, a rare attack on the mainland. In a significant shift in targeting by armed groups, a November attack on a mosque in North Sinai during Friday prayers killed at least 300 people.

HUMAN RIGHTS DEFENDERS

The authorities continued to curb the work of human rights defenders in an unprecedented manner as part of their relentless efforts to silence all critical voices. In February the authorities shut down the El-Nadeem Center, an NGO offering support to survivors of torture and violence. The criminal investigations into so-called "Case 173" against human rights defenders and NGOs were ongoing; investigative judges summoned at least 28 additional human rights defenders and NGO staff for interrogation during the year, bringing the total to 66 people summoned or investigated in the case since 2013. They were questioned in relation to charges that included "receiving foreign funding to harm Egyptian national security" under Article 78 of the Penal Code, which carries a sentence of up to 25 years' imprisonment. The investigative judges also ordered three additional travel bans, bringing to 25 the number of human rights defenders banned from travelling outside Egypt. In January a court ordered the freezing of the assets of the NGOs Nazra for Feminist Studies and the Arab Organization for Penal Reform and their directors.

In May, President al-Sisi signed a draconian new law giving the authorities broad powers to deny NGOs registration, dissolve NGOs and dismiss their boards of administration.

The law also provided for five years' imprisonment for publishing research without government permission.[2] The government had not issued the executive regulations to enable it to start implementing the law by the end of the year.

FREEDOMS OF EXPRESSION AND ASSEMBLY

Between January and May, courts sentenced at least 15 journalists to prison terms ranging from three months to five years on charges related solely to their writing, including defamation and the publication of what the authorities deemed "false information". On 25 September a court sentenced former presidential candidate and prominent human rights lawyer Khaled Ali to three months' imprisonment on charges of "violating public decency" in relation to a photograph showing him celebrating a court ruling ordering a halt to the handover of two islands to Saudi Arabia.[3] From May onwards, the authorities blocked at least 434 websites, including those of independent newspapers such as *Mada Masr* and human rights organizations such as the Arab Network for Human Rights Information. In March the Minister of Justice referred two judges, Hisham Raouf and Assem Abdelgabar, to a disciplinary hearing for participating in a workshop organized by an Egyptian human rights group to draft a law against torture.

Security forces arrested at least 240 political activists and protesters between April and September on charges relating to online posts the authorities considered "insulting" to the President or for participating in unauthorized protests. In April, a criminal court sentenced lawyer and activist Mohamed Ramadan to 10 years' imprisonment in his absence under the draconian Counter-terrorism Law.[4] In December, an Alexandrian court sentenced human rights lawyer Mahinour El-Masry to two years' imprisonment for her peaceful participation in a protest.

ARBITRARY ARRESTS AND DETENTIONS

Security forces continued to arrest hundreds of people based on their membership or perceived membership of the Muslim Brotherhood, rounding them up from their homes or places of work or, in one case, from a holiday resort.

The authorities used prolonged pre-trial detention, often for periods of more than two years, as means to punish dissidents. In October a judge renewed the pre-trial detention of human rights defender Hisham Gaafar, despite him having been detained for more than the two-year limit under Egyptian law. Photojournalist Mahmoud Abu Zeid, known as Shawkan, had already spent two years in pre-trial detention when his trial started in August 2015. Throughout 2017 he remained in detention alongside 738 co-defendants as their trial continued.

Upon release, political activists were often required to serve probation periods of up to 12 hours a day in a local police station, amounting to arbitrary deprivation of liberty.

EXTRAJUDICIAL EXECUTIONS AND ENFORCED DISAPPEARANCES

Forces of the Ministry of the Interior continued to subject to enforced disappearance and extrajudicially execute people suspected of engaging in political violence. According to the Egyptian Commission for Rights and Freedoms, security forces subjected at least 165 people to enforced disappearance between January and August for periods ranging from seven to 30 days.

The Ministry of the Interior claimed that more than 120 people were shot dead in an exchange of fire with security forces during the year. However, in many of these cases the people killed were already in state custody after having been subjected to enforced disappearance. In May the Ministry announced the death of schoolteacher Mohamed Abdelsatar "in an exchange of fire with the police". However, his colleagues had witnessed his arrest a month earlier from his workplace. In April, a leaked video showed military forces in North Sinai extrajudicially executing six unarmed men and a 17-year-old boy.

DETENTION

Torture and other ill-treatment remained routine in official places of detention and was systematic in detention centres run by the National Security Agency. In July, a Coptic man was arrested and detained in Manshyet Nasir police station in the capital, Cairo, in relation to a minor offence; 15 hours later, he was dead. Family members stated that they saw bruises on the upper part of his body, and the official autopsy report stated that his death was the result of a "suspected criminal act".

Prison authorities, including in Tora Maximum Security Prison and Wadi el-Natrun Prison, punished prisoners detained for politically motivated reasons by placing them in indefinite and prolonged solitary confinement. In February the Ministry of the Interior amended the prison regulations to allow solitary confinement to be increased up to six months; a practice that can amount to torture or other ill-treatment. Political activist Ahmed Douma spent his third year in solitary confinement in Tora Prison, confined to his cell for at least 22 hours a day. Muslim Brotherhood spokesman Gehad el-Hadad remained indefinitely detained in solitary confinement in Al Aqrab maximum security prison since his arrest on 17 September 2013.

Other forms of ill-treatment and medical negligence in prisons continued; dozens of prisoners died, often due to prison authorities refusing to transfer them to hospital for medical treatment. In September, former Muslim Brotherhood leader Mohamed Mahdi Akef died in prison from pancreatic cancer.

UNFAIR TRIALS

Hundreds were sentenced, some to death, after grossly unfair mass trials. In September a Cairo criminal court sentenced 442 people in the case of the August 2013 al-Fateh mosque protests to prison terms of between five and 25 years after a grossly unfair trial of 494 defendants. Courts continued to rely heavily on reports of the National Security Agency and unsound evidence, including confessions obtained under torture, in their sentencing. Civilians continued to face unfair trials before military courts; at least 384 civilians were referred to military trials during the year.

DEATH PENALTY

Ordinary and military courts continued to hand down death sentences following grossly unfair mass trials. In June the Court of Cassation upheld the death sentences of seven men in two different cases after grossly unfair trials. At least six of the men had been subjected to enforced disappearance and tortured to force them to "confess" and the court relied heavily on these coerced confessions in its verdict and sentencing. Also in June, the Military High Court upheld death sentences against four men following grossly unfair trials in which the court relied on "confessions" obtained under torture during 93 days of incommunicado detention.[5] On 26 December the authorities executed 15 men who had been convicted by a military court of killing nine military personnel in North Sinai in 2013.

WOMEN'S RIGHTS

Women and girls continued to face inadequate protection from sexual and gender-based violence, as well as gender discrimination in law and practice. The absence of measures to ensure privacy and protection of women reporting sexual and gender-based violence continued to be a key factor preventing many women and girls from reporting such offences. Many who did report offences faced harassment and retaliation from the perpetrators or their families. In some cases, state officials and members of parliament blamed victims of sexual violence and attributed the incidents to their "revealing clothing". In March a young student was attacked and sexually assaulted by a mob in Zagazig city, al-Sharkia governorate. Instead of arresting the perpetrators and bringing them to justice, the Security Directorate in al-Sharkia governorate issued a statement mentioning that by "wearing a short dress" the victim had "caused the mob attack".

Women continued to face discrimination in the judiciary. A number of women who attempted to apply to the State Council for appointment as judges were not given the papers needed to process their requests. One woman filed a suit against the State Council on grounds of discrimination.

REFUGEES' AND MIGRANTS' RIGHTS

Asylum-seekers and refugees continued to face arrest, detention and deportation for entering or exiting the country irregularly. Between January and April, immigration officials deported at least 50 asylum-seekers from Eritrea, Ethiopia and Sudan, including young children, to their countries of origin without giving them access to legal representation or to UNHCR, the UN refugee agency. The forced return of Eritrean asylum-seekers, as well as Ethiopian and Sudanese nationals with a well-founded fear of persecution, constituted *refoulement*. In July the authorities rounded up Chinese students, mostly of the Uighur ethnic minority, arresting at least 200 and deporting at least 21 men and one woman to China, in violation of Egypt's *non-refoulement* obligations.

RIGHTS OF LESBIAN, GAY, BISEXUAL, TRANSGENDER AND INTERSEX PEOPLE

In the worst crackdown in over a decade, the authorities across Egypt rounded up and prosecuted people on the grounds of their perceived sexual orientation after a rainbow flag was displayed at a concert in Cairo on 22 September. These prosecutions provoked a public outcry. Security forces arrested at least 76 people and carried out at least five anal examinations, a practice which amounts to torture. Those arrested included a man and a woman who were detained for three months for carrying the rainbow flag at the concert, as well as people who made online expressions of support for the raising of the flag. Many of those arrested were entrapped by security forces through online dating applications. Courts sentenced at least 48

people to prison terms of between three months and six years on charges that included "habitual debauchery". The other people arrested remained in detention facing questioning by prosecutors.

In late October, a group of parliamentarians proposed a deeply discriminatory law explicitly criminalizing same-sex sexual relations and any public promotion of LGBTI gatherings, symbols or flags. The proposed law carried penalties of up to five years' imprisonment, or 15 years' imprisonment for a person convicted of multiple charges.

FREEDOM OF RELIGION AND BELIEF

The authorities continued to violate the right to freedom of religion by discriminating against Christians. In August, security forces prevented dozens of Coptic Christians from praying in a house in Alforn village in Minya governorate, citing reasons of security. There was continued impunity for sectarian attacks on Christian communities, and the authorities continued to rely on customary reconciliation and settlements agreed by local authorities and religious leaders. Amid this impunity, violence by non-state actors against Christians increased significantly. Armed groups in North Sinai killed seven Coptic Christians between 30 January and 23 February, prompting an unprecedented internal displacement of at least 150 Coptic families living in North Sinai.[6] The authorities failed to offer them the necessary protection or appropriate compensation. In December, IS claimed responsibility for the shooting of 10 people in an attack on a church in Helwan in southern Cairo.

In November, an attack on a mosque in North Sinai during Friday prayers killed at least 300 worshippers. No group claimed responsibility for the attack.

WORKERS' RIGHTS

The authorities subjected dozens of workers and trade unionists to arrest, military trial, dismissal and a range of disciplinary measures, solely for exercising their right to strike and form independent trade unions. In June a Cairo Misdemeanours Appeal Court sentenced 32 workers from the privately owned Tora Cement Company to two months' imprisonment after they were convicted of participating in an unauthorized protest and "assaulting security forces", despite the peaceful nature of their 55-day sit-in to protest at their dismissal. In December, the Military Court in Alexandria resumed the trial of 25 workers from the military-run Alexandria Shipyard Company. The trial started in May 2016 on charges that included "inciting the workers to strike". The government and the official Egypt Trade Union Federation sought to deprive independent unions of the de facto recognition they had obtained in 2011 through a declaration issued by the then Minster of Manpower. The authorities continued to deny their legal recognition and hinder their ability to function freely through a range of measures.[7] On 5 December parliament passed a new trade union law, replacing Law 35 of 1976, creating excessive requirements for unions to have at least 150 members to obtain legal recognition or face automatic dissolution.

INDIGENOUS PEOPLES' RIGHTS

Despite an explicit constitutional provision recognizing the Nubian Indigenous people's right to return to their traditional lands, the government continued to deny displaced Nubians the right to access their traditional lands, posing a threat to the preservation of their cultural, historical and linguistic identity. On 3 September, Nubian activists held a protest calling on the authorities to repeal a 2014 presidential decree that classified 16 villages on traditional Nubian lands as military zones and prohibited residents from living there. The police arrested 25 activists and detained them for three months.[8]

1. New legislation threatens judicial independence in Egypt (Press release, 27 April)

2. Egypt: NGO law threatens to annihilate human rights groups (Press release, 30 May)

3. Egypt: Former presidential candidate given jail term in bid to stop him running in 2018 election (Press release, 25 September)

4. Egypt: 10-year prison term for insulting President an outrageous assault on freedom of expression (Press release, 13 April)

5. Egypt: Seven men facing imminent execution after being tortured in custody (Press release, 16 June); Egypt: Four men facing imminent executions after grossly unfair military trial (MDE 12/6590/2017)

6. Egypt: Government must protect Coptic Christians targeted in string of deadly attacks in North Sinai (Press release, 1 March)

7. Egypt: On Labour Day – relentless assault on labour rights (MDE 12/6154/2017)

8. Egypt: Release 24 Nubian activists detained after protest calling for respect of their cultural rights (Press release, 12 September)

EL SALVADOR

Republic of El Salvador
Head of state and government: **Salvador Sánchez Cerén**

El Salvador's high rate of gender-based violence continued to make it one of the most dangerous countries to be a woman. A total ban on abortion persisted, and women were convicted of aggravated homicide after suffering miscarriages or other obstetric emergencies. To combat violence, the government implemented a series of security measures, which did not comply with human rights standards. Measures were taken to address impunity for historical abuses; however, the executive and legislative branches of government admitted being in contempt of a 2016 Supreme Court judgment that declared the 1993 Amnesty Law unconstitutional.

BACKGROUND

El Salvador continued to have one of the world's highest murder rates, although the number of homicides fell from 5,280 in 2016 to 3,605 in 2017. The figure for 2017 included 429 femicides.

WOMEN'S RIGHTS

Abortion continued to be prohibited in all circumstances, and carried criminal penalties for women and health care providers. Women from poor backgrounds were disproportionately affected.

In March, the Inter-American Commission on Human Rights (IACHR) admitted a petition in the case of Manuela, a woman convicted of homicide after having a miscarriage, and who died from cancer in prison while serving her sentence.

On 5 July, Evelyn Beatriz Hernández Cruz was sentenced to 30 years' imprisonment after being convicted on charges of aggravated homicide after suffering obstetric complications resulting in a miscarriage. On 13 December, a court denied the release of Teodora del Carmen Vásquez; she had suffered a stillbirth in 2007 and was later sentenced to 30 years for aggravated homicide.

In August a parliamentarian for the opposition Nationalist Republican Alliance presented a new proposal to decriminalize abortion in two circumstances: when a woman's life is at risk or when the pregnancy is a consequence of rape of a minor. The proposal remained pending in Parliament. This followed previous, unsuccessful attempts at partial decriminalization of abortion in 2016.

In August, Congress approved a law banning child marriage, without exceptions.

In November, the IACHR admitted a petition on the case of "Beatriz", a woman who in 2013 was denied an abortion despite her life being put at risk by the pregnancy, and the foetus being diagnosed with fatal impairment, which would not have allowed its survival after birth.

HUMAN RIGHTS DEFENDERS

In June the home of human rights defender Sonia Sánchez Pérez was illegally searched by National Civilian Police officers. In 2015 the Office of the Human Rights Ombudsman had granted her precautionary measures for her environmental protection work.

RIGHTS OF LESBIAN, GAY, BISEXUAL, TRANSGENDER AND INTERSEX PEOPLE

In October, Karla Avelar, a human rights defender and founder of the first association of trans people in El Salvador, announced that she would claim asylum in Europe because of a lack of protection by the authorities, despite several security incidents,

threats, and being the victim of extortion by criminal gangs. Between January and September, the Association for Communicating and Training Trans Women in El Salvador (COMCAVIS TRANS) reported 28 serious attacks, most of them murders, perpetrated against LGBTI people.[1]

EXTRAJUDICIAL EXECUTIONS

In September the Human Rights Institute of José Simeón Cañas Central American University and the NGO Passionist Social Service reported before the IACHR that the armed forces and National Civilian Police were responsible for carrying out extrajudicial executions.

POLICE AND SECURITY FORCES

In November the UN High Commissioner for Human Rights urged El Salvador to end the extraordinary security measures adopted since 2016 to combat gang violence and organized crime, which failed to comply with international human rights standards. The measures included prolonged and isolated detention under inhuman conditions, and prolonged suspension of family visits to prisoners.

INTERNALLY DISPLACED PEOPLE

On 6 and 13 October, for the first time, the Constitutional Chamber of the Supreme Court of Justice issued two injunctions (amparo) to protect internally displaced people. The injunctions included protective measures for a family that had been forcibly internally displaced due to rape, threats, beatings and harassment by a gang. The decision was welcomed by the IACHR and the UN Special Rapporteur on the human rights of internally displaced persons.

IMPUNITY

Measures were adopted nationally and internationally to redress crimes under international law and punish perpetrators of human rights violations committed during El Salvador's armed conflict from 1980 to 1992.

In May, a court ordered the reopening of the case of Monseñor Óscar Arnulfo Romero y

Galdámez, Archbishop of San Salvador, who was murdered in 1980 by a death squad while celebrating mass.

Following a judgment by the Supreme Court in 2016 in which the 1993 Amnesty Law was ruled to be unconstitutional, the Court held a hearing in July to determine what steps the government had taken to comply with the ruling. In that hearing, both the executive and legislative branches of government admitted to being in contempt of the ruling.

In September the government created a commission to search for people who were subjected to enforced disappearance during the armed conflict.

In November, the Supreme Court of the USA cleared the way for Colonel Inocente Orlando Montano Morales to be tried in Spain on charges that he conspired in the killing of six Jesuit priests, their housekeeper and her daughter in El Salvador in 1989.

---

1. Americas: "No safe place" – Salvadorans, Guatemalans and Hondurans seeking asylum in Mexico based on their sexual orientation and/or gender identity (AMR 01/7258/2017)

EQUATORIAL GUINEA

Republic of Equatorial Guinea
Head of state and government: **Teodoro Obiang Nguema Mbasogo**

Harassment, intimidation and arbitrary detention of human rights defenders continued. The rights to freedom of association and assembly were curtailed; people attending peaceful gatherings were arbitrarily detained and beaten. Pregnant girls were barred from attending school.

BACKGROUND

On 27 October, Vice-President Teodoro Nguema Obiang Mangue, the President's son, was given a three-year suspended prison sentence, and a suspended EUR30 million fine by a court in Paris, France, for corruption and money laundering while he was Minister of Agriculture and Forestry.

In November's legislative and municipal elections, the ruling Democratic Party of Equatorial Guinea won 99 of 100 seats in the Chamber of Deputies, all elected seats in the Senate, and all but one seat in the municipal elections. Opposition parties denounced electoral irregularities and intimidation. Internet access was severely disrupted for at least five days.

HUMAN RIGHTS DEFENDERS

The authorities continued to harass, intimidate and arbitrarily detain human rights defenders.

On 17 April, Enrique Asumu and Alfredo Okenve, leaders of the Centre for Development Studies and Initiatives, were detained in the capital, Malabo, after they objected to the authorities' decision to prevent Enrique Asumu from boarding a plane to Bata city the previous day. Enrique Asumu was released eight days later on health grounds after paying a fine of CFA francs 2 million (USD3,500). Alfredo Okenve was released on 4 May after paying the same fine. The Ministry of Interior had suspended the Centre's activities in 2016.

On 16 September, state security agents arrested and detained Ramón Esono Ebalé, a cartoonist and critic of the government, and two Spanish nationals as they left a restaurant in Malabo. They were handcuffed, their mobile phones confiscated, and taken to the Office against Terrorism and Dangerous Activities where Ramón Esono Ebalé was questioned about his cartoons. The Spanish nationals were released the same day. Ramón Esono Ebalé was transferred three days later to the Black Beach prison in Malabo. National TV reported that he was accused of heading an organization involved in money laundering and counterfeiting money. On 27 November he was charged with counterfeiting money and remained in detention at the end of the year.

FREEDOMS OF ASSEMBLY AND ASSOCIATION

On 8 March, police arrested 47 women, four children and at least 12 men at an International Women's Day training session in Mbini city, southwest of Bata, in the office of the opposition Convergence for Social Democracy party. The police threatened to arrest Epifania Avomo, the party's executive women's officer, but when other women protested they were all arrested and taken to Mbini police station. Some of them were beaten at the police station, after which they were all released the same day.

In May, taxi drivers' organizations called for a three-day strike in Malabo to protest at the high prices of permits and papers. Security forces arbitrarily arrested at least 17 people and beat some of those believed to be participating in the strike, leaving several of them in need of medical assistance. They were released without charge about one week later.

On 27 May, security forces arbitrarily arrested rapper Benjamín Ndong, also known as "Jamin Dogg", in Malabo, for releasing two weeks ealier a song supporting the striking taxi drivers and denouncing government intimidation. He was released the same day without charge.

ECONOMIC, SOCIAL AND CULTURAL RIGHTS

In June, the NGO Human Rights Watch issued a report highlighting the lack of investment in health and education despite the increase, over two decades, of the per capita GDP which arose mainly from oil revenues. The government continued to focus spending on large infrastructure projects, from which some government officials profited, at the expense of health and education sectors.

Pregnant girls continued to be banned from school following a 2016 order issued by the Ministry of Education as a means to reduce adolescent pregnancies.

DEATH PENALTY

Death sentences continued to be handed down. On 16 September Raimundo Nfube Onva and Fausto Luis Nve Adugu were sentenced to death for a ritual killing committed in 2016.

ERITREA

State of Eritrea
Head of state and government: **Isaias Afwerki**

Thousands continued to flee Eritrea while the authorities severely restricted the right to leave the country. Indefinite mandatory national service continued to be imposed. Restrictions on the rights to freedom of expression and of religion remained. Arbitrary detention without charge or trial continued to be the norm for thousands of prisoners of conscience. Thousands were denied the right to an adequate standard of living.

BACKGROUND

Skirmishes broke out between the Eritrean and Ethiopian military periodically. Military hostilities with Djibouti escalated over ownership of the disputed territory of Ras Doumeira.

REFUGEES' AND MIGRANTS' RIGHTS

Thousands of Eritreans continued to flee the country. They faced serious human rights abuses while in transit and in destination countries. Sudan remained a key transit for Eritrean refugees. In one case in August, Sudanese courts deported 104 refugees to Eritrea where they were at risk of serious human rights violations. In a context where little is known about the fate of those deported across the border with Sudan, there were reports that 30 of them were deported from Kassala city, eastern Sudan, after being charged with illegal entry. Eritreans also risked arbitrary detention, abduction, sexual abuse and ill-treatment on their way to Europe.

Attempts to address the causes of migration from Eritrea continued at an international level. Following the High Level Dialogues on migration under the EU-Horn of Africa Migration Route Initiative (Khartoum Process), which involves the EU and African states and aims to address migration flows, the European Commission apportioned over EUR13 million for Eritrea in order to support employment opportunities and skills development in the country as a means of reducing migration. The EU channelled EUR100 million to Sudan through the European Union Emergency Trust Fund for Africa for use in addressing the root causes of migration and displacement in the region.

FREEDOM OF MOVEMENT

The imposition of indefinite military national service, along with the general human rights situation, created severe difficulties for many Eritreans. The right of people to leave the country was severely restricted. The authorities continued to prohibit those aged between five and 50 from travelling abroad, and anyone attempting to leave was subject to arbitrary detention. People seeking to leave to avoid indefinite national service and other human rights violations, or for family reunion with relatives abroad, had to travel by foot and use unofficial border crossings in order to take flights from other countries. If caught by the military, they were detained without charge until they paid exorbitant fines. The amount payable depended on factors such as the commanding officer making the arrest and the time of the year. People caught during national holidays to commemorate independence were subject to higher fines. The amount was greater for those attempting to cross the border with Ethiopia. A "shoot-to-kill" policy remained in place for anyone evading capture and attempting to cross the border into Ethiopia. Children close to conscription age caught trying to leave were sent to Sawa National Service training camp.

FORCED LABOUR AND SLAVERY

The mandatory national service continued to be extended indefinitely despite repeated calls from the international community on the government to limit conscription to 18 months. Significant numbers of conscripts remained in open-ended conscription, some for as long as 20 years. Despite a minimum legal conscription age of 18, children continued to be subjected to military training under the requirement that they undergo grade 12 of secondary school at Sawa National Service training camp, where they faced harsh living conditions, military-style discipline and weapons training. Women, in particular, faced harsh treatment in the camp including sexual enslavement, torture and other sexual abuse.

Men of up to 67 years of age were conscripted into the "People's Army", where they were given a weapon and assigned duties under threat of punitive repercussions, such as detention, fines or hard labour.

ARBITRARY ARRESTS AND DETENTIONS

Arbitrary detention and enforced disappearances continued, for which security forces were not held accountable. Thousands of prisoners of conscience and political prisoners, including former politicians, journalists and practitioners of unauthorized religions, continued to be detained without charge or trial and lacked access to lawyers or family members. Many had been detained for well over a decade.

FREEDOM OF RELIGION AND BELIEF

Bans on religious faiths, other than Islam, Orthodox Christianity, Protestant Lutheranism and Catholicism, remained in place. Many Evangelical Christians practised their religion in secret to avoid imprisonment.

Patriarch Antonios, head of the Eritrean Orthodox Church, was reported to have been seen attending mass in the capital, Asmara, in July. He had last been seen in public 10 years earlier just before he was sentenced to house arrest for objecting to government interference in church affairs.

RIGHT TO AN ADEQUATE STANDARD OF LIVING

UNICEF said that malnutrition rates had increased over the past few years in four out of six regions of Eritrea, and cited research which projected that 22,700 children under five would be affected by severe acute malnutrition during the year. It also noted national data indicating that half of all children had stunted growth. In her June report, the UN Special Rapporteur on the situation of human rights in Eritrea cited UNICEF's report. She further highlighted accounts from Eritreans living abroad describing their relatives at home as "struggling to meet their basic needs". Many of them could not afford "adequate and sufficient basic supplies" and were dealing with "acute water shortages, especially in Asmara". Reports suggested that more and more people were leaving "drought-affected regions in search of better living conditions." She noted that the government's draconian regulations that limited cash withdrawals from individuals' bank accounts prevented people from buying adequate food and other basic items.

ESTONIA

Republic of Estonia
Head of state: **Kersti Kaljulaid**
Head of government: **Jüri Ratas**

A draft amendment to the Asylum Act would increase the risk of *refoulement* for refugees sentenced to imprisonment for certain types of crimes. The Supreme Court ruled that the Family Law does not prohibit recognition of same-sex marriages registered in other countries.

REFUGEES AND ASYLUM-SEEKERS

By the end of the year, Estonia had relocated 141 asylum-seekers from Italy and Greece under the EU Emergency Relocation Scheme; however, of these, 71 people had left the country by the end of the year.

In accordance with the November 2016 decision of the Tallinn Appeal Court, which ruled against the blanket application of the "safe third country" concept for applications from asylum-seekers entering from the Russian Federation, the merits of eight individual asylum requests were assessed. These cases were pending at the end of the year.

In May, the government presented a draft amendment to the Asylum Act. The draft extended the exceptions under which *refoulement* – the forcible return of people to countries where they are at real risk of persecution – was allowed in situations where refugees have been sentenced to imprisonment for certain types of crimes. UNHCR, the UN refugee agency, raised concerns that the proposed amendment was not compliant with the UN Refugee Convention. In particular, it recommended that the government clarify the term "danger to the community of Estonia", which was included among the grounds for removal of a refugee from the country.

A number of refugees faced legal uncertainty and difficulty in accessing services as a consequence of the March 2016 Supreme Court decision which held that asylum-seekers who received a negative decision on their application immediately lose their status. The NGO Estonian Human Rights Centre raised concern over access to legal aid for asylum-seekers held in detention centres. This lack of access particularly affected asylum-seekers who entered the country via its border with Russia.

The lack of thorough investigations into racially motivated crimes against refugees and migrants persisted.

DISCRIMINATION – ETHNIC MINORITIES

80,000 people resident in Estonia remained stateless – almost 7% of the population, most of them Russian speakers. Roma continued to suffer discrimination across a range of social and economic rights.

RIGHTS OF LESBIAN, GAY, BISEXUAL, TRANSGENDER AND INTERSEX PEOPLE

In June, the Supreme Court held that although the Family Law does not provide for marriage of same-sex couples, it does not preclude recognition of same-sex marriages registered in other countries. The decision involved an Estonian-US lesbian couple initially forced to leave Estonia after the authorities had refused to provide one of the partners with a residence permit.

ETHIOPIA

Federal Democratic Republic of Ethiopia
Head of state: **Mulatu Teshome Wirtu**
Head of government: **Hailemariam Desalegn**

The government lifted the state of emergency in June. In August protests resumed in Oromia against income tax increases and calling for the release of Beqele Gerba, Merera Gudina and other political prisoners. In February, 10,000 people who had been arbitrarily detained were released. Reports of torture and other ill-treatment, unfair trials and violations of the rights to freedom of expression and of association continued.

BACKGROUND

The authorities failed to implement the reforms they had promised to address grievances raised during protests in 2015 and 2016 in Amhara and Oromia. The demonstrators had been protesting against the forced eviction of farmers from their lands in Oromia in the past 20 years; arbitrary arrests and detention of opposition political party leaders; and severe restrictions on the rights to freedom of expression and of association. Instead, the government declared a state of emergency in October 2016 after mobs torched farms and businesses in Oromia and Amhara following a stampede during the Oromo Thanksgiving Ceremony (Irrecha) in which at least 55 people were killed. The Ethiopian authorities have yet to conduct an independent and credible investigation into the cause and scale of the deaths.

TORTURE AND OTHER ILL-TREATMENT

Reports of torture and other ill-treatment of people accused of terrorism persisted. Detainees repeatedly complained to the courts that police tortured and ill-treated them during interrogations. Although, in some cases, judges ordered the Ethiopian Human Rights Commission (EHRC) to investigate the allegations, the investigations did not adhere to international human rights standards. Angaw Tegeny and Agbaw Seteny were tried under the 2009 Anti-Terrorism Proclamation (ATP) along with 35 others, in connection with a fire at Qilinto prison on the outskirts of the capital, Addis Ababa. The two men complained that the police suspended a water bottle from their scrotums and flogged them on the soles of their feet. However, an EHRC report to the Federal High Court did not refer to their torture complaints.

ARBITRARY ARRESTS AND DETENTIONS

Arbitrary detention continued under the state of emergency declaration which was lifted in June. On 2 February, the government ordered the release of 10,000 of the 26,000 people arbitrarily detained and arrested, under the declaration, in 2016.

Hundreds of people were detained under the ATP, which includes overly broad and vague definitions of terrorist acts punishable by up to 20 years' imprisonment. Detainees were held in excess of four months, the maximum period allowed under the law for pre-trial detention. Seven Oromo artists, for example, were detained for more than six months when the prosecutor finally charged them on 29 June.

UNFAIR TRIALS

Hundreds of political activists, dissenters and peaceful protesters faced unfair trials on charges brought under the ATP law. The trials were marked by prolonged pre-trial detention, undue delays and persistent complaints of torture and other ill-treatment.

Prominent leaders of opposition political parties such as Merera Gudina, Chairman of the Oromo Federalist Congress (OFC), and Beqele Gerba, Deputy Chairman of the OFC, were tried on charges under the ATP for their alleged role in organizing the November 2015 Oromia protest. Beqele Gerba's trial was repeatedly adjourned. Finally the court dismissed the terrorism charges against him. However, it ruled that his trial should proceed on charges of provocation and preparation for outrages against the Constitution or the Constitutional Order as per the Criminal Code.

FREEDOM OF EXPRESSION

The Federal High Court convicted journalists, bloggers and other activists on terrorism charges and handed down prison sentences. Yonatan Tesfaye was convicted of encouraging terrorism in his Facebook posts and sentenced to six-and-a-half years in prison. Getachew Shiferaw was sentenced to 18 months in prison for sending emails to leaders of a banned opposition political party based abroad. The court convicted him on charges including expressing appreciation of someone who, in 2012, publicly denounced the late Prime Minister Meles Zenawi.

ECONOMIC, SOCIAL AND CULTURAL RIGHTS

On 11 March, 115 people were killed as a result of a landslide at the Koshe rubbish dump, the largest dump in Ethiopia, located on the outskirts of Addis Ababa, in an area inhabited by hundreds of people. Most of the victims lived next to the site and supported themselves by recycling rubbish. The authorities had been aware that the landfill was full to capacity, and the residents had no option but to live and work there because the government failed to protect their right to adequate housing and decent work. More than 80 million birr (around USD3 million) was fundraised for rehabilitation of the victims. Although the municipal government managed the fund, the authorities had not

provided rehabilitation for victims and their families by the end of the year.

EXTRAJUDICIAL EXECUTIONS

The Ethiopian Somali Liyu Police (Liyu Police), a special force in Somali Regional State in eastern Ethiopia, and local Ethiopian militia, extrajudicially executed hundreds of Oromos living in the Somali Region. Among those killed were infants as young as six months. The Liyu Police also evicted at least 50,000 Oromos living in the Somali Region between September and October. It attacked the neighbouring Oromia Regional Districts and displaced thousands of residents in February, March, August, September and October.

ABDUCTION OF CHILDREN

The authorities failed to adequately protect people in Gambella Regional State from repeated attacks by armed members of the Murle ethnic group based in neighbouring South Sudan. The Murle gunmen crossed the border to Ethiopia on 12 March and abducted 22 children from the Anuwa community. The authorities were not known to have taken steps to ensure the return of the abducted children to their families.

IMPUNITY

The police and army continued to enjoy impunity for human rights violations committed in 2015 and 2016. During the year, the government rejected calls for independent and impartial investigations into human rights violations committed in the context of protests in various regional states. In the few cases where the EHRC conducted investigations and found that human rights violations had taken place, the government did not investigate or bring to justice suspected perpetrators.

FIJI

Republic of Fiji
Head of state: Jioji Konousi Konrote
Head of government: Josaia Voreqe Bainimarama

The government failed to ensure accountability for the torture and other ill-treatment of detainees by security forces. In two incidents, individuals were forcibly returned without due process to countries where they may be at risk of serious human rights violations. The increasing use of sedition charges, and the arrest of a lone peaceful protester on the International Day in Support of Victims of Torture highlighted the continuing restrictions on the rights to freedom of expression and peaceful assembly.

BACKGROUND

In June, the UN Special Rapporteur on racism published a report from his December 2016 mission to Fiji. The government had not implemented several of the report's recommendations by the end of the year, including calls to combat hate speech while protecting the right to freedom of expression, to facilitate meaningful dialogue to address past injustices and current inequalities and to strengthen the Human Rights and Anti-Discrimination Commission to ensure it complies with the Paris Principles.

FREEDOMS OF EXPRESSION AND PEACEFUL ASSEMBLY

The authorities used restrictive legislation to stifle the media and curtail the rights to freedom of expression and peaceful assembly, including by imposing sedition charges. In March, three senior staff at the *Fiji Times* and the author of a letter to its editor were charged with sedition, which carries a maximum prison sentence of seven years. In May, opposition MP Mosese Bulitavu and Fiji United Freedom Party leader Jagarth Karunaratne went on trial on sedition charges for their alleged role in posting anti-government graffiti in public places in 2011.

On 26 June, Jope Koroisavou, a youth leader from the opposition Social Democratic Liberal Party, was arrested and detained for 48 hours after he carried placards in the capital, Suva, calling for justice in torture cases.

TORTURE AND OTHER ILL-TREATMENT

Police and military officers charged in 2015 in connection with the torture of Iowane Benedito had not been brought to trial by the end of the year.

DEATHS IN CUSTODY

Vikrant Nand, aged 18, died in police custody in February. The police promptly announced an investigation into his death but by the end of the year it remained unclear what steps had been taken since the autopsy.

REFUGEES AND ASYLUM-SEEKERS

On two occasions, people were forcibly returned to countries where they may be at risk of serious human rights violations. In January, Iranian refugee Loghman Sawari fled Papua New Guinea for Fiji to seek asylum. On his way to meet Fiji's Director of Immigration, police intercepted his vehicle, arrested him and separated him from his lawyer. He said the police officers punched and attacked him with pepper spray. He was returned to Papua New Guinea without due process (see Papua New Guinea entry).

In August, 77 Chinese nationals were returned to China in co-operation with the Chinese authorities. The Fijian authorities claimed that they had committed "computer crimes" and breached the terms of their visas, charges which they were not given the opportunity to contest. They were not permitted to seek legal advice or appeal their forcible return.

FINLAND

Republic of Finland
Head of state: **Sauli Niinistö**
Head of government: **Juha Sipilä**

Changes to the asylum procedure continued to affect asylum-seekers negatively. Support services for women who experienced domestic violence remained inadequate. Legislation on legal gender recognition continued to violate the rights of transgender people. Draft legislative changes limiting the right to privacy were proposed.

REFUGEES AND ASYLUM-SEEKERS

Many changes in the law introduced in 2016, including restrictions of the right to free legal representation and reduced time frames for appeals, continued to affect refugees' and asylum-seekers' rights. The likelihood of asylum-seekers being forcibly returned to countries where they might be at risk of human rights violations (*refoulement*) was increased. The government had not evaluated the combined impact of these changes by the end of the year.

Family reunification remained difficult for most refugees due to both legislative and practical obstacles, including high income requirements.

Despite international NGOs raising concern, Finland continued to forcibly return asylum-seekers whose applications were rejected to Afghanistan.

Contrary to international standards, the authorities continued to detain unaccompanied children, and families with children, based on their immigration status. There was no time limit on detaining families with children. In February, "directed residence" was introduced as a new form of deprivation of liberty for asylum-seekers and migrants. It meant that asylum-seekers had to report to a reception centre up to four times a day.

RIGHTS OF LESBIAN, GAY, BISEXUAL, TRANSGENDER AND INTERSEX PEOPLE

Legislation on legal gender recognition continued to violate the rights of transgender people. They could obtain legal gender recognition only if they agreed to sterilization, were diagnosed with a mental disorder, and were aged over 18. Despite an April decision by the European Court of Human Rights condemning sterilization, the government did not consider amending the law.

VIOLENCE AGAINST WOMEN AND GIRLS

NGOs and state institutions working to combat violence against women and girls remained systematically under-resourced. Neither adequate and accessible walk-in services nor long-term support services for survivors of violence were in place. Existing legislation did not sufficiently protect institutionalized or hospitalized individuals from sexual violence.

In May, the first Sexual Assault Support Centre was opened at the Women's Hospital in the capital, Helsinki. Finland still lacked a nationwide, accessible service network for victims of all forms of sexual violence, which could also provide long-term support.

In January, an Administrative Committee on Coordination on violence against women, as required by the Istanbul Convention, started its work to enhance the implementation of the Convention and facilitate work to prevent violence against women. However, neither women's nor victims' support organizations were represented in the Committee and it was also inadequately resourced.

RIGHT TO PRIVACY

In April, draft civilian and military intelligence legislation was published. It enabled the acquisition of information on threats to national security by giving military and civilian intelligence agencies permission to conduct communications surveillance without any requirement for a link to a specific criminal offence.

CONSCIENTIOUS OBJECTORS

Conscientious objectors to military service continued to be punished for refusing to undertake alternative civilian service, which remained punitive and discriminatory in length. The duration of alternative civilian service was 347 days, more than double the shortest military service period of 165 days.

FRANCE

French Republic
Head of state: **Emmanuel Macron (replaced François Hollande in May)**
Head of government: **Édouard Philippe (replaced Bernard Cazeneuve in May)**

The state of emergency, introduced in 2015, was eventually lifted. A new law increased the government's powers to impose counter-terrorism measures on vague grounds and without full judicial scrutiny. Authorities continued to return Afghan nationals to Afghanistan in violation of the principle of *non-refoulement*. A new vigilance law imposing obligations on large companies entered into force.

COUNTER-TERROR AND SECURITY

In July, Parliament approved the government's proposal to extend the state of emergency until 1 November and then to end it. It had been in force since the attacks carried out in the capital, Paris, on 13 November 2015.

In October, Parliament adopted a governmental bill to introduce new counter-terrorism measures into ordinary law. The law increased the powers of the Minister of the Interior and the prefects to impose administrative measures on individuals, in cases where there was not sufficient evidence to open a criminal investigation. The measures included restrictions on freedom of movement, house searches, closure of places of worship, and the establishment of security zones where law enforcement officials were permitted to exercise enhanced stop-and-search powers.

The law required prefects to seek a judicial authorization only in respect of searches.

The UN Special Rapporteur on the promotion and protection of human rights and fundamental freedoms while countering terrorism had in September expressed concern that the bill included a vague definition of what constituted a threat to national security and had the effect of transposing emergency measures into ordinary law.

FREEDOM OF ASSEMBLY

Prefects continued to resort to emergency measures to restrict the right to freedom of peaceful assembly. In particular, they adopted dozens of measures restricting the freedom of movement of individuals to prevent them from attending public assemblies. Authorities imposed these measures on vague grounds and against individuals with no apparent connection with any terrorism-related offence. Prefects imposed 17 measures to prevent individuals from participating in the public assemblies calling for police accountability after a young man reported he had been raped by a police officer on 2 February. The Paris Prefect of Police imposed 10 measures to prevent protesters from attending the public assembly scheduled for International Workers' Day on 1 May.

On 5 January, a police officer was indicted for firing a sting-ball grenade that blinded protester Laurent Théron in one eye. The trial of the police officer was ongoing at the end of the year. The investigation into the alleged excessive use of force by police against dozens of protesters who had attended the public assemblies organized in 2016 against the reform of labour laws was still ongoing at the end of the year.

In March, a new law on the use of force and weapons by law enforcement officials entered into force. The law permitted the use of some weapons, including kinetic impact projectiles, in instances that did not fully comply with international standards.

In June, the Constitutional Court ruled that the emergency measure that had allowed prefects to restrict freedom of movement was unconstitutional. However, in July Parliament included the same measure in the law that extended the state of emergency. Prefects imposed 37 such measures between 16 July and 30 October.

REFUGEES' AND MIGRANTS' RIGHTS

Between January and July, the prefectural authorities of Alpes-Maritimes department stopped 28,000 refugees and migrants who had crossed the border from Italy. The authorities sent 95% of them back to Italy, including unaccompanied minors, without providing them with the right to seek asylum in France.

Between January and August, authorities placed more than 1,600 Afghan nationals in detention centres in view of returning them to other European countries under the Dublin III Regulation – a mechanism for allocating responsibility for the examination of asylum claims among EU member states – or to Afghanistan. In the same period, according to civil society organizations, authorities returned about 300 Afghan nationals to other EU countries and expelled at least 10 of them to Afghanistan. Authorities returned 640 individuals to Afghanistan in 2016. All returns to Afghanistan constituted a violation of the principle of *non-refoulement* – the principle according to which states are obliged not to return any person to a country where they would risk human rights violations – given the volatile security and human rights situation in Afghanistan.

In the aftermath of the eviction of the informal settlement near Calais, known as "The Jungle", in November 2016, authorities put in place punitive measures against the hundreds of migrants and refugees who had subsequently returned to Calais. They enhanced police stop-and-search operations, which raised concerns over ethnic profiling. In March, municipal authorities prohibited humanitarian organizations from distributing meals to migrants and asylum-seekers in the town. At the end of March, a court ruled that the decision constituted an inhumane and degrading treatment and suspended it.

Municipal authorities refused to fully comply with the ruling and only allowed the distribution of one meal a day. In June, the Public Defender of Rights (Ombudsperson) expressed concerns about the human rights violations experienced by migrants and asylum-seekers in Calais and called on authorities to ensure the respect of their social and economic rights, in particular access to water and to adequate housing, and to provide them with effective opportunities to seek asylum in France.

Authorities continued to prosecute and convict individuals who supported migrants and refugees in entering or staying in France irregularly, for example by providing food or shelter. In August, an appeal court convicted Cédric Herrou, a farmer living close to the French-Italian border, and sentenced him to a suspended sentence of four months' imprisonment for helping migrants and refugees to cross the border into France and for sheltering them.

DISCRIMINATION

In January, a law extending the moratorium on evictions of informal settlements during winter entered into force. Authorities continued to forcibly evict people from informal settlements, many of them Roma migrants. Civil society organizations reported that authorities had evicted 2,689 individuals in the first half of the year.

On 14 March, the Court of Justice of the EU failed to uphold Muslim women's rights to non-discrimination by ruling that a private French employer had not breached EU anti-discrimination law in dismissing a woman for wearing a headscarf.

CORPORATE ACCOUNTABILITY

In March, a law imposing a "duty of vigilance" on large companies entered into force. The law required companies to establish and implement a "vigilance plan" to prevent serious human rights abuses and environmental damage resulting directly or indirectly from their own activities and those of subsidiaries and other business partners. Victims of human rights abuses resulting from a company's failure to comply with the law could seek compensation before a French court.

ARMS TRADE

The government continued to license weapon transfers to governments that were likely to use them to commit serious violations of international human rights law and humanitarian law. The government continued to license weapon transfers to members of the Saudi Arabia-led coalition in Yemen and to Egypt.

In May, the Senate recommended the use of armed remotely piloted vehicles (drones) for the armed forces to improve their effectiveness in military operations. The Minister of Defence confirmed concrete plans to use armed drones from 2019, but the authorities were yet to articulate and implement clear policies on their use and transfer.

GABON

Gabonese Republic
Head of state: Ali Bongo Ondimba
Head of government: Emmanuel Issoze-Ngondet

The new Communications Code was criticized by journalists for its vague and overly broad provisions, and a newspaper was suspended. Prominent opposition supporters were arbitrarily arrested. The activities of the teachers' unions were severely restricted. Representatives of the ICC conducted a two-day visit.

BACKGROUND

Presidential candidate Jean Ping continued to contest the results of the August 2016 presidential elections, and in September 2017 he was temporarily denied the right to leave the country. Legislative elections were postponed until April 2018. In November, the report submitted by Gabon and parallel reports submitted by civil society organizations were examined under the UN UPR process.

FREEDOMS OF EXPRESSION, ASSOCIATION AND ASSEMBLY

In January, the new Communications Code came into force. The Code was criticized by journalists for its vague and overly broad provisions, including prohibitions on Gabonese nationals working for local media outlets outside the country, and provisions banning the use of pseudonyms, holding printers and distributors jointly responsible for any infractions, and an obligation for media to "contribute to the country's image and national cohesion".

On 17 March, the authorities suspended the activities of CONASYSED, the main teachers' union, citing "disturbance of public order" caused by strikes that began in October 2016. The Minister of Education also ordered the suspension of the payment of salaries to over 800 teachers in order to end the strike.

In June 2017 the National Council of Communication banned *Les Echos du Nord*, a newspaper considered to be close to the political opposition, for statements deemed defamatory against President Bongo and Prime Minister Issoze-Ngondet. The outlet reopened in August.

ARBITRARY ARRESTS AND DETENTIONS

On 14 April, Alain Djally, an assistant to opposition leader Jean Ping, was arrested without a warrant in the capital, Libreville. He was blindfolded and ill-treated by men in plain clothes, but allowed to see his lawyer the day after his arrest. After that he was denied access. He was detained at the Direction Générale de la Recherche, a facility run by the Gabonese intelligence services, before being transferred to the central prison in Libreville, where he was kept in solitary confinement for the entire period of his detention. He was charged with impersonating an active service member and illegal possession of firearms, for retaining his old military ID card and possessing a blank-firing gun. His lawyer claimed such a weapon did not require a permit, and that the charges were politically motivated. He was provisionally released on 23 June.

On 15 June, Marcel Libama, an adviser for CONASYSED and the union confederation Dynamique Unitaire, was arrested in Tchibanga city after discussing the case of a detained colleague, Cyprien Moungouli, during a Radio Massanga show. He was held for three days at a police station, and on 20 June transferred to the local prison. He was charged with insulting a magistrate, obstruction of justice and defamation. On 17 June, Juldas Biviga, a journalist from Radio Massanga, was also arrested for refusing to delete recordings of archived interviews, among other things. On 13 July, both Marcel Libama and Juldas Biviga were severely beaten by their prison guards. Suffering injuries to his ankles, ribs and ears, Juldas Biviga was transferred to hospital. They both received sentences of 184 days in prison and a EUR450 fine.

On 27 August, security forces arrested Hervé Mombo Kinga, an activist and prominent supporter of Jean Ping. He had publicly projected videos next to his internet café, and was charged with "instigating violence" and "insulting the Head of State", and spent one and a half months in solitary confinement. He remained in detention at the end of the year.

IMPUNITY

The ICC continued its preliminary examination into whether alleged crimes committed after May 2016, including in the context of the 2016 presidential elections, could amount to crimes under the Rome Statute, and whether the criteria for opening an investigation were met. In June, representatives of the ICC conducted a two-day visit.

GAMBIA

Republic of the Gambia
Head of state and government: **Adama Barrow (replaced Yahya Jammeh in January)**

The new government committed to reforming several repressive laws and reforming the security forces. Steps were taken to begin a transitional justice process.

BACKGROUND

Following mediation by regional leaders and the threat of a military intervention by ECOWAS,[1] former President Yahya Jammeh accepted the results of the December 2016 presidential elections and departed Gambia on 21 January for Equatorial Guinea.[2] ECOWAS had a coalition force stationed in Gambia scheduled to withdraw in mid-2018. Adama Barrow was inaugurated in Senegal's capital, Dakar, on 19 January during the impasse.

LEGAL, CONSTITUTIONAL OR INSTITUTIONAL DEVELOPMENTS

On 10 February, the government cancelled the planned withdrawal from the Rome Statute of the ICC which had been introduced under President Jammeh's rule.[3]

On 21 September, Gambia signed the Second Optional Protocol to the ICCPR, in an apparent step towards abolishing the death penalty.

Plans were initiated to begin a constitutional reform process and to reform other repressive laws implemented under the previous President.

Bills on the Constitutional Review Commission and Human Rights Commission were passed by the National Assembly on 13 December.

POLITICAL PRISONERS

Between December 2016 and January 2017, dozens of political prisoners and prisoners of conscience were released, including prisoners of conscience Amadou Sanneh and Ousainou Darboe. On 30 January, President Barrow pardoned Ousainou Darboe and dozens of others arrested for taking part in a peaceful protest in April 2016.

DETENTION

Prison conditions did not meet international standards due to inadequate sanitation, food and access to medical care. In February, 174 prisoners were released to commemorate independence celebrations and a further 84 were released in March in order to reduce prison overcrowding. Legal aid provision was limited, especially outside of the capital, Banjul. New judges were appointed, in order to address the need for a more independent judiciary.

FREEDOM OF EXPRESSION

The government committed to reforming several repressive media laws. A number of journalists returned to the country, having fled into exile due to harassment or threat of imprisonment under the previous government.

On 19 February, a woman was arrested and detained for breach of the peace after she allegedly insulted President Barrow. She was granted bail on 2 March, and the case was dismissed by the Brikama Magistrates Court on 3 April.

In November, at a symposium marking the International Day to End Impunity for Crimes against Journalists, the government announced that it would comply with judgments by the ECOWAS Community Court of Justice on state involvement in human rights violations against three journalists – Deyda Hydara, Chief Ebrima Manneh and Musa Saidykhan. This would include negotiating compensation payments with victims' families.

FREEDOM OF ASSEMBLY

Restrictive laws on freedom of peaceful assembly had not yet been amended. On 23 November, Gambia's Supreme Court ruled that Section 5 of the Public Order Act 1961, requiring police permission for peaceful assembly, did not violate the Constitution.

On 2 June, one person died and at least six were injured when the ECOWAS coalition force fired live ammunition to disperse demonstrators near Yahya Jammeh's former residence in the village of Kanilai. The government committed to holding an investigation, but no information had been made public by the end of the year.

The Occupy Westfield movement was initially authorized to peacefully protest against electricity and water shortages, but permission was denied on 11 November. The protest was dispersed on 12 November by riot police.

POLICE AND SECURITY FORCES

In February the National Intelligence Agency (NIA), which practised torture and arbitrary detention under the previous government, was renamed the State Intelligence Services and its powers of detention ended through a government policy decision. However, the changes were not supported by new legislation. During the following months, the heads of the police, prison, intelligence agency and military were replaced. However, there had not been systemic reform of these institutions, or any vetting of people who had committed serious human rights abuses. Civil society groups expressed concern that the government had not taken steps to preserve documentary and physical evidence of abuses by the security forces, particularly the NIA.

In July, 12 soldiers were arrested on allegations connected to "mutinous and seditious" posts on social media in support of former President Jammeh. They were held without charge in military detention until being brought to court on 17 November, in violation of detention time limits set in the Constitution. On 27 November, 10 were charged with treason and mutiny and two with negligent interference of lawful custody.

TRANSITIONAL JUSTICE

Ten soldiers were arrested and detained in January, accused of involvement in enforced disappearances and killings, but were not charged and remained in detention at the end of the year.

In February, criminal proceedings began against nine NIA officers, including the former director, accused of murdering opposition activist Solo Sandeng in April 2016.

In October, victims of human rights abuses, civil society organizations and international human rights groups formed a coalition to campaign for Yahya Jammeh and others who committed serious human rights abuses during his rule to be brought to justice.

Ousmane Sonko, Minister of Interior from 2006 until he fled the country in September 2016, faced investigation in Switzerland for crimes against humanity committed during President Jammeh's rule.

On 13 December, the Truth, Reconciliation and Reparation Commission (TRRC) bill to examine events during President Jammeh's rule, was passed by the National Assembly, following consultation on the bill with national and international actors.

On 10 August, a Commission of Inquiry was set up to investigate Yahya Jammeh's alleged mismanagement of public finances and abuse of office. The government also froze assets believed to belong to him.

A Panel on Missing Persons, a specialized police unit investigating enforced disappearances during President Jammeh's rule, was created in February. In March, the bodies of four people, possible victims of enforced disappearance, were exhumed, including that of Solo Sandeng. It is expected to submit the list of missing people to be investigated by the TRRC.

RIGHTS OF LESBIAN, GAY, BISEXUAL, TRANSGENDER AND INTERSEX PEOPLE

Same-sex relations remained criminalized. A law approved in October 2014, for example, imposed sentences of up to life imprisonment for "aggravated homosexuality" offences. LGBTI people continued to suffer discrimination and threats from non-state actors.

SEXUAL AND REPRODUCTIVE RIGHTS

In November, the government and development partners launched the Comprehensive Sexuality Education programme to be delivered in schools.

Despite laws criminalizing female genital mutilation (FGM), it remained widespread. The government and development partners developed a communication strategy to further educate communities about the harms of FGM.

Abortion remained a criminal offence, except in cases where the pregnant woman's life was at risk.

1. Gambia: Adama Barrow must not forget his big promises (News story, 19 January); Gambia: State of Emergency no licence for repression (News story, 18 January)

2. Gambia: Response to the departure of Yahya Jammeh (News story, 22 January)

3. Gambia: Progress in first 100 days of Barrow government requires major reform to break with brutal past (News story, 27 April)

GEORGIA

Georgia
Head of state: **Giorgi Margvelashvili**
Head of government: **Giorgi Kvirikashvili**

Continued impunity for human rights abuses committed by law enforcement officials emphasized the need for an independent investigation mechanism. A legal dispute over a pro-opposition TV channel caused concern about judicial independence and media freedom. The fencing of the de facto border around the breakaway regions of Abkhazia and South Ossetia continued to have a negative impact on local residents' economic and social rights.

BACKGROUND

The Parliament – under the majority ruling party Georgian Dream – adopted a new Constitution in October. It deferred until 2024 the introduction of a fully proportional electoral system, which the opposition had long been seeking, and ensured that from 2024 mandates won by political parties that fail to reach the election threshold are assigned to the winning party. Under the new rules, electoral blocs will no longer be allowed from 2020, and the president will no longer be elected by direct popular vote after 2018.

In December, Parliament started the process of changing the Constitution again to accommodate some of the opposition's demands which were excluded from the new Constitution.

Far-right movements organized xenophobic and homophobic marches in the capital Tbilisi.

The national currency, Lari, continued to devalue, adversely affecting living standards.

In February, Georgian nationals were granted visa-free travel to the Schengen Area after the government implemented several key institutional and legislative reforms demanded as a precondition by the EU.

IMPUNITY

Impunity for human rights abuses committed by law enforcement officers persisted, while the government continued to promise, but failed to deliver, an independent investigation mechanism. In June, instead of an independent investigation mechanism, the government proposed a new department within the Prosecutor's Office with a mandate to investigate alleged abuses by law enforcement officers.

In June, two members of the rap group Birja Mafia were arrested for alleged drug possession, and demonstrations erupted in their support. The arrested musicians said police had planted drugs on them in revenge for a YouTube video satirizing a police officer, and cited earlier threats from police demanding that they remove the video. The protests resulted in their release on bail pending trial. An investigation was launched into the musicians' allegations of police abuse and was ongoing at the end of the year.

In June, the first instance court in Kutaisi acquitted the police officer charged with "exceeding official capacity". The alleged victim, Demur Sturua, a 22-year-old resident of Dapnari, western Georgia, committed suicide on 8 August 2016. The prosecution's evidence included Demur Sturua's note blaming the police officer for his suicide, a postmortem examination confirming signs of ill-treatment, video footage showing the officer picking up Demur Sturua with his car on the day of the suicide, and phone call logs. NGOs criticized the court's decision, calling it unsubstantiated in light of the evidence. The prosecution appealed against the Court's decision.

LACK OF ACCOUNTABILITY

On 29 May, Azerbaijani investigative journalist Afghan Mukhtarli – who was exiled in Georgia – vanished from Tbilisi, and reappeared the following day in Azerbaijan in official custody, falsely accused of illegal border crossing and money smuggling. He told his lawyer that he had been abducted by Georgian-speaking men, some wearing Georgian criminal police uniforms, and trafficked across the border. The authorities denied the involvement of Georgian forces, and started an investigation into Afghan Mukhtarli's allegations. The investigation was not known to have produced substantial results; he remained in detention in Azerbaijan at the end of the year.

JUSTICE SYSTEM

The litigation over the ownership of Rustavi 2 Broadcasting Company, a pro-opposition TV channel, continued. On 2 March, the Supreme Court ruled to transfer the ownership of Rustavi 2 TV to its former co-owners – known to be government supporters – upholding previous rulings by the court of first instance and the Court of Appeals. Local NGOs raised concerns about possible government interference in the judicial process and called the trial unfair. In March, the European Court of Human Rights requested that enforcement of the Supreme Court's decision be suspended until it had considered the case.

FREEDOM OF MOVEMENT

Russian forces and de facto authorities in the breakaway regions of Abkhazia and South Ossetia continued to restrict movement across the de facto border, briefly detaining and fining dozens of people for "illegal" border crossing. The increased fencing along the administrative boundary lines continued to adversely affect the rights of local residents, including the rights to work, food and an adequate standard of living, owing to the loss of access to their orchards, pasture and farm land.

RIGHTS OF LESBIAN, GAY, BISEXUAL, TRANSGENDER AND INTERSEX PEOPLE

The new Constitution restricted the definition of marriage from "a voluntary union based on equality between the spouses" to "a union between a man and a woman". Same-sex couples were not legally recognized.

On 25 August, police arrested two LGBTI activists after a violent incident at a nightclub in Batumi, the second largest city. The activists questioned why they, the targets of violence, were arrested and charged with "disorderly conduct" and not their assailants, and complained of beating and verbal abuse by police. An investigation was opened into their complaint and was ongoing at the end of the year.

REFUGEES AND ASYLUM-SEEKERS

On 24 May, Mustafa Çabuk – a Turkish national resident in Georgia since 2002 – was detained under an extradition request from Turkey which claimed that he was "supporting terrorism" and had links with the Fethullah Gülen movement. Mustafa Çabuk was at real risk of torture and other ill-treatment if returned to Turkey. His application for refugee status in Georgia was rejected. Appeals were made against the decision; Mustafa Çabuk continued to be held in pre-extradition detention at the end of the year.

WORKERS' RIGHTS

Throughout the year, more than a dozen cases of fatal occupational accidents were reported, particularly among miners and construction workers. The need for stricter regulations and their effective monitoring by an independent labour standards regulatory authority remained.

GERMANY

Federal Republic of Germany
Head of state: **Frank-Walter Steinmeier (replaced Joachim Gauck in March)**
Head of government: **Angela Merkel**

Parliament passed a law granting same-sex couples the right to marry. The authorities continued to deport to Afghanistan asylum-seekers whose applications had failed despite the worsening security situation in the country. The federal Parliament extended police powers to conduct surveillance measures and to impose administrative measures on individuals identified as "potential attackers".

INTERNATIONAL JUSTICE

In March, September and November, 22 Syrian nationals residing in Germany submitted four criminal complaints to the office of the Federal Prosecutor General against 27 Syrian officials working for the military police and different intelligence services for their alleged involvement in torture as a war crime and a crime against humanity. The alleged crimes were committed in Saydnaya and other military prisons and in prisons of the Air Force Intelligence in Damascus and other places in Syria. In May, the Federal Prosecutor General carried out hearings with Syrian witnesses. Investigations were ongoing at the end of the year.

COUNTER-TERROR AND SECURITY

In April, the federal Parliament passed an amendment that expanded the control powers of the Federal Criminal Police to impose administrative measures for "potential attackers", such as electronic ankle tagging, assigned residency and telecommunication surveillance. These "potential attackers" were vaguely defined as "individuals who could be involved in committing a terrorism-related offence in the future".

In May, the federal Parliament passed a law that facilitated the detention of people representing a "significant security threat" to society, pending their deportation. The law also granted the Federal Office for Migration and Refugees the power to seize the electronic devices of asylum-seekers who do not possess identity documents.

In July, the state of Bavaria increased the period of administrative police detention without charge for "potential attackers" from 14 days to up to three months.

RIGHT TO PRIVACY

In June, the federal Parliament passed a law granting police authorities the power to use new surveillance techniques, including by installing surveillance software on computers and phones.

Also in June, a Higher Administrative Court ruled in an urgent procedure that the indiscriminate retention of data prescribed by a law that was due to enter into full force in July, was not in compliance with EU law. The law was not enforced pending the final ruling.

Also in June, a parliamentary committee of inquiry – established in 2013 following Edward Snowden's revelations regarding the USA's surveillance of its allies, including Germany – concluded that the Federal Intelligence Service had resorted to an overly broad interpretation of surveillance laws and had implemented surveillance measures, such as mass surveillance of foreign-to-foreign communications, without sufficient legal basis and oversight.

REFUGEES AND ASYLUM-SEEKERS

There were 222,683 asylum applications made, a drop by 70.1% compared to 2016, and the decisions on 68,245 claims were pending.

The right to family reunification for beneficiaries of subsidiary protection remained suspended throughout the year. This had a particularly negative impact on Syrian refugees who were increasingly granted subsidiary protection instead of full refugee status, providing them with fewer rights.

Despite the worsening security situation in Afghanistan, authorities continued to forcibly return Afghan nationals whose asylum claims had been rejected, in violation of the principle of *non-refoulement*. By the end of the year, 121 Afghan nationals had been forcibly returned.

In March, the Federal Council rejected a draft law from the government that sought to classify Algeria, Morocco and Tunisia as "safe" countries of origin and to establish a fast-track procedure to determine the refugee status of applicants from those countries.

Germany had relocated around 9,100 asylum-seekers who had arrived via Italy and Greece by the end of December. Germany also resettled almost 280 refugees from Egypt and Lebanon, and around 2,700 Syrian refugees from Turkey as part of the EU-Turkey deal.

DISCRIMINATION – HATE CRIMES

In June, the second Committee of Inquiry – established by Parliament in 2015 to address the authorities' failure to investigate the racist crimes perpetrated by the far-right group Nationalist Social Underground (NSU) between 2000 and 2007 – concluded that the authorities had to establish clear rules for infiltrating "far-right extremist" movements, provide long-term funding to civil society initiatives against racism and assist victims of racist crimes. The authorities continued to fail to launch an official investigation into the potential role of institutional racism behind Germany's failure to investigate the crimes committed by the NSU.

In the first nine months, the Interior Ministry reported 1,212 criminal offences against refugees and asylum-seekers, and 210 offences against asylum-seekers' accommodations. Federal and state authorities continued to fail to implement a comprehensive assessment strategy to identify the risks of attacks against asylum shelters, in order to provide adequate police protection if necessary.

In June, following a comprehensive consultation with civil society organizations, the federal government adopted a National

Action Plan against racism and other forms of discrimination, including homophobia and transphobia.

TORTURE AND OTHER ILL-TREATMENT
Authorities at both the federal and the state levels continued to fail to establish any independent complaints mechanism to investigate ill-treatment by police.

Civil society organizations continued to report discriminatory identity checks by police on members of ethnic and religious minorities.

In November, the central investigation unit in Hamburg was investigating complaints filed against 109 police officers for the alleged unlawful use of force during protests against the G20 summit in Hamburg in July.

In eight federal states, police officers remained under no legal obligation to wear identification badges. In October, the newly elected Parliament in North-Rhine Westphalia repealed the recently introduced requirement for law enforcement officials in the federal state to wear identification badges.

In October, prosecutorial authorities closed the new investigations opened in May into the death in custody of Oury Jalloh, a Sierra Leonean national who died in a fire in a cell of a police station in Dessau in 2005. In November, media reports revealed that months before the investigations were closed, fire experts meeting in February had unanimously excluded the possibility of Oury Jalloh setting fire to himself. In December, the Minister of Justice of Saxony-Anhalt newly assigned the investigations to the Prosecutor General of Naumburg.

ARMS TRADE
The selective post-shipment control system to improve the monitoring of German small arms exports to ensure compliance with end-use certificates entered its pilot phase. In May, a first control mission on the whereabouts of exported sniper rifles in India was conducted in agreement with the Indian authorities.

The federal government continued to license the export of arms and other related military equipment to countries, such as India and Turkey, where there was a risk that such arms could be used to commit or facilitate serious human rights violations.

CORPORATE ACCOUNTABILITY
In March, Parliament passed a law implementing the 2014 EU Directive on non-financial reporting, which required certain large companies to report on the human rights impacts of their global operations. However, the law was more limited than the Directive, requiring companies to report only on risks that were "very likely to cause severe negative consequences" on human rights and only to the extent necessary for an understanding of their business operations.

There continued to be a lack of a binding mechanism requiring business enterprises to exercise due diligence to ensure that they respect human rights throughout their operations and supply chain. Access to the justice system for victims of human rights abuses by or involving business enterprises remained burdensome.

RIGHTS OF LESBIAN, GAY, BISEXUAL, TRANSGENDER AND INTERSEX PEOPLE
In July, the federal Parliament passed a law granting same-sex couples the right to marry and to access adoption.

Children and adults with variations of sex characteristics continued to suffer human rights violations. Invasive and irreversible medical procedures carried out on children with variations of sex characteristics continued and had lifelong harmful effects. Guidelines drawn up by intersex activists and medical professionals for treatment of individuals with variations of sex characteristics had not been widely implemented.

In November, the Federal Constitutional Court ruled that individuals should be allowed to choose a legal gender other than male and female by the end of 2018.

GHANA

Republic of Ghana
Head of state and government: **Nana Addo Dankwa Akufo-Addo (replaced John Dramani Mahama in January)**

Concerns were raised around unfair trials and poor prison conditions for people on death row, as well as the shackling of people with psychosocial disabilities. LGBTI people continued to face discrimination, violence and police harassment.

BACKGROUND

Nana Addo Dankwa Akufo-Addo of the New Patriotic Party was inaugurated as President in January, following presidential and parliamentary elections in December 2016.

LEGAL, CONSTITUTIONAL OR INSTITUTIONAL DEVELOPMENTS

In July, Ghana signed the AU Convention on Cyber Security and Personal Data Protection, and the Protocol to the African Charter on Human and Peoples' Rights on the Rights of Older Persons in Africa.

WORKERS' RIGHTS

On 23 March, Ghana ratified the UN Minamata Convention on Mercury, which aims to protect workers from toxic liquid metal by reducing mercury use in artisanal and small-scale gold mining and protecting children from exposure. About 1 million people were working in Ghana's gold mines, and nearby communities were often directly exposed to mercury. In April, the government began a campaign to end illegal small-scale gold mining (known as "galamsey"), the negative impacts of which include increased crime, lost revenues and environmental damage as well as encouraging hazardous child labour. The government launched a five-year project to provide illegal miners with alternative livelihoods in the legal mining sector. More than 300 people were arrested on suspicion of illegal gold mining; one person was shot dead by police during the arrests. No official report concerning the death had been released by the end of the year.

CHILDREN'S RIGHTS

In May the Minister for Gender, Children and Social Protection launched a strategy for 2017-2026 to address the issue of child marriage. Some regions were disproportionately affected by child marriage; 34% of girls in northern Ghana were married before the age of 18. The strategy included accelerating access to quality education and sexual and reproductive health information and services, as well as enforcing the existing legal and policy frameworks in relation to child marriage.

DEATH PENALTY

Scores of people on death row, including six officially considered to have mental and intellectual disabilities, faced poor prison conditions. Inmates experienced overcrowding and lack of access to health care and educational and recreational facilities.

Many death row inmates reported that they had not received adequate legal representation at their trials. Fewer than one in four death row inmates interviewed by Amnesty International had been able to appeal against their conviction or sentence. Few inmates interviewed were aware of how to appeal or access legal aid, while most were unable to pay for private lawyers. The Ghana Prison Service reported that only 12 death row inmates had filed appeals since 2006 – half of which were successful.[1] Proposals made by the Constitutional Review Implementation Committee to abolish the death penalty continued to be stalled as a result of delays in the constitutional review process.

JUSTICE SYSTEM

Access to justice remained limited, especially for people from low income or marginalized backgrounds. The Ghana Legal Aid Scheme suffered from funding shortages; just 23 lawyers offering legal aid were available to the country's population of more than 28 million people.

RIGHT TO HEALTH

Shackling of people with psychosocial disabilities remained common, particularly in private "prayer camps" across the country. The practice involved restraining a person using chains or ropes and locking them in a confined space such as a room, shed or cage. In June the Mental Health Authority of Ghana released 16 people, including two girls, held in shackles at Nyakumasi Prayer Camp, a "spiritual healing centre" in the Central Region. Those freed, some of whom had mental health conditions, were taken to nearby Ankaful Psychiatric Hospital. A coalition of civil society organizations called on the government to adopt and enforce a ban on shackling and to invest in appropriate community-based services to support people with mental health conditions. They also called on the government to fully implement the Mental Health Act 2012, which, among other things, required the establishment of regional mental health committees responsible for monitoring mental health facilities across the country. Funding for mental health services remained lacking.

RIGHTS OF LESBIAN, GAY, BISEXUAL, TRANSGENDER AND INTERSEX PEOPLE

Consensual same-sex sexual relations between men remained a criminal offence. LGBTI people continued to face discrimination, violence and police harassment as well as extortion attempts by members of the public. In February the Speaker of Parliament stated in the media that the Constitution should be amended to make homosexuality completely illegal and punishable by law. In July he also stated in the media that Ghana would not decriminalize homosexuality as this could lead to bestiality and incest becoming legalized.

1. Locked up and forgotten: The need to abolish the death penalty in Ghana (ACT 50/6268/2017)

GREECE

Hellenic Republic
Head of state: **Prokopis Pavlopoulos**
Head of government: **Alexis Tsipras**

Thousands of asylum-seekers and migrants remained trapped on the Greek islands in appalling conditions. The European Court of Human Rights found that Greece failed to prevent human trafficking in the case of 42 migrant workers from Bangladesh. New legislation reforming legal recognition of gender identity was adopted.

BACKGROUND

Unemployment rates dropped but remained high, particularly for the 15-24 age group. In July, the unemployment rate was 20.5% and youth unemployment was at 39.5%. Also in July, Greece returned to the international bond market after a three-year hiatus.

According to the 2017 Gender Equality Index, Greece ranked last among EU states in terms of overall gender equality. In November, the Ministry of Justice presented a bill on the ratification of the Council of Europe Convention on Preventing and Combating Violence against Women and Domestic Violence.

REFUGEES' AND MIGRANTS' RIGHTS

Nearly 47,000 asylum-seekers remained trapped in Greece due to the closure of the Balkans migration route and the implementation of the EU-Turkey deal in March 2016. By the end of the year, 29,716 people had arrived by sea from Turkey in comparison with 173,450 in 2016. However, Greece continued to be one of the main entry points for refugees and migrants into Europe.
THE EU-TURKEY MIGRATION DEAL
The expectation that everyone arriving irregularly on the Greek islands, including asylum-seekers, would be returned to Turkey under the EU-Turkey deal of March 2016

continued to condemn many to extended asylum procedures while being stranded in appalling reception conditions on the islands.

In September, the Greek Council of State, the highest administrative court in the country, rejected the final appeals of two Syrian refugees, against previous decisions declaring their asylum claims inadmissible on the basis that Turkey was a safe third country. This decision could result in the first forcible returns of Syrian asylum-seekers under the EU-Turkey deal.

By the end of the year, 684 individuals were returned to Turkey from the Greek islands (1,485 in total since the EU-Turkey deal became effective). Out of those, five were Syrian nationals in detention who did not challenge their return after their claims were found inadmissible at second instance.

In October, NGOs, including Amnesty International, documented instances in which Syrian asylum-seekers were automatically detained upon arrival as the authorities expected them to be shortly returned to Turkey, under the EU-Turkey deal.

Greek authorities discriminated against asylum-seekers of certain nationalities. Due to the EU-Turkey deal, many of those with nationalities of countries prejudged to be producing "economic migrants" rather than "refugees" were automatically detained and expected to be returned to Turkey.

EU RELOCATION SCHEME

The EU relocation scheme continued to be one of very few formal options available, for those eligible, to safely leave Greece and move elsewhere in Europe. However, asylum-seekers who arrived in Greece since the EU-Turkey deal came into effect, were arbitrarily excluded from the scheme. A total of 21,703 asylum-seekers had been relocated from Greece to other European countries, out of the 66,400 that were foreseen to be relocated under the scheme.

RECEPTION CONDITIONS

Security continued to be a main concern in many of the remaining refugee camps, in particular in overcrowded "hotspots" on the islands.

In June, the three refugee camps in the Elliniko area in the capital Athens – which housed around 1,000 refugees and migrants, including many children – were evacuated. The majority of refugees and migrants were transferred to alternative camps. The conditions in the Elliniko camps, which occupied two former Olympic sites and the arrivals terminal of an unused airport, had been appalling and unsafe. NGOs had raised serious concern regarding security in Elliniko, especially for women and girls. Many women reported verbal harassment and being at risk of sexual and gender-based violence.

In January, three men died within one week in Moria camp on the island of Lesvos. Their deaths were suspected to be linked to carbon monoxide poisoning from makeshift heaters used to heat their tents. By the end of the year, the investigation into the deaths had not been concluded.

Following these deaths, the Greek authorities transferred thousands of vulnerable asylum-seekers from the islands to the mainland. However, in August, rising numbers of people arrived on the islands and reception facilities returned to being overcrowded. The authorities had not been able to provide reception conditions on the islands that met minimum standards under EU law by the end of the year.

The use of urban accommodation for asylum-seekers, largely flats, increased. By the end of the year, there were around 18,000 asylum-seekers and refugees staying in flats and other urban accommodation rather than in camps. The majority of those living in the urban accommodation were in mainland Greece; there were fewer than 1,000 asylum-seekers living in flats on the islands.

UNACCOMPANIED CHILDREN

In September, the Council of Europe Committee for the Prevention of Torture criticized the continued and routine detention of unaccompanied migrant and refugee children. As of 15 December, there were 2,256 unaccompanied children waiting to be placed in shelters, including 74 detained in police stations.

FORCED LABOUR AND SLAVERY

In March, in *Chowdury and Others v. Greece,* in a landmark judgment, the European Court of Human Rights found that 42 migrant workers from Bangladesh had been subjected to forced labour and human trafficking while working at a strawberry farm in the village of Manolada. The Court also found that Greece had failed to prevent human trafficking and to conduct an effective investigation into the offences committed.

CONSCIENTIOUS OBJECTORS

Conscientious objectors continued to be arrested, repeatedly prosecuted, tried in military courts and fined. In June, a 53-year-old conscientious objector who was prosecuted for having refused to enlist in 1990, was tried in a military court, but was acquitted.

According to the 2016 submissions of the Greek National Commission for Human Rights and the European Bureau for Conscientious Objection, the duration of alternative civilian service for certain categories of conscientious objectors was still not conforming with the European Social Charter. In July, the European Committee of Social Rights asked Greece to provide further information.

TORTURE AND OTHER ILL-TREATMENT

Allegations of ill-treatment and excessive use of force by law enforcement officials persisted. The majority of victims of the reported incidents were refugees and migrants trapped on the Aegean islands as a result of the EU-Turkey deal.

There were allegations that police used excessive force against asylum-seekers during an operation to arrest protesters who were clashing with the police in the Moria camp, on Lesvos, on 18 July. Police also allegedly ill-treated some of those arrested and detained in the island's main police station following the clashes. In July, a local prosecutor ordered a criminal investigation into the allegations. The investigation was ongoing at the end of the year.

RACISM

Numerous hate-motivated attacks were reported during the year. Between August 2016 and the end of 2017, over 50 attacks reportedly took place in the town of Aspropyrgos where groups of young locals attacked migrant workers from Pakistan. In June, representatives of national NGOs filed a complaint and authorities launched a criminal investigation. In October, police arrested three young men suspected of being linked to one of the violent attacks.

Sixty-nine individuals linked to the far-right party Golden Dawn, including the party's leader and MPs, were put on trial in 2015 for the murder of anti-fascist singer Pavlos Fyssas in 2013 and for participation in a criminal organization. In October, the Athens Court of Appeal completed hearing evidence from all prosecution witnesses called to testify in the trial.

RIGHTS OF LESBIAN, GAY, BISEXUAL, TRANSGENDER AND INTERSEX PEOPLE

Refugees and migrants stranded on the Aegean islands were also subjected to hate-motivated crimes. Some of the victims were transgender women and gay men.

In October, amid transphobic reactions inside and outside Parliament, the government passed a new law reforming legal recognition of gender identity. Law 4491/2017 expressly stated that transgender people could change their identity documents without the requirements of medical interventions, tests and psychiatric assessments. However, the new legislation also contained several flaws, including a single status requirement and the validation of gender recognition by a local court. While the procedure was open to individuals above the age of 15, blanket age restrictions remained and 15- to 16-year-old children seeking legal gender recognition faced the additional barrier of a psycho-medical assessment.

FREEDOM OF ASSOCIATION

In October, Parliament adopted a legislative amendment seeking to implement three

European Court of Human Rights judgments. The judgments were regarding the violation of the right to freedom of association in relation to the authorities' refusal to register associations of Greece's national minorities in 2007, 2008 and 2015. The new provision amended the Code of Civil Procedure to allow the possibility of reopening proceedings in these cases. However, the NGO Greek Helsinki Monitor expressed concern over the limitations placed by the law in relation to the reopening of such proceedings, including on grounds of national security and public order.

GUATEMALA

Republic of Guatemala
Head of state and government: **Jimmy Morales Cabrera**

Thousands continued to flee the country to escape high levels of inequality and violence. Human rights defenders, in particular those working on land, territorial and environmental issues, were at great risk and faced smear campaigns. Impunity and corruption persisted, undermining public trust in local authorities and hindering access to justice. Recent progress to consolidate the criminal justice system and the rule of law was challenged. High-profile cases of past crimes under international law remained stalled.

LEGAL, CONSTITUTIONAL OR INSTITUTIONAL DEVELOPMENTS

In August, Augusto Jordan Rodas took up office as Ombudsperson for Human Rights. In November, the last criminal provisions referring to the death penalty were declared unconstitutional.

TRANSITIONAL JUSTICE

Despite progress in the prosecution of some crimes against humanity committed during the internal armed conflict (1960-1996), efforts towards truth, justice and reparations remained halted, and the vast majority of cases continued to suffer setbacks and undue delays. Five former members of the military, including the former head of the High Command of the Guatemalan Army, were sent to trial charged with crimes against humanity and rape against Emma Guadalupe Molina Theissen, and the enforced disappearance of her younger brother, Marco Antonio Molina Theissen.

Criminal proceedings remained stalled against former members of the military on charges related to multiple cases of enforced disappearances and unlawful killings carried out in a military base, now known as Creompaz, in the northern Alta Verapaz region. Appeals filed against decisions affecting the victims' rights were pending and several officers remained at large. In both cases, victims and human rights defenders were intimidated and harassed inside or outside the court and online. After several failed attempts since 2015, the trials of former military head of state José Efraín Ríos Montt and former intelligence chief Rodríguez Sánchez resumed in October.

IMPUNITY

Judges and prosecutors continued to face intimidation and pressure. Efforts to fight impunity were at great risk of setbacks due to increased resistance from certain political actors. A constitutional reform introduced in Congress in November 2016, aimed at consolidating efforts towards justice and accountability and strengthening the independence of the judiciary, had not been approved at the end of the year. Mass protests took place in August and September and the country faced a political crisis when several members of the government resigned in September, in reaction to President Morales' attempt to expel the head of the International Commission against Impunity in Guatemala (an independent body established by the UN and the Guatemalan government in 2006 to strengthen the rule of law post-conflict).

HUMAN RIGHTS DEFENDERS

Human rights defenders faced continuous threats, stigmatization, intimidation and attacks.

The Guatemalan NGO Unit for the Protection of Human Rights Defenders in Guatemala said that defenders working on rights related to land, territory and the environment faced the highest number of attacks. In January, Sebastián Alonso Juan was killed during a peaceful protest against the construction of hydroelectric projects in the Ixquisis region of San Mateo Ixtatán.

In addition, human rights defenders were constantly subjected to smear campaigns to stigmatize and discredit them and their work in an attempt to force them to stop their legitimate activities. From the end of June, members of the Centre for Environmental, Social and Legal Action were targeted with smear campaigns after they challenged the licence of Minera San Rafael mining company in San Rafael Las Flores. The justice system was regularly misused to target and harass human rights defenders in an attempt to break up movements and organizations, and silence human rights defenders.

A General Instruction by the Public Prosecutor's Office containing guidelines to effectively investigate attacks against human rights defenders was under review pending its approval for several months. Despite some progress, the process to create, in consultation with civil society, a comprehensive public policy for the protection of human rights defenders had not concluded by the end of the year.

LAND DISPUTES

In September the Supreme Court recognized the lack of prior consultation with the Xinca Indigenous People of Santa Rosa and Jalapa, who had been negatively affected by the activities of the mine of San Rafael Las Flores. The Court ordered the Ministry of Energy and Mines to carry out a consultation, but it also allowed the company to continue mining operations. As a result, an appeal was filed before the Constitutional Court, which remained pending.

In September the Inter-American Commission on Human Rights ordered Guatemala to protect the rights of around 400 people, including children and elderly people, who were stranded at the northern border with Mexico from early June in poor sanitary conditions. They had abandoned their community situated in Laguna Larga hours before a massive eviction was carried out. By the end of the year the authorities had not facilitated their return.

REFUGEES' AND MIGRANTS' RIGHTS

Thousands of Guatemalans migrated to the USA through Mexico in an effort to escape the high levels of inequality and violence affecting marginalized groups. UNHCR, the UN refugee agency, said that between January and October 18,764 Guatemalans sought asylum in other countries. Unaccompanied children from Guatemala comprised the biggest group of arrivals apprehended at the US border. Although large numbers of people continued to be forcibly returned to Guatemala, there was no comprehensive mechanism or protocol in place to address the needs of returnees who were sent back to the same conditions and danger that they had fled.

CHILDREN'S RIGHTS

In March, 41 girls died in a fire in the Virgen de la Asunción government-run shelter in San José Pinula municipality while locked inside a classroom. The deaths revealed the lack of sufficient and adequate measures to protect children's rights in Guatemala. A number of public officials were charged, but delays in the investigation were reported.

High levels of child pregnancy remained a particular concern. The Observatory on Sexual and Reproductive Health registered 69,445 births by girls and young women aged from 10 to 19 between January and September.

GUINEA

Republic of Guinea
Head of state: **Alpha Condé**
Head of government: **Mamady Youla**

The security forces continued to use excessive force against demonstrators. Journalists, human rights defenders and others expressing dissent were arbitrarily arrested. Impunity was widespread. The right to adequate housing was not fulfilled.

BACKGROUND

The postponement of local elections until February 2018, along with speculation about whether President Condé would run for a third term, led to social and political tensions.

FREEDOM OF ASSEMBLY

At least 18 people were killed and dozens were injured during demonstrations. In February, seven people were killed in the capital, Conakry, during protests connected to a strike over the authorities' decision to review teachers' terms and conditions, and to school closures. The security forces dispersed the demonstrators with tear gas, batons and live ammunition.

On 20 February, the police arrested seven human rights defenders of the Voice of the People movement who had organized a sit-in in Conakry calling for schools to reopen. They faced charges of "disturbing public order", later amended to "participating in an unlawful assembly", and were released the same evening. Three days after his release, national television journalist Hassan Sylla – one of the seven – was suspended from his job for six months for gross misconduct; no explanation was given.

Security forces used live ammunition during violent protests against poor living standards in the Boké region in April, May and September. At least four people died from gunshot wounds.

On 22 August, former soldier and trade unionist Jean Dougou Guilavogui was arrested by gendarmes in Matoto, a Conakry neighbourhood, and taken to a gendarmerie detention centre. He was charged with "participating in an unlawful assembly" and was detained without trial at the Maison centrale, Conakry's main prison, until his release on bail on 21 December.

FREEDOM OF EXPRESSION

Journalists, human rights defenders and others expressing dissent were beaten and arbitrarily detained. At least 20 people were arrested solely for exercising their right to freedom of expression and 20 others were subjected to police violence.

In February, Radio Lynx FM reporter Mariam Kouyaté was arrested by security agents as she investigated health services at the Ignace Deen Hospital in Conakry. She was questioned at a police station after refusing to hand over her press badge and recording equipment, and released the same day without charge. In May, Gangan TV journalist Aboubacar Camara was beaten by gendarmes as he filmed a land dispute in a Conakry suburb where he believed the security forces were using excessive force. The officers forced him into their car, took him to the gendarmerie and released him later the same day after deleting his recordings.

In June, the High Authority of Communication suspended Espace FM radio presenter Mohamed Mara for one month on grounds that he had used "insulting" language during a radio debate on polygamy. In November, the Authority ordered that the radio station be taken off air for one week after the station discussed under-resourcing in the army which the authorities claimed could undermine national security and morale among the armed forces. In July, National Television suspended Alia Camara, one of their journalists, for criticizing the low pass rate in baccalaureate examinations.

On 27 June, gendarmes arrested guinéematin.com journalist Amadou Sadio Diallo in Lélouma for "disturbing public order" after he published what the authorities described as "false news" about a possible cholera outbreak. He was released the following day.

On 30 October, four Gangan TV journalists were arrested by gendarmes in Matam, a neighbourhood of Conakry, and charged with publishing false information and offending the head of state by spreading rumours of President Condé's death. Three of them were released hours later and one was released the following day. At least 18 journalists who gathered in solidarity with the arrested journalists at the Matam gendarmerie were beaten and had their equipment broken by security forces.

LEGAL DEVELOPMENTS

In June, the National Assembly adopted a new Military Code of Justice, which if promulgated would effectively abolish the death penalty. The Code also contained provisions that could undermine the rights to fair trial and justice, including by allowing the trials of civilians before military courts.

IMPUNITY

In February, an Anti-Crime Brigade captain in Kipé, a neighbourhood of Conakry, was arrested and charged with torturing a man in police custody in March 2016. At least 10 other gendarmerie and police officers were suspended over the incident, but were not brought to justice.

There was progress in the trial proceedings relating to the killing of over 150 peaceful demonstrators and the rape of at least 100 women in the Conakry Stadium in 2009. In March, Aboubacar Sidiki Diakité was extradited to Guinea from Senegal after being at large for several years, and faced charges in connection with the Stadium event. He was the former aide to Moussa Dadis Camara (leader of the military junta in 2009). Several people charged in connection with the killings and rapes retained influential positions, including Mathurin Bangoura, Moussa Tiégboro Camara and Claude Pivi who were senior officials in the military junta at the time. In November, the investigating judges announced that the judicial investigation had been completed; however,

none of the suspected perpetrators had been brought to trial by the end of the year.

In September, a group of victims filed a lawsuit against Sékouba Konaté, who served as Minister of Defence in 2009, as well as transitional President between 2009 and 2010.[1]

There was no progress in the judicial proceedings against security force members for the human rights violations committed during demonstrations in Conakry between 2011 and 2017, in Zogota in 2012 and during the occupation by the security forces of the village of Womey in 2014.

RIGHT TO HOUSING

In August, at least 10 people, including two children, were killed in a landslide at a rubbish dump site at Dar-Es-Salam, a neighbourhood of Conakry. In September, the government spokesperson acknowledged a failure in the sanitation services. The National Director of Humanitarian Actions at the Ministry of Territorial Administration said that the remaining inhabitants should be evicted immediately.

---

1. Guinea: 8 years later, justice for massacre needed (Press release, 27 September)

HAITI

Republic of Haiti
Head of state: **Jovenel Moïse (replaced Jocelerme Privert in February)**
Head of government: **Jack Guy Lafontant (replaced Enex Jean-Charles in March)**

Violence against women and girls, particularly sexual violence, continued. Legislators sought to approve openly discriminatory laws against LGBTI people.

BACKGROUND

In February, Jovenel Moïse assumed the presidency after being elected in November 2016 following an electoral crisis; a new Prime Minister was appointed.

In March, prompted by the Haitian government, the mandate of the UN Independent Expert on the situation of human rights in Haiti ended.

In October, UN Security Council resolution 2350 ended the mandate of the UN Stabilization Mission in Haiti (MINUSTAH) after 13 years. Peacekeepers left following years of controversy over their alleged responsibility for the cholera outbreak of 2010, and numerous reports of sexual violence. It was replaced by the UN Mission for Justice Support in Haiti (MINUJUSTH), mandated to strengthen the rule of law.

The authorities took steps to re-establish the army which had been dissolved in 1995. It was unclear what vetting processes would be established to recruit soldiers following the widespread allegations of human rights violations committed by previous forces.

INTERNALLY DISPLACED PEOPLE

The International Organization for Migration reported that by June, 37,867 people were internally displaced because of the 2010 earthquake; most of them lived in makeshift camps.

DISCRIMINATION – STATELESS PERSONS

In March, Parliament voted to accede to the 1954 and 1961 UN Conventions on Statelessness, following recommendations made during Haiti's examination under the UN UPR process in 2016.[1] Haiti had not signed or ratified the Conventions by the end of 2017.

REFUGEES' AND MIGRANTS' RIGHTS

In July, the UN Office for the Coordination of Humanitarian Affairs (OCHA) reported an increase in deportation cases at the Dominican-Haitian border.

Despite a request in October from the Haitian government for a further extension, the US Department of Homeland Security announced, in November, its decision to terminate the temporary protected status (TPS) for nearly 60,000 Haitians at risk of deportation from the USA. TPS for Haitian nationals was due to expire in January 2018 with a delayed effective date of 18 months which, according to the Department, would "allow for an orderly transition before the designation terminates on 22 July, 2019". TPS is granted to nationals from particular countries on the grounds that they cannot return safely to their country due to conditions there.

RIGHT TO HEALTH – CHOLERA EPIDEMIC

Between January and June, there were 7,623 new cases of suspected cholera and 70 related deaths, a decrease of more than 60% in comparison with the same period in 2016. Since the 2010 outbreak, more than 800,000 people had been infected and nearly 10,000 had died, according to the authorities.

The UN's "new approach to cholera in Haiti", presented in 2016, was severely underfunded. There were no consultations with cholera survivors, as planned. Individual assistance was consequently suspended. Victims' advocates objected to this on the grounds that it was inconsistent with the right to remedy.

According to the government, almost 70% of the Haitian population did not have access to health services.

VIOLENCE AGAINST WOMEN AND GIRLS

Sexual violence and violence against women and girls was prevalent although under-reported.

In April, the government tabled comprehensive reforms of the Criminal Code in Parliament. It contained new provisions to tackle sexual violence, including criminalizing rape in marriage. In July, the NGO Doctors Without Borders found that 77% of survivors of sexual and gender-based violence who were treated in its specialized clinic in the capital, Port-au-Prince, between May 2015 and March 2017, were under the age of 25; 53% were under 18.

RIGHTS OF LESBIAN, GAY, BISEXUAL, TRANSGENDER AND INTERSEX PEOPLE

The Senate supported bills which discriminated against LGBTI people; they were pending approval by the Chamber of Deputies at the end of the year. In July, the Senate voted for certificates to be issued which would vouch for an individual's "good moral" standing and from which anyone deemed to be "homosexual" would be excluded. In August, it approved a law making same-sex marriage and public support or advocacy for "homosexuality" illegal.

HUMAN RIGHTS DEFENDERS

Human rights defenders David Boniface and Juders Ysemé reported fearing for their lives following the sudden death in March of their colleague Nissage Martyr. He died a day after the three men filed a lawsuit in the USA against Jean Morose Viliena – former Mayor of Les Irois, their hometown in Haiti – for grave human rights violations. Jean Morose Viliena had fled to the USA from Haiti in 2009. The men said that they had been subjected to repeated death threats and to violent attacks by or on behalf of the former Mayor since 2007. However, the authorities did not implement adequate protection measures, although the Inter-American Commission on Human Rights granted them precautionary measures to ensure their safety in 2015.[2]

Sanièce Petit Phat reported that she had received death threats because of her work in defence of the rights of women and girls.[3]

RIGHT TO EDUCATION

In June, the UN Economic and Social Council Ad Hoc Advisory Group on Haiti criticized inefficiency in the education sector. It noted that most schools were privately managed, "making education an expensive, profit-based system" too expensive for many Haitian families. Illiteracy among over-15s was over 50%.

1. Following political crisis Haiti must urgently advance human rights agenda (AMR 36/5899/2017)

2. Haiti: Human rights defenders' lives in danger (AMR 36/6045/2017)

3. Haiti: Women's rights defender threatened with death: Sanièce Petit Phat (AMR 36/7598/2017)

HONDURAS

Republic of Honduras
Head of state and government: **Juan Orlando Hernández Alvarado**

The level of insecurity and violence remained high. Widespread impunity continued to undermine public trust in the authorities and the justice system. Protests in the aftermath of the presidential election were brutally repressed by security forces. Honduras remained one of the most dangerous countries in the Americas region for human rights defenders, especially for those working to protect land, territory and the environment. The government announced the creation of a Ministry for Human Rights and Justice, to become operational in 2018.

EXCESSIVE USE OF FORCE

Mass protests, which began on 29 November around the country to denounce the lack of transparency around the presidential election, were brutally repressed by security forces. Hundreds of people were arrested or detained and a 10-day curfew was implemented in December. Security forces used excessive force against protesters, including with lethal weapons. At least 31 people were killed, and multiple cases of people being injured by firearms or brutally beaten by security forces were also reported, as well as cases that could amount to torture and other cruel, inhuman and degrading treatment.

HUMAN RIGHTS DEFENDERS

Human rights defenders, particularly environmental and land activists, continued to be at risk of human rights abuses. They were subjected to smear campaigns by both state and non-state actors to discredit their work, and were regularly targeted with intimidation, threats, and attacks. In June, three members of the Civic Council of Popular and Indigenous Organizations of Honduras (COPINH) were attacked by armed assailants while they were in a car, returning from a meeting. Local NGOs said that the justice system continued to be misused to harass and discourage human rights defenders. Unnecessary and excessive use of force by security forces during peaceful protests was also reported.

The vast majority of attacks registered against human rights defenders remained unpunished, as a result of multiple obstacles hindering investigations and trials. There was little progress in the investigation into the killing in March 2016 of Berta Cáceres, the Indigenous environmental defender and co-founder of COPINH. The public hearings of eight suspects detained in relation to the case were postponed on multiple occasions. Independent experts revealed a lack of due diligence in the investigations, including a lack of prosecution of other individuals potentially involved in the crime. There was no information about any progress made by the Public Prosecutor in identifying those responsible for planning her killing.

Although some progress was made to protect human rights defenders through the National Mechanism to Protect Human Rights Defenders, Journalists, Social Commentators and Justice Officials, efforts to ensure their comprehensive protection remained insufficient.

New provisions of the Criminal Code on terrorism and related criminal offences approved by Congress in February and September were defined in an overly broad and vague manner, contrary to the principle of legality. The provisions could lead to the arbitrary and inadequate application of the Code against peaceful protesters and human rights defenders, which could further criminalize their work and obstruct social movements.

INDIGENOUS PEOPLES' RIGHTS

Several Indigenous Peoples continued to claim that their rights to consultation and to free, prior and informed consent were violated in the context of projects to explore and exploit natural resources in their territories. Killings, aggressions and cases of misuse of the justice system against those defending Indigenous Peoples were reported.

The Draft Framework Law on Free, Prior and Informed Consultation of Indigenous Peoples faced criticism, including of the insufficient participation of Indigenous and Garifuna (Afro-descendant) communities in the process.

Reparation measures ordered in 2015 by the Inter-American Court of Human Rights in two cases where Honduras had violated the collective land rights of the Garifuna communities had yet to be implemented.

LAND DISPUTES

Conflicts persisted due to the lack of secure land tenure. High levels of violence were reported in the Aguán Valley where long-standing land disputes remained unresolved. According to the Unified Campesino Movement of the Aguán, precautionary measures granted by the Inter-American Commission on Human Rights to protect the life and integrity of leaders in the Aguán Valley were not adequately implemented.

GENDER-RELATED VIOLENCE

Women, girls and LGBTI people continued to face high levels of gender-related violence. Between January and October, 236 violent deaths of women were registered by the Centre for Women's Rights. According to the Lesbian Cattrachas Network, killings of LGBTI people also increased, with a total of 35 people killed. Impunity remained high in these cases, as authorities lacked sufficient capacity and resources to investigate, prosecute and punish those responsible.

SEXUAL AND REPRODUCTIVE RIGHTS

The failure to protect women's and girls' rights and guarantee access to safe and legal abortion in any circumstances continued.

Despite recommendations from international human rights bodies and mechanisms, in April Congress decided to maintain the prohibition of abortion in all circumstances in the new Criminal Code.

REFUGEES AND ASYLUM-SEEKERS

Widespread violence across Honduras remained a key factor of forced migration from the country. According to UNHCR, the UN refugee agency, between January and October, 14,735 Hondurans sought asylum worldwide, mostly in Mexico and the USA. However, large numbers of Hondurans also continued to be forcibly returned from these countries to the same life-threatening situations which initially pushed them to escape. To date, there was no comprehensive mechanism or protocol to detect and address in a systematic manner the protection needs of deportees.

HUNGARY

Hungary
Head of state: **János Áder**
Head of government: **Viktor Orbán**

The systematic crackdown on the rights of refugees and migrants continued. Foreign-funded universities and NGOs faced restrictions under new legislation.

BACKGROUND

The government faced domestic protests and increased international scrutiny for its continued rollback on human rights and non-compliance with EU law. The European Commission launched and moved forward with four formal infringement proceedings following the introduction of legislation deemed incompatible with EU freedoms, and in May the European Parliament adopted a comprehensive resolution expressing alarm at the situation of human rights in the country. More than a quarter of the population remained at risk of poverty and social exclusion and 16% were severely materially deprived.

REFUGEES AND ASYLUM-SEEKERS

Hungary continued to severely restrict access to the country for refugees and asylum-seekers, limiting admission to its two operational border "transit zones" in which only 10 new asylum applications could be submitted per working day. Consequently, between 6,000 and 8,000 people were left in inadequate conditions in Serbia, in substandard camps and at risk of homelessness and of *refoulement* further south to Macedonia and Bulgaria.

In March, the European Court of Human Rights ruled in *Ilias and Ahmed v. Hungary* that the confinement of asylum-seekers in "transit zones", essentially heavily guarded container camps at Hungary's external land borders, amounted to arbitrary deprivation of liberty. The Court also found that, due to the poor conditions in which asylum-seekers were held for weeks and the lack of judicial remedies available against this form of detention, Hungary had failed to provide adequate protection against a real risk of inhuman and degrading treatment.

The same month, a package of amendments to five laws on migration and asylum was passed in the National Assembly, enabling the automatic detention, without judicial review, of all asylum-seekers in border "transit zones", including unaccompanied minors of 14-18 years of age. These amendments also allowed for the detention of asylum-seekers for the whole duration of their asylum processes, including any appeals, and for the summary expulsion of all irregular migrants found on Hungarian territory to the external side of Hungary's extensive border fences.

Consequently, most asylum-seekers in Hungary either absconded from the procedure or were detained in the border "transit zones" indefinitely. By the end of the year, almost 500 asylum-seekers were unlawfully detained at the border. The Hungarian authorities denied or provided extremely limited access to human rights monitors and NGOs providing legal aid. These draconian measures were originally supposed to apply during a "crisis situation caused by mass immigration". However, a "crisis situation" had been continuously invoked since September 2015 and was extended in August until March 2018, despite the lack of a factual or legal basis for its prolongation.

Hungary further enhanced its border fences and police presence at its southern borders. More than 20,000 people were summarily and sometimes violently returned to Serbia or otherwise prevented from entering Hungary without access to fair and efficient asylum processes and an examination of their protection needs. In March, the newspaper *Magyar Nemzet* revealed that, contrary to the government's statements refuting allegations of abuse, more than 40 investigations had been launched into instances of excessive use of force by police at the border over a period of 18 months; most of the investigations were closed without further action.

In September, Hungary lost a case at the Court of Justice of the European Union, which ruled that it could not absolve itself of participation in the EU Emergency Relocation Scheme for the relocation of asylum-seekers from Greece and Italy to other EU member states. Hungary continued to refuse to relocate any of its minimum quota of 1,294 asylum-seekers, or to participate in other regional solidarity mechanisms. By the end of the year, it had not resettled or relocated anyone.

FREEDOM OF ASSOCIATION

In April, the adoption in an emergency procedure of amendments to the National Higher Education Law prompted widespread protests and criticism from academic experts and the general public. The law, widely interpreted as targeting the operations of a particular educational institution, the Central European University (CEU), introduced new requirements for foreign universities operating in Hungary under an extremely tight deadline – including the requirement of a bilateral state-level agreement – putting at risk the continued functioning of those institutions. The same month, the European Commission took legal action against Hungary by launching infringement proceedings. In the Commission's assessment, the law was not compatible with fundamental EU freedoms, including the freedom to provide services, the freedom of establishment, and academic freedom. In October, the National Assembly voted to extend the deadlines by which the new requirements had to be met by one calendar year. By the end of the year the government had failed to strike an agreement with the State of New York that would allow for the continued operations of the CEU.

In June, the National Assembly passed a law effectively stigmatizing NGOs that received foreign funding. Under the law on the transparency of organizations funded from abroad, NGOs receiving more than EUR24,000 direct or indirect funding from abroad had to re-register as a "civic organization funded from abroad" and to put this label on every publication. Additionally, the law required NGOs to reveal the identity of their funders and supporters above a threshold of around EUR1,650. The law was adopted amid a government-sponsored communication campaign discrediting NGOs and accusing several of undermining national sovereignty and security. By only covering certain types of civil society organizations, the law directly discriminated against these organizations and imposed limitations on their right to association, including the right to seek, receive and utilize resources. In mid-July, the European Commission notified Hungary of another infringement procedure, based on an assessment that this law imposed measures at odds with the right to freedom of association and unjustified and disproportionate restrictions on the free movement of capital, and raised concerns in relation to the obligation of protecting private life and personal data.

In August, a coalition of more than 20 NGOs submitted a complaint to the Constitutional Court requesting that the law be annulled.

COUNTER-TERROR AND SECURITY

In June, an appeals court in the southern town of Szeged annulled the conviction of Ahmed H, a Syrian man sentenced to 10 years' imprisonment for allegedly committing "acts of terror" while participating in a riot by refugees and migrants at the Serbia-Hungary border in September 2015. On appeal, the court found that available evidence had not been properly assessed and ordered a retrial. In August, the Prosecutor General appealed against this decision to the Curia (the highest court in Hungary). In November, the Curia ruled that the appeals court should have delivered a binding judgment instead of ordering a retrial; this, however, did not affect ongoing proceedings. Ahmed H's case was pending before a newly appointed court of first instance at the end of the year.

VIOLENCE AGAINST WOMEN AND GIRLS

By October, allegations of abuse committed by men holding positions of power sparked a national debate on the recognition and prosecution of rape and other forms of sexual violence. Hungary had yet to ratify the Council of Europe Convention on preventing and combating violence against women and domestic violence, and prosecutions of these crimes remained limited.

INDIA

Republic of India
Head of state: **Ram Nath Kovind (replaced Pranab Mukherjee in July)**
Head of government: **Narendra Modi**

Religious minority groups, particularly Muslims, faced increasing demonization by hardline Hindu groups, pro-government media and some state officials. Adivasi communities continued to be displaced by industrial projects, and hate crimes against Dalits remained widespread. Authorities were openly critical of human rights defenders and organizations, contributing to a climate of hostility against them. Mob violence intensified, including by vigilante cow protection groups. Press freedom and free speech in universities came under attack. India failed to respect its human rights commitments made before the UN Human Rights Council. The Supreme Court and High Courts delivered several progressive judgments, but some rulings undermined human rights. Impunity for human rights abuses persisted.

ABUSES BY ARMED GROUPS

In January, three road construction workers were killed in an attack on a military camp by suspected members of the Jamaat-ud-Dawa armed group in Akhnoor, in the state of Jammu and Kashmir (J&K). The United Liberation Front of Asom (Independent) claimed responsibility for detonating seven bombs across Assam state on 26 January; no casualties were reported. In July, suspected members of the Lashkar-e-Taiba armed group attacked a bus carrying Hindu pilgrims in Botengoo, J&K, killing eight people and injuring 17.

Suspected armed group members in J&K threatened and attacked political workers and ransacked the homes of state police personnel. Armed groups in northeastern states were suspected of carrying out abductions and unlawful killings. The Communist Party of India (Maoist) armed group was suspected of killing suspected police "informants" in several states.

CASTE-BASED DISCRIMINATION AND VIOLENCE

Official statistics released in November stated that more than 40,000 crimes against Scheduled Castes were reported in 2016. Several incidents were reported of members of dominant castes attacking Dalits for accessing public and social spaces or for perceived caste transgressions.

In May, two Dalit men were killed, several injured, and dozens of Dalit homes burned by dominant caste men in Saharanpur, Uttar Pradesh, following a clash between members of the communities. In September, S. Anitha, a 17-year-old Dalit girl who had campaigned against the introduction of a uniform national exam for admission to medical colleges, committed suicide, sparking protests in Tamil Nadu. Protesters said the exam would disadvantage students from marginalized backgrounds.

Activists said that at least 90 Dalits employed as manual scavengers died during the year while cleaning sewers, despite the practice being prohibited. Many of those killed were illegally employed by government agencies. In August, the Delhi state government said that people who employed manual scavengers would be prosecuted for manslaughter. In November, the UN Special Rapporteur on safe drinking water and sanitation expressed concern that the government's emphasis on building new toilets as part of its Clean India Mission could prolong manual scavenging.

CHILDREN'S RIGHTS

In November, statistics were published stating that over 106,000 cases of violence against children were reported in 2016. In June, India ratified two key ILO conventions on child labour. Activists remained critical of amendments to child labour laws which allowed children to work in family enterprises.

According to national survey data released in March, nearly 36% of children aged below five were underweight, and more than 38% were short for their age. In September, 70 children died at a hospital in Gorakhpur, Uttar Pradesh, allegedly because of disruption to the oxygen supply. The share of public spending on health remained low at 1.2% of GDP. Spending on government programmes to provide nutrition and pre-school education to children under six remained inadequate.

COMMUNAL AND ETHNIC VIOLENCE

Dozens of hate crimes against Muslims took place across the country. At least 10 Muslim men were lynched and many injured by vigilante cow protection groups, many of which seemed to operate with the support of members of the ruling Bharatiya Janata Party (BJP). Some arrests were made, but no convictions were reported. In September,

Rajasthan police cleared six men suspected of killing Pehlu Khan, a dairy farmer who had named the suspects before he died. Some BJP officials made statements which appeared to justify the attacks. In September, the Supreme Court said that state governments were obligated to compensate victims of cow vigilante violence.

A special investigation team set up in 2015 to reinvestigate closed cases related to the 1984 Sikh massacre closed 241 cases and filed charges in 12 others. In August, the Supreme Court set up a panel comprising two former judges to examine the decisions to close the cases.

In March, mobs carried out with impunity a string of racist attacks against black African students in Greater Noida, Uttar Pradesh. In June, three people were killed in Darjeeling, West Bengal, in violent clashes between police and protesters demanding a separate state of Gorkhaland.

FREEDOM OF EXPRESSION

Journalists and press freedom came under increasing attack. In September, journalist Gauri Lankesh, an outspoken critic of Hindu nationalism and the caste system, was shot dead outside her home in Bengaluru by unidentified gunmen. The same month, journalist Shantanu Bhowmick was beaten to death near Agartala while covering violent political clashes. In September, photojournalist Kamran Yousuf was arrested in J&K for allegedly instigating people to throw stones at security forces, under a law which does not meet international human rights standards. In November, journalist Sudip Datta Bhowmik was shot dead, allegedly by a paramilitary force member, at a paramilitary camp near Agartala. In December, a French film-maker conducting research for a documentary on the Kashmir conflict was detained for three days in J&K, allegedly for violating visa regulations.

Journalists continued to face criminal defamation cases filed by politicians and companies. In June, the Karnataka legislature sentenced two journalists to one year's imprisonment each for allegedly writing defamatory articles about members of the state assembly.

Repressive laws were used to stifle freedom of expression. In June, 20 people were arrested for sedition in Madhya Pradesh and Rajasthan, following complaints that they had cheered the Pakistan cricket team's victory over India. In July, 31 Dalit activists were arrested and detained for a day in Lucknow for organizing a press conference about caste-based violence. State governments banned books, and the central film certification board denied the theatrical release of certain films, on vague and overly broad grounds. In November, five state governments banned the release of *Padmaavat*, a Hindi period film, on the grounds that it would "hurt community sentiments".

Freedom of expression in universities remained under threat. The student body of the Hindu nationalist organization Rashtriya Swayamsevak Sangh used threats and violence to block events and talks at some universities. In June, eight Lucknow University students were arrested and detained for 20 days for protesting against the Uttar Pradesh Chief Minister. In September, Uttar Pradesh police personnel baton-charged students, mostly women, protesting against sexual assault at Banaras Hindu University.

In August, India's Supreme Court ruled in a landmark judgment that the right to privacy was part of the constitutional right to life and personal liberty.

HUMAN RIGHTS DEFENDERS

In January, the Home Ministry said that it had refused to renew the foreign funding licence of the NGO known as People's Watch because it had allegedly portrayed India's human rights record in a "negative light" internationally.

In March, GN Saibaba, an activist and academic, was convicted with four others and sentenced to life imprisonment by a Maharashtra court for being a member of and supporting a banned Maoist group. The conviction was based primarily on letters,

pamphlets and videos, and used the provisions of the Unlawful Activities Prevention Act, a law which does not meet international human rights standards.

The same month, Jailal Rathia, an Adivasi activist, died in Raigarh, Chhattisgarh, after allegedly being poisoned by members of a land mafia he was campaigning against. In April, Varsha Dongre, an official at Raipur Central Jail in Chhattisgarh, was transferred after she posted on Facebook that she had seen police torturing Adivasi girls.

In May, four men were arrested in Chennai and held in administrative detention for more than three months for attempting to stage a memorial for Tamils killed in the civil war in Sri Lanka. The same month, the Odisha state police arrested Kuni Sikaka, an Adivasi activist opposing bauxite mining in the Niyamgiri hills, and released her only after presenting her to journalists as a surrendered Maoist.

In August, activist Medha Patkar and three others protesting against inadequate rehabilitation for families affected by the Sardar Sarovar dam project (see below) were arrested on fabricated charges and detained for more than two weeks.

INDIGENOUS PEOPLES' RIGHTS

In November, statistics were published stating that over 6,500 crimes were committed against Scheduled Tribes in 2016. Indigenous Adivasi communities continued to face displacement by industrial projects. The government acquired land for coal mining under a special law without seeking the free, prior and informed consent of Adivasis. In July, an Environment Ministry panel said that coal mines seeking to increase production capacity by up to 40% did not have to consult affected communities.

In September, activists protested against the inauguration of the Sardar Sarovar dam in Gujarat, saying that some 40,000 displaced families, including many Adivasi families, had not received adequate reparation. In June, 98 Adivasis in Raigarh, Chhattisgarh, tried to file criminal cases under the Scheduled Castes and Scheduled Tribes (Prevention of

Atrocities) Act, alleging that they had been forced into selling their land to agents of private companies, following intimidation and coercion. The police accepted the complaints but refused to register criminal cases.

JAMMU AND KASHMIR

In April, eight people were killed by security forces, some of them by the use of excessive force, following protests during a by-election for a parliamentary seat. One voter, Farooq Ahmad Dar, was beaten by army personnel, strapped to the front of an army jeep and driven around for over five hours, seemingly as a warning to protesters. In May, the officer suspected of being responsible received an army commendation for his work in counter-insurgency operations. In July, the J&K State Human Rights Commission directed the state government to pay Farooq Dar 100,000 INR (around USD1,500) as compensation. In November, the state government refused to pay.

Impunity for human rights abuses persisted. In June, a military court set up under the paramilitary Border Security Force acquitted two soldiers of killing 16-year-old Zahid Farooq Sheikh in 2010. The force had successfully prevented the case from being prosecuted in a civilian court. In July, the Supreme Court refused to reopen 215 cases in which over 700 members of the Kashmiri Pandit community were killed in J&K in 1989, citing the passage of time. The same month, an appellate military court suspended the life sentences of five army personnel convicted by a court-martial of the extrajudicial executions of three men in Machil in 2010. In November, the State Human Rights Commission repeated a directive issued to the state government in 2011 to investigate over 2,000 unmarked graves.

Security forces continued to use inherently inaccurate pellet-firing shotguns during protests, blinding and injuring several people. Authorities frequently shut down internet services, citing public order concerns.

POLICE AND SECURITY FORCES

In January, four Adivasi women in Dhar, Madhya Pradesh, said they had been gang-raped by police personnel. In March, Adivasi villagers in Sukma, Chhattisgarh, accused security force personnel of gang-raping a 14-year-old Adivasi girl. In September, two paramilitary personnel were arrested on suspicion of killing a woman and raping and throwing acid on her friend in Mizoram in July.

In April, a senior officer of the paramilitary Central Reserve Police Force alleged in writing to his commanding authorities that multiple security agencies had killed two suspected armed group members in an extrajudicial execution in Assam. The officer was transferred. In July, the Supreme Court directed the Central Bureau of Investigation to investigate more than 80 alleged extrajudicial executions by police and security force personnel in Manipur between 1979 and 2012. The court ruled that cases should not go uninvestigated merely because of the passage of time.

In June, the Madhya Pradesh police shot dead five farmers who were among protesters in Mandsaur demanding better prices for crops. In August, at least 38 people were killed, some of them by the use of excessive force, when they were fired on by police during protests in Haryana following the conviction for rape of a self-styled "godman", or guru.

REFUGEES' AND MIGRANTS' RIGHTS

An estimated 40,000 Rohingya people in India were at risk of mass expulsion. They included more than 16,000 who were recognized as refugees by UNHCR, the UN refugee agency. In August, the Home Ministry wrote to state governments asking them to identify "illegal immigrants", including Rohingya. In September, the Ministry said that all Rohingya in India were "illegal immigrants", and claimed to have evidence that some Rohingya had ties to terrorist organizations. In October, in response to a petition filed by two Rohingya refugees, the Supreme Court temporarily deferred expulsions.

In September, the Home Ministry said that it would grant citizenship to about 100,000 Chakma and Hajong refugees who had fled to India from Bangladesh in the 1960s.

TORTURE AND OTHER ILL-TREATMENT

Between January and August, 894 deaths in judicial custody and 74 deaths in police custody were recorded. In February, Uma Bharti, a central government minister, said she had ordered rape suspects to be tortured when she was Chief Minister of Madhya Pradesh. In August, Manjula Shetye, a woman prisoner at the Byculla jail in Mumbai, died after being allegedly beaten and sexually assaulted by officials for complaining about food in the prison. A team of parliamentarians that visited Byculla jail reported that prisoners were routinely beaten. In November, a committee set up by the Delhi High Court said that 18 prisoners in Tihar jail in New Delhi had been beaten after they had objected to their pillow covers being taken.

In September, during India's UN UPR process before the UN Human Rights Council, the government accepted for the third time recommendations to ratify the UN Convention against Torture, which it signed in 1997. India's Law Commission released a report in October recommending that the government ratify the Convention and enact a law criminalizing torture.

WOMEN'S RIGHTS

In November, statistics were published showing that over 338,000 crimes against women were registered in 2016, including over 110,000 cases of violence by husbands and relatives. Responding to petitions in courts seeking to criminalize marital rape, the central government stated that doing so would "destabilize the institution of marriage".

In August, the Supreme Court banned the practice of triple talaq (Islamic instant divorce), declaring that it was arbitrary and unconstitutional. However, in other cases,

court rulings undermined women's autonomy. In July, the Supreme Court weakened a law enacted to protect women from violence in their marriages, by requiring that complaints be initially assessed by civil society "family welfare committees". In October, the Supreme Court suggested that it would review its judgment. The same month, it ruled that sexual intercourse by a man with his wife, if she was under 18, would amount to rape.

Several rape survivors, including girls, approached courts for permission to terminate pregnancies over 20 weeks, as required under Indian law. Courts approved some abortions, but refused others. In August, the central government instructed states to set up permanent medical boards to decide such cases promptly.

INDONESIA

Republic of Indonesia
Head of state and government: **Joko Widodo**

Indonesia failed to address past human rights violations. The rights to freedom of expression, of peaceful assembly and of association continued to be arbitrarily restricted. Blasphemy provisions were used to imprison those who peacefully exercised their rights to freedom of religion and belief. At least 30 prisoners of conscience remained in detention for peacefully exercising their rights to freedom of expression or of religion and belief. The security forces carried out unlawful killings and used excessive force during protests and security operations. Two men were caned in public in Aceh after being convicted by a local Shari'a court of same-sex consensual sexual relations.

BACKGROUND

Indonesia's human rights record was examined in May under the UN UPR process. Although Indonesia accepted 167 out of 225 recommendations, it rejected, among other things, calls to investigate past human rights violations and to repeal blasphemy provisions in laws and regulations. These included several provisions of the Criminal Code and Law No. 1/PNPS/1965, which imposed restrictions on freedoms of expression and of religion and belief.[1]

IMPUNITY

Despite commitments made by the President, Indonesia failed to address past human rights violations. In February, the Administrative Court in the capital, Jakarta, overturned a decision by the Public Information Commission ordering the government to publish a report on the 2004 murder of human rights defender Munir Said Thalib, which reportedly implicated senior intelligence officers. The Court made the decision on the grounds that the current government had not received the report from the previous government. In August, the Supreme Court upheld the Administrative Court's decision.

During the UPR, Indonesia promised that the Attorney General would finalize a criminal investigation into alleged gross human rights violations in Wasior in 2001 and Wamena in 2003, both in Papua region, and forward the case to the Human Rights Court established under Law No. 26/2000. However, this had not happened by the end of the year.

FREEDOMS OF ASSEMBLY, ASSOCIATION AND EXPRESSION

The authorities continued to prosecute those participating in peaceful political activities, particularly in areas with a history of pro-independence movements such as Papua. Prisoner of conscience Oktovianus Warnares remained in detention because he refused to sign a document declaring his allegiance to the state of Indonesia, despite having served two thirds of his prison sentence and being eligible for release on parole. He had been convicted of "rebellion" (makar) in 2013 after taking part in activities peacefully marking the 50th anniversary of the handover of Papua to the Indonesian government by the UN Temporary Executive Authority.

In August Novel Baswedan, an investigator for the Corruption Eradication Commission, was reported to the police by the Commission's director of investigation under Article 27(3) of the Electronic Information and Transactions (ITE) Law, which concerns online defamation. The defamation report related to an email he had sent in his capacity as representative of the Commission's workers' union, criticizing the director's leadership. Novel Baswedan suffered an acid attack in Jakarta on 11 April that severely damaged his corneas. At the time of the attack he was leading an ongoing investigation into misappropriation by high-ranking government officials of funds for an electronic ID cards project.

On 10 July President Widodo signed Government Regulation in Lieu of Law (Perppu) No. 2/2017, amending the 2013 Law on Mass Organizations to remove judicial safeguards over the process of banning NGOs and other organizations. The new legislation, enacted by Parliament in October, would impose restrictions on the rights to freedom of association, expression, religion and belief, which were even more extensive than those currently set out in the Law on Mass Organizations. The Law already stifled the work of human rights defenders and reflected discriminatory attitudes towards certain groups.[2]

Security forces and vigilante groups broke up closed-door discussions and public events relating to serious human rights violations committed in 1965. On 1 August, the local police and military from East Jakarta disrupted a workshop in Jakarta concerning the findings of the International Peoples Tribunal 1965, a civil society initiative to raise international awareness about the mass human rights violations that occurred that year.

On 16 September the police banned a closed-door seminar at the office of the Indonesian and Jakarta Legal Aid Institute featuring a discussion by survivors of the 1965 violations. On the night of 17 September, a crowd of around 1,000 claiming to be "anti-communists" surrounded the office, trapping scores of artists and activists attending an event concerning the recent crackdown on the rights to freedom of expression and peaceful assembly. Early the following morning, the crowd threw rocks at the office and destroyed the fence surrounding the building. Hundreds of police officers used tear gas to disperse the crowd.[3]

FREEDOM OF RELIGION AND BELIEF

Blasphemy provisions in Articles 156 and 156(a) of the Criminal Code and Article 28(2) of the ITE Law were used to imprison those who peacefully exercised their rights to freedom of religion and belief. At least 11 people were convicted under blasphemy laws. Individuals belonging to minority religions or faiths or holding minority beliefs were often targeted for prosecution. On 9 May, Jakarta Governor Basuki Tjahaja Purnama, an ethnic Chinese Christian known as Ahok, was sentenced to two years' imprisonment for "insulting Islam" in a video posted on the internet. Ahok was the first high-ranking government official to be convicted of blasphemy.[4]

On 7 March, Ahmad Mushaddeq, Mahful Muis Tumanurung and Andry Cahya, leaders of the disbanded Fajar Nusantara religious movement known as Gafatar, were convicted of blasphemy by the East Jakarta District Court. The conviction was upheld by the Jakarta High Court on 3 July.

At the end of the year, at least 30 prisoners of conscience remained in detention for peacefully exercising their right to freedom of expression or of religion and belief.

On 4 June, the local government in Depok, West Java, sealed a mosque belonging to the Ahmadiyya religious minority, considered by many Islamic groups to be "deviant and outside of Islam". Authorities prevented the Ahmadis from using the mosque during Ramadan. The Depok Mayor argued that the legal basis for the closure of the mosque was a ministerial decree and a provincial regulation, both forbidding Ahmadiyya community members from promoting their activities and spreading their religious teachings. The Mayor also said that it was necessary to protect the Ahmadiyya community in Depok from violent attacks by other groups in the area.

POLICE AND SECURITY FORCES

Human rights groups reported unlawful killings and other serious human rights violations by security forces, primarily in the context of excessive use of force during mass protests or during security operations. No perpetrators were known to have been held to account, particularly for numerous incidents in Papua.

EXCESSIVE USE OF FORCE

Between September 2016 and January 2017, joint police and military forces carried out security operations in Dogiyai, Papua province, during the run-up to the 2017 local elections. On 10 January police officers arbitrarily arrested Otis Pekei when he refused to hand over a knife at a police checkpoint, and detained him at the Moanemani sub-district police station. Later that day, police delivered Otis Pekei's body to the home of his family; the family accused the police of torturing him during detention. No investigation was known to have been conducted.

On 1 August in Deiyai, Papua province, police officers arbitrarily opened fire into a crowd of protesters without warning, wounding at least 10 people, including children. Nine police officers were subjected to disciplinary action; no criminal proceedings were known to have been opened.

UNLAWFUL KILLINGS

The number of killings by police of suspected drug dealers increased sharply, from 18 in 2016 to at least 98 in 2017. Some of the officers involved in the incidents were seconded to the National Narcotics Agency. Police claimed that all the killings were in self-defence or because suspects tried to flee the scene. No independent investigations were known to have been conducted into these killings. The number of deaths escalated after several high-ranking Indonesian officials, including the President, advocated during the year for tougher measures to address drug-related crime, including calling for the application of unrestrained lethal force against suspected traffickers.

DEATHS IN CUSTODY

Deaths in custody and torture by police personnel were reported by human rights organizations.

On 27 August Rifzal Riandi Siregar was arrested in Batang Toru precinct in North Sumatra province after he was involved in a fight with a police officer. When his relatives visited him at the Batang Toru police station, he told them that he had been badly beaten at the station by four police officers, including the one with whom he had had the altercation. On 3 September, Rifzal Riandi Siregar was found dead in the police station. At the request of his family, the police transferred his body to a police hospital in Medan, where an autopsy was conducted. The police promised to give the autopsy report to the family within a week. They had not received it by the end of the year.

CRUEL, INHUMAN OR DEGRADING PUNISHMENT

At least 317 people were caned in Aceh during the year for offences such as adultery, gambling and drinking alcohol, as well as same-sex consensual sexual relations.

In May, two men were each caned 83 times in public after being convicted by the Banda Aceh Shari'a Court of consensual same-sex sexual relations (liwath) under the Aceh Islamic Criminal Code. Although Shari'a by-laws have been in force in Aceh since the enactment of the province's Special Autonomy Law in 2001, and are enforced by Islamic courts, this was the first time that gay men had been caned under Shari'a law in the province.[5]

RIGHTS OF LESBIAN, GAY, BISEXUAL, TRANSGENDER AND INTERSEX PEOPLE

On 25 May, 141 men were arrested in North Jakarta by local police after attending what police described as a "gay sex party". The next day the police released 126 men, but charged 10 of them with providing "pornography service" under Law No. 44/2008 on Pornography. On 6 October, 51 people, including seven foreign nationals, were arrested in a Central Jakarta sauna. Most of the customers were released the following day; five employees remained in detention at the end of the year. The police charged six people with providing pornography and prostitution services.[6]

With the exception of Aceh, consensual same-sex relations were not treated as crimes under the Indonesian Criminal Code.

ECONOMIC, SOCIAL AND CULTURAL RIGHTS – RIGHT TO WATER

On 10 October, the Supreme Court ordered the government to terminate a water privatization scheme in Jakarta. The Court approved an appeal filed by the Coalition of Jakarta Residents Opposing Water Privatization that the private provider had "failed to protect the right to water" of the residents. The Court ordered the government to immediately revoke its contracts with two private water utilities.

---

1. Indonesia: Human Rights Council must ensure strong recommendations at human rights review (ASA 21/6156/2017)

2. Indonesia: Amendments to the mass organizations law expand threats to freedom of association (ASA 21/6722/2017)

3. Indonesia: Offices of human rights defenders attacked (ASA 21/7113/2017)

4. Indonesia: Blasphemy conviction demonstrates intolerance - Basuki Tjahaja Purnama (Ahok) (ASA 21/6213/2017)

5. Indonesia: Revoke conviction and caning sentence for gay men in Aceh (ASA 21/6279/2017)

6. Indonesia: Arrest of 51 people fuels hostile environment for LGBTI people (ASA 21/7289/2017)

IRAN

Islamic Republic of Iran
Head of state: **Ayatollah Sayed Ali Khamenei (Supreme Leader of the Islamic Republic of Iran)**
Head of government: **Hassan Rouhani (President)**

The authorities heavily suppressed the rights to freedom of expression, association and peaceful assembly, as well as freedom of religion and belief, and imprisoned scores of individuals who voiced dissent. Trials were systematically unfair. Torture and other ill-treatment was widespread and committed with impunity. Floggings, amputations and other cruel punishments were carried out. The authorities endorsed pervasive discrimination and violence based on gender, political opinion, religious belief, ethnicity, disability, sexual orientation and gender identity. Hundreds of people were executed, some in public, and thousands remained on death row. They included people who were under the age of 18 at the time of the crime.

BACKGROUND

In March the UN Human Rights Council renewed the mandate of the UN Special Rapporteur on the situation of human rights in Iran; the Iranian authorities continued to deny her and other UN experts entry to the country.

In May, President Rouhani was elected to a second term in office, following an electoral process that discriminated against hundreds of candidates by disqualifying them on the basis of gender, religious belief and political opinion. The appointment of individuals allegedly involved in grave human rights violations to ministerial posts attracted public criticism.

The EU and Iran worked towards renewing a bilateral human rights dialogue while several human rights defenders served prison sentences imposed for communicating with EU and UN officials. Several governments including those of Australia, Sweden and Switzerland also started bilateral human rights dialogues with Iran.

At the end of December, thousands of Iranians took to the streets to protest against poverty, corruption and political repression, in the first anti-establishment demonstrations on such a scale since 2009.

FREEDOMS OF EXPRESSION, ASSOCIATION AND ASSEMBLY

The authorities continued to crack down heavily on the rights to freedom of expression, association and peaceful assembly, jailing scores of peaceful critics on spurious national security charges. Among those targeted were peaceful political dissidents, journalists, online media workers, students, filmmakers, musicians and writers, as well as human rights defenders including women's rights activists, minority rights and environmental activists, trade unionists, anti-death penalty campaigners, lawyers, and those seeking truth, justice and reparation for the mass executions and enforced disappearances of the 1980s.

Many prisoners of conscience undertook hunger strikes to protest against their unjust imprisonment.

The authorities arrested hundreds of protesters following anti-establishment demonstrations that began across the country at the end of December. Reports emerged that security forces killed and injured unarmed protesters by using firearms and other excessive force. On 31 December the Minister of Information and Communications Technology blocked access to Instagram and the popular messaging application Telegram, used by activists to promote and support the protests.

Earlier in the year, judicial officials had exerted persistent pressure on the Ministry of Information and Communications Technology to request that Telegram relocate its servers to Iran and close tens of thousands of Telegram channels, which according to the judiciary "threatened national security" or "insulted religious values". Telegram said it rejected both requests.

Other popular social media sites including Facebook, Twitter and YouTube remained blocked.

Journalists and online media workers faced a renewed wave of harsh interrogations and arbitrary arrests and detentions before the presidential election in May. Those using Telegram were particularly targeted for harsh prison sentences, some exceeding a decade.

Freedom of musical expression remained curtailed. Women were banned from singing in public and the authorities continued to forcibly cancel many concerts. In August, several hundred artists called on President Rouhani to end such restrictions.

The authorities continued their violent raids on private mixed-gender parties, arresting hundreds of young people and sentencing many to flogging.

Censorship of all forms of media and jamming of foreign satellite television channels continued. The judicial authorities intensified their harassment of journalists working with the Persian BBC service, freezing the assets of 152 former or current BBC journalists and banning them from conducting financial transactions.

The Association of Journalists remained suspended.

Scores of students continued to be barred from higher education in reprisal for their peaceful activism, despite President Rouhani's election promise to lift the ban.

Bans on independent trade unions persisted and several trade unionists were unjustly imprisoned. Security forces continued to violently suppress peaceful protests by workers, including on International Workers' Day.

Dozens of environmental activists were summoned for interrogation, detained and prosecuted for participating in peaceful protests against air pollution, disappearing lakes, river diversion projects and dumping practices.

Opposition leaders Mehdi Karroubi and Mir Hossein Mousavi and the latter's wife, Zahra Rahnavard, remained under house arrest without charge or trial since 2011.

TORTURE AND OTHER ILL-TREATMENT

Torture and other ill-treatment remained common, especially during interrogations. Detainees held by the Ministry of Intelligence and the Revolutionary Guards were routinely subjected to prolonged solitary confinement amounting to torture.

Failure to investigate allegations of torture and exclude "confessions" obtained under torture as evidence against suspects remained systematic.

The authorities continued to deprive prisoners detained for political reasons of adequate medical care. In many cases, this was done as a deliberate punishment or to extract "confessions", and amounted to torture.

Prisoners endured cruel and inhuman conditions of detention, including overcrowding, limited hot water, inadequate food, insufficient beds, poor ventilation and insect infestations.

More than a dozen political prisoners at Karaj's Raja'i Shahr prison waged a prolonged hunger strike between July and September in protest at their dire detention conditions. Some faced denial of medical care, solitary confinement and fresh criminal charges in reprisal.

CRUEL, INHUMAN OR DEGRADING PUNISHMENT

Judicial authorities continued to impose and carry out, at times in public, cruel and inhuman punishments amounting to torture.

Scores of individuals, including children, faced up to 100 lashes for theft and assault as well as for acts that, under international law, must not be criminalized – including extra-marital relationships, attending mixed gender parties, eating in public during Ramadan or attending peaceful protests.

In January, journalist Hossein Movahedi was lashed 40 times in Najaf Abad, Esfahan province, after a court found him guilty of inaccurately reporting the number of motorcycles confiscated by police in the city.

In August, a criminal court in Markazi province sentenced trade unionist Shapour Ehsanirad to 30 lashes and six months' imprisonment for participating in a protest against unjust work conditions.

In February, the Supreme Court upheld a blinding sentence issued by a criminal court in Kohgiluyeh and Boyer-Ahmad province against a woman in retribution for blinding another woman.

Dozens of amputation sentences were imposed and subsequently upheld by the Supreme Court. In April, judicial authorities in Shiraz, Fars province, amputated the hand of Hamid Moinee and executed him 10 days later. He had been convicted of murder and robbery. At least four other amputation sentences were carried out for robbery.

The authorities also carried out degrading punishments. In April, three men accused of kidnapping and other crimes were paraded around Dehloran, Ilam province, with their hands tied and watering cans used for lavatory washing hung around their necks. Eight men were similarly humiliated in Pakdasht, Tehran province, in July.

In May, a woman arrested for having an intimate extramarital relationship was sentenced by a criminal court in the capital, Tehran, to two years of washing corpses and 74 lashes. The man was sentenced to 99 lashes.

UNFAIR TRIALS

Trials, including those resulting in death sentences, were systematically unfair. There were no independent mechanisms for ensuring accountability within the judiciary. Serious concerns remained that judges, particularly those presiding over Revolutionary Courts, were appointed on the basis of their political opinions and affiliation with intelligence bodies, and lacked legal qualifications.

Fair trial provisions of the 2015 Code of Criminal Procedure, including those guaranteeing access to a lawyer from the time of arrest and during investigations, were routinely flouted. The authorities continued to invoke Article 48 of the Code of Criminal Procedure to prevent those detained for political reasons from accessing lawyers of their own choosing. Lawyers were told they were not on the list approved by the Head of the Judiciary, even though no official list had been made public.

Trials, particularly those before Revolutionary Courts, remained closed and extremely brief, sometimes lasting just a few minutes.

Foreign nationals and Iranians with dual nationality continued to face arbitrary arrest and detention, grossly unfair trials and lengthy imprisonment. The authorities claimed that they were countering foreign-orchestrated "infiltration projects". In reality, such individuals were often charged with vague national security offences in connection with the peaceful exercise of their rights to freedom of expression and association.

FREEDOM OF RELIGION AND BELIEF

Freedom of religion and belief was systematically violated, in law and practice. The authorities continued to impose codes of public conduct rooted in a strict interpretation of Shi'a Islam on individuals of all faiths. Non-Shi'a Muslims were not allowed to stand as presidential candidates or hold key political offices.

Widespread and systematic attacks continued to be carried out against the Baha'i minority. These included arbitrary arrests, lengthy imprisonment, torture and other ill-treatment, forcible closure of Baha'i-owned businesses, confiscation of Baha'i properties, bans on employment in the public sector and denial of access to universities. The authorities regularly incited hatred and violence, vilifying Baha'is as "heretical" and "filthy". There were renewed concerns that hate crimes could be committed with impunity after two men who had admitted to killing Farang Amiri because of his Baha'i faith were released on bail in June.

Other religious minorities not recognized under the Constitution, such as Yaresan (Ahl-e Haq), also faced systematic discrimination, including in education and employment, and were persecuted for practising their faith.

The right to change or renounce religious beliefs continued to be violated. Christian converts received harsh prison sentences, which ranged from 10 to 15 years in several cases. Raids on house churches continued.

Gonabadi dervishes faced imprisonment and attacks on their places of worship. A number were arbitrarily dismissed from employment or denied enrolment in universities.

Those who professed atheism remained at risk of arbitrary arrest and detention, torture and other ill-treatment and the death penalty for "apostasy".

Sunni Muslims continued to report discrimination, including restrictions on holding separate prayers for Eid al-Fitr celebrations and exclusion from high-ranking positions.

In a departure from Iranian law, the Court of Administrative Justice suspended the membership of Sepanta Niknam, a Zoroastrian man, from Yazd's City Council in October, based on an opinion from the head of Iran's Guardian Council who said it was against Shari'a law to allow the governance of non-Muslims over Muslims.

At least two people were sentenced to death for the peaceful exercise of their rights to freedom of religion and belief (see below).

DISCRIMINATION – ETHNIC MINORITIES

Ethnic minorities, including Ahwazi Arabs, Azerbaijani Turks, Baluchis, Kurds and Turkmen, remained subject to entrenched discrimination, curtailing their access to education, employment, adequate housing and political office.

Continued economic neglect of minority-populated regions further entrenched poverty and marginalization. In Sistan-Baluchistan province, residents of many villages reported a lack of access to water, electricity, schools and health facilities. The impoverished province retained high rates of illiteracy among girls and of infant mortality.

The Persian language remained the sole medium of instruction during primary and secondary education, contributing to higher drop-out rates in minority-populated areas.

There was ongoing criticism of the absence of measures ensuring minority self-government.

Members of minorities who spoke out against violations of their rights faced arbitrary arrest, torture and other ill-treatment, grossly unfair trials, imprisonment and the death penalty. Intelligence and security bodies frequently accused minority rights activists of supporting "separatist currents" threatening Iran's territorial integrity.

Iran's border guards continued to unlawfully shoot and kill, with full impunity, scores of unarmed Kurdish men known as Kulbars who work as cross-border porters between Iraqi and Iranian Kurdistan. In September, security forces violently suppressed protests in Baneh and Sanandaj over the fatal shootings of two Kulbars, and detained more than a dozen people.

There was a heavy police presence across Kurdistan province in September when members of Iran's Kurdish minority held rallies in support of the independence referendum in the Kurdish region of northern Iraq. More than a dozen people were reportedly arrested.

In June, security forces were deployed in Ahvaz in advance of the Eid al-Fitr holiday to prevent gatherings planned in solidarity with families of Ahwazi Arabs imprisoned or executed for political reasons. More than a dozen people were arbitrarily detained and many more were summoned for interrogation. Ahwazi Arab human rights defender Mohammad Ali Amouri remained on death row.

DISCRIMINATION – WOMEN AND GIRLS

Women remained subject to entrenched discrimination in law and practice, including in access to divorce, employment, equal inheritance and political office, and in family and criminal law.

Acts of violence against women and girls, including domestic violence and early and forced marriage, were widespread and committed with impunity. The authorities failed to criminalize gender-based violence; a draft bill remained pending since 2012. The legal age of marriage for girls remained at 13, and fathers and grandfathers could obtain permission from courts for their daughters to be married at an even younger age.

All 137 women who registered as presidential candidates were disqualified by the Guardian Council. President Rouhani included no woman ministers in his cabinet, despite civil society demands.

Compulsory veiling (hijab) allowed police and paramilitary forces to harass and detain women for showing strands of hair under their headscarves or for wearing heavy make-up or tight clothing. State-sanctioned smear campaigns were conducted against women who campaigned against the compulsory hijab.

Iran's Civil Code continued to deny Iranian women married to non-Iranian men the right to pass their nationality on to their children, a right enjoyed by Iranian men married to foreign spouses.

Authorities defied ongoing public pressure to open football stadiums to women spectators.

Women experienced reduced access to affordable modern contraception as the authorities failed to restore the budget for state family planning programmes cut in 2012. Parliament passed a law in October imposing severe restrictions on imparting information about contraception.

The authorities continued to monitor and restrict foreign travel of women's rights activists. Alieh Motalebzadeh was sentenced to three years' imprisonment in August for attending a workshop in Georgia on "Women's empowerment and elections".

DISCRIMINATION – PERSONS WITH DISABILITIES AND PEOPLE LIVING WITH HIV

The UN Committee on the Rights of Persons with Disabilities reviewed Iran's human rights record in March. The Committee condemned state discrimination and violence against people with physical and intellectual disabilities; poor implementation of accessibility standards; and denial of reasonable accommodation at the workplace. The Committee also expressed alarm at reports of forced institutionalization of people with disabilities and non-consensual medical treatments against people perceived to have a disability, including on the grounds of gender identity and sexual orientation. In December, parliament passed a proposed law on the Protection of the Rights of People with Disabilities which, if implemented fully, would enhance accessibility and access to education, housing, health care and employment.

In August the Ministry of Education adopted discriminatory criteria for disqualifying candidates for teaching positions. This included illnesses, crossed eyes, facial moles, short height and heavy weight. Following public outrage, the Ministry promised revisions but said that people living with HIV would still be barred as they lacked "moral qualifications".

DEATH PENALTY

The authorities continued to execute hundreds of people after unfair trials. Some executions were conducted in public.

The authorities continued to describe peaceful campaigning against the death penalty as "un-Islamic", and harassed and imprisoned anti-death penalty activists.

The majority of executions were for non-lethal drug-related offences. A new law adopted in October increased the quantities of drugs required for imposing the death penalty but retained mandatory death sentences for a wide range of drug-related offences. While the new law provided for retroactive applicability, it remained unclear how the authorities intended to implement it to commute the death sentences of those already on death row.

It was possible to confirm the execution of four individuals who were under 18 at the time of the crime and the cases of 92 other juvenile offenders who remained on death row. The real numbers were likely to be much higher. Several executions were scheduled and postponed at the last minute because of public campaigning. Retrials of juvenile offenders pursuant to Article 91 of the 2013 Islamic Penal Code continued to result in renewed death sentences following arbitrary assessments of their "maturity" at the time of the crime.

The death penalty was maintained for vaguely worded offences such as "insulting the Prophet", "enmity against God" and "spreading corruption on earth".

In August, spiritual teacher and prisoner of conscience Mohammad Ali Taheri was sentenced to death for the second time for "spreading corruption on earth" through establishing the spiritual group Erfan-e Halgheh; in October the Supreme Court quashed the death sentence. He remained in solitary confinement.

Prisoner of conscience Marjan Davari was sentenced to death in March for "spreading corruption on earth" in connection with her membership of the religious group Eckankar and for translating their materials. The Supreme Court subsequently quashed the death sentence and sent the case back to the Revolutionary Court in Tehran for retrial.

The Islamic Penal Code continued to provide for stoning as a method of execution.

Some consensual same-sex sexual conduct remained punishable by death.

IRAQ

Republic of Iraq
Head of state: **Fuad Masum**
Head of government: **Haider al-Abadi**

Iraqi and Kurdish forces, paramilitary militias, coalition forces and the armed group Islamic State (IS) committed violations of international humanitarian law, war crimes and gross human rights abuses in the armed conflict. IS fighters forcibly displaced thousands of civilians into active conflict, used them as human shields on a mass scale, deliberately killed civilians fleeing the fighting, and recruited and deployed child soldiers. Iraqi and Kurdish forces and paramilitary militias extrajudicially executed captured fighters and civilians fleeing the conflict and destroyed homes and other civilian property. Iraqi and Kurdish forces as well as government authorities arbitrarily detained, forcibly disappeared and tortured civilians suspected of being affiliated with IS. Courts subjected IS suspects and other individuals suspected of terrorism-related offences to unfair trials and sentenced them to death on the basis of "confessions" extracted under torture. Executions continued at an alarming rate.

BACKGROUND

By December, the Iraqi government, Kurdish forces, paramilitary militias and US-led coalition forces had recaptured the territory and population centres held by IS, including east Mosul in January, west Mosul in July, Tel Afar in August and Hawija in October. By November, more than 987,648 people in Nineveh governorate had been internally displaced as a result of the military operation to recapture Mosul and surrounding areas. More than 3 million people remained internally displaced across Iraq.

On 25 September the Kurdish Regional Government (KRG) held a referendum on independence in the Kurdistan Region of Iraq (KR-I) as well as in the "disputed areas" of Iraq, including areas in the governorates of Nineveh, Kirkuk, Salah al-Din and Diyala. Preliminary results showed that approximately 93% of votes were cast in favour of independence. The government of Iraq declared the referendum illegal and unconstitutional. Following the referendum, Iraqi government forces and pro-government forces including the Popular Mobilization Units (PMU) retook control of Kirkuk governorate as well as areas of Nineveh, Salah al-Din and Diyala governorates.

ABUSES BY ARMED GROUPS

IS committed gross human rights abuses and serious violations of international humanitarian law, some of which amounted to war crimes. It forcibly displaced thousands of civilians into zones of active hostilities in an attempt to shield their own fighters. IS deliberately killed civilians who were trying to flee the fighting and hanged their bodies in public areas as a warning to others who were contemplating escape. It carried out execution-style killings which targeted opponents, and recruited and deployed child soldiers. In Mosul, IS regularly denied medical care to civilians, and its fighters occupied several medical buildings and hospitals to avoid being targeted by Iraqi and coalition forces.

IS killed and injured civilians across Iraq in suicide bombings and other deadly attacks that deliberately targeted civilians in markets, Shi'a religious shrines and other public spaces. On 2 January, bombings by IS in the predominantly Shi'a neighbourhood of Sadr City in the capital, Baghdad, killed at least 35 people and injured more than 60. Suicide attacks on 30 May outside an ice-cream parlour and a government building in Baghdad killed at least 27 people and wounded at least 50. An IS attack on a restaurant frequented by Shi'a pilgrims in Nasiriya on 14 September killed at least 84 people and injured 93.

The UN reported in October that as many as 1,563 Yazidi women and children remained in IS captivity in Iraq and Syria. They were subjected to rape and other torture, assault and enslavement. Those who managed to escape or were freed after their relatives paid ransoms did not receive adequate remedies, including the necessary care and support required to help rebuild their lives. The UN stated in August that at least 74 mass graves had been discovered in areas previously controlled by IS in Iraq.

ARMED CONFLICT – VIOLATIONS BY GOVERNMENT FORCES, COALITION FORCES AND MILITIAS

Government forces, paramilitary militias and coalition forces committed repeated violations of international humanitarian law, some of which may amount to war crimes. In west Mosul, Iraqi and coalition forces launched a series of disproportionate or otherwise indiscriminate attacks. In one such attack, on 17 March in Mosul al-Jadida neighbourhood, at least 105 civilians were killed by a US air strike targeting two IS snipers.

In west Mosul, Iraqi forces consistently used explosive weapons with wide-area effects, such as improvised rocket-assisted munitions (IRAMs), which cannot be precisely targeted at military objectives or used lawfully in populated civilian areas. In east Mosul, hundreds of civilians were killed in air strikes launched by the coalition and Iraqi forces on their homes or places where they sought refuge as they followed Iraqi government instructions not to leave during the battle.

Iraqi and Kurdish government forces and paramilitary militias carried out extrajudicial executions of men and boys suspected of being affiliated with IS. In the final weeks of the Mosul battle between May and July, consistent reports emerged that Iraqi forces, including the Emergency Response Division, Federal Police and the Iraqi Security Forces, had detained, tortured and extrajudicially executed men and boys who were fleeing the fighting.

ARBITRARY ARRESTS AND DETENTIONS

Thousands of men and boys considered to be of fighting age (roughly 15 to 65) fleeing territories controlled by IS were subjected to security screenings by Iraqi security forces, Kurdish forces and paramilitary militias at temporary reception sites or in makeshift detention facilities. Men suspected of affiliation with IS were held for days or months, often in harsh conditions, or transferred onward. Iraqi forces, Kurdish forces and paramilitary militias, including the PMU, arrested thousands more alleged "terrorism" suspects without judicial warrant from their homes, checkpoints and camps for internally displaced people (IDPs).

TORTURE AND ENFORCED DISAPPEARANCES

Men and boys suspected of being members of IS were subjected to enforced disappearance – cut off from their families and the outside world – in facilities controlled by the Iraqi Ministries of the Interior and Defence, the KRG and in secret detention centres. Detainees were interrogated by security officers without lawyers present and were routinely tortured. Common forms of torture included beatings on the head and body with metal rods and cables, suspension in stress positions by the arms or legs, electric shocks, and threats of rape of female relatives. Detainees faced limited access to medical care, which led to deaths in custody and amputations. They also endured harsh conditions, including severe overcrowding, poor ventilation and lack of access to showers or toilets.

UNFAIR TRIALS

The criminal justice system in Iraq remained deeply flawed. Defendants, in particular "terrorism" suspects, were routinely denied the rights to adequate time and facilities to prepare a defence, to not incriminate oneself or confess guilt, and to question prosecution witnesses. Courts continued to admit "confessions" that were extracted under torture as evidence. Many of those convicted after these unfair and hasty trials were sentenced to death.

Between July and August, the Iraqi authorities issued arrest warrants for at least 15 lawyers who were defending suspected IS members, accusing the lawyers of being affiliated with IS. These arrests caused concern among other lawyers that they could be arrested simply for defending IS suspects.

INTERNALLY DISPLACED PEOPLE

More than 3 million people remained internally displaced across Iraq. The displaced sheltered in host communities, IDP camps, informal settlements and buildings under construction. By November, more than 987,648 people in Nineveh governorate had been displaced as a result of the Mosul military operation. Humanitarian agencies reported significant shortfalls in international funding.

Civilians in IDP camps experienced shortages of food, water, medicine and other basic needs. Freedom of movement in IDP camps was severely limited, and camp residents reported that civilians, including children, were recruited from camps by paramilitary militias – sometimes forcibly – and that family members had been forcibly disappeared from public areas in the camps

and from their tents. Families were separated for days or months due to screening procedures carried out at temporary reception centres. Women heads of households who sheltered in IDP camps – particularly those whose male relatives were suspected of affiliation with IS – reported being subjected to rape and other sexual abuse and exploitation and systematic discrimination, including having inadequate and unequal access to food, water and other basic supplies.

FORCED DISPLACEMENT AND DESTRUCTION OF PROPERTY

In the context of the armed conflict involving IS, Iraqi government forces and paramilitary militias forcibly displaced civilians and destroyed their homes on a mass scale. For example, early in the year Sunni tribal militias within the PMU known as the Hashad al-Ashari, alongside Iraqi government forces, forcibly displaced at least 125 families from Salah al-Din governorate perceived to be affiliated with IS, following a decree issued by local authorities authorizing their displacement. The families were then held against their will in an IDP camp functioning as a detention centre near Tikrit.

ARMS TRADE

Factions of the PMU, which had committed war crimes and other serious violations across central and northern Iraq since 2014, benefited from transfers of arms from a range of countries, including the USA, Russia and Iran. The transferred weapons included armoured vehicles and artillery as well as a wide range of small arms. Poor management of weapons stocks and a thriving in-country and cross-border illicit trade led to the arming of militia groups, further undermining security.

FREEDOM OF EXPRESSION – KURDISTAN REGION OF IRAQ

Journalists and online activists in the KR-I were subject to arbitrary arrest, beatings, surveillance, death threats, and smear campaigns intended to damage their reputations or the reputations of their family members. This trend of interference in the freedom of expression of journalists and online activists appeared to escalate in the run-up to the independence referendum in the KR-I; Amnesty International documented 12 cases of arbitrary arrests, beatings and intimidation of journalists and online activists between June and September.

On 14 March, security forces, including anti-riot police belonging to the KR-I and Syrian fighters under the command of the KRG ("Rojava Peshmerga"), used tear gas canisters and fired live ammunition to disperse Yazidi protesters. The protesters were calling for the Rojava Peshmerga forces to leave the area, following clashes between members of the Rojava Peshmerga and Sinjar Resistance Unit earlier that month. Protesters and witnesses reported that Nazeh Nayef Qawal, a Yazidi woman, was killed during the violent dispersal of protesters.

IMPUNITY

In response to allegations of serious violations of international humanitarian law and war crimes committed by Iraqi forces and pro-government militias – such as torture, extrajudicial execution and enforced disappearance – the Iraqi authorities established committees to evaluate the available evidence and launch investigations. Such committees consistently failed to release any findings publicly or to communicate their findings to international or national NGOs. More than a year since 643 men and boys from Saqlawiya in the Anbar governorate were abducted and forcibly disappeared by PMU militias, a committee established by the Office of the Prime Minister on 5 June 2016 had failed to publicly release any findings.

On 21 September the UN Security Council passed a unanimous resolution aimed at ensuring accountability for war crimes and human rights abuses committed by IS. However, the resolution crucially failed to include any provisions to ensure accountability for crimes committed by Iraqi forces, paramilitary militias such as the PMU, the US-led coalition and others responsible for grave violations of international law, including war crimes, during the conflict.

DEATH PENALTY

Iraq remained one of the world's most prolific users of the death penalty. Scores of people were sentenced to death by courts after unfair trials and executed by hanging. The death penalty continued to be used as a tool of retribution in response to public outrage after attacks claimed by IS. In January, dozens of men were hanged for their alleged role in the killing of 1,700 Shi'a cadets at Speicher military camp near Tikrit in 2014. The men, whose "confessions" were extracted under credible allegations of torture, were convicted following deeply flawed and hasty trials. These mass executions followed a similar mass execution in August 2016, also in relation to the Speicher massacre. On 25 September, dozens of men were executed on "terrorism" charges. This mass execution took place 11 days after an IS suicide attack in Nasiriya on 14 September that killed at least 84 people.

IRELAND

Ireland
Head of state: **Michael D. Higgins**
Head of government: **Leo Varadkar (replaced Enda Kenny in June)**

Historical abuses against women and girls were not adequately addressed. Access to and information about abortion remained severely restricted and criminalized. Concerns remained about "direct provision" accommodation provided to asylum-seekers.

WOMEN'S RIGHTS

In March, the CEDAW Committee published its concluding observations on Ireland's sixth and seventh reports. It expressed concern at Ireland's abortion laws, measures to combat violence against women, including funding cuts to non-governmental support services, and the impact of austerity measures on the funding for women's NGOs.

The Committee criticized the state's failure to establish an independent, thorough and effective investigation into all alleged human rights abuses against women and girls in the "Magdalene Laundries", children's institutions and mother and baby homes which operated with state funding and oversight between the 1930s and 1996. This concern was echoed by the UN Committee against Torture in its concluding observations on Ireland's second periodic report, published in August. In November, the Ombudsman published a report criticizing the exclusion of some women from the Magdalene Laundries redress scheme.

The CEDAW Committee also noted numerous recommendations by other UN human rights mechanisms on the unresolved issue of historical abuses of women and girls, including in respect of symphysiotomies performed on women without their consent.

SEXUAL AND REPRODUCTIVE RIGHTS

In June, the UN Human Rights Committee found in *Whelan v. Ireland* that Ireland's abortion law violated the applicant's rights to be free from cruel, inhuman and degrading treatment, as well as her rights to privacy and non-discrimination in forcing her to travel abroad for an abortion. In its August concluding observations, the UN Committee against Torture stated that Ireland's abortion law causes women and girls "severe physical and mental anguish and distress".

In June, the Citizens' Assembly, established by the government to make recommendations on possible constitutional reform, recommended the removal of the Eighth Amendment to Ireland's Constitution, which placed the right to life of the foetus on a par with that of the pregnant woman. It recommended that access to abortion be provided without restriction in early pregnancy, and in a broad range of circumstances thereafter. Its recommendations were considered and supported by a specially convened parliamentary committee, which also recommended decriminalizing women and medical professionals accessing or providing

abortion services. The government committed to holding a referendum on the Eighth Amendment in early 2018.

REFUGEES AND ASYLUM-SEEKERS

Concerns remained about poor living conditions in "direct provision" accommodation centres for asylum-seekers, in particular limited living space and privacy, lack of recreational facilities especially for children, and little personal spending money. In May, the Supreme Court ruled that the state's prohibition on employment during the asylum procedure, irrespective of its duration, was unconstitutional; it gave the legislature six months to address its decision. The Ombudsman and Ombudsman for Children were given statutory powers to consider complaints from "direct provision" residents.

In September, the government announced its commitment to developing a community sponsorship programme for resettling refugees.

RIGHT TO HOUSING

A growing number of people were experiencing homelessness, many as a result of reduced availability of affordable rental properties. The number of homeless families increased by 31% between October 2016 and October 2017, with many children living in unsuitable hostel-type accommodation. In October, the European Committee of Social Rights published a decision finding Ireland in violation of the Revised European Social Charter. The decision related to conditions in some local authority housing.

SEX WORKERS

In February, the Criminal Law (Sexual Offences) Act 2017 was enacted which, among other provisions, criminalized the purchase of sex. While the Act removed criminal penalties from sex workers for soliciting and loitering, several aspects of sex work remained criminalized, despite international evidence that this can place sex workers at high risk of stigmatization, isolation, violence and other human rights abuses.

The Council of Europe Group of Experts on Action against Trafficking in Human Beings noted reports of possible negative impacts of the criminalization of the purchase of sex on victims of trafficking. It urged Ireland to analyse such impacts on the identification, protection and assistance of trafficking victims, and the prosecution of traffickers.

DISCRIMINATION – TRAVELLERS

In March, the government granted formal recognition to the Traveller community as a distinct ethnic group within Ireland, following years of campaigning by Traveller groups. This was seen as a symbolic but significant step towards recognizing and countering the long-standing discrimination experienced by Travellers in Ireland.

FREEDOM OF EXPRESSION

Concerns emerged about the growing impact on civil society groups of the Electoral Act 1997, a law which regulates political funding. The Act, as amended in 2001, prohibits overseas donations, or domestic donations over EUR2,500, to "third party" organizations for vaguely defined "political purposes".

ISRAEL AND THE OCCUPIED PALESTINIAN TERRITORIES

State of Israel
Head of government: Benjamin Netanyahu
Head of state: Reuven Rivlin

June marked 50 years since Israel's occupation of the Palestinian Territories and the start of the 11th year of its illegal blockade of the Gaza Strip, subjecting approximately 2 million inhabitants to collective punishment and a growing humanitarian crisis. The Israeli authorities intensified expansion of settlements and related infrastructure across the West Bank, including East Jerusalem, and severely restricted the freedom of movement of Palestinians. Israeli forces unlawfully killed Palestinian civilians, including children, and unlawfully detained within Israel thousands of Palestinians from the Occupied Palestinian Territories (OPT), holding hundreds in administrative detention without charge or trial. Torture and other ill-treatment of detainees, including children, remained pervasive and was committed with impunity. Israel continued to demolish Palestinian homes in the West Bank and in Palestinian villages inside Israel, forcibly evicting residents. Conscientious objectors to military service were imprisoned. Thousands of African asylum-seekers were threatened with deportation.

BACKGROUND

Israeli authorities intensified settlement expansion and land appropriation in the OPT. US and international efforts to revive negotiations failed, and Israeli-Palestinian relations remained tense. In January, Israeli authorities passed the so-called "regularization law" that retroactively legalized the settler takeover of thousands of hectares of privately owned Palestinian land and an estimated 4,500 settler homes. In addition, Israeli authorities announced and issued tenders for tens of thousands of new settlement units in East Jerusalem and across the rest of the West Bank.

Palestinians carried out stabbings, car-rammings, shootings and other attacks against Israelis in the West Bank and in Israel. The attacks, mostly carried out by individuals unaffiliated to armed groups, killed 14 Israelis and one foreign national. Israeli forces killed 76 Palestinians and one foreign national. Some were unlawfully killed while posing no threat to life.

In March, the UN Economic and Social Commission for Western Asia issued, then withdrew, a report determining Israel to be "guilty of the crime of apartheid" against Palestinians. In May, a UNESCO resolution reaffirmed the occupied status of East Jerusalem and criticized Israel's conduct in the city. Following the killing of two Israeli policemen by Palestinians, in July Israel installed metal detectors to screen Muslim worshippers entering the Temple Mount/ Haram al-Sharif. The new security measures led to heightened tensions and mass protests by Palestinians, including collective prayers, across the West Bank. The prayer protests, often met with excessive force, ended once the metal detectors were removed.

In September, the Hamas de facto administration in Gaza and the "national consensus" government in the West Bank embarked on a reconciliation process, which was rejected by Israel.

In December, US President Donald Trump recognized Jerusalem as Israel's capital in violation of international law, sparking widespread protests across the OPT and globally.

FREEDOM OF MOVEMENT – GAZA BLOCKADE AND WEST BANK RESTRICTIONS

Israel's illegal air, land and sea blockade of the Gaza Strip entered its 11th year, continuing the long-standing restrictions on the movement of people and goods into and from the area, collectively punishing Gaza's entire population. Combined with Egypt's almost total closure of the Rafah border crossing, and the West Bank authorities' punitive measures, Israel's blockade triggered a humanitarian crisis with electricity cuts reducing access to electricity from an average of eight hours per day down to as little as two to four hours, affecting clean water and sanitation and diminishing health service access, and rendering Gaza increasingly "unlivable" according to the UN. Gaza's economy deteriorated further and post-conflict reconstruction of civilian infrastructure remained severely hindered; some 23,500 Palestinians remained displaced since the 2014 conflict. Many patients with life-threatening illnesses were unable to access treatment outside Gaza due to Israeli restrictions and delays by West Bank authorities in processing referrals. Israeli forces maintained a "buffer zone" inside Gaza's border with Israel and used live ammunition against Palestinians who entered or approached it, wounding farmers working in the area. Israeli forces also fired at Palestinian fishermen in or near the "exclusion zone" along Gaza's coastline, killing at least one and injuring others.

In the West Bank, Israel maintained an array of military checkpoints, bypass roads and military and firing zones, restricting Palestinian access and travel. Israel established new checkpoints and barriers, especially in East Jerusalem. In response to Palestinian attacks on Israelis, the military authorities imposed collective punishment; they revoked the work permits of attackers' family members and closed off villages and entire areas including Silwad, Deir Abu Mishal and Beit Surik.

In Hebron, long-standing prohibitions limiting Palestinian presence, tightened in October 2015, remained in force. In Hebron's Tel Rumeida neighbourhood, a "closed military zone", Israeli forces subjected Palestinian residents to oppressive searches and prevented the entry of other Palestinians while allowing free movement for Israeli settlers. In May, Israel erected a new checkpoint and a new fence barrier within Hebron's H2 area, arbitrarily confining the Palestinian Gheith neighbourhood and segregating a street alongside the area.

ARBITRARY ARRESTS AND DETENTIONS

Israel detained or continued to imprison thousands of Palestinians from the OPT, mostly in prisons in Israel, in violation of international law. Many detainees' families, particularly those in Gaza, were not permitted entry to Israel to visit their relatives.

The authorities continued to substitute administrative detention for criminal prosecution, holding hundreds of Palestinians, including children, civil society leaders and NGO workers, without charge or trial under renewable orders, based on information withheld from detainees and their lawyers. More than 6,100 Palestinians, including 441 administrative detainees, were held in Israeli prisons at the end of the year. Israeli authorities also placed six Palestinian citizens of Israel under administrative detention.

In April around 1,500 Palestinian prisoners and detainees launched a 41-day hunger-strike to demand better conditions, family visits, an end to solitary confinement and administrative detention, and access to education. The Israeli Prison Service punished hunger-striking detainees, using solitary confinement, fines, and denial of family visits.

Palestinians from the West Bank charged with protest-related and other offences faced unfair military trials, while Israeli civilian courts trying Palestinians from East Jerusalem or the Gaza Strip issued harsh sentences even for minor offences.

In April the Israeli High Court of Justice issued a decision to reduce excessive sentencing of Palestinians under the military judicial system and ordered that legislation be amended to apply shorter sentences as of May 2018. Despite the ruling, the sentences would remain harsher than those in the Israeli civilian judicial system.

Khalida Jarrar, a member of the Palestinian Legislative Council and board member of the NGO Addameer, and Addameer staff member Salah Hammouri, remained in administrative detention at the end of the year.

The trial of Mohammed al-Halabi, a Gaza-based humanitarian worker, began at Beer Sheva District Court on charges of embezzlement from the NGO World Vision to fund Hamas. Neither an Australian government review of World Vision Gaza nor an internal World Vision audit found any evidence to support the charges. Mohammed al-Halabi stated in court that he was tortured during interrogation and detention.

TORTURE AND OTHER ILL-TREATMENT

Israeli soldiers and police and Israel Security Agency officers subjected Palestinian detainees, including children, to torture and other ill-treatment with impunity, particularly during arrest and interrogation. Reported methods included beatings, slapping, painful shackling, sleep deprivation, use of stress positions and threats. No criminal investigations were opened into more than 1,000 complaints filed since 2001. Complaints of torture and other ill-treatment by the Israeli police against asylum-seekers and members of the Ethiopian community remained common.

In December the Israeli High Court of Justice accepted the Attorney General's decision not to open a criminal investigation into Asad Abu Ghosh's torture claims despite credible evidence, thus condoning the continued use of stress positions and sleep deprivation against Palestinian detainees by Israeli interrogators.

UNLAWFUL KILLINGS

Israeli soldiers, police and security guards killed at least 75 Palestinians from the OPT, including East Jerusalem, and five Palestinians with Israeli citizenship. Some of those killed were shot while attacking Israelis or suspected of intending an attack. Many, including children, were shot and unlawfully killed while posing no immediate threat to life. Some killings, such as that of Yacoub Abu al-Qi'an, shot in his car by police in Umm al-Hiran in January, appeared to have been extrajudicial executions.

EXCESSIVE USE OF FORCE

Israeli forces, including undercover units, used excessive and sometimes lethal force when they used rubber-coated metal bullets and live ammunition against Palestinian protesters in the OPT, killing at least 20, and injuring thousands. Many protesters threw rocks or other projectiles but were posing no threat to the lives of well-protected Israeli soldiers when they were shot. In July, in response to the tensions over Temple Mount/Haram al-Sharif, the authorities killed 10 Palestinians and injured more than 1,000 during the dispersal of demonstrations, and conducted at least two violent raids on al-

Makassed hospital in East Jerusalem. In December, wheelchair user Ibrahim Abu Thuraya was shot in the head by an Israeli soldier as he was sitting with a group of protesters near the fence separating Gaza from Israel.

FREEDOMS OF EXPRESSION, ASSOCIATION AND ASSEMBLY

The authorities used a range of measures, both in Israel and the OPT, to target human rights defenders who criticized Israel's continuing occupation.

In March the Knesset (parliament) passed an amendment to the Entry into Israel Law banning entry into Israel or the OPT to anyone supporting or working for an organization that has issued or promoted a call to boycott Israel or Israeli entities, including settlements. The authorities continued to obstruct human rights workers' attempts to document the situation by denying them entry into the OPT, including the UN Special Rapporteur on the human rights situation in the OPT. An Amnesty International staff member was denied entry after he was questioned about the organization's work on settlements.

Using public order laws in East Jerusalem, and military orders in the rest of the West Bank, Israeli authorities prohibited and suppressed protests by Palestinians, and arrested and prosecuted protesters and human rights defenders. In July, the military trials of Palestinian human rights defenders Issa Amro and Farid al-Atrash began on charges related to their role in organizing peaceful protests against Israel's settlement policies. Israeli authorities continued to harass other Hebron-based human rights activists, including Badi Dweik and Imad Abu Shamsiya, and failed to protect them from settler attacks.

From May to August, the Israeli authorities detained prisoner of conscience and writer Ahmad Qatamesh under a three-month administrative detention order solely on account of his non-violent political activities and writing.

Palestinian human rights NGOs, including Al-Haq, Al Mezan and Addameer, encountered increased levels of harassment by Israeli authorities. Israeli authorities initiated tax investigations against Omar Barghouti, a prominent advocate of the boycott, divestment and sanctions campaign, in what appeared to be an effort to silence his work.

Several Israeli human rights organizations, including Breaking the Silence, Gisha, B'tselem and Amnesty International Israel were also targeted by government campaigns to undermine their work, and faced smears, stigmatization and threats.

RIGHT TO HOUSING – FORCED EVICTIONS AND DEMOLITIONS

In the West Bank, including East Jerusalem, the Israeli authorities carried out a large number of demolitions of Palestinian property, including 423 homes and structures built without Israeli permits that remained virtually impossible for Palestinians to obtain, forcibly evicting more than 660 people. Many of these demolitions were in Bedouin and herding communities that the Israeli authorities planned to forcibly transfer. The authorities also collectively punished the families of Palestinians who had carried out attacks on Israelis, by demolishing or making uninhabitable their family homes, forcibly evicting approximately 50 people.

Israeli authorities forcibly evicted eight members of the Shamasneh family from their home in Sheikh Jarrah, East Jerusalem, allowing Jewish settlers to move in. The authorities also demolished dozens of Palestinian homes inside Israel that they said were built without permits, including in Palestinian towns and villages in the Triangle, the Galilee, and in "unrecognized" Bedouin villages in the Negev/Naqab region. In January the Israeli police forcibly demolished the Bedouin village of Umm al-Hiran, to begin building a Jewish town in its place. The Knesset passed a law in April that raised the fines for building without permits, charging punitive costs for the demolition to those whose homes have been demolished, and limited recourse to the courts for those challenging demolition or eviction orders. In August, the authorities demolished al-Araqib village in the Negev/Naqab for the 116th time. Residents were ordered to compensate the state 362,000 new shekels (approximately USD100,000) for the cost of demolition and lawyers' fees.

IMPUNITY

More than three years after the end of the 2014 Gaza-Israel conflict, in which some 1,460 Palestinian civilians were killed, many in evidently unlawful attacks including war crimes, the authorities had previously indicted only three soldiers for looting and obstructing an investigation.

In a rare move, in January an Israeli military court convicted Elor Azaria, a soldier whose apparent extrajudicial execution of a wounded Palestinian in Hebron was filmed, of manslaughter. His conviction and 18-month prison sentence, which was confirmed on appeal but reduced by four months by Israel's military Chief of Staff in September, failed to reflect the gravity of the crime. Israeli authorities failed to investigate, or closed investigations into, cases of alleged unlawful killings of Palestinians by Israeli forces in both Israel and the OPT.

The Prosecutor of the ICC continued her preliminary examination of alleged crimes under international law committed in the OPT since 13 June 2014.

VIOLENCE AGAINST WOMEN AND GIRLS

There were new reports of violence against women; Palestinian communities in Israel were particularly affected. In June, the Special Rapporteur on violence against women issued recommendations urging Israeli authorities to carry out law and policy reforms by integrating CEDAW standards; to combat and prevent violence against women in Israel and the OPT; and to investigate reported abuses.

DEPRIVATION OF NATIONALITY

On 6 August the Haifa District Court confirmed the citizenship revocation of Alaa Zayoud, who was stripped of his citizenship and rendered stateless by the Minister of the Interior following a conviction for attempted murder. An appeal against the decision was pending before the Supreme Court at the end of the year. The authorities also revoked the citizenship of dozens of Palestinian Bedouin residents of the Negev/Naqab region without process or appeal, leaving them as stateless residents.

REFUGEES AND ASYLUM-SEEKERS

The authorities continued to deny asylum-seekers, more than 90% of whom were from Eritrea or Sudan, access to a fair or prompt refugee status determination process. More than 1,200 asylum-seekers were held at the Holot detention facility and at Saharonim Prison in the Negev/Naqab desert at the end of the year. According to activists, there were more than 35,000 asylum-seekers in Israel; 8,588 asylum claims remained pending. In December, the Knesset passed an amendment to the anti-infiltration law that would force asylum-seekers and refugees to accept relocation to countries in Africa or face imprisonment. Tens of thousands were at risk of deportation.

CONSCIENTIOUS OBJECTORS

At least six Israeli conscientious objectors to military service were imprisoned, including Tamar Zeevi, Atalia Ben-Abba, Noa Gur Golan, Hadas Tal, Mattan Helman and Ofir Averbukh. Israeli authorities recognized Tamar Zeevi as a conscientious objector and released her from conscription after she served a total of 100 days in prison.

ITALY

Italian Republic
Head of state: **Sergio Mattarella**
Head of government: **Paolo Gentiloni**

Italy co-operated with the Libyan authorities and non-state actors to restrict irregular migration through the central Mediterranean. This resulted in refugees

and migrants being disembarked and trapped in Libya, where they faced human rights violations and abuse. Roma continued to be forcibly evicted and segregated in camps with sub-standard living conditions. The European Commission failed to take decisive action against Italy for discrimination against Roma in access to adequate housing. Legislation criminalizing torture was introduced; however, the new law did not meet all the requirements of the Convention against Torture.

REFUGEES' AND MIGRANTS' RIGHTS

Over 2,800 refugees and migrants were estimated to have died at sea while attempting to reach Italy from Libya on unseaworthy and overcrowded vessels. The numbers were down from more than 4,500 deaths registered in 2016. Over 119,000 people survived the crossing and reached Italy, compared to 181,000 arrivals in 2016.

In May, the Italian magazine L'Espresso published new information regarding the 11 October 2013 shipwreck in the Maltese search and rescue region of the central Mediterranean. Over 260 people died, mostly Syrian refugees, among them about 60 children. According to recorded phone conversations obtained by the magazine, in the period preceding the capsizing of the refugees' boat, Italian navy and coastguard officials were reluctant to deploy the Italian warship Libra which was the closest to the boat in distress, despite repeated requests by Maltese authorities to do so. In November, a judge of the Rome tribunal ordered that charges be brought against two high-ranking officials of the Italian navy and coastguard respectively and that further investigations be carried out into the conduct of the Libra's captain. The charges against four other navy and coastguard officials were dismissed. The trial was pending at the end of the year.

The government continued to fail to adopt the decrees required to abolish the crime of "illegal entry and stay", despite being instructed to do so by parliament in April 2014.

CO-OPERATION WITH LIBYA TO CONTROL MIGRATION

In February, to reduce arrivals, Italy signed a Memorandum of Understanding with Libya, committing to provide support to Libyan authorities responsible for official immigration detention centres. Torture and other ill-treatment remained widespread in these centres. Italy continued to implement measures to increase the Libyan coastguard's capacity to intercept refugees and migrants and take them back to Libya. This was done amidst growing evidence of the Libyan coastguard's violent and reckless conduct during interceptions of boats and of its involvement in human rights violations. In May, Italy provided the Libyan coastguard with four patrolling speedboats. Italy also continued to train Libyan coastguard and navy officials as part of the EU Naval Force Mediterranean (EUNAVFOR Med) operation. In July, following a request from the Libyan government, Italy deployed a naval mission to Libyan territorial waters to combat irregular migration and the smuggling of refugees and migrants.

In November, a Libyan coastguard vessel interfered in an ongoing rescue operation in international waters. Several people drowned. The Libyan coastguard's vessel – one of those donated by Italy – was recorded on video departing at high speed, ignoring people in the water, and with a man still holding on to ropes the Libyan officials had thrown off the vessel.

Between August and December, Italy's co-operation with Libyan authorities was criticized by various UN experts and bodies, including the UN High Commissioner for Human Rights as well as the Council of Europe's Commissioner for Human Rights. The Committee against Torture expressed concern over the lack of assurances that co-operation with the Libyan coastguard or other Libyan security actors would be reviewed in light of human rights violations.

NGOS' SEARCH AND RESCUE OPERATIONS

Many of those who reached Italy by sea – over 45,400 – were rescued by NGOs. In July, Italy, with support from the EU, imposed a code of conduct on NGOs operating at sea, limiting their capacity to rescue people and disembark them in Italy. During the year, rescue NGOs were targeted by some officials, claiming that they encouraged departures from Libya. Criminal investigations were opened and were ongoing at the end of the year against some NGOs for abetting irregular migration.

ASYLUM PROCEDURES

By the end of the year, nearly 130,000 people sought asylum in Italy, a 6% increase over the nearly 122,000 in 2016. Throughout the year, over 40% of applicants received some form of protection in the first instance.

In April, legislation was introduced to speed up asylum procedures and counter irregular migration, including by reducing procedural safeguards in appeals against rejected asylum applications. The new law failed to adequately clarify the nature and function of the hotspots set up by the EU and the government following agreements in 2015. Hotspots are facilities set up for the initial reception, identification and registration of asylum-seekers and migrants coming to the EU by sea. In its May report, the National Mechanism for the Prevention of Torture highlighted the continued lack of a legal basis and applicable norms regulating the detention of people in hotspots.

Also in May, the UN Human Rights Committee criticized the prolonged detention of refugees and migrants at hotspots. It also criticized the lack of safeguards against the incorrect classification of asylum-seekers as economic migrants, and the lack of investigations into reports of excessive use of force during identification procedures. In December, the UN Committee against Torture expressed concern about the lack of safeguards against the forcible return of people to countries where they could be at risk of human rights violations.

In September, the criminal trial started in Perugia against seven officials implicated in the illegal expulsion to Kazakhstan of Alma Shalabayeva and Alua Ablyazova, the wife and daughter of Kazakhstani opposition politician Mukhtar Ablyazov, in May 2013. The accused, charged with kidnapping, false statements and abuse of power, included three high-ranking police officers and the judge who validated the expulsion.

UNACCOMPANIED CHILDREN

Nearly 16,000 unaccompanied children reached Italy by sea. A new law to strengthen their protection was introduced in April. It covered access to services and introduced safeguards against expulsions. However, the authorities continued to struggle to ensure their reception in accordance with international standards.

RELOCATION AND RESETTLEMENT SCHEMES

Of the around 35,000 asylum-seekers who were to be transferred to other EU countries under the EU relocation scheme, only 11,464 had left Italy by the end of the year, while a further 698 were about to be transferred.

Italy continued to grant humanitarian access to people transferred through a scheme funded by the faith-based NGOs Comunità di Sant'Egidio, Federation of Evangelical Churches and Tavola Valdese. Over 1,000 people were received under the scheme since its beginning in 2016.

At the end of December, Italy also granted access to 162 vulnerable refugees evacuated from Libya to Italy by UNHCR, the UN refugee agency.

RIGHT TO HOUSING AND FORCED EVICTIONS

Roma continued to experience systemic discrimination in access to adequate housing. The European Commission still failed to take decisive action against Italy for breach of EU law for discrimination in its denial of the right to housing, including the lack of safeguards against forced evictions and the continued segregation of Roma in camps.

In April, hundreds of Roma living in the informal settlement of Gianturco in Naples were forcibly evicted after authorities failed to carry out any meaningful consultation with the affected families. The only alternative the authorities offered was the rehousing of 130 people in a new authorized segregated camp. The remaining adults and children were rendered homeless. Around 200 of them settled in a former market area in Naples and remained at risk of being forcibly evicted.

In August, the authorities forcibly evicted hundreds of people, including many children, from a building in the centre of Rome. Many of them were recognized refugees who had been living and working in the area for several years. The authorities failed to provide adequate housing alternatives, leaving scores of people to sleep in the open for days, before they were violently removed by police in riot gear. Several people were hurt by police using water cannons and batons. Some families were eventually rehoused temporarily outside Rome.

TORTURE AND OTHER ILL-TREATMENT

In July, Italy finally introduced legislation criminalizing torture, having ratified the Convention against Torture in 1989. However, in December, the Committee against Torture noted that the definition of torture in the new law was not in line with the Convention. The new law also failed to provide for the implementation of other key provisions, including the reviewing of interrogation policies and provision of redress to victims.

In September, the Council of Europe Committee for the Prevention of Torture (CPT) published the report of its visit to Italy in April 2016. The CPT received allegations of ill-treatment, including unnecessary and excessive use of force by law enforcement officials and prison officers in virtually all detention facilities it visited. The CPT noted that overcrowding persisted, despite recent reforms.

In October, the European Court of Human Rights found that the treatment of 59 people by police and medical staff during their detention, following the protests against the 2001 Genoa G8 summit, amounted to torture.

Also in October, 37 police officers, serving in the Lunigiana area in northern Tuscany, were charged in relation to numerous cases of personal injury and other abuses. Many of these abuses were against foreign nationals, on two occasions involving the use of electric batons. The trial was pending at the end of the year.

DEATHS IN CUSTODY

In July, following a second police investigation which started in 2016, five police officers were charged in relation to the death in custody of Stefano Cucchi in 2009. Three officers were charged with manslaughter and two with slander and making false statements. The trial was pending at the end of the year.

JAMAICA

Jamaica
Head of state: **Queen Elizabeth II, represented by Patrick Linton Allen**
Head of government: **Andrew Michael Holness**

Unlawful killings – some of which may amount to extrajudicial executions – continued to be carried out by the police with impunity. A review of national legislation related to sexual offences, domestic violence, child care and child protection was underway. NGOs raised concerns over the right to privacy after proposals to introduce national identity cards. Lesbian, gay, bisexual and transgender people continued to face discrimination in law and in practice. Gay and bisexual prisoners continued to be at heightened risk for HIV.

BACKGROUND

Despite committing to the establishment of a national human rights institution, Jamaica had not established the mechanism by the end of the year.

Jamaica continued to have one of the highest homicide rates in the Americas. Between January and June, homicides increased by 19% compared with the same period in 2016, according to police data.

POLICE AND SECURITY FORCES

Between January and March, the police oversight mechanism, the Independent

Commission of Investigations (INDECOM) received 73 new complaints of assault and documented 42 killings by law enforcement officials. During the year, 168 people were killed by law enforcement officials, compared with 111 people in 2016.

Female relatives of those allegedly killed by the police continued to battle an underfunded, sluggish court system in their fight for justice, truth and reparation.[1]

More than a year after a Commission of Enquiry published its findings into the events that took place in Western Kingston during the 2010 state of emergency that left at least 69 people dead, the government had still not officially responded on how it planned to implement the recommendations, or made a public apology. In June, the Jamaica Constabulary Force completed an internal administrative review into the conduct of officers named in the Commissioners' report. However, it found no misconduct or responsibility for human rights violations during the state of emergency.

In June, legislation was passed to create "zones of special operations" as part of a crime prevention plan.

INDECOM hosted a Caribbean Use of Force Conference to develop a region-wide Use of Force Policy consistent with best practice in human rights. Law enforcement officials from across the region participated in the forum, along with experts in policing and human rights.

VIOLENCE AGAINST WOMEN AND GIRLS

In March, women's movements and survivors of gender-based and sexual violence took to the streets in the capital, Kingston, to protest against impunity for sexual violence.

Jamaican NGOs made a series of recommendations to the Joint Select Committee of Parliament tasked with reviewing national legislation related to sexual offences, domestic violence, child care and child protection. These included, among other things, repealing marital rape exceptions under the Sexual Offences Act to protect women against rape, irrespective of their marital status.

RIGHT TO PRIVACY

The NGO Jamaicans for Justice (JFJ) raised concerns that the National Identification and Registration Authority Act could undermine the right to privacy and that Article 41 specifically could limit access to public goods and services.

CHILDREN'S RIGHTS

JFJ made a series of recommendations to the Parliamentary Joint Select Committee to strengthen the Child Care and Protection Act. Among other things, JFJ recommended expanding the list of authorities to which members of the public can make a legally mandated report of child abuse, to make reporting easier.

RIGHTS OF LESBIAN, GAY, BISEXUAL AND TRANSGENDER PEOPLE

There remained no legal protection against discrimination based on real or perceived sexual orientation or gender identity. As a result, LGBT people continued to face harassment and violence.

Consensual sex between men remained criminalized, and there was limited protection against intimate-partner violence for people in same-sex relationships. NGOs recommended that laws be amended to ensure that rape is treated as a gender-neutral offence.

As transgender people continued to be unable to change their legal name and gender, LGBTI organizations were concerned that the proposed national identification system could undermine the privacy of transgender people and expose them to stigma and discrimination, including from potential employers.

Jamaica's third annual Pride event took place in August and continued to increase visibility for the LGBTI community and create opportunities for engagement with wider society.

RIGHT TO HEALTH

In June, the NGO Stand up for Jamaica released *Barriers Behind Bars*, a report which analysed the high risk of sexual violence, human rights violations, and consequently HIV, faced by gay and bisexual men in Kingston's General Penitentiary, in which gay and bisexual men are segregated from the general prison population. The report aimed to generate discussion about best practices for reducing HIV in prisons.

INTERNATIONAL JUSTICE

Jamaica again failed to ratify the Rome Statute of the ICC, which it signed in September 2000, nor had it adhered to the UN Convention against Torture or the International Convention for the Protection of All Persons from Enforced Disappearance.

---

1. Jamaica: A thank you from Shackelia Jackson (News story, 15 December 2017)

JAPAN

Japan
Head of government: **Shinzo Abe**

Despite harsh criticism from civil society and academics expressing fears that human rights would be weakened, parliament passed a controversial law targeting conspiracies to commit "terrorism" and other serious crimes. Authorities in Osaka city approved a same-sex couple as foster parents, and two municipalities moved towards recognizing same-sex partnerships. Detention of a prominent peace activist raised fair trial concerns. A District Court supported tuition waivers for a Korean school that was excluded due to their alleged ties to the Democratic People's Republic of Korea (North Korea). Executions continued to be carried out.

RIGHTS OF LESBIAN, GAY, BISEXUAL, TRANSGENDER AND INTERSEX PEOPLE

While pervasive discrimination based on real or perceived sexual orientation and gender identity continued, some progress was made in local municipalities.[1] Under the foster care scheme providing support to children without guardians or children who are neglected or

abused, authorities in the city of Osaka approved a gay couple as foster parents. The couple had been looking after a teenage boy since February. This was the first case of a same-sex couple becoming foster parents and being considered as a single household by the city. Sapporo City and Minato Ward advanced towards recognizing same-sex partnerships, following the practices of five other municipalities in 2015 and 2016.

FREEDOM OF EXPRESSION

In June, the Diet (parliament) adopted an overly broad law targeting alleged conspiracies to commit "terrorism" and other serious crimes. The law gave authorities broad surveillance powers that could be misused to curtail the rights to freedom of expression, association and privacy, without sufficient safeguards.

The law also presented a threat to the legitimate work of independent NGOs, as the definition of "organized crime group" was vague and overly broad and not clearly limited to activities that would constitute organized crime or pose a genuine threat to national security. Protests were held in multiple locations against the law's potentially adverse effect on civil society.

FREEDOM OF ASSEMBLY

Prominent peace activist Hiroji Yamashiro was arrested and detained for five months from late 2016 until March 2017, under restrictive conditions and without access to his family, for his role in protests against new US military construction projects on Okinawa.[2] The protracted detention of one of the most vocal opponents of the US military construction on Okinawa, without respecting the presumption of release pending trial, had a chilling effect on others exercising their right to peaceful assembly. Some activists hesitated to join protests for fear of reprisals.

DISCRIMINATION – ETHNIC MINORITIES

In July the Osaka District Court ruled as illegal the government's exclusion of Osaka Korean High School from its high school education tuition waiver programme. The

Court found that this hindered the right to education of children of Korean origin. This was the first ruling in a number of similar lawsuits on the eligibility of such schools for the programme. Although public high schools had been exempt from tuition fees under the programme since 2010, the government excluded Korean schools due to concerns that the subsidies may be misused because of the schools' historical ties to North Korea.

WORKERS' RIGHTS – MIGRANT WORKERS

In November, the government began to accept the first of 10,000 Vietnamese nationals to be admitted over three years under the Technical Intern Training Program to meet Japan's labour shortage. The scheme had been harshly criticized by human rights advocates for causing a wide range of human rights abuses. Critics feared that expanding the scheme without addressing its problems would result in increased incidents of sexual abuse, work-related deaths and working conditions amounting to forced labour.

REFUGEES AND ASYLUM-SEEKERS

While the number of asylum applications continued to increase dramatically, the government reported in February that it had approved 28 out of 10,901 claims in 2016, which was a 44% increase in claims from the previous year.

VIOLENCE AGAINST WOMEN AND GIRLS

President Moon Jae-in of the Republic of Korea (South Korea) made a statement in December that the 2015 agreement between Japan and South Korea on Japan's Military Sexual Slavery System failed to solve the issue, following the findings of the task force appointed in July to review the deal. The agreement had been criticized by civil society organizations as well as historians for its failure to provide a fully victim-centred approach and to provide an official, unequivocal recognition of responsibility by Japan for serious human rights violations committed by its military against women and girls before and during World War II.

1. Japan: Human rights law and discrimination against LGBT people (ASA 22/5955/2017)

2. Japan: Prominent peace activist detained without bail - Hiroji Yamashiro (ASA 22/5552/2017)

JORDAN

Hashemite Kingdom of Jordan
Head of state: **King Abdullah II bin al-Hussein**
Head of government: **Hani Al-Mulki**

Parliament approved several reforms including the repeal of a law which allowed rapists to escape prosecution if they married their victims. Women continued to be discriminated against in law and in practice. Parliament passed a law that would guarantee certain rights for pre-trial detainees and reduce the length of custodial sentences. Local governors continued to issue orders to hold individuals in prolonged detention without charge. The rights to freedom of expression and of association continued to be restricted. Migrant workers were inadequately protected from exploitation and abuse. Around 50,000 refugees from Syria remained trapped in the desert on the border with Syria in appalling conditions. Death sentences were imposed and executions carried out.

BACKGROUND

Jordan remained part of the US-led military coalition fighting in Iraq and Syria against the armed group Islamic State (IS) (see Iraq and Syria entries), and of the Saudi Arabia-led coalition engaged in the armed conflict in Yemen (see Yemen entry).

In August, local elections were held which, for the first time, included local governorate-level councils in accordance with the 2015 Decentralization Law.

In February, the government adopted several measures to address the economic crisis amid public protests driven mainly by rising unemployment and low wages. They included subsidy cuts, and tax hikes on fuel and commodities as well as telecommunication services.

In May, the national Law on the Rights of Persons with Disabilities came into force; its provisions were largely in line with the UN Convention on the Rights of Persons with Disabilities, which Jordan ratified in 2008.

In July, Parliament held ordinary and exceptional sessions to discuss a 16-bill package of draft laws and by-laws proposed by the Royal Committee for Developing the Judiciary and Enhancing the Rule of Law, which was established by the King in October 2016.

DETENTION

In April, the National Centre for Human Rights published a report that detailed ongoing human rights violations by security forces during arrest, including late-night security raids where excessive force was used, and in pre-trial detention in temporary detention facilities. Detainees were denied access to a lawyer during interrogations, and faced torture and other ill-treatment. The report also documented poor detention conditions and the lack of a classification system to protect detainees' safety, including by holding incompatible categories of detainees in the same cell.

In mid-2017, Parliament enacted laws that guaranteed suspects the right of access to a lawyer on arrest, created a legal aid fund, and limited the use of pre-trial detention as an "exceptional measure" for specific purposes. The new laws set a maximum three-month period for those charged with minor offences, and up to 18 months for serious charges. The legislation also introduced alternatives to pre-trial detention, such as electronic monitoring, travel bans and house arrest but did not cover detention under the General Intelligence Directorate.

ADMINISTRATIVE DETENTION

The authorities continued to detain suspects under the 1954 Crime Prevention Law that allowed detentions of up to one year without charge or trial or any means of legal remedy. It was used particularly in cases related to

terrorism, espionage, treason, drugs and counterfeiting.

The NGO Sisterhood Is Global Institute in Jordan reported that women who were victims of domestic violence or at risk of so-called honour crimes were held under administrative detention for their protection. More than 1,700 such women were held in administrative detention, which represented a 16% decrease since 2015.

FREEDOM OF ASSOCIATION

In August, the Companies Control Department notified the Attorney General that the Center for Defending Freedom of Journalists (CDFJ) violated the 1997 Law on Companies by receiving foreign funding while registered as a "civil company" instead of a "non-profit company". CDFJ received a copy of the notification which ordered it to stop receiving foreign or domestic funding and calling itself a non-profit company.

Prior to this, CDFJ had not received an official warning about its funding although it had been active for 19 years with the stated mission to protect media freedoms, address violations of journalists' rights, and to reform legislation to protect press freedoms.

FREEDOM OF EXPRESSION

The Audiovisual Commission continued to block access to several websites and online platforms under Article 49 of the Press and Publications Law, which required any "electronic publication that engages in publication of news, investigations, articles, or comments, which have to do with the internal or external affairs of the Kingdom" to obtain a licence, and granted executive authorities the power to close unlicensed sites.

WOMEN'S RIGHTS

In February, the CEDAW Committee noted Jordan's efforts to address discrimination against women in marriage and the family, but remained concerned about the continued application of discriminatory provisions in the Personal Status Act, particularly in relation to the guardianship of women. It also raised concerns about the persistence of child marriage in accordance with legislation that allows Shari'a courts and legal guardians the discretion to allow marriage, in certain circumstances, of girls aged 15 and over. The Committee further noted the continued discrimination in inheritance law, and the tendency of Shari'a courts to rule in favour of husbands in divorce, alimony and child custody proceedings.

In July, Parliament abolished Article 98 of the Penal Code which was invoked in so-called honour killing cases and allowed a man to receive a reduced sentence if he killed a woman relative and the act was deemed to have been committed in a "fit of rage caused by an unlawful or dangerous act on the part of the victim". However, Article 340 remained; it allowed for a reduced sentence on grounds of mitigating circumstances in cases where a man murdered his wife or any woman relative after finding her in an "adulterous situation". Although this applied to both men and women, men remained less likely to face adultery charges in a polygamous system.

In August, Parliament repealed Article 308, which allowed rapists to escape prosecution if they married their victims.

WORKERS' RIGHTS – MIGRANT WORKERS

The NGO Tamkeen Fields for Aid said that almost 1.2 million migrant workers resided in Jordan although only 315,016 had work permits. Migrant workers continued to face exploitation and abuse, including confiscation of their passports by employers, poor working and living conditions, the denial of their right to change employment, forced labour, and human trafficking.

Migrant women domestic workers continued to be denied their annual leave entitlement, and were subject to ill-defined working hours, verbal, physical and sexual abuse, confinement to their employers' home and unpaid wages.

In February, the CEDAW Committee welcomed measures adopted to protect women migrant domestic workers' rights, such as the issuing of unified standard contracts, protection under Labour Code provisions, regulation of employment agencies, and the adoption of a law which criminalized trafficking in people. It remained concerned, however, that the measures were insufficient due to the lack of shelters, restricted access to justice, the largely ineffective application of the Labour Code and lack of regular inspection visits to the workplace.

REFUGEES AND ASYLUM-SEEKERS

Jordan hosted about 655,000 Syrian refugees registered by UNHCR, the UN refugee agency, in addition to over 13,000 Palestinian refugees from Syria, and over 2 million long-term Palestinian refugees, among others.

Some 50,000 refugees from Syria remained trapped at Rukban in the "berm", a desert area between Jordan and Syria, with humanitarian access effectively blocked since June 2016, apart from in June 2017 when the authorities permitted one round of aid distribution. Refugees were trapped in appalling humanitarian conditions: food, medical assistance and shelter were extremely limited, and they had sporadic access to water.

In October, Jordan ended even limited cross-border aid and said that aid could only be delivered from Syria. The international community and Jordan failed to agree to a long-term solution for the stranded refugees who were denied access to asylum procedures or opportunities for resettlement to third countries.

According to humanitarian agencies, by September the authorities had forcibly returned more than 2,330 refugees to Syria.

INTERNATIONAL JUSTICE

In December, the ICC ruled that Jordan failed to comply with its obligations as a state party to the Rome Statute of the ICC after it did not execute the Court's request for the arrest of Sudanese President Omar al-Bashir. The Court decided to refer Jordan's non-compliance to the Assembly of States Parties of the Rome Statute and to the UN Security Council. Jordanian authorities failed to arrest President al-Bashir when he visited the country in March for the Arab League summit. The ICC has issued two arrest warrants against him on charges of genocide, war crimes and crimes against humanity in Darfur, Sudan.

DEATH PENALTY

Courts continued to hand down death sentences and several people were executed.

KAZAKHSTAN

Republic of Kazakhstan
Head of state: **Nursultan Nazarbayev**
Head of government: **Bakytzhan Sagintayev**

Leading or participating in an unregistered organization continued to be an offence. Trade unions and NGOs faced undue restrictions. Torture and other ill-treatment in detention facilities persisted. Journalists were subjected to politically motivated prosecutions and attacks. Women and people with disabilities continued to face discrimination.

WORKERS' RIGHTS

Independent trade unions faced restrictive laws and closure. Trade unionists were prosecuted on fabricated charges of inciting illegal strikes or embezzlement.

On 4 January, a court ordered the dissolution of the Confederation of Independent Trade Unions of Kazakhstan (KNPRK), and two affiliates, the National Healthcare Workers' Union and National Domestic Workers' Union, on the grounds that they failed to meet a registration deadline. On 5 January, hundreds of oil workers began a hunger strike to protest against the dissolution, and three union leaders were arrested. On 7 April, Nurbek Kushakbaev was sentenced to two and a half years' imprisonment. On 16 May, Amin Yeleusinov was charged with misappropriation or embezzlement of

property and sentenced to two years' imprisonment, and on 25 July, Larisa Kharkova was sentenced for abuse of power and given a sentence of four years of restricted freedom by a court in Shymkent. In the period 19-24 January, 63 oil workers were prosecuted and fined for their participation in the hunger strike. In June, the Committee on the Application of Standards of the ILO expressed concern about the "grave issue" of the dissolution of the KNPRK and called on the authorities to ensure that the KNPRK and its affiliates "are able to fully exercise their trade union rights".

PRISONERS OF CONSCIENCE

On 20 January, the Atyrau Regional Court in western Kazakhstan upheld the sentence of human rights defenders and prisoners of conscience Maks Bokaev and Talgat Ayan to five years' imprisonment for their involvement in organizing peaceful demonstrations and for their posts on social media against the Land Code. At the end of January, they were transferred to a penal colony in Petropavlovsk, northern Kazakhstan, 1,500km from their home city. Maks Bokaev and Talgat Ayan were not informed in advance of their transfer and did not have adequate clothing for the winter weather conditions in northern Kazakhstan. On 13 April, the Supreme Court rejected Maks Bokaev's and Talgat Ayan's appeals. On 22 August, following his lawyer's successful petition, Talgat Ayan was transferred to a penal colony in Aktobe, in northwestern Kazakhstan, closer to his young children.

TORTURE AND OTHER ILL-TREATMENT

Following its second periodic report to the UN Human Rights Committee, in April Kazakhstan reported that the Prosecutor General's office received 700 allegations of torture in detention facilities in 2016, and that over the past five years 158 officials had been convicted of torture.

In June, the UN Committee against Torture found that Aleksei Ushenin had been subjected to torture and other ill-treatment and that the authorities failed to conduct a prompt, impartial and effective investigation into his complaint. Aleksei Ushenin claimed that he was beaten for two days in August 2011 to force him to confess to a robbery. Police officers put a plastic bag over his head until he lost consciousness, stubbed out cigarettes on his body, and repeatedly inserted a rubber baton into his anus.

IMPUNITY

The authorities had not fully and effectively investigated allegations of human rights violations committed in connection with the violent clashes between police and demonstrating oil workers in Zhanaozen in December 2011, during which at least 15 people were killed and over 100 were seriously injured when the police reportedly used excessive force against demonstrators.

FREEDOM OF ASSOCIATION

NGOs faced undue restrictions, stringent reporting requirements under legislation introduced at the end of 2015, and frequent tax inspections. Failure to regularly supply accurate information for the central database of NGOs led to fines or a temporary ban on activities.

The NGOs International Legal Initiative (ILI) and Liberty Foundation faced punitive fines for allegedly failing to pay tax. On 6 April, the Special Inter-District Economic Court of Almaty upheld the decision of the Tax Directorate that ILI should pay corporate income tax on grants received from foreign donors, although not-for-profit organizations were exempt from paying tax. On 31 May, the Special Inter-District Economic Court of Almaty rejected Liberty Foundation's appeal against the Tax Directorate's decision. The organizations paid fines of 1,300,000 tenge and 3,000,000 tenge (EUR4,000 and 8,300) respectively.

FREEDOM OF EXPRESSION

Independent journalists critical of the authorities were subjected to politically motivated prosecutions and attacks.

In September, Zhanbolat Mamai, editor of the independent newspaper *Sayasi Kalam*

Tribuna, which is critical of the authorities, was sentenced to three years of restricted freedom for money laundering. He claimed that the charges were politically motivated. Zhanbolat Mamai had been detained since February. On 14 May, Ramazan Yesergepov, journalist and chairman of the NGO Journalists in Trouble, was stabbed while travelling by train to the capital Astana to discuss Zhanbolat Mamai's case with foreign diplomats and international experts. He believed that the attack was linked to his critical reporting and interest in Zhanbolat Mamai's case.

FREEDOM OF ASSEMBLY

Organizing or participating in a peaceful demonstration without the authorities' prior authorization remained an offence under both the Administrative Offences Code and the Criminal Code, punishable by heavy fines or up to 75 days' detention.

On 13 July, the UN Human Rights Committee found that Andrei Sviridov's right to freedom of peaceful assembly had been violated in 2009 when he was prosecuted for holding a one-man picket to protest against the prosecution of human rights defender Yevgeny Zhovtis. He was found guilty of conducting a demonstration without prior authorization and fined 12,960 tenge (EUR33).

On 1 August, peaceful protesters Askhat Bersalimov and Khalilkhan Ybrahamuly were detained and sentenced to five and three days' administrative detention respectively for taking part in an unauthorized demonstration. They were part of a group of a dozen people who gathered in Mahatma Ghandi Park in the city of Almaty on 29 July, walked to the main post office and sent appeals to foreign governments and international organizations on behalf of Zhanbolat Mamai and other prisoners.

WOMEN'S RIGHTS

The Ministry of Internal Affairs said that during the first half of the year, 35,253 protection orders were applied in cases of domestic violence. However, NGOs reported that violence against women was under-reported and that there was a low rate of prosecution of cases of violence against women as well as in sexual harassment cases.

The authorities continued to refuse to acknowledge that Anna Belousova had been a victim of sexual harassment despite the CEDAW Committee ruling in 2015 that recommended that Kazakhstan provide her with adequate compensation. In March, the Supreme Court upheld a ruling by a court in Kostanai that she was not due compensation. In July, the Saryarkinsk District Court refused a claim for compensation against the Ministry of Finance. Anna Belousova had been employed at a primary school in Pertsevka since 1999. In January 2011, the school's new director threatened to dismiss her unless she engaged in sexual relations with him. She refused and her employment was terminated in March 2011.

INTERNATIONAL SCRUTINY

In April, the NGO Coalition for the Defence of Human Rights Defenders and Activists sent a petition to the President. It called for the adoption of legislation to allow for the implementation of decisions by UN treaty bodies relating to Kazakhstan. The Coalition stated that of 25 decisions taken in favour of applicants from Kazakhstan since 2011, none had been implemented due to the absence of necessary legislation.

In September, the UN Special Rapporteur on the rights of persons with disabilities visited the country. The Special Rapporteur called on Kazakhstan to bring its national legislation on legal capacity and mental health in line with international human rights law and standards. She highlighted the fact that under current legislation people with disabilities may be institutionalized and subjected to medical interventions without their free and informed consent.

KENYA

Republic of Kenya
Head of state and government: Uhuru Muigai Kenyatta

Police used excessive force against opposition protesters following the elections, leaving dozens dead. The ruling party made statements threatening the independence of the judiciary after the Supreme Court annulled the election results. The NGOs Coordination Board threatened organizations working on human rights and governance with closure and other punitive measures after they criticized the electoral process. Prolonged strikes by medical workers had an impact on access to public health care, disproportionately affecting the poor.

BACKGROUND

The general election held on 8 August was contested by the ruling Jubilee Party, led by incumbent President Kenyatta, and the opposition coalition, the National Super Alliance (NASA), led by former Prime Minister Raila Odinga. On 11 August, the Independent Electoral and Boundaries Commission declared that President Kenyatta had won 54% of the vote and Raila Odinga 44%. NASA rejected the presidential results citing irregularities in the counting process, and the way the results were transmitted. It filed a petition against the results with the Supreme Court on 18 August.

On 1 September, the Court ruled that the election results should be annulled because they were "invalid, null and void", and ordered a new presidential election to take place. NASA said they would not participate unless their demands were met including, among other things, the appointment of new returning officers in all 291 constituencies, and the engagement of independent international experts to monitor the electoral information and communication technology system. On 10 October Raila Odinga announced his withdrawal from the contest because the Commission had not made the necessary reforms.

The election re-run was planned for 26 October. On 30 October, the Commission declared that Uhuru Kenyatta had won with 98% of the vote from a turnout of under 40% – less than half the turnout recorded in August. On 31 October, Raila Odinga called for a "national resistance movement" and the formation of a "people's assembly" to bring civil society groups together to "restore democracy".

JUSTICE SYSTEM

High-ranking members of the Jubilee Party verbally attacked the Supreme Court after its 1 September ruling annulling President Kenyatta's August election victory. On 2 September, President Kenyatta announced that there was a problem with the judiciary. A record of telephone calls by one Court judge appeared in the media, prompting him to pursue legal action on defamation grounds against the Senior Director of Innovation, Digital and Diaspora Communication in the Office of the President.

On 24 October, an unidentified gunman shot and injured the Court Deputy Chief Justice's driver in the capital, Nairobi. The incident happened a day before the Court's ruling that there would be an election re-run on 26 October.

EXCESSIVE USE OF FORCE

In the run-up to the 8 August election, the police classified opposition stronghold areas of Nairobi, including Mathare, as likely "hotspots" for election-related violence.

In the period following the August election and the Supreme Court's decision to annul it, supporters of both parties took to the streets in protest.

The police used excessive force to disperse protesters who supported the opposition party and demonstrated against the electoral process, including with live ammunition and tear gas. Dozens died in the violence, including at least 33 people who were shot by police and of whom two were children. Meanwhile, pro-government protesters were permitted to demonstrate without interference.

On 19 September, Jubilee Party supporters protested outside the Supreme Court in Nairobi against its decision to annul the election; they accused the Court of "stealing" their victory.

They blocked a main highway and burned tyres. There were similar demonstrations in the towns of Nakuru, Kikuyu, Nyeri and Eldoret. The demonstrators, mostly young people, accused the judges of making an illegal judgment.

On 28 September, University of Nairobi students clashed with General Service Unit police during a protest outside the university premises against the arrest of MP and former student leader Paul Ongili. Paul Ongili was arrested the same day for abusive remarks he allegedly made about President Kenyatta in connection with the election. Following the protest, the police raided the university buildings and beat students with batons, injuring 27 of them. The Inspector General of Police said the university administration had invited the police to enter after the protesting students stoned motorists. The university Senate then closed the university on 3 October; it had not reopened by the end of the year.

Following the 26 October election, there were further killings when police fired live ammunition at protesters. The real number of deaths during this period was unknown; relatives of victims did not report the killings for fear of reprisals from the police.

FREEDOM OF ASSOCIATION

The authorities continued to use legal and administrative measures to restrict the activities of civil society organizations working on human rights and governance. In May the Nairobi High Court ruled that the government should publish the Public Benefit Organization (PBO) Act 2013. If implemented, the law could improve the working environment for civil society organizations and NGOs. It contains provisions, in line with the Constitution, guaranteeing the right to freedom of association. However, the authorities continued to use the Non-Governmental Organization (NGO) Law, which restricted the full realization of these rights.

Between 14 and 16 August, the NGOs Coordination Board (within the Ministry of Interior and Co-ordination of National Government) accused two human rights organizations – the Kenya Human Rights Commission and the Africa Centre for Open Governance (AfriCOG) – of financial and regulatory impropriety. It called upon the Kenya Revenue Authority, the Directorate of Criminal Investigations and the Central Bank of Kenya to take action against them, including by freezing their accounts and arresting and prosecuting AfriCOG's directors and board members.[1] On 16 August, the NGOs Coordination Board threatened to arrest the heads of both organizations, as well as a former UN Special Rapporteur on the rights to freedom of peaceful assembly and of association, who also served on AfriCOG's board of directors. The same day, Kenya Revenue Authority officials, accompanied by police, attempted to raid AfriCOG's offices with irregular search warrants. They stopped the raid on the orders of an official in the Ministry of Interior and Coordination of National Government who also suspended the closure threat for 90 days. AfriCOG and the Commission had been at the forefront of those exposing the electoral irregularities.

REFUGEES AND ASYLUM SEEKERS

Kenya continued to host almost 500,000 refugees, most of whom resided in Dadaab refugee camp in Garissa County, and Kakuma refugee camp in Turkana County. Other refugees were located in Nairobi. The majority of refugees in Dadaab were from Somalia; the majority of refugees in Kakuma were from South Sudan. By September, appeals for international support from UNHCR, the UN refugee agency, for the regional refugee crisis had secured only 27% of the necessary funding.

In February, the High Court declared the 2016 government directive to close Dadaab refugee camp by May 2017 to be in violation of the Constitution and Kenya's obligations under international law with regard to the principle of *non-refoulement* and the prohibition of discrimination on grounds of race or ethnicity. Thus, Dadaab refugee camp remained open. The ruling also stated that the government's move to revoke the assumed refugee status of Somalis who had fled to Kenya was unconstitutional and violated rights guaranteed in national and international instruments.

The authorities continued the voluntary repatriation of Somali refugees, initiated in 2014 under the Tripartite Agreement framework. Between May 2016 and September 2017, over 70,000 refugees were repatriated from Dadaab to Somalia.

On 17 February, the Court of Appeal upheld a 2013 High Court ruling which quashed government directives to round up all refugees living in urban areas and relocate them to refugee camps, as part of a plan to repatriate them.

On 25 April, a High Court in Garissa ordered the deportation of 29 Somali asylum-seekers to Somalia. The group had been arrested in Mwingi in March and charged before a Magistrate Court with being in Kenya unlawfully. The magistrate ordered that they be taken to Dadaab refugee camp and registered by the Refugee Affairs Secretariat (RAS); however, the RAS officer refused to register them. The magistrate's order was ultimately quashed by the High Court and all 29, including 10 children, were deported to Somalia on 4 May 2017.

INDIGENOUS PEOPLES' RIGHTS

Elias Kimaiyo, Indigenous Sengwer community leader and human rights defender, suffered a broken collar bone when he was beaten and shot at by a Kenya Forest Service guard in Embobut Forest on 5 April. He was attacked when he photographed guards burning Sengwer huts in violation of a 2013 injunction issued by the High Court of Eldoret to stop arrests and evictions of the Sengwer people.

On 26 May, the AU African Court on Human and Peoples' Rights ruled that the government had illegally evicted Ogiek Indigenous People from the Mau Forest, and failed to substantiate its claim that the eviction would serve to conserve the forest.

RIGHT TO HEALTH

The strike by doctors in public hospitals which began in December 2016 ended in March 2017. The strike followed the breakdown, after several years, of negotiations between the government and the Kenya Medical Practitioners, Pharmacists and Dentist Union regarding the Collective Bargaining Agreement signed in 2013. The strike took place against a background of alleged massive financial corruption at the Ministry of Health. It was followed in June by a strike by public hospital nurses which lasted until November, when the government and the nurses' union signed the 2013 Agreement.

The strikes adversely affected public health services across the country, and disproportionately impeded access to health care for people who could not afford private medical insurance cover, particularly those living in informal settlements.

---

1. Kenya: Attempts to shut down human rights groups unlawful and irresponsible (News story, 15 August)

KOREA (DEMOCRATIC PEOPLE'S REPUBLIC OF)

Democratic People's Republic of Korea
Head of state: **Kim Jong-un**
Head of government: **Pak Pong-ju**

Although the government took some positive steps to engage with international human rights mechanisms, the situation on the ground failed to show real progress. Up to 120,000 people continued to be arbitrarily detained in political prison camps, where conditions fell far short of international standards. Restrictions on the rights to freedom of expression and freedom of movement remained severe. Workers sent abroad suffered harsh working conditions.

BACKGROUND

The Democratic People's Republic of Korea (North Korea) conducted a nuclear test on 3 September, the sixth in its history, and carried out numerous medium- and long-range missile tests throughout the year. The military provocations resulted in the UN issuing unprecedentedly stringent sanctions on the country. Exchange of military and political threats between authorities of North Korea and the USA further escalated tensions. Concerns over the safety risks of nuclear tests increased after media reports of landslides near a nuclear test site, and people who had previously lived near sites showing signs of possible radiation exposure. The killing of Kim Jong-nam, half-brother of leader Kim Jong-un, in Malaysia on 13 February by two women allegedly using chemical agents raised questions about the possible involvement of North Korean state agents.

ARBITRARY ARRESTS AND DETENTIONS

Systematic, widespread and gross human rights violations continued as up to 120,000 people remained in detention in the four known political prison camps, and were subjected to forced labour as well as torture and other ill-treatment. Some of the violations amounted to crimes against humanity; no action to ensure accountability was known to have been taken during the year. Many of those living in the camps had not been convicted of any internationally recognized criminal offence; they were detained arbitrarily for being related to individuals deemed threatening to the state, or for "guilt-by-association".

Foreign nationals continued to be arrested and detained for extended periods. Tony Kim and Kim Hak-song, both US nationals and academics at the foreign-funded Pyongyang

University of Science and Technology, were arrested on 22 April and 6 May respectively for "hostile acts against the country". A US diplomat was allowed to meet them in June. North Korean authorities said that they were investigating their alleged crimes, and verdicts and sentences were pending in the courts. The two men remained in detention at the end of the year.

US national Otto Warmbier, imprisoned in 2016 for stealing a propaganda poster, died on 19 June, six days after he was returned to the USA in a coma. North Korean authorities failed to adequately explain the cause of his poor state of health. A coroner's report released on 27 September in his home state of Ohio noted no evidence of torture or other ill-treatment, but also did not rule out its possibility.

Lim Hyeon-soo, a Canadian pastor who was sentenced in 2015 to life imprisonment with hard labour, was released on 9 August for "humanitarian reasons", after more than two years of detention during which adequate medical treatment was not provided.[1]

WORKERS' RIGHTS – MIGRANT WORKERS

The authorities continued to dispatch workers to other countries, including China and Russia. The number of workers deployed was hard to estimate and believed to be in decline, as some countries, such as China, Kuwait, Poland, Qatar and Sri Lanka, stopped renewing or issuing additional work visas to North Koreans in order to comply with the new UN sanctions on North Korea's economic activities abroad. North Korea derived part of its state revenue from these workers, who did not receive their wages directly from their employers, but from their government after significant deductions. The North Korean authorities maintained tight control on the workers' communications and movement, and deprived them of information about workers' rights in the host countries.

Workers remaining in their host countries continued to be subjected to excessive working hours and were vulnerable in terms of occupational health and safety. The media

reported cases of North Koreans dying while working in Russia, which hosted at least 20,000 North Koreans. In May, two construction workers died in the Russian capital Moscow after complaining of breathing problems; they were believed to have suffered acute heart failure. A subcontractor of a World Cup stadium project in St Petersburg, where a worker died from heart failure in November 2016, said in a media interview that many workers suffered from severe fatigue due to working long hours continuously for months without rest days.

FREEDOM OF MOVEMENT

During the year, 1,127 North Koreans left the country and resettled in South Korea (the Republic of Korea), the lowest number since 2002. Tightened security on both sides of the Chinese-North Korean border could be a possible reason for the change. Some North Korean women were able to leave the country through deals with human traffickers, only to find themselves subjected to physical and sexual abuse or exploitative work conditions once on the Chinese side of the border.

The year saw larger numbers of North Koreans being detained in China or forcibly returned to North Korea, where they were at risk of forced labour or torture and other ill-treatment.[2] Media also reported that the North Korean government was actively requesting that China repatriate individuals suspected of leaving North Korea without prior approval.

A number of sources, including the UN Special Rapporteur on the situation of human rights in the Democratic People's Republic of Korea, reported cases of North Koreans who had left the country, but returned or expressed a wish to return after arriving in South Korea. Some individuals who returned appeared in state media testifying about the hardships they faced outside North Korea. As the procedures for these people to re-enter North Korea remained unclear, their appearance led to speculations about whether they had returned voluntarily or were abducted back to the country, and whether they had been persuaded by the North

Korean authorities to give fabricated testimonies.

FREEDOM OF EXPRESSION

The government continued to exercise severe restrictions over information exchange between North Koreans and the rest of the world. All telecommunications, postal and broadcasting services remained state-owned, and there were no independent newspapers, other media or civil society organizations. Apart from a select few in the ruling elite, the population had no access to the internet and international mobile phone services.

Despite the risk of arrest and detention, people close to the Chinese border continued to contact individuals abroad by connecting with the Chinese mobile network using smuggled mobile phones. Media reports said the authorities further strengthened efforts to trace mobile phone activity on Chinese networks and jam the signals through the installation of new radar detectors in the border areas.

INTERNATIONAL SCRUTINY

Following the state's ratification of the UN Convention on the Rights of Persons with Disabilities in December 2016, the Special Rapporteur on the rights of persons with disabilities conducted an official visit to North Korea between 3 and 8 May. This was the first visit to North Korea by an independent expert designated by the UN Human Rights Council.

The CEDAW Committee and the UN Committee on the Rights of the Child reviewed North Korea's human rights record in 2017. North Korea submitted state party's reports to the Committees, after an interval of 14 and nine years respectively, and responded to questions at the sessions. In its review, the Committee on the Rights of the Child noted the inability of North Korean children to regularly communicate with their parents and family members who live in a different country.[3] They also noted the exclusion of children aged 16 and 17 under the current domestic Act for the Protection of the Rights of the Child, and the requirement for some children to perform extensive amounts of strenuous labour.

---

1. North Korea: Pastor Lim Hyeon-soo released after more than two years of imprisonment (ASA 24/6921/2017)

2. China: Eight North Koreans at risk of forcible return (ASA 17/6652/2017)

3. North Korea: Amnesty International's submission to the United Nations Committee on the Rights of the Child (ASA 24/6500/2017)

KOREA (REPUBLIC OF)

Republic of Korea
Head of state and government: **Moon Jae-in (replaced acting President Hwang Kyo-an in May, who replaced Park Geun-hye in March)**

Large protest rallies took place in response to a corruption scandal involving former President Park Geun-hye. She was removed from office in March. Following the change of government, the Korean National Police Agency accepted recommendations for comprehensive reform that called for a change in the overall approach to policing assemblies so as to better respect freedom of peaceful assembly, although their full implementation remained pending at the end of the year. An increasing number of lower courts handed down decisions recognizing the right to conscientious objection. Discrimination against LGBTI people remained prevalent in public life, especially in the military. Arbitrary detention based on the vaguely worded National Security Law continued. A series of deaths of migrant workers raised concerns about safety in the workplace.

BACKGROUND

Moon Jae-in, a former human rights lawyer and leader of the Democratic Party, was elected President in May, following the decision by the Constitutional Court in March to uphold a parliamentary vote impeaching then President Park. Charges against her included bribery and abuse of power.[1]

FREEDOM OF ASSEMBLY

Han Sang-gyun, president of the Korean Confederation of Trade Unions, was held criminally responsible for sporadic clashes between protesters and police, and for his role in organizing a series of largely peaceful anti-government protests in 2014 and 2015. In May, the Supreme Court rejected his final appeal against a three-year jail sentence, despite an opinion by the UN Working Group on Arbitrary Detention that the charges against Han Sang-gyun violated his rights to freedom of expression and of peaceful assembly, and that his detention was arbitrary. The Working Group called for his immediate release.

In June, Lee Cheol-seong, commissioner general of the Korean National Police Agency (KNPA), offered an apology to the family of Baek Nam-gi, an activist farmer who died in 2016 as a result of injuries sustained when police used water cannons during protests against the government's agricultural policies. The family and civic groups criticized the belated apology that lacked a clear acknowledgement by police of their responsibility.

In September, following calls by civil society organizations, the KNPA accepted recommendations by the newly established Police Reform Committee.[2] These included a presumption that assemblies would be peaceful and that spontaneous and other urgent peaceful assemblies would be protected, marking a shift in the previous overall approach to policing. While the decision was an important step forward, the measures fell short in other regards, including not lifting the blanket ban on outdoor assemblies taking place at specific times and places. In addition, the adopted measures still needed to be firmly enshrined in law to bring them into line with international human rights law and standards.

CONSCIENTIOUS OBJECTORS

At the same time as the Constitutional Court was examining the legality of conscientious objection, an increasing number of lower courts ruled in favour of men who refused military service for reasons of conscience. They included at least 44 District Court decisions during the year.

In May and December, the Seoul Administrative Court ordered suspension of the practice of publicly disclosing personal information about conscientious objectors, including name, age and address, until it had made its final rulings on two cases brought against the Military Manpower Administration for issuing the lists. The Administrative Court noted the irrevocable damage to conscientious objectors caused by this public disclosure.

Calls to introduce an alternative to military service increased. In May, two additional bills to amend the Military Service Act by introducing an alternative service were submitted to the National Assembly. In June, the National Human Rights Commission of Korea again issued a recommendation to the Ministry of National Defense to introduce an alternative to military service.

RIGHTS OF LESBIAN, GAY, BISEXUAL, TRANSGENDER AND INTERSEX PEOPLE

Gay men faced considerable difficulties in fulfilling compulsory military service free from violence, bullying or verbal abuse. In May, a gay soldier was found guilty of violating Article 92-6 of the Military Criminal Act that prohibits military personnel from engaging in same-sex consensual sexual activity. Dozens of others were charged under the same Article.

The advocacy group Center for Military Human Rights Korea published screen shots of dating app conversations that the group said resulted from military pressure on targeted men to identify other supposedly gay men. The group said that military investigators had confiscated mobile phones belonging to up to 50 soldiers suspected of being gay and insisted that they identify other gay men on their contact lists and gay dating apps.

In September, the National Assembly rejected Kim Yi-su as chief justice of the Constitutional Court despite his nomination by President Moon Jae-in. He had been questioned during the National Assembly's public hearing about his support for LGBTI rights and there were active campaigns by some religious groups opposing his candidacy.

WORKERS' RIGHTS – MIGRANT WORKERS

Migrant workers continued to be vulnerable to exploitation under the Employment Permit System, including having to work long hours with little or no rest time, low and irregularly paid wages, and dangerous working conditions.

In May, two Nepalese migrant workers died from suffocation while cleaning a septic tank at a pig farm in North Gyeongsang Province. Two weeks later, two migrant workers from China and Thailand died after losing consciousness while cleaning excrement at a different pig farm in Gyeonggi Province.

In August, a Nepalese migrant worker in North Chungcheong Province committed suicide in a factory dormitory. He left a note stating that his employer had refused to allow him to either change his workplace or return to Nepal to receive treatment for severe insomnia.

ARBITRARY ARRESTS AND DETENTIONS

Arbitrary detention of individuals based on the vaguely worded National Security Law (NSL) continued. Lee Jin-young, owner of online library "Labour Books", was brought to court for alleged violations of the NSL after distributing online materials deemed to "benefit" the Democratic People's Republic of Korea (North Korea). A District Court acquitted him in July, but an appeal by the government to the High Court remained pending.

FREEDOM OF EXPRESSION

In April, the Seoul Administrative Court ruled as unlawful the decision by the Korea Communications Standards Commission, which censors internet content, to ban a blog entitled "North Korea Tech" covering IT development in North Korea. The Commission had claimed that the site breached the NSL, which had been used in the past to imprison people for "praising" or expressing sympathy for North Korea.

CORPORATE ACCOUNTABILITY

Courts handed down decisions acknowledging the responsibility of multinational corporations for the work-related death or illness of former or current employees. These included a Supreme Court judgment in August against Samsung Electronics that a former factory worker should be recognized as suffering from an occupational disease. The Supreme Court returned the case to the High Court, noting that the lack of evidence resulting from the company's refusal to provide information and an inadequate investigation by the government should not be held against the worker.

1. South Korea: 8-point human rights agenda for presidential candidates (ASA 25/5785/2017)

2. Mission failed: Policing assemblies in South Korea (ASA 25/7119/2017)

KUWAIT

State of Kuwait
Head of state: **Sheikh Sabah al-Ahmad al-Jaber al-Sabah**
Head of government: **Sheikh Jaber al-Mubarak al-Hamad al-Sabah**

The authorities continued to unduly restrict freedom of expression, including by prosecuting and imprisoning government critics and banning certain publications. Members of the Bidun minority continued to face discrimination and were denied citizenship rights. Migrant workers remained inadequately protected against exploitation and abuse. Courts continued to hand down death sentences and executions resumed after a hiatus of four years.

BACKGROUND

On 6 April, Parliament reversed a 2015 amendment to the Juvenile Law, once again raising the age of minors from 16 to 18 years. As such, those arrested below 18 years of age could be protected from life-term prison sentences and the death penalty.

In July the authorities reinstated mandatory military service, imposing punitive measures for those failing to register for military service within 60 days of reaching the age of 18.

Kuwait led mediation efforts seeking to resolve the Gulf crisis that erupted in early June, when Saudi Arabia, the United Arab Emirates (UAE) and Bahrain severed relations with Qatar. Kuwait remained part of the Saudi Arabia-led coalition engaged in armed conflict in Yemen (see Yemen entry).

FREEDOM OF EXPRESSION

The authorities continued to unduly restrict the right to freedom of expression, prosecuting and imprisoning government critics and online activists under penal code provisions that criminalized comments deemed offensive to the Emir or damaging to relations with neighbouring states.

In March, UK-based writer and blogger Rania al-Saad was sentenced on appeal and in her absence to three years in prison on charges of "insulting Saudi Arabia" on Twitter. The Appeal Court reversed her earlier acquittal rendering this verdict final.

In May the Cassation Court upheld an Appeal Court verdict in the "al-Fintas group" case of 13 men charged in connection with WhatsApp discussions about video footage that appeared to show government members advocating the Emir's removal from power. Six were acquitted and seven were sentenced to between one and 10 years' imprisonment, some in their absence. The trial was marred by irregularities.

In July the Cassation Court upheld a 10-year prison sentence against blogger Waleed Hayes on vaguely worded charges that included "defaming" the Emir and the judiciary. During his trial, Waleed Hayes claimed he was tortured to make him "confess" to offences he did not commit. He remained on trial on other similar charges.

Former MP Musallam al-Barrak was released in April after serving a two-year prison term for criticizing the government. He continued to face separate trials on other charges.

Bidun activist Abdulhakim al-Fadhli was released on 1 August after serving a one-year prison sentence in relation to a peaceful demonstration in 2012, after which he had been due to be expelled from Kuwait. In February, the Cassation Court had overturned his acquittal along with 25 other Bidun men for their participation in peaceful demonstrations in Taima. The court reinstated their two-year prison sentence, as well as a bail of 500 Kuwaiti dinars (about USD1,660) to halt the implementation of the prison sentence on condition that they signed a pledge to no longer take part in demonstrations. Abdulhakim al-Fadhli signed the pledge which, in his case, also annulled his expulsion order.

In August the Public Prosecutor ordered a ban on publications in connection with reporting on ongoing state security cases before the courts. The ban was despite the Cassation Court establishing in May that there were no provisions in the law criminalizing the breach of "confidentiality" or prohibiting the publication of such information.

COUNTER-TERROR AND SECURITY

On 18 July, the Cassation Court issued its verdict in the case against 26 defendants on charges that included "spying for Iran and Hizbullah". The court upheld the death sentence of one defendant in his absence and commuted that of another to life imprisonment. Thirteen men had their acquittals overturned and were sentenced to between five and 15 years in prison. During the trial, some of the 26 defendants reported that they had been tortured in pre-trial detention; their allegations were not investigated. In August the authorities re-arrested 14 men who had been acquitted and released on appeal.

DEPRIVATION OF NATIONALITY

In March the Emir ordered that the nationality of some government critics and their families be reinstated.

On 2 January the Court of Cassation suspended the Appeal Court's decision to restore the nationality of Ahmad Jabr al-Shamari and his family until it issued its verdict. In early March, Ahmad Jabr al-Shamari withdrew his appeal against the 2014 government decision to strip him of his nationality and in April the Cassation Court closed the case, declaring the dispute resolved.

DISCRIMINATION – BIDUN

More than 100,000 Bidun residents of Kuwait remained stateless. In May 2016, Parliament had approved a draft law that would grant Kuwaiti citizenship to up to 4,000 Bidun, but it had not been enacted by the end of 2017. In September the UN Committee on the Elimination of Racial Discrimination recommended that all Bidun should be guaranteed access to adequate social services and education on an equal footing with Kuwaiti nationals, and that in its next periodic report Kuwait should provide information on access to education for Bidun.

WORKERS' RIGHTS – MIGRANT WORKERS

Migrant workers, including those in the domestic, construction and other sectors, continued to face exploitation and abuse under the official *kafala* sponsorship system, which prevents them from changing jobs or leaving the country without their employers' permission.

WOMEN'S RIGHTS

In May, the UN Working Group on the issue of discrimination against women in law and in practice recognized improvements, including women's rights to vote, to stand for elections and to receive equal pay to men. Discrimination against women continued, however, with regard to laws on inheritance, marriage, child custody, nationality rights and domestic violence.

DEATH PENALTY

Executions were carried out on 25 January, the first since 2013. Courts continued to hand down death sentences for offences including murder, drugs offences and terrorism-related charges.

KYRGYZSTAN

Kyrgyz Republic
Head of state: **Sooronbai Jeenbekov (replaced Almazbek Atambaev in October)**
Head of government: **Sapar Isakov (replaced Sooronbai Jeenbekov in August)**

The authorities restricted the rights to freedom of expression and peaceful assembly, particularly in the run-up to the presidential elections. LGBTI people continued to face discrimination and violence from state and non-state actors. Vulnerable groups, including people with disabilities, faced additional difficulties accessing health care. The life sentence of prisoner of conscience Azimjan Askarov was upheld following his retrial.

PRISONERS OF CONSCIENCE

On 24 January, the Chui Regional Court completed the retrial of prisoner of conscience Azimjan Askarov, an ethnic Uzbek human rights defender, and upheld his conviction and life sentence for "participating in ethnic violence and the murder of a police officer" in 2010. In March 2016, the UN Human Rights Committee recommended that Azimjan Askarov be released immediately, recognizing that he had been tortured, denied the right to a fair trial and detained arbitrarily and under inhumane conditions. Following the 24 January decision, the UN Office of the High Commissioner for Human Rights stated that the Court's decision highlighted "serious shortcomings" in the country's judicial system.

In September, a court in the town of Bazar-Korgan overturned the 2010 court decision to confiscate Azimjan Askarov's family home. If approved, the confiscation order would have rendered his wife, Khadicha Askarova, homeless.

RIGHTS OF LESBIAN, GAY, BISEXUAL, TRANSGENDER AND INTERSEX PEOPLE

LGBTI people continued to face discrimination and violence from state and non-state actors. Labrys, an LGBTI rights group, continued its efforts to bring to justice the suspected perpetrators of a violent attack in 2015 on its office and on a private event to mark the International Day against Homophobia and Transphobia. Criminal trials against the members of a nationalist youth group behind the attacks collapsed when the victims named in the court documents "reconciled" with the perpetrators.

SEX WORKERS

Sex work was not criminalized but continued to be highly stigmatized, and sex workers faced discrimination and violence. Police operations targeting sex workers through arbitrary arrests for "petty hooliganism" and other purported administrative offences continued throughout the year. Police officers regularly extorted money from sex workers.

RIGHT TO HEALTH

Marginalized groups, including people living in rural areas, people living in poverty, and people with disabilities, continued to face barriers to accessing adequate health care. Although they were entitled to free or subsidized health care, they were routinely denied access to quality health care facilities, specialist treatment and medications. Informal payments to medical personnel, who were affected by low salaries, were commonplace.

LEGAL, CONSTITUTIONAL OR INSTITUTIONAL DEVELOPMENTS

Kyrgyzstan signed the UN Convention on the Rights of Persons with Disabilities in 2011, but had not ratified it, citing Kyrgyzstan's economic difficulties as the primary reason.

FREEDOMS OF EXPRESSION AND ASSEMBLY

The authorities imposed restrictions on the rights to freedom of expression and peaceful assembly, particularly in the run-up to the October presidential elections. Independent journalists, media outlets, human rights defenders and political activists faced intimidation and harassment, including prosecution on charges of spreading false information and destabilizing the country.

Between March and April, the General Prosecutor's Office initiated a number of civil court proceedings for defamation against online media outlet Zanoza.kg, its co-founders and independent journalists Narynbek Idinov and Dina Maslova, and human rights defender Cholpon Dzhakupova. This was in connection with media articles critical of the President. In June, the court ruled in favour of the plaintiff in two trials and ordered Zanoza.kg as well as the other three defendants to pay 3 million soms (USD44,000) each in moral damages. The Supreme Court upheld the rulings in November.

On 18 March, police disrupted a peaceful demonstration in the capital Bishkek and arrested a number of participants. Human rights defenders, journalists, and other activists had organized the march to protest against the deterioration of freedom of expression. The route had been previously agreed with the relevant authorities. Five demonstrators were charged and sentenced to five days' administrative detention for disrupting traffic. The hearing was closed, including to the defendants' lawyers who were denied access to the courtroom.

In July, a court in Bishkek accepted a request by the Mayor's Office for a blanket ban on all public demonstrations at key locations until after the presidential elections. The ban, however, did not apply to official events organized by the authorities.

LAOS

Lao People's Democratic Republic
Head of state: **Bounnhang Vorachith**
Head of government: **Thongloun Sisoulith**

The rights to freedom of expression, association and peaceful assembly remained severely restricted, and the state exercised strict control over media and civil society. Three activists were convicted in a trial concerning their participation in protests in Thailand and comments made on social media. There was no progress on investigations into a number of enforced disappearances.

BACKGROUND

Laos submitted state party reports to the UN Human Rights Committee, as well as to the CEDAW Committee and the UN Committee on the Rights of the Child.

ENFORCED DISAPPEARANCES

Despite signing the International Convention for the Protection of All Persons from Enforced Disappearance in 2008, Laos had yet to ratify the treaty.

The government failed to establish the fate or whereabouts of Sombath Somphone, a prominent civil society member who was abducted in 2012 outside a police post in the capital, Vientiane. CCTV cameras captured him being stopped by police and driven away. Authorities also failed to establish the fate or whereabouts of Kha Yang, a Lao ethnic Hmong arrested after his forced return from Thailand in 2011, and of Sompawn Khantisouk, an entrepreneur who was active on conservation issues and abducted in 2007 by men believed to be police.

In July, Ko Tee, a Thai political activist sought by the Thai government, disappeared in Laos. The Lao government made no apparent efforts to investigate his disappearance.

FREEDOMS OF EXPRESSION, ASSEMBLY AND ASSOCIATION

Various criminal code provisions and restrictive decrees were used to imprison activists and to suppress the rights to freedom of expression and assembly. Broadcast media, print media and civil society activity remained under stringent state control. Political parties other than the ruling Lao People's Revolutionary Party remained banned.

After a secret trial held in April, activists Soukan Chaithad, Somphone Phimmasone and Lodkham Thammavong were convicted on charges relating to co-operating with foreign entities to undermine the state, distributing propaganda, and organizing protests to cause "turmoil". They were sentenced to between 12 and 20 years in prison. The three had been arrested the previous year after returning from Thailand to renew their passports. They had previously participated in a protest outside the Lao embassy in the Thai capital, Bangkok, and posted a number of messages on Facebook criticizing the Lao government. In August, the UN Working Group on Arbitrary Detention declared that their detention was arbitrary. Also in August, the government passed a Decree on Associations that imposed onerous registration requirements and restrictions on NGOs and other civic groups and stipulated harsh criminal penalties for failure to comply.

ECONOMIC, SOCIAL AND CULTURAL RIGHTS

Villagers affected by development projects, including the construction of dams and a Laos-China railway, were forced to relocate. They claimed that they had not been adequately consulted or compensated. In April, the Prime Minister acknowledged problems with implementing land concession regulations. Activists expressed concerns about damage to livelihoods and the environment caused by the construction of hydropower dams.

LATVIA

Republic of Latvia
Head of state: **Raimonds Vējonis**
Head of government: **Māris Kučinskis**

Ill-treatment of detainees by law enforcement officials continued to be reported and prison conditions remained poor. A disproportionate fine imposed on a news portal for defamation gave rise to concerns about the right to freedom of expression. The government put forward draft legislation that would discriminate against women wearing full-face veils in public places.

UNFAIR TRIALS

In January, the European Court of Human Rights found that Latvia had violated the European Convention on Human Rights, including in relation to Article 6 because proceedings had exceeded a reasonable time in the case of a man seeking compensation for injuries inflicted on him by a police officer upon his arrest in 1995. The man alleged he had lost his sight as a result of being beaten and kicked by the officer. Although the perpetrator was convicted of ill-treatment in 2003, the complainant had not received adequate reparations.

DETENTION

In June, the European Committee for the Prevention of Torture called on the authorities to address inter-prisoner violence and improve prisoners' access to health care. It also expressed concerns about allegations of excessive use of force by police officers during the apprehension and questioning of suspects in the absence of their lawyers.

FREEDOM OF EXPRESSION

In January, the Riga Higher Court ordered the news portal Tvnet to pay a EUR50,000 fine for damaging the reputation of the Latvian National Opera and Ballet. Tvnet had published an article criticizing it for becoming a "public house of Putin's court". The Council of Europe Commissioner for Human Rights described the fine as disproportionate and raised concerns about the harmful effect of such a measure on the right to freedom of expression in the country.

DISCRIMINATION

In August, the government put forward draft legislation which effectively prohibits wearing the full-face veil in public. The Justice Ministry argued that the measure would protect people's welfare and morality, and facilitate the integration of immigrants. Critics called the legislation discriminatory and disproportionate.

REFUGEES AND ASYLUM-SEEKERS

Latvia continued to build a fence along its border with Russia, expected to be completed in 2019 and to cover a 90km area, with the stated aim of preventing an "influx of migrants".

Under the EU relocation and resettlement schemes, Latvia pledged to relocate 481 asylum-seekers from Greece and Italy. By May it had relocated 308.

WOMEN'S RIGHTS

In March, the Minister of Welfare announced that the government would ratify the Council of Europe Convention on preventing and combating violence against women and domestic violence (Istanbul Convention) by the end of 2018.

LEBANON

Lebanese Republic
Head of state: **Michel Aoun**
Head of government: **Saad Hariri**

Lebanon hosted more than 1 million refugees from Syria, in addition to several hundred thousand long-term Palestinian refugees and more than 20,000 refugees from other countries. The authorities maintained restrictions that effectively closed Lebanon's borders to people fleeing Syria. Parliament repealed a law allowing people accused of rape to escape punishment by marrying their victim, and passed a new law criminalizing torture. Access to essential services remained curtailed by the economic crisis. Authorities handed down death sentences; there were no executions.

BACKGROUND

The economic crisis continued. Access to basic services, including electricity and water, remained severely curtailed across the country. Public protests and strikes continued throughout the year, including by judges, public sector staff, parents and workers, as well as residents living near sites of unprocessed waste. Waste mismanagement, which had prompted the largest protests in years, remained unresolved.

On 4 November, Prime Minister Hariri announced his resignation in a speech delivered from the Saudi Arabian capital, Riyadh, under circumstances that remained unclear. President Aoun did not accept his resignation.

The Lebanese Armed Forces (LAF) and the armed group Hezbollah launched two military operations in the northern border town of Arsal against the armed groups Jabhat Al-Nusra and Islamic State (IS), in July and August respectively. By the end of August, the LAF had regained control of Arsal and the surrounding area, and retrieved the bodies of 10 Lebanese soldiers taken hostage by IS in 2014.

In the Palestinian refugee camp of Ein el-Helweh, in the southern city of Saida, clashes erupted between IS and IS-affiliated groups on the one hand, and Palestinian armed groups and the LAF.

In June, the Parliament approved a new electoral law and scheduled the twice-postponed parliamentary elections for May 2018, the first to take place since 2009.

REFUGEES AND ASYLUM-SEEKERS

A government decision from May 2015 continued to bar UNHCR, the UN refugee agency, from registering newly arrived refugees.

Syrian refugees faced financial and administrative difficulties in obtaining or renewing residency permits, exposing them to a constant risk of arbitrary arrest, detention and forcible return to Syria. In February the authorities introduced a waiver of the 300,000 Lebanese pound (USD200) residency fee for Syrian refugees registered with UNHCR, excluding those who had entered Lebanon after January 2015 or who had renewed their residency through work or a private sponsor, as well as Palestinian refugees from Syria. The waiver was not applied consistently by government officials, and many refugees were not able to renew their residency permits.

Refugees from Syria continued to face severe economic hardship. According to the UN, 76% of Syrian refugee households lived below the poverty line and more than half lived in substandard conditions in overcrowded buildings and densely populated neighbourhoods. Refugees faced restrictions to finding official work and were subjected to curfews and other restrictions on their movement in a number of municipalities. Several municipalities served refugees with eviction notices, forcing them to seek alternative places to live in an increasingly hostile and xenophobic environment. In March the LAF issued eviction notices to refugees living in camps in the vicinity of Riyak Airbase in the Bekaa region, affecting around 12,665 individuals.

The UN humanitarian appeal for Syrian refugees in Lebanon was only 56% funded by the end of the year and resettlement places in other countries remained inadequate.

On 30 June the LAF conducted raids on two informal tented settlements accommodating Syrian refugees in Arsal. At least 350 men were arrested during the raids. Most were subsequently released but there were reports that some detainees were tortured and otherwise ill-treated by soldiers and four men died while in custody. The authorities did not publish any findings from their investigations into these deaths.

Between June and August, thousands of Syrians returned from Arsal to Syria, mostly following agreements negotiated by Hezbollah with armed groups in Syria.

Palestinian refugees, including many long-term residents in Lebanon, remained subject to discriminatory laws excluding them from owning or inheriting property, accessing public education and health services, or working in at least 36 professions. At least 3,000 Palestinian refugees who did not hold official identity documents faced further restrictions denying them the right to register births, marriages and deaths.

Lebanon had not yet ratified the 1951 UN Refugee Convention and its 1967 Protocol.

TORTURE AND OTHER ILL-TREATMENT

In May, Lebanon made its first appearance before the UN Committee against Torture, following ratification of the UN Convention against Torture and its Optional Protocol in 2000 and 2008, respectively. A new anti-torture law came into effect on 26 October. The law was largely aligned with Lebanon's international obligations but failed to incorporate the Committee's observations with regards to the statute of limitations and penalties for committing the crime of torture. Moreover, the law failed to provide that army officers accused of torture would be tried before civilian courts.

WOMEN'S RIGHTS

In August, the Parliament repealed Article 522 of the Penal Code which allowed a person convicted of kidnapping or rape, including statutory rape, to escape prosecution if they proposed to marry the victim. Civil society organizations continued to call for the repeal of Articles 505 and 518, which allowed for marriage with minors aged between 15 and 18 as a way to escape prosecution.

Women's rights groups continued to advocate for the right of women married to foreign nationals to pass their nationality to their husband and children. The UN Committee on the Rights of the Child also included this recommendation in its concluding observations on Lebanon, in addition to calling on Lebanon to ensure that citizenship would be conferred to children who would otherwise be stateless.

Women migrant workers continued to suffer discriminatory laws and practices, restricting their rights to freedom of movement, education and health, including sexual and reproductive health.

RIGHTS OF LESBIAN, GAY, BISEXUAL, TRANSGENDER AND INTERSEX PEOPLE

The Internal Security Forces (ISF) continued to arrest people and press charges under Article 534 of the Penal Code, which criminalized "sexual intercourses which contradict the laws of nature" and was used to prosecute LGBTI people.

In May the ISF banned several activities that had been planned across the country to mark International Day against Homophobia and Transphobia, citing security concerns following threats made by radical Islamist groups.

FREEDOM OF EXPRESSION

The ISF Cybercrime and Intellectual Property Bureau continued to interrogate, arrest and hold in pre-trial detention peaceful activists for posting comments on social media. The Public Prosecution issued at least four arrest orders on charges that included "insulting the President... the flag or the national emblem", "defamation" and "libel and slander". During their pre-trial detention, which lasted several days, most of the activists were denied access to their lawyers and families.

RIGHT TO HEALTH

In August the governmental General Disciplinary Council confirmed that expired and fake drugs were being used to treat cancer at Beirut's Rafik Hariri University Hospital, the capital's largest public hospital, and took disciplinary action against the head of the hospital pharmacy.

Civil society raised a number of cases before the judiciary related to violations of the rights to health and clean water, including cases related to the sale of expired drugs in public hospitals and to waste mismanagement; these efforts were unsuccessful, either as a result of delayed court rulings or failure to implement rulings.

DEATH PENALTY

Courts continued to hand down death sentences; no executions were carried out.

LESOTHO

Kingdom of Lesotho
Head of state: **King Letsie III**
Head of government: **Thomas Motsoahae Thabane (replaced Pakalitha Mosisili in June)**

The continued political and security crisis led to a sharp increase in human rights violations. Allegations of torture and other ill-treatment continued. The right to freedom of expression remained severely restricted. There were unlawful killings.

BACKGROUND

On 1 March, after months of unrest, Parliament passed a vote of no confidence in then Prime Minister Pakalitha Mosisili. On 7 March, King Letsie announced Parliament's dissolution and elections were held on 3 June. A coalition government, led by Thomas Thabane of the All Basotho Convention party, was formed.

UNLAWFUL KILLINGS

On 28 April, Tumelo Mohlomi, a student from the University of Lesotho was killed when she was shot in the back of the head by a Lesotho Mounted Police Service (LMPS) officer while she was in a restaurant outside the campus. A police officer was arrested after the killing and apparently released on bail. The victim's family brought a civil case of murder against the LMPS, which sought an out-of-court settlement. The National Police Commissioner said that a criminal investigation into the case was ongoing.

In August the High Court ruled in favour of a habeas corpus application brought by the family of Mokalekale Khetheng who disappeared on 26 March 2016 after arrest on unspecified charges by four LMPS officers in Leribe District. In August, the police officers were arrested in connection with his murder; Mokalekale Khetheng's body was exhumed. The former Minister of Defence was then arrested in connection with the murder. He and the officers were also charged with conspiracy to cause a disappearance. The former Minister was released on bail in September. The former National Police Commissioner, who remained abroad throughout the year, was apparently implicated in the case although he was not charged.

On 5 September, Lesotho Defence Force (LDF) Commander Khoantle Motsomotso was shot dead in his office at the LDF headquarters in the capital, Maseru. Two suspects in the killing, LDF members Brigadier Bulane Sechele and Colonel Tefo Hashatsi, also died in retaliatory fire. The Prime Minister announced an investigation into the incident. No further information about the progress of the investigation had been received by the end of the year.

IMPUNITY

On 14 June, Lipolelo Thabane, the estranged wife of Prime Minister Thabane, was killed on the eve of his inauguration. The National Police Commissioner said that a criminal investigation into the case was ongoing.

In August, the Southern Africa Development Community (SADC) extended the tenure of an oversight committee, established in 2016 to ensure implementation of the recommendations made by its Commission of Inquiry. The Commission was set up in the light of heightened political instability in 2015 and, among other things, investigated the killing by LDF soldiers of former army chief Lieutenant-General Maaparankoe Mahao. The Commission found that he was deliberately killed and recommended a criminal investigation. In June his widow instituted a case for damages against the LDF's Commander, the Minister of Defence and National Security and the Attorney General. On 1 December, eight LDF members appeared before the Maseru Magistrates Court on charges connected to his killing.

UNFAIR TRIALS

In August, the Prime Minister postponed indefinitely the court-martial of 23 LDF officers accused of mutiny. Sixteen officers were released from prison in 2016; the remaining seven were released on 1 March 2017. All 23 were under "open arrest", a form of military bail,[1] for most of the year. In August, 22 of the officers had signed a petition to the government raising concerns that the deferred court-martial could undermine their rights to redress and requesting that due process be followed and that their open arrest be cancelled. In November, the High Court ordered the court-martial against one of them to be discontinued. On 18 December, a court-martial hearing found the remaining 22 soldiers not guilty on all charges.

TORTURE AND OTHER ILL-TREATMENT

Thato Makara said that he was tortured and otherwise ill-treated after he reported to the Maseru police headquarters in April; he had been summoned in connection with a murder case. He attended the police station with his employer, Thuso Litjobo, president of the Alliance for Democrats Youth League, who was released the same evening. Thato Makara said that he was taken to Ha Matela police holding cell in the Maseru area, and then to Lekhalo La Baroa where he was subjected to torture including waterboarding, rubber gloves tied over his mouth and nose, and beatings. After a habeas corpus application, Thato Makara appeared in court where he testified about his torture; he was released on 18 April. He was charged with murder the next day in connection with a death at a political rally. He was bailed on 20 April.

FREEDOM OF EXPRESSION

The right to freedom of expression continued to be threatened. Nkoale Oetsi Tsoana, a journalist with *Moeletsi Oa Basotho*, received death threats from Lesotho Congress for Democracy (LCD) supporters in August while he covered the Directorate on Corruption and Economic Offences' investigation into corruption allegations against LCD leader and former Deputy Prime Minister Mothetjoa Metsing. The same day, Palo Mohlotsane, a PC-FM radio journalist, received threats from the Deputy Leader and members of the LCD after he covered the same story.

Nthakoana Ngatane, South African Broadcasting Corporation correspondent, received repeated online death threats from June after she reported on possible motives for the killing of Lipolelo Thabane. On 16 June crowds gathered outside MoAfrika FM radio station's offices and threatened the owner, Sebonomoea Ramainoane, after the station implicated Prime Minister Thabane in the killing of his wife. On 8 September the Maseru Magistrate Court ordered Sebonomoea Ramainoane, also the station's editor-in-chief, to release to the LMPS the station's audio recordings of interviews aired between 28 August and 6 September. On 13 September, the authorities closed the station for 72 hours and on 15 September detained Sebonomoea Ramainoane for several hours. On 25 September, the Lesotho High Court cancelled the Magistrate Court's order.

On 29 August, exiled investigative journalist Keiso Mohloboli received online death threats for comments she posted on social media about human rights violations in Lesotho. She had received similar threats on 10 June.

On 13 December, five members of the LDF went on trial for the attempted murder of the *Lesotho Times* editor Lloyd Mutungamiri in July 2016. He suffered near fatal gunshot wounds after being attacked outside his home in Maseru. The shooting followed his newspaper's publication of an article claiming that the outgoing LDF head was to receive an exit package of USD3.5 million.

LIBERIA

Republic of Liberia
Head of state and government: **Ellen Johnson-Sirleaf**

Domestic violence, and sexual violence against women and girls remained widespread. Impunity for human rights violations persisted. Prison conditions did not meet international standards and individuals were frequently held in prolonged pre-trial detention.

BACKGROUND

Presidential and legislative elections began in October. George Weah, of the Congress for Democratic Change party, was elected as President on 26 December and was expected to take up his position in January 2018.

The practice of placing government schools under the control of a private company limited children's access to adequate education, a concern raised in 2016 by the UN Special Rapporteur on the right to education.

IMPUNITY

Most of the 2009 recommendations of the Truth and Reconciliation Commission were yet to be implemented, including a recommendation to establish a criminal tribunal to prosecute crimes under international law, and measures aimed at obtaining accountability and reparation for victims. The Commission was established following human rights violations and abuses carried out during the 14-year civil war which ended in 2003.

No one had been prosecuted in Liberia for human rights violations committed during the civil war. However, Mohammed Jabbateh was convicted of perjury and immigration fraud in the USA, in relation to his role in alleged war crimes. Investigations also continued in Switzerland and Belgium into alleged war crimes committed by Alieu Kosiah and Martina Johnson – commanders in rebel groups – who were arrested in Switzerland and Belgium respectively, in 2014.

DETENTION

Prisons continued to be overcrowded, partly because hundreds of people were held in prolonged pre-trial detention. Detainees had inadequate access to medical care and recreational facilities. In June, an inmate became pregnant by a male prisoner at Tubmanburg Central Prison after she was coerced into sex. The incident was facilitated by prison officers who then took her to have an abortion without her consent. Following an investigation, several prison officers were dismissed; however, none of them were known to have been prosecuted.

FREEDOM OF EXPRESSION

A bill was introduced in the House of Representatives to decriminalize press offences, particularly related to libel. It remained pending at the end of the year.

RIGHT TO EDUCATION

In August, 174 national and international organizations called on investors to stop supporting Bridge International Academies, a private company that runs 25 schools in Liberia and other African countries. Earlier, in March, the Coalition for Transparency and Accountability in Education highlighted concerns about the company's practices such as capping classroom numbers in government schools, a practice that left children without access to a local school. The running of these schools had been outsourced to the Bridge International Academies in 2016.

WOMEN'S RIGHTS

Domestic violence, rape and other forms of sexual violence against women and girls, including practices such as female genital mutilation and early marriage remained widespread. Impunity for rape and other forms of violence against women remained prevalent. However, a domestic violence bill was passed by the legislature in July and was awaiting the President's signature at the end of the year. The government, the UN and development partners continued to invest in sexual and gender-based violence units, located in police stations and government ministries to investigate sexual abuse and violence, as well as a specialized court to deal with such crimes in Montserrado County in the northwest. The authorities continued to run 12 one-stop centres in seven counties which offered medical and support services to survivors of sexual violence.

Affordable and accessible abortion services continued to be largely unavailable to rape survivors, despite legislation allowing for abortion in sexual violence cases where the attack is recorded with the police and authorization given by two medical professionals. Unsafe abortions continued to contribute to Liberia having one of highest rates of maternal deaths and injuries in Africa.

RIGHTS OF LESBIAN, GAY, BISEXUAL, TRANSGENDER AND INTERSEX PEOPLE

LGBTI people experienced discrimination, harassment and threats. The Penal Code criminalized consensual sexual activity between same-sex adults. A man arrested in June 2012 on allegations of "voluntary sodomy" remained in detention at the Monrovia Central Prison at the end of the year.

LIBYA

State of Libya
Head of state: Disputed
Head of government: Fayez Serraj

Forces affiliated to three rival governments, as well as armed groups and militias, committed serious violations of international law and abuses of human rights with impunity. All sides to the conflict carried out indiscriminate attacks in heavily populated areas leading to deaths of civilians and unlawful killings. Armed groups abducted, arbitrarily arrested and indefinitely detained thousands of people. Torture and other ill-treatment was widespread in prisons under the control of armed groups, militias and state officials. Migrants, refugees and asylum-seekers were subjected to widespread and systematic serious human rights violations and abuses at the hands of state officials, smugglers and armed groups. Women faced discrimination, including arbitrary restrictions on their right to travel. The death penalty remained in force; no executions were reported.

BACKGROUND

Three rival governments and hundreds of militias and armed groups continued to compete for power and control over territory, lucrative trade routes and strategic military locations. The UN-backed Government of National Accord (GNA) continued to reinforce its positions in the capital, Tripoli, gradually gaining territory through strategic alliances and often after armed clashes. In May, the Tripoli Revolutionaries Brigade and the Abu Salim Brigade, both affiliated to the GNA's Ministry of the Interior, removed the coalition of militias supporting the Government of National Salvation (GNS) from their key positions in Tripoli. These included the site of Hadba prison where former senior officials from the rule of Mu'ammar al-Gaddafi were detained, and Tripoli International Airport, where they took control of key strategic areas, including the airport road.

The self-styled Libyan National Army (LNA), led by Khalifa Haftar, consolidated its power and made significant gains in eastern Libya after defeating the Shura Council of Benghazi Revolutionaries (SCBR) in Benghazi and evicting the Benghazi Defence Brigades (BDB) from Benghazi, the oil port of Ras Lanuf and the desert military base of al-Jufra. In May, the Misrata 3rd force aided by the BDB attacked the Brak al-Shati air base, resulting in the deaths of 141 people including LNA soldiers. The LNA regained control of the air base, aided by air strikes from the Egyptian air force.

In July the Constitutional Drafting Assembly approved the new draft Constitution, an initiative that had begun in 2014. No date was set for the referendum on the Constitution.

In September and November, the USA carried out several strikes by remotely piloted vehicles (drones) in Libya including south of Sirte, targeting the armed group Islamic State (IS). In May, the armed group Ansar al-Shari'a in Libya announced its own dissolution.

In September, the UN Security Council extended the mandate of the UN Support Mission in Libya (UNSMIL) until 15 September 2018. Ghassan Salamé, the UN's newly appointed Special Representative for Libya, outlined his action plan, which included amending the UN-brokered Libyan Political Agreement (LPA), convening a national congress, and holding legislative and presidential elections in 2018. In December, the UN Security Council reiterated its commitment to the LPA as the only viable framework for the transition period.

INTERNAL ARMED CONFLICT

Armed clashes between rival forces continued to take place sporadically throughout the country, with armed groups and militias carrying out indiscriminate attacks in heavily populated areas leading to the deaths of civilians. In February, clashes between militias in the Abu Salim area of Tripoli resulted in two civilians being killed and three injured, including a child who was shot in the head by a stray bullet. In July, clashes broke out between two militias near Mitiga airport in Tripoli over the control of a local beach resort. The militias used explosive weapons with wide-area effects, including rocket propelled grenades (RPGs), in densely populated civilian areas. In one case, RPGs hit a nearby beach, killing five civilians – two women and three children – from the same family. A forensic doctor in Tripoli confirmed that the deaths were caused by shrapnel from an RPG.

In March, LNA forces broke the siege they had imposed on an apartment complex in the Ganfouda area of Benghazi by launching an attack to drive the BDB forces out of one of their last strongholds in the city. The two-month siege had cut off all supplies to the area, including food and water, and had trapped civilians and wounded fighters without access to medical care and other basic services. The attack on Ganfouda was indiscriminate and resulted in the deaths of at least five civilians. LNA fighters posed for photos with the bodies, including the exhumed body of a BDB commander who had been killed in air strikes and buried in the days prior to the ground attack.

In July the LNA tightened its siege on the city of Derna in its fight against the Derna Mujahideen Shora Council, hindering access to food, petrol and medical supplies, resulting in a rapid deterioration of the humanitarian situation in the city. A series of air strikes on Derna killed scores of civilians and injured others, including children.

UNLAWFUL KILLINGS

In March, LNA-affiliated fighters were filmed killing captured SCBR fighters, a serious violation of international humanitarian law and a war crime. In August, the ICC issued a warrant for the arrest of Mahmoud el-Werfelli for alleged war crimes committed while he was field commander of the Special Forces Brigade (Al-Saiqa) affiliated to the LNA, including for involvement in the March killings.

A number of mass graves were uncovered in Benghazi between February and October. On at least four occasions, groups of bodies were found in different parts of the city with their hands bound behind their backs, and in some cases blindfolded with signs of torture and execution-style killing. In August, the bodies of six unidentified men were found in a rubbish bin in the eastern Benghazi neighbourhood of Shabneh. The bodies showed signs of torture and had bullet wounds in the head and chest. On 26 October, the bodies of 36 men were found on a deserted road south of the town of al-Abyar, including a 71-year-old Sufi sheikh who had been abducted in August, and a medical student.

FREEDOMS OF EXPRESSION AND ASSOCIATION

Journalists, activists and human rights defenders were particularly vulnerable to harassment, attacks and enforced disappearance by armed groups and militias aligned with various authorities of rival governments.

In the west, Special Deterrence (Radaa) forces operating under the Ministry of the Interior of the GNA carried out a series of arrests, targeting people for peacefully exercising their right to freedom of association and other rights. In September, an imam in Tripoli was arbitrarily arrested by Radaa on suspicion of using his mosque to incite violence. He remained in detention at the end of the year. In November, Radaa forces raided a comic-book convention in Tripoli and arrested 20 people, including the organizers and some attendees. They were released at the end of November.

In the east, forces associated with the LNA targeted journalists and others deemed to have criticized Khalifa Haftar and LNA forces. Armed groups composed of adherents of the Madkhali doctrine, a strand of Salafism inspired by the Saudi Arabian sheikh Rabee al-Madkhali, burned books and abducted student members of a university group who had organized an Earth Day event on their campus in Benghazi. Those abducted included photographer Abdullah Duma, who was later released. In September a radio host from the city of al-Marj was detained for nearly three weeks for openly criticizing a decision made by Abdelraziq al-Nathouri, the LNA's military governor of eastern Libya.

ARBITRARY ARRESTS AND DETENTIONS

Militias, armed groups and security forces affiliated to rival governments continued to arbitrarily arrest and indefinitely detain thousands of people. In the east, militias operating as security forces associated with the LNA abducted people and imprisoned them without charge or trial. In June, an armed group in Bayda abducted cameraman Musa Khamees Ardia and transferred him to Grenada prison in the east. He was released without charge on 3 November.

Armed groups and militias abducted and unlawfully detained hundreds of people because of their opinions, origin, perceived political affiliations or perceived wealth. Those abducted included political activists, lawyers, human rights activists and other civilians. Militias carried out abductions with the aim of extracting ransoms from families, to negotiate an exchange of detainees, or to silence criticism. In April a militia abducted a university professor in Sayyad on the outskirts of Tripoli. He was held for 47 days in an undisclosed location with little access to food, water and medication. In August, unidentified militiamen abducted former Prime Minister Ali Zeidan from a hotel in Tripoli. He was released after eight days.

JUSTICE SYSTEM

An environment of impunity continued to prevail, leaving perpetrators of serious abuses emboldened and without fear of accountability, which in turn threatened prospects of political stability. Courts and prosecutors' offices were dysfunctional and often feared reprisals for their work. The post of Public Prosecutor remained vacant. In September, senior prosecutor Sadik Essour announced that 800 arrest warrants had been issued and 250 people had been referred to court for their involvement in political violence. In October, just hours before one of these trials was due to start, a gun and suicide-bomb attack on a court in GNA-controlled Misrata killed four people - two civilians and two security personnel - and injured at least 40. IS claimed responsibility for the attack.

Torture was widespread in prisons, where thousands were held without charge. Many detainees had been held since 2011 with no judicial oversight or means to challenge the legality of their detention.

None of the parties to the conflict implemented any of the human rights provisions in the UN-brokered Libya Political

Agreement of December 2015, including those obliging them to release detainees held without legal basis.

INTERNALLY DISPLACED PEOPLE

Some 40,000 former residents of the town of Tawargha, near Misrata, remained displaced for a sixth year. In June a political agreement was signed by the mayor of Misrata, the Tawargha local council and the Misrata-Tawargha Reconciliation Committee chairman, in the presence of Prime Minister Serraj, ostensibly to allow the displaced former residents to return to Tawargha. However, the agreement made no mention of accountability for past crimes. Three days later, a group of Tawargha families attempted to return but were threatened and intimidated at a checkpoint manned by residents of Misrata and forced to return to Tripoli. By the end of the year there had been no progress on the return of the Tawargha people or the implementation of the agreement.

MIGRANTS, REFUGEES AND ASYLUM-SEEKERS

Migrants, refugees and asylum-seekers were subjected to widespread and systematic serious human rights violations and abuses at the hands of detention centre officials, the Libyan Coast Guard, smugglers and armed groups. Some were detained after being intercepted by the Libyan Coast Guard at sea trying to cross the Mediterranean to Europe. It was estimated that up to 20,000 people were held in detention centres in Libya run by the Directorate for Combating Illegal Migration (DCIM), a division of the Ministry of the Interior of the GNA. They were held in horrific conditions of extreme overcrowding, lacking access to medical care and adequate nutrition, and systematically subjected to torture and other ill-treatment, including sexual violence, severe beatings and extortion. While the DCIM formally controlled between 17 and 36 centres, armed groups and criminal gangs ran thousands of illicit holding sites throughout the country as part of a lucrative people-smuggling business. In November, a video released by US media organization CNN showing the apparent sale of migrants into slavery caused international outrage. Libyan law continued to criminalize the irregular entry, stay or exit of foreign nationals, and still lacked a legal framework for asylum. In November, UNHCR, the UN refugee agency, announced that it had reached an agreement with the Libyan authorities to temporarily accommodate people from a transit centre who were in need of international protection. However, there was no progress on a Memorandum of Understanding that would formally recognize UNHCR's operations in Libya. The International Organization for Migration calculated that there were 416,556 migrants in Libya at the end of September. UNHCR stated that 44,306 people in Libya were registered as refugees or asylum-seekers as of 1 December, but the actual number of refugees was likely to be higher. The International Organization for Migration continued to assist in the "voluntary return" of 19,370 nationals to their home countries during the year, often from detention centres. In a significant development, UNHCR began evacuating refugees and asylum-seekers, taking 25 people to Niger for resettlement in France in November and 162 people to Italy in December.

WOMEN'S RIGHTS

Women were particularly affected by the ongoing conflict, which disproportionately affected their right to move freely and to participate in political and public life.

In February the military in eastern Libya issued Decree No. 6 of 2017, restricting Libyan women under the age of 60 from travelling abroad without a legal male guardian. Following a public outcry and calls from civil society for its removal, Decree No. 6 was replaced on 23 February with Decree No. 7, which stipulated that no Libyan male or female between the ages of 18 and 45 could travel abroad without prior "security approval". The Decree failed to specify the procedure required to obtain such approval or the criteria that would be used to grant or deny it.

In the face of intimidation and targeting, high-profile women activists continued to be forced to retreat from public and political engagement.

LITHUANIA

Republic of Lithuania
Head of state: **Dalia Grybauskaitė**
Head of government: **Saulius Skvernelis**

The President signed legislation which discriminated against lesbian, gay and bisexual people. Parliament considered a law which would severely restrict access to abortion. Lithuania offered visas to two gay men from the Russian republic of Chechnya who feared for their safety. In two separate cases, a district court ruled in favour of two transgender people seeking to change their identity documents without undergoing gender reassignment surgery.

INTERNATIONAL SCRUTINY

The case of *Abu Zubaydah v. Lithuania* remained pending before the European Court of Human Rights. Abu Zubaydah alleged he had been forcibly disappeared and tortured at a secret CIA detention centre in Antaviliai, a neighbourhood of Vilnius, Lithuania's capital, between 2005 and 2006. In September, the UN Committee on Enforced Disappearances urged Lithuania to investigate its involvement in US-led rendition and secret detention programmes; hold those responsible to account; and provide victims with appropriate redress and reparation.

REFUGEES AND ASYLUM-SEEKERS

In May, Lithuania offered visas to two Chechen men who were seeking international protection outside of Russia for fear of persecution based on their sexual orientation. This followed allegations of abductions, torture and other ill-treatment and in some cases even the killing of men suspected of being gay in Chechnya (see Russian Federation entry).

RIGHTS OF LESBIAN, GAY, BISEXUAL, TRANSGENDER AND INTERSEX PEOPLE

In April, the Vilnius City District Court ordered the Civil Registry Office to change the identity documents of a transgender individual who had applied for legal gender recognition, without them having to undergo gender reassignment surgery. In May, the Court ruled that the Civil Registry Office should change the gender marker and personal identity number of another transgender applicant.

In July, the President signed an amendment to the Law on Equal Opportunities which defines family members as "spouses or direct descendants", effectively excluding unmarried partners and thereby preventing – among others – same-sex couples from being legally considered as family members.

SEXUAL AND REPRODUCTIVE RIGHTS

In October, Parliament considered a draft law initiated by the Electoral Action of Poles in Lithuania, a political party. If implemented, it would restrict women's access to abortion in cases where the pregnancy poses a risk to the woman's life or health, or when it is the result of rape.

MACEDONIA

The former Yugoslav Republic of Macedonia
Head of state: **Gjorge Ivanov**
Head of government: **Zoran Zaev (replaced Emil Dimitriev in May)**

Impunity for war crimes persisted. Asylum-seekers and migrants were unlawfully detained. A court's judgment provided for legal gender recognition for transgender people.

BACKGROUND

Following elections in December 2016, the Internal Macedonian Revolutionary Organization - Democratic Party for Macedonian National Unity gained over half the seats, but could not form a government. The Social Democratic Union of Macedonia (SDSM) agreed to form a coalition with ethnic

Albanian parties and formed a government in May 2017 following a violent invasion of Parliament by former government supporters. In November, a former police chief and several MPs were arrested for their part in the disruption.

The election followed a political crisis triggered by the publication by SDSM in 2015 of audio recordings revealing unlawful surveillance and widespread corruption within the government.

The European Commission asked Macedonia to implement measures including ensuring the rule of law, the right to privacy, freedom of expression, an independent judiciary and an end to government corruption.

FREEDOM OF EXPRESSION

Until May, media freedom was seriously compromised by government interference in print and other media, including through the control of advertising and other revenues, resulting in widespread self-censorship and little investigative journalism. In March, 122 NGOs issued a statement protesting against the government's apparent campaign to undermine their work.

IMPUNITY

The Special Prosecution Office, established to investigate crimes arising from the audio recordings, opened an investigation into the 2011 murder of Martin Neshkovski and the subsequent government cover-up. In June, the Office indicted 94 former government officials, including former Prime Minister Gruevski and the former head of Security and Counter Intelligence.

Impunity for war crimes, including enforced disappearances and abductions, persisted.

JUSTICE SYSTEM

Following votes by the Council of Public Prosecutors and the Parliament, Public Prosecutor Marko Zvrlevski was removed from office in August for his lack of independence. In October, provisional Public Prosecutor Liljana Spasovska called for the retrial of six ethnic Albanians, convicted in June 2014 of the killing of five Macedonians at Easter 2012. The retrial was called on the grounds that the 2014 trial had not met international standards for fair trial.

REFUGEES' AND MIGRANTS' RIGHTS

Asylum seekers and migrants, including unaccompanied children, were unlawfully detained at the Reception Centre for Foreigners as witnesses in criminal proceedings against smugglers, for an average of two weeks, after which they were released. Most applied for asylum, but left the country shortly afterwards.

The European Court of Human Rights (ECtHR) considered the case of eight refugees from Syria, Iraq and Afghanistan who were among 1,500 refugees and migrants forcibly returned to Greece in March 2016 by the Macedonian authorities, who failed to examine their individual circumstances or provide an effective remedy.

RIGHTS OF LESBIAN, GAY, BISEXUAL, TRANSGENDER AND INTERSEX PEOPLE

In September, the Administrative Court ruled that a transgender person could change their gender marker in the official registry, providing for the legal recognition of gender identity.

SEXUAL AND REPRODUCTIVE RIGHTS

A court in Skopje, the capital, determined in July that the termination of a woman's employment contract, because she was pregnant for a second time, constituted direct discrimination.

Also in July, a local antenatal clinic in Suto Orizari, a predominatly Roma suburb of Skopje, was reopened after eight years. In September, four newborn babies died within two days in the Clinic of Gynaecology and Obstetrics in Skopje. A subsequent inspection found a shortage of medical staff, babies sharing intensive care incubators, faulty ventilation and a leaking roof. Between January and October, 127 babies died.

DEATHS IN CUSTODY

In March, the European Roma Rights Centre highlighted the deaths in custody of young Romani men from overdoses of methadone only available to prison guards, and the death of a Romani woman, allegedly after she had been ill-treated. In October the European Committee for the Prevention of Torture raised concerns about the failure since 2006 to improve the management of, and conditions in, Idrizovo Prison in Skopje, where nine prisoners died in 2016.

COUNTER-TERROR AND SECURITY

In December, the Committee of Ministers reviewed implementation of the judgment of the ECtHR in 2012 in the case of German national Khaled el-Masri, expressing concern at the failure to make a public apology and requesting information on any progress in implementing the judgment. The Court held Macedonia liable for Khaled el-Masri's detention, enforced disappearance, torture and other ill-treatment in 2003, and subsequent handover to the CIA which transferred him to a secret detention site in Afghanistan.

In November, 37 ethnic Albanian defendants were convicted of terrorism for their participation or assistance in a gun battle with police in Kumanovo in 2015, in which 18 people were killed.

MADAGASCAR

Republic of Madagascar
Head of state: **Hery Rajaonarimampianina**
Head of government: **Olivier Mahafaly Solonandrasana**

There was widespread poverty; access to food, water, health care and education was restricted. Prison conditions remained harsh; the excessive use of pre-trial detention persisted. The criminal justice system continued to be used to harass and intimidate human rights defenders and journalists, and restrict their freedom of expression, particularly those working on environmental and corruption issues.

BACKGROUND

An outbreak of pneumonic plague, first reported in August, continued throughout the year in rural and urban areas. Of 2,348 reported cases between 1 August and 22 November, 202 resulted in deaths.

INTERNATIONAL SCRUTINY

In July, the UN Human Rights Committee expressed concern about human rights violations including the excessive use of force by police against alleged cattle rustlers (*dahalos*); and revenge attacks by members of the security forces after two police officers were killed by villagers, in the northern town of Antsakabary.

The Committee called on Madagascar to immediately provide the National Human Rights Commission with an independent and sufficient budget to enable it to carry out its mandate. It also recommended that the government expedite the establishment of the High Council for the Defence of Democracy and the Rule of Law, whose mission included the promotion and protection of human rights, and provide it with financial autonomy.

JUSTICE SYSTEM

The criminal justice system remained seriously flawed and failed to guarantee due process. The excessive use of pre-trial detention continued despite provisions in the Constitution and the Code of Penal Procedure that limited its use as an exceptional measure for specific reasons; more than 50% of prison inmates were awaiting trial. Despite constitutional provisions guaranteeing the right to legal defence at all stages of the process, where lack of resources should not be an obstacle, lawyers reported that they were not paid for legal aid work, including trial attendance, and were prevented from fulfilling their duties. In practice, pre-trial legal aid was not available.

DETENTION

The government allowed international NGOs, as well as the National Human Rights Commission, to visit detention centres.

Prisons were severely overcrowded and conditions were inhumane. Food and medical care were inadequate. Toilets and showers did not work properly, and some prisons had open sewers putting inmates at risk of disease. Most of the country's prisons had not been adequately renovated for more than 60 years. Infrastructure was dilapidated and, in some instances, put prisoners' lives at risk. In July, four detainees were killed after a wall collapsed in the Antsohihy prison in the north.

Families of inmates reported being forced to pay bribes to visit their relatives and detainees relied on their families for food.

Antanimora prison in the capital, Antananarivo, held around 2,850 detainees, the highest number of inmates in the country, and three times its intended capacity. Overcrowding was mainly due to the large number of pre-trial detainees, the ineffective judicial system and lengthy trial delays. Some detainees had been held for up to five years before being brought to trial.

In contravention of international standards, convicted prisoners and pre-trial detainees were held together. As of July, Tsiafahy maximum security prison near Antananarivo hosted 396 pre-trial detainees alongside sentenced prisoners, in inhumane conditions, despite National Law 2006-015 stipulating that it should house only prisoners serving life sentences or those considered to be dangerous. The need to separate children from adults was not respected in all prisons.

FREEDOM OF ASSEMBLY

Peaceful protests were repressed. Civil society organizations claimed that the authorities banned protests on the grounds that they were likely to be a "high risk of public disorder". In June, civil society movements Wake-Up Madagascar and SEFAFI, which works to improve democratic processes in the country, criticized a one-month ban on public protests which the government said was necessary to protect public order during National Day celebrations on 26 June.

In July, police stopped a protest planned by the Movement for Freedom of Expression to mark the first anniversary of the passing of the new Code of Media Communication law which imposes heavy fines for offences such as contempt, defamation or insult against a government official.

HUMAN RIGHTS DEFENDERS

Human rights defenders who opposed projects to exploit natural resources, or who made allegations of corruption against government officials were particularly at risk of harassment, arrests on trumped-up charges, or other abuses under the criminal justice system. In June, after 10 months' pre-trial detention on charges of organizing a protest which became violent, environmental activist Clovis Razafimalala was released from Tamatave prison. In July, the Tamatave Tribunal sentenced him to a five-year suspended prison sentence.[1] On 27 September, environmental activist Raleva was detained in Mananjary police station, in the southeast, after he questioned the legality of a Chinese mining company in the Mananjary region.[2] He was later transferred to Mananjary prison. On 26 October, the Mananjary court found him guilty of using the false title of "Head of District", and gave him a two-year suspended sentence.

SEXUAL AND REPRODUCTIVE RIGHTS

Abortion remained criminalized in all cases under Article 317 of the Penal Code. Anyone providing or attempting to provide an abortion was subject to a heavy fine and imprisonment of up to 10 years. Medical personnel providing information on obtaining an abortion were subject to, in addition to imprisonment and fines, suspension from practice for between five years and life. Women who sought or had abortions were also subject to a heavy fine and up to two years' imprisonment. Several women were sent to prison for abortion-related offences during the year.

In July, the government stated that it was working on a bill which would make abortion a minor offence.

Later in July, the UN Human Rights Committee considered Madagascar's fourth periodic report. The Committee called for the decriminalization of abortion, and for greater efforts to make sexual and reproductive health services more accessible to women.

1. Madagascar: A Damocles sword on environmental activist's head (AFR 35/6841/2017)

2. Madagascar: Environmental rights defender falsely accused – Raleva (AFR 35/7248/2017)

MALAWI

Republic of Malawi
Head of State and Government: **Arthur Peter Mutharika**

Two people were killed as attacks against people with albinism resumed. Gender-based violence increased. Lesbian, gay, bisexual, transgender and intersex (LGBTI) people continued to live in fear of harassment and attacks. Draft legislation threatened to silence NGOs and civil society organizations working on governance and human rights issues.

DISCRIMINATION – PEOPLE WITH ALBINISM

Attacks against people with albinism resumed in January after an interval of seven months. Two people were killed. On 10 January, Madalitso Pensulo, a teenage boy, was killed in Mlonda village in the Tyolo District. In February, Mercy Zainabu Banda was found murdered in Lilongwe with her wrist, right breast and hair removed. In March, two brothers were stabbed in Nsanje. As of 30 August, 20 murders of people with albinism which have taken place since 2014 remained unresolved.

VIOLENCE AGAINST WOMEN AND GIRLS

Gender-based violence continued; seven women were reported to have been murdered in August and September alone. On 14 September, around 150 women participated in a national march to protest against the alarming levels of gender-based

violence. The Ministry of Gender, Children, Disability and Social Welfare publicly expressed its concerns about the killings. One of the protesters, Beatrice Mateyo, was arrested and charged with carrying a placard bearing "offensive and obscene words". She was charged with "insulting the modesty of a woman" under section 137(3) of the Penal Code and released on bail the same day. If convicted she faced up to one year's imprisonment.

RIGHTS OF LESBIAN, GAY, BISEXUAL, TRANSGENDER AND INTERSEX PEOPLE

Harassment of and attacks against LGBTI people continued. In January the People's Party spokesman, Kenneth Msonda, publicly said that "gays are worse than dogs and must be killed". Activists brought a case against him for inciting violence against gay and lesbian people. The Constitutional Court was considering whether charges should be brought against him at the end of the year.

In August, a 12-year-old boy stopped going to school after he faced repeated harassment and attacks, such as people throwing stones at him and urinating on him. He and his family lived in fear that he might be killed.

Same-sex sexual relations between consenting adults remained illegal. However, the solicitor general intervened in April after political and church leaders held a protest against LGBTI people. The Malawi Human Rights Commission indicated it would hold public consultations on whether to reform the law.

HUMAN RIGHTS DEFENDERS

Draft amendments to the NGO law remained before Parliament. The amendments, which introduced broad, excessive, intrusive and arbitrary controls on the activities of NGOs, could silence critics including human rights groups. If implemented, the law would establish an NGO Board under the Ministry of Gender, Children, Disability and Social Welfare with wide discretionary powers, including to approve NGOs' funding applications to donor agencies; and to demand that such applications fall in line with government policies and be designed to "advance the public interest". NGOs would be forced to register with the NGO Board which would have power to deregister them. They would also be required to sign Memorandums of Understanding with local government before operating in the community.

MALAYSIA

Malaysia
Head of state: **King Muhammad V**
Head of government: **Najib Tun Razak**

Civic space shrank further as a crackdown on civil and political rights continued. There was a rise in the use of open-ended and arbitrary travel bans to restrict and threaten the freedom of movement of human rights defenders. Indigenous rights activists and journalists were arrested and investigated for campaigning against and reporting human rights abuses.

FREEDOM OF EXPRESSION

The government continued to harass, detain and prosecute critics through the use of restrictive laws such as the Sedition Act and the Communications and Multimedia Act. More than 60 individuals were arrested, charged or imprisoned under various pieces of legislation. Four individuals were charged, and another convicted, under Section 233 of the Communications and Multimedia Act which criminalizes, among other things, the "misuse of network facilities" for criticizing the government or for government-related satire.

FREEDOM OF MOVEMENT

In July, the Court of Appeal ruled that the government has absolute discretion to bar any citizen from travelling abroad without needing to provide a reason.[1] This ruling facilitated continued violations of the right to freedom of movement and the work of human rights defenders, including cartoonist Zunar and activist Hishamuddin Rais. The authorities also barred several human rights defenders from entering Malaysia; they included Bangladeshi activist Adilur Rahman Khan[2] and Singaporean activist Han Hui Hui, who were deported after attempting to attend human rights conferences. Bans were secretive, arbitrary and not subject to appeal. No prior notice was given.

FREEDOMS OF ASSOCIATION AND ASSEMBLY

Human rights defenders and opposition parliamentarians continued to stand trial for participating in peaceful protests. In July, the Kota Kinabalu High Court reversed an earlier acquittal by the Magistrate's Court of activist Jannie Lasimbang who had been charged under Section 9 of the Peaceful Assembly Act 2012. Her trial was ongoing at the end of the year. Parliamentarians and activists were charged after joining the peaceful #KitaLawan (We Fight) protest rally; they included MP Sim Tze Tzin, Maria Chin Abdullah, Mandeep Singh and Adam Adli. Charges against Maria Chin Abdullah, Mandeep Singh and Sim Tze Tzin were initially dismissed by the courts, but brought again in October. Adam Adli was acquitted of his charges by the Magistrate's Court in November.

INDIGENOUS PEOPLES' RIGHTS

In January, following peaceful protests against logging licences granted by local authorities, 21 Indigenous human rights defenders from the Temiar people in the northern state of Kelantan were detained. Two journalists were also arrested.[3] They were released within 48 hours, but the rights of the Temiar to their customary lands remained under threat because logging activities continued without the free, prior and informed consent of the communities. In August, 11 Indigenous human rights defenders in Perak were arrested by police when peacefully protesting against a logging company.

ARBITRARY ARRESTS AND DETENTIONS

Preventive detention laws such as the Prevention of Terrorism Act and Security Offences (Special Measures) Act (SOSMA) continued to be used to detain, prosecute and imprison people alleged to have committed security offences. The maximum detention period of 28 days under the SOSMA was set to remain in force for five years from 31 July, following a parliamentary vote.

On 26 April, the Kuala Lumpur High Court sentenced Siti Noor Aishah to five years' imprisonment for possession of 12 books, under a sweeping provision of the SOSMA prohibiting the possession, custody or control of any item associated with any terrorist group or the commission of a terrorist act.[4] The books owned by Siti Noor Aishah had not been banned, which raised further concerns about the arbitrary nature of the law and the way it was applied.

POLICE AND SECURITY FORCES

Impunity for deaths in custody and excessive use of force and firearms persisted. There were at least five deaths in custody during the year. They included S. Balamurugan who, according to cellmates, was beaten by police during interrogation. A magistrate had earlier ordered that he be released and given medical attention. No police investigation into his death was known to have been carried out.

DEATH PENALTY

The death penalty continued to be retained as the mandatory punishment for offences including drug trafficking, murder and discharge of firearms with intent to kill or harm in certain circumstances. Executions continued to be carried out during the year and there remained no established procedure for notification of scheduled executions.[5] In November, Parliament amended the Dangerous Drugs Act, providing the judiciary with discretion on the mandatory death penalty in the event the accused is a drug courier and has co-operated with law enforcement in "disrupting

drug trafficking activities". The provision included a mandatory 15 whip lashes.

RIGHTS OF LESBIAN, GAY, BISEXUAL, TRANSGENDER AND INTERSEX PEOPLE

Discrimination against LGBTI people continued both in law and practice. Section 377A of the Penal Code criminalizes consensual sexual relations between adult men. In June, the Health Ministry received local and international criticism for its decision to launch a video competition for teenagers on how to "prevent gender confusion" which included "gay, lesbian, transgender, transvestite and tomboy". The wording was subsequently removed.

TORTURE AND OTHER ILL-TREATMENT

In July, Kelantan state assembly passed amendments to the Syariah Criminal Procedure Enactment 2002 which would allow caning of criminals to be carried out in public. Torture is not adequately defined or prohibited in the state Syariah Criminal Code or the Malaysian Penal Code.

1. Malaysia: Open-ended travel bans violate the rights of human rights defenders (ASA 28/6697/2017)

2. Malaysia: Bangladeshi human rights activist detained (News story, 20 July)

3. Malaysia: End harassment of Indigenous rights defenders (ASA 28/5549/2017)

4. Malaysia: Student convicted for possession of 'illegal' book – Siti Noor Aishah (ASA 28/6136/2017)

5. Malaysia: Stop execution of prisoners due to be hanged on Friday (News story, 23 March)

MALDIVES

Republic of Maldives
Head of state and government: **Abdulla Yameen Abdul Gayoom**

The crackdown on the rights to freedom of expression and peaceful assembly continued. Authorities used the criminal justice system to silence political opponents, as well as human rights defenders, journalists and civil society. The

lack of independence of the judiciary remained a concern. The President reaffirmed that executions would resume after more than 60 years.

JUSTICE SYSTEM

Political turmoil persisted as the President used the military and the judiciary to stifle the opposition. In July, the opposition initiated a no confidence motion to impeach the Speaker of Parliament, but proceedings were halted with the suspension of four opposition MPs. On 24 July, parliamentarians were denied entry into the Parliament and the President directed the military to use pepper spray and tear gas to disperse them. MPs Faris Maumoon and Qasim Ibrahim were arrested arbitrarily for allegedly bribing law makers to unseat the Speaker of Parliament.[1]

UNFAIR TRIALS

The authorities ignored constitutional provisions safeguarding the right to a fair trial, as evidenced by a string of criminal cases against political opponents. On 18 July, MP Faris Maumoon was arrested during a raid on his house for allegedly bribing law makers to sign the motion of no confidence against the Speaker. He was seeking to cancel the charges, claiming that the evidence was obtained unlawfully.

In April, Qasim Ibrahim, leader of the Jumhooree Party, was sentenced to 38 months' imprisonment after being convicted on charges including plotting to overthrow the government. After repeated requests for medical attention, in September the court granted him permission to travel abroad for treatment.

FREEDOM OF EXPRESSION

In April, popular political blogger and social media activist Yameen Rasheed was stabbed to death in his apartment building in the capital, Malé.[2] The year marked three years since the disappearance of journalist Ahmed Rilwan. By the end of the year, neither of the investigations had resulted in successful prosecutions of perpetrators, and were marred by political interference.

In March, journalists from Raajje TV reported to the Maldives Police Service that they had received threats of death if they sent journalists to Faafu Atoll to cover a visit by the King of Saudi Arabia. No additional security was granted by police. Around the same time, two journalists from the newspaper *Maldives Independent* were taken into "protective custody" by police after receiving threats from members of the ruling party. The journalists claimed that the police read their notes and treated them like suspects.

In July, seven journalists from Sangu TV and Raajje TV were arrested while covering a protest marking Independence Day. They were detained for several hours accused of obstructing police.

FREEDOM OF ASSEMBLY

Arbitrary restrictions on peaceful protesters and human rights defenders continued. On 24 July, the military used pepper spray and tear gas to disperse parliamentarians trying to enter the Parliament building. On 8 August, a march led by relatives and friends of Ahmed Rilwan to mark the third anniversary of his disappearance was blocked by Specialist Operations police officers who used pepper spray, snatched banners, tore up placards and briefly detained nine people. Several days later, Ahmed Rilwan's nephew and Yameen Rasheed's sister were dismissed from their posts as civil support staff at Maldives Police Service for joining the protest.

DEATH PENALTY

The government stated that the death penalty was to be implemented "by the end of September". Executions would be the first to be carried out in over 60 years. Three men – Hussain Humaam Ahmed, Ahmed Murrath and Mohamed Nabeel – remained at risk of imminent execution despite serious concerns about the fairness of the legal proceedings. These included the use of an apparently coerced "confession" by Hussain Humaam Ahmed, which he later retracted. The UN

Human Rights Committee made repeated requests to the government to stay the executions of the three men during 2016 and 2017, in accordance with Maldives' commitments under the Optional Protocol to the ICCPR.[3] Of the 17 prisoners on death row, at least five were sentenced to death for crimes committed when they were below 18 years of age.[4]

1. Maldives: Opposition MP must get a fair trial (News story, 22 September)

2. Maldives: Killing of popular blogger an attack on freedom of expression (News story, 23 April)

3. Maldives: Halt first execution in more than 60 years (News story, 20 July)

4. Maldives to resume executions by September (ASA 29/7007/2017)

MALI

Republic of Mali
Head of state: **Ibrahim Boubacar Keïta**
Head of government: **Soumeylou Boubeye Maiga**
(replaced Abdoulaye Idrissa Maïga in December, who replaced Modibo Keïta in April)

A bill for the protection of human rights defenders was adopted by the National Assembly in December. The government postponed the revision of the Constitution following protests. Full implementation of the 2015 Algiers peace agreement remained delayed. Joint operations between the Malian army and some armed groups began in Gao under the Operational Coordination Mechanism.

INTERNATIONAL SCRUTINY

The UN Independent Expert on the situation of human rights in Mali and the UN Multidimensional Integrated Stabilization Mission in Mali (MINUSMA) raised concerns about serious security threats in the northern and central regions, which put civilians at risk and hampered their access to basic social services. During the year MINUSMA documented 252 cases of human rights violations by security forces and armed groups involving more than 650 victims. The cases included 21 instances of extrajudicial executions and deliberate and arbitrary killings, 12 cases of enforced disappearance and 31 cases of torture and other ill-treatment.

The French authorities opened an inquiry into the death of a child during the November 2016 Operation Barkhane involving French soldiers. The results had not been made public by the end of 2017. In December the spokesman for the French Army said that the internal inquiry did not reveal any individual or collective responsibility.

ABUSES BY ARMED GROUPS

Attacks in the central regions of Mopti and Ségou increased during the year. A rise in the presence of armed groups and in local recruitment aggravated tensions between different ethnic groups. In February, 20 people were killed and 18 others injured when unidentified assailants attacked members of the Fulani community. The attack followed the killing of a well-known opponent of radical influences in Ségou region.

Between January and September, MINUSMA recorded at least 155 attacks against its own peacekeeping forces, the Malian security forces and French soldiers involved in Operation Barkhane. Throughout the year, more than 30 MINUSMA-related personnel, including civilians and contractors, were killed by armed groups. Most attacks were claimed by the Group for the Support of Islam and Muslims. Victims included eight children.

In June, five people were killed and 10 wounded during an attack by an armed group on a hotel on the outskirts of the capital, Bamako.

In July, armed men beat 10 women who were part of a wedding party. In August, 12 women who were not wearing a veil were flogged in Mopti.

At the end of the year at least eight people remained held hostage by armed groups following their abductions in Mali, Burkina Faso and Niger over the last three years. The eight included three women – Beatrice

Stockly, a Swiss missionary, Gloria Cecilia Agoti Narvaez, a Colombian missionary, and Sophie Petronin (French) – as well as Julian Ghergut (Romanian); Jeffery Woodke (US); Ken Eliott (Australian); and Malian nationals Mamadou Diawara and Soungalo Koné.

FREEDOM OF EXPRESSION

Freedom of speech was under threat in the run-up to a referendum on amendments to the Constitution.

In June, at least eight people were injured when protesters against the constitutional changes clashed with police using tear gas and batons.

Physical and verbal threats against opponents of the referendum were reported in July. Also in July, Maliba FM radio journalist Mohamed Youssouf Bathily, known as Ras Bath, was sentenced to one year's imprisonment for "incitement to military disobedience" following criticisms of the army in 2016. In November, he was acquitted by the Bamako Court of Appeal.

DETENTION

Prisons remained overcrowded and conditions were poor. At the end of the year, the Bamako Central Prison housed 1,947 detainees despite a capacity of 400. Of those held, 581 had been convicted and 1,366 were awaiting trial. Detainees held since 2013 on terrorism charges were not permitted to leave their cramped and poorly ventilated prison cells, even for exercise.

Detainees continued to be held at an unofficial detention centre known as the "Sécurité d'Etat".

IMPUNITY

Efforts to tackle impunity faltered as several high-profile trials related to abuses committed in northern Mali during the 2012-2013 occupation failed to make significant progress. The 2015 peace agreement, which recommended the establishment of an international commission of inquiry to investigate crimes under international law including war crimes, crimes against humanity and human rights

violations, had not been implemented by the end of the year.

In August, the former head of the police unit of the Movement for Oneness and Jihad in West Africa, Aliou Mahamane Touré, was convicted of "violation of internal security, illegal possession of weapons of war, criminal conspiracy and aggravated assault" by the Bamako Assizes Court and sentenced to 10 years' imprisonment.

The trial of General Amadou Haya Sanogo in relation to the abduction and murder of 21 soldiers in April 2012 had not recommenced after it was postponed in December 2016. The postponement followed a ruling that DNA tests were held inadmissible because the correct legal procedure had not been followed.

RIGHT TO EDUCATION

The UN Independent Expert on the situation of human rights in Mali expressed concern about the high number of schools closed due to insecurity in central and northern parts of the country, depriving more than 150,000 children of their right to education.

Throughout the year, more than 500 schools in Gao, Kidal, Ségou, Mopti and Timbuktu remained closed. Many schools, notably in Niono, Macina and Tenenkou, were threatened with attack by armed groups if they did not either close or convert to Qur'anic teaching. In May, an armed group burned down a school in Mopti, threatening further attacks against non-Qur'anic schools.

Despite Article 39 of the peace agreement committing all signatories to pay particular attention to education for all, armed groups continued to occupy some schools.

INTERNATIONAL JUSTICE

In August, the International Criminal Court held Ahmad Al Faqi Al Mahdi liable for €2.7 million in individual and collective reparations. He was convicted in 2016 of the war crime of intentionally directing attacks against religious and historic buildings in Timbuktu, and sentenced to nine years' imprisonment. ICC investigations into alleged war crimes committed since January 2012 in Mali were ongoing.

MALTA

Republic of Malta
Head of state: Marie-Louise Coleiro Preca
Head of government: Joseph Muscat

New information emerged regarding the 2013 shipwreck in which many Syrian refugees died. It exposed Italy's reluctance to assist Maltese authorities in rescuing the boat in distress. Malta denied three Libyan asylum-seekers who were rescued within its search and rescue region permission to disembark. The authorities admitted 168 asylum-seekers under the EU relocation programme, a higher number than they had committed to. Marriage rights were extended to same-sex couples. Abortion remained prohibited in all circumstances.

BACKGROUND

In October, journalist Daphne Caruana Galizia was killed in a car bomb explosion. She had been critical of the government and investigated organized crime, corruption including against politicians, and the Maltese chapter of the so-called "Panama Papers" – leaked files from an offshore law firm regarding tax havens and their users. The government was under pressure from the EU and others to ensure a thorough and independent investigation into Daphne Caruana Galizia's death. In December, three men were charged with her murder and remanded in custody.

REFUGEES AND ASYLUM-SEEKERS

In May, the Italian magazine L'Espresso published new information regarding the shipwreck that occurred on 11 October 2013 in the Maltese search and rescue region of the central Mediterranean. Over 260 people died, mostly Syrian refugees, many of them children. The magazine reported that phone conversations held in the period immediately preceding the capsizing of the refugees' boat showed that Italian navy and coastguard officials were reluctant to deploy the Italian warship Libra which was the closest to the boat in distress, notwithstanding repeated requests by Maltese authorities to do so. Criminal proceedings and investigations against some of the Italian navy and coastguard officials involved were ongoing in Italy at the end of the year. No investigation was known to have been initiated by the Maltese authorities into the incident.

In August, Maltese authorities denied authorization to disembark three Libyan asylum-seekers from the rescue boat Golfo Azzurro, operated by the NGO Proactiva Open Arms. The three men had been rescued within Malta's search and rescue region in the central Mediterranean. After three days of negotiations between Malta and Italy over which country should take the asylum-seekers, Italy accepted the request and the three men were taken to Sicily.

Malta received 168 refugees and asylum-seekers from Greece and Italy, more than the 131 it legally committed to accept under the EU relocation programme, which closed on 26 September.

RIGHTS OF LESBIAN, GAY, BISEXUAL, TRANSGENDER AND INTERSEX PEOPLE

In July, marriage equality legislation was approved by Parliament. The new law extended full marriage rights to same-sex couples.

SEXUAL AND REPRODUCTIVE RIGHTS

Abortion remained prohibited in all circumstances. Women were denied access to abortion even when the life of the pregnant woman was at risk.

MAURITANIA

Islamic Republic of Mauritania
Head of state: Mohamed Ould Abdel Aziz
Head of government: Yahya Ould Hademine

Human rights defenders, bloggers, anti-slavery activists and other opponents of the government were intimidated, attacked and prosecuted for their peaceful activities. Freedoms of expression, association and peaceful assembly were restricted. International human rights activists were refused entry to the country. Torture and other ill-treatment in custody was common. Haratine and Afro-Mauritanian people faced systematic discrimination. Slavery practices persist.

BACKGROUND

In March, the Senate rejected a proposal to amend the 1991 Constitution. The authorities called a referendum for August; the majority voted to abolish the Senate.

FREEDOMS OF EXPRESSION, ASSOCIATION AND ASSEMBLY

Security forces continued to intimidate and attack bloggers, human rights defenders and others who criticized the government.

Anti-slavery activists, among them prisoners of conscience, were detained. Abdallahi Abdou Diop was released in January after serving a six-month prison sentence. Abdallahi Maatalla Seck and Moussa Biram remained in Bir Moghrein prison, more than 1,000km from their homes, since July 2016. The three prisoners of conscience were convicted on charges including participating in an unauthorized gathering and membership of an unauthorized association.

In April, the security forces used tear gas and batons to repress a peaceful protest in the capital, Nouakchott, that was organized by youth groups calling for policies to address youth unemployment and to support young people. At least 26 people were arrested. Most of them were released the same day, but 10 were detained for four days, charged with participating in an unauthorized gathering. The court in Nouakchott gave one woman a three-month suspended prison sentence, which was overturned on appeal. The others were acquitted.

On 23 April, police arrested seven people, of whom four were foreign nationals and two were children, in connection with their attending a religious service in Nouakchott.

One of them was released without charge after three days; the others were charged with belonging to an unauthorized organization and released six days later.

Ahead of the August referendum, the Office of the UN High Commissioner for Human Rights expressed concern about the authorities' apparent suppression of dissent and the reported use of excessive force against protest leaders.

Five days after the referendum, Senator Mohamed Ould Ghadda, who opposed the vote, was arrested and charged with corruption. He remained in detention without trial at the end of the year. Three weeks later, 12 Senators and four journalists were questioned by a judge regarding allegations that they received financial support from a businessman. They were required to sign weekly at the police station while the police were investigating the allegations.

In November, the Appeal Court of Nouadhibou commuted the death sentence of blogger Mohamed Mkhaïtir to two years' imprisonment. He was convicted in December 2014 of apostasy for writing a blog critical of those who used Islam to foster discrimination against Moulamines (blacksmiths) and had been held since January 2014. Although he was scheduled for release at the end of the year, he remained in custody; his family and his lawyers were not able to visit him or confirm his whereabouts.

In November, 15 human rights defenders were arrested in the southern town of Kaédi by plain clothes men who identified themselves as members of the Battalion for Presidential Security. They had been distributing leaflets and holding banners calling for justice for their relatives who had been unlawfully killed between 1989 and 1991. They were taken to a military base and questioned about their activities. Ten were released the same day and five were transferred to a police station and detained for six days, without access to a lawyer, before being released without charge.

International human rights activists and NGOs were refused access to Mauritania throughout the year. In May, a foreign lawyer and journalist carrying out research into slavery were asked to leave the country. In September, US anti-slavery activists were denied entry visas when they arrived at Nouakchott International Airport. In November, the authorities refused an Amnesty International delegation access to the country.

TORTURE AND OTHER ILL-TREATMENT

Detainees reported that they were tortured during pre-trial detention in order to extract confessions and to intimidate them. People held in police stations including the Commissariat in Nouakchott were routinely placed in prolonged solitary confinement – a type of detention condemned by the UN Human Rights Committee as a violation of the prohibition of torture or other cruel, inhuman or degrading treatment.

In his March report, the UN Special Rapporteur on torture acknowledged that while torture and other ill-treatment was no longer "rampant", it occurred frequently. He expressed concern that the "culture of torture" persisted in police and gendarmerie units, and that torture continued to be used to extract confessions. The Special Rapporteur noted that the practice of detaining terrorism suspects for up to 45 days without access to legal representation was excessive; oversight mechanisms for the investigation of allegations of torture and other ill-treatment lacked due diligence and were slow; existing laws and safeguards needed to be expanded and implemented; and that there was no significant improvement in detention conditions, such as overcrowding, poor sanitation and inadequate nutrition.

ECONOMIC, SOCIAL AND CULTURAL RIGHTS

In his report in March the UN Special Rapporteur on extreme poverty and human rights concluded that while the government had made progress in alleviating poverty in recent years, a large proportion of the population continued to live in poverty

without adequate access to food, education, water, sanitation and health care. The Special Rapporteur stressed that despite Mauritania's obligations under international human rights treaties, there was a complete absence of prenatal and postnatal care in rural areas. He also highlighted that Haratines and Afro-Mauritanians, who constituted an estimated two thirds of the population, were excluded from many areas of economic and social life. In addition, the fact that the government had not collected statistics on the numbers of Haratine and Afro-Mauritanian people in the country, served to render their needs and rights invisible.

REFUGEES' AND MIGRANTS' RIGHTS

In his March report, the UN Special Rapporteur on torture expressed concerns about the collective expulsion of irregular migrants and refugees who were often abandoned on the southern border with Senegal which could contravene the principle of *non-refoulement*. During a visit to a site where irregular migrants were held in Nouakchott, he said that the 20 to 30 detainees had no toilet facilities and had insufficient room to lie or even sit down to sleep.

MEXICO

United Mexican States
Head of state and government: Enrique Peña Nieto

Violence increased throughout Mexico. The armed forces continued to undertake regular policing functions. Human rights defenders and journalists were threatened, attacked and killed; digital attacks and surveillance were particularly common. Widespread arbitrary detentions continued to lead to torture and other ill-treatment, enforced disappearances and extrajudicial executions. Impunity persisted for human rights violations and crimes under international law. Mexico received a record number of asylum claims, mostly from nationals of El Salvador, Honduras,

Guatemala and Venezuela. **Violence against women remained a major concern; new data showed that two thirds of women had experienced gender-based violence during their lives. The rights to housing and education were compromised by two major earthquakes.**

BACKGROUND

Early in the year an increase in gas prices caused social unrest, including road blockages, lootings and protests throughout the country, leading to hundreds of arrests and some fatalities. Throughout the year, security forces carried out a number of operations to crack down on a spate of clandestine robberies of petroleum. At least one of these security operations resulted in a likely extrajudicial execution by the army in May. The National Human Rights Commission raised concerns over deficient security measures in prisons that affected the rights of people deprived of their liberty. There were riots in prisons including in the states of Nuevo León and Guerrero, and a hunger strike in the federal maximum security prison at Puente Grande, Jalisco state.

The new adversarial criminal justice system, fully operational since June 2016, continued to replicate problems from the old inquisitorial system, including violations of the presumption of innocence and the use of evidence collected in violation of human rights and other illicit evidence. Bills were introduced in Congress that would weaken fair trial guarantees and expand the scope of mandatory pre-trial detention without a case-by-case assessment by a judge.

Congress approved long-overdue laws against torture and other ill-treatment and against enforced disappearance by state actors and disappearances committed by non-state actors. Legal reforms allowed the use of cannabis for medical purposes. Sustained public debates over the transformation of the federal Attorney General's Office, responsible for law enforcement and prosecution, into an independent body were conducted during

the year. In August, civil society organizations and opinion leaders presented a proposal for the design of this institution.

In October, the acting Attorney General removed the Special Prosecutor for Electoral Crimes, regarded as independent by different political forces, after he publicly reported being subjected to political pressure to disregard a high-profile corruption case.

POLICE AND SECURITY FORCES

There was a marked increase in the number of homicides, with 42,583 recorded nationally, the highest annual number of homicides registered by authorities since the start of the presidential term in December 2012. The real number may be higher, with some crimes not being reported to police, and not all of those reported triggering official action.

In December, Congress passed a Law on Interior Security enabling the prolonged presence of the armed forces in regular policing functions without any effective provisions for transparency, accountability or civilian oversight.

ARBITRARY ARRESTS AND DETENTIONS

Arbitrary arrests and detentions remained widespread, and often led to further human rights violations including torture and other ill-treatment, enforced disappearances and extrajudicial executions. Arbitrary arrests often included the planting of evidence, commonly guns and illicit drugs, by law enforcement officials. Authorities appeared to especially target those who had historically faced discrimination, in particular young men living in poverty.

The police routinely disregarded their obligations during and following an arrest. They usually did not inform the persons of the reasons for the arrest or of their rights, such as the right to legal counsel and to communicate with their families. Unjustified delays in bringing the detainee before the relevant authorities were common and often enabled other human rights violations. Police reports of arrests often contained significant errors, fabricated information and other serious flaws, including inaccuracies in recording date and time of arrest.

The reasons for arbitrary arrests were varied, but included: to extort money from detainees; to detain a particular individual in return for payment from a third party; for politically motivated reasons; and to investigate detainees in connection with another crime by detaining them for a misdemeanour that they usually had not committed.

There was no unified and accessible register of detention, consistent with international human rights law and standards, in which every detention by law enforcement officials is recorded in real time.[1]

TORTURE AND OTHER ILL-TREATMENT

In February, the UN Special Rapporteur on torture issued a follow-up report to a previous visit to Mexico in 2014; the report concluded that torture and other ill-treatment remained widespread, including the alarming use of sexual violence as a frequent method of torture.

In June, a new general law on torture came into force, replacing existing state and federal laws with nationwide application. Civil society organizations welcomed it as an advance that better incorporated international standards compared to the previous legislation. The Special Unit on Torture of the Federal Attorney General's Office reported 4,390 cases of torture under revision at the federal level and commenced 777 investigations under the new adversarial justice system. Federal authorities did not announce any new criminal charges against public officials, nor provide any information on arrests made for the crime of torture. In Quintana Roo state, a federal judge sentenced a former policeman to five years' imprisonment for the crime of torture.

ENFORCED DISAPPEARANCES

Enforced disappearances with the involvement of the state and disappearances committed by non-state actors continued to be common and those responsible enjoyed

almost absolute impunity. The official National Register of Missing and Disappeared Persons indicated that the fate or whereabouts of 34,656 people (25,682 men and 8,974 women) remained unclarified. The actual numbers were higher because the official figure excluded federal pre-2014 cases and cases classified as other criminal offences such as hostage-taking or human trafficking.

Investigations into cases of missing persons continued to be flawed and authorities generally failed to immediately initiate searches for the victims. Impunity for these crimes continued, including in the case of 43 students from the Ayotzinapa teacher training college who were forcibly disappeared in Guerrero state in 2014. The investigations into the case made little progress during the year. In March, in a hearing before the Inter-American Commission on Human Rights, state representatives reasserted the government's version of events that the students had been killed and burned in a local rubbish dump – a theory that was proved to be scientifically impossible by the Interdisciplinary Group of Independent Experts appointed by the Commission.

In October, Congress passed a general law on disappearances that defined the crime in accordance with international law and provided tools to prevent and prosecute it. The implementation of the law was expected to require a sufficient budget allocation in the following years.

EXTRAJUDICIAL EXECUTIONS

Cases of extrajudicial executions were not properly investigated and perpetrators continued to enjoy impunity. For the fourth consecutive year, the authorities failed to publish the number of people killed or wounded in clashes with the police and military forces. No information was made available regarding criminal charges in the cases of Tlatlaya, Mexico state, where soldiers killed 22 people in 2014; Apatzingán, Michoacán state, where federal police and other security forces killed at least 16 people in 2015; and Tanhuato,

Michoacán state, where the security forces killed 43 people during a security operation in 2015.

On 3 May, military personnel carried out public security operations in Palmarito Tochapan town, Puebla state, and reported that seven people died, including four soldiers. Days later, video footage from security cameras installed at the location were published on the internet. One of the videos clearly showed a person in military uniform shooting dead a man lying on the floor. Amnesty International independently verified the video and concluded that there was sufficient reason to believe that an extrajudicial execution took place.[2]

REFUGEES' AND MIGRANTS' RIGHTS

A total of 8,703 asylum claims were lodged between January and August, a similar number as for the whole of 2016. The percentage of claims that resulted in the granting of refugee status decreased from 35% in 2016 to 12% in 2017. The majority of asylum claims came from Honduran and Venezuelan nationals, the latter surpassing for the first time the number of refugees and asylum-seekers from El Salvador and Guatemala.

Between January and November, 88,741 irregular migrants were detained and 74,604 deported, in most cases without the opportunity to challenge their deportation. Of those deported, 94% were from Honduras, Guatemala and El Salvador, countries which have registered some of the highest homicide rates in the world in recent years, and 20% of those deported to these countries were children. In February, Mexico's Foreign Minister announced that Mexico would not receive foreign nationals turned back from the USA under the US Border Control Executive Order announced by US President Donald Trump on 25 January.

In June, the government met with North American and Central American governments, ostensibly to tackle the root causes of the regional refugee crisis; they did not publish any agreements reached.

The Unit for the Investigation of Crimes against Migrants of the Attorney General's Office marked two years in operation, yet remained marred by institutional challenges in its operation and problems in co-ordinating with other authorities. These problems limited advances in criminal investigations, including into massacres of migrants, that remained shrouded by impunity.

In August, a citizen consultative body published research demonstrating the involvement of the National Migration Institute in a number of human rights violations against those deprived of liberty in migration detention centres run by the Institute. Violations included overcrowding, lack of access to adequate medical services, solitary confinement used as punishment, allegations of torture and other ill-treatment. The authorities denied allegations of torture committed by the Institute, despite the National Human Rights Commission having also confirmed evidence of torture on prior occasions.

HUMAN RIGHTS DEFENDERS AND JOURNALISTS

Human rights defenders and journalists continued to be threatened, harassed, attacked and killed.

At least 12 journalists were killed, the highest number recorded in one year since 2000. They included prize-winning journalist Javier Valdez, founder of the newspaper *Ríodoce*, who was killed on 15 May in Sinaloa state. Many of the killings of journalists occurred in daylight in public places. The authorities made no significant advances into the investigations of these killings. The Special Prosecutor's Unit for Attention to Crimes against Freedom of Expression failed to investigate the journalists' work as a possible motive in the majority of cases of attacks. The federal Mechanism to Protect Human Rights Defenders and Journalists left human rights defenders and journalists inadequately protected.

Former Goldman Prize winner Isidro Baldenegro López and Juan Ontiveros Ramos, two Indigenous human rights defenders of the Raramuri (Tarahumara) Indigenous People, were killed in January and February respectively. In May, Miriam Rodríguez, a human rights defender leading the search for her daughter and other disappeared persons in Tamaulipas, was killed. In July, Mario Luna Romero, leader of the Indigenous Yaqui People in Sonora state and beneficiary of protection measures from the federal protection mechanism, was subjected to an intrusion in his house by unidentified assailants who set fire to his partner's car.

In January, it became known that a network of people was using the internet to harass and threaten human rights defenders and journalists throughout Mexico.[3] In June, evidence emerged of surveillance against journalists and human rights defenders using software that the government was known to have purchased. The federal Mechanism to Protect Human Rights Defenders and Journalists provided no strategy to respond to digital attacks and unlawful surveillance for those who have been granted protection measures.

VIOLENCE AGAINST WOMEN AND GIRLS

Gender-based violence against women and girls was widespread. Most of the cases were inadequately investigated and perpetrators enjoyed impunity. Sufficient and current data on gender-based killings was not available. However, official data for 2016 was published indicating that 2,668 women were considered to be victims of homicide, pending further investigations.

In August, the National Institute of Statistics and Geography published a survey estimating that 66.1% of girls and women aged 15 or above had experienced gender-based violence at least once in their lives, and that 43.5% of women had experienced gender-based violence committed by their partners.

Mechanisms known as "Alerts of gender-based violence against women" were active in 12 states. Established by the General Law on Women's Access to a Life Free from Violence, the Alert mechanisms relied on co-ordinated efforts to confront and eradicate violence against women and girls. By the end of the year, the Alerts mechanisms were not shown to have reduced gender-based violence against women and girls.

RIGHTS OF LESBIAN, GAY, BISEXUAL, TRANSGENDER AND INTERSEX PEOPLE

Same-sex couples were able to marry in Mexico City and 11 states without recourse to judicial proceedings. Couples in states where laws or administrative practice did not allow for same-sex marriage had to file a constitutional complaint (*amparo*) before federal tribunals to have their case reviewed and their rights recognized.

Supreme Court rulings continued to uphold same-sex couples' rights to marry and to adopt children without being discriminated against on the basis of sexual orientation and gender identity. In March, the Supreme Court ruled unconstitutional the Law of the Institute of Security and Social Services for State Workers because it protected only different-sex couples' rights.

ECONOMIC, SOCIAL AND CULTURAL RIGHTS

Two earthquakes in September had a serious impact on vast areas, mostly in central and southern Mexico. More than 360 people died; in Mexico City the majority of fatalities were women. According to official figures, more than 150,000 households were affected and at least 250,000 people were made homeless.

The government implemented survivor rescue and emergency care actions with the participation of both civil and military personnel and with the support of the international community. However, several reports emerged of inadequate co-ordination among authorities, inaccurate and untimely information on the rescue and recovery of bodies, illegal commandeering of food and other essential services meant for survivors, and insufficient aid deliveries to many devastated areas, especially in small, impoverished communities.

Expert preliminary assessments published in the media suggested that some of the collapsed structures might have been in breach of building regulations. There was no comprehensive strategy to guarantee that people made homeless were provided with safe and adequate housing options. On 6 October, President Peña Nieto called on affected families to organize themselves to rebuild their houses.

Educational services, including many primary schools, were disrupted for weeks or months while safety checks and reconstruction of schools were underway. Thousands of national monuments and other culturally significant public buildings were destroyed or damaged by the earthquakes.

---

1. False suspicions: Arbitrary detentions by police in Mexico (AMR 41/5340/2017)

2. Mexico: Open letter to the President on a possible extrajudicial execution by the military (AMR 41/6347/2017)

3. Mexico's misinformation wars: How organized troll networks attack and harass journalists and activists in Mexico (News story, 24 January)

MOLDOVA

Republic of Moldova
Head of state: **Igor Dodon**
Head of government: **Pavel Filip**

The government recalled a draft law on NGOs which contained undue restrictions for organizations that receive foreign funding. Nine activists were convicted of attempting to organize mass disturbances in 2015 and given conditional prison sentences in an unfair trial. In May, the LGBTI Pride in the capital Chişinău was stopped by police due to alleged security concerns, while President Igor Dodon made homophobic statements. Public spending on health, education and social protection continued to fall; discrimination against Roma persisted.

BACKGROUND

In July, the Parliament adopted controversial changes to the Electoral Law despite public protests and international condemnation. The changes were widely seen as benefiting the two biggest parties in Parliament, the ruling Democratic Party of Moldova and the opposition Socialist Party of Moldova. On 19 June, the Venice Commission of the Council of Europe issued a highly critical opinion on the amendments. Most of the mainstream media remained effectively controlled by and biased towards the Democratic Party of Moldova.

FREEDOM OF ASSOCIATION

A draft law on NGOs was agreed by a Working Group which included representatives of the Ministry of Justice, the Office of the UN High Commissioner for Human Rights, and several NGOs. The law was widely welcomed by civil society. However, in July, the Ministry of Justice unexpectedly introduced three articles into the draft without consulting the Working Group. These articles would compel NGOs involved in broadly defined "political activities" to publish financial reports and disclose the origin and use of their funding, among other requirements. Non-compliance would incur severe penalties, including hefty fines, exclusion from the government-run financial mechanism that facilitates and encourages voluntary donations to NGOs by taxpayers, and potential closure of the NGO. The amendments met strong opposition from civil society and international organizations who regarded them as undue restrictions on NGOs receiving foreign funding. Critics foresaw a stigmatizing effect on human rights defenders and civil society, particularly for those critical of the authorities. In September, the government recalled the draft law.

UNFAIR TRIALS

In June, the former leader of the "Our Home – Moldova" political party, Grigore Petrenco, and eight fellow political activists were convicted of attempting to organize mass disturbances on 6 September 2015, received conditional prison sentences and were prohibited from attending public events. The sentences ranged from three to four and a half years. On the day of the alleged offence, they had attempted to forcibly enter a government building during an otherwise peaceful rally. Their trial faced multiple delays and procedural infringements.

Grigore Petrenco's lawyers, Ana Ursachi and Eduard Rudenco, who also defended other high-profile clients in politically sensitive cases, continued to be subjected to smear campaigns in pro-government media, and reported harassment by the authorities in connection with their work.

TORTURE AND OTHER ILL-TREATMENT

Allegations of torture and other ill-treatment in places of detention and in the criminal justice system continued to be reported.

On the night of 26 August, Andrei Braguta, a driver who had been arrested for speeding, died in police custody. The authorities claimed that he had died of pneumonia and later admitted that Andrei Braguta had been beaten up by two fellow cell mates. Three police officers who were on duty that night and the two cell mates were arrested as criminal suspects in the case. One of the cell mates claimed that Andrei Braguta had already been severely beaten when placed in the cell, and protested his and the other cell mate's innocence. The criminal investigation was ongoing at the end of the year.

RIGHTS OF LESBIAN, GAY, BISEXUAL, TRANSGENDER AND INTERSEX PEOPLE

The police cut short the 21 May Pride march after the demonstrators had walked just a few hundred metres, stating that they were unable to guarantee their security in the event of violent attacks by counter-demonstrators.

The President publicly criticized the LGBTI community, described the Pride march as being contrary to the country's "traditional values", and participated in a parallel demonstration named the "Traditional Family Festival".

ECONOMIC, SOCIAL AND CULTURAL RIGHTS

Moldova's third periodic report on its implementation of the International Covenant on Economic, Social and Cultural Rights was considered by the UN Committee on Economic, Social and Cultural Rights in September. Particular concerns raised during the review included the continually falling rate of public spending on health, education and social protection, and the persistent discrimination and marginalization of Roma. The Committee described the situation of Roma as a "glaring problem" and "the failure in many aspects" of the National Action Plan on Roma for 2011-2015 as "a serious cause for concern".

MONGOLIA

Mongolia
Head of state: **Khaltmaa Battulga (replaced Tsakhia Elbegdorj in July)**
Head of government: **Ukhnaa Khurelsukh (replaced Jargaltulga Erdenebat in September)**

The death penalty was abolished as the new Criminal Code and Code of Criminal Procedure came into force. Impunity for torture and other ill-treatment of detainees and attacks against human rights defenders continued. The economic, social and cultural rights of people living in rural areas affected by mining activities, and in *ger* areas – areas without adequate access to essential services – were at risk of being violated.

DEATH PENALTY

The death penalty was abolished for all crimes when the new Criminal Code came into force on 1 July, after its adoption in December 2015.[1] However, in November, the newly elected President proposed reinstatement to the Ministry of Justice in response to two violent rape and murder cases.

HUMAN RIGHTS DEFENDERS

Human rights defenders continued to report physical attacks and harassment by law enforcement authorities and private corporations. These human rights defenders included students with disabilities acting as whistleblowers exposing discrimination and sexual abuse in a school, and journalists trying to report human rights issues such as gender-based violence. Existing laws failed to protect them from harassment and unjustified interference with their privacy.

TORTURE AND OTHER ILL-TREATMENT

Impunity and under-reporting of torture and other ill-treatment of individuals in detention, including people with disabilities and foreign nationals, continued in the absence of an independent, dedicated investigation mechanism. The new Criminal Procedure Code becoming effective in July did not re-establish the previously disbanded independent investigation unit, despite advocacy efforts by civil society.

FREEDOM OF EXPRESSION

On 1 July, a new Administrative Offence Act came into effect, allowing for increased administrative fines including when false information was published that could damage the reputation of individuals or business entities. A media professionals' organization criticized the law for being vague and overly broad, and feared it could be excessively used to suppress freedom of expression. Media companies staged a media blackout on 26 April to protest against the law, which was subsequently passed with reduced fines.

ECONOMIC, SOCIAL AND CULTURAL RIGHTS

Authorities failed to protect traditional herders from the operations of mining companies that negatively affected their livelihoods, traditional culture, and access to land and clean water. The influx of mining companies and transporting trucks in the Dalanjargalan subdivision of Dornogovi province caused heavy dust which severely degraded pastures and threatened the health and safety of livestock and people. Media workers filmed mining company representatives intimidating journalists and herders. Following his visit to Mongolia in September, the UN Special Rapporteur on human rights and the environment called for consultation with local communities before mining permits were issued, and for improved standards to ensure safe operation.

RIGHT TO HOUSING AND FORCED EVICTIONS

Residents in the ger areas of the capital, Ulaanbaatar, continued to live with the possibility of forced eviction due to urban redevelopment, without updated information on redevelopment plans, genuine consultation or adequate compensation. Residents complained that the new local government elected in June 2016 had failed to implement redevelopment plans agreed with the previous government; the new government claimed it lacked funds. These plans included the provision of essential components of adequate housing such as safe drinking water, sanitation and energy.

---

1. Mongolia: Death penalty confined to history as new criminal code comes into effect (ACT 50/6646/2017)

MONTENEGRO

Montenegro
Head of state: Filip Vujanović
Head of government: Duško Marković

Past murders and attacks on journalists and media workers were not resolved. The Constitutional Court found that investigations into alleged torture and ill-treatment failed to meet international standards. The funding of NGOs was threatened and human rights defenders were subjected to smear campaigns by media supportive of the government.

BACKGROUND

Montenegro joined NATO in June. Serious concerns continued about criminal proceedings against 14 men, including Russian intelligence officers and opposition leaders, who were indicted in May for "violent overthrow of the government" and "preventing NATO accession" on election day in October 2016.

LACK OF ACCOUNTABILITY

The State Prosecutor's Office reportedly reviewed seven war crimes cases, in which all but four defendants had been acquitted, to determine whether grounds existed to reopen proceedings. In September, the government reported it would pay the victims EUR1.35 million in compensation.

Proceedings opened in September against Vlado Zmajević, who was arrested in Montenegro in 2016 and indicted – originally by Serbia – for war crimes in Kosovo.

TORTURE AND OTHER ILL-TREATMENT

In June and again in July, the Constitutional Court found that the State Prosecutor's Office had failed to conduct effective investigations into the alleged torture and ill-treatment during demonstrations in November 2015 of Branimir Vukčević and Momčilo Baranin, and Milorad Martinović, respectively.

Proceedings against prison officers indicted in 2016 for abusing prisoners continued to be delayed by their lawyers, with no verdict by December.

FREEDOM OF EXPRESSION

In June, the government proposed to amend the Law on Gatherings to prohibit protests in front of Parliament. NGOs feared that amended legislation on sources of NGO income would potentially reduce their funding, and allow the government to decide whether new NGOs could be registered.

JOURNALISTS

Civil society members of a commission charged with monitoring investigations into violence against journalists continued to be denied security clearance to classified documents.

Investigative journalist Jovo Martinović, detained in 2015, was released in February after international appeals, but proceedings –

alleging his membership of a drug-trafficking gang that he had been investigating – continued at the end of the year.

In October, the Constitutional Court awarded journalist Tufik Softić EUR7,000 in compensation for the ineffective investigation into the 2007 attack on his life, continued threats and his fear of another attempt on his life.

RIGHTS OF LESBIAN, GAY, BISEXUAL, TRANSGENDER AND INTERSEX PEOPLE

In April, activists proposed a model law on gender identity. In August, members of the NGO LGBT Forum Progress were attacked; one was hospitalized.

ECONOMIC, SOCIAL AND CULTURAL RIGHTS

In January, the government cut by 25% a lifetime benefit, provided under the 2016 Law on Social and Child Protection, to mothers with three or more children who gave up employment. Protests followed, including a 14-day hungerstrike in March. In June, the government abolished the benefit completely. Although the law was potentially discriminatory, beneficiaries feared that, with insufficient support to enable them to return to work, the lost benefit would have a drastic impact on their family income.

REFUGEES AND ASYLUM-SEEKERS

Almost 1,000 Roma and Egyptian refugees who fled Kosovo in 1999 remained at Konik camp outside the capital, Podgorica, awaiting resettlement into adequate EU-funded apartments, 120 of which were completed in November.

Around 800 Roma and Egyptians remained at risk of statelessness, their applications for regular status pending. Some 379 had only three years' temporary residence. In May, the government withdrew a procedure to determine statelessness from a draft Law on Foreigners.

Four men convicted in May of grave offences against general safety, for overloading a boat in 1999, resulting in the deaths of 35 Roma refugees, were sentenced in December to between six and eight years' imprisonment.

MOROCCO/ WESTERN SAHARA

Kingdom of Morocco
Head of state: **King Mohammed VI**
Head of government: **Saad-Eddine El Othmani (replaced Abdelilah Benkirane in March)**

Journalists and protesters calling for social justice and political rights were imprisoned, often following unfair trials. Judicial authorities did not adequately investigate reports of torture in detention. Impunity persisted for past human rights violations. Migrants continued to face excessive force and detention. Courts imposed death sentences; there were no executions.

BACKGROUND

Significant and sustained social justice protests took place in Morocco's northern Rif region. In January, Morocco rejoined the African Union. In February, Morocco submitted a request to join ECOWAS. In March, King Mohammed VI appointed Saad-Eddine El Othmani as head of government following a government reshuffle. In April, the UN Security Council extended the mandate of the UN Mission for the Referendum in Western Sahara (MINURSO) for another year without human rights monitoring.[1] In September, the UN Human Rights Council adopted recommendations following a review of Morocco's human rights record under the UN UPR process.[2]

FREEDOMS OF EXPRESSION AND ASSOCIATION

The authorities used Penal Code provisions on insult and on incitement to protest or rebellion to prosecute and imprison journalists, bloggers and activists who criticized officials or reported on human rights violations, corruption or popular protests. In the second half of the year, prosecutors investigated at least one protester for "false reporting" after he claimed that the police had tortured him. Courts also convicted and imprisoned journalists and activists on vague and overly broad state security and terrorism offences in what amounted to punishment for their criticism of the authorities.

Between May and August, security forces arrested and detained eight journalists and bloggers over critical coverage or online commentary of the protests in Rif. Prosecutors charged them with protest-related, state security offences. Hamid El Mahdaoui was convicted of inciting others to take part in an unauthorized protest and sentenced to three months' imprisonment and a fine of 20,000 dirhams (around USD2,100), increased to one year's imprisonment on appeal.

Seven people, including journalists, activists and the academic Maati Monjib, remained on trial on charges including "threatening state security" for promoting a mobile application for citizen journalism that protected users' privacy. Journalist Ali Anouzla remained on trial on trumped-up charges of "advocating, supporting and inciting terrorism" for an article he had published on the website lakome.com in 2013.

The authorities imposed restrictions on some organizations in Morocco and Western Sahara perceived to be critical of the authorities. Restrictions included continuing obstruction of the registration of associations, banning the activities of associations, and expelling foreign nationals invited by such associations.

FREEDOM OF ASSEMBLY

Authorities tried and imprisoned hundreds of activists involved in social or environmental justice protests on assembly-related charges. Courts also used trumped-up criminal charges for offences under ordinary law and charges under vaguely defined state security and terrorism provisions to try protesters.

In February, gendarmes violently arrested peaceful environmental protesters including

Mohamed Akkad, causing significant sight loss in his right eye. He and 13 other people who had protested peacefully against a stone quarry near their village in Beni Oukil were convicted by a court in Oujda city of "obstructing public officials" and sentenced to a one-month suspended prison term and fines which totalled 10,000 dirhams (around USD1,050). In a separate protest, gendarmes arrested environmental activist Abderrahmane Akhidir from Imider in the Atlas Mountains. In March, a court convicted him on trumped-up charges of assault and theft and sentenced him to a four-month prison term.

In April, gendarmes arrested human rights defenders Mahjoub El Mahfoud, Miloud Salim and Saif Saifeddine after they participated in a protest organized by Zohra El Bouzidi, who self-immolated to protest against her forced eviction from her home in the town of Sidi Hajjaj. Gendarmes also arrested Zohra El Bouzidi's sister, Khadija El Bouzidi. A court convicted the four of assaulting and insulting public officers and sentenced the three men to two-year prison terms reduced on appeal to four months, and Khadija El Bouzidi to 10 months' imprisonment, reduced on appeal to two months, as well as fines of 500 dirhams (around USD50) each. Zohra El Bouzidi died from her injuries in October.

From May onward, the authorities deployed security forces on a scale unmatched in recent years to prevent protests in the Rif region, and conducted mass arrests of largely peaceful protesters, including children.[3] On some occasions, security forces used excessive or unnecessary force. Judicial authorities failed to conduct adequate investigations into the circumstances of the deaths in August of two protesters, Imad El Attabi and Abdelhafid Haddad.

Between July and November, courts convicted many protesters in relation to protests in Rif, sentencing them to terms of up to 20 years' imprisonment on charges ranging from unauthorized protest to plotting to undermine state security. Throughout the year, the authorities routinely used excessive and unnecessary force to disperse peaceful protests in Western Saharan cities including Laayoune, Smara, Boujdour and Dakhla, particularly against those demanding Sahrawi self-determination and calling for the release of Sahrawi prisoners. Several protesters, bloggers and activists were imprisoned, often after unfair trials on trumped-up charges.

In September, Sahrawi blogger Walid El Batal was released from prison in Smara after serving a 10-month sentence and receiving a fine of 1,000 dirhams (around USD105) on trumped-up charges of insulting and assaulting public officers, damaging public property and taking part in an armed gathering.

In July, a court in Laayoune convicted Sahrawi activist Hamza El Ansari on trumped-up charges of assaulting and insulting public officers and criminal damage for his participation in a protest in February, and sentenced him to one year's imprisonment and a fine of 10,000 dirhams (around USD1,050). The court failed to investigate his allegation that police had ill-treated him and forced him to sign a statement while blindfolded. He was released after his sentence was reduced to three months on appeal in September.

TORTURE AND OTHER ILL-TREATMENT

In October, the UN Subcommittee on Prevention of Torture visited Morocco. Morocco had yet to establish a National Preventive Mechanism against torture.

Courts continued to rely on statements made in custody in the absence of a lawyer to convict defendants, without adequately investigating allegations that statements were forcibly obtained through torture and other ill-treatment.

Between July and November, courts in Al Hoceima and Casablanca tried and convicted many Rif protesters, drawing on statements that defendants claimed were coerced, without adequately investigating their allegations that they were tortured and otherwise ill-treated in custody.[4]

In July, a civilian court convicted 23 Sahrawi activists in connection with deadly clashes in

Gdim Izik, Western Sahara, in 2010, and handed down heavy sentences, including some of life imprisonment, following their grossly unfair trial by a military court in 2013.[5] The civilian court failed to adequately investigate allegations that they were tortured in custody and did not exclude information tainted by torture as evidence from the proceedings.[6] From September, at least 10 of the 19 Sahrawi activists who remained imprisoned went on hunger strike against prison conditions after being separated into different prisons in Morocco.

Detainees reported torture and other ill-treatment in police custody both in Morocco and in Western Sahara. Judicial authorities failed to adequately investigate these allegations and hold those responsible to account.

Authorities kept several detainees in prolonged solitary confinement, which constitutes torture or other ill-treatment. Prisoner Ali Aarrass was held in isolation for more than one year.[7]

IMPUNITY

The authorities failed to take any steps towards addressing impunity for grave violations including systematic torture, enforced disappearances and extrajudicial executions in Morocco and Western Sahara between 1956 and 1999, despite recommendations by the Equity and Reconciliation Commission transitional justice body.

RIGHTS OF LESBIAN, GAY, BISEXUAL, TRANSGENDER AND INTERSEX PEOPLE

Courts continued to imprison men under Article 489 of the Penal Code that criminalizes consensual same-sex sexual relations. At least two men were sentenced to six months' imprisonment under Article 489. Victims of homophobic attacks reported being afraid to approach the police to file complaints because of the risk of arrest under Article 489.

REFUGEES' AND MIGRANTS' RIGHTS

Morocco did not adopt a law on asylum but maintained its policy of allowing refugees access to basic rights and services, including education. The authorities issued asylum-seekers and refugees registered by UNHCR, the UN refugee agency, with documents protecting them against *refoulement* – forcible return of individuals to a country where they risk serious human rights violations – without taking a decision on their definitive status.

The authorities left a group of 25 Syrian refugees stranded in the buffer zone of the border area with Algeria for three months before giving them protection in July.[8]

Security forces continued to participate in the summary expulsion of migrants and asylum-seekers from the Spanish enclaves of Ceuta and Melilla to Morocco, and to use excessive or unnecessary force against them. Courts imprisoned migrants for unlawful entry, stay or exit from Moroccan territory, including some who had applied to regularize their status, and on some occasions put them on trial without access to a lawyer.

In September, two Burkina Faso nationals died after Moroccan security forces used tear gas against migrants attempting to enter the Spanish enclave of Melilla.

DEATH PENALTY

Courts continued to hand down death sentences. No executions had been carried out since 1993.

POLISARIO CAMPS

The Polisario Front again failed to hold to account those responsible for committing human rights abuses in camps under its control during the 1970s and 1980s.

1. UN peacekeeping force in Western Sahara must urgently monitor human rights (News story, 18 April)

2. Human Rights Council adopts Universal Periodic Review outcome on Morocco (MDE 29/7141/2017)

3. Morocco: Rif protesters punished with wave of mass arrests (News story, 2 June)

4. Morocco: Dozens arrested over mass protests in Rif report torture in custody (News story, 11 August)

5. Morocco/Western Sahara: Verdict in Sahrawi trial marred by failure to adequately investigate torture claims (News story, 19 July)

6. Morocco/Western Sahara: Grant Sahrawi defendants a fair trial (MDE 29/5753/2017)

7. Morocco: Further information: Health risks for detainee in isolation for 232 days – Ali Aarrass (MDE 29/6303/2017)

8. Syrian refugees trapped in desert on Moroccan border with Algeria in dire need of assistance (News story, 7 June)

MOZAMBIQUE

Republic of Mozambique
Head of state and government: **Filipe Jacinto Nyusi**

The government's hidden borrowing plunged the country into economic crisis. Food insecurity deepened because of large-scale land acquisition for mining which pushed people off land on which they depended for subsistence. People expressing dissenting or critical views continued to face attacks and intimidation by unidentified individuals or security forces. An estimated 30,000 people with albinism faced discrimination and feared for their lives, and at least 13 were killed. Violence against women and girls remained widespread.

BACKGROUND

The Administrative Tribunal and the Parliamentary Commission of Inquiry into the Situation of the Public Debt stated in 2016 that the guarantees on the undisclosed borrowing by the government of USD2.2 billion for use in security and defence spending was illegal and unconstitutional. The undisclosed loans were revealed in April 2016; it was projected that they would drive the public debt to 135% of GDP during 2017. Local currency lost value and prices increased substantially, a situation which was compounded by the country's dependence on imports.

Senior government officials obstructed a forensic audit of the loans which had been demanded by international donors in order to restore trust and to resume aid support. Consequently, donors withheld aid pending the government's co-operation and its full disclosure.

The December 2016 truce reached between the government, led by the Mozambique Liberation Front (FRELIMO), and the main opposition party, Mozambique National Resistance (RENAMO), continued to hold in 2017, after three years of violent clashes. Peace negotiations continued on decentralization of government powers. The relationship between the two leaders remained tense; RENAMO leader Afonso Dhlakama accused President Nyusi of failing to withdraw government troops from the Gorongosa region by the agreed time.

LAND DISPUTES

Mining companies acquired land used by residents, exacerbating already existing food insecurity which affected over 60% of people in rural areas who depended on the land for their livelihoods, and for food and water.

Coal mining company Vale Mozambique began in 2013 to fence off land used by local residents to graze their livestock and collect firewood, including in the Nhanchere area in the Moatize district of Tete province. On 13 June 2017, Hussen António Laitone was shot dead by police in Nhanchere during the community's peaceful protest against land acquisition for mining; he had not participated in the protest.

FREEDOMS OF EXPRESSION AND ASSOCIATION

Intimidation and harassment of and attacks against people who expressed dissenting or critical views continued.

Journalist and human rights activist Armando Nenane was severely beaten on 17 May in the capital, Maputo, by riot police. He was attacked for his views on the so-called G40, a group allegedly created under the government of former President Guebuza to discredit opponents in favour of the government. Prior to the beating, Armando Nenane received anonymous death threats by telephone. No one had been held accountable for the attack by the end of the year.

On 4 October, Mahamudo Amurane, Mayor of the northern city of Nampula, was shot dead in front of his house by an unidentified gunman. Following disagreements with the leadership of the Mozambique Democratic Movement (MDM), Mahamudo Amurane had announced his intention to leave the party to form his own party and seek re-election in October 2018 municipal elections.

On 2 December, a gunman threatened to kill Aunício da Silva, an investigative journalist and editor of *Ikweli*, a weekly publication, in Nampula. The gunman accused him of publishing articles that tarnished the image of Carlos Saíde, the MDM mayoral candidate for Nampula.

DISCRIMINATION – PEOPLE WITH ALBINISM

An estimated 30,000 people with albinism experienced discrimination and were ostracized; many lived in fear of their lives. Incidents of persecution increased; at least 13 people with albinism were known to have been killed although figures are likely to have been greater. The killings were fuelled by superstition or myths about the magical powers of people with albinism. Most killings took place in the central and northern provinces, the country's poorest regions.

A seven-year-old boy with albinism was murdered on 31 January by four unidentified men who broke into his house and abducted him while the family slept, in Ngaúma district, Niassa province. On 28 May, a group of unidentified assailants abducted a three-year-old boy from his mother in Angónia district, Tete province. On 13 September, a 17-year-old youth was killed for his body parts and organs in Benga area, Moatize district, in Tete province. The attackers removed his brain, hair, and arm bones. None of those responsible for the killings were arrested or brought to justice by the end of the year.

Despite public outcry, the government did little to address the problem. A strategy was designed to stop the killings; however, this was not implemented, allegedly because of a lack of resources.

VIOLENCE AGAINST WOMEN AND GIRLS

There were high rates of women murdered, often by men intimately known, or related, to them. In several cases, the perpetrators attempted to justify their actions by claiming the victim used witchcraft against them.

On 10 January, a 31-year-old man stabbed his 27-year-old wife to death with a kitchen knife in Inhagoia neighbourhood on the outskirts of Maputo. In February, in Vanduzi district, Manica province, a 27-year-old man decapitated his mother with a machete saying she had refused to serve him food. In May, a man killed his mother in Guru district, Manica province, claiming she had cast a spell of sexual impotence on him. In August, two brothers killed their 70-year-old grandmother in the Messano locality, Bilene district, Gaza province, after accusing her of casting a bad luck spell on them. In September, in the Centro Hípico neighbourhood located on the outskirts of Chimoio, Manica province, a man killed his 80-year-old mother with an iron bar after accusing her of bewitching him.

Although, in all these cases, the suspected perpetrators admitted that they carried out the killings, the authorities failed to develop, resource and implement an effective strategy to combat violence against women.

MYANMAR

Republic of the Union of Myanmar
Head of state and government: Htin Kyaw

The human rights situation deteriorated dramatically. Hundreds of thousands of Rohingya fled crimes against humanity in Rakhine State to neighbouring Bangladesh; those who remained continued to live under a system amounting to apartheid. The army committed extensive violations of international humanitarian law. Authorities continued to restrict humanitarian access across the country. Restrictions on freedom of expression remained. There was increased religious intolerance and anti-

Muslim sentiment. Impunity persisted for past and ongoing human rights violations.

BACKGROUND

The civilian-led administration, headed de facto by State Counsellor Aung San Suu Kyi, completed its first year in office in March. Economic reforms stagnated, while the peace process – aimed at bringing an end to decades of internal armed conflicts – stalled. The military retained significant political power and remained independent of civilian oversight. On 6 October, Myanmar ratified the ICESCR, due to come into force in the country on 6 January 2018.

CRIMES UNDER INTERNATIONAL LAW – CRIMES AGAINST HUMANITY

Rakhine State was plunged into crisis when security forces unleashed a campaign of violence against the predominantly Muslim Rohingya ethnic minority in the northern part of the state, following co-ordinated attacks in late August by the armed group Arakan Rohingya Salvation Army (ARSA) on approximately 30 security posts. The attacks took place just hours after a commission headed by former UN Secretary-General Kofi Annan presented its recommendations to "prevent violence, maintain peace and foster reconciliation" in the state.

The military, often working with Border Guard Police and local vigilantes, killed an undetermined number of Rohingya women, men and children; tortured and otherwise ill-treated Rohingya women and girls, including with rape and other forms of sexual violence; laid landmines; and burned hundreds of Rohingya villages in what the UN High Commissioner for Human Rights described as a "textbook example of ethnic cleansing". The conduct of the security forces amounted to crimes against humanity.[1]

More than 655,000 Rohingya fled to Bangladesh as a result of the violence. Other ethnic minority communities were also affected, with an estimated 30,000 people temporarily displaced to other parts of Rakhine State. There were reports of abuses, including killings of informants and the enforced disappearance of ethnic Rakhine and Mro villagers by ARSA.

Rohingya who remained in Rakhine State continued to live under a system amounting to apartheid, which severely restricted virtually every aspect of their lives and segregated them from the rest of society.[2] Their rights to nationality, freedom of movement, the highest attainable standard of health, education, work, food, freedom of religion and belief, and to participate in public life were routinely and systematically violated on a discriminatory basis.

The government dismissed allegations of human rights violations and ignored calls for investigations and accountability. It signed a deal with Bangladesh to repatriate refugees subject to a verification process, and announced that it would work to implement Kofi Annan's recommendations and bring development to Rakhine State.

INTERNAL ARMED CONFLICT

Fighting between the Myanmar Army and ethnic armed groups intensified in northern Myanmar. The Army committed wide-ranging human rights violations against ethnic minority civilians, including extrajudicial executions and other unlawful killings, enforced disappearances, arbitrary detentions, torture and other ill-treatment and forced labour. The Army regularly fired mortar and artillery shells when fighting ethnic armed groups, which often landed in civilian areas. In May, an 81-year-old woman was killed when a mortar exploded near her home in Namhkan township, northern Shan State.[3] Several of these violations were likely to amount to war crimes.

Ethnic armed groups committed violations of international humanitarian law, including enforced disappearances, forcible recruitment and extortion. Both the Myanmar Army and ethnic armed groups laid anti-personnel landmines or landmine-like weapons. Many displaced people were afraid to return to their homes as a result.

LACK OF HUMANITARIAN ACCESS

Both the civilian government and the military continued to severely and arbitrarily restrict humanitarian access, placing hundreds of thousands of people at risk.

In Rakhine State, authorities restricted aid access in the wake of the August ARSA attacks, suspending it entirely in the north of the state. The authorities later allowed the Red Cross Movement and the World Food Programme to operate in the area. However, their access was limited and insufficient to meet needs. In other parts of Rakhine State, access was further impaired by local tensions and hostility towards international aid groups.[4]

The authorities further restricted access to displaced populations in northern Myanmar, especially to people living in territory that was not under government control. In February, the Myanmar Army prevented the delivery of 200 UN-stamped "dignity kits" – which included basic sanitary supplies – for women and girls displaced in areas controlled by the Kachin Independence Organization.

REFUGEES AND INTERNALLY DISPLACED PEOPLE

Civilians were displaced as a result of conflict, violence and natural disasters. More than 106,000 people remained internally displaced by the conflicts in northern Myanmar. Some 120,000 people, mostly Rohingya, continued to live in squalid displacement camps in Rakhine State where they have been confined for five years following violence in 2012.

By the end of the year more than 655,000 Rohingya refugees had fled to Bangladesh following unlawful and disproportionate military operations in northern Rakhine State. In November, Myanmar and Bangladesh signed an agreement to repatriate refugees to Myanmar even as people continued to flee across the border. The entrenched and ongoing regime amounting to apartheid in Rakhine State ensured that any returns would not be safe or dignified.

Some 100,000 additional refugees from Myanmar continued to live in camps in Thailand, where they faced decreasing humanitarian assistance. Many expressed concerns about returning to Myanmar, citing ongoing instability, militarization in ethnic areas and lack of access to essential services.

PRISONERS OF CONSCIENCE

Despite prisoner amnesties in April and May, prisoners of conscience remained in detention. The authorities continued to use a range of vaguely worded laws that restricted the rights to freedom of expression, association and peaceful assembly to arrest and imprison people solely for peacefully exercising their rights.

Prisoner of conscience Lahpai Gam, an ethnic Kachin farmer, remained in prison, suffering from serious health conditions. He was tortured at the time of his arrest in 2012.

The government failed to provide restitution to former prisoners of conscience and their families, such as compensation, assistance in gaining access to education and employment opportunities, and other forms of reparation.

FREEDOMS OF EXPRESSION, ASSOCIATION AND ASSEMBLY

The rights to freedom of expression, association and peaceful assembly remained subject to severe restrictions. There was a surge in the number of people charged with "online defamation" under Section 66(d) of the 2013 Telecommunications Act.[5] Following national and international pressure, Parliament adopted minor amendments to the law. However, "online defamation" remained a criminal offence.

Human rights defenders, lawyers and journalists – in particular those speaking out about the situation of the Rohingya, religious intolerance and violations by the military – faced surveillance, intimidation and attacks. On 29 January, Ko Ni, a lawyer, was shot dead at Yangon International Airport while returning from an interfaith conference in Indonesia. At the end of the year, the trial of four alleged perpetrators was still ongoing; a fifth suspect remained at large. In November, ethnic Kachin pastor Dumdaw Nawng Lat and his assistant Langjaw Gam were imprisoned for providing assistance to journalists reporting on military air strikes near the town of Monekoe in late 2016. Both men were sentenced to two years' imprisonment under the Unlawful Associations Act. Dumdaw Nawng Lat was sentenced to an additional two years for "defamation".

The operations of independent media outlets were increasingly restricted, and in some cases journalists were subjected to criminal prosecution for carrying out their work. In June, three media workers were arrested and charged with contacting an "unlawful association" after returning from an area controlled by an armed ethnic group operating in northern Myanmar. They were released after charges against them were dropped in August.[6] In December, two Reuters reporters were detained under the Official Secrets Act in connection with their work reporting on the situation in Rakhine State. Both were held incommunicado for two weeks and remained in detention at the end of the year.

FREEDOM OF RELIGION AND BELIEF

There was a sharp rise in religious intolerance and anti-Muslim sentiment in the wake of the August attacks in Rakhine State. The government exacerbated the situation by both allowing and directly producing hate speech inciting discrimination and violence in print and online. State media published derogatory anti-Rohingya articles; government officials published inflammatory posts on social media.

Throughout the year religious minorities, in particular Muslims, continued to face discrimination. In April, two madrassas (religious schools) in Yangon were closed by local authorities and police following pressure from a mob of Buddhist hardline nationalists. In September, the Kayin State authorities issued an order requiring all Muslims in the state to report to local authorities before travelling. Although the Kayin State Chief Minister later said that the order was an "administrative error", travel restrictions

reportedly remained in place at the end of the year.

CORPORATE ACCOUNTABILITY

Thousands of families living near the Letpadaung copper mine in Sagaing region remained at risk of losing their homes and farmland under plans to expand the project.[7] Villagers living close to the mine continued to protest against the project. In March, at least 10 people were injured after police fired rubber bullets at a group of villagers protesting about the impact of trucks transporting materials to the mine. According to local authorities, six police officers were wounded by protesters using catapults.[8]

In August, the Ministry of Defence rejected a proposal to relocate a factory producing sulphuric acid to supply the mine. Severe risks were posed to the health of the community living nearby. Environmental and human rights concerns related to the project had not been addressed by the end of the year.

DEATH PENALTY

Courts continued to impose death sentences under legal provisions allowing for the imposition of the death penalty. No executions were carried out.

LACK OF ACCOUNTABILITY

A persistent culture of impunity remained for human rights violations committed by the security forces. Most perpetrators of past and current human rights violations, including crimes under international law, had not been held accountable for their actions.

The government failed to adequately investigate and hold to account perpetrators of serious human rights violations in Rakhine State, including crimes against humanity. In August, an Investigation Commission established by the President to probe the October 2016 attacks and their aftermath published a summary of its findings in which it acknowledged casualties, destruction of buildings, loss of property and displacement. However, it failed to establish responsibility for these acts, or to state whether any action had been taken to prosecute perpetrators. The investigation lacked independence.[9] In November, a military investigation concluded that no human rights violations had been committed in Rakhine State following the 25 August ARSA attacks and subsequent military campaign.

INTERNATIONAL SCRUTINY

In March the UN Human Rights Council established an independent, international Fact-Finding Mission to "establish the facts and circumstances" about human rights violations and abuses, in particular in Rakhine State. The Council requested the Mission to present its findings in September 2018. The move was met with strong opposition by the government, which disassociated itself from the investigation and refused to allow the team into the country.

A significant increase in international attention was focused on Myanmar and the crisis in Rakhine State following the August attacks. On 6 November, the UN Security Council issued a presidential statement calling for an end to the violence and for the restrictions on humanitarian aid to be lifted. Also in November, the UN General Assembly adopted a resolution on the situation of human rights in Myanmar. In December, the Human Rights Council held a special session on the situation of the Rohingya and other minorities. The EU and the USA suspended invitations to senior military officials.

The UN Special Rapporteur on the situation of human rights in Myanmar faced increasing restrictions on her access, and by the end of the year had been barred from the country for the remainder of her tenure. She had previously raised concerns about the deteriorating situation in the country.

1. "My world is finished": Rohingya targeted by crimes against humanity in Myanmar (ASA 16/7288/2017)

2. "Caged without a roof": Apartheid in Myanmar's Rakhine State (ASA 16/7484/2017)

3. "All the civilians suffer": Conflict, displacement and abuse in northern Myanmar (ASA 16/6429/2017)

4. Myanmar: Restrictions on international aid putting thousands at risk (News story, 4 September)

5. Myanmar: Repeal Section 66(d) of the 2013 Telecommunications Law (ASA 16/6617/2017)

6. Myanmar: Release journalists immediately (News story, 26 June)

7. Mountain of trouble: Human rights abuses continue at Myanmar's Letpadaung mine (ASA 16/5564/2017)

8. Myanmar: Investigate police use of force against protesters at troubled mine (ASA 16/5983/2017)

9. Myanmar: National efforts to investigate Rakhine State violence are inadequate (ASA 16/5758/2017)

NAMIBIA

Republic of Namibia
Head of state and government: **Hage Gottfried Geingob**

The right to adequate housing was restricted and the situation was exacerbated by high levels of unemployment, poverty and inequality. Eight prisoners of conscience in the long-running Caprivi trial were held 14 years after their arrest, on treason and sedition charges.

RIGHT TO HOUSING

Housing remained inadequate; the government failed to ensure accessible, affordable and habitable housing. Over 500,000 people lived in shacks or makeshift settlements in urban areas while only 10% of the population could afford to buy a house which cost on average 800,000 Namibian dollars (USD58,474) per household. Rural to urban migration, high unemployment levels, low salaries, high rents and lack of available and affordable land plots with residential services led to inadequate housing particularly in the capital, Windhoek. On 28 March, 15 families were rendered homeless when Windhoek City Police arbitrarily evicted them, without an eviction notice, from their informal settlements in Agste Laan, Windhoek. Although the residents took their case to the High Court seeking to be allowed to stay in the settlement and have their shacks rebuilt while their case was finalized, the Court ruled against them on grounds that they were not legally resident on the site.

The inadequate housing in informal settlements was highlighted between 25 and

31 August when five children in the Erongo and Oshikoto regions died in their homes in separate fires after their parents left them alone in corrugated shacks.

The UN Independent Expert on the enjoyment of all human rights by older persons noted that, while housing conditions for older people in rural areas had improved since the country gained independence in 1990, it had worsened in urban areas because of the growth of informal settlements where access to essential services like sanitation facilities and water and electricity supplies were inadequate.

CAPRIVI DETAINEES
The trial of eight prisoners of conscience, accused in the long-running Caprivi case, resumed in May. Progress Kenyoka Munuma, Shine Samulandela, Manuel Manepelo Makendano, Alex Sinjabata Mushakwa, Diamond Samunzala Salufu, Hoster Simasiku Ntombo, Fredderick Ntamilwa and John Mazila Tembwe were charged and convicted of treason and sedition in 2007. In 2013, the Supreme Court set aside their convictions and sentences ranging from 30 to 32 years and ordered a retrial. However, they remained in detention pending trial, in violation of international fair trial standards, at the end of the year.

NAURU

Republic of Nauru
Head of state and government: **Baron Waqa**

Refugees and asylum-seekers remained trapped on Nauru. They had been forcibly sent there by the Australian government, despite widespread reports of physical, psychological and sexual abuse. In September, 27 refugees were sent to the USA; over 1,000 remained on the island.

REFUGEES AND ASYLUM-SEEKERS
In April, an Australian Senate Committee report described numerous allegations of physical and sexual abuse, self-harm and neglect of refugees and asylum-seekers in Nauru and Papua New Guinea. The committee found that the main contributing factors were a harmful living environment, uncertainty about the future, an inadequate regulatory framework (including child protection policies), a lack of transparency in operations affecting refugees, and a failure to hold authorities accountable for abuses. By the end of the year, neither the Australian nor the Nauruan authorities had taken steps to remedy the situation.

Reports emerged during the year that the Spanish multinational company Ferrovial and its Australian subsidiary Broadspectrum were complicit in the abuse of refugees on Nauru, and that they reaped vast profits from Australia's refugee policies. Ferrovial stated that it would not renew its contract when it expired in October.[1]

In August, a medical professional reported that four refugee women were being denied transfer to Australia to have abortions, which are illegal on Nauru.

In November, a refugee died after a motorcycle accident; a police investigation was under way. Later in the same month, another refugee received head injuries in a motorcycle accident.

FREEDOMS OF EXPRESSION AND ASSEMBLY
In May, three suspended parliamentarians, who were charged and convicted for peaceful protests in 2015, had their prison sentences substantially increased on appeal: from three months to 22 months for two defendants, and to 14 months for the third defendant. Their lawyer announced the intention of the three defendants to appeal their conviction and sentences to the High Court of Australia, which is the ultimate court of appeal under Nauru's legal system.

Journalists seeking to visit Nauru remained subject to a non-refundable visa fee of USD6,089. This severely restricted media freedom and hampered independent scrutiny of Nauru's policies and practices.

1. Treasure i$land – how companies are profiting from Australia's abuse of refugees on Nauru (ASA 12/5942/2017)

NEPAL

Federal Democratic Republic of Nepal
Head of state: **Bidhya Devi Bhandari**
Head of government: **Sher Bahadur Deuba (replaced Pushpa Kamal Dahal in June)**

Nearly 70% of people made homeless by the 2015 earthquake remained in temporary shelters. Thousands of people affected by monsoon floods in the Tarai region were not provided with adequate assistance, including housing. Concerns by Indigenous and Madhesi people about clauses they viewed as discriminatory in the 2015 Constitution remained unaddressed. No effective investigations took place into the use of excessive force against protesters in the Tarai. Efforts toward ensuring truth, justice and reparations for thousands of victims of human rights violations committed during the decade-long armed conflict were inadequate. Nepali migrant workers continued to be subjected to extortion, fraud and bonded labour, and were put at risk of further human rights abuse in employment abroad.

BACKGROUND

Local elections were held for the first time in more than two decades. Parliamentary and provincial elections took place in November and December. In October, Nepal was elected to the UN Human Rights Council.

RIGHT TO HOUSING

Hundreds of thousands of survivors from the 2015 earthquake (nearly 70% of those affected) were still living in temporary shelters. The government stipulated proof of land ownership as a condition for receiving a rebuilding grant. However, since up to 25% of the population were considered not to have met this criterion, tens of thousands of the earthquake survivors were ineligible for these grants. The situation primarily affected marginalized and disadvantaged groups, including women, Dalits and other caste-based and ethnic minorities.

In August, a vast area of the southern Tarai was flooded by monsoon rains that killed 143 people and affected 1.7 million others. More than 400,000 people were forced out of their homes, with more than 1,000 homes being completely destroyed. Victims were given inadequate assistance by the government, which blocked attempts to distribute aid privately. Many continued to live in inadequate housing and poor conditions.

EXCESSIVE USE OF FORCE

Security forces continued to use unnecessary or excessive force in response to protests in the Tarai, particularly over grievances relating to the Constitution. In March, five protesters were killed and 16 others injured when police used firearms to disperse Madhesi protesters in Saptari district.

WORKERS' RIGHTS – MIGRANT WORKERS

The government failed to deliver effective protection for migrant workers and end the culture of impunity for unlawful and criminal recruitment practices. Migrant workers were systematically subjected to unlawful and criminal conduct by recruitment businesses and agents. Recruiters routinely charged migrant workers illegal and excessive fees; deceived them about the terms and conditions of their work abroad; and manipulated their consent to overseas work through the accumulation of recruitment debts. Some recruiters were directly involved in labour trafficking, which is punishable under Nepal's Human Trafficking and Transportation (Control) Act.

Migrants trapped in forced-labour situations abroad faced extreme difficulty in accessing support from Nepalese embassies in order to return home. Recruiters rarely provided repatriation assistance to workers when they encountered problems abroad despite their obligations under the Foreign Employment Act. The authorities failed to investigate – including through autopsies – the high number of migrant worker deaths during foreign employment.

No improvements were made in the implementation of the government's "Free visa, free ticket" policy, which was intended to curtail recruitment charges by agencies. Although the government made repeated public commitments to reduce migration costs for workers and to protect them from incurring debt, it increased the burden on migrants by raising pre-departure costs. In July, the Foreign Employment Promotion Board increased the amount migrant workers were required to contribute to the government-administered welfare fund.

Fewer than 100 recruitment agencies were fined or referred to the Foreign Employment Tribunal for violations of Nepal's foreign employment laws, even though more than 8,000 migrant workers filed cases against recruitment agents. The Foreign Employment Act 2007 stipulates that victims must file their complaints with the Department of Foreign Employment and restricts police from actively investigating recruitment businesses for their violations of Nepal's criminal legislation. Recruitment businesses continued to use their political influence to prevent investigation, prosecution and redress for their routine abuse and exploitation of migrants.

TORTURE AND OTHER ILL-TREATMENT

The criminal investigation system remained archaic and draconian. Torture and other ill-treatment was widespread in pre-trial detention to extract "confessions".

The new Criminal Code passed by Parliament in August contained provisions criminalizing torture and other ill-treatment, with a maximum of five years' imprisonment. A separate anti-torture bill, which remained pending in Parliament, fell far short of international legal requirements.

TRANSITIONAL JUSTICE

The government did not amend the Investigation of the Disappeared Persons, Truth and Reconciliation Commission Act 2014 as ordered by the Supreme Court in 2014 and 2015. By the end of the year, two bodies – the Truth and Reconciliation Commission and the Commission of Investigation on Enforced Disappeared Persons – had respectively collected over 60,000 and 3,000 complaints of human rights violations, such as murder, torture and enforced disappearances committed by state security forces and Maoists during the conflict from 1996 to 2006. Effective investigations did not take place. An acute shortage of resources and capacity adversely affected the ability of the two bodies to deliver truth, justice and reparation.

IMPUNITY

Impunity remained entrenched. Political parties resisted amending transitional justice laws in what was widely perceived as a prioritization of reconciliation and monetary compensation over truth, justice and other reparations, including guarantees of non-repetition. No effective investigations had taken place into the hundreds of killings of demonstrators by security forces since 1990 in various parts of the country, including the Tarai.

DISCRIMINATION

Discrimination persisted on the bases of gender, caste, class, ethnic origin, sexual orientation, gender identity and religion. Constitutional amendments did not fully guarantee equal rights to citizenship for women, nor provide protection from discrimination to marginalized communities including Dalits and other caste-based and ethnic minorities, and lesbian, gay, bisexual, transgender and intersex people.

The provisions for punishment and the statutory limitations relating to rape in the new Criminal Code were still far short of international law and standards. Gender-based discrimination continued to undermine women's and girls' ability to control their sexuality and make informed choices related to reproduction; to challenge early and forced marriages; and enjoy adequate antenatal and maternal health care.

NETHERLANDS

Kingdom of the Netherlands
Head of state: **King Willem-Alexander**
Head of government: **Mark Rutte**

Undocumented migrants continued to be deprived of their rights. New security legislation threatened to undermine human rights and the rule of law. Ethnic profiling by police continued to be a pressing concern, as was the use of Tasers in day-to-day policing.

REFUGEES' AND MIGRANTS' RIGHTS

The number of people in immigration detention increased, after years of decline. Insufficient attention was given by the authorities to alternatives to detention, while the necessity and proportionality of an individual's (continued) detention were also insufficiently assessed. A draft law on amending immigration detention rules was pending at the end of the year. Although the bill offered minor improvements, the detention regime would remain "prison-like" in terms of facilities, detention conditions and the use of disciplinary measures, including isolation cells and use of handcuffs.

Despite a deteriorating security situation in Afghanistan, the Netherlands continued to forcibly return asylum-seekers whose claims were rejected to Afghanistan, including families with children, in breach of the principle of *non-refoulement*.

RIGHT TO AN ADEQUATE STANDARD OF LIVING

The authorities remained unwilling to implement a recommendation by the UN Committee on Economic, Social and Cultural Rights to put in place a comprehensive strategy to ensure that everyone, including undocumented migrants, enjoys the minimum essential levels of all Covenant rights (such as the rights to food, housing, health, water and sanitation) and ensure this is supported by adequate funding.

COUNTER-TERROR AND SECURITY

In March, two anti-terrorism laws came into force for individuals suspected of being a threat to national security. The first allowed for administrative control measures on individuals, including travel bans and restrictions on movement and contact with certain persons, without providing sufficient safeguards against arbitrary and discriminatory use. The second administrative law enabled the revocation of Dutch nationality of dual citizens who are suspected of having travelled abroad to join an armed group. The laws did not provide for a meaningful and effective appeal.

In July, the law on the Intelligence and Security Services was adopted. It gave sweeping surveillance powers to intelligence and security services, threatening the rights to privacy, freedom of expression and non-discrimination. Safeguards against abuse of these powers were insufficient. Serious concerns remained about the possibility of information-sharing with intelligence agencies in countries that might use such information to target human rights defenders and government opponents.

Any person suspected or convicted of terrorism-related offences continued to be automatically placed in a specialized high-security prison where they were subjected to inhuman and degrading treatment.

POLICE AND SECURITY FORCES

In order to address ongoing ethnic profiling, the police introduced a professional standard and a training module to promote the fair and effective use of their stop-and-search powers. However, the impact of this remained unclear, as there was no systematic monitoring and recording of how these stop-and-search powers were executed in practice.

In February, the police began piloting the use of Taser X2 electro-shock weapons. Police records between February and August showed that Tasers were used in situations where there was no imminent threat of death or serious injury. In almost half of the cases, persons were tasered in direct contact mode, including when already handcuffed, inside a police cell or vehicle, and in a separation cell in a psychiatric hospital. This usage is inconsistent with international human rights standards.

FREEDOM OF RELIGION AND BELIEF

A government proposal for a ban on face-coverings in certain public spaces was pending before the Senate at the end of the year. The ban would restrict the rights to freedom of religion and of expression, particularly of Muslim women.

NEW ZEALAND

New Zealand
Head of state: **Queen Elizabeth II, represented by Patricia Lee Reddy**
Head of government: **Jacinda Ardern (replaced Bill English in October)**

New Zealand received criticism about its mental health services, detention facilities, high rates of Indigenous Māori representation in the criminal justice system, and about poor health and wellbeing among children.

JUSTICE SYSTEM

The Waitangi Tribunal, a permanent commission of inquiry, found that the government had failed to prioritize the reduction of the high rate of recidivism among Māori and had breached its Treaty of Waitangi obligations. The commission called for urgent practical action to reduce the number. The National Preventive Mechanism found that Māori were disproportionally represented in all detention centres. Mental health and disability in detention continued to be a concern. Separate reviews by the Ombudsman and an independent expert commissioned by the Human Rights Commission highlighted the high use of prolonged solitary confinement and restraint practices in places of detention and the over-representation of ethnic minority groups in these incidents. The use of "tie-down beds"

and/or waist restraints in at-risk units was found to amount to cruel, inhuman or degrading treatment or punishment. The separation of children and young people in "secure care" units in "care and protection" residences was found to be inappropriate.

REFUGEES AND ASYLUM-SEEKERS

The government announced the framework for its pilot community sponsorship programme for refugee resettlement, to begin at the end of the year. The new refugee category allows community groups to sponsor 25 refugees to enter New Zealand.

CHILDREN'S RIGHTS

A UNICEF report raised concern over the health and wellbeing of children in New Zealand, due to the high rates of teen pregnancy, neonatal mortality and the high teen suicide rate. The UN Committee on the Elimination of Racial Discrimination recommended the establishment of an independent inquiry into abuse suffered by children, the vast majority Māori, in state care between the 1950s and 1990s.

INTERNATIONAL JUSTICE

The authorities declined to hold an independent inquiry into allegations that the New Zealand Defence Force committed crimes under international law during a raid in Afghanistan in 2010, resulting in civilian deaths. Lawyers filed a civil lawsuit calling for a judicial review on behalf of the alleged Afghan victims.

RIGHT TO HEALTH

The Auditor-General found that problems with access to housing, rehabilitation and other services led to patients being kept in mental health units for years.

NICARAGUA

Republic of Nicaragua
Head of state and government: **Daniel Ortega Saavedra**

Gender-based killings became increasingly brutal. Attacks against human rights defenders persisted. A total ban on abortion remained in place. Impunity persisted for perpetrators of violence against Indigenous Peoples. The authorities continued to deny a genuine and effective consultation process for communities likely to be affected by the construction of the Grand Interoceanic Canal.

BACKGROUND

In January, Daniel Ortega assumed office as President for a third consecutive term. Rosario Murillo, his wife, assumed office as Vice-President for the first time.

WOMEN'S RIGHTS

Between January and December, there were 55 gender-based killings of women, according to the NGO Catholics for the Right to Decide. The NGO found that the killings were more brutal than in previous years and tended to be committed by perpetrators acting in groups.

In June 2017, the National Assembly approved an amendment to the Comprehensive Law on Violence against Women; the amendment reduced the scope of the definition of femicide to the private sphere, limiting the crime to relations between spouses and partners. Critics said the new definition denied the reality of femicides, which were also committed in public places.

Abortion remained banned in all circumstances. Nicaragua continued to have one of the highest teenage pregnancy and maternal mortality rates in the Americas region, according to the UN Population Fund (UNFPA).

INDIGENOUS PEOPLES' RIGHTS

Impunity persisted for crimes such as killings, rapes, kidnappings, enforced disappearances, death threats and forced displacement of Indigenous Peoples in the North Atlantic Autonomous Region, even though both the Inter-American Commission on Human Rights (IACHR) and the Inter-American Court of Human Rights had ordered Nicaragua in 2015 to adopt all necessary measures to investigate those crimes.

HUMAN RIGHTS DEFENDERS

Attacks against women human rights defenders continued, as reported at a public hearing before the IACHR in September. Women's civil society organizations reported receiving death threats as well as being arbitrarily detained and attacked with the complicity or acquiescence of state officials.

In March, the Inter-American Court of Human Rights issued its judgment in *Acosta et al. v. Nicaragua*; it found the state responsible for having violated the rights to access to justice, truth and physical integrity of human rights defender María Luisa Acosta, following the murder of her husband Francisco García Valle.[1] The authorities had yet to take steps to comply with the judgment, in particular to put an end to the impunity in the case and ensure the rights to justice and truth of María Luisa Acosta.

In August the IACHR granted precautionary measures to Francisca Ramírez and her family after they were victims of death threats, harassment and attacks in retaliation for her activism in opposition to the construction of the Grand Interoceanic Canal.

GRAND INTEROCEANIC CANAL

There continued to be no genuine and effective consultation process for those who would be affected by the construction of the Grand Interoceanic Canal, in violation of international human rights principles.[2]

According to the Centre for Legal Assistance for Indigenous Peoples, the right to free, prior and informed consent of the Indigenous and Afro-descendant Rama Kriol people relating to the project had not been guaranteed, despite several appeals lodged with the courts. Civil society organizations noted that the scale of the project, which would include an oil pipeline and two ports, among other infrastructure, would affect hundreds of thousands of people and would put them at risk of eviction.

Human rights organizations and peasant farmer communities continued to call for the repeal of Law 840, the law regulating the Canal, due to its insufficient safeguards to protect Indigenous Peoples' rights. Their demands continued to be rejected and the authorities had yet to open a meaningful dialogue with the communities likely to be affected by the construction of the Canal.

FREEDOMS OF EXPRESSION, ASSOCIATION AND ASSEMBLY

In November, municipal elections took place in a context of violence, with at least five people reported to have been killed and 30 wounded in six municipalities.

There were also reports of unnecessary and excessive use of force by the police against people peacefully protesting against the construction of the Canal, as well as reports of arbitrary detention of protesters. Human rights defenders were also reported to have been harassed and intimidated for their opposition to the project.

---

1. Nicaragua: The state must uphold, without delay, the judgment issued by the Inter-American Court of Human Rights (AMR 43/6173/2017)

2. Danger: Rights for sale – the Interoceanic Grand Canal project in Nicaragua and the erosion of human rights (AMR 43/6515/2017)

NIGER

The Republic of Niger
Head of state: **Mahamadou Issoufou**
Head of government: **Brigi Rafini**

Armed conflict continued and armed groups carried out at least 70 attacks, killing tens of civilians. The humanitarian situation continued to deteriorate. Over 700 suspected Boko Haram members went on trial. Hundreds of people, including prisoners of conscience, were arrested and prosecuted for exercising their rights to freedom of expression and association. Security forces used excessive force against protesters. The rights of refugees and migrants were violated.

BACKGROUND

In March, the government declared a state of emergency in the western areas bordering Mali and extended the security forces' powers after attacks by armed groups in Tillabéry and Tahoua. It renewed the state of emergency in the Diffa region, where attacks by armed groups continued.

FREEDOMS OF EXPRESSION AND ASSOCIATION

Hundreds of people, including prisoners of conscience, were arbitrarily arrested and prosecuted for exercising their rights to freedom of expression and association.

In May, Insar Abdourahmane, a member of the Association of Action for Democracy and Human Rights, was arrested and detained for more than 20 days in Agadez town for criticizing the authorities on Facebook. He was given a six-month suspended prison sentence for inciting violence.

In April, security forces used excessive force to repress a student protest in Niamey, the capital, against the suspension of bursary payments and new age restrictions on welfare payments. One student, Mala Bagallé, was killed after being shot in the back with a tear gas canister, and dozens were wounded. In May, a commission of inquiry found that the gendarmerie was responsible for the killing; and a judicial investigation was opened.

At least 300 students, including board members of the Niger Union of Students, were arrested throughout the country, detained for a few days and released without charge for participating in a protest and blocking traffic.

In May, Amadou Ali Djibo, leader of the opposition coalition Front for the Restoration of Democracy and the Defence of the

Republic, was convicted of inciting revolt and, after 11 days' detention, was given a 90-day conditional suspended sentence.

In April, Baba Alpha, an outspoken journalist working for private television channel Bonferey, and his father, who was born in Mali, were arrested and charged with forgery and illegal status. In July they were sentenced to two years' imprisonment for forgery.

In June, Ibrahim Bana, a member of opposition party Moden Fa Lumana, and Gamatié Mahamadou Yansambou, Secretary General of the Union of Taxi Drivers, were arrested and charged for attempting to influence a judicial investigation after they denounced, on social media, corruption in the judicial system. In July, Ibrahim Bana was sentenced to three months' imprisonment, including two months suspended, and Mahamadou Yansambou was released after more than 15 days.

In July, 43 members of the teachers' union SYNACEB were convicted of disrupting public safety and inciting a riot, after they boycotted substitute teacher evaluations. They spent more than 15 days in detention and were sentenced to suspended prison terms of between one and three months.

ARMED CONFLICT

Armed groups including Boko Haram carried out at least 70 attacks on soldiers and villages in the Diffa, Mainé-Soroa, Tillabéry and Bosso regions. At least 30 people, including civilians, were killed and others wounded; over 60 people were abducted. In June, suspected Boko Haram members killed nine people and abducted 37 women in the region of Nguigmi.

The trial of 700 people accused of supporting Boko Haram began on 2 March. Most had been arrested in the Diffa region since 2013, although some had been detained since 2012. Among them were Nigerians, including refugees from areas affected by Boko Haram.

In July, 13 people, including two Niger nationals and 11 Nigerian nationals, were killed by Niger soldiers in a village near Abada on the Nigeria border, when they were mistaken for members of an armed group. An investigation was launched into the killings.

ECONOMIC, SOCIAL AND CULTURAL RIGHTS

The UN CEDAW Committee expressed concern that 82% of the population lived in extreme poverty. Women were particularly affected by food insecurity in rural areas, a fact linked to, among other things, their socioeconomic status and the impact of climate change and extractive industries. The Committee also expressed concern that temporary measures to achieve greater gender equality were inadequately applied, including in employment, education and health.

As the humanitarian situation deteriorated due to conflict, the UN estimated that 2.2 million people, including 408,000 in Diffa, were in need of humanitarian assistance; 1.8 million were estimated to be severely food insecure. Over 73% of children under five and almost 46% of women of reproductive age suffered from anaemia.

REFUGEES' AND MIGRANTS' RIGHTS

Over 60,000 refugees and migrants transited Niger on the way to Libya and Algeria where many suffered serious abuses including rape, unlawful detention in harsh conditions, ill-treatment and extortion, and unknown numbers died. Operations to arrest perpetrators pushed smugglers to use more dangerous routes to Libya or Algeria.

In May, eight migrants from Niger, including five children, died of thirst after they were abandoned on the way to Algeria; and 92 migrants were found close to death by the Niger Army after being beaten and abandoned by their driver in the desert near Bilma in the north. In June, 44 migrants, including babies, were found dead in the desert near Agadez, central Niger, after their vehicle broke down on the way to Libya.

NIGERIA

Federal Republic of Nigeria
Head of state and government: **Muhammadu Buhari**

The armed group Boko Haram continued to carry out attacks, resulting in hundreds of deaths. Reports continued of extrajudicial executions, enforced disappearances, and torture and other ill-treatment, which, in some cases, led to deaths in custody. Conditions in military detention conditions were harsh. Communal violence occurred across the country. Thousands of people were forcibly evicted from their homes.

ARMED CONFLICT

BOKO HARAM

Boko Haram carried out at least 65 attacks causing 411 civilian deaths, and abducted at least 73 people. Sixteen women, including 10 policewomen, were abducted in June when Boko Haram ambushed an army-escorted convoy on the Maiduguri-Damboa road. In July, Boko Haram ambushed a team of oil prospectors in a village in Magumeri. Three oil workers were abducted and at least 40 other people were killed, including soldiers and members of the Civilian Joint Task Force. On 6 May, 82 Chibok schoolgirls, abducted in 2014, were released by Boko Haram fighters in an exchange deal; 113 girls remained in captivity. In November, six farmers in Dimge village in Mafa were abducted and beheaded.

INTERNALLY DISPLACED PEOPLE

There remained at least 1.7 million internally displaced people (IDPs) in the northeastern states of Borno, Yobe and Adamawa; 39% lived in camps or similar settings and 61% in host communities. The UN said that 5.2 million people in the northeast remained in urgent need of food assistance; 450,000 children under five were in urgent need of nutrition. In July, Doctors without Borders reported that 240 children had died from malnutrition in Borno state.

On 17 January, the Nigerian Air Force bombed an IDP camp in Rann, headquarters of Kala Balge local government, in Borno state, killing at least 167 civilians, including many children. The military said the bombing was an accident as Rann was not identified as a humanitarian camp.

ARBITRARY ARRESTS AND DETENTIONS

The military arbitrarily arrested and held thousands of young men, women and children in detention centres around the country. Detainees were denied access to lawyers and family members. The army released 593 detainees in April and 760 in October.

By April, the military detention facility at Giwa barracks, Maiduguri, held more than 4,900 people in extremely overcrowded cells. Disease, dehydration and starvation were rife and at least 340 detainees died. At least 200 children, as young as four, were detained in an overcrowded and unhygienic children's cell. Some children were born in detention.

The military detained hundreds of women unlawfully, without charge, some because they were believed to be related to Boko Haram members. Among them were women and girls who said they had been victims of Boko Haram. Women reported inhuman detention conditions, including a lack of health care for women giving birth in cells.

On 24 September, the Minister of Justice announced that the mass trial of Boko Haram suspects held in different detention centres had commenced. The first phase of trials was handled by four judges in secret, between 9 and 12 October. Fifty defendants were sentenced to various terms of imprisonment. An interim report of the Director of Public Prosecutions showed that 468 suspects were discharged and the trial for the remainder was adjourned to January 2018.

LACK OF ACCOUNTABILITY

In June, the Special Board of Inquiry to investigate allegations of gross violations of human rights, established by the Chief of Army Staff, found that Giwa barracks was extremely overcrowded, with poor sanitation and insufficient ventilation, factors which resulted in detainees' deaths. It cleared senior military officers, alleged to have committed crimes under international law, of wrongdoing.

In August, acting President Yemi Osinbajo set up a presidential investigation panel to probe allegations of human rights violations carried out by the military. Between 11 September and 8 November, the panel sat in the capital, Abuja, and in the cities of Maiduguri, Enugu, Port Harcourt, Lagos and Kaduna.

In its December preliminary report, the Office of the Prosecutor of the ICC announced that it would continue to assess the admissibility of the eight potential crimes it had previously identified as having been allegedly committed in Nigeria.

TORTURE AND OTHER ILL-TREATMENT

Torture and other ill-treatment and unlawful detention by the police and the State Security Service (SSS) continued. In February, Nonso Diobu and eight other men were arrested and detained by Special Anti-Robbery Squad (SARS) officers in Awkuzu, Anambra state. They were tortured and all, except Nonso Diobu, died in custody. Nonso Diobu was charged with robbery and released four months after arrest.

In May, a high court ordered the SSS to release Bright Chimezie, a member of the Indigenous People of Biafra (IPOB). Instead, the SSS included his name in another case. Bright Chimezie had not been brought to court by the end of the year; the SSS had held him in incommunicado detention for more than one year.

Ibrahim El-Zakzaky, leader of the Islamic Movement of Nigeria (IMN), and his wife remained in incommunicado detention without trial since their arrest in December 2015 despite a court ordering their release and compensation.

In September, the Nigerian police launched Force Order 20 which sought to reduce the excessive use of pre-trial detention by providing free legal advice to suspects at police stations. In December, the Anti-Torture Bill – intended to prohibit and criminalize the use of torture – was signed into law.

UNLAWFUL KILLINGS

At least 10 IPOB members were killed and 12 others wounded by soldiers in Umuahia, Abia state on 14 September. The military claimed that they were killed when they tried to resist the arrest of leader Nnamdi Kanu at his home. Witnesses say that, in addition to those killed, at least 10 IPOB members were shot and taken away by soldiers. The government subsequently banned the IPOB.

On 9 March, a court in Abuja sentenced two police officers to death for their part in the extrajudicial execution of six traders in Apo, Abuja, in 2005. Three other police officers including the leader of the police team were acquitted. In 2005, a Judicial Commission of Inquiry had indicted six police officers for the murders and recommended their trial as well as compensation for the victims' families. One of them allegedly escaped from custody in 2015.

In September, the High Court in Port Harcourt convicted five SARS policemen for the extrajudicial executions of Michael Akor and Michael Igwe in 2009. The court also awarded 50 million naira (USD143,000) in compensation to the victims' families.

In December, after huge pressure on social media, the Inspector General of Police agreed to reform SARS.

COMMUNAL VIOLENCE

Inter-communal violence linked to lingering clashes between herdsmen and farming communities resulted in more than 549 deaths and the displacement of thousands in 12 states. In February, 21 villagers were killed in an attack by suspected herdsmen in three communities in the Atakad district of Kaura, Kaduna state. Witnesses said the herdsmen killed, looted, and burned the villagers' houses. In June, a communal clash in the Mambilla Plateau of Taraba state left scores of people dead, mostly herdsmen and their families. In September, at least 20 people were killed when suspected herdsmen invaded Ancha village in the Miango district of Jos, Plateau state, after a misunderstanding between villagers and herdsmen residing in the community. In

October, 27 people were killed by suspected herdsmen in a classroom where they were sheltering after three days of attacks in the Nkyie-Doghwro community of Bassa, Plateau state. In December, herdsmen attacked at least five villages in Demsa LGA in Adamawa state to avenge the massacre of up to 57 people, mostly children, in November in nearby Kikan community. Residents described being attacked by a fighter jet and a military helicopter as they attempted to flee. At least 86 people were killed by the herdsmen and air force bombing.

RIGHT TO HOUSING AND FORCED EVICTIONS

Authorities in Lagos, Imo and Rivers states continued to forcibly evict thousands of residents, without adequate notice, compensation, or the provision of alternative accommodation and resettlement.

In Lagos state, at least 5,000 people were forcibly evicted from Otodo-Gbame and Ilubirin waterfront communities between March and April, in violation of previous Lagos State High Court orders. The orders restrained state authorities from demolishing the homes of affected communities consisting of at least 300,000 residents, and ordered them to consult with residents. In March, the Lagos state government pulled out of the consultations saying the communities' demand for resettlement was unreasonable.

During the forced eviction of Otodo-Gbame community on 9 April, at least two people were shot, one fatally, as the police fired at unarmed residents. There were no investigations into the shootings. On 13 June, Lagos state authorities forcibly evicted hundreds of people from Ijora-Badia community.

On 15 June, Rivers state authorities forcibly evicted hundreds of people from Ayagologo waterfront community in Port Harcourt.

On 15 November, police in Lagos arrested and detained 158 residents, including six women one of whom was pregnant, who were protesting against forced evictions in the state.

On 2 February, a High Court in Abuja declared threats of forced evictions without the service of statutory notices illegal. It urged state authorities to take measures to confer security of tenure on affected residents. The judgment prevented the Abuja authorities from forcibly evicting hundreds of thousands of residents in Mpape community. On 21 June, a Lagos State High Court found that forced evictions and their threat were unconstitutional and amounted to cruel, inhuman or degrading treatment.

WOMEN'S RIGHTS

Nigeria's federal Parliament and Adamawa and Gombe states continued to debate the Gender and Equal Opportunities Bill. In October, ECOWAS Court held that Nigeria violated the right to dignity of three women by wrongly accusing them of being sex workers, and unlawfully arresting and verbally abusing them.

IDP women and girls reported gender-based violence including rape and sexual exploitation, often in exchange for food and other necessities, by military officers and members of the Civilian Joint Task Force in the northeast. Households headed by women reported discrimination in access to food assistance and livelihood opportunities in some locations.

A group of women who were previously confined to Bama IDP camp campaigned for the release of their husbands from military detention, and for justice for rape and other abuses they suffered while in the camp between 2015 and 2016. The Chief of Army Staff was reported to have ordered an investigation in June into misconduct by soldiers in the camp.

HUMAN RIGHTS DEFENDERS

Human rights defenders continued to face intimidation for their work. Parliament debated a bill to regulate and restrict the work of NGOs. If passed, it would establish an NGO Regulatory Commission to keep a register of all NGOs, co-ordinate their activities, and monitor their budgets and funding. A public hearing on the bill took place in December.

On 19 July, police arrested and detained Maurice Fangnon for six days for calling for investigations into alleged killings and assaults of residents in Otodo-Gbame community. He was rearrested on 12 December with Bamidele Friday; they were released on bail on 22 December. Raymond Gold faced criminal charges carrying a maximum three-year prison sentence for demanding that an oil company conduct an Environmental Impact Assessment on activities which harmed the environment. On 6 June, police officers harassed, beat and injured Justus Ijeoma at Onitsha Area Command. In October, he received a written apology from the Area Command.

FREEDOM OF EXPRESSION

Journalists were harassed, intimidated and arrested. On 19 January, police raided the offices of *Premium Times* and arrested publisher Dapo Olorunyomi and correspondent Evelyn Okakwu for several hours, after the Chief of Army Staff accused the newspaper of offensive publications.

On 19 April, Kaduna state police arrested and detained Midat Joseph, a journalist with *Leadership* newspaper, for a WhatsApp comment. He was taken to court the next day on charges of criminal conspiracy, inciting disturbance and injurious falsehood. On 31 July, the court dismissed the case on grounds of lack of diligent prosecution.

On 19 September, the Katsina state police arrested three bloggers, Jamil Mabai, Bashir Dauda and Umar Faruq, for criticizing the Governor. Bashir Dauda and Umar Faruq were released after one week and Jamil Mabai was detained for 22 days.

On 27 October, Audu Maikori, who was arrested for publishing false information online, was awarded 40 million naira (USD112,700) in compensation for unlawful arrest and detention.

FREEDOMS OF ASSEMBLY AND ASSOCIATION

The security forces disrupted, in some cases violently and with excessive force, peaceful protests and assemblies.

The police continued to deny IMN, which was banned by the Kaduna state government in 2016, the right to peaceful protest. On 25 January, the Abuja police arrested nine IMN members in connection with a peaceful protest demanding the release of Ibrahim El-Zakzaky.

On 25 July, police in Kano city prevented a group of women from protesting against the persistent rape of women and children in the state. On 8 August, police violently dispersed peaceful protesters who demanded the return of President Buhari who was in the UK for medical treatment.

CORPORATE ACCOUNTABILITY

In June, the widows of four men from the Ogoni region in the Niger Delta who were executed following an unfair trial in 1995, filed a lawsuit in the Netherlands against Shell, demanding compensation and a public apology. They accused Shell of complicity in the unlawful arrest and detention of their husbands during a brutal crackdown by the then military authorities on the Movement for the Survival of the Ogoni People. International organizations called for Shell to be investigated for involvement in these crimes.

Environmental pollution linked to the oil industry continued to undermine the economic, social and cultural rights of the Niger Delta communities.

The government took limited steps to address pollution in the Ogoni region of the Niger Delta, as recommended by the UN Environment Programme (UNEP) in 2011. However, local communities expressed frustration at the slow progress of the initiative and because operations on the ground had not begun. Shell failed to comply with some of UNEP's key recommendations.

In September, operations to clean up the pollution caused by two large oil spills in 2008 began in the Bodo community in the Ogoni region.

RIGHTS OF LESBIAN, GAY, BISEXUAL, TRANSGENDER AND INTERSEX PEOPLE

Arrest, public shaming, extortion of and discrimination against individuals based on their sexual orientation were reported in several parts of the country. In April, the Nigerian police arraigned 53 men in a magistrate court in Zaria, Kaduna state, for conspiracy and unlawful assembly and for belonging to an unlawful society. They were accused of attending a gay wedding and granted bail.

In August, about 42 men and boys between 12 and 28 years old were arrested at a hotel in Lagos while attending an HIV intervention programme organized by an NGO. They were charged with "engaging in gay activities". The police paraded the victims to the media.

DEATH PENALTY

Death sentences continued to be imposed; no executions were recorded. In July, at the National Economic Council, state governors agreed to either sign execution warrants or commute death sentences as a way of addressing overcrowding in prisons. Death row prisoners reported that execution gallows were being prepared for executions in Benin and Lagos prisons.

In August, the Ogun state government announced that it would no longer maintain an informal commitment to refrain from authorizing executions.

In September, the Senate passed a bill prescribing the death penalty for kidnapping.

NORWAY

Kingdom of Norway
Head of state: **King Harald V**
Head of government: **Erna Solberg**

Serious concerns remained about the prevalence of, and inadequate state response to, rape and other violence against women. The rights of refugees and asylum-seekers continued to be restricted; Afghan asylum-seekers faced forced returns to Afghanistan.

REFUGEES AND ASYLUM-SEEKERS

There was a dramatic decrease in the number of people claiming asylum. By November, only 3,378 people had claimed asylum, compared to 31,145 in 2015, according to government statistics.

The government continued to take initiatives to restrict the rights of asylum-seekers and refugees. The practice of "Dublin" returns – requiring any asylum claim to be processed by the country in which the applicant first arrived – to Italy continued, and restarted to Greece.

Afghan nationals represented the fifth biggest group of people who claimed asylum by the end of November. They continued to face obstacles in accessing asylum and forced return to Afghanistan. According to Eurostat, there was a dramatic drop in asylum recognition rates for Afghan nationals, down to 24% by August; Norway had the highest number of persons being forcibly returned to Afghanistan.

VIOLENCE AGAINST WOMEN AND GIRLS

Gender-based violence, including rape and sexual violence, remained a serious concern. The Norwegian Penal Code was still not in accordance with international human rights standards as the definition of rape was not based on consent. The number of rape cases reported to the police had been increasing steadily over the years. In 2016, 1,663 cases of rape were reported to the police, an increase of nearly 21.9% since 2015. Shortcomings in police investigations contributed to the low level of rape prosecutions. In April, the Director of Public Prosecutions reviewed the quality of investigations in 275 nationally reported rape cases. The review concluded that there was considerable room for improvement in the quality of police investigations, and pointed especially at weaknesses in the initial phase, where the necessary steps to secure evidence were not always taken.

Following the consideration of Norway's ninth periodic report, the Committee on the Elimination of Discrimination against Women expressed concerns about the high level of gender-based violence against women, and recommended a number of measures including the adoption of a legal definition of rape in the Penal Code that places lack of free consent at its centre. In addition, the Committee expressed concern at the consequences of the criminalization of the purchase of sexual services from adults. The committee recommended a white paper on prostitution with a comprehensive framework which ensured that women who engage in sex work are not prosecuted for the selling of sexual services, including for acts that currently amount to criminal acts of "promotion of prostitution".

RIGHTS OF LESBIAN, GAY, BISEXUAL, TRANSGENDER AND INTERSEX PEOPLE

The Penal Code still did not classify violence motivated by discriminatory attitudes towards transgender people as a hate crime.

INTERNATIONAL JUSTICE

On 1 March, a 44-year-old Rwandan national accused of complicity in the 1994 genocide in Rwanda was released after four years in custody. The Ministry of Justice had previously concluded that he could be extradited to Rwanda. The investigation into an allegation by his defence lawyer – that two witnesses were pressured into giving false testimonies to the prosecutors – led to the conclusion that their testimonies were not sufficiently credible.

OMAN

Sultanate of Oman
Head of state and government: **Sultan Qaboos bin Said Al Said**

The authorities curtailed the rights to freedom of expression and association, using flawed legal procedures to suspend newspapers and to arrest, prosecute and convict journalists on criminal and administrative grounds. Family members of human rights defenders faced harassment and intimidation from the authorities.

Women remained subject to discrimination in law. Migrant workers were exposed to exploitation and abuse. The death penalty remained in force; no executions were reported.

BACKGROUND

Oman maintained a neutral stance in the regional crisis in which Saudi Arabia, the UAE, Bahrain and Egypt severed relations with Qatar, as well as in relation to the Saudi Arabia-led coalition fighting in Yemen since 2015.

There was a marked decline in coverage of human rights issues in the country. Oman's economy continued to be impacted by: lower oil prices, Oman's main source of income; a relatively high deficit; the removal of subsidies, notably on petroleum; a rise in fees for some government services; and a temporary hiring freeze for public sector positions.

FREEDOM OF EXPRESSION

The government continued to unduly restrict freedom of expression. In January the authorities ordered the dismissal of a journalist who was reporting on sex trafficking in the country, and revoked the licence of another journalist who was covering reports that Oman had sought financial support from its neighbours. In February, the annual Muscat International Book Fair suspended the participation of two writers, apparently in connection with their criticism of the government. In April, the authorities arrested at least two people in connection with Facebook posts; they were subsequently released. In May, the government blocked the online publication of the *Mowaten* newspaper; it remained blocked at the end of the year.

The chilling effect of the trials against *Azamn* newspaper and its journalists continued to reverberate following *Azamn*'s publication in 2016 of two reports detailing allegations of corruption in the government and the judiciary. The government renewed a rolling, temporary suspension of the newspaper, despite a court ruling overturning the suspension. In January the Public Prosecutor appealed against the December 2016 acquittal of *Azamn* journalist Zaher al-'Abri. He was released on bail in August. Editor-in-chief Ibrahim al-Maamari and deputy editor-in-chief Youssef al-Haj were released in April and October respectively after completing their prison sentences. In June, *Azamn* staff members approached the government for financial support following its closure.

In January the High Court in the capital, Muscat, overturned a three-year prison sentence on journalist Hassan al-Basham, partly because of his ill-health, and ordered the case back to the Appeal Court. In November the initial three-year prison sentence was upheld. In June 2016 the Court of Appeal in Sohar had upheld the verdict, which was based on charges of "insult" to God and the Sultan.

In January a Muscat Appeal Court overturned the three-year prison sentence and fine of 1,000 Omani Riyals (about USD2,600) handed down in October 2016 to writer Hamoud al-Shukaily, a member of the Omani Society for Writers and Authors, on charges of incitement to protest or disturbing public order relating to a 2016 Facebook post.

The Appeal Court verdict in the case of writer and film critic Abdullah Habib was postponed several times. In November 2016 he had been sentenced to three years' imprisonment and a fine of 2,000 Omani Riyals (about USD5,200).

On 23 May a lower instance court sentenced writer and researcher Mansour al-Mahrazi to three years' imprisonment and a fine on charges of "undermining the state" and violating publication laws by writing and publishing a book in Lebanon without permission. He was appealing the case at the end of the year.

WOMEN'S RIGHTS

Women faced discrimination in criminal law and in personal status or family law, in relation to matters including divorce, child custody, inheritance, and passing their nationality on to their children.

WORKERS' RIGHTS – MIGRANT WORKERS

Migrant workers continued to face exploitation and abuse. Domestic workers, mainly women from Asia and Africa, complained that employers to whom they were tied under the official *kafala* sponsorship system confiscated their passports, forced them to work excessive hours without time off, and denied them their full wages and adequate food and living conditions. The *kafala* system did not provide domestic workers with the protections available under the Labour Law.

DEATH PENALTY

The death penalty remained in force for a range of crimes. No convictions or executions were reported.

PAKISTAN

Islamic Republic of Pakistan
Head of state: **Mamnoon Hussain**
Head of government: **Shahid Khaqan Abbasi (replaced Muhammad Nawaz Sharif in August)**

The crackdown on freedom of expression intensified. The Prevention of Electronic Crimes Act, 2016 was used to intimidate, harass and arbitrarily detain human rights defenders for online comments. Enforced disappearances were widespread; impunity was prevalent. Blasphemy-related violence claimed the life of a student, triggering rare condemnation from the government. Large demonstrations took place in support of blasphemy laws, which were used to convict people expressing opinions online. Journalists were attacked by unidentified assailants. Minorities continued to face discrimination in the enjoyment of economic and social rights. Attempts to restrict child marriage were blocked by Parliament. Killings of women continued

in so-called "honour" crimes, despite the 2016 law criminalizing the practice.

BACKGROUND

The Supreme Court disqualified Prime Minister Nawaz Sharif from office in July for failing to disclose a source of foreign income. Following his resignation, the government's authority progressively weakened as members of the Sharif family and ministers in the government became the subject of fresh corruption probes. The Minister for Law and Justice resigned in November after weeks of protests in which he was accused of blasphemy. The military took an increasing lead on foreign policy, national security and daily governance ahead of elections due by August 2018.

Tensions endured between India and Pakistan against the backdrop of firing from both sides across the Line of Control that divides the disputed territory of Kashmir. Relations with Afghanistan deteriorated as the two countries accused each other of using their territory as a launching pad for armed attacks. Under its new South Asia policy, the USA singled out Pakistan as a source of instability in Afghanistan, raising the prospect of a rupture in relations. Turning away from the West, Pakistan drew closer to China with the expansion of the China-Pakistan Economic Corridor, a multi-billion dollar infrastructure project.

Pakistan was elected to the UN Human Rights Council in October. Pakistan's human rights record was examined by UN bodies during the year: the Committee on Economic, Social and Cultural Rights, the Human Rights Committee and under the UPR process.

FREEDOM OF EXPRESSION

Attacks on freedom of expression continued, particularly against those posting comments online. In January, five bloggers who made anonymous online comments said to be critical of the military were subject to enforced disappearances. Four of the bloggers were later released; two of them later said they had been tortured while in military intelligence custody; the fifth remained disappeared. The draconian Prevention of Electronic Crimes Act of 2016 was used to carry out a number of arrests throughout the year including, in June, the arrest of journalist Zafarullah Achakzai, a reporter for the newspaper *Daily Qudrat*. Over subsequent weeks, supporters of different political parties were arrested for social media posts critical of the authorities. No action was taken against social media accounts belonging to armed groups that incited discrimination and violence.

People were prosecuted after being accused, particularly over social media, for alleged breaches of vague and broad blasphemy laws, which criminalized peaceful expression if deemed to offend religious sensibilities. In June, Taimoor Raza was sentenced to death by an anti-terrorism court in Punjab, southern province, for allegedly blasphemous posts on Facebook. In September, Nadeem James, a Christian, was sentenced to death by a court in Gujrat city for sharing a "blasphemous" poem over WhatsApp.

Accusations of committing blasphemy triggered the execution-style killing of Mashal Khan, a university student, in Mardan city. In April, a mob of students stormed his hostel, stripped him naked and beat him repeatedly before shooting him. Then Prime Minister Nawaz Sharif vowed to take action against those who "misuse" the blasphemy laws. Six days later, a "faith healer" accused of blasphemy was similarly killed by three attackers inside his home in Sialkot city. Two days after that, a mob in Chitral city attacked a man accused of blasphemy, injuring police officers trying to protect him. In May, a 10-year-old boy was killed and five others were injured as a mob in Hub town in Balochistan tried to attack Prakash Kumar, a Hindu, for allegedly posting an offensive image online.

Senior government officials exacerbated tensions around blasphemy-related offences. In March, then Interior Minister Nisar Ali Khan deemed so-called blasphemers "enemies of humanity". In February and March, the Islamabad High Court ordered the removal of allegedly blasphemous content online and directed the government to initiate proceedings against people responsible for uploading them.

HUMAN RIGHTS DEFENDERS

Bloggers, journalists, lawyers, activists and other human rights defenders faced harassment, intimidation, threats, violence and enforced disappearance. The five bloggers who were forcibly disappeared and activists who campaigned for their release were subject to a smear campaign accusing them of being "blasphemers", "anti-Pakistan", "anti-Army" and "anti-Islam". Human rights defenders criticized on television and on social media faced death threats, forcing some to self-censor and to seek protection for their physical safety.

In May, Rana Tanveer, a journalist covering abuses against religious minorities, found death threats sprayed on his home in Lahore city. A few weeks later, he was knocked off his motorbike and severely injured after a car deliberately crashed into him. In September, Matiullah Jan, a journalist who had regularly been critical of the military's interference in politics, was attacked by men on motorbikes who hurled a large piece of concrete at the car in which he was travelling with his children, shattering the windscreen. In October, Ahmad Noorani, an outspoken political journalist, was attacked by men on motorbikes who stopped his car and beat him, including with iron rods. At the end of the year no one was known to have been held accountable for any of these attacks.

Defenders continued to be subjected to enforced disappearances, but some also reappeared. Raza Khan, a Lahore-based peace activist, was subjected to an enforced disappearance in December. Punhal Sario, a campaigner against enforced disappearances in Sindh province, went missing in August. He returned home in October. Zeenat Shahzadi, the first female journalist to be forcibly disappeared, was found near the Afghanistan border in October, 26 months after she went missing in Lahore. She disappeared again in November; her whereabouts remained unknown at the end of the year. In October and November, dozens of Sindhi and Baloch defenders were subjected to enforced disappearances by Pakistani security forces. Some returned to their homes days later, but others remained missing at the end of the year.

Space for civil society continued to shrink as the Interior Ministry used broad powers to undermine the ability of human rights defenders and NGOs to work independently. In November, the Ministry of the Interior ordered 29 international NGOs to halt their operations and leave the country within days.

ECONOMIC, SOCIAL AND CULTURAL RIGHTS

Around 58% of households were food insecure, according to the National Nutrition Survey, and an estimated 44% of children remained underdeveloped or short for their age. The percentage was significantly higher in Federally Administered Tribal Areas and Balochistan.

The government failed to take action against those who held people in bonded labour in rural areas. The 1992 Bonded Labour Abolition Act was still not adequately enforced; reasons included a lack of clarity regarding the law on the part of lower court judges and lack of action by police when complaints were filed.

In its 2017 review, the UN Committee on Economic, Social and Cultural Rights noted that more than 73% of workers, a majority of them women, were in the informal economy with no labour or social protection. The Committee called on Pakistan to address the gender pay gap, which rose from 34% in 2008 to 39% in 2015. The Committee also noted an urgent need to increase spending in the social sector, especially for health and education. It further stated that adequate steps must be taken to reduce the gap between girls and boys in enrolment for education.

RIGHTS OF LESBIAN, GAY, BISEXUAL, TRANSGENDER AND INTERSEX PEOPLE

In an historic advance for LGBTI rights, the government recognized those who wished to register as a "third gender" on national identity cards. Transgender people were recognized for the first time in the national census, on the orders of the Lahore High Court.

Despite this symbolic victory, transgender people continued to suffer harassment and violent attacks. In August, a 25-year-old transgender woman called Chanda was shot dead in Karachi. In September, five men broke into a house rented by a group of transgender women in Karachi city and subjected them to sexual violence, including the gang rape of two of the women.

WOMEN'S RIGHTS

Key legislation to protect women's rights failed to be passed and existing legislation was not enforced. The draft Sindh Criminal Law (Protection of Minorities) that criminalized forced conversions of women from religious minority groups remained unratified. A bill that would have equalized the age of consent to marriage for men and women by raising the minimum age of marriage for girls from 16 to 18 was blocked by the upper house of Parliament.

VIOLENCE AGAINST WOMEN AND GIRLS

Violence continued against women and girls, including killings by relatives committed in the name of so-called "honour". In Khyber Pakhtunkhwa northwest province, 94 women were murdered by close family members. In several cases, there was a failure to conduct investigations and hold the perpetrators accountable.

Parallel and informal justice systems continued to undermine the rule of law and to issue unjust "verdicts" that punished women and girls. In July, a village council in Multan district ordered and carried out the rape of a teenage girl in "revenge" for a crime allegedly committed by her brother. In August, the bodies of a teenage couple in Karachi were exhumed to reveal evidence of electric shocks. The couple had been sentenced to death by a *jirga* (tribal council). In September, a man in Peshawar city killed his two daughters because he suspected they had boyfriends.

The 2016 law, which brought the penalties for so-called "honour" crimes in line with murder, proved ineffective. The law, which provides for the death penalty, allows the judge to decide whether the crime was "honour-based". In some cases in 2017, the accused successfully claimed another motive and was pardoned by the victim's family under *qisas* and *diyat* laws, which allow for "blood money" and forgiveness instead of punishment.

REFUGEES AND ASYLUM-SEEKERS

The expulsion of Afghan refugees continued, albeit at a far slower rate. According to UNHCR, the UN refugee agency, 59,020 registered Afghan refugees were involuntarily returned to Afghanistan, compared to more than 380,000 in 2016 (the mass deportations triggered by escalating tensions between the Pakistani and Afghan governments). More than 2 million Afghans remained at risk of being forcibly returned as their legal residency status was due to expire at the end of the year.

POLICE AND SECURITY FORCES

The mandate of military courts to try civilian "terrorism" suspects was extended for a further two years. Reports continued that security forces were involved in human rights violations, including torture and other ill-treatment, arbitrary detention, extrajudicial executions and enforced disappearances. Impunity remained in the absence of independent, impartial mechanisms to investigate and bring perpetrators to justice. While the number of attacks by armed groups fell in 2017, scores of people died in bombings that targeted the security forces, religious minorities and others.

PALESTINE (STATE OF)

State of Palestine
Head of state: **Mahmoud Abbas**
Head of government: **Rami Hamdallah**

The Palestinian authorities in the West Bank and the Hamas de facto administration in the Gaza Strip escalated their restrictions on freedom of expression. In both areas, security forces tortured and otherwise ill-treated detainees with impunity. The authorities in the West Bank took punitive actions against the Hamas administration that further restricted the civilian population's access to vital services, exacerbating the humanitarian crisis resulting from Israel's military blockade of Gaza. Women in both areas continued to face discrimination and violence. Courts in Gaza handed down death sentences and Hamas carried out public executions; no executions were carried out in the West Bank.

BACKGROUND

Gaza remained under an Israeli air, sea and land blockade, in force since June 2007. Continuing restrictions on exports crippled the economy and exacerbated widespread impoverishment among Gaza's 2 million inhabitants. Egypt continued to enforce an almost total closure of the Rafah border crossing with Gaza, compounding the impact of the Israeli blockade.

Divisions between the Ramallah-based "national consensus" government and the Hamas de facto administration in Gaza persisted for much of the year. In an apparent effort to regain control of the Gaza Strip, the Palestinian authorities introduced a series of punitive measures against Hamas, which remained in place at the end of the year.

In October, the "national consensus" government held a cabinet meeting in Gaza, mediated by the Egyptian authorities, after Hamas announced its readiness to dismantle its committee administering Gaza, and called for legislative and presidential elections to be held in the West Bank and Gaza. Later that month, the two rival political parties Hamas and Fatah signed a reconciliation agreement in Cairo, Egypt, aimed at ending the decade-long split between the West Bank and Hamas-run Gaza. In November, the "national consensus" government took over control of the border crossing between Gaza and Egypt, and checkpoints near crossings with Israel.

FREEDOMS OF EXPRESSION AND ASSEMBLY

As political in-fighting continued, authorities in the West Bank and Gaza used threats and intimidation against activists and journalists to suppress peaceful expression, including reporting and criticism. According to the NGO Palestinian Centre for Development and Media Freedoms, the Palestinian authorities in the West Bank were responsible for 147 attacks on media freedom during the year. These included arbitrary arrests, ill-treatment during interrogations, confiscation of equipment, physical assaults, bans on reporting and the banning of 29 websites critical of the West Bank authorities. Hamas authorities in Gaza were responsible for 35 such attacks.

In January, security forces in Gaza violently dispersed a protest in Jabalia refugee camp against Hamas' mismanagement of the electricity crisis (see below). Activists and organizers were detained, threatened and in some cases tortured for organizing the demonstrations. Activist Mohammad al-Talowli was arrested on three occasions throughout the year for his role in organizing the protests, and received death threats.

Journalists working with media affiliated with the West Bank authorities were barred from working freely in Gaza. Palestine TV correspondent Fouad Jaradeh was arrested by Hamas Internal Security Forces on 6 June and tried before a military court for "collaborating with Ramallah". He was released in August.

The Electronic Crimes Law (Law 16 of 2017) was adopted in July. It permitted the arbitrary detention of journalists, whistle-blowers and others who criticize the authorities online. The law allowed for prison sentences and up to 25 years' hard labour for anyone deemed to have disturbed "public order", "national unity" or "social peace". An amended draft proposed removing several repressive provisions, but left in place others that allowed arbitrary restrictions on the rights to freedom of expression, privacy and protection of data. The draft had not been made public by the end of the year.

Six Palestinian journalists were charged under the Electronic Crimes Law in August. In June and July, at least 10 journalists were summoned for interrogation by Preventative Security Forces for publicly criticizing the law. Human rights defenders were subjected to interrogation, harassment and threats in relation to their human rights work, including criticism of the Electronic Crimes Law.

Prominent human rights defender Issa Amro was detained for a week in September and charged with several offences under the Electronic Crimes Law and the 1960 Jordanian Penal code, which remained in force in the West Bank.

TORTURE AND OTHER ILL-TREATMENT

Torture and other ill-treatment of detainees remained common and was committed with impunity by Palestinian police and security forces in the West Bank, and by Hamas police and security forces in Gaza. The Independent Commission for Human Rights (ICHR), Palestine's national human rights institution, received hundreds of allegations of torture and other ill-treatment of detainees held in the West Bank and Gaza.

In September, a 16-year-old boy and another detainee died in unclear circumstances in Hamas-controlled detention centres in Gaza City. The Public Prosecution in Gaza announced that it would carry out an investigation; this had not been concluded by the end of the year.

At least one activist detained in relation to his role leading the protests against Hamas'

mismanagement of the electricity crisis said that Hamas' internal security forces tortured him in custody. He reported being beaten with a plastic pipe, blindfolded, and forced to sit in strenuous positions with his hands cuffed for around four days. Others reported ill-treatment.

EXCESSIVE USE OF FORCE

Security forces used excessive force to disperse protests in the West Bank and Gaza.

On 12 March, Palestinian security forces used excessive force to violently suppress a peaceful protest outside the Ramallah District Court in the West Bank. At least 13 men and eight women were injured; among them were four journalists covering the protest. Seventeen people were hospitalized. Those injured suffered bruises from heavy beatings with wooden batons or after being struck by tear gas canisters. Farid al-Atrash, a lawyer, human rights defender and the head of ICHR's Bethlehem office, reported being beaten to the ground by police using wooden batons.

A Fact-Finding Commission established by Prime Minister Hamdallah to investigate the incident found that the use of force to disperse the protest violated government regulations. It made a series of recommendations, including reparation and accountability measures. Despite the Prime Minister's stated commitment to uphold the recommendations, these remained unimplemented, and none of the officers responsible for the violence were brought to justice.

WOMEN'S RIGHTS

Women and girls continued to face discrimination in law and in practice, and were inadequately protected against sexual and other gender-based violence, including so-called "honour" killings. At least 28 women and girls were reported to have been killed by male relatives in "honour" killings, according to civil society.

Under provisions of the Jordanian Penal Code, judges were able to use stereotypes of women's sexuality to justify minimizing the sentences of those convicted of "honour" killings.

Article 308 of the Jordanian Penal Code, which allows for those who commit rape or sexual assault to escape punishment by marrying the victim, remained in force.

More than three years after the State of Palestine acceded to CEDAW, national legislation had not been amended in line with CEDAW. The applicable Jordanian Personal Status law continued to discriminate against women with regard to marriage, inheritance, divorce, guardianship and property rights.

ECONOMIC, SOCIAL AND CULTURAL RIGHTS

The Palestinian government based in Ramallah imposed several punitive measures against Gaza in a bid to pressure the Hamas administration to give up control of Gaza. These measures impeded the civilian population's access to medical care, essential services including water and electricity, and education. This contributed to violations of the rights to health, an adequate standard of living, and education.

In May, the West Bank authorities informed Israel that they would cover only 70% of the monthly cost of Israeli electricity supplies to Gaza due to Hamas' failure to reimburse them. As a result, access to electricity in Gaza was reduced from an average of eight hours per day to between two to four hours per day.

The West Bank authorities cut the salaries of some 60,000 civil servants in Gaza by 30%, undermining their right to an adequate standard of living and prompting mass protests.

According to the UN Office for the Co-ordination of Humanitarian Affairs, in March the West Bank authorities suspended the payments for transfers of people in need of medical treatment outside Gaza, delaying the referrals of some 1,400 patients. NGOs reported that procedural delays resulted in the deaths of several patients, including babies. The UN reported delays in the transfer of essential medicines and medical supplies to hospitals in Gaza, affecting patients' long-term health. Hamas authorities reported a shortage of baby formula, blaming West Bank authorities.

DEATH PENALTY

The death penalty was applied in Gaza. Six people were executed after civil and military courts sentenced them to death after convicting them of "collaboration with Israel" or other offences.

In May, Hamas executed three men in Gaza for allegedly assassinating a senior Hamas commander. They were sentenced to death in a trial that lasted one week and consisted of four brief sessions only. The sentences were carried out in a public square in Gaza City; two men were hanged and one executed by firing squad. The executions were shown live on social media.

No one was sentenced to death or executed in the West Bank.

IMPUNITY

Impunity for human rights abuses including unlawful killings and torture in the West Bank and Gaza persisted. No criminal investigations were launched into the apparent extrajudicial executions of Fares Halawa and Khaled al-Aghbar by Palestinian security forces in Nablus in August 2016, nor was anyone brought to justice for the death of Ahmad Izzat Halawa under torture in Jneid prison in the same month.

In Gaza, Hamas authorities took no steps to prosecute members of its forces and Hamas' military wing, the 'Izz al-Din al-Qassam Brigades, for extrajudicial executions they carried out in 2014 and 2016.

PAPUA NEW GUINEA

Independent State of Papua New Guinea
Head of state: **Queen Elizabeth II, represented by Robert Dadae (replaced Michael Ogio in February)**
Head of government: **Peter Charles Paire O'Neill**

Violence by security forces remained endemic; prisoners, refugees and women were the most frequent victims. Disputes about elections led to violent clashes and deaths in some parts of the country. More than 800 refugees and asylum-seekers remained trapped in Papua New Guinea after being forcibly sent there by the Australian authorities. Two refugees with serious mental health issues died, raising concerns about inadequate health care.

REFUGEES AND ASYLUM-SEEKERS

Australia's policy of detaining and processing refugees on Manus Island, Papua New Guinea (PNG), resulted in the systematic violation of the rights of hundreds of individuals. In February, Iranian refugee Loghman Sawari was detained and charged after he was forcibly returned to PNG from Fiji, where he had fled to seek asylum. Papua New Guinea claimed he had provided false information to obtain a passport. However, by September all charges against him had been dismissed by the courts for lack of evidence.

Two refugees died (in August and October) in suspected suicides. The circumstances of the deaths were being investigated by the PNG Coroner.

In September, around 25 refugees were transferred to the USA. The vast majority of refugees and asylum-seekers remained trapped on Manus Island.

On 23 and 24 October, refugees were forcibly removed from the Lombrum refugee centre by PNG immigration and police officers armed with metal poles and transferred to Hillside Haus, West Lorengau Haus or the East Lorengau Transit Centre; some sustained minor injuries. Facilities at Hillside Haus and West Lorengau Haus were inadequate, with frequent water and power cuts. Refugees were subject to threats and attacks following the transfers.

POLICE AND SECURITY FORCES

In April, PNG navy officers fired shots at the Manus Island refugee centre at Lombrum after a dispute about use of a nearby football field. Initial reports by PNG and Australia suggested that only one shot was fired into the air and was not a serious security breach. However, after forensic evidence established that multiple shots had been fired directly into the centre, putting the lives of refugees, immigration officials and private contractors at risk, Australia confirmed that nine people were injured, including three refugees. No investigation had taken place by the end of the year.

In May, PNG security forces shot and killed 17 detainees during an escape attempt from a prison in Lae city. The prison had previously been noted for poor conditions, lack of sanitation and overcrowding. The authorities stated that investigations would be conducted into the incident but no further information was received by the end of the year. Around half of those detained at the facility were being held on remand and many had waited years for their trials.

ELECTION-RELATED VIOLENCE

National elections were held from late June to August. Allegations of corruption, mismanagement, widespread exclusion of voters and a heavy-handed response by the authorities led to a tense atmosphere, in some cases involving violence or arrests.

By mid-August, violence over disputed seats following the election resulted in the deaths of at least 20 people and the burning down of some 120 houses in Enga and Southern Highlands provinces.

GENDER-RELATED VIOLENCE

Gender-related violence continued to be a major issue. On 14 October, prominent journalist Rosalyn Albaniel Evara died. Family members and close friends claimed she was a victim of domestic violence. No charges had been brought by the end of the year.

In November, a six-year-old girl was cut and burned following accusations of sorcery in Enga. Her mother, Kepari Leniata, had been publicly burned to death in Mount Hagen in 2013; no perpetrators have been brought to justice. Authorities often failed to adequately investigate or prosecute cases of violence following sorcery accusations because of the deeply held customary beliefs of police officers and the community.

In November, the PNG government announced 25 million Kina (USD7.8m) in funding to end violence against women, set up child protection, and to address violence following sorcery accusations.

PARAGUAY

Republic of Paraguay
Head of state and government: **Horacio Manuel Cartes Jara**

Indigenous Peoples continued to be denied their rights to land and to free, prior and informed consent on projects affecting them. A bill to eliminate all forms of discrimination was pending approval at the end of the year. There were reports that human rights defenders and journalists were persecuted amid violations of the right to freedom of expression, and that police used excessive force to repress demonstrations.

FREEDOMS OF EXPRESSION AND ASSEMBLY

In March, journalists Menchi Barriocanal and Oscar Acosta reported on a secret attempt by senators to amend the Constitution to allow presidential re-elections. Protests erupted on 31 March and 1 April, with some protesters setting fire to the Congress building.

President Cartes and ruling party representatives publicly accused the two journalists of inciting violence and threatened them with arrest. Other media workers critical of the government's reaction to the protests also reported being harassed by the authorities.

On 1 April, opposition activist Rodrigo Quintana was killed by police in the context of the protests. Dozens of people were injured, more than 200 were detained, and local organizations reported allegations of torture and other ill-treatment by security forces.

In June, in response to allegations that 23 journalists had been attacked by police during the protests in March, National Police adopted a security protocol for journalists at risk.

INTERNATIONAL SCRUTINY

In September, the UN Committee against Torture issued concluding observations and recommendations on Paraguay, including to ensure that all persons deprived of their liberty enjoy all legal safeguards from the beginning of the detention, including the rights to access a lawyer of their choice, to be promptly examined by a doctor respecting their confidentiality and privacy, and to be given access to an independent medical practitioner if they so request.

The Committee also recommended prompt, impartial and effective investigations into all allegations of excessive use of force, arbitrary detention and acts of torture and other ill-treatment by law enforcement officials, including those reported during the demonstrations of 31 March and 1 April, and to ensure that the perpetrators are prosecuted and the victims receive adequate reparation.

In addition, the Committee recommended that an independent, effective, exhaustive and impartial investigation be conducted into allegations of disproportionate use of lethal force, torture and other ill-treatment during the confrontation in Curuguaty in 2012, as well as alleged violations of due process during the judicial proceedings against 11 *campesinos* (peasant farmers) related to this case.

On 16 August, Congress approved a law to implement the Rome Statute of the International Criminal Court (ICC) and ensure co-operation with the ICC. On 23 August the Executive sent to Congress for ratification the Kampala Amendments on the crime of aggression and on Article 8 of the Rome Statute.

INDIGENOUS PEOPLES' RIGHTS

Negotiations began between the government and representatives of the Ayoreo Totobiegosode Indigenous Peoples living in voluntary isolation, with a view to implementing the precautionary measures granted by the Inter-American Commission on Human Rights (IACHR) to protect these communities from third parties seeking to access their ancestral land, and to reach a friendly settlement in a case pending before the IACHR for the violation of their rights.

The Yakye Axa community remained without access to their lands despite a ruling from the Inter-American Court of Human Rights ordering the government to construct an access route. The case regarding the ownership of land expropriated from the Sawhoyamaxa community, which has a similar ruling from the Inter-American Court in their favour, had also not been resolved by the government.

RIGHT TO HOUSING AND FORCED EVICTIONS

In September, the Chamber of Deputies upheld the Executive's veto of a bill that would have expropriated 900 hectares of land from its current occupants to return it to the Guahory *campesino* community, who were forcibly evicted in 2016.

In October, human rights organizations reported that one year after the forced eviction of the Avá Guaraní de Sauce community in connection with the Itaipu hydroelectric dam, no progress had been made regarding the restitution of their lands. As a result, the community withdrew from dialogue with the authorities.

DETENTION

In September, two boys held at a juvenile detention centre in Ciudad del Este died in a fire, and 12 others were injured. The National Mechanism for the Prevention of Torture had reported in 2016 the lack of fire protection and evacuation protocols in the centre.

SEXUAL AND REPRODUCTIVE RIGHTS

In July, President Cartes vetoed Bill No. 5833/2017, which aimed to establish a civil registry record of "deaths of conceived unborn children". In August, the Chamber of Deputies and the Senate rejected the veto and approved the bill, which was promulgated by the President at the end of the year. The bill was denounced by human rights organizations as introducing an almost absolute protection of the foetus, which could potentially take precedence over the rights to life, physical integrity and health of women and girls.

In October, the Ministry of Education and Science passed a resolution banning public education materials on "gender theory", which in practice restricted materials related to gender equality, reproductive rights, sexuality and non-discrimination.

PERU

Republic of Peru
Head of state and government: Pedro Pablo Kuczynski Godard

Land and territory-related rights continued to be threatened by the adoption of laws weakening the protection framework for the rights of Indigenous Peoples and undermining the right to free, prior and informed consent. Violence against women and the rate of pregnancy among girls continued to increase without an effective response from the state. A presidential pardon and grace granted to former Peruvian president Alberto Fujimori on humanitarian grounds raised serious concerns regarding impunity and the respect of due process guarantees.

HUMAN RIGHTS DEFENDERS

Both state and non-state actors continued to threaten and harass human rights defenders, particularly those working on issues related to land, territory and the environment, in the absence of policies for their effective protection or public recognition of the importance of their work. Human rights defenders were criminalized and harassed through judicial proceedings with high penalties, and they usually lacked financial resources for adequate legal representation.

In May, the Supreme Court confirmed the acquittal of Máxima Acuña, putting an end to an unfounded criminal proceeding for land seizure that had lasted for more than five years. Máxima Acuña and her family continued to report acts of intimidation, while the ownership of the lands on which they lived was still pending judicial resolution.

INDIGENOUS PEOPLES' RIGHTS

The issuance of a series of regulations lowering environmental standards and procedures for access to land aimed at promoting extractive or infrastructure projects continued to conflict with the protection framework for Indigenous Peoples' rights.

Indigenous Peoples of the Cuninico community in Loreto region and the communities of Espinar in Cusco region were still suffering a health crisis due to their only water sources being contaminated with toxic metals, while the government failed to undertake necessary actions to provide them with specialized medical attention or access to clean and safe water.

No substantial progress was made in the case of four Asháninka Indigenous leaders who were killed in Ucayali region in 2014 after reporting death threats from illegal loggers to the authorities.

IMPUNITY

One year after its approval, the National Plan for the Search for Disappeared Persons was still not implemented.

On 24 December, President Kuczynski granted a humanitarian pardon and grace to former president Alberto Fujimori who, since 2009, had been serving a 25-year sentence for crimes against humanity. The decision was seriously flawed by lack of transparency,

impartiality, respect for due process and participation of the victims and their families, notably given the severity of the crimes under international law.

In June, the Supreme Court of Chile confirmed the extension of Alberto Fujimori's extradition request to include the killing of six residents of Pativilca district in the department of Lima in January 1992. In July, the Third National Criminal Prosecutor's Office of Peru accused Alberto Fujimori of responsibility for this crime, committed by his subordinates in complicity with others. Nevertheless, the grace granted to him on 24 December lifted any criminal proceedings against him, therefore raising concerns of impunity in the Pativilca case.

In August, military officers were sentenced for the torture, enforced disappearance and extrajudicial execution of 53 people in Los Cabitos military barracks in Ayacucho in 1983.

In September, the trial began of former navy personnel charged with killing more than 100 people during a riot in El Frontón prison in 1986, a charge which could amount to a crime against humanity.

VIOLENCE AGAINST WOMEN AND GIRLS

Between January and September the Attorney General's Office registered 17,182 complaints of "crimes against sexual freedom", which include rape and other forms of sexual violence. Only 2,008 (11%) of the complaints were followed up by the judiciary. The registry of complaints did not list the gender of complainants.

In the same period, the Ministry for Women reported 94 cases of femicide.

There were no concrete advances in policy or legislation to combat violence against women and girls.

SEXUAL AND REPRODUCTIVE RIGHTS

Pregnancy rates among girls remained high. Official records showed that at least 12 girls aged 11 and under, and 6,516 girls aged between 12 and 17, gave birth between January and March.

Abortion continued to be criminalized in all circumstances except when the health or life of the pregnant woman or girl is at risk. The debate on a bill for decriminalization of abortion in cases of rape was pending before Congress.

More than 5,000 women had been included in the Registry of Victims of Forced Sterilization. Despite this, there was no progress in obtaining justice and providing reparation.

RIGHTS OF LESBIAN, GAY, BISEXUAL, TRANSGENDER AND INTERSEX PEOPLE

Peru continued to lack specific legislation recognizing and protecting the rights of LGBTI people, who continued to face discrimination and violence based on their sexual orientation or gender identity.

In May, Congress partially repealed Legislative Decree 1323, including the section which established "sexual orientation and gender identity" as aggravating grounds for certain crimes and as elements of the crime of discrimination.

Transgender people continued to lack social and legal recognition of their gender identity, and were deprived of their rights to freedom of movement, health, work, housing and education, among others.

PHILIPPINES

Republic of the Philippines
Head of state and government: **Rodrigo Roa Duterte**

Thousands of unlawful killings by police and other armed individuals continued as part of the government's anti-drugs campaign. Human rights defenders critical of the campaign were singled out and targeted by the President and his allies. A state of martial law was declared and extended twice on the island of Mindanao, raising fears of further human rights abuses. Attempts to reintroduce the death penalty stalled at the Senate after a bill was passed by the House of Representatives.

EXTRAJUDICIAL EXECUTIONS AND SUMMARY KILLINGS

The deliberate, unlawful and widespread killings of thousands of alleged drug offenders appeared to be systematic, planned, organized and encouraged by the authorities, and may have constituted crimes against humanity. Most of those killed were from poor urban communities.[1] Despite evidence that police and gunmen with links to the police killed or paid others to kill alleged drug offenders in a wave of extrajudicial executions, authorities continued to deny any unlawful deaths. In January, the President suspended the violent anti-drugs campaign for one month following the killing in police custody of a Republic of Korea national. In March, the unlawful killings of suspected drug offenders in police operations resumed, as did drug-related killings by other armed individuals. The number of killings on a single day in police anti-drug operations reached 32 in August. Police continued to rely on unverified lists of people allegedly using or selling drugs. In September, the killings of three teenagers within a few weeks sparked a national outcry. CCTV footage and witness statements contradicted police accounts of the killing of one of the three, 17-year-old Kian delos Santos, who according to forensic experts and witnesses appeared to have been extrajudicially executed.[2]

In October, President Duterte announced that the Philippine Drug Enforcement Agency would take over the anti-drugs campaign from the Philippine National Police. However, it was announced less than two months later that police might rejoin anti-drug operations, despite unresolved issues. Meaningful investigations into killings of alleged drugs offenders failed to take place; no police officers were known to have been held to account. Relatives of victims continued to be fearful of reprisals if they filed complaints against police.

FREEDOM OF EXPRESSION

Human rights defenders, in particular those critical of the government, faced threats and intimidation. Journalists worked in dangerous and at times deadly environments. In August, radio broadcaster Rudy Alicaway and columnist Leodoro Diaz were shot dead in the provinces of Zamboanga del Sur and Sultan Kudarat respectively. Radio broadcaster Christopher Iban Lozada was killed by unidentified gunmen in Surigao del Sur in October.

HUMAN RIGHTS DEFENDERS

Attacks against human rights defenders increased, as the President encouraged police to "shoot" human rights defenders who were "obstructing justice". In February, Senator Leila de Lima, former justice secretary and former chair of the Philippines Commission on Human Rights, was arrested on charges of drug trafficking. At the end of the year she remained in detention at the Philippine National Police headquarters in the capital, Manila, and faced between 12 years' and life imprisonment if convicted. It was believed that the charges were politically motivated and that she had been deliberately targeted by the government since emerging as the most prominent critic of the "war on drugs".[3] Attacks against the Commission on Human Rights also intensified, as lawmakers accused it of "siding with suspected criminals" in the anti-drugs campaign and caused uproar by approving a budget of just USD20, before the decision was overturned in the Senate. Human rights groups expressed concern at reports of increased numbers of arbitrary arrests and detention, and extrajudicial executions of political activists and individuals aligned with the left, following a declaration of martial law in the island of Mindanao, and as peace talks between communist rebels, the New People's Army and the government broke down.

DEATH PENALTY

International groups called on the government to abandon its plan, proposed in 2016, to reintroduce the death penalty, citing the Philippines' international obligations and in particular as a state party to the Second Optional Protocol to the ICCPR, aiming at the abolition of the death penalty. A draft law to reintroduce the punishment was adopted by the House of Representatives in March but stalled in the Senate after facing opposition.

INTERNAL ARMED CONFLICT

President Duterte declared martial law in the island of Mindanao on 23 May. Fighting had erupted in the city of Marawi between government forces and an alliance of militants, including the Maute group, which pledged allegiance to the armed group Islamic State (IS). The conflict ended in October when the military killed several militant leaders.[4] Militants allied with IS targeted Christian civilians, committing at least 25 extrajudicial killings and carrying out mass hostage-taking and extensive looting of civilian property, which may have amounted to war crimes. Philippine armed forces detained and ill-treated fleeing civilians, and also engaged in looting. Their extensive bombing of militant-held areas of Marawi city wiped out entire neighbourhoods and killed civilians, which highlighted the need for an investigation into their compliance with international humanitarian law. In response, the Philippine armed forces said they would probe allegations of war crimes. Martial law was extended for a second time in December, amid concerns that military rule could allow for further human rights abuses.

TORTURE AND OTHER ILL-TREATMENT

In April a secret detention cell was found in a police station in Manila. The Philippines Commission on Human Rights referred the discovery, along with allegations of torture and other ill-treatment, to the Office of the Ombudsman for investigation.

Security forces were accused of torture and extrajudicial executions of those rounded up during five months of fighting between the Philippine armed forces and the Maute group in Marawi.

A bill to establish a National Preventative Mechanism in accordance with the Philippines' obligations under the Optional Protocol to the UN Convention against Torture had not been adopted by the end of the year.

CHILDREN'S RIGHTS

President Duterte pledged to lower the minimum age of criminal responsibility, generating wide condemnation from children's rights organizations and the UN. A bill to amend the Juvenile Justice and Welfare Act, which was adopted on 23 May by the Sub-Committee on Correctional Reforms, retained the minimum age of criminal responsibility as 15, but introduced provisions that placed children as young as nine in crowded and often unsanitary short-term institutions for rehabilitation or as they awaited court disposition. An additional bill by a lawmaker was filed later in the year, seeking to lower the minimum age of criminal responsibility to 12, but remained pending.

RIGHT TO HEALTH

The nationwide anti-drugs campaign undermined people's right to the enjoyment of the highest attainable standard of physical and mental health. Many drug users were forced into compulsory and inadequate treatment and rehabilitation initiatives, which prevented them from accessing essential health services and harm reduction programmes.

SEXUAL AND REPRODUCTIVE RIGHTS

In January, President Duterte signed an executive order to strengthen the implementation of the Reproductive Health Act of 2012 which promised to provide greater access to family planning and birth control services.

---

1. 'If you are poor, you are killed': Extrajudicial executions in the Philippines' war on drugs (ASA 35/5517/2017)

2. Philippines: State hearing highlights deadly consequences for children in , war on drugs' (News story, 24 August)

3. Philippines: Impending arrest of Senator politically motivated (ASA 35/5772/2017)

4. 'Battle of Marawi': Death and destruction in the Philippines (ASA 35/7427/2017)

POLAND

Republic of Poland
Head of state: **Andrzej Duda**
Head of government: **Mateusz Morawiecki (replaced Beata Szydło in December)**

The government continued its efforts to exert political control over the judiciary, NGOs and the media. Hundreds of protesters faced criminal sanctions for participating in peaceful assemblies. Women and girls continued to face systemic barriers in accessing safe and legal abortion.

LEGAL, CONSTITUTIONAL OR INSTITUTIONAL DEVELOPMENTS

In July, the European Commission stated that the independence of the Constitutional Tribunal had been "seriously undermined" and raised concerns that the constitutionality of Polish laws "could not be effectively guaranteed". The government also attempted to extend its influence over other branches of the judiciary, including the Supreme Court, the National Council of the Judiciary and Common Courts.

Between May and July, Parliament adopted four laws on the reform of the judiciary. These provoked a strong response from the public, intergovernmental organizations and NGOs which expressed alarm over the waning independence of the judiciary and rule of law. The changes would have given the Minister of Justice control over the Supreme Court and would have also undermined the independence of the National Council of Judiciary, a self-regulating body of judges. On 24 July, the President vetoed two of the adopted laws, the amendment of the Law on the National Council of Judiciary and of the Law on the Supreme Court.

The President did, however, sign the amendment to the Law on Common Courts, which entered into force in August. The amendment empowered the Minister of Justice to appoint and dismiss presidents and vice-presidents of courts. In response, the European Commission started infringement proceedings against Poland for breaching EU law on the grounds that the law, which introduced different retirement ages for men and women judges, was discriminatory. The proceedings were pending at the end of the year. The Commission stated that it would also trigger proceedings under Article 7(1), which could result in sanctions if any law giving the Minister of Justice control over the Supreme Court were adopted.

In October, the daily *Gazeta Wyborcza* reported that six prosecutors faced disciplinary proceedings for criticizing a 2016 reform that merged the functions of the national Prosecutor General and the Minister of Justice, giving the Minister undue influence over judicial proceedings.

In December, the Parliament adopted amendments to the Law on the National Council of Judiciary and of the Law on the Supreme Court which subjected the judiciary to the political control of the government. On 20 December, the European Commission, in an unprecedented move, triggered Article 7.1 of the EU Treaty against Poland. The process could lead to sanctions for undermining human rights and the rule of law in Poland.

FREEDOM OF ASSEMBLY

Public protests continued throughout 2017 in opposition to government policies and legislation on the judiciary, the right to peaceful assembly, the functioning of NGOs, media freedom, sexual and reproductive rights, and the right to housing. The largest demonstrations occurred in July, when thousands of people in over 100 cities took to the streets to protest against the reform of the judiciary. Law enforcement officials responded with heavy-handed security measures in the area around Parliament and at the Presidential Palace, inhibiting the demonstrators' ability to protest. The police contained groups of peaceful protesters; used constant and varied forms of monitoring and surveillance at the protests by surveillance teams that also asked protesters to provide identification; used threats of sanctions; and, for some, the pursuit of criminal charges and prosecutions. Dozens of protesters faced proceedings in court under the Code of Petty Offences and in some cases also under the Criminal Code; proceedings were still pending at the end of the year. Hundreds of others were summoned to police stations in relation to their participation in protests.

In April, an amendment to the Law on Assemblies that prioritized "cyclical" assemblies in central Warsaw, entered into force. The law had been used to ban alternative or counter-demonstrations in favour of monthly pro-government assemblies and to grant a pro-government group regular access to the public space near the Presidential Palace.

FREEDOM OF EXPRESSION – JOURNALISTS

Using new powers conferred by the 2015 media law, the Minister of Treasury dismissed a number of directors and supervisory councils of public TV and radio stations. The Minister appointed new directors without consulting the independent National Broadcasting Council, resulting in government control over all public media outlets. By October, over 234 journalists working in public broadcasting, including trade union leaders, had been demoted, dismissed, or forced to resign.

Investigative journalist Tomasz Piątek was at risk of criminal charges for his book published in June that alleged a link between the Minister of National Defence and the Russian intelligence services. In late June, the Minister filed a criminal complaint against Tomasz Piątek, alleging a violation of the laws on "using violence or unlawful threat [which] affects a government authority performing its duty" and "insulting a public official in the course and in connection with the performance of [their] duties". On 26 June, the complaint was forwarded to the Regional Prosecutor's Office in Warsaw. In October, the Minister publicly accused the journalist of aiming to prevent the reform of Poland's army and that the allegations presented in the book were "an integral part of the hybrid war against Poland". No charges against Tomasz Piątek had been formally pressed by the end of the year.

SEXUAL AND REPRODUCTIVE RIGHTS

In October, the President expressed support for a legislative proposal drafted by anti-choice groups which would prohibit abortion in cases of severe or fatal fetal impairment.

In June, Parliament adopted an amendment to the Law on State Funded Health Services under which emergency contraception became accessible only on prescription, contrary to international recommendations on emergency contraception.

FREEDOM OF ASSOCIATION

On 4 October, one day after a national protest against restrictive policies on abortion, the police simultaneously raided four offices of women's rights NGOs in different cities that had supported the action. The police confiscated hard drives and computer data, including databases with information on individuals and medical reports of victims of domestic violence. The authorities claimed that the action was part of an investigation of former staff members of the Ministry of Justice for alleged maladministration of funds.

In October, Parliament adopted the Law on the National Freedom Institute, a body that will decide on state funding to NGOs. Civil society groups raised serious concerns that the law provided for the Institute to be under the effective control of the government, which would potentially undermine the ability of organizations that were critical of the government to access such funds.

COUNTER-TERROR AND SECURITY

The Council of Europe Commissioner for Human Rights and NGOs raised concerns over the lack of due process in cases of deportations where national security grounds were invoked.

In April, an Iraqi student was deported to Iraq after the Refugee Board rejected his asylum application alleging that he represented a "threat to national security". The evidence against him, collected by the Internal Security Agency, was not made available to his legal representatives. The NGO Helsinki Foundation for Human Rights argued that the denial of access to the case files had effectively prevented the applicant from knowing the detailed grounds for the rejection of his asylum claim. In August, the Foundation appealed against the decision.

REFUGEES AND ASYLUM-SEEKERS

There were ongoing reports of push-backs of asylum-seekers at a border crossing with Belarus. The European Court of Human Rights requested information from Poland regarding four cases in which the applicants claimed that they were repeatedly denied entry to seek international protection and that this put them at risk of *refoulement* – forcible return to a country where they were at real risk of persecution. In late August, the NGO Human Constanta, which is based in Belarus, filed another case against Poland with the UN Human Rights Committee for the breach of the *non-refoulement* principle. The cases remained pending at the end of the year.

In June, the European Commission started infringement procedures against Poland, as well as the Czech Republic and Hungary, for refusing to participate in the refugee relocation scheme from EU member states such as Greece and Italy. In December, the European Commission decided to step up the action against all three countries and referred them to the Court of Justice of the European Union.

PORTUGAL

Portuguese Republic
Head of state: **Marcelo Rebelo de Sousa**
Head of government: **António Costa**

Housing conditions for Roma and people of African descent remained inadequate. Portugal relocated fewer asylum-seekers

than it was required to under the EU Relocation Programme. The government proposed legislation to strengthen the protection of transgender and intersex people's rights. Parliament extended protection against hate speech and discrimination.

RIGHT TO HOUSING AND FORCED EVICTIONS

In February, in her report of a December 2016 visit to Lisbon, the capital, and Porto, the UN Special Rapporteur on the right to adequate housing noted that many Roma and people of African descent were living in substandard conditions and often faced discrimination in accessing adequate housing. She urged the authorities, among other things, to address inadequate housing in informal settlements as a priority and to ensure that evictions and demolitions did not result in homelessness and were carried out in compliance with international standards.

In March, the Council of Europe Commissioner for Human Rights visited Lisbon and Torres Vedras; he also expressed concern about the substandard and often segregated Roma settlements and called for new social housing programmes for all vulnerable groups to be developed.

Residents of the informal settlement of Bairro 6 de Maio in the Amadora municipality, near Lisbon, feared their houses could be demolished and they could be forcibly evicted without access to adequate processes. Many of the residents were of African and Roma descent.

TORTURE AND OTHER ILL-TREATMENT

In July, the Public Prosecutor of the Amadora municipality charged 18 police officers for the ill-treatment of six men of African descent in February 2015 (the charges against one officer were struck out in December). The officers were accused of torture, unlawful imprisonment, grave abuse of power and other offences aggravated by racism. In September, the investigating judge rejected the Public Prosecutor's request that the officers be suspended pending trial.

DETENTION

The publication of the Council of Europe Committee for the Prevention of Torture's report of its visit to Portugal in September-October 2016 was pending at the end of the year. The visit focused on the application of safeguards against torture and other ill-treatment of persons in custody; conditions of detention in prison and on remand; and the situation of patients in forensic psychiatric units.

REFUGEES AND ASYLUM-SEEKERS

Portugal relocated 1,518 asylum-seekers from Greece and Italy, leaving over 1,400 places to fill according to the legal commitment it had made under the EU Relocation Programme. However, the authorities reported that of those relocated, over 720 persons had left the country by the end of the year.

RIGHTS OF LESBIAN, GAY, BISEXUAL, TRANSGENDER AND INTERSEX PEOPLE

In April, a government-sponsored bill aiming to bring the protection of LGBTI people's rights in line with international standards was presented to Parliament. The bill was being considered at the end of the year. The bill proposed removing the requirement for psychological assessments and introduced the requirement for expressed consent to any medical treatment aimed at determining the gender for intersex people, including children.

DISCRIMINATION

In August, Parliament approved legislation strengthening protection against discrimination. The criminal code was amended to include descent and physical and mental disability among the grounds for criminal liability for discriminatory conduct. A separate offence of incitement to hatred and violence based on discriminatory motives was also introduced.

VIOLENCE AGAINST WOMEN

In October, the Porto Court of Appeal upheld the suspended sentence of two men convicted in 2015 of assaulting a woman. The woman's former partner abducted her and her former husband beat her with a nail-spiked bat. The judges justified their decision by referring to religious beliefs and gender stereotypes, stating that "the adultery of the woman was a very serious attack on the honour and dignity of a man." In December, the Superior Council of the Judiciary opened disciplinary proceedings, which were pending at the end of the year, against the two judges responsible for the ruling.

PUERTO RICO

Commonwealth of Puerto Rico
Head of state: Donald Trump (replaced Barack Obama in January)
Head of government: Ricardo Rosselló Nevares

Hurricane Maria caused deaths and widespread damage to infrastructure, housing and essential services. Protections for transgender people and of freedoms of expression and association suffered setbacks. Austerity measures put human rights at risk. Police used excessive force to quell protests on International Workers' Day.

BACKGROUND

On 20 September, Hurricane Maria caused the largest natural disaster on the island in modern history. According to the authorities, at least 64 people died, but due to uncertainties regarding the actual number, the Governor announced that a new investigation would be carried out. The hurricane destroyed infrastructure and buildings, leaving many people without housing and access to potable water, food, and essential services including medical treatment and education. The slow response of the local and federal government resulted in a deepening of the humanitarian crisis caused by the hurricane. In October, UN human rights experts noted that the lack of an effective emergency response came in the context of an "existing dire situation caused by debt and austerity measures". In

December, the Inter-American Commission on Human Rights expressed concern over the emergency and reconstruction efforts.

RIGHTS OF LESBIAN, GAY, BISEXUAL, TRANSGENDER AND INTERSEX PEOPLE

In February, the Department of Education eliminated the curriculum for gender perspective in public schools, which was established by the previous administration to ensure equality between genders in education and in all Department of Education projects; the new curriculum would only have a binary conception of gender. The Department also removed guidelines allowing public-school students to wear school uniform according to their gender identity.

Protections for transgender people suffered a further setback when the President of the Senate signed an administrative order eliminating protective measures that previously allowed employees of the legislative branch to dress and use bathrooms according to their gender identity.

In July, Governor Rosselló signed an executive order for the creation of an LGBTI advisory council to promote and implement initiatives for LGBTI people across governmental departments and in collaboration with civil society.

FREEDOMS OF EXPRESSION AND ASSEMBLY

On 19 May, Governor Rosselló signed into law several amendments to the Criminal Code, making illegal certain conduct such as blocking entry to construction sites or educational institutions – tactics traditionally used by peaceful protesters – thus potentially undermining the rights to freedom of expression and peaceful assembly. The amendments were rushed through Parliament with limited consultation with civil society and entered into force immediately after their approval, without the usual 90-day waiting period. The amendments appeared to be a direct attempt by the government to discourage peaceful protests.

ECONOMIC, SOCIAL AND CULTURAL RIGHTS

Puerto Rico continued to face a serious financial crisis as a result of crippling external debt of more than USD70 billion, according to figures from the authorities.

The Financial Oversight and Management Board, established by US authorities in 2016, implemented several austerity measures during the year. These measures could have negative consequences on human rights, in particular access to health care, housing, education and work. On 9 January, the UN Independent Expert on foreign debt and human rights publicly expressed concerns over the adverse effects that further austerity measures would have on the enjoyment of economic, social and cultural rights. The government of Puerto Rico continued to refuse to conduct a thorough audit of its debt despite calls from local civil society organizations.

In December, the UN Special Rapporteur on extreme poverty and human rights visited Puerto Rico. He expressed concern regarding the lack of consideration given to social protections in the projected austerity measures.

EXCESSIVE USE OF FORCE

Excessive and unnecessary use of force by police was reported during protests related to the fiscal crisis. On 1 May, International Workers' Day, the American Civil Liberties Union documented the indiscriminate use of tear gas against protesters without prior dispersal orders, contrary to international law and standards. Observers collected canisters which revealed that expired tear gas had been used. Additionally, video evidence showed the use of rubber bullets against largely peaceful protesters. Other concerns were raised concerning police officers not being properly identifiable during the protests, and undercover police infiltrating protests and making arrests without identifying themselves.

DEATH PENALTY

Although the death penalty was abolished in Puerto Rico in 1929, it can still be imposed for crimes under US federal law that are punishable by death penalty. In February, the Office of the US Attorney for the District of Puerto Rico announced that it would again seek the death penalty against Alexis Candelario-Santana at his retrial, due to begin on 1 August 2018. In 2013 he had been sentenced to life imprisonment.

QATAR

State of Qatar
Head of state: **Sheikh Tamim bin Hamad bin Khalifa Al Thani**
Head of government: **Sheikh Abdullah bin Nasser bin Khalifa Al Thani**

Severance of relations with Qatar by several of its regional neighbours imposed arbitrary restrictions on Qatar that resulted in human rights violations. The government continued to unduly restrict freedom of expression. Steps were taken to improve access to compensation for abused migrant workers. The government committed to revise its laws and reform the sponsorship system, as part of an agreement with the ILO. After years of delays, migrant domestic workers' labour rights were protected for the first time, though the new law contained flaws. Discrimination against women remained entrenched in both law and practice. The courts imposed death sentences; no executions were reported.

BACKGROUND

On 5 June, Saudi Arabia, UAE, Bahrain and Egypt severed relations with Qatar, accusing it of financing and harbouring "terrorists" and interfering in the domestic affairs of its neighbours. Saudi Arabia closed Qatar's only land border while the four countries closed their airspace to flights to Qatar. Saudi Arabia, Bahrain and UAE arbitrarily banned their nationals from visiting or living in Qatar, and ordered Qataris to leave within 14 days, threatening fines or other unspecified consequences for non-compliance. Despite statements in response to international outcry, it was unclear what practical steps the three states had taken to mitigate negative impacts on families and those in education or undergoing medical treatment. As a result of the dispute, Qatari forces were expelled from the Saudi Arabia-led coalition in Yemen (see Yemen entry) and a UN mission to Djibouti, while the government accelerated efforts to increase its military capacity, including through military co-operation with Turkey and other states. In July, the Emir issued a decree amending some provisions of the 2004 Law on Combating Terrorism, which included redefining some terms and enabling individuals and groups accused of "terrorist activities" to appeal before the courts. In November the Emir announced that the first ever legislative elections would be held in 2018 and appointed four women to the Consultative Council (Shura Council).

FREEDOMS OF EXPRESSION, ASSOCIATION AND ASSEMBLY

The authorities maintained restrictions to the rights to freedom of expression, association and peaceful assembly that were not in conformity with international law and standards. The authorities did not permit the existence of independent political parties, and workers' associations were only permitted for Qatari citizens if they met strict criteria. Laws criminalizing expression deemed offensive to the Emir were maintained.

In January, the government arbitrarily imposed a travel ban on human rights lawyer Najeeb al-Nuaimi, who was initially informed by text message. The ban remained in place at the end of the year, limiting the lawyer's right to free movement.

TORTURE AND OTHER ILL-TREATMENT

On 25 May, although he was at risk of torture, the government forcibly returned Saudi Arabian human rights activist Mohammad al-Otaibi to Saudi Arabia, where he faced trial. Mohammad al-Otaibi had arrived in Qatar in

February 2017. On 24 May he was travelling with his wife to Norway, where he had been granted asylum, when Qatari officials detained him at Doha airport.

Filipino national Ronaldo Lopez Ulep, whose conviction on espionage charges was upheld in 2016, continued to be detained despite an unfair trial and allegations of torture.

WORKERS' RIGHTS – MIGRANT WORKERS

In January, the Emir signed an amendment to Qatar's new sponsorship law, which had come into effect in December 2016. Law No. 1 of 2017 confirmed that migrant workers would continue to require the permission of their employer to leave the country, by requiring workers to "notify" their employer. In October the cabinet reportedly approved a new amendment to the exit permit; it was not published during the year.

The ILO complaint against Qatar was closed on 8 November after the government committed to revising its laws in line with international labour standards and the guidance of ILO experts. If implemented in full, the agreement would enhance the protection of migrant workers' rights.

On 18 August, the Emir approved the establishment of a new, judge-led Labour Dispute Resolution Committee (Law No.13 of 2017) to settle labour disputes within three weeks of a worker filing a complaint. If operated fairly and effectively, the new committee could address some of the barriers to migrant workers accessing justice. At the end of the year the dispute resolution courts had not yet begun operating.

A new law providing legal protections for domestic workers' labour rights was passed for the first time. Law No.15 of 2017 included a limit to working hours per day, at least 24 consecutive hours off every week and three weeks' paid leave per year. However, the law failed to provide adequate safeguards to restrict the abuse of a provision allowing domestic workers to work beyond the legal limit if they "agreed".

Third-party auditors highlighted some progress on projects for the football World

Cup in 2022, but identified abuses of migrant workers at all 10 of the contractors they investigated.

The dispute with neighbouring countries affected some migrant workers. Low-paid workers were disproportionately impacted by increases in food prices. Workers in the hospitality and tourism sectors reported being forced to take extended leave without pay. Some foreign workers had annual leave cancelled and exit permits revoked.

WOMEN'S RIGHTS

Women continued to face discrimination in law and practice. Personal status laws continued to discriminate against women in relation to marriage, divorce, inheritance, child custody, nationality and freedom of movement.

In June, the UN Committee on the Rights of the Child (CRC) urged the authorities to investigate crimes related to gender-based violence and to bring perpetrators to justice. The Committee called on the authorities to amend the Nationality Act in order to allow women to confer nationality to their children on an equal basis with Qatari men. Despite the approval of a draft law providing permanent residency rights for the children of Qatari women married to non-Qataris, discrimination persisted with women unable to pass on nationality and citizenship to their children.

CHILDREN'S RIGHTS

In June, the CRC expressed concern over gender discrimination of children, violence against children in schools and at home, and laws limiting the right to nationality of children born in Qatar. The Committee called for the enactment of measures to end these practices. It also called for ending child marriage and raising the age of criminal responsibility, which remained at seven years of age in contravention of international standards. The Committee reiterated concerns about discrimination against the children of migrant workers and recommended the abolition of the *kafala* sponsorship system "without delay".

DEATH PENALTY

The courts reportedly imposed at least two new death sentences that were upheld by the Court of Cassation, Qatar's highest court. No executions were reported.

ROMANIA

Romania
Head of state: **Klaus Iohannis**
Head of government: **Mihai Tudose (replaced Sorin Grindeanu in June)**

Laws extending pardons and amnesties for corruption and official misconduct were put forward, sparking protests across the country. European and international institutions criticized overcrowding in prisons and inadequate detention conditions. Amendments were proposed to the law regulating civil society organizations and foundations. Roma continued to face discrimination.

BACKGROUND

In January, tens of thousands of people protested against two emergency ordinances adopted without substantial discussion by the then recently formed government. The bills extended a pardon of persons sentenced for certain corruption offences and decriminalized official misconduct. National institutions, some foreign embassies and the European Commission criticized the laws which were then repealed in February. In April, a new draft law – granting an amnesty for sentences of less than five years, including for corruption – was put forward, sparking more protests throughout the country during the year. The bill had not been adopted by the end of the year.

LEGAL, CONSTITUTIONAL OR INSTITUTIONAL DEVELOPMENTS

Amendments were proposed to the law regulating NGOs and foundations introducing additional administrative and financial obligations. National NGOs criticized the new measures as arbitrary, unnecessary and vague. The Conference of international NGOs of the CoE highlighted in December shortcomings regarding compliance with international standards and best practices. The proposals, adopted by the Senate in November, remained pending before the Parliament's Chamber of Deputies at the end of the year.

The proposal for a new National Strategy for Housing remained pending.

In March, the Senate rejected a draft law calling for the repeal of part of the Anti-discrimination Law that instituted the national equality body. The draft law was proposed by a former MP who was fined by the body in 2016 for homophobic statements.

DETENTION

In April, the European Court for Human Rights (ECtHR) advanced recommendations aimed at reducing overcrowding in prisons in a "pilot judgment" issued against Romania. It imposed an obligation on the state to resolve the highlighted structural dysfunctionalities or risk sanctions.

DISCRIMINATION – ROMA

In February, the European Commission stated that the risk of living in poverty was almost three times higher for Roma than for the rest of the population.

RIGHT TO HOUSING AND FORCED EVICTIONS

In September, according to NGOs, around 30 Roma, half of them children, living in the town of Eforie Sud in Constanta county, were verbally threatened by local authorities with eviction from a publicly owned property. They had occupied the building since October 2013 when they had been repeatedly forcibly evicted by local authorities from a long-standing settlement and rendered homeless.

In May, around 35 of the Roma families from the Pata Rat informal settlements – located on the outskirts of Cluj-Napoca, near a waste and chemical dump – received new homes across the city's neighbourhoods and nearby villages as part of a multi-stakeholder desegregation project. This included around 20 families from the former Coastei Street community, forcibly evicted in December

2010 by local authorities. The legal case brought by the community against the municipality challenging the forced eviction remained pending in national courts at the end of the year.

RIGHT TO EDUCATION

New legislation aiming to prevent, combat and prohibit segregation in primary and secondary education entered into force after its adoption in December 2016 by the Ministry of National Education and Scientific Research. Two ministerial orders established a public policy against segregation in schools on a wide range of grounds, including ethnic origin, disability and socio-economic status of families, and a related action plan scheduled to be implemented by October.

RIGHTS OF LESBIAN, GAY, BISEXUAL, TRANSGENDER AND INTERSEX PEOPLE

The Senate's decision on a national referendum on the possible restriction of the constitutional definition of "family" from "marriage between spouses" to "marriage between a man and a woman" remained pending at the end of the year. The Coalition for Family – a group of some 30 associations and foundations – has been promoting such restriction since 2016.

The case of the same-sex couple seeking recognition of their marriage officiated in Belgium remained under examination by the Constitutional Court. The Court had sought a preliminary ruling from the European Court of Justice on the harmonic interpretation of EU legislation on freedom of movement and residence for same-sex couples.

COUNTER-TERROR AND SECURITY

The case of Abd al-Rahim al-Nashiri, a Saudi Arabian national currently held in the US detention facility at Guantánamo Bay, Cuba, remained pending before the ECtHR. The case was lodged against Romania in 2012 for allegations of the enforced disappearance and torture of Abd al-Rahim al-Nashiri at a secret CIA detention facility in Bucharest, the capital, between 2004 and 2006.

DISCRIMINATION – PEOPLE WITH DISABILITIES

Living conditions in social care and psychiatric institutions for people with disabilities remained extremely precarious. The monitoring mechanism required by the UN Convention on the Rights of Persons with Disabilities, ratified by Romania in 2011, was not fully operational at the end of the year.

VIOLENCE AGAINST WOMEN AND GIRLS

In July, the UN Committee on the Elimination of Discrimination against Women recommended broadening existing legislation to address all forms of gender-based violence, strengthening women's access to justice and remedies, disaggregated data collection, and improved access to sexual and reproductive health and rights.

In May, the ECtHR noted that despite existing legislation and a national strategy there was insufficient commitment from the government to take appropriate action to prevent and combat domestic violence. The ECtHR also criticized the limited number of shelters for women victims of domestic violence available across the country.

RUSSIAN FEDERATION

Russian Federation
Head of state: **Vladimir Putin**
Head of government: **Dmitry Medvedev**

There were further restrictions to the rights to freedom of expression, association and peaceful assembly. Harassment and intimidation of human rights defenders and independent NGOs continued. Cultural rights were reduced, including through reprisals and self-censorship. Religious minorities continued to face harassment and persecution. The right to a fair trial was frequently violated. Torture and other ill-treatment persisted; the work of independent monitoring bodies for places of detention was further eroded. Serious
human rights violations continued in the North Caucasus. Russia used its veto to block UN Security Council resolutions on Syria. Migrants and refugees were denied protection of their rights. Some forms of domestic violence were decriminalized. LGBTI people continued to face discrimination and violence; gay men in Chechnya were targeted through a co-ordinated campaign of abduction, torture and killings by the Chechen authorities.

LEGAL, CONSTITUTIONAL OR INSTITUTIONAL DEVELOPMENTS

On 10 February, the Constitutional Court ruled that the mere fact of holding an "unauthorized" peaceful gathering did not constitute a criminal offence under Article 212.1 of the Criminal Code, which made repeated violation of protest rules a crime.[1] On 22 February, activist Ildar Dadin, who had received a prison sentence for his peaceful protest, had his sentence under Article 212.1 reviewed; the Supreme Court ordered his release.

In July, provisions were enacted allowing the authorities to deprive of Russian citizenship individuals who had acquired it while "intending" to "threaten the foundations of [Russia's] constitutional order". NGOs criticized the language of the law, which they said was open to arbitrary application.

VIOLENCE AGAINST WOMEN AND GIRLS

In February, a law was enacted decriminalizing domestic violence committed by "close relatives" that caused pain but no injury or loss of ability to work. This prompted an increase in violent incidents mainly targeting women in several regions.

FREEDOM OF ASSEMBLY

Across the country, the biggest protests in years took place. Hundreds of peaceful protesters, bystanders and journalists were arrested; many were subjected to cruel, inhuman or degrading treatment, prolonged arbitrary detention, and unfair trials resulting in heavy fines and "administrative detention" for several days.

In March, anti-corruption rallies took place in at least 97 cities and towns. In many places, police dispersed peaceful protesters using unnecessary and excessive force. More than 1,600 people were arrested, including at least 14 journalists covering the protests. Many of those arrested faced unfair trials on politically motivated charges and hundreds were detained solely for peacefully exercising their rights to freedom of expression and assembly. Fourteen employees and volunteers of the Anti-Corruption Foundation, who had organized a widely watched live internet broadcast of the protests, were arbitrarily arrested at their office in Moscow, the capital. On 27 and 28 March, 12 of them were sentenced to "administrative detention".[2]

Since 26 March, criminal convictions were pressed against at least eight protesters for violent offences allegedly committed while trying to protect themselves or others from police violence in Moscow, Petrozavodsk and Volgograd. Criminal proceedings were initiated against more protesters; some of them faced further questionable charges.

Many who took part in the largest protests were teenagers and young students. The authorities put pressure on them through schools and universities, using informal warnings and expulsions, and in some cases threatened to challenge custodial rights of parents of under-age protesters.

On 7 February, the European Court of Human Rights (ECtHR) ruled in *Lashmankin and Others v. Russia* – a case concerning 23 applicants from different regions. The ECtHR found that the restrictions on location, time and manner of conduct of street protests violated their right to freedom of assembly, without effective remedy being available to them. The applications concerned events of 2009-2012 when restrictions on protests were less strict than in 2017.

FREEDOM OF ASSOCIATION

NGOs were affected by the law on "foreign agents". Thirteen NGOs receiving foreign funding were added to the Ministry of Justice's list of "foreign agents". Several dozen organizations were removed from the list following their closure or after their foreign funding or their "political activity", as defined by the "foreign agents" law, ceased, bringing the number of organizations that remained in the list to 85 at the end of the year. However, NGOs affected by the "foreign agents" law, among them leading human rights groups, did not perceive this as an improvement.

In March, the ECtHR combined and communicated the complaints of 61 Russian NGOs against the "foreign agents" law; and Russian authorities filed their comments in September. The case was pending before the Court at the end of the year.

On 19 June, the charge of "malicious evasion" of obligations arising from the "foreign agents" law – in the first and only such criminal case – against human rights defender Valentina Cherevatenko was dropped due to the absence of elements of a crime.

Four more foreign organizations were declared "undesirable", making them and working for or supporting them, illegal in Russia. There were 11 "undesirable" organizations at the end of the year.

Between September and November, administrative proceedings were initiated against the NGO SOVA Centre, Andrey Rylkov Foundation for Health and Social Justice, the Centre for Independent Social Research, and the Centre for Social Partnership, for allegedly distributing materials of "undesirable" organizations. The NGOs did not remove old mentions of "undesirable" organizations and hyperlinks to their websites. Administrative proceedings against SOVA Centre were terminated because of the expiration of the statute of limitations. Other NGOs were fined 50,000 roubles (USD871) each.

FREEDOM OF EXPRESSION

Most of the media remained under effective state control and were used by the authorities to smear human rights defenders, political opponents and other dissenting voices. Throughout the country, protest leaders and political activists supporting critical voices faced harassment, administrative and criminal proceedings and physical violence by pro-government activists and "unidentified" individuals, believed to be security officials or others acting in collusion with them.

In a further crackdown on freedom of expression online, the authorities banned anonymizers and virtual private networks, among other new restrictive measures. In May, the President approved the Strategy for the Development of the Information Society for 2017-2030 which stated "priority of traditional Russian spiritual-ethical values" in the use of information and communication technologies.

Anti-extremism legislation was further extended and used arbitrarily against protected speech. In August, the UN CERD Committee expressed concern over its use to silence individuals belonging to groups vulnerable to discrimination and reiterated its recommendations that the legislation contain a clear legal definition of extremism and abandon the Federal List of Extremist Materials.

Artistic expression was restricted on occasions under pressure from conservative groups that regarded specific artistic productions as an offence to their religious belief. Performances were cancelled and individuals associated with them faced harassment and violence. Criminal proceedings were initiated against a number of prominent theatre workers in Moscow and were widely condemned by their devotees as politically motivated.

In November, a law was enacted allowing authorities to recognize as "foreign agents" media outlets that were both registered abroad and foreign-funded, which stigmatized them and imposed restrictive reporting requirements. At the end of the year, nine mass media outlets were recognized as "foreign agents".

FREEDOM OF RELIGION AND BELIEF

Religious minority groups continued to be harassed, including by banning, blocking of their websites, and the inclusion of their publications on the Federal List of Extremist Materials.

On 20 April, the Supreme Court banned the Jehovah's Witnesses' central organization and all its affiliates in Russia, ruling that the group comprising 395 local organizations and over 170,000 followers was "extremist". Jehovah's Witnesses who continued to manifest their beliefs risked being criminally prosecuted and faced up to 12 years' imprisonment.

Restrictions on missionary activities introduced in 2016 were indiscriminately applied, ranging from the attempted prosecution of a yoga instructor in St Petersburg in January for giving a public lecture to the confiscation of copies of the Salvation Army's Bible in Vladivostok as they did not feature the prescribed official marking of the distributing organization.

On 11 May, a court in Yekaterinburg imposed on blogger Ruslan Sokolovsky a three-and-a-half-year conditional prison sentence, reduced to two years and three months on appeal, for "inciting hatred" and "offending believers' feelings" by posting a video in which he played the reality game Pokémon Go in a cathedral.

RIGHTS OF LESBIAN, GAY, BISEXUAL, TRANSGENDER AND INTERSEX PEOPLE

State-sponsored discrimination and persecution of LGBTI people continued unabated, and the homophobic "propaganda law" was actively enforced. On 18 October, activist Evdokia Romanova was found guilty of the administrative offence of "propaganda of non-traditional sexual relationships among minors using the Internet". She was fined 50,000 roubles (USD871) by a court in Samara, for the links to the international Youth Coalition for Sexual and Reproductive Rights website she had shared on social media in 2015 and 2016.[3]

In April, independent *Novaya Gazeta* newspaper reported that over 100 men in Chechnya who were believed to be gay were abducted, tortured and otherwise ill-treated in secret prisons, and that some were killed. Escaped survivors reported a campaign of violence co-ordinated by the authorities.

Eyewitnesses stated that a number of captives were killed, and some handed over to their families for "honour killings" under local "traditions".

The federal investigative authorities were slow to respond to these reports. They refused to open a formal investigation after a protracted pre-investigation failed to recognize the allegations as well founded, despite the efforts by the federal Ombudsperson to establish and check the relevant facts. No investigation was known to have been initiated by the end of the year.

NORTH CAUCASUS

Reports continued of serious human rights violations, including enforced disappearance, unlawful detention, torture and other ill-treatment of detainees, and extrajudicial executions in the North Caucasus. The situation in Chechnya was further deteriorating. Impunity remained for past violent incidents against human rights defenders in Chechnya.

In January, Magomed Daudov, speaker of the Chechen Parliament, issued personal threats through his Instagram account against Grigory Shvedov, editor-in-chief of the independent online news project Caucasian Knot.[4] In April, *Novaya Gazeta* journalists received threats from Chechnya for their coverage of the anti-gay campaign in Chechnya. Radio Ekho Moskvy journalists also received such threats for expressing solidarity with *Novaya Gazeta* journalists.[5]

Novaya Gazeta reported the unlawful detention of dozens of people, starting in December 2016, and secret execution of at least 27 captives by the security forces on 26 January. No one was known to have been investigated or held accountable for these incidents by the end of the year.

UNFAIR TRIALS

Independent trial monitors reported systematic violations of the right to a fair trial at criminal and administrative hearings, including in the cases brought against peaceful protesters. Most administrative trials relied heavily on widely disputed police

reports as sole evidence. The trials resulted in lengthy detentions and hefty fines. Trails were often swift; after the 26 March protest, Tverskoi District Court in Moscow considered 476 cases in 17 working days.

On 22 August, Aleksandr Eivazov, former Secretary of the October District Court in St Petersburg and also a whistle-blower, was arrested for purportedly "interfering in the work of the court", on account of his refusal to sign and backdate records of a court hearing that someone else compiled. He was a witness to numerous violations of court procedures, judicial ethics and workers' rights in the court, and had sent complaints about all violations to the authorities and shared this information on social media. Aleksandr Eivazov's complaints were not known to be addressed. He remained in detention despite his asthma at the end of the year.[6]

TORTURE AND OTHER ILL-TREATMENT

Reports of torture and other ill-treatment in prisons and detention centres across Russia persisted. The conditions during prisoner transports amounted to torture and other ill-treatment, and in many instances, to enforced disappearance.[7] Some prisoners faced journeys lasting a month or more, while being transferred in overcrowded train carriages and vans, and spending weeks in transit cells at various stages on their way to remote prison colonies. Their families and lawyers had no information about their fate and whereabouts.

Prisoner of conscience Ildar Dadin was forcibly disappeared for a month while being transferred to another prison; his whereabouts became known in January. He made allegations of torture in Segezha prison colony in October 2016 and as a consequence the authorities transferred him to another prison colony. During his transfer, the authorities refused to provide any information on his whereabouts to his family and lawyers until after his arrival at the colony.

In May, the ECtHR ruled on the cases of eight applicants from Russia, that the condition of their transport by the penitentiary service amounted to inhuman and degrading treatment. This included the cases of Anna Lozinskaya and Valery Tokarev who were repeatedly transported in single-person van compartments measuring 0.3m².

The role and effectiveness of Public Oversight Commissions, an independent monitoring mechanism for places of detention, was further eroded, including through continued under-funding. The rules governing the nomination of their members by Public Chambers – consultative bodies consisting of state-appointed members of civil society organizations – were changed. This led to a reduction in the membership of some of the Commissions, which in some cases had an impact on their independence by effectively precluding certain human rights defenders from becoming members.

There were reports of independent monitors, including members of Public Oversight Commissions and of the Presidential Human Rights Council, being arbitrarily denied access to prison colonies by prison administrations.

ARMED CONFLICT – SYRIA

Russia five times used its veto in the UN Security Council to block resolutions that would have imposed sanctions for the production and use of chemical weapons in Syria, condemned the reported chemical weapons attack on the town Khan Shaykhun, called on the Syrian government to grant access to and the right to inspect any sites, and renewed the mandate of the Joint Investigative Mechanism, formed to determine the perpetrators of chemical-weapons attacks.

REFUGEES' AND MIGRANTS' RIGHTS

Russia continued to return asylum-seekers and refugees to countries where they were at risk of torture and other ill-treatment.

On 1 August, a court in Moscow ruled that Uzbekistani national and journalist Khudoberdi Nurmatov (also known as Ali Feruz) was violating Russia's immigration laws and should be deported to Uzbekistan.

Khudoberdi Nurmatov fled Uzbekistan years earlier to avoid persecution by security services for refusing to act as a secret informer. He would also be subject to prosecution under Uzbekistani law which criminalized homosexuality. Following the ECtHR's decision granting Khudoberdi Nurmatov urgent interim measures, the Moscow City Court on 8 August stayed his deportation but remanded him in a detention centre for foreign nationals, where he remained at the end of the year. In December, the ECtHR communicated his complaint.

Registration with local police at the place of residence remained a precondition for labour and other migrants to access health care and education. But the registration was routinely refused by many landlords who were required to consent to it.

In September, human rights defender Tatiana Kotlyar was convicted of fictitiously registering 167 migrants at her address to enable them to comply with immigration regulations and to be able to access essential services. The court sentenced Tatiana Kotlyar to a fine of 150,000 roubles (USD2,619). The fine was waived on account of the expiration of the statute of limitations for this crime.

1. Russia: Court offers "chink of light" in case brought by jailed protester Ildar Dadin (News story, 10 February)

2. Russian Federation: Detained members of corruption watchdog are prisoners of conscience and should be freed immediately (EUR 46/5998/2017)

3. Russia: Homophobic legislation used to persecute activist who shared LGBTI articles on Facebook (News story, 18 October)

4. Russian Federation: Journalist threatened by Chechen official – Grigory Shvedov (EUR 46/5442/2017)

5. Russian Federation: Newspaper threatened for reports on abductions (EUR 46/6075/2017)

6. Russian Federation: Whistle-blower detained on spurious charges – Aleksandr Eivazov (EUR 46/7200/2017)

7. Prison transportation in Russia – travelling into the unknown (EUR 46/6878/2017)

RWANDA

Republic of Rwanda
Head of state: **Paul Kagame**
Head of government: **Edouard Ngirente (replaced Anastase Murekezi in August)**

The clampdown on political opponents continued before and after presidential elections, with cases of severe restrictions on freedoms of expression and association, as well as unlawful killings and unresolved disappearance cases.

BACKGROUND

Presidential elections were held in August. President Kagame was re-elected with 98.79% of the vote. The Democratic Green Party of Rwanda won 0.48% of the vote and the independent candidate 0.73%.

The National Electoral Commission (NEC) decided that three aspiring independent candidates did not fulfil the eligibility requirements. One of them, Diane Rwigara, was accused of submitting forged signatures. On 14 July, she launched a new activist group, the People Salvation Movement.

Several diplomatic missions and civil society observers found that the electoral process had been peaceful; however, they raised concerns about irregularities including in the counting of ballots and vote tabulation.

FREEDOMS OF ASSOCIATION AND ASSEMBLY

Opposition political parties and independent candidates faced challenges in the lead-up to and following the August elections.

Shortly after Diane Rwigara announced her candidacy in May, nude photos allegedly of her appeared on social media. She complained to the police and the NEC that her representatives were intimidated as they travelled the country collecting the signatures needed to stand as an independent candidate.

Police interrogated Diane Rwigara and her relatives at their home in Kigali, the capital, on 29 August and prevented them from leaving their house. On 30 August, the police confirmed that an investigation was under way and that the family was not in detention. For several weeks the family was questioned by police and their movement restricted; they were unable to communicate freely. On 23 September, the police arrested Diane Rwigara, her mother Adeline and sister Anne. On 3 October, the Public Prosecutor confirmed that they were being charged with "inciting insurrection or trouble among the population", that Diane Rwigara would be charged with using counterfeit documents and her mother charged with discrimination and sectarian practices. Anne Rwigara was granted bail on 23 October; Diane and Adeline Rwigara were remanded in custody and remained in detention awaiting trial at the end of the year.

On 26 September, eight leaders and members of the unregistered United Democratic Forces-Inkingi (FDU-Inkingi) party were charged with forming an irregular armed group and with offences against the President. Théophile Ntirutwa, the party's Kigali representative, was detained on 6 September and held incommunicado until 23 September. He was later charged with supporting an armed group.

Those arrested in September included FDU-Inkingi's assistant treasurer Léonille Gasengayire. She had been arrested in March 2016 and remained in police detention for several days; she was rearrested in August 2016 and prosecuted on charges of "inciting insurrection or trouble among the population". On 23 March 2017, she was acquitted and released.

FREEDOM OF EXPRESSION

In April, the NEC issued election regulations requiring presidential candidates to submit campaign materials to be published on social media networks for approval 48 hours in advance, leading to considerable debate in May. The Rwanda Utilities Regulatory Authority announced on 31 May that the NEC "has no mandate to regulate or interrupt the use of social media by citizens". The next day, the NEC announced that it would adjust the regulations based on public feedback. This requirement was not implemented.

ENFORCED DISAPPEARANCES

Possible enforced disappearances were reported. Several cases of disappearances remained unresolved, and may potentially have amounted to enforced disappearances. There was no news on the fate or whereabouts of FDU-Inkingi member Illuminée Iragena, who went missing in March 2016 in Kigali.

Violette Uwamahoro, a British national and wife of a member of the outlawed Rwanda National Congress (RNC) opposition group, went missing as she arrived by bus in Kigali on 14 February. She had travelled from the UK to attend her father's funeral in Rwanda. The authorities initially denied knowledge of her whereabouts. However, she was held in incommunicado detention until 3 March when the police announced that she was in their custody. She and her cousin, Jean Pierre Shumbusho, a police officer, were charged with revelation of state secrets, formation of an irregular armed group and offences against the established government or President. She denied all charges; she was provisionally released on 27 March, after a judge ruled that there was insufficient evidence against her. She was allowed to return to the UK on 12 April.

CRIMES UNDER INTERNATIONAL LAW

Léopold Munyakazi, a university professor deported from the USA to Rwanda in 2016, was found guilty of genocide charges in July. The Intermediate Court of Muhanga sentenced him to life imprisonment in solitary confinement – a detention practice condemned by the UN Human Rights Committee as a violation of the prohibition of torture or other cruel, inhuman or degrading treatment.

Jean Twagiramungu, a former teacher, was extradited to Rwanda from Germany in August to stand trial. He was accused of planning and committing genocide in Gikongoro Prefecture (now in Southern Province).

The genocide trial of Ladislas Ntaganzwa, whose case was transferred from the International Criminal Tribunal for Rwanda (ICTR), continued at the Rwandan High Court's Chamber of International Crimes. In December, the Chamber found Emmanuel Mbarushimana, extradited from Denmark in 2014, guilty on genocide charges and sentenced him to life imprisonment.

Bernard Munyagishari, whose case was transferred from the ICTR to Rwanda in 2013, was convicted in April and sentenced to life imprisonment for genocide and crimes against humanity.

Henri Jean-Claude Seyoboka, who was deported from Canada in 2016 accused of involvement in the genocide, was denied bail by the Military High Court in February.

Enoch Ruhigira, who was arrested in Germany in 2016 on genocide charges, was released in March. The German General Prosecutor's Office cancelled the arrest warrant after a submission from the Ministry of Foreign Affairs stating that the Rwandan prosecution of Enoch Ruhigira was likely to be politically influenced.

WOMEN'S RIGHTS

Rwanda was reviewed by the CEDAW Committee in February. The Committee welcomed anti-discrimination legislation; however, it was concerned that certain discriminatory legal provisions remained. For example, while rape convictions ordinarily carry a prison sentence of at least five years, the punishment for marital rape is only two to six months' imprisonment and a fine. The Committee also expressed concern that maternal mortality was exacerbated by unsafe abortions. Abortion was allowed only in exceptional cases, requiring a court order in cases of rape, incest or forced marriage and the authorization of two doctors, if the health of the pregnant woman or the fetus is in danger. Proposed amendments to the Penal Code would end the requirement for a court order.

REFUGEES AND ASYLUM-SEEKERS

Rwanda continued to receive and host refugees from Burundi, with numbers reaching 89,146 at the end of the year.

INTERNATIONAL SCRUTINY

The UN Subcommittee on Prevention of Torture suspended its visit to Rwanda in October citing obstructions by the authorities, including limitations on access to places of detention and confidentiality of some interviews. The head of delegation reported that many of those interviewed expressed fear of reprisals. The Subcommittee suspended visits to only three countries in the past 10 years.

SAUDI ARABIA

Kingdom of Saudi Arabia
Head of state and government: **King Salman bin Abdul Aziz Al Saud**

The authorities severely restricted freedoms of expression, association and assembly. Many human rights defenders and critics were detained and some were sentenced to lengthy prison terms after unfair trials. Several Shi'a activists were executed, and many more were sentenced to death following grossly unfair trials before the Specialized Criminal Court (SCC). Torture and other ill-treatment of detainees remained common. Despite limited reforms, women faced systemic discrimination in law and practice and were inadequately protected against sexual and other violence. The authorities used the death penalty extensively, carrying out scores of executions. The Saudi-led coalition continued to commit serious violations of international law in Yemen.

BACKGROUND

In June, Saudi Arabia, Bahrain, Egypt and the United Arab Emirates severed relations with Qatar, negatively affecting thousands of nationals and migrant workers.

The same month, King Salman reshuffled the security and political landscape, considerably reducing the Ministry of Interior's powers. On 17 June the King stripped the Ministry of its powers to investigate and prosecute crimes, transferring these powers to the Public Prosecution, which he placed under his direct authority. In July, the Ministry's mandate was further reduced when a royal decree established the Presidency of State Security, mandated to address all state security matters including "terrorism", and reporting directly to the King. A number of changes in senior positions also took place during this time, but the most significant change happened on 21 June, when King Salman named his son Mohammed bin Salman as Crown Prince, unseating his nephew Mohammed bin Naif Al Saud.

In May, the UN Special Rapporteur on human rights and counter-terrorism concluded that Saudi Arabia's anti-terrorism law did not comply with international standards, and urged the government "to end the prosecution of people including human rights defenders, writers and bloggers simply for expressing non-violent views".

US President Donald Trump visited Saudi Arabia in May to participate in the Riyadh summit, attended by representatives of more than 55 mostly Arab or Muslim-majority states. A USD300 billion arms deal between the USA and Saudi Arabia was announced during the visit.

The Saudi Arabia-led military coalition supporting the internationally recognized government in Yemen continued to bomb areas controlled or contested by Huthi forces and their allies, killing and injuring civilians. Some attacks amounted to war crimes. A UN report, released in September, found that the Saudi-led coalition continued to be the leading cause of civilian casualties in the conflict (see Yemen entry). In October, the UN Secretary-General listed the Saudi Arabia-led coalition in his annual Children and Armed Conflict report, creating a new category specifically designed to limit condemnation of the coalition.

DISCRIMINATION – SHI'A MINORITY

Members of the Shi'a Muslim minority continued to face discrimination because of their faith, limiting their right to express religious beliefs and their access to justice, and arbitrarily restricting other rights, including the rights to work and to state services. Shi'a activists continued to face arrest, imprisonment and in some cases the death penalty following unfair trials. Four Shi'a men sentenced to death for protest-related offences were executed in July.

Between May and August, security forces began evacuating al-Masoura district, in the town of al-Awamiyah in the Eastern Province where Shi'a form the majority of the population, in order to build development projects. Armed clashes, marked by the use of heavy artillery and shelling, erupted between security forces and armed men who refused to leave the area, leading to the deaths and injury of scores of residents and significant damage to the town. The authorities accused the men of "terrorism activities" and other criminal offences, vowing to crack down on them. Residents reported that the authorities banned ambulances and medical aid from entering the area, and many families who remained lacked food, water, medical treatment and other basic goods. Scores of people were reportedly arrested and detained during this operation, including activists.

For example, human rights defender Ali Shaaban was arrested on 15 May following Facebook posts expressing solidarity with al-Awamiyah's residents. He remained in detention at the end of the year.

In July, families of 15 Shi'a men accused of spying for Iran and sentenced to death after a grossly unfair mass trial learned that the SCC's court of appeal had upheld their sentences. In December, some relatives were told that the sentences were upheld following the Supreme Court's review, leaving the men at risk of imminent execution.

The SCC continued to try Shi'a activists for their alleged participation in protests in 2011 and 2012. The death sentence continued to be used against political dissenters. At least 38 Shi'a men remained at risk of execution, including four who were sentenced to death for participating in protests in 2012 when they were under the age of 18.

FREEDOMS OF EXPRESSION, ASSOCIATION AND ASSEMBLY

The authorities continued to repress peaceful activists and dissidents, harassing writers, online commentators and others who exercised their right to freedom of expression by expressing views against government policies.

Following the announced decision to sever ties with Qatar, the Saudi authorities warned people against expressing sympathy towards Qatar or criticizing government actions, stating that this would be considered an offence punishable under Article 6 of the Anti-Cyber Crime Law. All public gatherings, including peaceful demonstrations, remained prohibited under a 2011 order by the Ministry of the Interior.

HUMAN RIGHTS DEFENDERS

Two years after the law on association was passed, no new independent human rights organizations had been established under its provisions. Independent human rights organizations that were forcibly shut down, including the Saudi Civil and Political Rights Association (ACPRA), the Union for Human Rights, the Adala Center for Human Rights, and the Monitor for Human Rights in Saudi Arabia, remained inactive. Almost all their members were convicted and sentenced, fled the country, or were brought to trial before the SCC.

In October, the authorities passed a new Counter-Terrorism Law replacing the February 2014 law, introducing specific penalties for "terrorist" crimes, including the death penalty. The law continued the use of a vague and overly broad definition of acts of terrorism, allowing it to be used as a tool to further suppress freedom of expression and human rights defenders.

The authorities continued to arrest, prosecute and sentence human rights defenders on vaguely worded charges that extensively drew on the Counter-Terrorism

Law of February 2014. For instance, all 11 founding members of ACPRA, which the authorities closed down in 2013, were sentenced to prison terms.

In September Abdulaziz al-Shubaily, a human rights defender and founding member ACPRA, was detained to begin serving his sentence of eight years' imprisonment to be followed by an eight-year travel ban and a ban from writing on social media, after his sentence was upheld by the court of appeal. He was convicted of, among other charges, "insulting the integrity of the judicial system and the judges" and "violating Article 6 of the Anti-Cyber Crime Law" by "inciting public opinion against the rulers of this country and signing statements that were published online that call on people to demonstrate".

In early January, computer engineer and human rights activist Essam Koshak was summoned for interrogation and repeatedly questioned about his Twitter account. On 21 August his trial began before the SCC. He faced several charges related to his online activism.

On 21 August, human rights defender Issa al-Nukheifi's trial began before the SCC. He faced several charges relating to his Twitter posts. He had been arrested on 18 December 2016 and remained in detention in Mecca General Prison at the end of 2017.

ARBITRARY ARRESTS AND DETENTIONS

Security authorities continued to carry out arbitrary arrests and detentions without charge or trial for prolonged periods without referrals to a competent court, in breach of the Code of Criminal Procedures. Detainees were frequently held incommunicado during interrogation and denied access to lawyers, in violation of international fair trial standards. In February, the UN Working Group on Arbitrary Detention found that Ali al-Nimr, Abdullah al-Zaher and Dawood al-Marhoon, three young men arrested on protest-related charges and at risk of imminent execution, were detained arbitrarily. The Working Group stated that the men had been deprived of their liberty without any legal basis, as they were prosecuted and sentenced on the basis of laws enacted two years after their arrest, contrary to international law.

In September, the authorities carried out a wave of arrests detaining more than 20 prominent religious figures, writers, journalists and academics.

In November, the authorities detained hundreds of current and former officials and businessmen without disclosing details about any charges that had been brought against them. Some were later freed, reportedly after making financial settlements.

TORTURE AND OTHER ILL-TREATMENT

Torture and other ill-treatment of detainees remained common and widespread. Courts continued to convict people and uphold death sentences on the basis of contested pre-trial "confessions". Security officials continued to torture and otherwise ill-treat detainees with complete impunity.

In July, the families of 14 men sentenced to death for protest-related charges learned by telephone that their relatives' sentences had been upheld. Court documents showed that the 14 men were subjected to prolonged pre-trial detention and that they reported having been tortured and ill-treated during interrogation in order to extract "confessions" from them. In sentencing, the SCC appeared to have relied mostly on the "confessions" for evidence against the men and failed to investigate their allegations of torture.

WOMEN'S RIGHTS

Women and girls continued to face discrimination in law and practice, despite the government's promised reforms. Women were required to have permission from a male guardian – their father, husband, brother or son – to enrol in higher education, seek employment, travel or marry. They also remained inadequately protected against sexual and other forms of violence.

In April, King Salman issued a royal decree calling on government entities to refrain from requesting the authorization of a male guardian for any services unless stipulated in the regulations. The decree also ordered government entities to review their existing regulations and to prepare a list of procedures that would require a guardian's permission. The decree could improve women's freedom to control their own lives; however, it had not been implemented by the end of the year. The same month, Saudi Arabia was elected as a member of the UN Commission on the Status of Women.

In September, the King issued another royal decree allowing women to drive, due to enter into force after 23 June 2018. The decree stated that it would be implemented according to "established legal regulations", without providing clarification, which raised questions about how it would be implemented in practice. Following this announcement, women's rights activists who had campaigned against the driving ban reported receiving telephone calls warning them against publicly commenting on the development or risk facing interrogations.

Maryam al-Otaibi, a 29-year-old activist who had actively participated in the campaign to end the male guardianship system, was arrested and detained in the capital, Riyadh, on 19 April after fleeing an abusive home environment in al-Qassim. She was interrogated after her father – also her legal guardian – filed a complaint against her for leaving the family home. On 30 July, she was released on bail. At the end of the year her case was ongoing in court and she was at risk of being detained again.

Loujain al-Hathloul, a prominent human rights defender who had been detained for defying the driving ban, was rearrested and detained on 4 June upon arrival at Dammam airport. She was questioned about her activism and released four days later. The conditions of her release remained unclear.

WORKERS' RIGHTS – MIGRANT WORKERS

The authorities continued to crack down on migrant workers with irregular status, arresting, detaining and deporting thousands. In March, the Ministry of Interior launched a campaign called "A Nation without Violations", giving migrant workers 90 days to regularize their status or leave the country without penalties.

DEATH PENALTY

Courts continued to impose death sentences for a range of crimes, including drug offences or for conduct that under international standards should not be criminalized, such as "sorcery" and "adultery". Many defendants were sentenced to death after unfair trials by courts that convicted them without adequately investigating allegations of coerced "confessions", including under torture. The authorities routinely failed to inform families of their relatives' imminent execution, or failed to inform them immediately after executions had been carried out.

On 11 July, father-of-two Yussuf Ali al-Mushaikhass was executed along with three other men for terror-related offences in connection with anti-government protests in the Eastern Province between 2011 and 2012. His family only found out about the execution after it had happened when they saw a government announcement on television. The court appeared to have based the conviction largely on "confessions" which Yussuf al-Mushaikhass told the court had been obtained under torture and other ill-treatment.

Said al-Sai'ari was executed on 13 September. He had been sentenced to death by the General Court in Najran in 2013, although the court concluded that there was insufficient evidence to convict him. In passing its verdict, the court relied on the sworn statements of the victim's father, who believed that Said al-Sai'ari was responsible for the murder of his son, even though the victim's father was not present at the crime scene.

SENEGAL

Republic of Senegal
Head of state: **Macky Sall**
Head of government: **Mahammed Dionne**

The rights to freedom of peaceful assembly and of expression were restricted. Conditions of detention remained harsh. Children were forced into begging on the street. Impunity for human rights violations was not addressed.

UNFAIR TRIALS

Khalifa Sall, opposition leader and Mayor of Dakar, the capital, was detained on 7 March, on charges including criminal conspiracy, forgery and falsification of records, misappropriation of public funds, fraud and money laundering. He was denied bail on several occasions. In July, while in detention, he was elected to Parliament. In November, the National Assembly lifted his parliamentary immunity at the Public Prosecutor's request. His lawyers and opposition and civil society groups expressed concerns that the judiciary showed a lack of independence in his case. Seven others were charged in the same case, five of whom remained, along with Khalifa Sall, in detention without trial in Rebeuss prison in Dakar.

FREEDOM OF ASSEMBLY

The authorities banned peaceful demonstrations and arrested protesters, particularly in the run-up to the July elections.

In June, security forces shot and injured two women, and beat several others, during a protest in the city of Touba against the ill-treatment of a 14-year-old boy by members of a religious association, often described as the "religious police". The police denied opening fire on the protesters but opened an investigation into the incident.

About 20 members of the "collective of 1,000 youth for the release of Khalifa Sall" were arrested in June and November for "public disorder" after they held peaceful demonstrations in Dakar calling for Khalifa Sall's release. All but one were released the same day.

In July, the security forces used tear gas and batons to repress a peaceful demonstration organized by former President and opposition leader Abdoulaye Wade. The authorities stopped the protest under a 2011 decree banning all assemblies in city centre areas.

FREEDOM OF EXPRESSION

Journalists, artists, social media users and others who expressed dissent were arbitrarily arrested.

On 30 June, journalist Ouleye Mané and three others were arrested for "publishing pictures which offended morality" and "criminal conspiracy" after sharing photographs of the President on WhatsApp. They were released on bail on 11 August.

Ami Collé Dieng, a singer, was arrested in Dakar on 8 August and charged with "offending the head of state" and "spreading false news", after she sent an audio-recording criticizing the President on WhatsApp. She was released on bail on 14 August.

In August, the Public Prosecutor issued a formal warning to anyone posting "offensive" comments or images on the internet, as well as to site administrators, that they faced prosecution for cybercrimes under the Criminal Code.

The new Press Code, adopted by the National Assembly in June, was vaguely worded and provided for custodial sentences for press offences. It allowed the Ministers of Interior and of Communication to ban foreign newspapers and periodicals, and provided for prison terms and fines for anyone defying the ban. Article 192 empowered administrative authorities to order the seizure of property used to publish or broadcast information, to suspend or stop a television or radio programme, and to provisionally close a media outlet on national security or territorial integrity grounds, among other things. It provided for prison sentences for offences including "offending" the head of state, defamation, insults, the transmission or distribution of images contrary to morality, and spreading false news. It criminalized various techniques used by whistleblowers, for which prison terms would be imposed. Article 227 allowed for restriction of access to online content deemed to be "contrary to morality", to "degrade honour" or to be "patently unlawful", in certain cases.

DETENTION AND DEATHS IN CUSTODY

Prison conditions remained harsh and overcrowded. At least four people died in custody, including two who were believed to have hanged themselves.

Dozens remained in prolonged pre-trial detention on terrorism-related charges. Imam Ndao had been detained for over two years on charges including "acts of terrorism" and "glorifying terrorism" before being brought to trial on 27 December. He was denied adequate medical treatment for his deteriorating health.

RIGHTS OF LESBIAN, GAY, BISEXUAL, TRANSGENDER AND INTERSEX PEOPLE

The Criminal Code continued to criminalize consensual same-sex sexual relations between adults. LGBTI people faced discrimination, particularly in accessing health services and justice.

CHILDREN'S RIGHTS

In July, Human Rights Watch reported that over 1,000 of the approximately 1,500 children taken off the streets between July 2016 and March 2017 had returned to their traditional Qur'anic boarding schools. They were taken out of the schools under a 2016 government initiative to protect them from forced begging and other abuses by Qur'anic schoolteachers. Official inspections were not conducted in most of these schools, and many children were forced to beg on the streets again. Few investigations into or prosecutions of those responsible for the abuses were carried out.

IMPUNITY

In April the UN Committee on Enforced Disappearances issued its concluding observations on Senegal. It recommended that criminal legislation and investigation procedures be brought in line with the International Convention for the Protection of All Persons from Enforced Disappearance and that the Senegalese Human Rights Committee be strengthened in line with the Principles relating to the Status of National Institutions (Paris Principles).

INTERNATIONAL JUSTICE

In April, the Extraordinary African Chambers in Senegal upheld the conviction and sentence of life imprisonment of former Chadian President Hissène Habré for war crimes, crimes against humanity and torture committed in Chad between 1982 and 1990.

SERBIA

Republic of Serbia, including Kosovo
Head of state: Aleksandar Vučić (replaced Tomislav Nikolić in May)
Head of government: Ana Brnabić (replaced Aleksandar Vučić in June)

Impunity continued for crimes under international law. Slurs by officials and media close to the government created a toxic environment for transitional justice activists and independent media.

BACKGROUND

Mass demonstrations, protesting against electoral corruption and media bias, followed the presidential elections won by the ruling party in April. Former Serbian military leaders released after serving sentences handed down by the International Criminal Tribunal for the former Yugoslavia (ICTY) were increasingly afforded influential positions. In December, despite a UN Committee against Torture ruling against his extradition, Serbia returned a Kurdish activist, Cevdet Ayaz, to certain imprisonment in Turkey.

CRIMES UNDER INTERNATIONAL LAW

In November, Ratko Mladić, former Commander of the Republika Srpska Army, was convicted and sentenced to life imprisonment by the ICTY for genocide, crimes against humanity and war crimes in Bosnia and Herzegovina (BiH). In August, the Appeal Court acquitted 10 people indicted for concealing Ratko Mladić, arrested in Serbia in 2011.

In May, Snežana Stanojković was elected Chief War Crimes Prosecutor. Only three prosecutions, all resulting in acquittals, were concluded at the Special War Crimes Chamber. The retrial continued of former soldiers indicted for war crimes in Kosovo, including the first indictment for rape.

In July, the trial of eight former Bosnian Serb special police – accused of killing 1,313 Bosniak civilians near Srebrenica in July 1995 – was halted because the 2016 indictment had been filed in the absence of a Chief Prosecutor. On appeal, the indictment was reinstated; proceedings started afresh in November. In October, the Appeals Court similarly dismissed charges against five former Bosnian Serb paramilitaries indicted for the February 1993 abduction of 20 people from a train at Štrpci station in BiH and their murder.

ENFORCED DISAPPEARANCES

Relatives of the disappeared were denied recognition as civilian victims of war, if their missing family member had died outside Serbia.

In May, relatives of missing Kosovo Serbs called on the government to make progress in recovering their bodies. There was no progress towards the prosecution of those responsible for the transfer and subsequent burial of bodies of Kosovo Albanians in Serbia in 1999.

HUMAN RIGHTS DEFENDERS

Transitional justice NGOs were attacked by senior government officials, including Aleksandar Vučić, by media supportive of the government and on social media. In January, intruders left bags of fake bank notes at the Youth Initiative for Human Rights (YIHR) office, and messages accusing the NGO of being "foreign mercenaries". Also in January, YIHR activists were physically attacked at a ruling party meeting where Veselin Šljivančanin, convicted for war crimes in Croatia, was speaking.

FREEDOM OF EXPRESSION – JOURNALISTS

Investigative journalists were subjected to smear campaigns by ministers and media close to the government. The ruling party's private security staff physically attacked six journalists reporting on demonstrations held during the presidential inauguration on 31 May. In July, journalists working for the Network for Investigating Crime and Corruption (KRIK) received death threats, and the flat of investigative reporter Dragana Pećo was broken into. In September, the Defence Minister's political party accused KRIK editor-in-chief, Stevan Dojčinović, of being a drug addict and paid by foreigners. This followed KRIK's investigation into the minister's property.

RIGHTS OF LESBIAN, GAY, BISEXUAL, TRANSGENDER AND INTERSEX PEOPLE

The appointment of Ana Brnabić, a lesbian, as Prime Minister, and her presence at the Belgrade Pride in the capital in September was welcomed by some as progress. However, the authorities failed to protect LGBTI individuals and organizations from discrimination, threats and physical attacks. In April, the UN Human Rights Committee urged Serbia to implement hate crime legislation effectively, and to introduce a procedure for legal gender recognition compatible with international standards.

DISCRIMINATION – ROMA

Roma families in Belgrade continued to live in informal settlements. They were denied access to social and economic rights, including health, education, water and sanitation, and were at risk of forced eviction. Some 44 of over 100 Roma families forcibly evicted in 2012 were still living in containers awaiting resettlement; planned apartments for 22 families were not due to be completed until February 2019; by November, two of the remaining families due to be moved to villages north of Belgrade had been rehoused.

Roma continued to face ill-treatment by police. In April, a Roma couple, who reported that their car had been stolen, were detained by the police for 13 hours, denied access to a lawyer, severely ill-treated, and threatened that their children would be taken to an orphanage.

REFUGEES' AND MIGRANTS' RIGHTS

Refugees and migrants were trapped in the country; those trying to enter the EU via Hungary and Croatia were repeatedly and violently returned to Serbia.

In January, up to 1,800 refugees and migrants were still living in abandoned warehouses, often in sub-zero temperatures. By May, they had all been evicted and transferred to government-run centres, where conditions were inadequate and overcrowded. There were continued obstacles and delays in registering, interviewing and providing identification for asylum-seekers. By August, out of 151 asylum applications that were received, two were accepted and 28 rejected; 121 asylum applications were being processed.

The EU negotiated an agreement with Serbia, enabling the European Border and Coast Guard Agency (FRONTEX) to operate within Serbia.

VIOLENCE AGAINST WOMEN AND GIRLS

In May, Serbia adopted 18 May as Remembrance Day for women killed by their husbands or partners. In July, women's organizations protested at the authorities' failure to protect two women and one of their children, who were killed by their former husbands in two separate incidents at the Belgrade Centre for Social Work. In November, Serbia ratified the Istanbul Convention on preventing and combating violence against women.

KOSOVO
CRIMES UNDER INTERNATIONAL LAW

Under 2014 legislation, the competencies of the EU-led Police and Justice Mission (EULEX) for the prosecution of crimes under international law were limited, although some prosecutions continued. The absence of any agreement on mutual legal assistance between Kosovo and Serbia hampered the prosecution of Serbs suspected of crimes under international law during the 1998-99 armed conflicts, including conflict-related sexual violence (CRSV).

Hundreds of unresolved case files were due to be transferred by June 2018 to Kosovo's Special Prosecution Office. Prosecutors, NGOs and survivors of CRSV were concerned that testimonies, known to have been gathered after the armed conflict by the UN Mission in Kosovo (UNMIK), had not been promptly or adequately investigated. In June, former president Atifete Jahjaga was denied entry to Serbia, where she was due to present a book of testimonies from survivors of CRSV.

REPARATION

Progress was made in implementing legislation introduced in 2014, which provided some reparation for survivors of CRSV. A commission was appointed to consider applications from survivors, who were due to be able to apply for monthly compensation payments from January 2018. Other reparation measures did not meet international standards, failing to provide survivors with free health care or adequate rehabilitation. Stigma associated with war-time rape continued to overshadow survivors.

ENFORCED DISAPPEARANCES

Little progress was made in locating people still missing from the armed conflict and its aftermath. Of the few remains recovered, the body of a man buried by Albanian villagers, who had found him in a river flowing from Kosovo, was exhumed in September. Some 1,658 people were still missing.

The Kosovo Specialist Chambers opened in The Hague on 28 June. It had been established to investigate the alleged abduction, torture and murder of Kosovo Serbs and some Kosovo Albanians, transferred to Albania by members of the Kosovo Liberation Army (KLA) during and after the war. In December, MPs failed to revoke the law governing the Specialist Chambers, which they considered discriminated against the KLA.

DETENTION
In May, the Kosovo Rehabilitation Centre for Torture Victims, authorized to monitor the treatment of the people in detention, was refused access to prison hospitals after these had been transferred to the Ministry of Health. Some detainees were held for long periods before and during trial; one defendant was detained for over 31 months, in violation of the Criminal Procedure Code. The Ministry of Justice failed to provide an explanation for the death in detention of Astrit Dehari, a member of the Vetëvendosje opposition party, in November 2016.

FREEDOM OF EXPRESSION
In October, the first Pride took place with government support. Hate crimes investigations were opened after a speaker on transgender rights subsequently received serious threats.

The Association of Kosovo Journalists reported an increase in attacks, especially on investigative journalists.

RIGHT TO HEALTH
In May, the UN Secretary-General agreed to set up a voluntary trust fund, but refused to pay compensation, apologize or accept responsibility – as recommended in 2016 by the UNMIK Human Rights Advisory Panel – for the lead poisoning of 138 Roma, Egyptians and Ashkali who were relocated by UNMIK to an internally displaced persons camps in northern Kosovo in 1999. The Panel found that the right to life, health and non-discrimination of the 138 internally displaced people had been violated. They had suffered from lead poisoning and other health conditions, including seizures, kidney disease, and memory loss, after they had been placed in the camps on land known to be contaminated.

VIOLENCE AGAINST WOMEN AND GIRLS
In April, a National Strategy for Protection from Domestic Violence was launched. In May, the Law on Compensation for Crime Victims was extended to victims of domestic violence, trafficking, rape and child sexual abuse. However, few received adequate protection from the authorities.

SIERRA LEONE

Republic of Sierra Leone
Head of state and government: **Ernest Bai Koroma**

Restrictions were imposed on the rights to freedom of expression, of peaceful assembly and of association. Hundreds of people died and thousands were left homeless following a mudslide. Prison conditions fell far below international standards. Pregnant girls were excluded from school.

FREEDOM OF EXPRESSION

Abdul Fatoma of the Campaign for Human Rights and Development International was arrested in the capital, Freetown, on 31 January after he participated in a radio discussion in which he criticized the government and Anti-Corruption Commission for their lack of accountability. He was released on bail on 1 February but his passport was withheld for 45 days.[1]

Three journalists from the *Salone Times* and *New Age* newspapers were summoned to court on 22 September to respond to various charges of seditious libel under the Public Order Act 1965, after they published stories criticizing plans by the National Telecommunications Commission to increase telecommunications prices. Their preliminary hearing was adjourned twice and they had not been summoned to appear in court by the end of the year.

FREEDOM OF ASSEMBLY

On 23 March, security forces killed a teenage boy of around 16 and seriously injured two students when they opened fire on a Njala University student protest in Bo, southern region. The students were protesting against a lecturers' strike during which time the university was closed for several months. Police said that the students did not obtain a permit to protest, and that they burned tyres and blocked roads. Seven students were arrested but released without charge after being detained for two days. The Independent Police Complaints Board launched an investigation into allegations that police used excessive force.

On the same day, police fired tear gas to disperse students protesting against the strike in front of the President's residence in Freetown. Fourteen students were arrested and charged with riotous conduct, and fined and released by the Magistrate Court. Two other students were arrested that day at State House and charged with conspiracy and possession of an offensive weapon. They were released on bail and their case was ongoing at the end of the year.

On 21 September, police prevented the Malen Land Owners and Users Association (MALOA) from holding a peaceful assembly in Pujeheun town. The gathering had been organized to coincide with a meeting between MALOA members and the District Security Committee on the International Day against monoculture tree plantations. The police blocked the road and prevented them from joining the assembly, but allowed six members to attend the meeting.

In October, the District Security Committee denied MALOA permission to hold a meeting in Pujeheun on the grounds that the association was not registered in the Chiefdom. The Paramount Chief had refused to register the group since 2013, even though they were registered with the Registrar General in Freetown.

HUMAN RIGHTS DEFENDERS

In February, the Human Rights Defenders Network submitted a draft bill to protect human rights defenders to the Attorney General's office.

ECONOMIC, SOCIAL AND CULTURAL RIGHTS

On 14 August, a mudslide in the Regent community of Freetown left more than 400 people dead and around 3,000 homeless. Most of the victims had been living in informal settlements. Poor planning, and a failure to implement relevant legislation or provide adequate housing exacerbated the scale of the disaster.[2] The authorities provided immediate support and temporary shelter for survivors but closed these camps in mid-November. Households were given cash and other benefits to help them relocate. No public enquiry had been established into the incident by the end of the year.

In August, the UN Special Rapporteur on human rights and hazardous substances and wastes visited Sierra Leone. He raised concerns about the human rights impact of hazardous substances and waste, and called on the government to adopt and enforce laws and policies related to waste reduction and labour inspection requirements.

CHILDREN'S RIGHTS

In October, civil society organizations reiterated calls on the government to allow pregnant girls to attend mainstream schools and sit exams. Part-time education schemes for pregnant girls, available three days a week with a reduced curriculum, ended in July and were due to resume in January 2018. Many girls who had given birth were unable to return to school due to costs such as child care, school fees or other associated costs like uniforms.

DETENTION

Prisons remained overcrowded, largely due to prolonged pre-trial detention periods, and fell far below international standards. Civil society organizations raised concerns about delayed access to health care for inmates; inadequate food and basic items; poor conditions in police cells, including inadequate sanitation; and extended detention periods which violated detainees' constitutional rights.

In November, civil society organizations called for the decriminalization of petty offences, such as fraudulent conversion (criminalization of debt), and loitering, which were used disproportionately against women and marginalized communities. They also contributed to prison overcrowding. Legislation on these offences was vaguely worded and allowed for arbitrary arrests.

In May, new bail and sentencing guidelines to reduce the use of pre-trial detention were approved by the Rules of Court Committee and became binding on the courts.

ARBITRARY ARRESTS AND DETENTIONS

On 1 June, Mohamed Kamaraimba Manasary, leader of the Alliance Democratic Party, was arrested on allegations that he was in possession of a stun gun. He was charged with possession of an offensive weapon and released on bail on 7 June. On 21 June, the charges were dropped and a new charge was brought of unlawful possession of small arms under the Arms and Ammunition Act 2012 which does not specifically cover stun guns. His bail was revoked and he was detained for another week before being released on 28 June. His trial was ongoing at the end of the year. He and his lawyers claimed that his arrest was politically motivated.

DEATH PENALTY

Death sentences continued to be handed down. In September, six police officers were sentenced to death by firing squad for conspiracy and robbery with aggravation.

LEGAL, CONSTITUTIONAL OR INSTITUTIONAL DEVELOPMENTS

On 10 November, the government issued a White Paper in response to the Constitutional Review Committee's recommendations. It rejected over 100 of the Committee's 134 recommendations, including abolition of the death penalty, and constitutional provisions to protect economic, social and cultural rights and equal rights for women.[3]

---

1. Sierra Leone: Anti-corruption activist's detention an attempt to stifle freedom of expression (News story, 1 February)

2. Sierra Leone: Housing and environmental failures behind shocking scale of mudslide deaths (News story, 18 August)

3. Sierra Leone: Government rejection of important constitutional review recommendations a missed opportunity to strengthen human rights protection (News story, 6 December)

SINGAPORE

Republic of Singapore
Head of state: Halimah Yacob (replaced Tony Tan Keng Yam in September)
Head of government: Lee Hsien Loong

Amendments to Singapore's Public Order Act gave authorities greater powers to restrict or ban public assemblies. Freedom of expression and assembly suffered another blow as charges were brought against those who participated in peaceful protests.

FREEDOM OF ASSEMBLY

In April, amendments to the Public Order Act to impose more regulations on organizers of public events passed into law. The amended law stipulated that organizers must apply for a permit at least 28 days in advance of an event and inform the police of the estimated size of the gathering. Punishments laid down for breaches of the regulations included a fine of up to S$20,000 (USD14,297), imprisonment for up to a year, or both. Permit applications could be rejected if the gathering was for a political purpose or was attended, organized or funded by foreign nationals.[1]

Human rights defenders were investigated by police for participating in peaceful public assemblies. In June, nine activists who held a silent protest were investigated for assembly without a permit under the Public Order Act. In September, 10 activists were investigated for holding a peaceful vigil for Prabagaran Srivijayan on the eve of his execution in July.[2] In November, activist Jolovan Wham faced seven charges for his role in several peaceful assemblies over a one year period, including the silent protest and vigil for Prabagaran Srivijayan.[3]

FREEDOM OF EXPRESSION

In August, lawyer Eugene Thuraisingam was fined S$7,000 (USD5,122) for contempt of court after posting a poem about the execution of his client, Muhammed Ridzuan

Mohd Ali. Contempt of court proceedings were initiated against US-based academic Li Shengwu for a Facebook post suggesting Singapore's courts were not independent. In September, artist and activist Seelan Palay was arrested under the Public Order Act for performing a political art piece outside Parliament.

DEATH PENALTY

Execution by hanging continued to be carried out for murder and drug trafficking. On 14 July, Malaysian national Prabagaran Srivijayan was executed despite an appeal pending on his case in Malaysia.[4]

RIGHTS OF LESBIAN, GAY, BISEXUAL, TRANSGENDER AND INTERSEX PEOPLE

LGBTI people continued to suffer discrimination. In July, organizers were required by authorities to conduct identity checks at the annual Pink Dot LGBTI event. Foreigners were officially banned from taking part.[5]

WORKERS' RIGHTS – MIGRANT WORKERS

Housing conditions for foreign workers were criticized by NGOs and at least one construction firm was fined for housing workers in unhygienic conditions.

COUNTER-TERRORISM AND SECURITY

Arrests continued under the Internal Security Act, which allows detention without charge or trial for indefinitely renewable two-year periods.

---

1. Singapore: Authorities given broad new powers to police protests (News story, 4 April)

2. Singapore: Investigation into peaceful assembly is the latest effort to intimidate human rights defenders (ASA 36/7076/2017)

3. Singapore: Activist faces seven charges for peaceful protest (ASA 36/7516/2017)

4. Singapore: Malaysian man hanged in hurried, secretive manner (ASA 36/6740/2017)

5. Singapore: Restrictions to LGBT gathering another attempt to suppress activism (ASA 36/6386/2017)

SLOVAKIA

Slovak Republic
Head of state: **Andrej Kiska**
Head of government: **Robert Fico**

The Court of Justice of the European Union (CJEU) rejected Slovakia's complaint against mandatory refugee relocation quotas. The discrimination of Roma remained widespread, and the European Commission continued an infringement procedure against Slovakia for discrimination against Roma pupils in schools.

DISCRIMINATION – ROMA
POLICE AND SECURITY FORCES

In January, a new crime prevention strategy was adopted aimed at strengthening policing in Roma settlements; it triggered concern by NGOs over ethnic profiling and discrimination. In September, the European Roma Rights Centre filed a civil complaint against the Ministry of Interior for the breach of anti-discrimination law for enhanced policing in Roma settlements.

In March, four Roma who had alleged the excessive use of force by police in April 2015 in the village of Vrbnica filed a complaint with the Constitutional Court with the support of the NGO Centre for Civil and Human Rights. The Department of Control and Inspection Service (SKIS) had pressed charges against the chief of the police operation in December 2016, but failed to hold the individual police officers who had participated in the action to account. The complaint remained pending at the end of the year.

In May, the European Roma Rights Centre published a video of police officers beating Roma residents with batons during a police operation in the village of Zborov on 16 April. The residents did not appear to resist or engage in violence. In May, the police president stated that a number of the operation's aspects seemed inappropriate. In July, the Ministry of Interior opened an investigation into the case.

In May and August, the police opened investigations targeting six victims of alleged excessive use of force by the police in the Roma settlement in the village of Moldava nad Bodvou in June 2013. The police accused the victims of having committed the criminal offence of falsely accusing the police of wrongdoing.

In May, the District Court in Košice again acquitted the police officers accused of the ill-treatment of six Roma boys at a police station in 2009. The Court held that there was insufficient evidence. The Prosecutor appealed against the decision.

RIGHT TO EDUCATION

The infringement proceeding launched in 2015 by the European Commission against Slovakia for the systemic discrimination and segregation of Roma children in education remained open. In March, the Minister of Education stated that complex reform plans were under way, but it was unclear what these consisted of. The 2016 amendments to the School Act had limited impact since entering into force.[1] They failed to address the systemic over-representation of Roma children in special schools and classes for children with mild disabilities. Mainstream primary schools lacked the human and financial resources to tackle the segregation of Roma pupils.

In February, the NGOs eduRoma and European Roma Rights Centre criticized the results of the Ministry of Education's 2016 funding reforms for schools educating students from socially disadvantaged backgrounds. The responsibility for classifying students as having a "social disadvantage" was given to psychologists rather than social services. There were cases of misclassifications of students and consequently insufficient resources were allocated to schools. The Ministry temporarily suspended the measure, and at the end of the year, pupils were assessed on the basis of their parents' situation.

In September, following the 2016 closure of the ethnically segregated Primary School Hollého Street in the town of Žilina, Roma pupils were transferred to a number of other schools. This potentially positive move was undermined by the authorities failing to provide sufficient support for Roma pupils, notably transport costs. In March, some non-Roma parents at one of the schools protested against the transfer of Roma children to the school.

REFUGEES AND ASYLUM-SEEKERS

In September, the CJEU rejected the application submitted in 2015 by Slovakia and Hungary against the mandatory relocation scheme which aimed to relocate refugees from EU member states such as Greece and Italy. The CJEU held that the EU institutions can adopt the provisional measures necessary to respond effectively and swiftly to an emergency situation characterized by a sudden inflow of displaced persons. By the end of 2017, Slovakia had accepted only 16 asylum-seekers of the 902 that it was assigned.

---

1. Slovakia: A lesson in discrimination – segregation of Romani children in primary education (EUR 72/5640/2017)

SLOVENIA

Republic of Slovenia
Head of state: **Borut Pahor**
Head of government: **Miro Cerar**

Amendments to the Aliens Act undermined the rights of asylum-seekers. There was no progress in addressing the long-standing human rights violations against those known as the "erased". Roma continued facing widespread discrimination and social exclusion, particularly regarding the right to housing.

REFUGEES AND ASYLUM-SEEKERS

In January, the National Assembly adopted amendments to the Aliens Act allowing special measures to be triggered after threats to public order and national security occur. Under these measures, Slovenia would be able to deny entry to people arriving at its borders and automatically expel migrants and refugees who enter irregularly without assessing their asylum claims. Such measures had not been invoked by the end of the year.

In July, the Court of Justice of the European Union ruled that two Afghan families and a Syrian national who had sought asylum could be deported back from Austria and Slovenia respectively to Croatia, the first EU country they had entered. The ruling upheld the requirement of the so-called 2013 Dublin regulation which imposes that refugees seek asylum in the first country they reach, even in exceptional circumstances. Slovenia's Ministry of Interior stated its intention to deport the Syrian asylum-seeker referred to in the ruling; he had not been deported by the end of the year. Refugees struggled to support themselves as a consequence of the 2016 amendments to the International Protection Act. The amendments ended the short-term financial assistance designed to help refugees bridge the gap before they received social support, leaving many of them without funds in the first month after they were granted international protection.

Slovenia had committed to accept 567 asylum-seekers by September 2017 from Greece and Italy under the EU relocation scheme; by the end of the year it had resettled only 232 people.

DISCRIMINATION

In September, the National Assembly amended the Ombudsman Act to provide it with a broad mandate to combat discrimination, and to establish a National Centre for Human Rights with capacity for research and education under the Ombudsman's Office. Alongside the Advocate for Equality, an independent anti-discrimination body established in 2016, these steps were welcomed by civil society. However, human rights organizations warned that the anti-discrimination framework as a whole still lacked monitoring, policy-making and executive powers as well as adequate resources to be fully effective.

THE 'ERASED'

Long-standing human rights violations continued to persist against the "erased", an estimated 25,000 former permanent residents of Slovenia mostly originating from other former Yugoslav republics. They were removed from the official registry following the country's independence. The authorities failed to offer new options to the remaining "erased" in terms of restoring their legal status and related rights since the expiry of the Legal Status Act in 2013. In September and November, the European Court of Human Rights ruled as inadmissible complaints by some of those whose applications for restoring legal status had been rejected under the Legal Status Act provisions.

ROMA

Roma continued to face widespread discrimination and social exclusion. Many were living in segregated settlements in inadequate housing, lacking security of tenure and access to water, electricity, sanitation and public transport. The government had yet to adopt a comprehensive National Roma Strategy as recommended by the parliamentary commission for human rights in 2015. In February, approximately three quarters of the Roma political representation, led by the Forum of Roma council members, adopted a platform of political demands, including immediate access to basic services and infrastructure, and the strengthening of their political participation. Other Roma organizations followed suit. In October, they held the first Roma-organized public demonstrations echoing similar demands.

SOMALIA

Federal Republic of Somalia
Head of state: **Mohamed Abdullahi Mohamed (replaced Hassan Sheikh Mohamud in February)**
Head of government: **Hassan Ali Khayre (replaced Omar Abdirashid Ali Sharmarke in March)**
Head of Somaliland Republic: **Muse Bihi Abdi (replaced Ahmed Mohamed Mahamoud Silanyo in November)**

Drought led to mass displacement and emergency levels of food insecurity. Up to three civilians were reported to have been killed in US air and drone strikes. Kenya continued its voluntary repatriation scheme for Somalis from Dadaab refugee camp and stopped registering new arrivals from Somalia. The armed group al-Shabaab and the authorities severely restricted journalists in their work. While women made small strides in the political sphere, sexual and gender-based violence remained prevalent.

BACKGROUND

The Somali Parliament, which represented all regions of Somalia, including Somaliland and Puntland, elected Mohamed Abdullahi Mohamed (also known as Farmajo) President in February. In February, President Mohamed appointed Hassan Ali Khayre as Prime Minister. Some presidential candidates were accused of using millions of US dollars of campaign finances to bribe MPs to vote for them. MPs were elected according to a system that allowed male elders belonging to the four main clans one vote per person while male elders from minority clans were allowed half a vote. This effectively denied young people, women and men from minority clans equal voting rights. Elections also took place in Somaliland territory, where Muse Bihi Abdi was elected President.

The peacekeeping forces AMISOM (AU Mission in Somalia) withdrew from key locations in Somalia throughout the year, after which al-Shabaab regained control over towns in conflict areas, including in El Buur, Bardere and Lego, located in southern and central Somalia.

COUNTER-TERROR AND SECURITY

Soon after he took office, President Mohamed declared that reform of the security forces and the defeat of al-Shabaab would be among his main priorities. Attacks on civilians by al-Shabaab intensified over the year; the most serious took place at a hotel in Mogadishu, the capital, on 14 October in which, according to the government, over 512 people were killed.

According to media reports, the US government made secret changes to its rules on the use of lethal force in counter-terror operations, and included Somalia as one of its designated areas for "active hostilities". This effectively meant that US forces could target those thought to be al-Shabaab fighters wherever they were located, regardless of whether they posed an imminent threat to life, and without obtaining high-level authorization. According to the Bureau of Investigative Journalism, a UK-based NGO, up to three civilians were killed in 31 US air strikes and strikes by remotely piloted vehicles (drones) during the year.

REFUGEES' AND MIGRANTS' RIGHTS

On 9 February, the High Court in Kenya declared that the Kenyan government's 2016 directive to close Dadaab refugee camp in Garissa County was unconstitutional and in violation of Kenya's obligations under international and national law (see Kenya entry). The majority of refugees housed at the camp were from Somalia. From January to November 2017, according to UNHCR, the UN refugee agency, approximately 32,500 Somali refugees were voluntarily repatriated from Kenya to Kismayo, Baidoa, Mogadishu, Luuq, and Afmadow in south- central Somalia under the Tripartite Agreement between Kenya, Somalia and UNHCR. By the end of the year, there were 229,592 Somalis registered as refugees in Dadaab refugee camp. However, Kenya continued not to register new arrivals from Somalia.

FREEDOM OF EXPRESSION

Al-Shabaab prohibited journalists from operating in areas under its control. The group continued to detain, threaten and harass media workers throughout the country.

In July, the Somali Cabinet passed a repressive law that established a statutory regulatory body – whose members were appointed by the Minister of Information and which oversaw the content of print and broadcast media. The law established a blanket prohibition on news deemed to be false and on the publication of "propaganda" without providing a clear definition of those terms. The legislation was vaguely worded and included broad restrictions on journalists; and gave the authorities wide discretion to prosecute media workers.

The Somaliland Journalist Association said that more than 30 journalists were arrested and detained by authorities in Somaliland for criticizing the government.

WOMEN'S RIGHTS

The Somali election quota system reserved 30% of seats for women. As a result, the level of women's representation improved and amounted to 24% of the lower house and 22% of the upper house.

Sexual and gender-based violence continued to be widespread although it was under-reported. The Integrated Management System of Somalia, a government agency, documented at least 271 and 312 cases of gender-based violence against displaced women and girls in Somaliland and Puntland respectively, and at least 400 cases in south-central Somalia. The drought led to more women being separated from their families, which put them at greater risk of sexual and gender-based violence, particularly because they were perceived as lacking "male protection".

ECONOMIC, SOCIAL AND CULTURAL RIGHTS

There was an unprecedented drought that led to a significant increase in the numbers of internally displaced people, estimated to be 943,000 by the end of the year. Over 3 million people experienced emergency levels of food insecurity. Malnutrition reached emergency levels in the southern and central regions, primarily among displaced populations, but also among those directly affected by the protracted conflict. In August, the UN Office for the Coordination of Humanitarian Affairs (OCHA) estimated that 388,000 children were malnourished and 87,000 were in need of life-saving support.

SOUTH AFRICA

Republic of South Africa
Head of state and government: **Jacob G. Zuma**

Profound inequalities continued to undermine economic, social and cultural rights, including in access to sexual and reproductive health services. Failures in the criminal justice system obstructed access to justice for victims of hate crimes and gender-based violence. Investigations into police conduct following excessive use of force during protests were ongoing.

BACKGROUND

Protests against corruption were widespread. Political tension was heightened after President Zuma made substantial changes to members of government in March, including the dismissal of Finance Minister Pravin Gordhan.

Despite increased public spending on health, education and essential services, the national statistical service reported that the country was unable to reduce poverty and inequality.

EXCESSIVE USE OF FORCE

The Independent Police Investigative Directorate reported an increase in abuse of power by the police, including 394 deaths as a result of police action and 302 deaths in police custody in 2016-2017, both figures higher than for the previous year. It also reported 173 cases of torture, 112 of rape by police officers – including 35 cases committed by officers on duty – and 3,827 of assault by police. At the end of the year, it concluded its investigation into the fatal shooting by police officers of journalist Godknows Nare in April in Johannesburg, and handed the case to the Director of Public Prosecution. Godknows Nare was reported to have been shot at by the officers, who thought he had stolen a car, after he exited his car with his arms raised.

On 23 May, 17-year-old Leonaldo Peterson was shot at his home by police officers with a rubber bullet at close range in Gauteng province, during a protest in the neighbourhood. His wounded hand required multiple surgeries.

On 27 May, Samuel Mabunda, a migrant from Mozambique, died as a result of injuries following beatings by the "Red Ants", a private security company hired by the police to carry out evictions in Ivory Park, Johannesburg. A police investigation into the case was ongoing at the end of the year.

On 12 September, 14-year-old Ona Dubula was shot at by police officers at close range with rubber bullets in his face and ribs at an informal settlement in Hout Bay town, Western Cape province, during protests over fishing licences; the injuries left him with speaking difficulties. A Directorate investigation into the incident was ongoing at the end of the year.

UNLAWFUL KILLINGS

The Department of Police said that killings of local councillors persisted, as did murders and attempted murders at Durban's Glebelands hostel complex – leading to several arrests in relation to the crimes. A Commission of Inquiry into the root causes of political killings in KwaZulu-Natal province commenced its hearings in March and was extended until March 2018.

GENDER-RELATED VIOLENCE

Violence against women and girls, including gender-related killings, remained widespread. Over 39,000 cases of rape were reported to the police between April 2016 and March 2017, although such cases were believed to be grossly under-reported. In September, the Medical Research Council stated that only 8.6% of rape cases opened by the police in

2012 had resulted in convictions, citing a lack of resources and training for police officers, as well as failures to investigate the crimes and gather forensic evidence.

In May, the Department of Justice published the South African Law Reform Commission report on adult prostitution. The Commission recommended that the sale and purchase of sex remain criminalized, contradicting the testimonies and recommendations of sex workers and activists, the South African Commission for Gender Equality, as well as human rights and public health experts. In June, Zwelethu Mthethwa was sentenced to 18 years' imprisonment for the murder of sex worker Nokuphila Kumalo in 2013. The case highlighted the delays faced by sex workers in accessing justice.

SEXUAL AND REPRODUCTIVE RIGHTS

Gross inequalities in women's access to sexual and reproductive health services persisted, with less than 7% of the country's 3,880 health facilities offering abortion services. The government failed to address health care professionals' refusal to provide abortion services as well as information on the location of those services, contrary to international human rights standards. Lack of access to information on sexual and reproductive health and rights – including how and where to access legal abortion services – and inequalities in access to those services for marginalized groups of women and girls exacerbated existing barriers to safe abortion.

RIGHT TO HEALTH

Official statistics stated that almost one in three boys and one in four girls suffered from stunting.

Despite health policies aimed at reducing the spread of HIV, incidence rates remained particularly high among women and girls, with an estimated 2,000 new HIV infections occurring every week among young women and girls aged 15 to 24.

Reporting to Parliament in September, the Health Minster highlighted that the politicization of provincial health departments and poor management had resulted in "a shortage of medical staff, medicines, equipment and other medical necessities" in public health facilities. The chairperson of the Portfolio Committee on Public Service and Administration was reported to have received death threats in March, following her investigation into the poor performance of health facilities in Mpumalanga province. In June, the South African Human Rights Commission (SAHRC) found that the Department of Health in KwaZulu-Natal province had violated cancer patients' rights to life, health and human dignity, due to the lack of oncologists and functional equipment for screening and treating patients.

In October, an arbitration hearing began in relation to the deaths of over 118 patients with mental illnesses who died after the Department of Health in Gauteng province moved over 1,300 patients from the Life Esidimeni health care facility to facilities managed by NGOs, because of resource constraints. However, the SAHRC emphasized that "[all] of the 27 NGOs where the patients were relocated were unlicensed, under-resourced and had no capacity to take on mentally ill people". In February, the Health Ombudsman found that the relocation breached the rights of the patients and their families, including their rights to life and to human dignity.

INTERNATIONAL JUSTICE

On 6 July, the ICC Pre-Trial Chamber found that South Africa should have executed the arrest warrant against Sudanese President Omar Al-Bashir when he visited the country in June 2015. South Africa's Supreme Court of Appeal ruled in March 2016 that the government's failure to arrest President Al-Bashir was unlawful.[1]

Following the conclusion of South Africa's domestic legal processes, the Pre-Trial Chamber convened a hearing in April 2017.

A draft bill to repeal the Rome Statute Domestication Act was introduced to Parliament in early December, signalling the government's intention to pursue its decision to leave the ICC.

FREEDOM OF EXPRESSION

On 7 July, the South Gauteng High Court granted the South African National Editors' Forum (SANEF) and 11 journalists an interdict against Black First Land First (BLF), a political party, and Andile Mngxitama, its leader, after journalists covering allegations of corruption involving President Zuma and the Indian-born Gupta family reported threats and harassment. On 17 July, Micah Reddy, a journalist at the amaBhungane Centre for Investigative Journalism, said that he was harassed by a group of BLF supporters and members, following his participation in a panel discussion with Andile Mngxitama at the South African Broadcasting Corporation.

On 27 July, amaBhungane organized a public event in Johannesburg to discuss the "GuptaLeaks" emails, which exposed alleged corruption by the political elite. The meeting was disrupted by BLF members and a group of about 20 people believed to be from the MK Inkululeko Foundation, a veterans' association. On 11 August, the South Gauteng High Court found that BLF and Andile Mngxitama were in contempt of the 7 July court order, following an application by journalists Sam Sole, Ferial Haffajee and the SANEF. The Court also ordered that the interdict be extended to cover all journalists. On 29 September, BLF and Andile Mngxitama launched an appeal, which SANEF and the journalists opposed.

RIGHTS OF LESBIAN, GAY, BISEXUAL, TRANSGENDER AND INTERSEX PEOPLE

LGBTI people continued to face harassment, discrimination and violence.

On 4 April, the burned body of Matiisetso Alleta Smous, a lesbian woman, was discovered in Kroonstad, Free State province. An eyewitness said she was raped, stabbed in the chest, and then burned to death. Three suspects were arrested on 5 April and released later that month due to insufficient evidence against them. An investigation into the murder was ongoing at the end of the year.

On 15 May, the body of Lerato Moloi, a lesbian woman, was found in a field in

Soweto, Gauteng province. The postmortem examination showed that she had been raped and stabbed in the neck. Two suspects were arrested in May. The National Prosecuting Authority referred the case to the Johannesburg High Court.

On 11 August, the Potchefstroom High Court sentenced David Shomolekae to life imprisonment for strangling Lesley Makousa, a 16-year-old gay student, to death in August 2016. David Shomolekae was found guilty of murder, robbery and housebreaking.

The Prevention and Combating of Hate Crimes and Hate Speech Bill, which included homophobic hate crimes, that was introduced in October 2016 had yet to be approved by members of the government before going to the National Assembly.

On 6 September, the Western Cape High Court ruled that the refusal by the Department of Home Affairs to allow transgender people who had transitioned after they got married to change the gender markers on their official documents infringed couples' rights to equality and human dignity. The Department of Home Affairs previously required transgender couples to get divorced before their gender markers could be changed on their official documents.

REFUGEES' AND MIGRANTS' RIGHTS

Human rights violations and discrimination against refugees, asylum-seekers and migrants continued.

On 29 June, the Constitutional Court declared section 34(1)(b) and (d) of the Immigration Act 13 of 2002 – including the provision to hold an "illegal foreigner" in custody for up to 120 days without a court hearing – inconsistent with sections 12(1) and 35(2)(d) of the Constitution and therefore invalid. The declaration was however suspended for two years to enable Parliament to pass corrective legislation.

In July, the Department of Home Affairs published a white paper on international migration intended to update migration policy. The white paper proposed the creation of detention facilities at South Africa's borders, which would house asylum-seekers while their applications were processed, and also limit their rights to work and movement while awaiting a decision on their application. It also proposed the establishment of a Border Management Authority – a centralized border control body – which would include police and customs. The related Border Management Authority Bill was passed by the National Assembly on 8 June and was before the National Council of Provinces for consideration.

In July, the SAHRC strongly condemned comments made by the Deputy Police Minister as "irresponsible" and "xenophobic", after he said that most foreign nationals in Johannesburg were engaged in various crimes.

On 29 September, the Supreme Court of Appeal declared the 2012 decision by the Department of Home Affairs to close the Cape Town Refugee Reception Office unlawful and ordered it to reopen the Office by March 2018.

On 30 November, the Refugee Amendment Bill was passed by the National Assembly. It amended the Refugees Act 130 of 1998 and restricts refugees' right to seek and enjoy asylum from persecution. In December, President Zuma assented to the Refugee Amendment Act (11 of 2017).

---

1.   ICC rules against South Africa on shameful failure to arrest President Al-Bashir (News story, 6 July)

SOUTH SUDAN

Republic of South Sudan
Head of state and government: **Salva Kiir Mayardit**

The armed conflict expanded and new armed opposition groups emerged. Parties to the conflict continued to commit crimes under international law and human rights violations and abuses with impunity. Fighting between government and opposition forces had a devastating humanitarian impact on the civilian population. Conflict and hunger displaced hundreds of thousands of people.

BACKGROUND

The Sudan People's Liberation Movement/ Army in Opposition (SPLM/A-IO), the main opposition group, remained split between those loyal to Riek Machar and those loyal to Taban Deng Gai. Taban Deng Gai had replaced Riek Machar as first Vice-President in July 2016 after fighting between government and opposition forces in Juba, the capital, forced Riek Machar to flee South Sudan. New opposition groups emerged including the National Salvation Front, led by General Thomas Cirillo Swaka, former deputy chief of general staff who resigned from South Sudan military in February 2017.

During the year, the legitimacy and relevance of the 2015 Agreement on the Resolution of the Conflict in the Republic of South Sudan waned due its failure to improve security. In June, the Intergovernmental Authority on Development announced that it would convene a high-level forum which would work to restore a permanent ceasefire and the implementation of the Agreement. Between August and November, the Authority consulted with parties to the Agreement, other opposition groups, and key stakeholders including civil society, on the forum's design and its expected outcomes. A cessation of hostilities agreement was signed in December but, soon afterwards, renewed fighting broke out in different parts of the country.

INTERNAL ARMED CONFLICT

Hostilities between government and opposition forces under Riek Machar, as well as other armed opposition groups, affected most of the country. Parties to the conflict committed violations and abuses of international human rights and humanitarian law, including targeted killings of civilians often based on ethnicity or perceived political allegiance; systematic looting and destruction of civilian property; abductions; and crimes of sexual violence.

In Upper Nile, for example, government forces, aided by ethnic Dinka Padang militias, carried out repeated attacks on territory held by opposition-aligned Shilluk forces on the west bank of the White Nile, throughout the year. They indiscriminately attacked civilian towns and villages, including Wau Shilluk, Lul, Fashoda, Kodok and Aburoc, and were responsible for deliberate killings of civilians, looting of property, and the displacement of tens of thousands of civilians.[1]

Fighting throughout the year in the Equatoria region also resulted in numerous civilian deaths. Cases of deliberate killings of civilians, sexual violence crimes, looting and destruction of civilian property in Yei and Kajo Keji counties, mostly by government forces, were documented.

SEXUAL VIOLENCE

Sexual violence continued to be a common feature of the conflict. All sides subjected women, girls, men and boys to rape, gang rape, sexual slavery, sexual mutilation including castration, and forced nudity during attacks on villages, searches of residential areas, on roads and at checkpoints, and following abduction or during detention. Government forces targeted women and girls living in camps under the protection of the UN Mission in South Sudan (UNMISS) peacekeepers, when they went to buy or search for basic necessities such as food and firewood. Survivors of sexual violence had little access to appropriate medical and psychological treatment because of limited availability or because they were unable to reach services. Perpetrators of crimes of sexual violence were rarely held accountable.[2]

LACK OF HUMANITARIAN ACCESS

The hostile environment in which humanitarian workers operated significantly undermined their ability to address food, health care, education and emergency shelter needs. Parties to the conflict regularly obstructed humanitarian access by threatening, harassing, detaining or committing acts of violence against humanitarian workers; at least 25 aid workers were killed during the year, according to the UN Office for the Coordination of Humanitarian Affairs (OCHA). On numerous occasions fighting between armed groups forced humanitarian workers to relocate from areas of operation and suspend services. Humanitarian supplies were looted by parties to the conflict, including, according to OCHA, more than 670 tons of food from humanitarian compounds in June and July.

RIGHT TO FOOD

An estimated 4.8 million people, almost half the population, were severely food insecure as a result of obstructions to humanitarian access, armed conflict, mass displacement, and the economic crisis. In February, localized famine was declared in the Leer and Mayendit counties in Unity state. By June, the situation had improved following a large-scale humanitarian response.

In the Equatoria region, formerly rich in food, government and opposition forces imposed restrictions on civilian access to food as a way to control their movement or force them from their homes and land.[3] Those who remained faced acute food shortages, and malnutrition levels increased.

Across the country, displacement and the threat of violence hampered agriculture and prevented civilians from tending livestock or receiving sustained and adequate food aid.

The deteriorating economic situation also exacerbated the food crisis. Government revenues fell due to low oil prices and oil production. The depreciation of local currency and the shortage of imported commodities caused food prices to soar. The government repeatedly failed to pay employees their salaries.

REFUGEES AND ASYLUM-SEEKERS AND INTERNALLY DISPLACED PEOPLE

More than 3.9 million people – approximately one third of the population – had been displaced since the beginning of the conflict in December 2013; 1.9 million of them were internally displaced, including over 200,000 who lived on UN bases under the protection of UNMISS peacekeepers.

More than 640,000 fled the country during the year, bringing the total number of refugees from South Sudan to over 2 million. Most of them were hosted by neighbouring Ethiopia, Uganda (see Uganda entry) and Kenya (see Kenya entry), with approximately 1 million refugees in Uganda.

ARBITRARY DETENTIONS AND TORTURE AND OTHER ILL-TREATMENT

In March, President Kiir announced plans to release all political detainees. At least 30 detainees were released during the year; however, the National Security Service (NSS) and the Military Intelligence Directorate continued to conduct arbitrary arrests and hold perceived government opponents in prolonged detention without charge or trial. Individuals were denied the right to have their detention reviewed by a court and were often subjected to torture and other ill-treatment. Detention conditions were harsh; detainees were regularly denied access to their family members, adequate food and clean water. The conditions, including inadequate medical care, contributed to the deaths of some detainees.

The NSS released 21 detainees without charge from prolonged arbitrary detention in a prison in the NSS headquarters compound in the Jebel neighbourhood of Juba; one was released in January, two in March, one in April, two in May, and 15 in August. Most had been detained for between two and three years. At least five others remained in detention in the compound, accused of communicating with or supporting the opposition. A sixth man, James Gatdet, former SPLM/A-IO spokesperson, detained in the same facility, was charged with inciting violence, "treason" and "publishing or communicating false statements prejudicial to Southern Sudan". He was detained after he was forcibly returned from Kenya to South Sudan in November 2016.[4]

Mike Tyson, Alison Mogga Tadeo, Richard Otti, and Andria Baambe, also held without charge for alleged links with the opposition, died in the same facility between February and July as a result of harsh conditions of detention and inadequate access to medical care. They had been held since 2014.

The government failed to investigate the use of arbitrary detention and related violations by government security agencies, or to hold those suspected of criminal responsibility accountable, or provide victims with reparation, such as financial compensation and rehabilitation.

ENFORCED DISAPPEARANCES

The NSS and the Military Intelligence Directorate subjected people believed to be opponents of the government to enforced disappearance.

Dong Samuel Luak and Aggrey Idri, both vocal critics of the government, went missing on 23 and 24 January respectively in Nairobi, Kenya. They were forcibly returned to South Sudan and taken to the prison facility at the NSS headquarters in Juba. They were reported to have been removed from this facility on 27 January. Their fate and whereabouts remain unknown.[5]

FREEDOM OF EXPRESSION

Journalists, human rights defenders, political opposition members and others who spoke out about the conflict were subjected to harassment, arbitrary arrests and detentions, and torture and other ill-treatment. This led to their self-censorship and a political environment in which people could not work or speak freely.

On 10 July, the NSS arrested Adil Faris Mayat, director of the South Sudan Broadcasting Corporation, after he failed to broadcast President Kiir's Independence Day speech. He was held without charge in a facility at the NSS headquarters in Juba for nine days and subsequently dismissed from his job. On 17 July, the South Sudan National Communication Authority blocked the websites of four news outlets. According to the media, the Information Minister said that the websites had published information that was "hostile" to the government.

LACK OF ACCOUNTABILITY

There were no credible investigations into crimes under international law and human rights violations or abuses, or prosecutions of those suspected of criminal responsibility in fair trials before civilian courts. The military said that some crimes carried out by government soldiers against civilians were prosecuted before military courts. This happened despite the provision under South Sudan's SPLA Act requiring that if military personnel commit an offence against a civilian, the civil court should assume jurisdiction over the offence. In May, for example, the trial of 12 government soldiers accused of rape, murder and looting at the Terrain hotel in Juba in 2016 commenced before a special military tribunal.

Three transitional justice bodies, provided for in the Agreement on the Resolution of the Conflict in the Republic of South Sudan in 2015, had not been established by the end of the year. In July, the AU Commission and the government agreed on the content of a statute and a memorandum of understanding for the establishment of one of the bodies, the Hybrid Court for South Sudan, although they were not formally approved or adopted. A technical committee for the Commission for Truth, Reconciliation, and Healing began consultations on the Commission's design and legislative framework.

South Sudan's legislative framework failed to define or criminalize torture, enforced disappearance, or crimes against humanity.

LEGAL, CONSTITUTIONAL OR INSTITUTIONAL DEVELOPMENTS

The General Assembly of Justices and Judges went on strike in April, demanding salary increases, improved working conditions, and the Chief Justice's resignation following poor leadership. President Kiir responded with a decree on 12 July removing 14 judges from office, and invoking a constitutional provision that allowed for judges to be removed for "misconduct". On 11 September, the judges ended their strike on grounds including a pledge from the President that he would deal with their demands and reinstate the dismissed judges. The judges were not reinstated by the end of the year. In November, a Supreme Court judge resigned, citing lack of judicial independence.

In October, the Transitional National Legislative Assembly voted to ratify the Protocol to the African Charter on Human and Peoples' Rights on the Rights of Women in Africa (Maputo Protocol).

---

1. South Sudan: "It was as if my village was swept by a flood": Mass displacement of the Shilluk population from the West Bank of the White Nile (AFR 65/6538/2017)

2. "Do not remain silent": Survivors of sexual violence in South Sudan call for justice and reparations (AFR 65/6469/2017)

3. South Sudan: "If men are caught, they are killed. If women are caught, they are raped": Atrocities in Equatoria Region turn country's breadbasket into a killing field (AFR 65/6612/2017)

4. South Sudan: Several men arbitrarily held in poor conditions (AFR 65/6747/2017); South Sudan: Fifteen released, five still arbitrarily detained (AFR 65/7144/2017)

5. South Sudan: Fate and whereabouts of two men unknown: Dong Samuel Luak and Aggrey Idri (AFR 65/6298/2017)

SPAIN

Kingdom of Spain
Head of state: **King Felipe VI de Borbón**
Head of government: **Mariano Rajoy**

The rights to freedom of expression and peaceful assembly of Catalan independence supporters were disproportionally restricted. Dozens of people were prosecuted for "glorification of terrorism" and "humiliation of victims" on social media. Law enforcement officials used excessive force against demonstrators peacefully resisting the enforcement of the High Court of Justice of Catalonia's ruling stopping the Catalan independence referendum. Spain relocated fewer asylum-seekers than it had pledged to under the EU relocation scheme, and resettled fewer refugees than it had committed to. Thousands of people continued to face forced evictions. The authorities continued to close investigations into crimes under international law committed during the Civil War and the Franco regime.

BACKGROUND

Two violent attacks took place in Catalonia in August, leaving 16 people dead and several others wounded. The armed group Islamic State (IS) claimed responsibility. Six people believed to be responsible were killed by security forces, and four others were arrested and prosecuted for being implicated in the attacks and as members of the group that carried out the attacks.

On 1 October, the government of Catalonia, an autonomous region in the northeast, held a referendum on the region's independence, in defiance of several Constitutional Court rulings. On 17 October, the Constitutional Court declared unconstitutional the regional law on which the referendum was based and confirmed its precautionary measure which it had adopted on 7 September, aimed at preventing the referendum. On 27 October, the pro-independence political groups in the Catalonian regional parliament unilaterally declared the independence of Catalonia. On the same day, the Senate authorized the Spanish government to adopt measures pursuant to Article 155 of the Spanish Constitution, effectively suspending the region's autonomy. On 21 December, new regional elections in Catalonia took place. The party which obtained more votes than any other single party was a non-independence party, but overall the elections delivered the majority in the regional parliament to the combined pro-independence parties.

FREEDOMS OF EXPRESSION AND ASSEMBLY

Following the Constitutional Court decision of 7 September aimed at preventing the referendum, some authorities disproportionately restricted the rights to freedom of expression and peaceful assembly. Courts in Madrid and Vitoria in the Basque country prohibited two public assemblies aimed at supporting the referendum. The municipality of Castelldefels in Catalonia adopted a blanket ban on the use of public spaces for assemblies aimed at supporting or protesting against the referendum.

On 16 October, a High Court judge ordered the pre-trial detention of Jordi Cuixart and

Jordi Sànchez, the presidents of two pro-Catalan-independence organizations. They were detained and charged with sedition, a broadly defined offence, in connection with protests they organized in Barcelona on 20 and 21 September to, according to a judge, oppose a lawful police operation. In November, the Supreme Court took charge of the proceedings against Jordi Sánchez and Jordi Cuixart. The Supreme Court extended the investigation against them to the offence of rebellion.

Dozens of people were prosecuted for "glorification of terrorism" and "humiliation of victims" on social media networks. In many instances, authorities pressed criminal charges against people who had expressed opinions that did not constitute incitement to a terrorism-related offence and fell within the permissible forms of expression under international human rights law. Twenty people were convicted in the course of the year. In March, Cassandra Vera was convicted and given a suspended sentence of one year`s imprisonment for "humiliation of victims of terrorism". She had published jokes on Twitter about ETA´s 1973 killing of Carrero Blanco, a Prime Minister under the Franco regime.

In January, the investigating judge dismissed charges of incitement to hatred against Alfonso Lázaro de la Fuente and Raúl García Pérez, professional puppeteers who in February 2016 were subjected to pre-trial detention for five days on charges of "glorifying terrorism" and incitement to hatred. The charges of "glorifying terrorism" were dismissed in 2016.

Administrative penalties continued to be imposed on private individuals, human rights activists and journalists on the basis of the Law on Public Security, which could constitute unlawful restrictions on the rights to freedom of expression, peaceful assembly and information.

Mercé Alcocer, a journalist at Catalunya Radio, was fined EUR601 for disobeying a police order. She crossed an unmarked police line in her attempt to interview a witness when she was covering a corruption case which was being investigated by the High Court. She appealed, arguing she had stepped back when told to and that her account could be substantiated by footage from security cameras. The footage was not admitted as evidence, and her appeal was pending at the end of the year.

TORTURE AND OTHER ILL-TREATMENT

In September, the High Court dropped the request for the extradition from Switzerland of Nekane Txapartegi. The term for enforcing a December 2009 conviction against her had expired. In April, the Special Rapporteur on torture had urged the Swiss authorities to oppose the extradition. Nekane Txapartegi said she was subjected to torture and other ill-treatment when she was held incommunicado for five days in a police station in Madrid in 1999. She had been arrested on suspicion of terrorism-related offences and of being an ETA member. Investigations into her torture allegations had not been conducted thoroughly in the past.

In May, the Constitutional Court declared admissible an appeal by the government against a Basque Parliament law on the recognition of and reparation for victims of human rights violations in the Basque Country.

EXCESSIVE USE OF FORCE

Law enforcement officials policing protests on 1 October in Catalonia used excessive force against peaceful protesters who were opposing a police operation. The police fired blank cartridges and rubber bullets, seriously injuring one person and causing him to lose the sight in one eye.

REFUGEES' AND MIGRANTS' RIGHTS

Spain failed to meet its commitment to relocate 15,888 asylum-seekers under the EU emergency relocation scheme; 1,328 were relocated by the end of the year, of which 592 were Syrian nationals. Spain also failed to meet its commitment to resettle 1,449 refugees from the Middle East and North Africa; 1,360 refugees were resettled, all Syrian nationals, except one refugee from Palestine, by 31 December.

Between January and December, 25,853 asylum claims were submitted, and 34,655 applications were still pending at the end of October. Asylum-seekers continued to face delays in receiving decisions on their claims. For many, the period during which they were entitled to access government support pending the outcome of their asylum application expired long before the decision was reached.

According to the EU border agency FRONTEX, there were 21,663 irregular border crossings via the Western Mediterranean route up to September, more than double the figure for the same period in 2016.

In October, the European Court of Human Rights held that the immediate return to Morocco of sub-Saharan migrants who were attempting to enter Spanish territory in Melilla in 2014 amounted to a collective expulsion of foreign nationals.

COUNTER-TERROR AND SECURITY

Judicial authorities continued to use counter-terrorism legislation disproportionately. Three of the seven people detained and charged with terrorism-related offences for their alleged participation in an attack against two off-duty civil guards and their partners in Alsasua (Navarra) in a pub in October 2016, were in pre-trial detention pending a hearing due in April 2018.

VIOLENCE AGAINST WOMEN

According to the Ministry of Health, Social Services and Equality, 48 women (and eight children) were killed by their partners or former partners.

In September, Parliament approved a plan to combat gender-based violence, encompassing a review of legislation and other measures to meet the obligations enshrined in the Istanbul Convention on violence against women.

RIGHT TO HOUSING

Thousands of people were forcibly evicted without adequate judicial safeguards or provision of alternative accommodation by the state. These included 26,767 rental evictions and 16,992 mortgage evictions. Public spending on housing continued to decrease, even though the demand for affordable social housing remained high. Single mothers and survivors of gender-based violence were particularly affected by the lack of affordable alternative housing. In July, the UN Committee on Economic, Social and Cultural Rights upheld a complaint against Spain for not having provided an evicted family with alternative housing.

IMPUNITY

Spanish authorities continued to close investigations into crimes under international law committed during the Civil War and the Franco regime. They argued that it would not be possible to investigate the crimes reported, such as enforced disappearances and torture, in view of, among other things, the Amnesty Act and the statute of limitations. The authorities continued to fail to take measures to locate and identify the remains of victims of enforced disappearances and extrajudicial executions, leaving families and organizations to undertake exhumation projects without state support.

In February, Mexico's Attorney General's Office started an investigation into the so-called "stolen babies" case, making Mexico the second country to investigate crimes under international law committed in Spain during the Civil War and the Franco regime. The investigation concerned the case of a woman born in Spain in 1968 and handed over to a Mexican family, reportedly after having been abducted from her family. In September, the UN Working Group on Enforced or Involuntary Disappearances stated that this case constituted a new opportunity for Spain to fully co-operate in the investigations carried out by other states into enforced disappearances which occurred in Spain.

The 2014 amendments to universal jurisdiction legislation were invoked by the Spanish judiciary to not investigate crimes under international law, such as enforced disappearances and torture, committed in Syria and Venezuela in 2017 against Spanish nationals.

SRI LANKA

Democratic Socialist Republic of Sri Lanka
Head of state and government: **Maithripala Sirisena**

Sri Lanka continued to pursue its 2015 commitments to deliver justice, truth, reparation and guarantees of non-recurrence for alleged crimes under international law, but progress slowed and there was evidence of backsliding. Parliament passed an amended Office on Missing Persons Act, intended to assist families of the disappeared seeking missing relatives. The Prevention of Terrorism Act (PTA) was not repealed; it was still used to arrest and detain suspects. Torture and other ill-treatment in police custody continued. Threats against religious and ethnic minorities and human rights defenders were reported.

BACKGROUND

Enforced disappearances, extrajudicial executions, torture and other serious human rights violations and abuses were committed with impunity before, during and in the aftermath of the armed conflict between government forces and the Liberation Tigers of Tamil Eelam (LTTE) that ended in 2009. Commitments made by Sri Lanka in 2015 – through its co-sponsorship of UN Human Rights Council resolution 30/1 – to establish truth, justice and reparation mechanisms and reforms aimed at non-recurrence of these crimes, had not been implemented by the end of the year. Sri Lanka's constitutional reform process, initiated in 2016, also faltered as lawmakers differed over issues such as the fate of the executive presidency, the place of Buddhism in the new

Constitution, and whether economic, social and cultural rights would be included in the Bill of Rights.

ARBITRARY ARRESTS AND DETENTIONS

The authorities continued to detain Tamils suspected of links to the LTTE under the PTA, which permitted extended administrative detention and shifted the burden of proof to a detainee alleging torture or other ill-treatment. During his visit to Sri Lanka in July, the UN Special Rapporteur on the promotion and protection of human rights and fundamental freedoms while countering terrorism stated that over 100 unconvicted prisoners (pre- and post-indictment) remained in detention under the PTA, some of whom had been held for over a decade. Sri Lanka failed to follow through on its 2015 commitment to repeal the PTA and replace it with legislation that complied with international standards.

TORTURE AND OTHER ILL-TREATMENT

Reports of torture and other ill-treatment in detention continued. In March, Sri Lanka's human rights record was examined under the UPR process; the Human Rights Commission of Sri Lanka said that it had continued to document widespread incidents of violence against detainees, including torture and other ill-treatment, which it described as "routine" and practised throughout the country, mainly by police. The Special Rapporteur on the promotion and protection of human rights and fundamental freedoms while countering terrorism found that 80% of those arrested under the PTA in late 2016 had complained of torture and other ill-treatment.

EXCESSIVE USE OF FORCE

Impunity persisted for excessive use of force against protesters. Killings by the army of unarmed demonstrators demanding clean water in August 2013 had yet to be prosecuted. In August, a Criminal Investigation Department investigator told the Gampaha Chief Magistrate that all evidence related to the shootings had been "destroyed" by previous investigators.

ENFORCED DISAPPEARANCES

By the end of the year Sri Lanka had not passed legislation criminalizing enforced disappearance in domestic law, despite ratifying the International Convention against Enforced Disappearance in 2016. A parliamentary debate on a bill criminalizing enforced disappearance scheduled for July was postponed without explanation.

The amended Office on Missing Persons Act was passed by Parliament in June; the amendments limited the Office's power to seek outside assistance. It was signed by the President on 20 July but had not come into operation by the end of the year. The Office was proposed to help many thousands of families of the disappeared trace missing relatives.

In June, President Sirisena promised families of the disappeared that he would order the release of lists of those who surrendered to, or were detained by, the armed forces during and after the armed conflict that ended in 2009. The lists were not made public by the end of the year.

IMPUNITY

Impunity persisted for alleged crimes under international law committed during the armed conflict. Impunity also remained for many other human rights violations. These included the January 2006 extrajudicial executions of five students in Trincomalee by security personnel and the killing of 17 aid workers with NGO Action Against Hunger in Muttur in August 2006; the December 2011 disappearances of political activists Lalith Weeraraj and Kugan Muruganandan; the 2010 disappearance of dissident cartoonist Prageeth Eknaligoda; and the 2009 killing of newspaper editor Lasantha Wickrematunge.

HUMAN RIGHTS DEFENDERS

In June, the then Minister of Justice threatened to have human rights lawyer Lakshan Dias disbarred if he did not apologize for speaking publicly about reported attacks against Christians.

Tamil human rights defenders and activist community members, including relatives of the disappeared, continued to report surveillance and harassment by law enforcement officials. Women human rights defenders in the north and east reported that interactions with police were often degrading and sexualized.

FREEDOMS OF EXPRESSION, ASSEMBLY AND ASSOCIATION

Attempts by families to arrange stones as memorials for lost relatives were stopped by security forces. Catholic priest Elil Rajendram was detained and other residents of Mullaitivu were subjected to police harassment following their efforts to hold memorials for family members who died during the armed conflict.

LEGAL, CONSTITUTIONAL OR INSTITUTIONAL DEVELOPMENTS

An expected parliamentary debate on the proposed draft Constitution aimed at ensuring checks on executive power and more equitable ethnic power sharing had not taken place by the end of the year.

Despite repeated promises, Sri Lanka failed to repeal the PTA and to pass legislation criminalizing enforced disappearances.

In December, Sri Lanka ratified the Optional Protocol to the Convention Against Torture (OPCAT).

DISCRIMINATION

Law enforcement officials continued to subject members of the Tamil minority, particularly former members of the LTTE, to ethnic profiling, surveillance and harassment.

Police failed to take action in response to continued threats and physical violence against Christians and Muslims by members of the public and supporters of a hardline Sinhala Buddhist political group.

In March, the UN CEDAW Committee asked Sri Lanka to amend all personal laws to remove discriminatory provisions. The Committee expressed particular concern about the Muslim Marriage and Divorce Act of 1951, which failed to specify a minimum age for marriages and permitted girls aged under 12 to marry with the permission of a religious adjudicator (Qazi). The Act also restricted women from serving on Qazi Boards, and did not recognize marital rape unless the couple was legally separated; this included statutory rape of a girl under 16 by an adult spouse.

VIOLENCE AGAINST WOMEN AND GIRLS

Impunity persisted for various forms of violence against women and girls, including child marriage, domestic violence, human trafficking, rapes by military or law enforcement officers or assaults by private actors. In a rare exception, the trial began on 28 June in Jaffna's High Court of nine men accused of involvement in the May 2015 gang rape and murder of Sivaloganathan Vidya, an 18-year-old school student, in Punkuduthivu. The trial was still ongoing at the end of the year. The nature of the crime and police mishandling of the case sparked widespread protests in 2015. In July 2017 a serving Senior Deputy Inspector General of Police was arrested for allegedly assisting one of the suspects to evade arrest.

DEATH PENALTY

Death sentences were imposed for murder, rape and drug trafficking. No executions have been carried out since 1976. On 4 February, Sri Lankan Independence Day, President Sirisena commuted the sentences of 60 death row prisoners to life imprisonment.

SUDAN

Republic of the Sudan
Head of state and government: **Omar Hassan Ahmed al-Bashir**

Security forces targeted opposition party members, human rights defenders, students and political activists for arbitrary arrest, detention and other abuses. The rights to freedom of expression, association and peaceful assembly were arbitrarily restricted. The security and humanitarian situation in Darfur, Blue Nile and South Kordofan states remained dire, with widespread violations of international humanitarian and human rights law.

BACKGROUND

In January, the US government partially lifted economic sanctions imposed on Sudan since 1997, which included unfreezing assets and banking, commercial and investment transactions. The US government agreed to lift all economic sanctions in October, stating that Sudan's government demonstrated its commitment to achieving progress in five key areas including: a marked reduction in offensive military activity culminating in a pledge to maintain a cessation of hostilities in conflict areas in Sudan; and improved humanitarian access throughout Sudan.

On 15 January, the Council of Ministers extended the unilateral ceasefire in Darfur, Blue Nile, and South Kordofan for a further six months. The Sudanese Armed Forces and the Sudan People's Liberation Movement-North (SPLM-N) exchanged accusations over ceasefire violations in South Kordofan State on 21 February. In March, the SPLM-N split into two rival factions which threatened to delay peace talks between the government and the SPLM-N, trigger wider conflict and cause additional displacement in SPLM-N-controlled areas in Blue Nile. However, in October the government extended the unilateral ceasefire to 31 December which held at the end of the year.

FREEDOMS OF ASSOCIATION AND ASSEMBLY

The activities of civil society organizations and political opposition parties were extensively restricted. The National Intelligence Security Service (NISS) prevented many civil society organizations and opposition parties from holding events. For example, on 17 February it banned a meeting of the Teachers Central Committee at the Umma National Party offices in Omdurman city. It prohibited the Umma National Party from holding a public meeting in Wad Madani in Al Jazeera State on 18 March. In April, it prevented the committee for the Sudanese Dramatists from holding a public event to address the impact on Sudanese society of an absence of dramatic arts. Also in April, it stopped the opposition Sudan Congress Party holding a memorial service for one of its members; and an event organized by the "No to women's oppression" initiative at Al-Ahfad University without providing a reason. In May, the NISS cancelled a symposium on Sufism entitled "Current and Future Prospects" at the Friendship Hall in the capital, Khartoum. In June, the Humanitarian Aid Commission (HAC) suspended the activities of Shari Al-Hawadith, an organization providing medical support in Kassala State.

FREEDOM OF EXPRESSION

In the second half of the year, authorities confiscated print-runs belonging to six newspapers on 26 occasions. Restrictions on freedom of expression continued with newspaper editors and journalists regularly instructed not to cover any subjects considered a security threat. Twelve journalists were repeatedly summoned and investigated by the NISS, and two others were convicted for reporting on issues said to be a threat to security. For example, in May, the Press and Publications Court in Khartoum convicted Madiha Abdala, former Editor of Sudanese Communist Party newspaper *Al-Midan*, of "dissemination of false information" and fined her 10,000 Sudanese pounds (around USD1,497), for publishing an article on the conflict in South Kordofan in 2015.

In September, Hanadi Alsiddig, Editor-in-Chief of *Akhbar Alwatan* newspaper, was briefly arrested and beaten by NISS for covering land dispute issues.

ARBITRARY ARRESTS AND DETENTIONS

NISS officials and other security forces targeted opposition political party members, human rights defenders, students and political activists for arbitrary arrest, detention and other abuses.[1] Three political opposition activists were held in detention without charge following their arrests in January and February by the NISS in Khartoum, and were

released at the end of April. They were arrested because they supported the civil disobedience protests in November and December 2016 against economic austerity measures.[2]

Dr Hassan Karar, former chairperson of the Central Committee of Sudanese Doctors (CCSD), was rearrested on 20 April and detained for four days at the office of the NISS Prosecutor of Crimes Against the State. He was held for his role in supporting a nationwide doctors' strike to protest against the deteriorating health service. Dr Mohamed Yasin Abdalla, also a former chairperson of the CCSD, was arrested and detained on 22 April in Khartoum at the office of the Prosecutor of Crimes Against the State. He was released without charge on 28 April. Both were accused of, but not formally charged with, forming an illegal entity and threatening the health system of the country.

In May, activists Dr Mudawi Ibrahim Adam and his colleague Hafiz Idris Eldoma were charged with six offences, two of which are punishable by life imprisonment or death.[3] They were arrested by the NISS along with a third activist in 2016 in connection with their work for the Sudan Social Development Organization-UK (SUDO-UK) which works on humanitarian and development projects across the country. They were subjected to ill-treatment on arrest. Dr Mudawi Ibrahim Adam and Hafiz Idris Eldoma were released on 29 August after eight months of wrongful imprisonment.[4]

Nabil Mohamed El-Niwari, a Sudanese political activist and member of the opposition party Sudan Congress, was arrested by the NISS in Khartoum on 5 September in connection with his political activities.[5]

ARMED CONFLICT

DARFUR

There was a reduction in armed conflict between the Sudanese Armed Forces and opposition armed groups at the beginning of the year. However, there were reports of renewed fighting in North Darfur on 28 May between, on one side, the Sudan Liberation

Movement (SLM-MM), led by Minni Minawi, and the SLM-Transitional Council against, on the other side, the Sudanese Armed Forces and the Rapid Support Forces (RSF). There was no clear progress in the peace process or mechanisms to address the causes and consequences of the Darfur conflict. There were at least 87 incidents of unlawful killing of civilians, including of internally displaced persons (IDPs), mainly by pro-government militia, and there were reports of widespread looting, rape and arbitrary arrests across Darfur. On 22 September, President al-Bashir announced a visit to Kalma IDP camp in South Darfur. Sudanese security forces used live ammunition to break up protests by IDPs against the visit. Five people were killed and dozens wounded. In June, the UN Security Council renewed the mandate of UNAMID (UN Mission in Darfur) until 30 June 2018. The mandate also included the restructuring of the UNAMID presence into two six-month phases, which had wider implications for the protection of civilians in Darfur.

SOUTH KORDOFAN AND BLUE NILE

The Famine Early Warning Systems Network (FEWS-NET) reported that the humanitarian situation in SPLM-N-controlled areas in South Kordofan was dire. The rate of chronic malnutrition was estimated at 38.3% due to long-term food deprivation and recurrent illness. FEWS-NET estimated that 39% of households in Blue Nile were severely food insecure. Meanwhile, the simmering leadership dispute within SPLM-N heightened tension among Sudanese refugees in Maban County in South Sudan and triggered violent ethnic clashes between the two rival SPLM-N factions in Blue Nile, resulting in the displacement of thousands of people from the SPLM-N-controlled area to government-controlled areas in Sudan, and to refugee camps in South Sudan and Ethiopia.

1. Courageous and resilient: Activists in Sudan speak out (AFR 54/7124/2017)

2. Opposition activists arbitrarily held in Sudan (AFR 54/6000/2017)

3. Sudan: Human rights defender facing death penalty: Dr Mudawi Ibrahim Adam (AFR 54/6300/2017)

4. Sudan: Dr Mudawi released after eight months of wrongful imprisonment (Press Release, 30 August)

5. Sudan: Detained opposition activist denied lawyer visits: Nabil Mohamed El-Niwari (AFR 54/7101/2017)

SWAZILAND

Kingdom of Swaziland
Head of state: **King Mswati III**
Head of government: **Barnabas Sibusiso Dlamini**

Forced evictions continued to be carried out. The Public Order Act and the Suppression of Terrorism Act (STA) severely limited the rights to freedom of expression, association and peaceful assembly. A ban on opposition parties continued. Gender-related violence remained prevalent and Parliament failed to enact the Sexual Offences and Domestic Violence Bill.

BACKGROUND

Student protests continued throughout the year following government cuts to state-funded tertiary scholarships in 2016. Ten students were arrested in September in connection with the protests.

RIGHT TO HOUSING AND FORCED EVICTIONS

Communities continued to be at risk of forced evictions. Around 85 families in at least two communities faced imminent evictions without being provided with alternative housing or adequate compensation. Although the Constitution prohibited arbitrary deprivation of property without compensation, in practice the lack of legal security of tenure left people vulnerable to forced evictions. In a judgment in April, a High Court ruled that the constitutional provision of compensation to evicted residents was limited to evictions carried out by the state; residents affected by forced evictions carried out by private actors were excluded from access to certain remedies.

In Madonsa in the Manzini region, at least 58 families were at risk of imminent eviction after the Swazi National Provident Fund (SNPF), a government parastatal, claimed ownership of the land on which they resided. After a protracted seven-year legal process, the High Court ordered in 2011 that the families be evicted without compensation or alternative accommodation. They remained on the land at the end of the year.

In Mbondzela, in the Shiselweni region, 27 families threatened with eviction began proceedings against a private company which sought to appropriate their land for the development of a game park. On 19 October, the Central Farm Dwellers Tribunal dismissed their case and allowed the eviction, ruling that the private company should provide the residents with building material to construct homes elsewhere.

FREEDOMS OF ASSEMBLY AND ASSOCIATION

King Mswati approved the Public Order Act on 8 August, which curtailed the rights to freedom of assembly and association, imposing far-reaching restrictions on organizers of public gatherings. The Act also failed to provide mechanisms to hold law enforcement officials accountable for using excessive force against protesters or public gatherings.

The government continued to ban opposition parties.

LEGAL, CONSTITUTIONAL OR INSTITUTIONAL DEVELOPMENTS

In August, the King approved the STA, which amended the 2008 Act. The amendments limited the definitions of what constitutes a terrorist act although the wording was overly broad and vague in relation to terrorism-related acts. The law also contained provisions that undermined the rights to freedom of expression, association and assembly.

An appeal by the government against a 2016 High Court ruling that found that the original STA, as well as the Sedition and Subversive Activities Act, were invalid on the grounds that they infringed the constitutionally guaranteed rights to freedom of expression, association and assembly, was due to be heard in October 2017. However, the government failed to submit its arguments on time and the Court withdrew their appeal.

VIOLENCE AGAINST WOMEN AND GIRLS

The Sexual Offences and Domestic Violence Bill, first introduced in Parliament in 2009, was not passed, despite ongoing reports of gender-related violence. In October, the Deputy Prime Minister's office introduced proposed amendments, which included the removal of clauses which criminalized incest, unlawful stalking, abduction and indecent exposure, on the grounds that these provisions compromised Swazi cultural practices.

IMPUNITY

Under the Game Amendment Act of 1991, game rangers continued to enjoy immunity from prosecution related to carrying out their duties, including in cases where they killed alleged poachers. During the year police investigated at least six such killings by rangers; no one was known to have been brought to justice.

More than two years after the death in police custody of Luciano Reginaldo Zavale, a Mozambican national, the authorities had still not made public findings from an inquest into his death.

SWEDEN

Kingdom of Sweden
Head of state: **King Carl XVI Gustaf**
Head of government: **Stefan Löfven**

The authorities failed to adopt effective strategies to prevent racist and xenophobic attacks. Rape and other forms of sexual violence against women and girls remained widespread but there were few convictions. Roma people continued to face discrimination. Courts convicted individuals for serious crimes under international law committed in Syria and Rwanda.

REFUGEES AND ASYLUM-SEEKERS

Emergency temporary measures introduced in 2016 prevented asylum-seekers who had been granted subsidiary protection from having the right to family reunification. During his visit to Sweden in October, the Council of Europe Commissioner for Human Rights recommended that Sweden lift the measures.

CRIMES UNDER INTERNATIONAL LAW

In February, Svea Court of Appeal upheld the sentence of life imprisonment of a Swedish citizen of Rwandan origin, convicted in Sweden of genocide and other crimes committed in Rwanda in 1994.

In May, Svea Court of Appeal confirmed the sentence of life imprisonment of a Syrian citizen convicted in Sweden of war crimes for the extrajudicial execution of seven Syrian army soldiers.

In September a Syrian man who had served in the Syrian army was convicted of war crimes by the Södertörn District Court and sentenced to eight months' imprisonment for violating the dignity of five dead or severely injured persons by posing for a photograph with his foot on one victim's chest.

Sweden had yet to make torture a crime under national law.

DISCRIMINATION

Roma citizens from Romania and Bulgaria supporting themselves through begging continued to be subjected to harassment and denial of basic services including shelter, water and sanitation, education and subsidized health care. In September, Vellinge in southern Sweden became the first Swedish municipality to ban begging, and one of the main political parties declared its intent to do the same nationally. The decision in Vellinge was later declared non-conforming with the Law on Public Order; the matter was subject to appeal. Anti-Roma prejudice towards Roma from other EU countries was widespread.

VIOLENCE AGAINST WOMEN AND GIRLS

Rape and other forms of sexual violence against women and girls remained widespread. In December, based on a proposal by the 2014 Sexual Offences Committee, the government presented draft legislation to the legal council which included a consent-based definition of rape and sexual abuse.

Serious concerns remained about rape attrition rates. The number of rapes reported to the police increased by 14% during the first half of the year compared with the same period in 2016 (from 2,999 to 3,430). Between January and June 2017, decisions to prosecute were taken in just 111 cases, according to preliminary official statistics.

SWITZERLAND

Swiss Confederation
Head of state and government: **Doris Leuthard (replaced Johann Schneider-Ammann in January)**

Migrants and asylum-seekers with rejected asylum claims were returned in violation of the *non-refoulement* principle. Concerns remained regarding the use of disproportionate force during the deportation of migrants. Government proposals for the creation of a National Human Rights Institution continued to be criticized for failing to guarantee the Institution's independence.

LEGAL, CONSTITUTIONAL OR INSTITUTIONAL DEVELOPMENTS

In August, the UN Human Rights Committee expressed concerns regarding the "Initiative for auto-determination", a referendum that was likely to be scheduled for 2018 and which would lead to supremacy of the Federal Constitution over international treaties. The Committee urged Switzerland to introduce a control mechanism to ensure that referendums comply with international human rights law before being presented for a popular vote.

The Council of Europe Commissioner for Human Rights and the UN Human Rights Committee urged Switzerland in May and June respectively to establish a fully independent National Human Rights Institution with a sufficiently broad mandate and adequate resources to comply with the Principles relating to the Status of National Institutions (Paris Principles). NGOs raised concerns about the lack of full independence of the Human Rights Institution proposed by the Federal Council (government) in June.

REFUGEES AND ASYLUM-SEEKERS

The authorities returned several asylum-seekers to other Schengen Area Member States by applying the Dublin III Regulation (EU law that determines the EU member state responsible to examine an application for asylum) but without duly taking into account their family ties in Switzerland.

In April, the Federal Court ruled that the detention of two Afghan parents with their infant, and the placement of their three other children in an orphanage in 2016, with the purpose of returning the whole family to Norway, had disproportionately violated their right to family life.

In October, the Council of Europe Commissioner for Human Rights called on Switzerland to improve the identification and protection of the most vulnerable migrants and asylum-seekers, and to apply a gender and child-sensitive approach to all migration and asylum-related decisions and measures. Child asylum-seekers in federal reception centres continued to be denied access to education.

In several cases, the European Court of Human Rights and the UN Committee against Torture ruled that the return of people with failed asylum claims or undocumented migrants to Sri Lanka, Sudan and Turkey violated the principle of *non-refoulement* (forcible return of individuals to a country where they risked serious human rights violations).

POLICE AND SECURITY FORCES

In August, the UN Human Rights Committee urged Switzerland to introduce an independent complaint mechanism to examine allegations of unlawful use of force by police and to collect comprehensive and disaggregated data on the number of complaints, investigations and convictions. It also recommended the introduction of a provision expressly prohibiting and criminalizing torture as a separate offence in the Criminal Code.

In July, while noting some improvements, the National Commission for the Prevention of Torture raised concerns about the excessive use of force by police, in particular in the context of deporting migrants.

DISCRIMINATION

In March, the Upper Chamber of the Federal Parliament (Council of States) rejected a bill to ban full-face veils at the national level.

In August, the Human Rights Committee urged Switzerland to introduce comprehensive legislation against discrimination. It also recommended that Switzerland not subject intersex children without consent to medically unnecessary interventions to determine their gender.

WOMEN'S RIGHTS

In August, the Human Rights Committee recommended that Switzerland continue to combat domestic violence, female genital mutilation and forced marriages, to train justice professionals to address cases of domestic violence, and to facilitate the stay of migrant women who had suffered domestic violence. In December, Switzerland ratified the Council of Europe Convention on preventing and combating violence against women and domestic violence (Istanbul Convention).

SYRIA

Syrian Arab Republic
Head of state: **Bashar al-Assad**
Head of government: **Imad Khamis**

Parties to the armed conflict committed war crimes and other grave violations of international humanitarian law and human rights abuses with impunity. Government and allied forces, including Russia, carried

out indiscriminate attacks and direct attacks on civilians and civilian objects using aerial and artillery bombing, including with chemical and other internationally banned weapons, killing and injuring hundreds. Government forces maintained lengthy sieges on densely populated areas, restricting access to humanitarian and medical aid to thousands of civilians. Government forces and foreign governments negotiated local agreements which led to the forced displacement of thousands of civilians following prolonged sieges and unlawful attacks. Security forces arrested and continued to detain tens of thousands of people, including peaceful activists, humanitarian workers, lawyers and journalists, subjecting many to enforced disappearances, torture or other ill-treatment and causing deaths in detention. Armed opposition groups indiscriminately shelled civilian areas and subjected predominantly civilian areas to prolonged sieges, restricting access to humanitarian and medical aid. The armed group Islamic State (IS) unlawfully killed and shelled civilians and used them as human shields. US-led coalition forces carried out attacks on IS in which civilians were killed and injured, at times violating international humanitarian law. By the end of the year, the conflict had caused the deaths of more than 400,000 people and displaced more than 11 million people within and outside Syria.

BACKGROUND

The armed conflict in Syria entered its seventh year. Government forces and their allies, including Iranian and Hezbollah fighters, captured the majority of areas previously held by IS and other armed groups in Homs and Deir el-Zour governorates and other areas. They were supported by Russian armed forces, which carried out attacks on IS and other armed groups fighting the government, reportedly killing and injuring civilians. The Syrian Democratic Forces, consisting of Syrian-Kurdish and Arab armed groups, captured Raqqa governorate from IS

in October. They were supported by a US-led international coalition of states which carried out air strikes against IS in northern and eastern Syria, killing and injuring hundreds of civilians. Other armed opposition groups primarily fighting government forces, such as Ahrar al-Sham Islamic Movement, Hay'at Tahrir al-Sham and Jaysh al-Islam, controlled or contested areas in the governorates of Damascus Countryside, Idleb and Aleppo, sometimes fighting each other. Several suspected attacks by Israel inside Syria targeted Hezbollah, Syrian government positions and other fighters.

Russia continued to block efforts by the UN Security Council to pursue justice and accountability. On 12 April, Russia vetoed a resolution condemning the use of chemical weapons in Syria and calling for those responsible to be held accountable. On 17 November, Russia vetoed a resolution to extend the mandate of the Organization for the Prohibition of Chemical Weapons-UN Joint Investigative Mechanism established by the UN Security Council in 2015 to investigate chemical weapons attacks and determine responsibility for the use of chemical weapons in Syria.

Efforts by the UN to broker peace were unsuccessful as parties to the conflict and their allies shifted diplomatic discussions to Kazakhstan's capital, Astana. The diplomatic talks sponsored by Russia, Iran and Turkey aimed to strengthen the nationwide ceasefire agreement negotiated in December 2016 and enforce the "road map to peace" outlined in UN resolution 2254 of 2015. In May 2017 the Russian-brokered talks established four de-escalation zones across Syria, including the governorates of Idleb, Deraa, Homs and Damascus Countryside.

The Independent International Commission of Inquiry on the Syrian Arab Republic, established by the UN Human Rights Council in 2011, continued to monitor and report on violations of international law committed by parties to the conflict, although it remained barred by the government from entering Syria.

In July, Catherine Marchi-Uhel was appointed head of the International Impartial and Independent Mechanism established in December 2016 by the UN General Assembly to assist in the investigation and prosecution of the most serious crimes under international law committed in Syria since March 2011.

ARMED CONFLICT – VIOLATIONS BY SYRIAN GOVERNMENT FORCES AND ALLIES, INCLUDING IRAN AND RUSSIA

INDISCRIMINATE ATTACKS AND DIRECT ATTACKS ON CIVILIANS AND CIVILIAN OBJECTS

The Syrian government and allied forces continued to commit war crimes and other serious violations of international humanitarian law, including indiscriminate attacks and direct attacks on civilians and civilian objects including homes, hospitals and medical facilities. Government forces attacked areas controlled or contested by armed opposition groups, unlawfully killing and injuring civilians and damaging civilian objects through aerial bombardment and artillery shelling.

According to the NGO Physicians for Human Rights, government forces carried out air strikes on three hospitals in Idlib governorate on 19 September, killing a staff member, destroying ambulances and damaging the facilities. On 13 November, Syrian and Russian forces carried out air strikes during the day on a large market in Atareb, an opposition-held town in Aleppo governorate, killing at least 50 people, mostly civilians. On 18 November, government forces carried out air strikes and artillery attacks on civilians besieged in Eastern Ghouta in Damascus Countryside, killing at least 14.

On 4 April, government warplanes carried out an attack using internationally banned chemical weapons on Khan Sheikhoun in Idlib countryside, killing more than 70 civilians and injuring hundreds. On 30 June, the Organization for the Prohibition of Chemical Weapons concluded that people in Khan Sheikhoun were exposed to sarin, a banned nerve agent, in the attack.

SIEGES AND DENIAL OF HUMANITARIAN ACCESS

The government continued to maintain lengthy sieges of predominately civilian areas. The UN Office for the Co-ordination of Humanitarian Affairs (OCHA) reported that, out of a total of 419,920 people besieged in Syria, almost 400,000 were besieged by government forces in Eastern Ghouta. Government forces deprived residents in besieged areas of access to medical care, other basic goods and services and humanitarian assistance, while subjecting them to repeated air strikes, artillery shelling and other attacks. In October, UNICEF announced that 232 children in Eastern Ghouta suffered from severe acute malnutrition.

FORCED DISPLACEMENT OF CIVILIANS

The government and armed opposition groups negotiated four so-called reconciliation agreements between August 2016 and March 2017 that led to the forced displacement of thousands of residents from five besieged areas: Daraya, eastern Aleppo city, al-Waer neighbourhood in the city of Homs, and the towns of Kefraya and Foua. The government, and to a lesser extent armed opposition groups, subjected these densely populated areas to prolonged sieges and unlawful bombardment, compelling the armed opposition groups to surrender and negotiate a deal resulting in the evacuation of fighters and the mass displacement of civilians. The unlawful sieges and bombardment leading to the forced displacement of civilians were part of a systematic, widespread attack by the government on civilians and amounted to crimes against humanity.

ARMED CONFLICT – ABUSES BY ARMED GROUPS

INDISCRIMINATE ATTACKS AND DIRECT ATTACKS ON CIVILIANS

IS forces carried out direct attacks on civilians as well as indiscriminate attacks, killing and injuring civilians. During the operation launched mid-year by the Syrian Democratic Forces and the US-led coalition to recapture Raqqa city, IS forces prevented residents from fleeing the city and used civilians as human shields.

IS claimed responsibility for a series of suicide and other bomb attacks that directly targeted civilians, including one in February in Aleppo city that killed 50 people and one in October in the capital, Damascus, that killed 17 civilians. Hay'at Tahrir al-Sham claimed responsibility for two suicide bombings near a Shi'a pilgrimage site in Damascus on 11 March in which 44 civilians were killed and 120 injured.

In May, in-fighting between armed opposition groups erupted in Eastern Ghouta. It lasted several days, killing more than 100 civilians and fighters. Armed opposition groups in Eastern Ghouta also carried out indiscriminate rocket and mortar attacks on government-controlled neighbourhoods, killing and injuring several people during the year. In November, armed opposition groups fired imprecise rockets into the government-held town of Nubul, Aleppo governorate, killing three civilians.

UNLAWFUL KILLINGS

According to the Syrian Observatory for Human Rights, IS summarily killed more than 100 civilians accused of collaborating with the government in the town of al-Qaryatan, Homs governorate, before government forces recaptured the town.

SIEGES AND DENIALS OF HUMANITARIAN ASSISTANCE

Armed opposition groups maintained lengthy sieges of predominantly civilian areas, restricting access to humanitarian and medical aid and other essential goods and services. OCHA reported that Hay'at Tahrir al-Sham and Ahrar al-Sham Islamic Movement besieged 8,000 people in the towns of Kefraya and Foua, Idleb governorate.

ARMED CONFLICT – AIR STRIKES BY US-LED FORCES

The US-led coalition continued its campaign of air strikes against IS. The air strikes, some of which violated international humanitarian law, killed and injured civilians. In June, coalition forces unlawfully used white phosphorous munitions on civilian neighbourhoods in the outskirts of Raqqa. In May, a series of US-coalition strikes on a farm northwest of Raqqa killed 14 members of a family – eight women, one man and five children – and severely wounded two other children. Also in May, an air strike that targeted houses in the northern outskirts of Raqqa killed 31 people. In July, a coalition attack on a residential building 100m from an IS target killed a family including three children. The coalition forces also struck boats crossing the Euphrates River, south of Raqqa, killing dozens of civilians attempting to flee the intense fighting in the city. The coalition failed to adequately investigate reports of civilian casualties and allegations of violations of international humanitarian law.

ARMED CONFLICT – ABUSES BY THE PYD-LED AUTONOMOUS ADMINISTRATION

The Autonomous Administration, led by the Syrian-Kurdish Democratic Union Party (PYD), continued to control most of the predominantly Kurdish northern border regions. It arbitrarily arrested and detained a number of Syrian-Kurdish opposition activists, including members of the Kurdish National Council in Syria. Many were held in prolonged pre-trial detention in poor conditions.

REFUGEES AND INTERNALLY DISPLACED PEOPLE

Between 2011 and 2017, 6.5 million people were displaced within Syria and more than 5 million people sought refuge outside Syria, including 511,000 people who became refugees during 2017, according to UNHCR, the UN refugee agency, and OCHA. The authorities in the neighbouring states of Turkey, Lebanon and Jordan, which hosted nearly all of the refugees (including Palestinians displaced from Syria), restricted the entry of new refugees, exposing them to further attacks, violations and deprivation in Syria. The number of resettlement places and other safe and legal routes for refugees offered by European and other states fell far below the needs identified by UNHCR.

Some of the people displaced within Syria were living in makeshift camps with limited access to aid, other basic necessities, or opportunities to make a living.

ENFORCED DISAPPEARANCES

The Syrian security forces held thousands of detainees without trial, often in conditions that amounted to enforced disappearance. Tens of thousands of people remained subject to enforced disappearance, some since the outbreak of the conflict in 2011. They included peaceful critics and opponents of the government as well as family members detained in place of relatives wanted by the authorities.

TORTURE AND OTHER ILL-TREATMENT

Torture and other ill-treatment of detainees by government security and intelligence agencies and in state prisons remained systematic and widespread. Torture and other ill-treatment continued to result in a high incidence of detainee deaths. For example, large numbers of detainees at Saydnaya Military Prison died after being repeatedly tortured and systematically deprived of food, water, ventilation, medicine and medical care. Their bodies were buried in mass graves.

EXTRAJUDICIAL EXECUTIONS

Government forces carried out unlawful killings of detainees held in their custody in Saydnaya Military Prison near Damascus. As many as 13,000 prisoners from Saydnaya Military Prison were extrajudicially executed in night-time mass hangings between 2011 and 2015. The victims were overwhelmingly civilians perceived to oppose the government and were executed after being held in conditions amounting to enforced disappearance. Before they were hanged, the victims were condemned to death at the Military Field Court in the al-Qaboun neighbourhood of Damascus, in "trials" which lasted between one and three minutes. The Court was notorious for conducting closed proceedings that fell far short of the minimum international standards for a fair trial.

In August, the family of software developer Bassel Khartabil learned that he had been killed in 2015 after being "tried" and "sentenced to death" by the Military Field Court in al-Qaboun. Bassel Khartabil had been arrested on 15 March 2012 by Syrian Military Intelligence and held in incommunicado detention for eight months before being moved to 'Adra prison in Damascus in December 2012. He remained at 'Adra until 3 October 2015, when he was transferred to an undisclosed location prior to his execution.

DEATH PENALTY

The death penalty remained in force for many offences. The authorities disclosed little information about death sentences passed, and no information on executions.

TAIWAN

Taiwan
Head of state: **Tsai Ing-wen**
Head of government: **William Lai Ching-te (replaced Lin Chuan in September)**

Taiwan's Constitutional Court ruled that the current marriage law is unconstitutional as it discriminates against same-sex couples. The government held its second review of the implementation of the ICCPR and the ICESCR and its first review regarding the Convention on the Rights of People with Disabilities (CRPD) and the Convention on the Rights of the Child (CRC). The Supreme Court rejected the Prosecutor-General's extraordinary appeal for Chiou Ho-shun who remained on death row. From mid-February to early June when they were dispersed, Indigenous people and supporters staged a 100-day sit-in near the Presidential Office protesting against government guidelines, proposed by the cabinet-level Council of Indigenous Peoples, on changing the designation of traditional Indigenous

territory. Media reported that migrant workers were sexually harassed at work.

RIGHTS OF LESBIAN, GAY, BISEXUAL, TRANSGENDER AND INTERSEX PEOPLE

On 24 May, the Grand Council of Judges (Constitutional Court) ruled that sections on marriage in the current Civil Code were unconstitutional as they discriminated against same-sex couples. It gave the authorities two years to revise the law in order to achieve equal protection of freedom of marriage for same-sex couples. In late 2016, the Legislative Yuan, Taiwan's Parliament, had started discussion of a draft bill on revising the Civil Code to allow same-sex marriage but the bill had not progressed by the end of 2017. If passed, Taiwan would become the first jurisdiction in Asia to legalize same-sex marriage.

LEGAL, CONSTITUTIONAL OR INSTITUTIONAL DEVELOPMENTS

In January, the government convened independent international human rights experts to conduct its second review of the implementation of the ICCPR and the ICESCR.[1] The government initiated this parallel review process as Taiwan is not a member of the UN. The second review was to examine progress since the last one in 2013.

During the second review, the Taiwan government announced that it will establish a national human rights institution meeting the standards set out in the Paris Principles.

In late October and November, the government also convened international experts to conduct its first reviews of the implementation of the CPRD and CRC respectively.

DEATH PENALTY

The Supreme Court rejected the Prosecutor-General's extraordinary appeal for Chiou Ho-shun in July, a year after the application. Chiou Ho-shun, who has been on death row since 1989, is the longest-serving death row inmate in modern Taiwan history. The appeal application cited the failure of previous courts to omit evidence from a coerced "confession". Chiou Ho-shun claims he was tortured in custody and forced to "confess" during police interrogations before being found guilty of robbery, kidnapping and murder in 1989.

The Taichung Branch of the Taiwan High Court held a retrial of the case of Cheng Hsing-tse, who was released on bail in 2016. The court cleared his name in October, overturning his convictions. He had served 14 years in prison after he was convicted of the murder of a police officer during an exchange of gunfire at a karaoke parlour in Taichung in 2002.

REFUGEES AND ASYLUM-SEEKERS

By the end of the year there had been no progress on the refugee bill since its second reading in July 2016. This was despite international experts concluding recommendations in January, which urged the speedy adoption of a refugee law to include the principle of *non-refoulement*.

---

1. Taiwan: Government must act on human rights review (ASA 38/5531/2017)

TAJIKISTAN

Republic of Tajikistan
Head of state: **Emomali Rahmon**
Head of government: **Qokhir Rasulzoda**

The authorities continued to impose sweeping restrictions on the rights to freedom of expression and of peaceful assembly to silence critical voices. Police and security services continued to persecute human rights lawyers and their families. A human rights lawyer was tortured in detention and had his sentence extended to 28 years' imprisonment following three unfair trials. Lesbian, gay, bisexual, transgender and intersex (LGBTI) people were subjected to violence, arbitrary arrest and discrimination. The authorities forced thousands of women to remove their hijabs to comply with the law on traditions.

BACKGROUND

Public order and counter-terrorism concerns, real and perceived, dominated the political agenda. The authorities relentlessly invoked national security issues to justify ever harsher restrictions on perceived dissent, on the grounds that these measures ensured stability and preserved cultural traditions.

The UN Special Rapporteur on the right to freedom of opinion and expression noted in his June report that since his 2016 visit to Tajikistan the "draconian restrictions on opposition voices and the squeezing of civil society" had continued to worsen. He concluded that "the Government is obligated under human rights law to reconsider its entire approach to restricting the opposition, the media, the Internet, and civil society as a whole."

JUSTICE SYSTEM

By December, less than half of the 2,000 lawyers registered nationwide had managed to requalify and were licensed to practise. Amendments introduced in 2015 to the law on the legal profession increased government control over the licensing of lawyers and significantly cut the total number of lawyers licensed to practise, drastically reducing citizens' access to justice.

PERSECUTION OF DEFENCE LAWYERS

Defence lawyers who took up politically sensitive cases, or cases related to national security and counter-terrorism, faced increasing harassment, intimidation and undue pressure in connection with their legitimate professional activities. Human rights lawyers faced arbitrary arrests, prosecutions on politically motivated charges, harsh prison sentences and the harassment of their families and colleagues. Many human rights lawyers fled the country for safety.[1]

THE CASE OF BUZURGMEKHR YOROV

In February, the Supreme Court in Dushanbe, the capital, turned down the appeals against the prison sentences of human rights lawyers Buzurgmekhr Yorov and Nuriddin Makhkamov who had represented several members of the banned Islamic Renaissance Party of Tajikistan.

Dushanbe City Court had sentenced them to 23 and 21 years' imprisonment respectively in October 2016, following a blatantly unfair trial. Both lawyers were found guilty of "arousing national, racial, local or religious hostility" and "public calls for violent change of the constitutional order of the Republic of Tajikistan", charges they consistently denied. The state media portrayed Buzurgmekhr Yorov as a "terrorist sympathizer" and therefore a "terrorist" himself.

In February, Firdavs District Court in Dushanbe started hearings into a third criminal case brought by the authorities against Buzurgmekhr Yorov on new fraud charges, allegedly in response to complaints made against him by members of the public.

In March, in the second trial of Buzurgmekhr Yorov, the Supreme Court found him guilty of disrespecting the Court and insulting government officials in his final statement to Dushanbe City Court in October 2016. He was sentenced to an additional two years' imprisonment. The trial was opened in December 2016 when he was in the pre-trial detention centre number 1 (SIZO) in Dushanbe.

In April, Buzurgmekhr Yorov's wife was informed of a fourth criminal case brought against her husband for allegedly insulting "the leader of the Nation". In August, he was sentenced to an additional three years' imprisonment on charges of fraud and of insulting "the leader of the Nation" in statements he made in court during his original trial in response to the fraud charges brought against him. The total length of his sentence was 28 years. The family could not find any lawyers willing to represent Buzurgmekhr Yorov as they feared reprisals from the authorities after human rights lawyer Muazzamakhon Kadirova, who represented him in 2016, had to seek protection abroad.

In September, the authorities allowed Buzurgmekhr Yorov's mother to visit him in SIZO 1. He told her that the guards subjected him and other cellmates to regular beatings, including to the head, using their legs, arms and batons while insulting, humiliating and threatening them. He spent several days in the SIZO medical centre following one of the beatings. Buzurgmekhr Yorov was put in solitary confinement at least four times as punishment for what the SIZO Director explained to the media were "violations of the detention regime". The SIZO Director denied all allegations of torture and other ill-treatment of Buzurgmekhr Yorov.

RIGHTS OF LESBIAN, GAY, BISEXUAL, TRANSGENDER AND INTERSEX PEOPLE

Consensual same-sex sexual relations were not criminalized but continued to be highly stigmatized. Since 2014, the Ministry of Internal Affairs (MIA) included "homosexuality and lesbianism" in its list of "amoral crimes, prostitution and procurement". LGBTI people were targeted in two public campaigns to prevent and combat "amoral behaviour" and crimes against "morality" launched in 2015 by the Office of the Prosecutor General, MIA and the State Committee on Women's Affairs and Family. LGBTI individuals were subjected to violence, arbitrary arrests, detention and discrimination, including being forcibly registered on MIA lists. In October, the Minister of Internal Affairs announced that the names and personal details of 367 individuals suspected of being LGBTI had been entered on an MIA register ostensibly to protect them and to "prevent the transmission of sexually transmitted diseases, including HIV/AIDS". The authorities accused NGOs working with LGBTI people in the context of sexual health of undermining traditional cultural values.

DISCRIMINATION

In August, President Rahmon signed into law amendments to the Law on Traditions regulating the practice of cultural traditions and celebrations. The amendments compelled citizens to wear traditional dress at cultural celebrations or ceremonies, such as weddings and funerals. Women in particular were prohibited from wearing black at funerals.

In the same month, police and local officials approached over 8,000 women who were wearing the Islamic headscarf (hijab) in public places, ordered them to remove it because it was against the law and asked them instead to wear a headscarf tied behind the head in the "traditional Tajik way". Dozens of women were briefly detained, many had their hijabs forcibly removed. Women wearing western-style dress were not targeted. Government officials claimed that the hijab was a form of "alien culture and tradition" and a sign of "extremism". Shops selling Islamic clothing were raided by security forces and many were forced to close.

REPRESSION OF DISSENT

Dozens of members and associates of banned opposition groups, such as Islamic Renaissance Party of Tajikistan and Group 24, and their families sought protection abroad. Party and Group 24 activists in exile reported that in retaliation for their actions abroad, such as conducting peaceful protests at international meetings and conferences, police and security services threatened, detained, questioned and in some cases beat family members, including elderly relatives and children, in Tajikistan. Local authorities publicly shamed relatives branding them as "traitors" and "enemies of the state".

FREEDOM OF EXPRESSION

The authorities continued to impose sweeping restrictions on freedom of expression and the media and controlled virtually all forms of access to information. Journalists continued to be subjected to intimidation and harassment by police and security services. Tens of journalists were forced to flee the country fearing reprisals for their critical reporting.

In May, the authorities unblocked access to some social media sites and search platforms, such as Facebook, Vkontakte and YouTube. However, access to media platforms considered to be promoting "extremism", such as BBC, CNN and Ferghana.ru, continued to be blocked.

In July, Parliament adopted new legislation granting the police and security services new powers to obtain information about internet sites visited by individuals. The law was proposed following claims, which were not substantiated, by some officials that over 80% of internet users accessed sites with "extremist" content.

1. In the line of duty: Harassment, prosecution and imprisonment of lawyers in Tajikistan (EUR 60/6266/2017)

TANZANIA

United Republic of Tanzania
Head of state: **John Magufuli**
Head of government: **Kassim Majaliwa**
Head of Zanzibar government: **Ali Mohamed Shein**

The authorities restricted the rights to freedom of expression and association, and failed to address discrimination on grounds of gender and sexual orientation. Refugees and asylum-seekers faced overcrowding, insufficient rations, and bureaucratic obstacles put in place by the state authorities.

RIGHTS OF LESBIAN, GAY, BISEXUAL, TRANSGENDER AND INTERSEX PEOPLE

The government continued its crackdown against LGBTI people, closing down health centres and threatening to deregister organizations that provided services and support to them. On 17 February, the Health Minister closed down 40 private health centres, accusing them of promoting same-sex relations which is punishable by up to 30 years' imprisonment. On 25 June, the Home Affairs Minister threatened to deport any foreign national, or prosecute anyone, working to protect LGBTI rights.

In Zanzibar 12 women and eight men – were detained on 18 September while receiving HIV/AIDS training at a hotel. The government accused them of promoting LGBTI rights. On 17 October the authorities arrested 13 health and human rights activists, including two South Africans and one Ugandan, during a consultative meeting to discuss the Tanzanian government's decision to limit provision of certain health services for LGBTI people. The activists were released without charge on 27 October, after a court found that there was insufficient evidence for the prosecutor to sustain the case.

FREEDOM OF EXPRESSION

Opposition MPs who were perceived as critical of the government faced harassment, intimidation and arrest. On 21 September, Zitto Kabwe, leader of the Alliance for Change and Transparency party, was arrested following comments he made on social media. These concerned the House Speaker's handling of reports by two parliamentary committees formed to investigate tanzanite and diamond mining before they were debated in Parliament. He appeared before the Parliamentary Privileges, Ethics and Powers Committee on 22 September and was subsequently released. The Committee had not sent their report to the Speaker by the end of the year.

On 31 October, Zitto Kabwe was again detained by police for allegedly issuing false statistics on the national economic growth figures. According to Section 37(5) of the Statistics Act of 2017, any agency or person who publishes or communicates official statistical information which may result in the distortion of facts, commits an offence. This can be punishable by a fine or imprisonment of not less than three years, or both. Zitto Kabwe was released on 31 October without charge.

Tundu Lissu, President of Tanganyika Law Society and an MP for the opposition Chadema party, was arrested on 21 October and charged with "hate speech" after he criticized President Magufuli. In a public speech on 17 July, he said that the government was discriminating along family, tribal and regional lines when employing government officials, and issuing work permits along religious lines. He also referred to the President as a dictator. He was released the same day after interrogation by the police.

Media freedom deteriorated significantly. President Magufuli stated in January that the days of newspapers viewed as "unethical" were numbered. From June to September, three newspapers – *MwanaHalisi*, *Mawio* and *Raia Mwema* – were either closed or temporarily banned from publishing because of "unethical" reporting and inciting violence. On 15 June the Information, Sports and Culture Minister banned *Mawio* for two years over articles it published linking two former presidents with alleged improprieties in mining deals signed in the 1990s and early 2000s. On 19 September, the Information Service Directorate issued a two-year ban on *MwanaHalisi*, after accusing it of insulting the President and publishing unethical stories. This was the second time the newspaper had been suspended in three months.

On 17 March, Dar es Salaam's Regional Commissioner led a raid on Clouds Media Group, allegedly for their decision not to broadcast a video aimed at undermining a popular local pastor.

The Electronic and Postal Communications (Online Content) Regulations, 2017, passed in September, curtailed online freedom. According to the regulations, social media users and online content producers are held liable for materials deemed "indecent, obscene, hate speech, extreme violence or material that will offend or incite others, cause annoyance, threaten harm or evil, encourage or incite crime, or lead to public disorder". Those found guilty face a fine of 5 million Tanzanian shillings (USD2,300), a minimum of 12 months in jail, or both.

RIGHT TO EDUCATION

On 22 June, President Magufuli issued a statement banning pregnant girls from returning to public-funded schools. He stated: "As long as I'm President, no pregnant students will be allowed to return to school." He said that young mothers could opt for vocational training or become entrepreneurs, but should not be permitted to pursue formal education in public schools. On 25 June, the Home Affairs Minister threatened to deregister organizations that challenged the President's ban on schooling for pregnant girls and teenage mothers.

REFUGEES AND ASYLUM-SEEKERS

According to UNHCR, the UN refugee agency, by the end of October, 359,494 Burundian refugees resided in Tanzania (see Burundi entry). On 20 January, the Home Affairs Ministry revoked prima facie refugee status recognition of Burundian asylum-seekers, and new arrivals had to undergo individual refugee status determination processes. UNHCR warned that the situation in Nduta camp in Tanzania, in particular, was "alarming". Originally designed to hold 50,000 people, at the end of 2017 it was home to over 127,000. UNHCR and its partners also lacked sufficient capacity to prevent, or respond adequately to, sexual and gender-based violence. UNHCR raised concerns about risks to health and safety caused by overcrowding. On 27 August, the World Food Programme warned that the already insufficient food rations for refugees in Tanzania would have to be further reduced unless there was urgent funding from donors. Regular food and water shortages in the camps in Tanzania were seen by some refugees as an attempt to force them to return home. This was particularly in the light of comments made in July by President Magufuli during a visit by Burundian President Pierre Nkurunziza, encouraging refugees to return to Burundi.

Tanzania operated a de facto encampment policy by which refugees who left the camps without permission faced fines or arrest.

THAILAND

Kingdom of Thailand
Head of state: **King Maha Vajiralongkorn Bodindradebayavarangkun**
Head of government: **Prayut Chan-o-Cha**

Activists, journalists, politicians, human rights lawyers and human rights defenders were arrested, detained and prosecuted for peacefully expressing opinions about the

government and monarchy. **The government maintained systematic and arbitrary restrictions on human rights, including the rights to freedom of expression, peaceful assembly and association. It failed to fulfil its promise to pass a law prohibiting torture and enforced disappearances. Refugees and asylum-seekers continued to be denied formal legal status; they were vulnerable to arrest, detention and deportation.**

BACKGROUND

The country remained under the authority of the military National Council for Peace and Order (NCPO). A new Constitution, drafted by a military-appointed body and approved in an August 2016 national referendum, came into effect in April. Authorities prosecuted former government officials for a rice subsidy scheme. Former Prime Minister Yingluck Shinawatra secretly left the country in August; she was subsequently tried in her absence on charges of negligence and sentenced to five years' imprisonment. King Maha Vajiralongkorn Bodindradebayavarangkun was crowned in December.

JUSTICE SYSTEM

Throughout the year, the Head of the NCPO continued to use extraordinary powers under Article 44 of the interim Constitution to arbitrarily restrict peaceful political activities and the exercise of other human rights. Military officials exercised sweeping law enforcement powers, including to detain individuals in unofficial places of detention without charge for a broad range of activities. A number were held incommunicado. Hundreds of civilians continued to face lengthy and unfair trials before military courts for violations of NCPO orders, offences against "national security" and allegedly insulting the monarchy.

FREEDOMS OF EXPRESSION, ASSEMBLY AND ASSOCIATION

The government continued to systematically and arbitrarily restrict the rights to freedom of expression, peaceful assembly and association. Student activists, media workers, human rights lawyers, politicians and others were prosecuted for peacefully exercising these rights, including in unfair trials in military courts.

Authorities initiated criminal proceedings against participants in peaceful public protests, academic seminars and civil society activities under a 2015 decree providing for criminal penalties for "political gatherings" of five or more people. In November authorities initiated criminal proceedings against protesters seeking to petition about the construction of a coal-fired power plant in Songkhla, southern Thailand.

Three opposition politicians and a journalist were among several individuals charged with sedition under Article 116 of the Penal Code for criticizing the government or voicing support for opposition politicians, including in comments made on social media.

Activists, journalists and workers faced criminal defamation charges initiated by government officials and private companies for publicizing information about rights violations, environmental concerns and official misconduct. In October, charges filed in 2016 against three human rights defenders – Pornpen Khongkachonkiet, Somchai Homla-or and Anchana Heemmina – in relation to their reporting on torture by military officers were formally withdrawn. The Supreme Court, overturning rulings by lower courts, sentenced two opposition politicians to one year's imprisonment for the criminal defamation of former Prime Minister Abhisit Vejjajiva in two separate cases in April and July.

Authorities continued to vigorously prosecute cases under Article 112 of the Penal Code – lèse-majesté provision – which penalized criticism of the monarchy. Individuals were charged or prosecuted under Article 112 during the year, including some alleged to have offended past monarchs. Trials for lèse-majesté were held behind closed doors. In June, the Bangkok Military Court sentenced a man to a record 35 years' imprisonment – halved from 70 years after he pleaded guilty – for a series of

Facebook posts allegedly concerning the monarchy.[1] In August, student activist and human rights defender Jatupat "Pai" Boonpattararaksa was sentenced to two and a half years' imprisonment after being convicted in a case concerning his sharing a BBC profile of Thailand's King on Facebook. Authorities brought lèse-majesté charges against a prominent academic for comments he made about a battle fought by a 16th century Thai king.

Authorities pressured Facebook, Google and YouTube to remove online content, including material deemed critical of the monarchy. The authorities also threatened to prosecute internet service providers that did not remove content, as well as individuals communicating with or sharing posts from exiled government critics. Six people were subsequently arrested for sharing Facebook posts concerning the removal of a plaque commemorating events in 1932 that brought an end to absolute monarchy. At the end of the year they remained imprisoned, facing charges on multiple counts of violation of Article 112.

Authorities proposed cybersecurity legislation and other measures that would allow for increased online surveillance and censorship without prior judicial authorization.

IMPUNITY

In August, the Supreme Court dismissed murder charges against former Prime Minister Abhisit Vejjajiva and Deputy Prime Minister Suthep Thaugsuban. The charges related to the deaths of at least 90 people in 2010 during clashes between protesters and security forces.

REFUGEES AND ASYLUM-SEEKERS

Thailand continued to host more than 100,000 refugees and asylum-seekers; they included Myanmar nationals in camps along the Thailand-Myanmar border, and refugees in the capital, Bangkok, and other cities. Refugees and asylum-seekers had no formal legal status in Thailand, leaving them vulnerable to arrest, detention and deportation.[2] In May, Thai authorities assisted in the extradition of Turkish national Muhammet Furkan Sökmen from Myanmar to Turkey via Bangkok, despite warnings from UN agencies that he was at risk of human rights violations if returned. At the end of the year, hundreds of refugees and asylum-seekers remained in immigration detention centres, where many had been held for years.

In January, the Cabinet authorized the development of a system for screening refugees and irregular migrants which, if implemented in a fair and non-discriminatory manner, could represent a major step towards advancing refugee rights. The system had not been finalized by the end of the year.

EXTRAJUDICIAL EXECUTIONS AND ENFORCED DISAPPEARANCES

In March, Chaiyaphum Pasae, a 17-year-old Indigenous Lahu youth activist, was shot dead at a checkpoint staffed by soldiers and anti-narcotics officers, who claimed to have acted in self-defence. By the end of the year, an official investigation into his death had made little progress; the authorities failed to produce CCTV footage from cameras known to have been present at the time of the incident.[3]

The government failed to make progress in resolving open cases of enforced disappearance. A Thai delegation told the UN Human Rights Committee in March that it was considering forwarding the cases of the enforced disappearances of Somchai Neelapaijit and Porlajee "Billy" Rakchongcharoen to the Department of Special Investigation, but had not done so by the end of the year.[4]

In March, the National Legislative Assembly approved proceeding with the ratification of the International Convention for the Protection of All Persons from Enforced Disappearance, which Thailand signed in 2012. However, by the end of the year Thailand had neither ratified the treaty nor provided a timeframe for doing so.

ARMED CONFLICT

There was little progress in government negotiations to resolve armed conflict with ethnic Malay separatists in southern Thailand. Insurgents carried out numerous attacks on military and civilian targets, including execution-style killings and the use of improvised explosive devices.

Martial law and a 2005 Emergency Decree remained in place in far south provinces. Individuals were arrested and detained in unofficial places of detention without judicial oversight.

TORTURE AND OTHER ILL-TREATMENT

Local organizations and community members reported that the military arbitrarily arrested, tortured and otherwise ill-treated Muslim men following attacks by militants in southern Thailand. Human rights defenders working with victims of torture were harassed by military authorities and threatened on social media.

In February, the National Legislative Assembly returned a draft Prevention and Suppression of Torture and Enforced Disappearance Act to the Cabinet for "more consultations".[5] The latest draft addressed gaps in the current legal framework relating to torture and enforced disappearances. Further amendments were needed to bring the bill into line with Thailand's obligations under international law.[6]

TRAFFICKING IN HUMAN BEINGS

In July, a criminal court convicted 62 individuals, including senior military, police and other government officials, for their involvement in human trafficking operations. They were sentenced to between four and 94 years' imprisonment. Human rights groups raised concerns that witnesses, translators and police investigators were threatened during the investigation and trial, and that the investigation had been terminated prematurely.

1. Thailand: Continuing crackdown on free online expression (ASA 39/6480/2017)

2. Between a rock and a hard place: Thailand's refugee policies and violations of the principle of non-refoulement (ASA 39/7031/2017)

3. Thailand: Ensure accountability for killing of 17-year-old Lahu activist (ASA 39/5915/2017)

4. Thailand: Joint statement on the International Day of the Victims of Enforced Disappearances (ASA 39/7015/2017)

5. Thailand: Prioritize the amendment and passage of legislation on torture and enforced disappearances (ASA 39/5846/2017)

6. Thailand must follow through on commitments to prevent torture and ill-treatment (ASA 39/6589/2017)

TIMOR-LESTE

Democratic Republic of Timor-Leste
Head of state: **Francisco Guterres (replaced Taur Matan Ruak in May)**
Head of government: **Mari Alkatiri (replaced Rui Maria de Araújo in September)**

Victims of serious human rights violations committed during the Indonesian occupation (1975-1999) continued to demand justice and reparations. Security forces were accused of ill-treatment. Journalists faced defamation charges for carrying out their work.

BACKGROUND

Presidential and parliamentary elections, held respectively in March and July, took place without incident. In June, Timor-Leste accepted fully 146 out of 154 recommendations made under the UPR process and noted the eight remaining recommendations. Those that were accepted included recommendations to address past human rights violations and ensure the delivery of reparations to victims.

IMPUNITY

A new government body, the Chega! National Centre – From Memory to Hope (CNC), was established through Decree Law No. 48/2016. The CNC's purpose was to facilitate the implementation of recommendations made by Timor-Leste's truth commission (CAVR) in 2005 and the bilateral Timor-Leste and Indonesia Commission of Truth and Friendship in 2008. The main planned activities of the CNC included memorialization, education, solidarity with victims of past human rights violations, and outreach. However, the CNC did not have a mandate to address the CAVR's recommendations on justice and reparations for victims of serious human rights violations.

POLICE AND SECURITY FORCES

Timorese human rights groups continued to express concern over allegations of unnecessary or excessive use of force and torture and other ill-treatment by security forces, and a lack of accountability. On 22 April, it was reported that members of the Public Order Battalion (BOP) Unit of the National Police beat and kicked a man in Bobonaro District causing bleeding from the nose, ear and mouth. At the end of the year, the alleged abuse was under investigation by the Office of the Public Prosecutor of Suai District.

FREEDOM OF EXPRESSION – JOURNALISTS

On 1 June, a court in the capital, Dili, cleared journalists Raimundos Oki and Lourenco Vicente Martins of all charges against them. The charges had been filed by the Public Prosecutor on 17 May in a defamation lawsuit, following assertions made in January 2016 by the then Prime Minister Araújo that the journalists had made false accusations or a "slanderous denunciation" under Article 285(1) of the Criminal Code. The charges were in relation to an article in the *Timor Post* newspaper alleging official interference during the tendering process for a government IT project.

TOGO

Togolese Republic
Head of state: **Faure Gnassingbé**
Head of government: **Komi Sélom Klassou**

The authorities continued to curtail the rights to freedom of expression and of assembly during mass demonstrations organized by opposition groups. Security forces used excessive force against demonstrators with at least 11 people killed during protests. Arbitrary arrests and detentions, torture and other ill-treatment, and impunity for human rights violations persisted.

INTERNATIONAL SCRUTINY

Togo accepted various recommendations that arose from the examination of its human rights record under the UPR process, including to take steps to prevent torture and other human rights violations by the security forces, and to ensure adequate investigation and prosecution of anyone suspected of being responsible. It rejected recommendations including to amend or repeal laws used to crack down on journalists and human rights defenders, including laws criminalizing defamation; and to ensure the protection of lesbian, gay, bisexual, transgender and intersex people.[1]

EXCESSIVE USE OF FORCE

The security forces, including the army, continued to suppress and disperse peaceful protests using excessive and lethal force. They violently dispersed protests, beat opposition members and subjected journalists to ill-treatment.

On 28 February, security forces used live ammunition to disperse a spontaneous protest against oil price rises in the capital, Lomé, killing one person and wounding several others.[2]

In June, the security forces repressed demonstrations organized by a University of Lomé student union which called for improved living conditions. Internet videos showed security force members, armed with shotguns, battering students on the ground with batons. Some students threw rocks at security forces. At least 19 students were arrested, 10 of whom were released shortly after being brought before the prosecutor. On 19 June, seven were released after the Tribunal of Lomé acquitted them of acts of rebellion and destruction of property. On 26 June, Foly Satchivi, President of the Togolese League of Student Rights, and Marius

Amagbégnon, received a 12-month suspended prison sentence for aggravated disturbance of public order as the court considered them to be the organizers of the demonstration. After their release on 27 June, they appealed against their convictions. Several students told the court that they were beaten by security forces during arrest and transfer.

Between August and December, the political opposition held mass demonstrations in major cities. The security forces dispersed them with tear gas, batons, water cannons and live ammunition and there were sporadic violent clashes between opposition groups and supporters of the ruling party. The security forces raided houses and places of prayer, beating people, including those who had not participated in demonstrations. At least 10 people were killed, including two members of the armed forces and three children aged between 11 and 14. Hundreds were injured, including members of the security forces. More than 200 people were arrested, including the Secretary General of the opposition Pan African National Party (PNP). At least 60 people were sentenced to prison terms of up to 60 months on charges including rebellion, wilful destruction, assault, violence against state officials, aggravated disruption of the public order and aggravated theft.[3]

FREEDOM OF EXPRESSION

The authorities continued to curtail the right to freedom of expression. They arbitrarily closed media outlets and arrested community and opposition leaders for expressing dissent. They cut off the internet to prevent activists and journalists from reporting violations.

On 6 February, the High Authority for Audiovisual and Communication (HAAC) withdrew the frequencies of radio station CityFM and TV station La Chaîne du Futur for breaching licensing rules. The HAAC statute did not provide any mechanism to appeal against the decision.[4]

On 7 February, journalist Robert Kossi Avotor was beaten with batons and handcuffed by gendarmes to prevent him from photographing an eviction in Lomé. He was detained and his photographs deleted, before being released on the same day without charge. He filed a complaint with the prosecution services in Lomé to which he said he had received no response by the end of the year. On 22 February, the General Prosecutor issued a warning that anyone who reported on the attack on Robert Kossi Avotor would risk criminal prosecution for "disseminating false news".

Kombate Garimbité, a member of the opposition Alliance of Democrats for Integral Development (ADDI), was arrested on 4 April after he criticized a call made by the chief of the Yembour locality for students' relatives to pay for damages caused during a protest in March. The authorities accused him of organizing the March protest and he was charged with aggravated disturbance of public order. He claimed that he was not involved in the protests and was in Lomé, 630km away from Yembour, at the time. By the end of the year, he remained in detention without trial.[5]

Salomée T. Abalodo was arrested by gendarmes in Pagouda, a town in the Kara region, on 13 April after she took pictures of wounded protesters and asked local authorities to stop security forces using excessive force against peaceful demonstrators. She was charged with "rebellion" and "participation in an unauthorized protest". She was released on 12 May when the Tribunal of Pagouda dropped the charges.[6]

The authorities shut down the internet for nine days in September amid opposition-led protests, disrupting the organization of the protest and impeding the work of human rights defenders and journalists who were monitoring the protests.

IMPUNITY

The authorities continued to fail to take steps to identify those suspected of responsibility for human rights violations, including the deaths of nearly 500 people, during the violence surrounding the presidential election in 2005. Of the 72 complaints filed by the victims' families with the Atakpamé, Amlamé and Lomé courts, none are known to have been fully investigated.

1. Amnesty International urges Togo to expressly commit to protecting the rights to freedom of association, freedom of expression and peaceful assembly (AFR 57/5884/2017)

2. Togo. Un mort par balle et plusieurs blessés lors d'une manifestation dispersée par l'armée (Press release, 1 March)

3. Togo. Les autorités doivent s'abstenir de tout recours injustifié ou excessif à la force lors des manifestations de l'opposition (Press release, 6 September); Togo. Un enfant de neuf ans tué par balle lors des manifestations (Press release, 20 September)

4. Togo. Le retrait des fréquences de deux médias est une attaque contre la liberté d'expression (Press release, 6 February)

5. Togo. Un militant politique détenu pour ses opinions doit être libéré (Press release, 12 April)

6. Togo: Detained community leader wrongly charged: Salomée T. Abalodo (AFR 57/6193/2017)

TUNISIA

Republic of Tunisia
Head of state: **Béji Caïd Essebsi**
Head of government: **Youssef Chahed**

The authorities continued to renew the state of emergency and used it to justify imposing arbitrary restrictions on freedom of movement. Torture and other ill-treatment of detainees continued in an environment of impunity. Police carried out arbitrary arrests and house raids without judicial warrants. Lesbian, gay, bisexual, transgender and intersex people were arrested and prosecuted for consensual same-sex sexual relations. Prosecutions of peaceful protesters increased in several regions.

BACKGROUND

The authorities renewed the nationwide state of emergency five times during the year for periods of one to three months. A major cabinet reshuffle in September brought 13 new ministers into government.

Protests against unemployment, poor living conditions and marginalizing development policies continued, particularly in underdeveloped regions.

In May, Parliament adopted an amendment to the Passport Law introducing positive provisions requiring that people affected by a travel ban be informed of the decision promptly, and guaranteeing that they have the right to challenge the decision.[1]

In May, Tunisia's human rights record was examined for the third time under the UN UPR process. Recommendations to Tunisia were adopted by the UN Human Rights Council in September.

Local municipal elections scheduled to take place in December were postponed to May 2018 because of delays in making appointments to the National Independent Elections Commission. Parliament failed to elect its allotted quota of Constitutional Court members as required by law, thereby impeding the establishment of the Court.

COUNTER-TERROR AND SECURITY

Emergency measures in place since November 2015 continued to give the Minister of the Interior broad additional powers, including the ability to conduct house raids without judicial warrants and impose restrictions on freedom of movement. The Ministry of the Interior continued to restrict freedom of movement through arbitrary and indefinite S17 orders that confined hundreds to their governorate of residence, justifying this as a measure to prevent Tunisians from travelling to join armed groups. Human rights lawyers reported instances of arbitrary arrest and short-term detention of people subjected to S17 border control measures. The Minister of the Interior told Parliament in April that 134 individuals had filed complaints with the Administrative Court challenging S17 orders. In April, the Minister announced that 537 individuals were facing trial for "terrorism-related" activities.

Family members of individuals suspected of joining or supporting armed groups faced harassment and intimidation by the police. The Malik family's home in Tozeur was regularly raided by police because they suspected one member of the family of affiliation to armed groups abroad. In May, two members of the family, journalists Salam and Salwa Malik, were prosecuted and sentenced to six months' imprisonment, later reduced to a fine, after they criticized the conduct of police during a particularly violent raid on their home.[2]

Police harassed individuals on account of their appearance, arresting and interrogating men with beards and men and women dressed in what officials deemed to be conservative religious clothing.

TORTURE AND OTHER ILL-TREATMENT

Human rights lawyers continued to report cases of torture and other ill-treatment of detainees, mostly during arrest and in pre-charge detention in regular criminal cases and national security cases. In March and April, the Parliamentary Committee on Rights, Liberties and External Relations invited Amnesty International to brief them after the Prime Minister said that the government would investigate claims made by Amnesty International regarding abuses by security forces, including torture.[3] It subsequently held four further sessions on torture: one session each with Amnesty International, two Tunisian NGOs, and the Minister of the Interior.

The work of Tunisia's National Preventive Mechanism (NPM) – the National Body for the Prevention of Torture, which was established in 2013 as part of Tunisia's obligations as a party to the Optional Protocol to the UN Convention against Torture – continued to be hampered by a lack of co-operation from the Ministry of the Interior and inadequate financial support from the government. In April, police at Tunis Carthage International Airport denied members of the NPM access to monitor the handover of a "terrorism" suspect deported from Germany.

RIGHTS OF LESBIAN, GAY, BISEXUAL, TRANSGENDER AND INTERSEX PEOPLE

LGBTI people continued to be at risk of arrest under Article 230 of the Penal Code, which criminalizes consensual same-sex sexual relations. Police arrested at least 44 individuals who were later charged and prosecuted under Article 230. In June, a judge in Sousse sentenced a 16-year-old boy in his absence to four months' imprisonment under Article 230.

LGBTI people also faced violence, exploitation and sexual and other abuse by police, including when they tried to seek a remedy for violations of their rights. In July, police officers in Sousse arbitrarily arrested and beat two men because of their perceived sexual orientation. In August, police officers in Sidi Bousaid, near the capital, Tunis, assaulted a transgender resident of Tunis when he went to the police station to file a complaint for harassment on the grounds of his gender.

The police continued to subject men accused of same-sex sexual relations to forced anal examinations, in violation of the prohibition of torture. In September, Tunisia accepted a recommendation under the UN UPR process to end the use of anal examinations.

FREEDOMS OF EXPRESSION, ASSOCIATION AND ASSEMBLY

On 10 May, President Essebsi announced the deployment of the army to protect key economic installations from disruption by social and labour protests. In the following days, police forces used excessive force including tear gas against peaceful protesters in the southern city of Tataouine. A young protester was killed when a National Guard vehicle ran him over in what the Ministry of Health said was an accident. On 18 September, a group of officers beat journalist Hamdi Souissi with batons while he was covering a sit-in in Sfax. Throughout the year, courts increasingly prosecuted peaceful protesters. In Gafsa alone, courts tried hundreds of individuals, at least 80 of them in their absence, on charges of "disrupting the freedom of work" following social protests related to unemployment.

Courts continued to use arbitrary Penal Code provisions to prosecute people for conduct protected by the right to freedom of expression. In May, the Court of First Instance in Sousse sentenced two young men to two months' imprisonment for "public indecency" for designing and wearing a T-shirt with a slogan suggesting that police officers are morally corrupt. In July, rap singer Ahmed Ben Ahmed was assaulted by a group of police officers who were supposed to be providing security for his concert, because they were offended that his songs were insulting to the police. A police union later filed a complaint before the Court of First Instance in Mahdia against Ahmed Ben Ahmed for the Penal Code crime of "insulting state officials".

In June, the Court of First Instance in Bizert convicted at least five people of "public indecency" for publicly smoking during the day during Ramadan.[4]

On 8 September, the authorities arbitrarily expelled Prince Hicham Al Alaoui, a cousin and vocal critic of Morocco's King Mohamed VI, from Tunisia as he arrived to attend a conference on democratic transitions.

WOMEN'S RIGHTS

In July, Parliament adopted the Law on Eliminating Violence against Women which brought several guarantees for the protection of women and girls from gender-based violence. It repealed Penal Code Article 227 bis that had allowed men accused of raping a woman or girl under the age of 20 to escape prosecution by marrying her.

In August, President Essebsi called on Parliament to reform the discriminatory inheritance law and created a commission mandated to propose legal reforms to ensure gender equality. The commission had not delivered its report by the end of the year. In September, the Ministry of Justice repealed the 1973 directive prohibiting marriage between a Tunisian woman and a non-Muslim man.

In a cabinet reshuffle in September the number of women ministers was decreased from four to three out of 28 ministerial posts, leaving women severely under-represented in government.

TRANSITIONAL JUSTICE

The Truth and Dignity Commission (IVD), created in 2013 to address human rights violations committed between July 1955 and December 2013, held 11 public sessions during the year. During these sessions, victims and perpetrators testified on a range of violations including election fraud, enforced disappearance and torture. There was no progress on the adoption of a memorandum of understanding between the IVD and the Ministry of Justice to allow for the referral of cases to specialized judicial chambers. Government institutions including the Ministries of the Interior, Defence, and Justice continued to fail to provide the IVD with the information it requested for its investigations. The Military Justice system refused to hand over to the IVD the case files of the trials of those accused of killing protesters during the 2011 uprising and of victims of police repression during Siliana protests in 2012.

In September, Parliament passed a controversial Administrative Reconciliation Law, first proposed by President Essebsi in 2015. The law had been long opposed by opposition political parties, civil society groups and the campaign group Manich Msameh ("I will not forgive") because it offers immunity to public servants involved in corruption and misappropriation of public funds if they were obeying orders and had derived no personal benefit. A group of MPs filed a challenge before the Provisional Authority for the Examination of the Constitutionality of Draft Laws, arguing that the law was unconstitutional; the Provisional Authority's inability to reach a majority decision resulted in the law being enacted.

RIGHT TO WATER

The water shortage in Tunisia became more acute with water supplies to dams falling 42% below the annual average. In August, the Minister of Agriculture, Water Resources and Fisheries stated that the government did not have a national strategy for water distribution, thereby making it impossible to ensure equitable access.

Water shortages in recent years disproportionately affected the distribution of water and resulted in repeated water cuts in marginalized regions leading to local protests throughout 2017. In September, residents of the small town of Deguech in Tozeur region organized a protest in front of the local authority's office demanding a solution to the regular cuts in running water that the region had suffered throughout the summer. In July, some neighbourhoods of Redeyef in the region of Gafsa suffered more than one month without running water, and towns including Moulares had running water for only a few hours per day. In March, the NGO Tunisian Water Observatory announced that it had registered 615 water cuts and 250 protests related to access to water.

DEATH PENALTY

Courts handed down at least 25 death sentences following trials related to national security. Defence lawyers appealed against the sentences. No executions have been carried out since 1991.

1. Tunisia: Changes to passport law will ease arbitrary restrictions on travel (News story, 26 May)
2. Tunisia: Journalists prosecuted for criticizing conduct of security forces (News story, 15 May)
3. "We want an end to the fear": Abuses under Tunisia's state of emergency (MDE 30/4911/2017)
4. Tunisia: Fifth man facing jail term for breaking fast during Ramadan (News story, 13 June)

TURKEY

Republic of Turkey
Head of state: **Recep Tayyip Erdoğan**
Head of government: **Binali Yıldırım**

An ongoing state of emergency set a backdrop for violations of human rights. Dissent was ruthlessly suppressed, with journalists, political activists and human rights defenders among those targeted. Instances of torture continued to be reported, but in lower numbers than in the weeks following the coup attempt of July 2016. Any effective investigation of human rights violations by state officials was prevented by pervasive impunity. Abuses by armed groups continued, including two attacks in January. However, there were no further bombing attacks targeting members of the general population that had been such a regular occurrence in previous years. No resolution was found for the situation of people displaced within the southeast of the country. Turkey continued to host one of the largest refugee populations in the world, with more than 3 million registered Syrian refugees alone, but risks of forcible return persisted.

BACKGROUND

The state of emergency, imposed following an attempted coup in July 2016, remained in force throughout the year. It paved the way for unlawful restrictions on human rights and allowed the government to pass laws beyond the effective scrutiny of Parliament and the courts.

After having been remanded in prison detention in 2016, nine parliamentarians from the Kurdish-rooted leftist Peoples' Democracy Party (HDP), including the party's two leaders, remained in prison during the whole year. Sixty elected mayors of the Democratic Regions Party, the sister party of the HDP, representing constituencies in the predominantly Kurdish east and southeast of Turkey, also remained in prison. The unelected officials who replaced them continued in office throughout 2017. In October, six elected mayors, including those representing the capital, Ankara, and Istanbul, were left with no option but to resign after being requested to do so by the President. As a result, a third of Turkey's population was not being represented by the people they had elected at the 2016 local elections.

Over 50,000 people were in pre-trial detention on charges linked to membership of the "Fethullahist Terrorist Organization" (FETÖ), which the authorities blamed for the 2016 coup attempt. A similar number were released on bail and were subjected to reporting requirements. Only a tiny minority of them were accused of taking part in the actual events of the attempted coup. The judiciary, itself decimated by the dismissal or detention of up to a third of Turkey's judges and prosecutors, remained under extreme political pressure. Arbitrary, lengthy and punitive pre-trial detention and fair trial violations continued routinely.

Armed clashes continued between the Kurdistan Workers' Party (PKK) and state security forces. Turkish armed forces also carried out military operations against armed groups within Syria and Iraq; in September, the mandate to do so for another year was approved by Parliament.

In April, constitutional amendments granting extensive powers to the office of President were passed by referendum. Opponents of the proposed amendments had complained that they had vastly less access to state media and were prevented from demonstrating their opposition in public. The authorities dismissed allegations of irregularities in the counting of votes.

FREEDOM OF EXPRESSION

Civil society representatives, as well as the general population, widely practised self-censorship, deleting social media posts and refraining from making public comments for fear of dismissal from their jobs, closure of their organizations or criminal prosecution. Thousands of criminal prosecutions were brought, including under laws prohibiting defamation and on trumped-up terrorism-related charges, based on peoples' peaceful exercise of their right to freedom of expression. Arbitrary and punitive lengthy pre-trial detention was routinely imposed. Confidential details of investigations were frequently leaked to government-linked media and splashed across the front pages of newspapers, while government spokespeople made prejudicial statements regarding cases under investigation. Prosecutions of journalists and political activists continued, and prosecutions of human rights defenders sharply increased. International journalists and media were also targeted.

Criticism of the government in the broadcast and print media largely disappeared, with dissent mainly confined to internet-based media. The government continued to use administrative blocking orders, against which there was no effective appeal, routinely, to censor internet content. In April, the Turkish authorities blocked all access to the online encyclopedia Wikipedia due to a page that cited news reports alleging links between the Turkish government and several armed groups in Syria. Wikipedia refused to edit the page. The website remained blocked at the end of the year.

JOURNALISTS

Among the more than 100 journalists and media workers in pre-trial detention at the end of the year, three were from the secular opposition newspaper *Cumhuriyet*; during the course of the year eight of their colleagues who had been in pre-trial detention were released pending the outcome of their trial. Journalists from media outlets closed by state of emergency decrees continued to face prosecution, conviction and imprisonment. Former *Taraf* editor Ahmet Altan and his brother Mehmet Altan remained in pre-trial detention following their detention in September 2016 on grounds of membership of the Gülen movement, as did 34 media workers who worked for Zaman group newspapers. Zehra Doğan, a journalist for the Kurdish women's Jinha news agency, was imprisoned in June following her conviction and sentencing to two years, nine months and 22 days for terrorist propaganda. İnan Kızılkaya, editor of the Kurdish *Özgür Gündem* newspaper, was released in October after 440 days in pre-trial detention pending the outcome of his trial for membership of the PKK.

Deniz Yücel, correspondent for the German *Die Welt* newspaper, was arrested in February and at the end of the year was still in detention without being indicted, much of it in solitary confinement. *Wall Street Journal* journalist Ayla Albayrak was convicted of terrorist propaganda and in October was given a prison sentence of two years and one month for a 2015 article about armed clashes between state forces and PKK-affiliated youths.

HUMAN RIGHTS DEFENDERS

In July, police raided a human rights workshop on Büyükada Island near Istanbul, detaining all 10 human rights defenders present, including two foreign nationals. Eight, including Amnesty International Turkey Director İdil Eser, were held in pre-trial detention until a trial under trumped-up charges for "membership of a terrorist organization" based on their work as human rights defenders began in October. The court also decided to join the prosecution of Taner Kılıç, Chair of Amnesty International Turkey. Detained in June, Taner Kılıç stood accused of "membership of FETÖ" on the grounds that he had downloaded onto his phone the ByLock messaging application, said by the authorities to be used for the group's communications. Despite two independent forensic reports showing that he had not downloaded the application, and without credible evidence being presented by the prosecution, he remained in pre-trial detention at the end of the year.

In August, veteran human rights defender Murat Çelikkan was imprisoned following his conviction for terrorist propaganda; this related to the 2016 solidarity action with the now closed *Özgür Gündem* newspaper. He was released on parole in October after serving two months of an 18-month prison sentence. A further 16 activists received suspended sentences for taking part in the action, while prosecutions were continuing against 18.

In October, civil society leader Osman Kavala was detained and accused of "attempting to overthrow the constitutional order" in connection with the 2016 coup attempt. At the end of the year, he was still in pre-trial detention without being indicted.

In November, Raci Bilici, Deputy Chair of the national Human Rights Association (İHD) and Chair of its Diyarbakır branch, went on trial accused of membership of a terrorist organization. More than 20 other İHD officials were being prosecuted for alleged terrorism-related offences.

Five representatives of the Progressive Lawyers Association (ÇHD), which took on human rights cases and was closed by emergency decree in 2016, were remanded in pre-trial detention following police operations across the country. They had been accused of offences linked to the PKK or the Revolutionary People's Liberation Party–Front (DHKP-C), an armed group. In November, Selçuk Kozağaçlı, ÇHD's national Chair, was detained. He remained in pre-trial detention at the end of the year.

ACTIVISTS

Activists were targeted for their criticism of the authorities. Nuriye Gülmen and Semih Özakça were detained in May and remanded in custody on the basis of court orders citing their peaceful protests; they had been on hunger strike since March in protest against their arbitrary dismissal by a state of emergency decree. Semih Özakça was released in October, but Nuriye Gülmen remained in detention until December when she was convicted of membership of the DHKP-C, pending the outcome of an appeal. Semih Özakça was acquitted of the same charge. Police routinely detained protesters demanding their release.

Over 70 Academics for Peace were indicted for making PKK propaganda following their January 2016 petition calling for an end to military operations in the southeast of Turkey. The first trials began in December.

Activist Barbaros Şansal was remanded in custody in January following posts he had made on social media criticizing the government. He was convicted in June of "denigrating the Turkish Nation" under Article 301 of the Penal Code and given a suspended sentence of six months and 20 days.

FREEDOM OF ASSEMBLY

Public demonstrations dwindled as provincial governors imposed arbitrary and blanket bans, citing powers under the state of emergency, and police used excessive force against the small number of individuals who demonstrated despite the risks. The "Justice March" led by the main opposition

Republican People's Party (CHP), which went ahead peacefully, provided a notable exception to this trend. Traditional May Day demonstrations in Istanbul were held outside the centre of the city, with the agreement of the major trade unions.

The annual Istanbul Pride march was banned for a third successive year on spurious security grounds. Police used unnecessary and excessive force, firing rubber bullets, and made arbitrary arrests, targeting small groups of people attempting to celebrate Pride. In November, the authorities in Ankara imposed an indefinite ban on events organized by lesbian, gay, bisexual, transgender and intersex (LGBTI) solidarity organizations ahead of a planned LGBTI-themed film festival which was due to take place in the city. Again, the authorities cited spurious security reasons.

In June and July, more than 200,000 people took part in a 400km "Justice March" between Ankara and Istanbul. The march was announced following the conviction and sentencing to 25 years' imprisonment of CHP parliamentarian Enis Berberoğlu; he had been charged with espionage after passing on to journalists a video that purportedly showed the transfer of weapons to Syria in National Intelligence Organization trucks. In October, his conviction was overturned on appeal and a retrial ordered.

TORTURE AND OTHER ILL-TREATMENT

Instances of torture and other ill-treatment, especially in police custody, continued to be reported, although at a markedly lower level than in the weeks following the July 2016 coup attempt. The Turkish authorities continued to deny permission for the European Committee for the Prevention of Torture to publish its report on torture allegations following the coup attempt. There was no effective national preventive mechanism with a mandate for monitoring places of detention. There were no available statistics regarding investigations into allegations of torture. There was no evidence that allegations of torture were being effectively investigated.

In August, NGOs reported that soldiers and police officers beat at least 30 people in the village of Altınsu/Şapatan in Hakkari province in southeast Turkey following a clash with the PKK in which two members of the security forces died. Witnesses reported that villagers were taken out of their homes, arbitrarily detained and beaten in the village square, and that 10 of them were taken into police custody. Images of the villagers' injuries resulting from their beatings were shared on social media. A statement from the Governor's office denied the allegations of torture, and maintained that news reports supporting the allegations were "terrorist propaganda".

IMPUNITY

In the face of extreme political pressure, prosecutors and judges were even less inclined than in previous years to investigate alleged human rights violations by law enforcement officials or bring to justice those responsible. Intimidation of lawyers, including detentions and the bringing of criminal cases against them, further deterred lawyers from bringing criminal complaints. No progress was made to investigate pervasive allegations of human rights violations during round-the-clock curfews in the southeast of Turkey during 2015 and 2016. More than five years after Turkey's ratification of the Istanbul Convention to Combat Violence against Women, its implementation remained flawed, and reports of violence against women continued to rise.

In April, the trial of a police officer accused of killing Berkin Elvan began in Istanbul. Berkin Elvan died of his injuries after being hit by a tear gas canister at the scene of a Gezi Park protest in June 2013. The investigation had been severely delayed by the failure to obtain CCTV footage from the scene.

More than two years after the fatal shooting on 28 November 2015 of Tahir Elçi, human rights lawyer and Chair of the Diyarbakır Bar Association, no suspects had been identified. Delays or failure to obtain CCTV footage continued to hamper the investigation.

In July, the government submitted information in regard to 34 cases brought to the European Court of Human Rights; these cases involved alleged violations of the right to life, prohibition of torture and the right to liberty and security in the southeast of Turkey during the curfews in 2015 and 2016.

The organization We Will Stop Femicide reported that murders of women were increasing, while media attention to such cases declined. It reported that 392 women had been killed in the year up to 25 November.

ABUSES BY ARMED GROUPS

Abuses by armed groups continued, although the number of indiscriminate attacks, and attacks targeting the general population, was lower than in recent years.

In January, 39 people were killed and over 70 injured after a gunman opened fire in a popular nightclub in Istanbul. The armed group Islamic State (IS) claimed responsibility for the attack.

Also in January, two people were killed and 10 injured by attackers targeting the İzmir Courthouse. The Kurdistan Freedom Falcons (TAK), an offshoot of the PKK, claimed responsibility for the attack.

In June, the PKK claimed responsibility for the killing of Necmettin Yılmaz, a teacher, after his kidnapping from the province of Tunceli/Dersim in southeast Turkey.

SUMMARY DISMISSALS

Under emergency decrees, public sector workers continued to face summary dismissal for alleged unspecified links to terrorist groups. Nearly 20,000 workers were dismissed during the course of the year, bringing the total number since July 2016 to 107,000. Many workers were effectively prevented from continuing their professions, and struggled to find other jobs after being branded "terrorists" as a result of their dismissal. In January, the authorities announced a seven-person appeal Commission to assess the dismissals. The Commission was not established until July, and at the end of the year had ruled on fewer than 100 of the reported 100,000 appeals submitted to it. There was widespread criticism that the Commission lacked the necessary independence and capacity to carry out the task. In June, rejecting the *Köksal v. Turkey* application as inadmissible, the European Court of Human Rights ruled that there was no reason to believe that the Commission would not be an effective remedy. The decision of the Court left the door open to a future reassessment by the Court of the effectiveness of the Commission.

INTERNALLY DISPLACED PEOPLE

Many of the estimated 500,000 people displaced from their homes in areas under the curfews across the southeast of Turkey in 2015 and 2016 lacked access to adequate housing and livelihoods. Many were unable to return to their homes that had been destroyed during or after military operations during which state security forces clashed with armed individuals affiliated to the PKK. The authorities lacked a comprehensive plan as to how the residents would be able to return to their homes.

In the Sur district of Diyarbakır, residents who had already been displaced from their homes during the curfew lost their homes a second time when they were forcibly evicted as part of a redevelopment scheme affecting the whole district. In May, hundreds of residents had their water and electricity supplies cut off in an apparent attempt to force them out.

REFUGEES AND ASYLUM-SEEKERS

Turkey continued to host one of the world's largest refugee populations, with over 3,300,000 registered Syrian refugees alone. Despite new initiatives to improve the situation of refugees, many faced insufficient access to livelihoods, housing, health care, and education for their children. Except for Syrians, refugees did not have access to fair and efficient procedures for the determination of their status. There were continued reports of forced returns of refugees and asylum-seekers, including to Syria. International humanitarian NGOs working with refugees found their work in Turkey was increasingly impeded as the authorities placed restrictions on, and in some cases withdrew, permission for them to work in the country.

Collective forced expulsions of Syrian and Iraqi refugees and asylum-seekers to their respective countries of origin from the Removal Centre in Van, eastern Turkey, were reported to have taken place during the final days of May and early June. According to reports, around 200 Iraqis and around 300 Syrians were forcibly returned after officials forced individuals to sign forms agreeing to "voluntary return".

TURKMENISTAN

Turkmenistan
Head of state and government: **Gurbanguly Berdymukhamedov**

The right to freedom of expression remained severely restricted. Torture and other ill-treatment was committed in pre-trial detention and prisons, sometimes resulting in death. There was no attempt to address enforced disappearances and incommunicado detention. The right to housing was widely violated. Consensual same-sex relations between men remained a criminal offence.

BACKGROUND

In February, President Berdymukhamedov was re-elected for a further seven-year term with 98% of the vote; the OSCE Election Assessment Mission found "serious irregularities". The economic crisis in the country deepened, and in June the President asked the Parliament to prepare an austerity proposal to cut benefits, including free gas and electricity supplies. There were reports that employees in state-run enterprises were not receiving their salaries; and there were shortages of cash.

LEGAL, CONSTITUTIONAL OR INSTITUTIONAL DEVELOPMENTS

In March, the Parliament elected the first Human Rights Commissioner (Ombudsperson) from a list provided by the President, calling into question the independence of the institution and its compliance with the UN Principles relating to the Status of National Institutions.

FREEDOM OF EXPRESSION

There was no independent media and the few independent journalists – typically working in secret for outlets based abroad – faced harassment and arrest.

On 15 February, independent journalist Khudayberdy Allashov and his mother Kurbantach Arazmedova were released, after being given three-year conditional sentences for possessing chewing tobacco. They had been in detention since 3 December 2016; there were allegations that they had been subjected to torture and other ill-treatment.

In March, the EU and the OSCE called for the immediate release of freelance journalist Saparmamed Nepeskuliev who was sentenced to three years' imprisonment in 2015 on drug charges. He was believed to be suffering from life-threatening health conditions.

In April, the UN Human Rights Committee expressed concern over, among other things, the absence of an independent media, undue restrictions on access to the internet, and the use of politically motivated charges against journalists and others expressing criticism of the government.

TORTURE AND OTHER ILL-TREATMENT

In January, the UN Committee against Torture noted its concern at "consistent allegations of widespread torture and ill-treatment, including severe beatings, of persons deprived of their liberty, especially at the moment of apprehension and during pre-trial detention, mainly in order to extract confessions".

In February, 18 men were convicted under various articles of the Criminal Code and sentenced to between five and 12 years' imprisonment for their suspected links to Turkmen-Turkish schools understood to have been previously affiliated to Fethullah Gülen. The men were allegedly tortured and held in inhumane conditions in pre-trial detention. A 19th man detained at the same time was thought to have died as a result of torture. The trial held at the pre-trial detention centre in the town of Yashlyk, Ahal Province, reportedly fell far short of international standards of fairness.

DEATHS IN CUSTODY

Alternative Turkmenistan News reported that on 24 June the body of Aziz Gafurov was delivered to his family in the village of Urgendzhi, near Turkmenabat. An eyewitness described the body as emaciated and covered in bruises. Aziz Gafurov was one of dozens of practising Muslims who were sentenced in recent years for conspiracy to overthrow the state, violent calls to overthrow the constitutional order, and incitement of social, national and religious enmity.

ENFORCED DISAPPEARANCES

The fate and whereabouts of at least 80 prisoners subjected to enforced disappearance after an alleged assassination attempt on then President Saparmurat Niyazov in November 2002 remained unclarified.

The bodies of three former senior state officials, who were forcibly disappeared following their arrest and criminal prosecution in connection with the assassination attempt, were delivered to their relatives in the course of the year. Tirkish Tyrmyev reportedly died on 13 January; Bairam Khasanov died in May; and on 18 August, the Russian NGO Human Rights Centre Memorial reported that Akmurad Redzhepov had died on 10 August.

On 26 January, the EU Delegation to the International Organizations in Vienna published a statement expressing concern about Tirkish Tyrmyev's death and called on Turkmenistan to immediately and effectively address and eradicate enforced disappearances.

RIGHT TO HOUSING AND FORCED EVICTIONS

Reports continued of mass house demolitions and forced evictions in connection with construction and development projects, including those implemented in preparation for the Asian Indoor and Martial Arts Games that were held in September. On 21 February, a group of women gathered in Ashgabat to demand the alternative housing that they had been denied due to the lack of documentation confirming ownership of their demolished homes. The authorities had not issued them with such documents because many of the women were not registered in Ashgabat.

RIGHTS OF LESBIAN, GAY, BISEXUAL, TRANSGENDER AND INTERSEX PEOPLE

Consensual same-sex relations between men remained a criminal offence punishable by up to two years' imprisonment. LGBTI people were subjected to discrimination including violence, arbitrary arrests and detention.

UGANDA

Republic of Uganda
Head of state and government: **Yoweri Kaguta Museveni**

The rights to freedom of expression, association and assembly were restricted. Journalists and others who criticized the President or his family were arrested, detained and harassed. There was a sharp rise in the number of women killed, some of whom were subjected to sexual violence. The government said it would investigate and prosecute those responsible. Draft constitutional amendments to the land laws gave the government authority to expropriate private land. Uganda hosted the largest number of refugees in the region, including over 1 million from South Sudan.

FREEDOM OF EXPRESSION

On 19 March, immigration officials at Entebbe International Airport prevented academic Stella Nyanzi from boarding a flight to the Netherlands to attend a conference. This followed her criticism of the President and his wife, the Education Minister, for the government's failure to fulfil a 2015 commitment to provide sanitary towels in girls' schools.

On 8 April, police arrested Stella Nyanzi for insulting President Museveni on social media. She was charged under the Computer Misuse Act of 2011 and detained for 33 days in Luzira Maximum Security Prison in the capital, Kampala, before being released on bail. The charges against her were later dropped.

On 8 April, Nation TV journalist Gertrude Tumusiime Uwitware was abducted, blindfolded and interrogated by unknown assailants for several hours, after she had posted her support for Stella Nyanzi on social media. The spokesperson for the Kampala Metropolitan Police promised to investigate the incident but there was no further information on its progress by the end of the year.

On 27 September, the Ugandan Communications Commission threatened to revoke or suspend licences of media outlets which broadcast live parliamentary debates on a proposed constitutional amendment to remove the presidential age limit of 75 which was passed by Parliament in December and, according to the government, became law in the same month. The Commission said that such broadcasts promoted a "culture of violence". The opposition viewed the amendment as a means to enable President Museveni to stand for re-election in 2021. He had already been in power for 31 years.

On 10 October, the police summoned editors Arinaitwe Rugyendo of the *Red Pepper* newspaper and the online Daily Monitor, and Charles Bichachi of the Nation Media Group which owns the Daily Monitor, about stories they published on the age limit debate. Police questioned them after an MP, who was leading on moves to remove the age limit, filed a complaint claiming that the stories tarnished his reputation. They were

charged in connection with these allegations under Section 27A of the Police Act.

On 24 November, after *Red Pepper* published an article alleging that the President was involved in a plot to overthrow Rwanda's President, the police searched the newspaper's office including computers and mobile phones, and closed it down. At the same time, they arrested Arinaitwe Rugyendo and other members of staff Richard Kintu, James Mujuni, Patrick Mugumya, Richard Tusiime, Johnson Musinguzi, Ben Byarabaha and Francis Tumusiime. They remained in detention at the end of the year.

FREEDOM OF ASSOCIATION
On 2 and 20 September, approximately 20 police officers and security officials raided ActionAid Uganda's offices in Kansanga, an area of Kampala, preventing staff from leaving the premises for several hours. The police warrant stated that ActionAid was being investigated for "illicit transfers of funds to support unlawful activities". The police removed documents and confiscated the organization's laptops and mobile phones belonging to staff members. On 9 October, the Bank of Uganda froze ActionAid's bank accounts. On 13 October, the NGO Bureau, under the Ministry of Internal Affairs, sent a letter to 25 development NGOs demanding their bank account details.

On 20 September, police raided the Great Lakes Institute for Strategic Studies offices with a warrant to search computers and mobile phones as well as financial and banking documents. The raid came after the organization's executive director, Godber Tumushabe, spoke against the proposal to lift the presidential age limit.

VIOLENCE AGAINST WOMEN AND GIRLS
According to the police, 28 women were killed in Entebbe town in Wakiso District. The media reported that a man had confessed to killing eight of the women on the orders of a local businessman. In a public statement on 3 September the police spokesperson said that four categories of murder had been identified and that 13 people had been

arrested and charged in connection with the 28 killings. Twelve of the victims had been raped or sexually assaulted before they were killed; four of them were killed by their husbands or partners; one woman was killed by her two brothers in what the police classified as a revenge killing; the other cases were described as "ritual murders".

The body of one of the victims, Rose Nakimuli, was discovered on 24 July in a banana plantation in Wakiso District.

RIGHT TO HOUSING AND FORCED EVICTIONS

In July, the government tabled a bill to amend Article 26(2) of the Constitution. This would allow compulsory acquisition by the government of private land for infrastructure projects without providing prompt, prior and fair compensation to the owners, and potentially while negotiations on compensation were pending.

Under existing law, the government can acquire private land only after the payment of "fair and adequate" compensation has been made. If the owner disputes the compensation amount, a High Court can block the government from acquiring the land until a resolution is reached. If passed, the new law would increase the risk of forced evictions and undermine the ability of those facing eviction to participate in consultations over acquisitions. It would also frustrate transparent and fair negotiations on compensation, and the possibility of appeal. Marginalized groups, including people living in poverty, and in rural areas, would be particularly affected.

RIGHT TO HEALTH

On 10 October, the doctors' union Uganda Medical Association (UMA) declared an indefinite strike protesting against low salaries and shortages of essential supplies. However, they continued to provide services to children, pregnant women and emergency accident victims.

President Museveni said the strike was illegal and ordered the doctors to return to work or face disciplinary action. The government said it would increase doctors' salaries only after the outcome of a salary review conducted by a commission set up by the President to review salaries of all civil servants.

REFUGEES AND ASYLUM-SEEKERS

As of 10 November, Uganda hosted around 1,379,768 refugees and asylum-seekers. Some 1,037,359 were from South Sudan, 348,782 having arrived between January and September; 61% of them were children, mostly unaccompanied or separated from their parents. Around 236,572 of the refugees were from the Democratic Republic of the Congo (DRC); 39,041 were from Burundi (see Burundi entry); 35,373 were from Somalia; and the rest were from various other countries.

Asylum-seekers from South Sudan and the DRC were granted prima facie refugee status, and those of other nationalities underwent an individual refugee status determination process conducted by the Refugee Eligibility Committee. The government had revoked the automatic refugee status for Burundian asylum-seekers in June.

Under the 2006 Refugee Act and the 2010 Refugee Regulations, refugees were allowed relative freedom of movement, equal access to basic services, such as primary education and health care, and the right to work and establish a business.

In May, the World Food Programme was forced to cut cereal rations by half for over 800,000 South Sudanese refugees.

Appeals for funding from international donors to address the regional refugee crisis failed to secure adequate funds. This proved to be the most significant challenge to Uganda's refugee response. In June, the Uganda Solidarity Summit on Refugees had rallied for international support, but as of November 2017, the South Sudan Refugee Response Plan (a joint government/UNHCR initiative) secured only 68% of the funds needed; and the Burundi Refugee Response Plan secured only 20%.

In October, there was a temporary 50% reduction in food assistance to refugees due to donors' payment delays. The cuts led to riots and protests by refugees in Nyumanzi settlement in Adjumani district.

UKRAINE

Ukraine
Head of state: **Petro Poroshenko**
Head of government: **Volodymyr Hroysman**

The investigation into the Security Service of Ukraine (SBU) for its alleged secret prisons failed to make any progress. Law enforcement officials continued to use torture and other ill-treatment.
The Ukrainian authorities increased pressure on their critics and independent NGOs, including journalists and anti-corruption activists. The authorities launched criminal investigations and passed laws aimed at restricting the rights to freedom of expression and freedom of association, among other things.
The de facto authorities in the separatist-controlled territories continued to unlawfully detain and imprison their critics. In November, the de facto Supreme Court in Donetsk ordered a man to be put to death. In Russian-occupied Crimea, critics of the authorities faced intimidation, harassment and criminal prosecution.
The LGBTI Pride march was held in the capital Kyiv, under effective police protection. The number of attacks on LGBTI events rose across the country. The government failed to adequately address sexual and domestic violence. The authorities announced that Ukraine was freezing all arms supplies to South Sudan.

BACKGROUND

Social discontent continued to grow. Mounting economic problems, the slow pace of reforms and pervasive corruption sparked regular protests in Kyiv that occasionally turned violent. Some of the protests brought together several hundred people. In April, the World Bank reported that the Ukrainian economy had stopped contracting, projected a 2% growth for 2017, and urged further reforms. On 14 June, the EU lifted its visa requirements for Ukrainian citizens. The government adopted wide-ranging medical and educational reforms, which for the first time included human rights as part of the future school curriculum.

In eastern Ukraine, the separatist and government forces continued fighting, in violation of the 2015 ceasefire agreement. Casualties among the forces and civilians continued to grow, and according to the UN had reached 10,225 dead by 15 August, including 2,505 civilians. On 27 December, the two sides exchanged prisoners, releasing a total of 380 people.

According to the September report of the UN Monitoring Mission in Ukraine, "increased levels of poverty and unemployment coupled with record-high food prices have affected the lives of 3.8 million people in the conflict-affected zones, in addition to daily hardships caused by the armed hostilities and related policies imposed by all sides." Laws introduced in previous years further impeded access to social rights and pensions for people living in the conflict-affected areas.

Crimea remained under Russian occupation. Russia continued to deny international human rights mechanisms access to the peninsula.

TORTURE AND OTHER ILL-TREATMENT

Members of law enforcement agencies continued to use torture and other ill-treatment, and committed other human rights violations; there was continued impunity for past and ongoing violations of international humanitarian law.

On 15 August, the SBU apprehended Daria Mastikasheva, a Ukrainian citizen resident in Russia who was visiting her mother in Ukraine, and held her incommunicado for two days. She was accused of treason and illegal weapons possession. Photos taken by her lawyer of her outside the court showed signs of beatings and possible torture by SBU officers. Her lawyer also reported that she was issued with threats targeting her mother and son, until she agreed to read out a self-incriminating statement on camera. At the end of the year she was still in detention awaiting trial.

On 16 November, the head of the State Investigation Bureau (SIB), a stand-alone agency created to undertake investigations independently of other law enforcement agencies, was finally appointed. However, the SIB was still not fully staffed and unable to begin its work by the end of the year.

CONFLICT-RELATED SEXUAL VIOLENCE

In a report published in February, the UN Human Rights Monitoring Mission to Ukraine documented cases of conflict-related sexual violence, and criticized Ukraine's justice system for failing its survivors and highlighted a lack of adequate care and counselling. The majority of the documented cases concerned sexual violence against men and women who had been detained by government forces or armed groups.

DETENTION

The Chief Military Prosecutor's investigation into the allegations of secret detention by the SBU in eastern Ukraine was ineffective. Evidence published in 2016 by international NGOs showing the existence of this practice was largely ignored by the authorities.

DETENTIONS OF CIVILIANS IN THE CONFLICT ZONE

On 27 April, the UN Subcommittee on Prevention of Torture (SPT) published its report on its 2016 visit to Ukraine. The report noted that the SBU had obstructed the SPT's mandate by denying it access to some facilities, forcing it to suspend a visit in May 2016. When the SPT resumed the visit in September, it "was left with the clear impression that some rooms and spaces had been cleared in order to suggest that they had not been used for detention". The facilities in question, particularly in the city Kharkiv, had allegedly been used as secret prisons, and their inmates moved to another unofficial facility before it was opened to visitors.[1] The SPT was denied any access to detention facilities in the territories controlled by the self-proclaimed, Russian-backed Donetsk People's Republic (DNR) and

Luhansk People's Republic (LNR) in eastern Ukraine.

The de facto authorities in the DNR and LNR continued to detain and imprison critics and individuals suspected of supporting Ukraine. On 4 May, a de facto court in Donetsk sentenced well-known academic Ihor Kozlovsky to two years and eight months in prison under trumped-up charges of weapons possession. Ihor Kozlovsky had been in detention since January 2016 and was released on 27 December 2017 in a prisoner exchange.

On 31 January, Russian activists and performance artists Seroe Fioletovoe and Viktoriya Miroshnichenko were held in incommunicado detention for two weeks after crossing into the DNR-controlled territory. Following an international campaign for their release on 14 February, the de facto Ministry of State Security (MGB) escorted them to the Russian border and released them.

On 2 June, freelance journalist Stanislav Aseev, who had been reporting anonymously from the DNR, was subjected to enforced disappearance in Donetsk. For weeks, the de facto authorities denied that they were holding him; on 16 July, a member of the MGB told his mother that her son was in their custody and accused of espionage. Stanislav Aseev remained in detention and under investigation at the end of the year.

FREEDOM OF ASSOCIATION

Civil society activists and members of NGOs, particularly those working on corruption, were regularly harassed and subjected to violence. These incidents were often not effectively investigated, and members of the authorities, including security services in some instances, were widely suspected to have instigated them.

A law adopted in March obliged anti-corruption activists, including members of NGOs and journalists, to file annual income declarations – something that state officials have to do – or face criminal charges and imprisonment.

In July, the Presidential Administration proposed two draft laws that sought to impose onerous and intrusive public financial reporting on NGOs whose annual budget exceeded 300 times the so-called "living minimum" – defined in law and regularly reviewed, as UAH1,700 (USD63) at the end of the year. NGOs were also required to publicly report on all payments made to members of staff or consultants. Non-compliance carried severe penalties, including the loss of the non-profit status and freezing of accounts. The two draft laws were under consideration in the Ukrainian Parliament at the end of the year.

On 11 October, tax police raided the offices of Patients of Ukraine, and the All-Ukrainian Network of People Living with HIV/AIDS (PLWH), two NGOs known for exposing questionable schemes in the state medical procurement system. The authorities alleged that the NGOs had misused their international funding – despite their having passed independent financial audit – and, according to court documents, accused them of "supporting terrorism" by funding partner patient organizations in Crimea.

FREEDOM OF EXPRESSION

The investigations into the killings of journalists Oles Buzina in 2015, and Pavel Sheremet in 2016, had yielded no results. The authorities continued their attempts to limit the right to freedom of expression by instigating trumped-up criminal cases against journalists who criticized the government over its failure to implement reforms and its policies in eastern Ukraine. On 7 June, the Supreme Special Court of Ukraine overturned the July 2016 decision by a court of appeal to acquit prisoner of conscience Ruslan Kotsaba, a journalist who had been prosecuted for treason and harming Ukraine's armed forces after he had criticized the conflict in eastern Ukraine.

In June, the office of the online newspaper *Strana.ua* was searched as part of an investigation into an alleged disclosure of state secrets, followed in August by searches at the homes of its editor-in-chief Ihor Guzhva and another journalist. In July, the office of the media holding company Vesti was searched in a fraud investigation. Both news outlets were known for their critical reporting on the Ukrainian authorities and their policies in the conflict-affected Donbass region.

In three separate instances in August, the SBU expelled four international journalists, two Spanish and two Russian, for "harming Ukraine's national interests" and barred them from returning to Ukraine for three years. The SBU spokesperson Olena Gitlyanska accused the Russian journalist Anna Kurbatova, expelled on 30 August, of producing material "harmful to Ukraine's national interest" and warned that this would happen to everyone "who dares to disgrace Ukraine". In October, the SBU lifted the ban on the Spanish journalists entering Ukraine.

Also in August, the SBU arrested freelance journalist Vasily Muravitsky from the city of Zhytomyr. He had contributed to a number of Russian media. The SBU accused him of preparing and distributing "anti-Ukrainian" materials on orders from Moscow. If convicted, he could face up to 15 years in jail. Vasily Muravitsky was in pre-trial detention at the end of the year.

RIGHTS OF LESBIAN, GAY, BISEXUAL, TRANSGENDER AND INTERSEX PEOPLE

On 18 June, thousands joined the biggest march yet of Equality, the annual LGBTI Pride demonstration, in Kyiv, as well as several dozen counter-protests. Police provided effective protection from those protesting against the march and no incidents were reported during the rally. After the march, members of far-right groups attacked and beat several participants. Overall, the number of violent attacks against LGBTI people rose in 2017. In September, a group of right-wing protesters severely beat a number of participants of an LGBTI festival in the city of Zapporizhhya.

VIOLENCE AGAINST WOMEN AND GIRLS

Parliament had still not ratified the Council of Europe Convention on preventing and combating violence against women and domestic violence (Istanbul Convention), which it signed in 2011.

CRIMEA

The clampdown on the rights to freedom of expression, association and assembly continued in Crimea. The authorities continued to predominantly target ethnic Crimean Tatars. The arbitrary ban on the Mejlis of the Crimean Tatar People, a self-governing body representing the ethnic Crimean Tatars, continued. The Russian Security Services raided dozens of Crimean Tatar homes, purportedly looking for illegal weapons, drugs or "extremist" literature, as part of their campaign to intimidate critics of the peninsula's occupation. The few lawyers willing to take up cases in defence of critical voices in Crimea faced harassment by the Russian authorities.

On 26 January, lawyer Emil Kurbedinov was arrested and sentenced by a de facto court in the Crimean capital, Simferopol, to 10 days of administrative detention. He was accused of violating Russian anti-extremist legislation with a social media post predating the Russian occupation of Crimea. In the post, he had shared a video about a protest held by the Muslim organization Hizb ut-Tahrir, which is banned in Russia but not in Ukraine. On 8 August, police in Simferopol used excessive force and arrested Server Karametov for holding a placard outside the Crimean Supreme Court to protest at reprisals against Crimean Tatars. He was sentenced to 10 days in prison. On 22 September, Ukrainian journalist Mykola Semena was convicted for "threatening [the] territorial integrity of the Russian Federation" in his publications and given a two-and-a-half-year conditional sentence and a three-year ban on participating in "public activities". In September, Crimean Tatar leaders Akhtem Chiygoz and Ilmi Umerov were given jail terms for their peaceful activism. On 25 October, both were flown to Turkey and released, without an official explanation. Akhtem Chiygoz had spent 34 months in detention, and Ilmi Umerov had been forcibly held in a psychiatric institution since August or September 2016. Both were prisoners of conscience.

ARMS TRADE

On 28 September, the Secretary of the National Security and Defence Council, Oleksandr Turchinov, announced that Ukrainian state companies had decided to freeze arms transfers to South Sudan. The announcement came days after Amnesty International published a report which included contract documents and end-user certificates listing the Ukrainian state-owned arms exporter Ukrinmash as the prospective supplier of USD169 million worth of small arms and light weapons to the South Sudanese Ministry of Defence.[2] In response to the report, the State Service of Export Control issued a statement saying that the contract in question had not been executed, and that no weapons had been shipped from Ukraine to South Sudan. In previous years, Ukraine had consistently reported exports of small arms, light weapons and major weapons to the government of South Sudan.

Ukraine had not yet ratified the Arms Trade Treaty, which it signed in September 2014.

---

1. Put an end to impunity for detention-related abuses in the context of the armed conflict in Ukraine (EUR 50/5558/2017)

2. From London to Juba, a UK-registered company's role in one of the largest arms deals to South Sudan (ACT 30/7115/2017)

UNITED ARAB EMIRATES

United Arab Emirates
Head of state: **Sheikh Khalifa bin Zayed Al Nahyan**
Head of government: **Sheikh Mohammed bin Rashed Al Maktoum**

The authorities continued to arbitrarily restrict freedoms of expression and association, using criminal defamation and anti-terrorism laws to detain, prosecute, convict and imprison government critics and a prominent human rights defender. Scores of people, including prisoners of conscience, who were sentenced following unfair trials remained in prison. Authorities held detainees in conditions that could

amount to torture and failed to investigate allegations of torture made in previous years. Women continued to face discrimination in law and in practice. Migrant workers remained vulnerable to exploitation and abuse. Courts continued to hand down death sentences; there was one execution.

BACKGROUND

The United Arab Emirates (UAE) remained part of the Saudi Arabia-led international coalition engaged in armed conflict in Yemen. Along with Saudi Arabia, the UAE trained, funded and supported forces in Yemen, some of which were under its direct report. These forces engaged in arbitrary and illegal detention practices, including in Aden where they perpetrated a campaign of arbitrary detention and enforced disappearances (see Yemen entry). The UAE joined Saudi Arabia, Bahrain and Egypt in severing ties with Qatar (see Qatar entry).

In September, the UN CERD Committee reiterated its call on the UAE to establish a national human rights institution, in line with the Paris Principles. The authorities rejected or took no action on statements and recommendations from UN human rights bodies, including those issued jointly by special procedures, the High Commissioner for Human Rights and the Working Group on Arbitrary Detention.

In June, a Belgian court convicted in their absence eight women from Abu Dhabi's ruling Al Nahyan family of trafficking in persons and of the degrading treatment of up to 23 women domestic workers.

FREEDOMS OF EXPRESSION AND ASSOCIATION

Authorities continued to arbitrarily restrict freedoms of expression and association, using the Penal Code and anti-terrorism and cybercrime laws that criminalized peaceful criticism of state policies or officials. At least 13 people were arrested or tried on such grounds. In Dubai, two men were arrested for "dressing in a feminine way", in violation of their right to freedom of expression.

In March, the government announced the creation of the Federal Public Prosecution for Information Technology Crimes, whose mandate to investigate and prosecute crimes included peaceful expression. In August, authorities in Dubai imposed a one-month suspension of the news website Arabian Business for publication of "false information" regarding unsuccessful real estate projects.

Also in March, leading human rights defender Ahmed Mansoor was arrested. He had had no access to a lawyer by the end of the year. He was held in solitary confinement and, except for two family visits, in incommunicado detention, in violation of the prohibition of torture and other ill-treatment.

Also in March, the Federal Appeal Court in the capital, Abu Dhabi, upheld the 10-year prison sentence of Dr Nasser Bin Ghaith, a prisoner of conscience. He was arbitrarily detained in 2015 and stated during his trial that he had been tortured. In April, he went on hunger strike to protest against not being permitted to see the verdict of the appeal court or meet with his lawyer.

In June, UAE's Attorney General announced that anyone expressing sympathy with Qatar could face up to 15 years' imprisonment and fines. In July, Ghanim Abdallah Matar was detained for a video he posted online in which he expressed sympathy towards the people of Qatar.

The Federal Supreme Court upheld the three years' imprisonment, a fine of Dh500,000 (USD136,135) and deportation sentence against Jordanian journalist and prisoner of conscience Tayseer al-Najjar. He had been detained since December 2015 for Facebook posts deemed "damaging [to] the reputation and prestige of the Emirati state".

Human rights defender and prisoner of conscience Dr Mohammad al-Roken remained in prison, serving a 10-year sentence imposed after an unfair mass trial in 2013 (known as the "UAE 94" trial). In May, he was awarded the Ludovic Trarieux International Human Rights Prize.

TORTURE AND OTHER ILL-TREATMENT

Reports of torture and other ill-treatment, including denial of medical care to detainees, remained common. No independent investigations were carried out into detainees' allegations of torture.

In May, detainees in al-Razeen Prison in Abu Dhabi, including Imran al-Radwan, undertook a hunger strike to protest against enforced strip searches, alleged sexual harassment and other ill-treatment by prison guards.

JUSTICE SYSTEM

The authorities refused to release at least five prisoners on completion of their sentence, including Osama al-Najjar, a prisoner of conscience arrested in 2014. Prison authorities at al-Razeen Prison, where those convicted in the UAE 94 case were detained, routinely harassed family members and prevented them from visiting their imprisoned relatives.

WOMEN'S RIGHTS

Women remained subject to discrimination in law and in practice, notably in matters of marriage and divorce, inheritance and child custody. They were inadequately protected against sexual violence and violence within the family.

WORKER'S RIGHTS – MIGRANT WORKERS

Migrant workers, who comprised the vast majority of the private workforce, continued to face exploitation and abuse. They remained tied to employers under the *kafala* sponsorship system and were denied collective bargaining rights. Trade unions remained banned and migrant workers who engaged in strike action faced deportation and a one-year ban on returning to the UAE.

In September, Federal Law No.10 of 2017 came into effect, limiting working hours and providing for weekly leave and 30 days' paid annual leave as well as the right to retain personal documents. The law appeared to enable employees to end their contract of employment if the employer violated any of its terms, and stipulated that disputes would be adjudicated by specialized tribunals as well as by courts. However, workers remained vulnerable to employers accusing them of overly broad and vague crimes such as "failing to protect their employer's secrets", which carry fines of up to Dh100,000 (USD27,225) or a six-month prison sentence.

In September the UN CERD Committee expressed concern over the lack of monitoring and enforcement of measures to protect migrant workers, and over barriers faced by migrant workers in accessing justice, such as their unwillingness to submit complaints for fear of adverse repercussions.

DEATH PENALTY

Courts handed down death sentences; one execution was carried out on 23 November.

UNITED KINGDOM

United Kingdom of Great Britain and Northern Ireland
Head of state: **Queen Elizabeth II**
Head of government: **Theresa May**

Women in Northern Ireland continued to face significant restrictions on access to abortion. Counter-terrorism laws continued to restrict rights. Full accountability for torture allegations against UK intelligence agencies and armed forces remained unrealized.

LEGAL, CONSTITUTIONAL OR INSTITUTIONAL DEVELOPMENTS

In March, the Prime Minister triggered Article 50 of the Treaty on the European Union, officially starting the withdrawal by the UK from the EU (Brexit). In July, the EU (Withdrawal) Bill received its first reading in the House of Commons. The Bill threatened to significantly reduce existing human rights protections. It excluded both the EU Charter of Fundamental Rights (in its entirety) and the right of action for violations of EU General Principles from domestic law after the UK's withdrawal. It also handed sweeping powers to ministers to alter legislation without appropriate parliamentary scrutiny, placing current rights and equality laws at risk.

JUSTICE SYSTEM

In January, the government committed itself to completing the post-implementation review of the Legal Aid, Sentencing and Punishment of Offenders Act 2012, by April 2018. Legal aid in civil cases had dropped drastically since the Act was introduced. In October, an internal post-legislative review memorandum was published and plans for completion of the review proper were announced for mid-2018.

In July, Lady Hale was appointed the first woman president of the Supreme Court. There was only one other woman Justice at the Court, and just 28% of all court judges were women. Representation of ethnic minorities among judges also remained a concern; only 7% declared to be a member of an ethnic minority.

COUNTER-TERROR AND SECURITY

Between March and June, 41 people were killed, including the attackers, and many others injured in attacks in London, the capital, and Manchester. In June, the government announced that it would review its counter-terrorism strategy and commission an independent "assurance" of the internal reviews conducted by the Security Service (MI5) and the police around the attacks. In June, plans for a "Commission for Countering Extremism" were announced.

In May, the UN Special Rapporteur on the rights to freedom of peaceful assembly and of association issued a report warning that the government's approach to "non-violent extremism" risked violating both freedoms.

In October, the government announced its intention to propose amendments to Section 58 of the Terrorism Act 2000 regarding the collection, recording or possession of information likely to be useful to a person committing or preparing an act of terrorism. The proposals sought to expand the scope of the offence to include repeated viewing or streaming of online material, and making such viewing punishable by up to 15 years'

imprisonment. Similar uplifts to discretionary sentences were also proposed to the offence of eliciting information about the armed forces.

In September, Muhammed Rabbani, Director of the advocacy group CAGE, was convicted of "wilfully obstructing or seeking to frustrate an examination or search" under Schedule 7 of the Terrorism Act 2000. He had refused to disclose the passwords for his laptop and phone to police at Heathrow Airport in London. By June, police had stopped 17,501 people under Schedule 7 powers, which did not require any suspicion of wrongdoing.

TORTURE AND OTHER ILL-TREATMENT
TORTURE IN NORTHERN IRELAND

The 2014 request by the Irish government to review the 1978 judgment in *Ireland v. UK*, on torture techniques used in internment in Northern Ireland in 1971-1972, remained pending before the European Court of Human Rights (ECtHR). In October, the High Court in Northern Ireland quashed a decision by the Police Service of Northern Ireland to end preliminary inquiries into torture of the 14 "Hooded Men", who were abused while in detention in Northern Ireland by the British army and the Royal Ulster Constabulary in 1971.

RENDITION

In January, the Supreme Court issued a judgment in the joined appeals in *Belhaj and Others v. Jack Straw and Others* and *Rahmatullah v. Ministry of Defence and Another*. It ruled that the government could not rely on the legal doctrines of "sovereign immunity" and "foreign act of state" to escape civil claims in the two cases alleging UK involvement in human rights violations by foreign governments. The first case concerned allegations by former Libyan opposition leader Abdul-Hakim Belhaj and his wife Fatima Boudchar that they had been subjected to rendition, torture and other ill-treatment in 2004 by the US and Libyan governments, with the knowledge and co-operation of UK officials. The second case was brought by Yunus Rahmatullah, detained by UK forces in Iraq in 2004 before being handed over to US forces and allegedly tortured and imprisoned without charge for over 10 years.

ARMED FORCES

Allegations of war crimes committed by UK armed forces in Iraq between 2003 and 2008 remained under preliminary examination by the Office of the Prosecutor of the ICC. On 3 December, the Office declared that there was a reasonable basis to believe that members of the UK armed forces committed war crimes within the jurisdiction of the Court against persons in their custody. An admissibility assessment was ongoing.

In April, the House of Commons Defence Select Committee issued a report in which it proposed to introduce a Statute of Limitations with regard to alleged crimes committed by British soldiers and other security forces personnel in Northern Ireland before 1998.

SURVEILLANCE

Proceedings brought by Amnesty International and other applicants were pending before the ECtHR regarding the legality of the pre-Investigatory Powers Act, mass surveillance regime and intelligence sharing practices. The judgment was pending at the end of the year.

NORTHERN IRELAND – LEGACY ISSUES

In January, the Historic Institutional Abuse Inquiry published findings from the investigation into 22 residential children's institutions in Northern Ireland, covering the period from 1922 to 1995. It found widespread and systemic failings by the UK and institutions in their duties towards the children in their care. The government had not implemented any of the recommendations at the end of the year.

The government continued to refuse funding to implement plans by the Lord Chief Justice of Northern Ireland to address the backlog of "legacy" coroners' inquests.

The government continued to refuse to establish an independent public inquiry into the 1989 killing of Patrick Finucane, despite having acknowledged previously that there had been "collusion" in the case.

SEXUAL AND REPRODUCTIVE RIGHTS

Abortion remained criminalized in Northern Ireland in almost every circumstance. Abortion was permitted only where the life or health of the woman or girl was at risk. Women faced criminal prosecution for taking WHO-approved medication to induce abortions. To access abortions, 724 women from Northern Ireland travelled to England and Wales in 2016.

In June, in the case of a 15-year-old girl who travelled to England for an abortion, and her mother, the Supreme Court ruled that women resident in Northern Ireland were not entitled to free abortions on the National Health Service. In September, the threat of prosecution against medical professionals in Northern Ireland who made abortion referrals to Great Britain was lifted.

The UK Supreme Court case challenging Northern Ireland's abortion law was ongoing. The case considered whether the law breached women's rights by prohibiting abortions in cases of rape or incest and serious/fatal foetal impairment. A ruling was expected in early 2018.

Arrangements for women resident in Northern Ireland to access free abortion services in England and Scotland were confirmed in October and November respectively.

DISCRIMINATION

In January, the Scottish government set up an independent review into hate crime laws in Scotland.

Northern Ireland remained the only part of the UK to deny same-sex couples the right to marriage. In July, thousands of people took part in a march in the city of Belfast calling for marriage equality.

In September, an independent review into ethnic minority individuals in the criminal justice system in England and Wales was published. It found that ethnic minorities were disproportionately represented in prisons, with 25% of prisoners (despite making up 14% of the population in the counties reviewed), and that 40% of young people in custody were from ethnic minority backgrounds.

In August, the UN Committee on the Rights of Persons with Disabilities severely criticized the UK for failing to ensure the rights of people with disabilities with respect to, among other things, education, employment, and an adequate standard of living and social protection.

RIGHT TO LIFE

During the night of 13-14 June, at least 71 people died and dozens were injured in a fire at the Grenfell Tower social housing block in London. In September, a public inquiry into the cause of the fire, the emergency services' and authorities' responses, the building's construction and modifications, as well as the adequacy of the regulatory framework began. The fire raised questions concerning the authorities' and private actors' compliance with their human rights obligations and responsibilities including protection of the right to life and guaranteeing an adequate standard of living, including the right to adequate housing.

REFUGEES' AND MIGRANTS' RIGHTS

The government continued to extend immigration-related controls across public and private life, collecting children's nationality and country of birth data from schools and widening nationality and immigration checks on access to free health care.

In July, the government ended its so-called "Dubs Amendment" scheme under which 480 unaccompanied refugee children who were already in Europe were to be resettled in the UK. No children were resettled in 2017, despite 280 local authority places available for them. A legal challenge to the government's limited implementation of the scheme, brought by the NGO Help Refugees, was unsuccessful before the High Court and an appeal was lodged.

In September, the government introduced a Data Protection Bill that included a provision to exclude basic safeguards on taking, holding and using personal data for the purpose of "effective immigration control".

In October, the High Court ruled that the Home Office's "Adults at Risk" policy on the detention of victims of torture was unlawful.

VIOLENCE AGAINST WOMEN AND GIRLS

In June, the Prime Minister announced plans for adopting a new Domestic Violence and Abuse Bill and appointing a Domestic Violence and Abuse Commissioner. The government was yet to ratify the Council of Europe Convention on Violence against Women and Domestic Violence (Istanbul Convention), which it signed in 2012.

Concerns remained about the impact of austerity-led cuts on funding for specialist services for women who had experienced domestic violence or abuse.

ARMS TRADE

The UK continued to supply arms to Saudi Arabia despite ongoing serious violations of international humanitarian law by the Saudi Arabia-led coalition in Yemen.

UNITED STATES OF AMERICA

United States of America
Head of state and government: **Donald Trump**
(replaced Barack Obama in January)

Executive orders to suspend travel to the USA from several Muslim-majority countries sparked legal challenges, which continued through the year. There were major attacks on the rights of women and girls. Eighteen detainees were transferred from the US naval base at Guantánamo Bay, Cuba; 41 detainees remained at the base and pre-trial military commission proceedings continued. Gun violence remained high. Death sentences were handed down and executions were carried out.

BACKGROUND

On 20 January, Donald Trump was sworn in as President, following an election campaign in which he made comments and promised policies that were discriminatory or otherwise contradicted international human rights principles.

REFUGEES' AND MIGRANTS' RIGHTS

A number of executive orders affecting migrants, asylum-seekers and refugees were signed by President Trump during the year. Two orders dated 25 January called for a wall to be built along the USA-Mexico border, allowed for *refoulement* (forcible return) and the increased detention of asylum-seekers and their families, increased the functions and number of immigration and customs enforcement agents, prioritized deportation of migrants, especially those suspected of crimes, and cancelled funding for "sanctuary cities" that did not co-operate with federal authorities in apprehending irregular migrants.

A third executive order signed on 27 January banned entry of foreign nationals from Iran, Iraq, Libya, Somalia, Sudan, Syria and Yemen for 90 days, suspended the US Refugee Admissions Program (USRAP) for 120 days, reduced the number of refugees eligible for entry during the 2017 fiscal year from 110,000 to 50,000, and imposed an indefinite ban on the resettlement of refugees from Syria. The order immediately led to chaos, protests and legal challenges on the basis of discrimination towards Muslims. A week later a federal judge issued a nationwide temporary injunction, which was upheld on appeal. The government issued a revised version of the order on 6 March, again suspending USRAP for 120 days, repeating the limit of 50,000 refugees, and imposing a 90-day ban on entry into the USA of nationals of six countries (the original seven minus Iraq). Federal judges in the states of Maryland and Hawaii issued nationwide injunctions temporarily blocking its implementation. On 26 June, the Supreme Court allowed a limited version of the order to take effect. The Court also ruled that the ban

could be applied to refugees being supported by resettlement agencies.

A second revision of the order, signed on 24 September, indefinitely banned immigration into the USA by nationals of seven countries: Chad, Iran, Libya, North Korea, Somalia, Syria and Yemen. It also banned the issuance of certain types of non-immigrant visas to nationals of Chad, Iran, Libya, North Korea, Syria and Yemen, and specifically barred visas for Venezuelan officials from certain government agencies and their families. On 17 October, federal judges in Hawaii and Maryland again ruled against the measure, blocking the government from enforcing it on nationals from six of the countries. On 13 November, a federal appeals court panel allowed the third ban to take effect for people with no legitimate ties to the USA.

On 24 October, President Trump issued an executive order to resume USRAP "with enhanced vetting procedures". On 4 December the Supreme Court granted the administration's request to temporarily allow the latest so-called "Muslim ban" to take full effect as the case continued to be litigated.

On 16 August, the federal Department of Homeland Security terminated the Central American Minors programme. The programme had allowed those under 21 years of age fleeing violence in El Salvador, Guatemala and Honduras, whose parents had regular status in the USA, to apply for refugee resettlement interviews before travelling to the USA. Children from those three countries who did not qualify for refugee status and had no other means of reuniting with their parents had also been able to apply for entry under the programme.

On 5 September, the government announced that it would end the Deferred Action for Childhood Arrivals (DACA) programme in six months if Congress did not find a legislative solution regarding the immigration status of those protected by the programme, placing more than 800,000 individuals at risk of deportation. DACA's aim was to protect from deportation migrant youth who came to the USA as children and met certain eligibility criteria. Congress introduced the DREAM Act to provide DACA beneficiaries with a means to obtain regular migration status; it had not been passed into law at the end of the year.

More than 17,000 unaccompanied children and 26,000 people travelling as families were apprehended after irregularly crossing the border with Mexico between January and August. Families were detained for months, many without proper access to medical care and legal counsel, while pursuing claims to remain in the USA.

WOMEN'S RIGHTS

Attacks on the rights of women and girls were broad and multi-faceted. President Trump's administration overturned policies that required universities to investigate sexual violence as gender discrimination and suspended equal pay initiatives that had helped women to identify whether they were being paid less than male colleagues. Attacks on women's reproductive health and rights were particularly virulent. There were repeated efforts by the government and Congress to withdraw funding from Planned Parenthood – a health organization providing vital reproductive and other health services, particularly to women on low incomes. The government issued rules exempting employers from providing health insurance coverage for contraception if it conflicted with their religious or moral beliefs, putting millions of women at risk of losing access to contraception. Gross inequalities remained for Indigenous women in accessing care following rape, including access to examinations, forensic evidence kits for use by medical staff, and other essential health care services. The government also introduced the so-called "global gag rule", prohibiting any US financial assistance to any hospitals or organizations that provide information about, or access to, safe and legal abortion care.

RIGHTS OF LESBIAN, GAY, BISEXUAL, TRANSGENDER AND INTERSEX PEOPLE

Murders of LGBTI people increased during the year, against a background of continuing discrimination against LGBTI people in state and federal law. Further discriminatory measures by the government against LGBTI people increased. The USA continued to lack federal protections banning discrimination on the grounds of sexual orientation and gender identity in the workplace, housing or health care. Transgender people continued to be particularly marginalized. President Trump's administration overturned guidelines that protected transgender students in public schools who used facilities that corresponded with their gender identity. In August, President Trump ordered a reversal in the policy announced in 2016 to allow openly transgender individuals to enlist in the military, which had been due to take effect on 1 January 2018. On 30 October, a federal judge issued a preliminary injunction blocking implementation of the directive. In December, a judge ruled that transgender people would be allowed to enlist in the military from 1 January 2018, as legal cases proceeded.

COUNTER-TERROR AND SECURITY

On 28 November, a federal jury in Washington DC convicted Libyan national Ahmed Abu Khatallah on terrorism charges relating to an attack on a US diplomatic compound in Benghazi, Libya, in 2012 in which four US nationals were killed. The jury acquitted him of murder. In August, the judge had ruled that any statements made by Ahmed Abu Khatallah while held incommunicado for nearly two weeks on board a US naval vessel after being seized by US forces in Libya could be admitted as evidence. On 29 October, US forces seized another Libyan national, Mustafa al-Imam, in Libya. He was flown to the USA and appeared in federal court on 3 November after five days' incommunicado detention. At the end of the year he was facing trial for terrorism offences in relation to the Benghazi attack.

After an attack in New York on 31 October in which eight people died and 12 were injured, Uzbek national Sayfullo Habibullaevic Saipov was charged and due to be tried in federal court, despite calls from two senior Senators for his transfer to military custody as an "enemy combatant" and comments from President Trump that he would consider sending him to Guantánamo Bay. President Trump flouted the presumption of innocence in a series of posts on Twitter in which he called for the death penalty for Sayfullo Saipov.

In January, under the administration of President Barack Obama, 18 detainees were transferred from Guantánamo Bay detention centre to Oman, Saudi Arabia and United Arab Emirates. Most of the remaining 41 Guantánamo Bay detainees were held without charge or trial. President Trump had made a pre-election pledge to keep the detention facility open and increase the numbers of detainees held there; no further detainee transfers were made into or out of Guantánamo Bay during the year.

Refusal in October by the Supreme Court to consider two jurisdictional challenges allowed military commission proceedings to continue at Guantánamo Bay, in contravention of international fair trial standards.

In October, Ahmed Mohammed Ahmed Haza al-Darbi, a Saudi Arabian national, was sentenced by military commission to 13 years' imprisonment after pleading guilty in 2014 to conspiracy, terrorism and other offences. He had been arrested in Azerbaijan in June 2002 and handed over to US agents two months later.

TORTURE AND OTHER ILL-TREATMENT

In an interview on 25 January, President Trump expressed his support for torture while stating that he would "rely" upon the Secretary of Defense, the CIA Director and others in deciding whether the USA should use it. No action was taken to end impunity for the systematic human rights violations, including torture and enforced disappearance, committed in a secret detention programme operated by the CIA after the attacks on 11 September 2001.

At least three people alleged to have been involved in the secret detention programme were nominated by President Trump for senior government roles: Gina Haspel, selected in February for the role of Deputy Director of the CIA; Steven Bradbury, nominated for General Counsel at the Department of Transportation; and Steven Engel, nominated to head the Office of Legal Counsel (OLC) at the Department of Justice. Gina Haspel was believed to have been CIA Chief of Staff in Thailand in 2002 when the CIA ran a so-called "black site" in which at least two detainees were subjected to torture and enforced disappearance. She was later Chief of Staff to the Director of the Counterterrorism Center, the branch of the CIA that ran the secret detention programme. As Acting Assistant Attorney General at the OLC between 2005 and 2009, Steven Bradbury authored a number of memorandums to the CIA giving legal approval to methods of interrogation and conditions of detention that violated the international prohibition of torture and other ill-treatment. As Deputy Assistant Attorney General at the OLC in 2007, Steven Engel was also involved in the writing of one of those memorandums. On 7 November, the Senate confirmed his appointment by 51 votes to 47. On 14 November, by 50 votes to 47, the Senate confirmed the appointment of Steven Bradbury. Gina Haspel's appointment did not require Senate confirmation.

A civil jury trial of James Mitchell and John "Bruce" Jessen, two CIA-contracted psychologists who had leading involvement in its detention programme, was due to begin on 5 September. However, in August an out-of-court settlement was reached.

On 19 June, the Supreme Court ruled in a case brought against former US officials by individuals of Arab or South Asian descent who were among the hundreds of foreign nationals taken into custody in the USA in the wake of the attacks of 11 September 2001. Following the attacks, detainees were held for months in harsh conditions and reported a range of abuses. The Supreme Court stated that if the allegations were true, then what happened to the detainees "was tragic", and "nothing in this opinion should be read to condone the treatment to which they contend they were subjected". However, it ruled that the case largely could not proceed, thus continuing a pattern of judicial remedies being blocked in cases involving human rights violations in the counter-terrorism context since the 2001 attacks.

EXCESSIVE USE OF FORCE

The authorities continued to fail to track the exact number of people killed by law enforcement officials across the USA. Data collected by *The Washington Post* newspaper put the total at 987 individuals killed during the year by law enforcement agents using firearms. According to the data, African Americans – who comprised 13% of the population – represented nearly 23% of the victims in 2017. Of those killed, 24% were known to have mental health problems. A proposal by the Department of Justice to create a system to track these deaths under the Deaths in Custody Reporting Act was not compulsory for law enforcement agencies and therefore risked leading to under-reporting. No information was released on whether the reporting process had been initiated during the year.

At least 40 people across 25 states died after police used projectile electro-shock weapons on them, bringing the total number of such deaths since 2001 to at least 802. Most of the victims were not armed and did not appear to pose a threat of death or serious injury when the electro-shock weapon was deployed.

In September, the acquittal of a former police officer for shooting dead Anthony Lamar Smith in 2011 sparked weeks of protests across the city of St Louis, Missouri, and hundreds of arrests. There were allegations by local civil rights organizations that police unlawfully detained people and that their use of chemical irritants against protesters amounted to excessive use of force. St Louis police used heavy-duty riot gear and military-grade weapons and equipment to police the demonstrations. In August, President Trump annulled restrictions put in place by the previous government that limited the transfer of some military-grade equipment to law enforcement agencies.

GUN VIOLENCE

In October a gunman used "bump stocks" – accessories that modify firearms to allow rapid firing similar to that of fully automatic firearms – against a crowd of concert-goers in Las Vegas, Nevada, killing 58 people. In response to the massacre, Congress considered legislation and regulations banning such devices, but the measures were not enacted. In November, Congress introduced but failed to pass a separate piece of legislation aimed at preventing gun violence.

Two pieces of federal legislation were pending at the end of the year that would make it easier for people to obtain firearm silencers and carry concealed weapons. Legislation in place since 1996 continued to deny funding to the Center for Disease Control and Prevention to conduct or sponsor research into the causes of gun violence and ways to prevent it.

President Trump's administration considered relaxing restrictions on the export of small arms, including assault rifles and ammunition, by shifting the responsibility for processing international non-military firearms sales from the Department of State to the Department of Commerce. The move would severely weaken oversight of arms sales and risked increasing the flow of firearms to countries suffering high levels of armed violence.

DEATH PENALTY

Twenty-three men were executed in eight states, bringing to 1,465 the total number of executions since the US Supreme Court approved new capital laws in 1976. Approximately 39 new death sentences were passed. Around 2,800 people remained on death row at the end of the year.

Arkansas conducted its first executions since 2005. Ohio resumed executions after a hiatus of more than three years. Florida conducted its first executions since January 2016, when the US Supreme Court ruled its capital sentencing statute unconstitutional. The Florida Supreme Court's decision that the ruling applied only retroactively to about half of those on death row allowed the state to begin executing those deemed not to benefit. During the year, the first death sentences were handed down under a new sentencing statute.

During the year, four inmates were exonerated of the crimes for which they were originally sentenced to death in the states of Delaware, Florida, Arkansas and Louisiana, bringing to 160 the number of such cases since 1973.

URUGUAY

Eastern Republic of Uruguay
Head of state and government: **Tabaré Vázquez**

Pre-trial detention continued to be imposed widely. Impunity persisted for past crimes; human rights defenders investigating such crimes received death threats. Sexual and reproductive health services were difficult to access in rural areas and objectors to providing abortion continued to obstruct access to legal abortions.

BACKGROUND

The Monitoring System for Recommendations (SIMORE), which since December 2016 has collected information on Uruguay's implementation of recommendations by international bodies, still had no effective mechanism for civil society participation. There had yet to be full implementation of the Inter-institutional Network for the Elaboration of Reports and Monitoring of the Implementation of Recommendations and Observations in the Field of Human Rights, also established in 2016.

DETENTION

The National Human Rights Institute, through the National Mechanism for the Prevention of Torture, continued to document and report human rights violations in prisons, including overcrowding and access to health services and education.

Pre-trial detention continued to be imposed in the majority of cases and conditional releases pending trial were often denied.

A proposed amendment to the Code on Children and Adolescents threatened to increase the proportion of cases subject to mandatory pre-trial detention and eliminate time limits for such detentions, endangering the rights of young people in the juvenile penal system.

People with psychosocial disabilities continued to be held against their will and in isolation in psychiatric institutions.

ECONOMIC, SOCIAL AND CULTURAL RIGHTS

The UN Committee on Economic, Social and Cultural Rights made several recommendations to Uruguay including increasing the direct applicability of these rights in the judicial system; strengthening legislation against discrimination; adopting a law on mental health in line with international standards; approving the comprehensive bill against gender-based violence; and ensuring the right to work for persons with disabilities.

IMPUNITY

In February, human rights defenders investigating human rights violations that occurred during the military regime (1973-1985) reported receiving death threats; the sources of these threats were not investigated. In May, human rights defenders denounced these threats at a hearing before the Inter-American Commission on Human Rights, which the Uruguayan authorities did not attend.

The national Working Group on Truth and Justice, implemented in 2015, had not achieved concrete results regarding reparations for victims of past crimes under international law.

In October, the Supreme Court ruled that statutory limitations apply to crimes against humanity, hindering victims' access to justice, and preventing the prosecution of those suspected of criminal responsibility.

RIGHTS OF LESBIAN, GAY, BISEXUAL, TRANSGENDER AND INTERSEX PEOPLE

There remained no comprehensive anti-discrimination policy protecting LGBTI people from violence in schools and public spaces and ensuring their access to health services.

VIOLENCE AGAINST WOMEN AND GIRLS

There were 27 femicides between January and November, according to official data. The adoption and implementation of a comprehensive law against gender-based violence, as part of Uruguay's 2016-2019 Action Plan on gender-based violence, was still pending.

SEXUAL AND REPRODUCTIVE RIGHTS

The lack of public policies to ensure access to health services in rural areas continued and access to sexual and reproductive health services in these areas remained limited.

Obstacles to accessing abortions persisted due to a lack of regulation of conscientious objection by physicians and other health personnel.

High rates of child and adolescent pregnancy continued, due in part to the absence of adequate sexual and reproductive health services and information to prevent unplanned pregnancies.

UZBEKISTAN

Republic of Uzbekistan
Head of state: **Shavkat Mirzioiev**
Head of government : **Abdulla Aripov**

The authorities eased some undue restrictions on the media and the right to freedom of expression. Several prisoners of conscience and other prisoners serving long sentences on politically motivated charges were released; their right to freedom of movement remained restricted. National Security Service (NSS) officers arbitrarily detained an independent journalist and tortured him to "confess" to anti-state crimes. The authorities continued to seek the return of people they considered a threat to national security. Local authorities continued to draft thousands of medical personnel and teaching staff to work in the cotton fields. Consensual sexual relations between men remained a criminal offence.

BACKGROUND

President Mirzioiev continued to introduce a number of wide-ranging political and economic reform proposals, designed to end past isolationist and repressive policies. An action strategy on judicial reform was approved in February. It set out several priorities for systemic reform, including ensuring genuine judicial independence, increasing the effectiveness and authority of the judiciary, and ensuring robust judicial protection of the rights and freedoms of citizens.

One of the legislative changes reduced the maximum time a person could be detained before being brought before a judge from 72 to 48 hours.

In May, at the end of the first ever visit by the UN Office of the High Commissioner for Human Rights to Uzbekistan, the Commissioner called on the President to translate his reform pledges into action for the effective protection of human rights.

In November, the President issued a decree explicitly prohibiting the use of torture to obtain confessions and their admission as evidence in court proceedings.

FREEDOM OF EXPRESSION – HUMAN RIGHTS DEFENDERS AND JOURNALISTS

The authorities eased some undue restrictions on the right to freedom of expression. They allowed some critical reporting by the media and released several prisoners convicted on politically motivated charges. However, the government retained firm control of access to information. Independent and international media platforms considered critical of the authorities remained inaccessible.

In February, the authorities released Muhammad Bekzhanov, after he served 17 years in prison on politically motivated charges. He remained under curfew and close police supervision. In July, Erkin Musaev, a former military official and staff member of the UN Development Programme, was released early. He had been sentenced to 20 years on fabricated espionage charges in 2006. Prisoners of conscience Azam Farmonov and Salidzhon Abdurakhmonov, human rights lawyer Agzam Turgunov and two other human rights defenders were released in October. All of them had been tortured in detention. Prisoner of conscience Isroil Kholdorov remained in prison.

In July, during a visit to the EU, the Foreign Minister extended invitations to international NGOs and international media to visit Uzbekistan. The authorities granted limited access to some representatives of international NGOs and media.

Despite these positive developments, human rights defenders and independent journalists, both exiled and in Uzbekistan, as well as their families, continued to be subjected to smear campaigns online, on national television and in the print media.

Surveillance by the authorities in Uzbekistan and abroad reinforced the repressive environment for human rights defenders, journalists and others. Technical and legal systems facilitated unlawful surveillance and failed to provide effective controls and remedies against abuse.[1]

On 27 September, NSS officers detained independent journalist Bobomurod Abdullayev as he was leaving his home in the capital, Tashkent. He was held incommunicado for two weeks in an NSS pre-trial detention facility, which is well known for the use of torture. The NSS accused him of using a pseudonym to publish online articles that called for the overthrow of the government and instigating unrest in Uzbekistan, crimes punishable by up to 20 years in prison. NSS officers warned his family not to contact human rights organizations or the media, and allowed him only limited and supervised access to a lawyer of his choice ten weeks after he was detained. In November, the authorities extended his pre-trial detention for another three months. On 26 December, the NSS accused his lawyer of misrepresenting the case to the public and forced Bobomurod Abdullayev to dismiss him in favour of a state-appointed one.

FREEDOM OF MOVEMENT

In August, the President announced that the legal requirement for Uzbekistani nationals to obtain permission to leave the country would be abolished by 2019. Nevertheless, the authorities continued to impose travel restrictions on newly released prisoners who had been convicted on politically motivated charges. Some former prisoners continued to be prevented from travelling abroad for urgent medical treatment.

Human rights lawyer Polina Braunerg who used a wheelchair, died in May from a stroke after being repeatedly refused permission to travel abroad for medical treatment.

In October, Murad Dzhuraev, a former Member of Parliament, who was released in November 2015 after serving 20 years in prison on politically motivated charges, was finally allowed to travel to Germany for urgent medical treatment following mounting international pressure. On 4 December, he died suddenly before being able to leave the country.

On 22 February, journalist Muhammad Bekzhanov was released after 17 years in prison. His sentence was handed down after an unfair trial and torture, and arbitrarily extended. At the end of the year, he had not been granted permission to apply for an exit visa to join his family abroad. He was not allowed to travel to Tashkent for urgent medical treatment that he required as a consequence of the torture and other ill-treatment he was subjected to.

RIGHTS OF LESBIAN, GAY, BISEXUAL, TRANSGENDER AND INTERSEX PEOPLE

The authorities repeatedly stated that they had no intention of decriminalizing consensual sexual relations between men, which constituted a crime punishable by a prison term of up to three years.

Same-sex consensual sexual relations remained highly stigmatized, and LGBTI people were regularly subjected to violence, arbitrary arrests, detention and discrimination by state and non-state actors.

FORCED LABOUR AND SLAVERY

In August, a presidential decree formally banned the forcible recruitment of children, students, medical personnel and teaching staff to work in the cotton fields. During his speech to the UN General Assembly in September, President Mirzioiev acknowledged the use of forced labour in the cotton industry in Uzbekistan and pledged to end it.

Nevertheless, human rights defenders and independent monitors detailed cases of hundreds of medical personnel and teaching staff being forced to work in the cotton fields, in poor working conditions. In some regions, they documented children harvesting cotton, despite the August ban. The authorities threatened those who refused to work in the cotton fields with large fines, dismissal or the loss of social benefits.

Police and local authorities tried to stop human rights activists from monitoring the work in the cotton fields, in some cases using intimidation, force, and arbitrary detention.

In March, police detained human rights defender Elena Urlaeva and forcibly confined her in a psychiatric hospital for a month. This was to prevent her from attending a scheduled meeting with visiting delegations from the World Bank and the ILO in Tashkent to discuss her findings of the common practice of forced labour in the cotton industry. Between August and November, police repeatedly detained her for brief periods of time to stop her talking to medical and teaching staff in the cotton fields.

FREEDOM OF RELIGION AND BELIEF

In August, the President publicly called for a review of the charges against people detained on suspicion of possessing banned religious or "extremist" materials. He also called for people who regretted joining unregistered Islamic movements, to be "rehabilitated". The authorities also announced that they had removed more than 15,000 names from a "blacklist" of up to 18,000 people suspected of membership of banned or unregistered religious movements and groups.

However, security forces continued to detain dozens of people accused of being members of banned "extremist" groups, including labour migrants returning from abroad. Relatives and human rights activists reported that police and NSS officers tortured many of the people accused of illegal membership to "confess" to fabricated charges, and that judges continued to ignore credible allegations, even when confronted with physical signs of torture in the court room, and admitted them as evidence.

In October, the UN Special Rapporteur on freedom of religion or belief visited Uzbekistan at the invitation of the authorities. He was the first representative of the UN Special Procedures to be granted access to Uzbekistan since 2002. In his preliminary findings he noted that religious practice was "subject to excessive regulations that prioritize security over freedom".

COUNTER-TERROR AND SECURITY

The authorities continued to secure forcible returns, including through extradition proceedings, of Uzbekistani nationals they identified as threats to the "constitutional order" or national security.

NSS officers continued to abduct wanted individuals (so-called renditions) from abroad.

Those abducted or otherwise forcibly returned were placed in incommunicado detention, often in undisclosed locations, and tortured or otherwise ill-treated to force them to confess or incriminate others. In many cases, security forces pressured relatives not to seek support from human rights organizations, and not to file complaints about alleged human rights violations.

---

1. "We will find you, anywhere": The global shadow of Uzbekistani surveillance (EUR 62/5974/2017)

VENEZUELA

Bolivarian Republic of Venezuela
Head of state and government: **Nicolás Maduro Moros**

Venezuela remained in a state of emergency, repeatedly extended since January 2016. A National Constituent Assembly was elected without the participation of the opposition. The Attorney General was dismissed under irregular circumstances. Security forces continued to use excessive and undue force to disperse protests. Hundreds of people were arbitrarily detained. There were many reports of torture and other ill-treatment, including sexual violence against demonstrators. The judicial system continued to be used to silence dissidents, including using military jurisdiction to prosecute civilians. Human rights defenders were harassed, intimidated and subject to raids. Conditions of detention were extremely harsh. The food and health crises continued to worsen, especially affecting children, people with chronic illness and pregnant women. The number of Venezuelans seeking asylum in other countries increased.

BACKGROUND

The year was marked by growing public protests due to rising inflation and shortages of food and medical supplies. The state of emergency declared in January 2016 remained in force, providing the government with special powers to attend the economic situation. Despite the political dialogue processes initiated between the government and the opposition during the year, there was no concrete progress in advancing human rights issues.

FREEDOM OF EXPRESSION

The Office of the Special Rapporteur for freedom of expression of the Inter-American Commission on Human Rights (IACHR) expressed concern about the closure of 50 radio stations by the National Telecommunications Commission. Other media outlets also faced the threat of closure, despite a 2015 ruling by the Inter-American Court of Human Rights declaring that such closures violated freedom of expression.

Anti-government protesters and some opposition leaders were accused by the government of being a threat to national security.

The government ordered the removal of some foreign news channels including CNN, RCN and CARACOL from national television cable operators. In September, journalists from the online news and research portal Armando.Info were threatened by unidentified actors for their investigations into cases of administrative corruption.

FREEDOM OF ASSEMBLY

Between April and July in particular, there were mass protests for and against the government in various parts of the country. The right to peaceful assembly was not guaranteed. According to official data, at least 120 people were killed and more than 1,177 wounded – including demonstrators, members of the security forces and bystanders – during these mass demonstrations.

There were also reports from the Attorney General's Office that groups of armed people with the support or acquiescence of the government carried out violent actions against demonstrators.

According to the local NGO Venezuelan Penal Forum, 5,341 people were arrested in the context of the protests, of which 822 were tried. Of these, 726 civilians were subjected to military justice and charged with military crimes for demonstrating against the government. At the end of the year, 216 people remained in pre-trial detention.

EXCESSIVE USE OF FORCE

In January the government relaunched its public security programme, previously named Operation Liberation of the People, under the new name Operation Humanist Liberation of the People. Reports continued of excessive use of force by security agents.

In the context of the demonstrations that took place between April and July, the government announced the activation of the "Zamora Plan", with the objective to "guarantee the functioning [of the] country [and] its security" by mobilizing civilians alongside police and military forces to "preserve internal order". However, the details of the plan were not made public.

The Bolivarian National Police and the Bolivarian National Guard – among other civil and military security forces – continued to use excessive and undue force against demonstrators. Between April and July there was an increase in the deployment of military forces to repress protests, resulting in an increase in the excessive use of less-lethal force and undue use of lethal force, including firing tear gas directly at people's bodies, shooting multiple munitions such as rubber bullets, beatings, and use of firearms, all of which put protesters at risk of serious harm or death.

According to the Attorney General's Office, Jairo Johan Ortiz Bustamante was killed by gunshot wounds during a protest in Miranda state on 6 April and Juan Pablo Pernalete was killed by the impact of a tear gas bomb to his chest during a protest in the capital, Caracas, on 26 April. David Vallenilla, Neomar Lander and Rubén Darío González also died from injuries sustained during the protests between April and July.

During this period, the civil society organization Micondominio.com recorded at least 47 illegal raids on multiple communities and homes in 11 states across the country. These raids were characterized by illegal use of force, threats and mass arbitrary arrests, and were often linked to police and military operations against protests that took place near the communities. The actions of the security forces during these raids were illegal and arbitrary and had indiscriminate effects. Groups of armed people also harassed and intimidated residents during the raids with the acquiescence of the state security forces present.

In August, the UN High Commissioner for Human Rights published a report highlighting the systematic and widespread use of excessive force during the protests between April and July, pointing to a pattern of violent home raids and torture and other ill-treatment of detainees. The report also expressed concern regarding difficulties faced by international organizations in accessing the country, and victims' fears of reporting abuses.

ARBITRARY ARRESTS AND DETENTIONS

Amnesty International documented 22 emblematic cases of people arbitrarily detained for political reasons through the implementation of various unlawful mechanisms since 2014. These mechanisms included the use of military justice, arrests without a warrant, and the use of ambiguous and discretionary criminal definitions, among others, that demonstrated a much broader pattern of efforts to silence dissent.[1] At the end of the year, 12 of these people were granted alternative measures to detention; the other 10 remained arbitrarily detained, although the courts had ordered the release of many of them.

These documented cases included those of MP Gilber Caro and activist Steyci Escalona, both members of the opposition party Popular Will, who were arbitrarily detained in January after senior government authorities publicly accused them of carrying out "terrorist activities". Despite Gilber Caro's trial requiring authorization by Parliament, he remained arbitrarily detained and his case was submitted to military courts. Steyci Escalona was granted conditional release from pre-trial detention in November. By the end of the year, neither had been brought to trial.

Hundreds of people reported that they were arbitrarily detained during the protests that took place between April and July. Many were denied access to medical care or a lawyer of their choice and in many cases were subjected to military tribunals. There was a notable increase in the use of military justice to try civilians.

In December, 44 people arbitrarily detained for what local NGOs considered to have been politically motivated reasons were released with alternative restrictions on their freedom.

TORTURE AND ILL-TREATMENT

Many new reports of torture and other ill-treatment were received. Wilmer Azuaje, a member of the Legislative Council of Barinas state, was arrested in May. His family reported that during his detention he was locked in a noxious-smelling room, handcuffed for long periods of time and sometimes kept incommunicado, conditions that constitute cruel treatment. In July, the Supreme Court of Justice ordered his transfer to house arrest; however, at the end of the year Wilmer Azuaje remained at the 26 July Detention Centre without any charges against him or any improvement in his conditions of detention.

During the demonstrations between April and July, there were reports of ill-treatment by state officials during arrests of protesters, including kicking, beatings and sexual violence.

HUMAN RIGHTS DEFENDERS

Human rights defenders and individuals who sought justice for human rights violations continued to be subjected to attacks and smear campaigns, in an apparent attempt to halt their human rights work.

In February, transgender lawyer Samantha Seijas was threatened by a police official while filing a complaint at a police station in Aragua state accompanied by his daughter.[2]

In May, authorities raided the home of human rights defender Ehisler Vásquez in the city of Barquisimeto, Lara state. When he requested information on the reason for the raid, the Public Prosecutor's Office threatened to charge him with a crime.[3] Later that month in the same city, a group of unidentified people stormed the home of human rights defenders Yonaide Sánchez and Nelson Freitez.[4]

Human rights defenders were intimidated by state media and high-ranking government officials, who publicly announced their names and contact details while accusing them of "terrorism".

Lawyers representing people on trial before military courts reported being harassed and intimidated by government authorities, putting great pressure on those defending people critical of the government.

JUSTICE SYSTEM

The justice system continued to be subject to government interference, especially in cases involving people critical of the government or those who were considered to be acting against the interests of the authorities. The Bolivarian National Intelligence Service continued to ignore court decisions to transfer and release people in its custody.

Two police officers from the Chacao municipality remained arbitrarily detained since June 2016, despite a warrant being issued for their release in August 2016. Twelve other officers accused in the same criminal case who had also been arbitrarily detained since June 2016 were released in December. In June 2017, the 14 officers went on hunger strike, some for 23 days, in order to demand that the authorities release them in compliance with the judicial order.[5]

In August, four opposition officials who had been elected to public office were arrested and five others had arrest warrants issued against them. These warrants were issued by the Supreme Court in a proceeding that was not enshrined in law. A total of 11 officials elected by popular vote were removed from office in irregular proceedings.

PRISONERS OF CONSCIENCE

Leopoldo López, leader of the opposition party Popular Will and a prisoner of conscience, was moved to house arrest in August. During his detention at the National Centre for Military Proceedings in Ramo Verde, Caracas, there had been several reports of abuses against him, including torture and denial of visits from his lawyers and family.

Villca Fernández, a student and political activist from the state of Mérida and a prisoner of conscience, remained arbitrarily detained by the Bolivarian National Intelligence Service in Caracas. He had been repeatedly denied urgent medical care and had reported other ill-treatment since his detention in January 2016.[6]

INTERNATIONAL SCRUTINY

In May, Venezuela announced that it was withdrawing from the Organization of American States and therefore from the authority of the IACHR, further limiting the protection for victims of human rights violations in Venezuela.

Decisions and rulings from international human rights monitoring mechanisms were still not implemented at the end of the year, especially regarding the investigation and punishment of those responsible for human rights violations.

In November, Venezuela received a visit from the UN Independent Expert on the promotion of a democratic and equitable international order. Visits from the UN Special Rapporteur on the right to development, and the UN Special Rapporteur on the negative impact of unilateral coercive measures on the enjoyment of human rights, were announced for 2018.

ENFORCED DISAPPEARANCES

Former Minister of Defence and detained government critic Raúl Isaías Baduel was unexpectedly taken from his cell at the National Centre for Military Proceedings in Ramo Verde, Caracas, on the morning of 8 August; he remained disappeared for 23 days. The authorities then acknowledged that he was being held at the facilities of the Bolivarian National Intelligence Service in Caracas, where he was held incommunicado and denied access to his family and lawyers for more than a month.[7]

IMPUNITY

Most victims of human rights violations continued to lack access to truth, justice and reparation. Victims and their families were often subjected to intimidation.

In April, two officers of the Bolivarian National Guard were sentenced for killing Geraldine Moreno during demonstrations in Carabobo state in 2014. The majority of victims of murder, torture and other violations by state actors were yet to receive justice or reparation.

The Attorney General's Office announced investigations into killings in the context of protests between April and July 2017. The National Constituent Assembly, established on 30 July, appointed a Truth Commission to investigate cases of human rights violations during the protests; there were concerns about its independence and impartiality. There were reports of victims or their families being pressured by authorities to testify and agree on facts that could waive the responsibility of state agents for these violations, as well as obstacles to the work of defence lawyers working with human rights organizations.

DETENTION

Despite reforms to the penitentiary system in 2011, prison conditions remained extremely harsh. Lack of medical care, food and drinking water, insanitary conditions, overcrowding and violence in prisons and other detention centres continued. During clashes inside penitentiary centres, the use of firearms remained commonplace among inmates. Many detainees resorted to hunger strikes to protest against the conditions of their detention.

The IACHR expressed concern over the deaths of 37 detainees at the Amazon Judicial Detention Centre in August during clashes that took place when the Bolivarian National Guard and the Bolivarian National Police reportedly attempted to search the premises.

RIGHT TO FOOD

The Documentation and Analysis Centre for Workers reported that in December the basket of consumer goods for a family of five, which is used to define the consumer price index, was 60 times the minimum wage, representing a 2123% increase since November 2016. The humanitarian organization Caritas Venezuela found that 27.6% of children studied were at risk of malnutrition and 15.7% of them suffered mild to acute malnutrition.

The government failed to acknowledge the worsening food shortage caused by the economic and social crises. In its *Global Report on Food Crises 2017*, the UN Food and Agriculture Organization stated that it lacked reliable official data on Venezuela and that the deepening of the critical economic situation could lead to a greater absence of consumer goods such as food and medical supplies.

RIGHT TO HEALTH

After almost two years of publishing no official data, in May the Ministry of Health published the weekly epidemiological bulletins from 2016. The data revealed that during 2016, there were 11,466 reported deaths of children under the age of one, an increase of 30.1% from 2015, when this figure stood at 8,812. The most common causes of infant mortality were neonatal sepsis, pneumonia and premature birth. In addition, the bulletins showed that 324 cases of diphtheria were reported in 2016.

WOMEN'S RIGHTS

The Ministry of Health bulletins indicated an increase in instances of maternal mortality of 65.8% from 2015 to 2016, with a total of 756 deaths recorded in 2016, 300 more than in 2015.

Lack of official data made it almost impossible to monitor the rate of femicides and other crimes against women. However, the NGO Women's Metropolitan Institute estimated that there were at least 48 femicides between January and May.

Ten years after the implementation of the Organic Law on Women's Right to Live a Life Free of Violence, local NGOs reported that prosecutors, judges, police officers and other officials remained poorly equipped to protect women's rights, and women often suffered re-victimization because of institutional violence. Other obstacles to implementing the law included a lack of official data to plan and programme public policies to prevent and eradicate violence against women.

SEXUAL AND REPRODUCTIVE RIGHTS

The economic crisis continued to limit access to contraception. In June, in an online survey carried out by the local NGO AVESA, 72% of respondents had not been able to access any contraceptives during the previous 12 months, and 27% said that they could not afford to buy contraceptives from pharmacies.

REFUGEES AND ASYLUM-SEEKERS

There was a notable increase in the number of Venezuelans seeking asylum in Brazil, Costa Rica, the USA, Spain, Peru, and Trinidad and Tobago. Other countries in the region, including Colombia and Ecuador, also continued to receive large numbers of Venezuelans seeking refuge.

---

1. Silenced by force: Politically motivated arbitrary detentions in Venezuela (AMR 53/6014/2017)

2. Venezuela: Trans man and daughter threatened by police (AMR 53/5651/2017)

3. Venezuela: Human rights defender harassed – Ehisler Vásquez (AMR 53/6252/2017)

4. Venezuela: Defenders' home invaded, safety at risk (AMR 53/6324/2017)

5. Venezuela: Arbitrary detainees on hunger strike (AMR 53/6758/2017)

6. Venezuela: Prisoner of conscience needs medical care: Villca Fernández (AMR 53/7464/2017)

7. Venezuela: Detainee held incommunicado again: Raúl Isaías Baduel (AMR 53/7051/2017)

VIET NAM

Socialist Republic of Viet Nam
Head of state: Trần Đại Quang
Head of government: Nguyễn Xuân Phúc

Arbitrary restrictions on the rights to freedom of expression, association and peaceful assembly continued. A crackdown on dissent intensified, causing scores of activists to flee the country. Human rights defenders, peaceful political activists and religious followers were subjected to a range of human rights violations, including arbitrary detention, prosecution on national security and other vaguely worded charges in unfair trials, and long-term imprisonment. Prominent activists faced restrictions on movement and were subject to surveillance, harassment and violent assaults. Prisoners of conscience were tortured and otherwise ill-treated. Suspicious deaths in police custody were reported, and the death penalty was retained.

BACKGROUND

Dozens of state company officials were arrested and prosecuted during an anti-corruption campaign, including those also holding government and Communist Party of Viet Nam positions. Several were sentenced to death for embezzlement. In July, state security officials abducted a former businessman and government official while he was seeking asylum in Germany, and forcibly returned him to Viet Nam to stand trial for embezzlement and economic mismanagement; Vietnamese authorities maintained that he had returned voluntarily.

During the assessment of Viet Nam's human rights record under the UN UPR process, the government stated that by February it had implemented 129 out of 182 recommendations made during the review in 2014. No amendments were made to vaguely worded national security legislation used against peaceful dissidents to bring it into line with international law and standards.

Viet Nam hosted meetings of the Asia-Pacific Economic Cooperation (APEC) forum throughout the year, including the leaders' summit in November.

REPRESSION OF DISSENT

The crackdown on freedom of expression and criticism of government actions and policies intensified, causing scores of peaceful activists to flee the country. At least 29 activists were arrested during the year, and others went into hiding after arrest warrants were issued. They were charged mostly under vaguely worded provisions in the national security section of the 1999 Penal Code or detained on other spurious charges. Bloggers and pro-democracy

activists were particularly targeted, as well as social and environmental activists campaigning in the aftermath of the 2016 Formosa Plastics toxic spill that killed tonnes of fish and destroyed the livelihoods of thousands of people. At least five members of the independent Brotherhood for Democracy, co-founded by human rights lawyer and prisoner of conscience Nguyễn Văn Đài, were arrested between July and December.[1] They were charged under Article 79 (activities aimed at overthrowing the People's Administration), which carried a punishment of up to life imprisonment or the death penalty. Several were previous prisoners of conscience. In August, the same additional charge was brought against Nguyễn Văn Đài and his associate Lê Thu Hà, who had been held incommunicado since their arrests in December 2015 on charges of "conducting propaganda against the state" under Article 88.

At least 98 prisoners of conscience were detained or imprisoned, an increase on previous years despite some releases on completion of sentences. They included bloggers, human rights defenders working on land and labour issues, political activists, religious followers and members of ethnic minority groups. The authorities continued to grant early release to prisoners of conscience only if they agreed to go into exile. Đặng Xuân Diệu, a Catholic social activist and blogger arrested in 2011, was released in January after serving six years of a 13-year prison sentence. He was immediately flown into exile in France. In July, Pastor Nguyễn Cong Chinh was released four years before the end of his 11-year sentence and immediately flown to exile in the USA. Both men were tortured and otherwise ill-treated while imprisoned.

Trials of dissidents routinely failed to meet international standards of fairness; there was a lack of adequate defence as well as denial of the presumption of innocence. Human rights defender and blogger Nguyễn Ngọc Như Quỳnh, also known as Mẹ Nấm, (Mother Mushroom), was sentenced to 10 years' imprisonment for "conducting propaganda" (Article 88) in June. Land and labour activist Trần Thị Nga received a nine-year sentence on the same charge with five years' house arrest upon release in July.[2] In October, after a trial lasting just a few hours, student Phan Kim Khánh was sentenced to six years' imprisonment and four years' house arrest upon release, after conviction under Article 88. He had criticized corruption and lack of freedom of expression in Viet Nam on blogs and social media. He was also accused of being in contact with "reactionaries" overseas.

In May, the authorities revoked the Vietnamese citizenship of former prisoner of conscience Phạm Minh Hoàng, a member of Viet Tan, an overseas-based group peacefully campaigning for democracy in Viet Nam. He was forcibly deported to France in June.

TORTURE AND OTHER ILL-TREATMENT

Reports continued of torture and other ill-treatment, including beatings and other assaults, of peaceful activists by individuals believed to be acting in collusion with security police. In September, Viet Nam's initial report on implementation of the UN Convention against Torture, ratified in November 2014, acknowledged challenges and difficulties in implementation due to an "incomplete legal framework on human rights", among other reasons.

Prisoners of conscience were routinely held incommunicado during pre-trial detention, lasting up to two years. Detainees were denied medical treatment and transferred to prisons distant from their family home.

The whereabouts of Nguyễn Bắc Truyển, a human rights defender arrested in secret in July, were not disclosed to his family until three weeks later. He was held incommunicado and denied access to medication for pre-existing medical conditions.[3]

Denial of medical treatment was used to try to force prisoners of conscience to "confess" to crimes. Đinh Nguyễn Kha, an activist sentenced to six years' imprisonment for distributing leaflets critical of Viet Nam's response to China's territorial claims in the region, was denied follow-up treatment after a medical operation.[4] Hòa Hảo Buddhist and land rights activist Trần Thị Thúy continued to be denied adequate treatment for serious medical conditions since April 2015.

FREEDOM OF ASSEMBLY

The authorities used unnecessary or excessive force to disperse and prevent peaceful gatherings and protests, in particular those relating to the Formosa Plastics toxic spill in April 2016. In February, police and plain-clothes men attacked around 700 mainly Catholic peaceful protesters gathered in Nghệ An province before marching to present legal complaints against Formosa Plastics. Several individuals were injured and required hospital treatment, and others were arrested.[5]

DEATHS IN CUSTODY

Deaths in police custody in suspicious circumstances continued to be reported. Hòa Hảo Buddhist Nguyễn Hữu Tấn died after his arrest in May. Police claimed that he committed suicide, but his father said that the injuries on his body suggested that he was tortured before being killed.

DEATH PENALTY

A Ministry of Public Security report published in February revealed the extent of implementation of the death penalty, with an average of 147 executions annually between August 2013 and June 2016. The report stated that five new lethal injection centres were to be built. Only one execution was reported by official media during 2017, but more were believed to have been carried out. Death sentences were handed down for drug offences and embezzlement.

1. Viet Nam: Four peaceful activists arrested in connection with long-detained human rights lawyer (ASA 41/6855/2017)

2. Viet Nam: Female activist sentenced to nine years in prison (ASA 41/6833/2017)

3. Viet Nam: Missing human rights defender at risk of torture – Nguyễn Bắc Truyển (ASA 41/6964/2017)

4. Viet Nam: Necessary medical treatment denied to prisoner – Đinh Nguyễn Kha (ASA 41/5733/2017)

5. Viet Nam: Hundreds of peaceful marchers attacked by police (ASA 41/5728/2017)

YEMEN

Republic of Yemen
Head of state: **Abd Rabbu Mansour Hadi**
Head of government: **Ahmed Obeid bin Daghr**

All parties to the continuing armed conflict committed war crimes and other serious violations of international law, with inadequate accountability measures in place to ensure justice and reparation to victims. The Saudi Arabia-led coalition supporting the internationally recognized Yemeni government continued to bomb civilian infrastructure and carried out indiscriminate attacks, killing and injuring civilians. The Huthi-Saleh forces indiscriminately shelled civilian residential areas in Ta'iz city and fired artillery indiscriminately across the border into Saudi Arabia, killing and injuring civilians. The Yemeni government, Huthi-Saleh forces and Yemeni forces aligned to the United Arab Emirates (UAE) engaged in illegal detention practices including enforced disappearance and torture and other ill-treatment. Women and girls continued to face entrenched discrimination and other abuses, including forced and early marriage and domestic violence. The death penalty remained in force; no information was publicly available on death sentences or executions.

BACKGROUND

Yemen's territorial divisions and controls became deeply entrenched as the armed conflict continued between the internationally recognized government of President Hadi, supported by the Saudi Arabia-led coalition, and the Huthis and allied forces, which included army units loyal to former President Ali Abdullah Saleh. The Huthi-Saleh authorities continued to control large parts of the country including the capital, Sana'a, while President Hadi's government officially controlled southern parts of Yemen including the governorates of Lahj and Aden. On 4 December, Ali Abdullah Saleh was killed by Huthi forces consolidating their control over Sana'a.

Meanwhile, rival armed factions proliferated and vied to assert control against a background of economic collapse and widespread lawlessness, in the absence of functioning state institutions.

The authority of President Hadi, weak or absent in large swathes of the country, continued to wane and faced challenges from multiple actors and entities. Through its Supreme Political Council, the Huthi-Saleh alliance undertook, in the areas under their control, responsibilities and functions of the state. This included the formation of a government, the appointment of governors and the issuing of governmental decrees.

In May, former Governor of Aden Aidarous al-Zubaydi, and Hani bin Brik, a former Minister of State, formed a 26-member Southern Transition Council. The Council, which expressed the aim of an independent South Yemen and which enjoyed public support, held several meetings and established headquarters in the city of Aden.

The continued conflict led to a political and security vacuum and the establishment of a safe haven for armed groups and militias, assisted by outside states. Some of these forces were trained, funded and supported by the UAE and Saudi Arabia. Some local security forces, including the Hadrami Elite Forces and Security Belt Forces, were armed and trained by and reported directly to the UAE. Such forces were characterized by in-fighting and competing agendas.

The armed group al-Qa'ida in the Arabian Peninsula (AQAP) continued to control parts of southern Yemen and to carry out bomb attacks in the governorates of Aden, Abyan, Lahj and al-Bayda. Air strikes and strikes by remotely piloted vehicles (drones) against AQAP by US forces increased threefold. US forces also carried out at least two ground assault raids. The armed group Islamic State (IS) continued to operate in parts of the country, albeit on a small scale.

There was no progress in political negotiations nor any cessations of hostilities during the year. As military operations and fighting continued in and around the port cities of Mokha and Hodeidah, all parties to the conflict refused to engage with the UN-led process at different times depending on military gains on the ground.

ARMED CONFLICT

According to the Office of the UN High Commissioner for Human Rights, 5,144 civilians, including more than 1,184 children, had been killed and more than 8,749 civilians wounded since the conflict began in March 2015 until August 2017. The UN Office for the Coordination of Humanitarian Affairs (OCHA) reported that more than two thirds of the population were in need of humanitarian assistance and at least 2.9 million people had fled their homes. The WHO reported that more than 500,000 people were suspected of having cholera due to lack of clean water and access to health facilities. Nearly 2,000 people had died of cholera since the outbreak began in 2016. The ongoing conflict was a major factor in the prevalence of cholera in Yemen.

VIOLATIONS BY HUTHI-SALEH FORCES AND PRO-GOVERNMENT MILITIAS

Huthi and allied forces, including army units loyal to former President Saleh, continued to employ tactics that appeared to violate the prohibition of indiscriminate attacks. They indiscriminately fired explosive munitions with wide-area effects, including mortars and artillery shells, into residential areas controlled or contested by opposing forces, killing and injuring civilians. The city of Ta'iz was particularly affected, with such attacks intensifying at particular times including in January and May. The UN reported that a series of attacks from 21 May to 6 June between Huthi and anti-Huthi forces killed at least 26 civilians and injured at least 61. The Huthis and their allies also continued to lay internationally banned anti-personnel landmines that caused civilian casualties. On 15 September, the UN reported a further series of apparently indiscriminate attacks launched by Huthi-Saleh forces in Ta'iz, including shelling on a house in the Shab al-Dhuba district and al-Sameel Market, killing three children and injuring seven others.

The Huthis and allied forces, as well as pro-government forces, continued to recruit and deploy child soldiers.

VIOLATIONS BY THE SAUDI ARABIA-LED COALITION

The UN reported that the Saudi Arabia-led coalition supporting President Hadi's government continued to be the leading cause of civilian casualties in the conflict. The coalition continued to commit serious violations of international human rights law and humanitarian law with impunity.

Coalition aircraft carried out bomb attacks on areas controlled or contested by Huthi forces and their allies, particularly in the Sana'a, Ta'iz, Hajjah, Hodeidah and Sa'da governorates, killing and injuring thousands of civilians. Many coalition attacks were directed at military targets, but others were indiscriminate, disproportionate or directed against civilians and civilian objects, including funeral gatherings, schools, markets, residential areas and civilian boats.

In March, a helicopter attacked a boat carrying 146 Somali migrants and refugees off the coast of the port city of Hodeidah, killing 42 civilians and injuring 34 others. Another attack in August on a residential neighbourhood in southern Sana'a killed 16 civilians and injured 17 others, the majority of whom were children.

Coalition forces used imprecise munitions in some attacks, including large bombs with a wide impact radius that caused casualties and destruction beyond their immediate strike location. They also continued to use cluster munitions in attacks in Sa'da governorate, despite such munitions being widely prohibited internationally because of their inherently indiscriminate nature. Cluster munitions scattered explosive bomblets over wide areas and presented a continuing risk because of their frequent failure to detonate on initial impact. In February, the coalition fired Brazilian-manufactured rockets containing banned cluster munitions on residential areas and farmland in Sa'da city, injuring two civilians and causing material damage.

AERIAL AND NAVAL BLOCKADE

The coalition continued to impose a partial sea and air blockade that was tightened in November, purportedly to enforce the UN-sanctioned arms embargo on the Huthis and Saleh-aligned forces. Throughout the year, these blockades curtailed the movement of people and goods, deepening the humanitarian crisis caused by the conflict and contributing to violations of the right to health and to an adequate standard of living, including adequate food. This contributed to pervasive food insecurity and what became the world's worst cholera epidemic. In March, the NGO Save the Children reported that the coalition prevented three of its aid shipments from reaching the port of Hodeidah, forcing them to reroute to Aden and delaying the delivery of aid for three months. In August, OCHA reported that four vessels carrying more than 71,000 tonnes of fuel were denied access to Hodeidah by the coalition. In November, 29 ships carrying essential supplies were prevented by the coalition from reaching Hodeidah port, according to OCHA.

ARBITRARY ARRESTS AND DETENTIONS

The Huthi-Saleh forces, Yemeni government and Yemeni forces aligned with the UAE engaged in arbitrary and illegal detention practices. Amnesty International documented a few cases in Sana'a and Marib of civilians being detained solely to be used as leverage in future prisoner exchanges, which amounts to hostage-taking and is a violation of international humanitarian law.

In Sana'a and other areas they controlled, the Huthis and their allies continued to arbitrarily arrest and detain critics and opponents as well as journalists, private individuals, human rights defenders and members of the Baha'i community, subjecting scores to enforced disappearance. Five Baha'i men remained in detention at the end of the year. One of the men had been held for nearly four years, accused by the Huthis of apostasy, which carries the death penalty under Yemeni law.

UAE-backed Yemeni forces in Aden perpetrated a campaign of arbitrary detention and enforced disappearances. Amnesty International documented 13 cases of arbitrary detention during the year; some of these detainees were held incommunicado or had been subjected to enforced disappearance. Members of the Baha'i community were also arbitrarily detained at Aden International Airport by local forces aligned with the UAE and were held without charge for nine months.

Professor and political figure Mustafa al-Mutawakel was arbitrarily arrested by the internationally recognized Yemeni government forces in Marib on 27 April. He remained in detention without charge.

IMPUNITY

Since the conflict began, all parties committed serious violations of international humanitarian law and violations and abuses of human rights law with absolute impunity.

Since its inception in September 2015, the National Commission to Investigate Alleged Violations of Human Rights, established by the Yemeni government, failed to conduct prompt, impartial and effective investigations consistent with international standards into alleged human rights violations committed by all parties to the conflict in Yemen. Similarly, the Saudi Arabia-led coalition investigative mechanism continued to appear to lack the necessary impartiality and independence to carry out its work credibly.

With the proliferation of armed groups and security forces without command and control and the lack of effective control of the central government over its security forces and territories, the space for impunity further widened. In its mid-term report, the UN Panel of Experts on Yemen expressed concern that member states of the coalition were expressly shielding themselves from accountability and individual responsibility by hiding behind the umbrella of the coalition.

In a positive development, the UN Human Rights Council passed a resolution in September mandating a group of experts to investigate abuses by all parties in Yemen.

This constituted a first step towards justice for victims of human rights abuses and grave violations of international law.

FREEDOMS OF EXPRESSION AND ASSOCIATION

The Huthis and their allies, as well as armed factions in Ta'iz, Aden and Sana'a, waged a campaign against journalists and human rights defenders, curtailing freedom of expression in areas under their de facto administration.

The Huthis and allied forces continued to hold at least nine journalists without charge; they had been arbitrarily detained for more than two years. Meanwhile in Aden and Ta'iz, armed groups and security forces assassinated, harassed, intimidated, detained and in some cases tortured human rights defenders and journalists, forcing some to exercise self-censorship and others to flee Yemen.

The Saudi Arabia-led coalition and the Yemeni government prevented journalists from entering Yemen, including by preventing the UN from allowing journalists onto their flights into Yemen, minimizing coverage and effectively imposing a media blackout. This ban was also extended to human rights organizations in May.

WOMEN'S RIGHTS

The protracted conflict exacerbated existing discrimination and inequality for women and girls and gave rise to the adoption of negative coping mechanisms, such as child marriage, especially in the governorates of Ta'iz, Hajjah, Hodeidah, Ibb and Sana'a. Societal and legal protection mechanisms – however inadequate – broke down. This left women and girls with less protection from, and fewer avenues of redress for, sexual and other violence, including female genital mutilation, forced marriage and other abuses.

DEATH PENALTY

The death penalty remained in force for many crimes; no information was publicly available about death sentences or executions. On 12 April, the Huthi-Saleh authorities in Sana'a convicted journalist Yahya al-Jubaihi and sentenced him to death on charges of spying. This was the first time the Huthi-Saleh authorities had sentenced somebody to death. Yahya al-Jubaihi was released in September.

ZAMBIA

Republic of Zambia
Head of state and government: **Edgar Chagwa Lungu**

The authorities cracked down on critics, including human rights defenders, journalists and opposition political party members. The Public Order Act was used to repress rights to freedom of expression, association and assembly. The police used unnecessary and excessive force against peaceful protesters and failed to address violence by groups close to the government. The judiciary came under verbal attack from the President. Levels of food insecurity in rural areas remained high.

BACKGROUND

There was heightened tension between supporters of the President and of Hakainde Hichilema, leader of the opposition United Party for National Development (UPND), following the disputed election results in 2016. Hakainde Hichilema refused to recognize Edgar Chagwa Lungu as President. The Constitutional Court rejected Hakainde Hichilema's petition against the results on procedural grounds. The Court was also expected to deliver a judgment during 2018 on whether President Lungu could run for president in the 2021 elections.

FREEDOMS OF ASSEMBLY AND ASSOCIATION

The space for civil society, human rights defenders, journalists and opposition political parties was increasingly restricted. The authorities continued to use the Public Order Act to prevent political parties and civil society organizations from gathering. Section 5(4) of the Act provided that anyone intending to assemble or convene a public meeting or demonstration was required to give the police seven days' notice. However, the police interpreted the law as imposing a requirement to obtain prior authorization for any public assembly to proceed. On 24 August, police dispersed a prayer meeting convened to welcome Hakainde Hichilema's release from Mukobeko Maximum Security Prison in Kabwe city where he had been held for four months on charges of treason, which were dropped.

On 10 January, UK lawyer Oliver Holland was arrested and charged under the Public Order Act with unlawful assembly for meeting with a community in Chingola city who was challenging in court environmental pollution allegedly caused by a mining company. He was released the same day and charges against him were dropped; however, he was later charged with conduct likely to breach the peace and ordered to pay a USD5 fine.

Police frequently used unnecessary and excessive force to disperse protesters.

In April, police stopped a UPND rally in Kanyama Township in the capital, Lusaka, on "security" grounds. Although the UPND had notified the police in advance of the rally, they unlawfully dispersed the rally, shooting 20-year-old Stephen Kalipa, one of the protesters. He died later from gunshot wounds at the hospital. An investigation was opened, but no one had been arrested in connection with the incident by the end of the year. The police claimed that he died of knife stab wounds at the hands of an unidentified assailant.

On 23 June, police arrested senior UPND officials on charges of unlawful assembly alleging that they held a press briefing at the UPND's secretariat offices without obtaining prior authorization. On 29 September, police arrested six human rights defenders who gathered outside Parliament and protested peacefully against the government's purchase, at the inflated cost of USD42 million, of 42 fire engines; they were charged with refusing to obey police orders. The protesters were beaten during the protest by members of the ruling Patriotic Front.

EXCESSIVE USE OF FORCE

On 8 April, Hakainde Hichilema and other UPND members – Lastone Mulilandumba, Muleya Haachenda, Wallace Chakwa, Pretorius Haloba and Hamusonde Hamaleka – were arrested and charged with treason and disobeying a lawful order following an earlier incident in which Hakainde Hichilema's motorcade refused to give way to President Lungu's convoy. Police raided Hakainde Hichilema's house without a warrant, using tear gas against him and his family. On 28 April, his wife, Mutinta, was threatened with arrest after she reported the police's use of excessive force. No charges had been brought against the police in connection with the incident by the end of the year. On 15 August, the Director of Public Prosecutions withdrew all charges against Hakainde Hichilema and the other UPND members.

FREEDOM OF EXPRESSION

Security forces and political activists affiliated with the Patriotic Front subjected media workers, political activists and others who criticized the government to harassment and intimidation.

Staff of the Law Association of Zambia were harassed and intimidated because of their work in defence of human rights. On 3 March, for example, Patriotic Front loyalists stormed the Association's offices demanding the resignation of its president, Linda Kasonde.

Later the same month, the Association joined a High Court petition to prevent the liquidation of Post Newspapers – known to be highly critical of the government – in proceedings in which the Zambia Revenue Authority, among others, sought the company's liquidation, alleging that it had failed to pay taxes.

On 3 August, police arrested Saviour Chishimba, president of the United Progressive People party on defamation charges after he criticized President Lungu for declaring a threatened state of emergency. Saviour Chishimba was detained for seven days, without being brought before a judge; he was released without charge.

In October, the Independent Broadcasting Authority summoned Prime Television Zambia's management to answer allegations that they had violated the provisions of their broadcasting licence when they covered a story about the UPND's parliamentary candidate for Kalulushi town, Everisto Mwalilino, who had accused government officials of electoral corruption. The station had also highlighted corruption allegations against former Information Minister, Chishimba Kambwili.

JUSTICE SYSTEM

The government verbally attacked the judiciary, which undermined the independence of the institution. At the same time, there was a growing public perception of the judiciary as a polarized institution in which some judges were not politically independent. In September, while on a visit to South Africa, Hakainde Hichilema accused the judiciary of corruption and of being under the control of the President. On 2 November, President Lungu warned judges against blocking him from running for President in 2021. In November, on a trip to Solwezi, he warned judges against following Kenyan judges who, in September, had ruled to annul the results of Kenya's presidential elections.

RIGHT TO FOOD

The 2017 Global Hunger Index reported that food insecurity and undernourishment remained alarmingly high. Many subsistence farmers were affected because they were denied access to their land due to ongoing land disputes. In Mpande, Northern Province, over 300 people were locked into a legal dispute with the government after they were forcibly evicted from their land to an arid region where they could not produce food. In Kaindu, Mumbwa District, the owners and employees of a German-owned safari company shot at, and verbally abused, members of a 700-strong community, preventing them from fishing in the Kafue River and gathering food from the forest. The community was not fully consulted over the use of its land for safaris.

ZIMBABWE

Republic of Zimbabwe
Head of state and government: Emmerson Dambudzo Mnangagwa (replaced Robert Gabriel Mugabe in November)

Activists and human rights defenders continued to mobilize to hold the government to account through protests on the streets and via social media. The state continued to use the law to crack down on dissenting voices. The authorities continued with forced evictions despite constitutional provisions prohibiting the practice. Independence of the judiciary remained under threat following amendments to the Constitution.

BACKGROUND

The economic situation worsened with no solution to the liquidity crisis in sight.

In October, the Ministry of Cyber Security, Threat Detection and Mitigation was established in response to social media activism.

Factionalism and succession battles within the ruling Zimbabwe African National Union–Patriotic Front (ZANU-PF) party intensified; President Mugabe dismissed the then First Vice-President Emmerson Mnangagwa on 6 November, for allegedly plotting against the government and exhibiting "disloyalty, deceitfulness, disrespect and unreliability". On 14 November, the military took power and after public support for the military action, and Parliament's impeachment process, Robert Mugabe resigned on 21 November. Emmerson Mnangagwa was sworn in as President on 24 November.

FREEDOMS OF ASSOCIATION AND ASSEMBLY

The police dispersed meetings or peaceful protests using excessive force.

On 26 June, police arrested Pastor Evan Mawarire in the capital, Harare, after he held prayers with University of Zimbabwe medical students during a protest against fee increases. He was held in Harare Central Police Station for two days before being released on bail on charges of inciting public violence and disorderly conduct. He was acquitted on 29 September, although separate charges remained against him relating to a different arrest (see below "Freedom of expression").

In July, Darlington Madzonga and Edmund Musvubi were arrested by police during a peaceful protest in Harare, held by the opposition Movement for Democratic Change youth against the Zimbabwe Electoral Commission's failure to implement reforms. They were charged with killing a police officer during the protest and they remained in detention in Harare at the end of the year while their case was pending in court.

On 10 November, the police disrupted a meeting in Marange Village, in the east, of 22 activists from Latin American and Southern African countries to commemorate the ninth anniversary of the killing of 200 people by the military. The 200 had been killed after they took control of the diamond fields in protest at government plans to hand over diamond mines to Chinese businesses. The 22 activists were arrested and charged with entering a protected area without a government permit. They were released on 11 November after pleading guilty and were each fined USD100.

FREEDOM OF EXPRESSION

The state restricted the right to freedom of expression particularly of human rights defenders and other activists.

On 16 January, Pastor Philip Mugadza was arrested by police in Harare and charged with criminal nuisance after he said that President Mugabe would die on 17 October. He was released on bail on 10 March. His case was pending in the Constitutional Court at the end of the year. If convicted, he faces a jail sentence of up to six months.

Pastor Evan Mawarire was targeted for various public statements he made criticizing the government. He had fled the country in July 2016, but was arrested by police in Harare, upon his return on 31 January, on charges of subversion and insulting the national flag. He was released on bail on 8 February. On 24 September, Pastor Mawarire was arrested again and charged with subverting a constitutionally elected government after he published a video on 23 September in which he complained about fuel shortages and rising prices. He was released from the Harare Central Police Station on 26 September. On 29 November, the Harare High Court acquitted him of all the charges.

On 10 August, Energy Mutodi, a businessman and supporter of Emmerson Mnangagwa, was arrested in Harare by police officers of the Criminal Investigation Department for suggesting on Facebook that a coup was likely if President Mugabe did not choose his successor carefully. He was charged with undermining the President's authority and causing disaffection among the police and defence forces. On 23 August, he was released from Harare Remand Prison on bail but his case was ongoing at the end of the year.

Victor Matemadanda, an executive member of the National Liberation War Veterans' Association, was detained by police at Harare Central Police Station in August on charges of undermining the office of the President and causing disaffection among the police and defence forces. He had called on President Mugabe to step down. He was released on bail after several days but his case remained pending at the end of the year.

On 2 October, journalist Kenneth Nyangani was arrested by police in the city of Mutare for reporting that the President's wife donated clothing, including used underwear, to ZANU-PF supporters in Mutare. He was bailed on 4 October and was awaiting trial until 13 December when the state failed to bring him to trial.

On 3 November, journalist Martha O'Donovan, a US national, was arrested at home by the Harare Police and charged with insulting the President and attempting to subvert a constitutionally elected government. She was alleged to have insulted Robert Mugabe on Twitter. She was released on bail from Chikurubi Maximum Security Prison on 10 November; she had not been brought to trial by the end of the year.

ARBITRARY ARRESTS AND DETENTIONS

The military police arrested a number of suspects on charges of fraud and corruption. Those arrested included senior state officials, implicated in corruption, whose rights were denied on arrest, including by being denied access to lawyers.

During the military takeover in November, army personnel detained several members of a ZANU- PF faction who were alleged to support Emmerson Mnangagwa's dismissal. They were held for more than the constitutionally permitted 48 hours before being brought to court. Former Finance Minister Ignatius Chombo, ZANU-PF Youth League Commissar Innocent Hamandishe, and ZANU-PF Youth League secretary Kudzanayi Chipanga, were arrested and detained by military police on 14 November. During their detention they were denied access to their lawyers and were not taken to court until 25 November. Ignatius Chombo was charged with corruption and criminal abuse of office; Kudzanayi Chipanga and Innocent Hamandishe were charged with publishing or communicating falsehoods after they claimed at a press conference that Army Commander General Chiwenga stole money from the sale of Marange diamonds.

FORCED EVICTIONS

In April, police used excessive force to evict around 15 families from Manzou Farm in the Mashonaland Central Province which consists of several small farms. The evictions contravened a High Court order on 24 March which directed the government to end the practice of arbitrary evictions and home demolitions without providing compensation or alternative land to those evicted. The residents had lived on the farmland since 2000; the forced evictions from Manzou have left over 200 families homeless and without compensation.

LEGAL, CONSTITUTIONAL OR INSTITUTIONAL DEVELOPMENTS

In August, Parliament passed a bill amending section 180 of the 2013 Constitution. MP Jessie Majome challenged the bill in court on the basis that the vote did not meet the required two-thirds majority and threatened judicial independence. The bill gives the President power to unilaterally appoint the most senior judicial positions.

ECONOMIC, SOCIAL AND CULTURAL RIGHTS

Economic instability, drought, high poverty levels and unemployment put obstacles in the way of access to education, health and adequate food. In July, Zimbabwe reported to the Voluntary National Review of Sustainable Development Goals for the UN High Level Political Forum that over 76% of children in Zimbabwe lived in consumption poverty, and a quarter lived in extreme poverty. Difficulties in paying basic school fees were widespread; the national Food and Nutrition Council found that at least 63% of school-age children were turned away from school for non-payment of fees. An estimated 4.1 million people in rural areas were reported to be food insecure.

The right to health was increasingly threatened as allocation of budget to health decreased to only 8.2% of the national budget. The Auditor General's June report highlighted a crisis in health service delivery, and noted shortages of essential medicines and equipment, unavailability of water and specialized personnel.

SEXUAL AND REPRODUCTIVE RIGHTS

In October, UNICEF reported that 34% of girls and women were married by the age of 18. The government was yet to amend the Marriage Act or related legislation to comply with the Constitutional Court's 2016 judgment under which marriage under 18 was unconstitutional. NGOs and girls and women giving birth reported that those who had babies in public health facilities were not allowed to leave until their fees were paid.

Despite the Ministry of Health policy guidance that maternal health services should be provided for free, local authorities continued to charge fees for such services in public health facilities. Marginalized women and girls experienced severe delays in accessing maternal health services or received no care at all.